HOME NETWORKING

IFIP – The International Federation for Information Processing

IFIP was founded in 1960 under the auspices of UNESCO, following the First World Computer Congress held in Paris the previous year. An umbrella organization for societies working in information processing, IFIP's aim is two-fold: to support information processing within its member countries and to encourage technology transfer to developing nations. As its mission statement clearly states,

> *IFIP's mission is to be the leading, truly international, apolitical organization which encourages and assists in the development, exploitation and application of information technology for the benefit of all people.*

IFIP is a non-profitmaking organization, run almost solely by 2500 volunteers. It operates through a number of technical committees, which organize events and publications. IFIP's events range from an international congress to local seminars, but the most important are:

- The IFIP World Computer Congress, held every second year;
- Open conferences;
- Working conferences.

The flagship event is the IFIP World Computer Congress, at which both invited and contributed papers are presented. Contributed papers are rigorously refereed and the rejection rate is high.

As with the Congress, participation in the open conferences is open to all and papers may be invited or submitted. Again, submitted papers are stringently refereed.

The working conferences are structured differently. They are usually run by a working group and attendance is small and by invitation only. Their purpose is to create an atmosphere conducive to innovation and development. Refereeing is less rigorous and papers are subjected to extensive group discussion.

Publications arising from IFIP events vary. The papers presented at the IFIP World Computer Congress and at open conferences are published as conference proceedings, while the results of the working conferences are often published as collections of selected and edited papers.

Any national society whose primary activity is in information may apply to become a full member of IFIP, although full membership is restricted to one society per country. Full members are entitled to vote at the annual General Assembly, National societies preferring a less committed involvement may apply for associate or corresponding membership. Associate members enjoy the same benefits as full members, but without voting rights. Corresponding members are not represented in IFIP bodies. Affiliated membership is open to non-national societies, and individual and honorary membership schemes are also offered.

HOME NETWORKING

*First IFIP WG 6.2 Home Networking Conference
(IHN'2007), Paris, France, December 10-12, 2007*

Edited by

Khaldoun Al Agha
University of Paris XI
France

Xavier Carcelle
OpenPattern
France

Guy Pujolle
University of Paris VI
France

 Springer

Library of Congress Control Number: 2007940535

Home Networking

Edited by Khaldoun Al Agha, Xavier Carcelle, and Guy Pujolle

p. cm. (IFIP International Federation for Information Processing, a Springer Series in Computer Science)

ISSN: 1571-5736 / 1861-2288 (Internet)
ISBN: 978-0-387-77215-8
eISBN: 978-0-387-77216-5

Printed on acid-free paper

Printed in the United States of America.

9 8 7 6 5 4 3 2 1

springer.com

Table of Contents

WiMAX, Wi-Fi

Very high throughput Home

Management, control & energy

Autonomic management and discovery

Autonomic and Routing

Autonomic and Routing 2

Autonomic management and discovery 2

Normalization

Services

An emission/reception chain modelling of the WiMAX access network

N. Fourty, T. Val

LATTIS – EA4155
Université de Toulouse, France
name@iut-blagnac.fr

P. Fraisse

Department of Robotics
CNRS LIRMM
Université Montpellier 2, France
fraisse@lirmm.fr

Abstract — This work describes the simulation under the Simulink environment of Matlab of an IEEE802.16 complete transmitter/receiver chain. Because of its superior performance the WirelessMAN OFDM 256 PHY layer is the most implemented in WiMAX compliant devices. The first part of the paper concerns the validation of a transmitter model using that PHY layer while the second part of the article deals with a complete transmitter/receiver model proposed. An example with a 20 MHz channel using adaptive modulation is considered and analyzed. This model takes into account several constraints and problem of the standard translation: reducing ambiguity in the standard and providing a reference for compliance testing.

Index Terms— 802.16, MATLAB, access network, PHY layer, wireless network

1   Introduction

The IEEE 802.16 Standards are a family of standards designed to establish interfaces for fixed, portable and even mobile Broadband Wireless Access (BWA) systems. In the first part of this article we describe how we have performed our validation (capture implementation, test) using Simulink. The validation model presented is designed as an interactive Simulink test file. In the second part of the article we present simulations of an entire 802.16 emission/reception chain.

Please use the following format when citing this chapter:

Fourty, N., Val, T., Fraisse, P., 2007, in IFIP International Federation for Information Processing, Volume 256, Home Networking, Al Agha, K., Carcelle, X., Pujolle, G., (Boston: Springer), pp. 1-14.

2 Interpreting the standard

2.1 Brief history

The first version of the 802.16 standard was released in October 2001. The specification described a Single Carrier air interface for fixed point-to-multipoint (PMP) BWA systems operating between 10-66 GHz [1].

Next amendment, 802.16a (2003) extends the physical environment towards lower frequency bands below 11 GHz. Moreover the amendment defines two other physical interfaces in order to fit this new frequency band: the Wireless-MAN OFDM PHY and the WirelessMAN OFDMA PHY. While the first is using a 256-carrier Orthogonal Frequency Division Multiplexing (OFDM), the second is using a 2048-carrier Orthogonal Frequency Division Multiple Access (OFDMA) scheme [2]. An optional mesh topology is also added to the mandatory PMP architecture.

The most recently approved version 802.16-2004 [3], enables us to have a comprehensive reading of the standard incorporating previous versions and amendments. The last amendment 802.16e-2005 [4] released on February 2006, propose a modification of Physical (PHY) and Medium Access Control (MAC) Layers described by 802.16-2004 for Combined Fixed and Mobile Operation in Licensed Bands.

While 802.16e [5] was amended, the first products to complete the rigorous test procedures required for 802.16-2004 certification have been released on the market. The WiMAX Forum is responsible for the interoperability of WiMAX devices, the certification being based on the 802.16 Standard document. The document, about 900 pages long, is describing in detail PHY and MAC layers for WiMAX systems, guaranteeing the compatibility and interoperability between broadband wireless access components.

However the complexity of the standard makes it difficult for designers to create standard-compliant components. For this kind of problems model-based simulations using network simulators often come to the rescue of designers. Although network simulators like Opnet, Network Simulator 2 (NS2), Qualnet, etc..., allow a network entire representation describing precisely the channel and upper layers of the OSI Stack representation, the PHY layer and specially real component constraints aren't well taken into account. That's why we have chosen the Simulink tool under the MATLAB environment to validate our system. The standard is the key element of the model development process but as in every document-based design product, every translation or new amendment can introduce errors and omissions. These errors can have a tremendous importance in compliance testing that is why we have decided first to design a validating tool for WiMAX compliance testing.

2.2 Simulink validating tool

Because of its superior performance in multipath fading wireless channels [6], the WirelessMAN OFDM 256 PHY layer is the most implemented in WiMAX compliant devices. That is why, the PHY layer we are going to validate is this one. In the rest of the paper we will only talk about this interface.

Unlike many other OFDM-based systems such as 802.11 [7], the 802.16 standard supports variable bandwidth sizes between 1.25 and 20 MHz. This feature and the support of combined fixed and mobile usage models, require a scalable OFDM signalling protocol.

Although the problem of the translation of the WiMAX standard into a Simulink model is a difficult job, the section 8.3.3 of the 802.16 standard gives some ways to handle the job dividing it into three steps: data randomization, forward error correction (FEC) and interleaving. In order to have a good understanding we include in our model the modulation and the OFDM symbol creation.

2.2.1 Randomization

Randomization is performed by a Pseudo Random Binary Sequence PRBS. The generator polynomial of the PRBS is $1+X^{14}+X^{15}$.

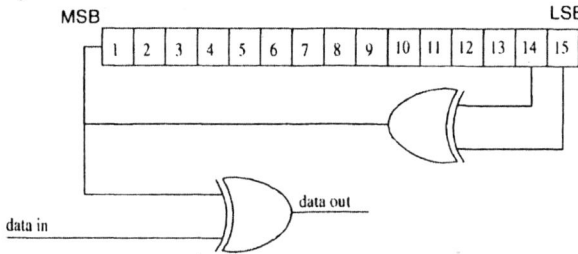

Figure 1. PRBS Generator

Under the Simulink environment the randomization is performed by a PN Sequence Block. The initial state of the PN sequence is given in all test sequences. It is also important to note that a '0x00' tail byte is appended after the randomization

2.2.2 Forward Error Correction

The FEC consists of the concatenation of a Reed-Solomon outer code and a rate compatible convolutional inner code. The support of block and convolutional Turbo Codes are optional. The encoding is performed by first passing the data in block format through the RS encoder and then passing it through a zero-terminating convolutional encoder.

Reed Solomon codes are a subset of Bose, Ray-Chaudhuri, Hocquenghem

(BCH) codes and are linear block codes. A Reed-Solomon code is specified as RS(n, k, t).

This means that the encoder takes k data symbols and adds parity symbols to make an n symbol codeword. The code rate is Rc= k/n and n-k parity symbols are added. A Reed-Solomon decoder can correct up to t symbols that contain errors in a codeword, where $2t = n$-k. This is known as a Systematic code because the data is left unchanged and the parity symbols are appended. The amount of processing "power" required to encode and decode Reed-Solomon codes is related to the number of parity symbols per codeword. A large value of t means that a large number of errors can be corrected but requires more computational power than a small value of t.

The standard states that the Reed-Solomon encoder is derived from a systematic RS(255, 239, 8) code using shortening techniques in order to achieve different rates. Reed-Solomon shortening consists in inserting a number of data symbols zero at the encoder, not transmitting them, and then re-inserting them at the decoder.

A convolutional code is generated by passing the information sequence through a linear finite state shift register. In general the register consists of K stages and n linear algebraic function generators. The parameter K is called the constraint length and the code rate is Rc=1/n.

In our case the data is then encoded by the binary convolutional encoder with a native rate of 1/2, a constraint length equal to 7 and polynomials codes given in octal: G1=171, G2=133. The code is then punctured with a mask in order to achieve the good redundancy.

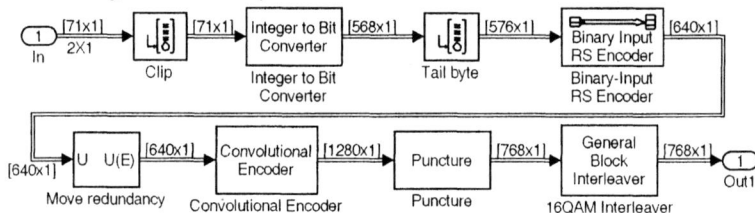

Figure 2. System overview

2.2.3 Interleaving

The standard defines the interleaver using a pair of permutation:

$$m_k = (N_{cbps}/12).k_{\mod 12} + floor(k/12) \tag{1}$$

$$j_k = s.floor(m_k/s) + (m_k + N_{cbps} - floor(12.m_k/N_{cbps}))_{\mod(s)} \tag{2}$$

$$s = ceil(N_{cpc}/2) \quad ; \quad k = 0,1,\cdots,N_{cbps}-1$$

With N_{cbps} being the number of coded bits per subchannel, N_{cpc} the number of coded bits per carrier.

The first ensures that adjacent coded bits are mapped onto nonadjacent OFDM subcarriers and the second map adjacent coded bits alternately onto less or more significant bits of the constellation. It is important to note that m_k and j_k are write addresses and *intrlv* MATLAB function need read addresses. This problem is solved using the *sort* MATLAB function to obtain the required permutation vector. Once we have the good permutation vector we can use the General interleaver block of the Communication blockset library of Simulink [8].

This kind of problem is typically a source of errors due to the standard translation, and without the test vectors the implementation wouldn't have been seen in bit error rate (BER) analysis and other system-level tests but it would have produced a non-interoperable device.

2.2.4 Modulation and OFDM symbol creation

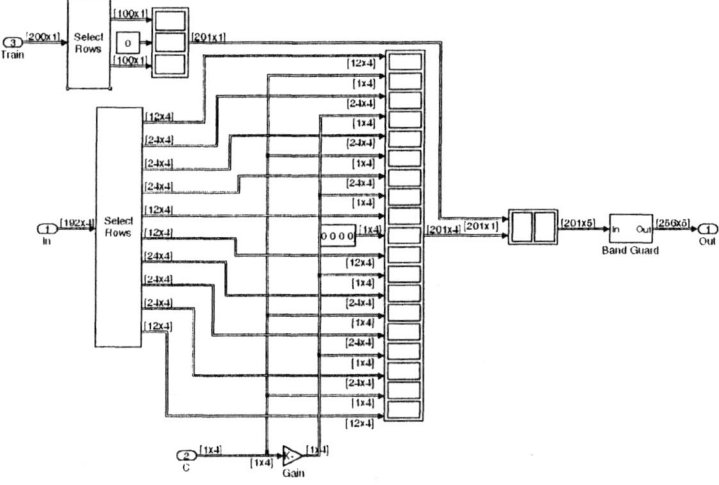

Figure 3. OFDM Symbol creation

After bit interleaving, the data bits are passed through the constellation mapper. Four constellations are defined BPSK, Gray mapped QPSK, 16QAM and 64QAM. 64QAM is optional in unlicensed frequency bands. The constellations are normalized with a factor to achieve equal average power.

Once data is correctly mapped the data has to be modulated onto all allocated data subcarriers according to the order of increasing frequency offset index. This job is performed by the FFT block. However before this stage pilot subcarriers should be inserted. A preamble can also be inserted in order to simulate a short frame.

The value of the pilot modulation is generated by a PRBS generator with the generator polynomial $1+X^9+X^{11}$. The value is then complemented according to the subcarrier index.

The result of all this succession of operations is a vector of 200 complex numbers, representing amplitude and phase information of the associated subcarrier created by the FFT block.

2.2.5 The validation stage

The validation is performed by passing the test vector into the Matlab environment and then verifying at each step the output of all precedent blocks. Fig.4 shows the validation of our transmitter with the first test vector given by the standard. This first WIMAX test vector is a 35 byte long data vector given in hex notation. This example using the pair modulation/coding QPSK-3/4, doesn't use subchannelisation and all initial states of the Pseudo Random Binary sequence PRBS used are well described.

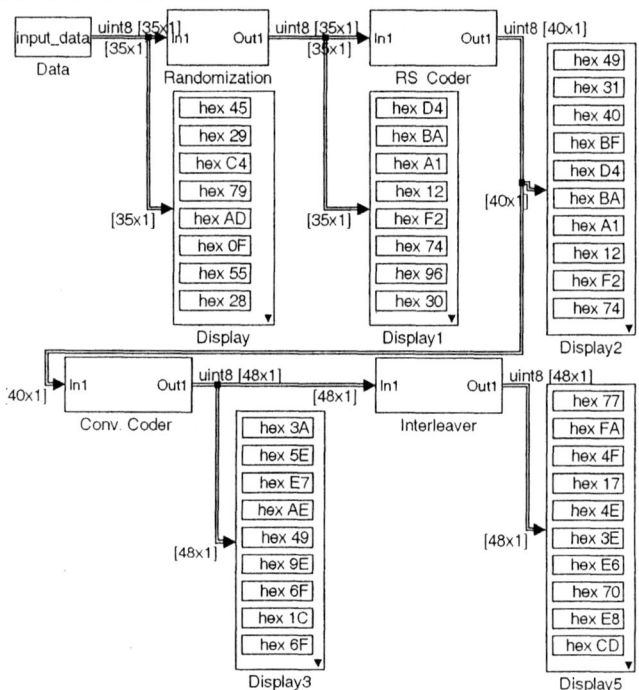

Figure 4. Validation stage

Once we have validated a test sequence we are now going to generate data continuously.

3 Receiver design

Like most communication standards, 802.16 specifies the signal processing in the transmitter only. This enables manufacturers to have an implementation margin without sacrifying interoperability. Once we have a complete Simulink model of the WiMAX transmitter, we are going to design a standard compliant receiver. The Fig.5 shows the complete model.

3.1 Structure of the model

This section is going to describe block by block the structure we have implemented, assumptions we have made and other simplifications we have performed.

3.1.1 Data Source

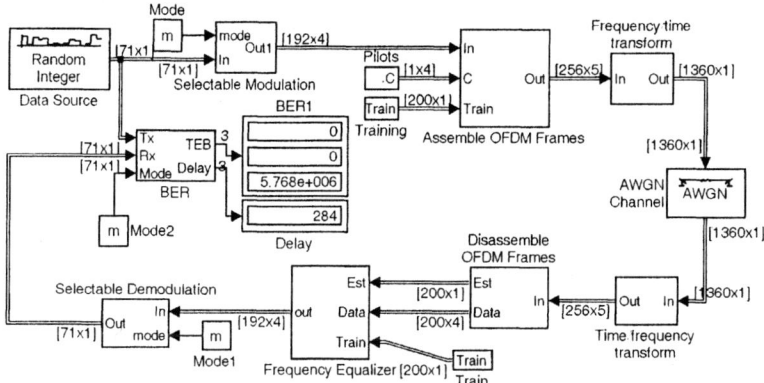

Figure 5. Complete system

The generation of random data is now achieved by a random integer generator. The generator creates a fixed frame of 71 bytes with a bit frame time of 12 µs when using a channel bandwidth of 20 Mhz. This time corresponds to the symbol time defined by the 8.3.2.2 section of the standard.

$$F_S = floor(n.BW / 8000).8000 \qquad (3)$$

$$T_S = (1 + G).1 / \Delta f \qquad with \ \Delta f = F_s / N_{FFT} \qquad (4)$$

If the pair modulation/coding requires a different amount of data the random data is clipped according to the standard. This operation is performed inside the modulation block.

3.1.2 Coding, interleaving and modulation

Modulation/coding	Ncbps	Throughput
BPSK	96	8 Mbit/s
QPSK1/2	192	16 Mbit/s
QPSK3/4	288	24 Mbit/s
16QAM1/2	384	32 Mbit/s
16QAM3/4	576	48 Mbit/s

Table 1. Throughput

The coding, interleaving, and modulation are simulated according to the standard. In particular, each modulator block performs these tasks: convolutional coding and puncturing using code rates of 1/2 and 3/4, data interleaving, BPSK, QPSK and 16-QAM modulation.

Each pair modulation/coding corresponds to a specific rate. If we keep the same conditions as above rates are summarised in the table 1.

The number of data symbols in each packet has been fixed to four OFDM symbol per frame. Pad bits have been omitted and buffering for frame transmission is performed at the end of the block.

3.1.3 Transmission, channel and equalisation

OFDM transmission uses 200 subcarriers, 8 pilots, 256-point FFTs, and a 16-sample cyclic prefix. The channel block is configurable as a simple AWGN channel or a dispersive multipath fading channel. However for simplicity, we have fixed the transmit power level to 1W.

The receiver equalization is based on a standard frequency-domain equalization. The principle is, in a first step, to find the transfer function of the channel for each subcarrier $H(\square)$. This operation is performed by a comparison of well known training sequences. And then multiplying the data by $1/H(\square)$ annihilating phase and gain in the subchannel, considered flat.

3.1.4 Demodulation, deinterleaving and decoding

The demodulation and decoding block perform the inverse operations of modulation and coding. The decoding of the convolutional coding is performed by a Viterbi algorithm.

Also, the simulation model does not model these aspects of the IEEE 802.16 standard: data scrambling, which is unnecessary in this model because the data is random, subchanelisation and time windowing of OFDM symbols

3.2 Test mechanism and validation of the transmitter/receiver chain.

Tests and validation presented in this paragraph were made with a manual selection of Modulation/Demodulation in order to qualify each pair coding modulation.

3.2.1 Test mechanisms

For our experimentation we ran simulation and sent 10 Mbits of data by the Data source described above. The pair modulation/coding has been selected manually and the channel chosen for characterization was an AWGN channel.

For each pair modulation/coding we have performed several measures of the residual BER after correction, varying the SNR.

3.2.2 Validation of the reception chain

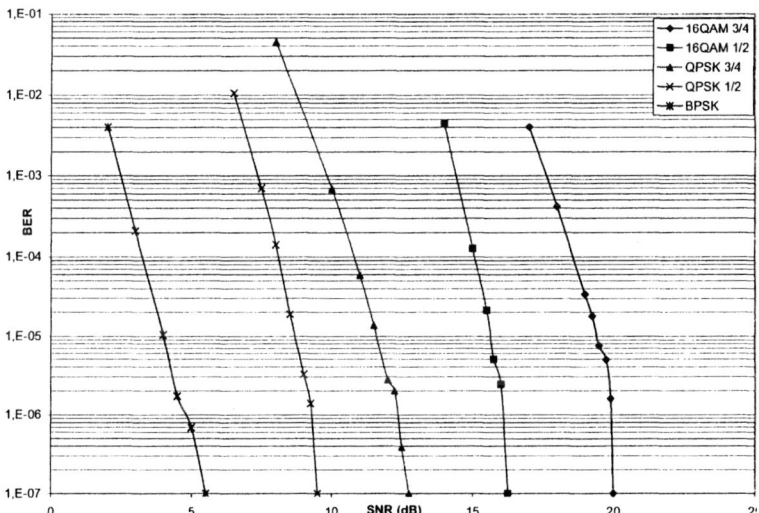

Figure 6. Residual BER varying SNR

The Fig.6 gives the result of our experimentation. This figure describes how the BER after FEC evolves when the SNR, modelled in the channel block, increase for different pairs modulation/coding.

The chapter 8.3.11 of the standard gives several constraints about the receiver sensitivity. The most important criterion is the residual BER after the FEC. Under several conditions such as an AWGN, in calibrated environments, certain packet formats and SNR assumptions, the standard defines a minimum residual BER of 10^{-6} at a given power level.

This power level is given by the equation:

$$R_{SS} = -102 + SNR_{Rx} + 10.\log(F_S . \frac{N_{used}}{N_{FFT}} . \frac{N_{subchannels}}{16})$$ (5)

With SNR_{Rx} being the SNR assumption in Table2, F_S being sampling frequency Eq(3), $N_{subchannels}$ the number of allocated subchannels.

Our approach is quite the same; since we have fixed our input signal strength to 1W we are going to verify SNR assumptions. The results show that all assumptions aren't verified especially the assumptions made for coding efficiency of 3/4 while pairs using a 1/2 redundancy satisfy easily their assumptions. However it seems that residual BER of 3/4 coded pairs decrease less quickly when the SNR goes down than 1/2 coded.

We can conclude for this first experiment that, apart from some assumptions and simplifications of the model, the receiver can be validated as a 802.16 compliant model. Although the chapter 8.3.11 of the standard gives several other constraints such as maximum input and maximum tolerable signal for the receiver, these parameters aren't modelled since our Simulink blocks are considered ideals. The table 2 presents a comparison between SNR assumed by the Table 266 of the standard and those measured by our model.

Modulation	SNR assumed	SNR with 10^{-6} BER	R_{SS}
BPSK	6,4 dB	4,7 dB	-23,1 dB
QPSK1/2	9,4 dB	9,2 dB	-20,1 dB
QPSK3/4	11,2 dB	12,5 dB	-18,3 dB
16QAM1/2	16,4 dB	15,9 dB	-13,1 dB
16QAM3/4	18,2 dB	19,8 dB	-11,3 dB

Table 2. Verifying SNR assumptions

3.3 Adaptive Modulation

The ability of WiMAX networks to offer a high performance within elevated distance with high spectral efficiency and signal tolerance is based on a strong adaptive modulation mechanism. This first experiment has fixed the border of each pair modulation/coding, now we are going to describe how the switching is done.

3.4 Channel quality estimating

Channels with variable signal-to-interference plus noise ratio (SINR) often use, like 802.11[9], several adaptive data rate schemes for increasing throughput[10]

These variations of SINR due to path loss, fading, or interferences have to be taken into account in order to satisfy the minimum BER fixed by the 802.16 standard. The symbol rate being fixed, the throughput may be varied by changing the bandwidth efficiency (bits/symbol) using a choice of coded modulation schemes. This variation may be assumed or coded systems by fixing the modulation and varying the code rate. Another possibility is to fix the code rate and adapt the constellation size. The last possibility, and it is our case, is to make a combination of the two former possibilities defining pairs modulation/coding and switching between them. It is also important to note that quality measurements are also essential for purposes of handoff and power control

In an OFDM system, the temporal comparison of ideal and corrupted signals can be replaced by comparing the modulation symbols, which is performed in frequency domain.

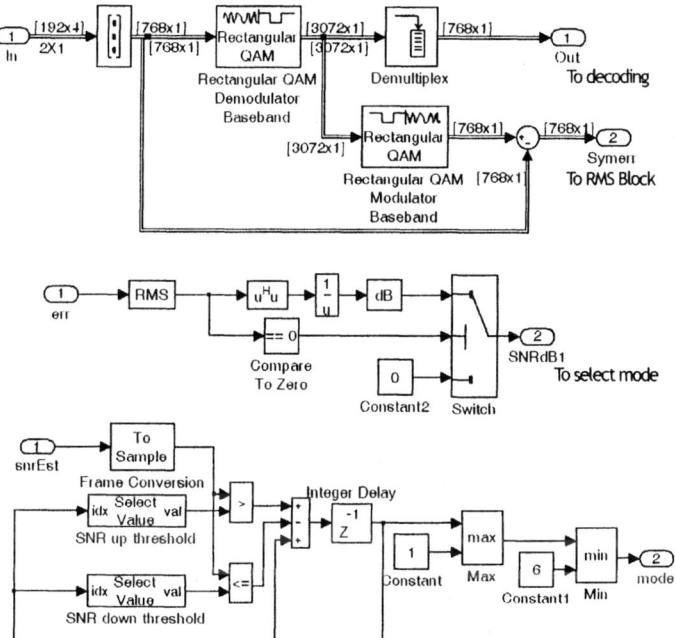

Figure 7. Quality estimation

The noise $Z_{n,k}$ for the kth sub-carrier of nth OFDM symbol can be formulated as [11]:

$$Z_{n,k} = Y_{n,k} - S_{n,k} H_{n,k} \qquad\qquad (6)$$

Where $S_{n,k}$ is the noiseless sample of the received symbol and $H_{n,k}$ is the channel estimate.

The computation is quite simple for an OFDM system, since a large frequency offset is not likely due to the frequency synchronization requirement of the OFDM system itself.

Under Simulink environment, the signal is received along with noise and interference by the demodulator block. After the demodulation, the ideal signal is remodulated using the same modulation. The complex sum is then computed and passed through the RMS block computing the quality.

The figure 7 describe the system

The channel quality estimated is then passed through the adaptive mode selection block selecting according to SNR threshold defined above.

3.5 Running the model

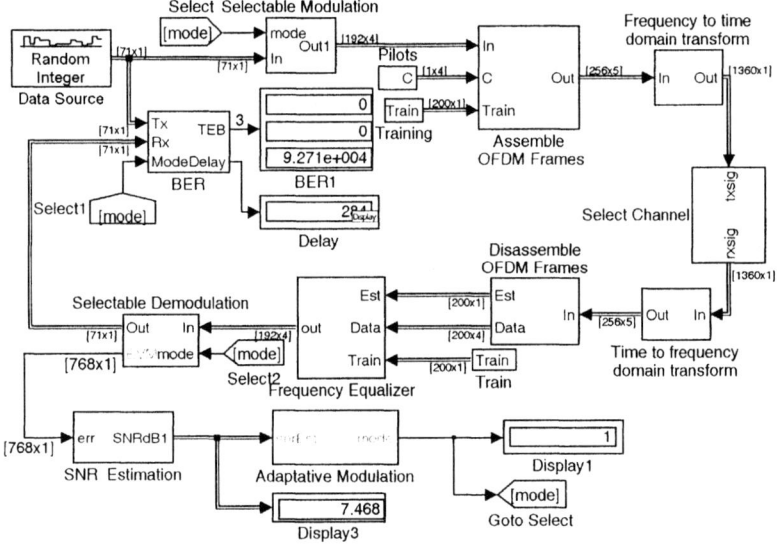

Figure 8. Adaptive Modulation

The complete model shown in Fig. 8 runs without any manual selection. Tests of the model using an ideal channel have proved that no errors without BER calculation time window errors were measured. Using an AWGN channel and varying manually the SNR we have found the same results as in III.B.2). More experiments with a Rayleigh fading channel have only shown a well known weakness of

OFDM systems: the sensitivity to carrier frequency offset. This offset destroys the orthogonality of the sub-carriers, causing sub-carrier offset and Inter Carrier Interference (ICI).

4 Conclusion

The WiMAX wireless network is thought to be used as an access network for the "last mile" and few engineering tools are currently available for this technology. In this work, we have implemented in a first stage a 802.16 compliant transmission chain validated by test vectors described in the standard. In a second stage we have developed a receiver according to advices and constraints of the standard. We have noticed during the implementation that all the conditions weren't observed due to our assumptions and simplification of the Standard. This work has been developed as an engineering tool to design 802.16 standard compliant devices because finally the 802.16 work group, as designers, confronts the challenge of standard translations. The best example is all amendments and corrigenda adopted in the 802.16 standard history. This model can help reducing ambiguity in the standard and providing a reference for compliance testing. In the continuation of this work, we envisage using these results including them in a PHY and MAC layer model. A work using a NS2 model of the 802.16 MAC framing is currently being performed in our laboratory. In a next stage, we aim at validating the WiMAX QoS mechanisms in order to assess the performances available for wireless Voice and Telephony over IP.

References

1. N. Fourty, T. Val, P. Fraisse, JJ. Mercier "Comparative analysis of new high data rate wireless communication technologies 'From Wi-Fi to WiMAX'" IEEE ICAS05, October 2005
2. H. Yaghoobi, Intel Communications Group, Intel Corporation "Scalable OFDMA Physical Layer in IEEE 802.16 WirelessMAN" Intel Technology Journal, Volume 8, Issue 3, 2004
3. 802.16-2004 IEEE Standard for Local and metropolitan area networks Part 16: Air Interface for Fixed Broadband Wireless Access Systems, October 2004
4. 802.16e-2005 IEEE Standard for Local and metropolitan area networks Part 16: Air Interface for Fixed Broadband Wireless Access Systems, February 2006
5. J. Sun, Y. Yao, H. Zhu "Quality of Service Scheduling for 802.16 BroadbandWireless Access Systems" IEEE VTC 2006_spring, May 2006
6. R. Prasad and R. Van Nee "OFDM for Wireless Multimedia Communications" Boston, London: Artech House Publishers, 2000.
7. L. Berlemann, C. Hoymann, G. R. Hiertz, S. Mangold "Coexistence and Interworking of IEEE 802.16 and IEEE 802.11(e)" IEEE VTC 2006_Spring, May 2006
8. M. Mulligan "Executable specification for the WiMAX Standard" The MathWorks News&Notes, October 2006, p18-19.

9. 802.11a-1999 IEEE Standard for Information technology Telecommunications and information exchange between systems Local and metropolitan area networks Part 11: Wireless LAN Medium AccessControl (MAC) and Physical Layer (PHY) specifications
10. D. R.. Pauluzzi and N. C. Beaulieu "A Comparison of SNR Estimation Techniques for the AWGN Channel" IEEE Transactions on communications, vol. 48, no. 10, October 2000
11. S. He and M. Torkelson, "Effective SNR estimation in OFDM system simulation" IEEE Global Telecommunications Conf., November 1998, pp. 945–950.

IEEE 802.11 Goodput Analysis for Mixed Real Time and Data Traffic

Alex Grote, Walter Grote, Rodolfo Feick

Electronics Department of Universidad Tecnica Federico Santa Maria,

Casilla 110-V, Av. España 1680 Valparaiso, Chile

{agrote, wgrote, feick} @elo.utfsm.cl

Abstract An IEEE 802.11 analytical performance evaluation model for ad-hoc WLAN's comprising terminals with different traffic source characteristics is presented. Although some publications address this issue, most of them propose to modify the original standard by some means that will affect the probability of transmission of a device when the network reaches congestion. The approach of this publication is to be able to establish a set of equations such that an intelligent choice of configuration parameters of standard home devices may improve the performance of the wireless network. Actually, two models are presented and compared, a simple one based on stationary behavior of the network assuming collisions have a negligible effect on network performance, and a second model based on a stationary stochastic model of a network, where devices have a packet ready for transmission at all times.

1 Introduction

Wireless Local Area Networks (WLAN) have expanded massively since the original IEEE 802.11 standard [1] was published in 1999. The amount of devices that use this wireless technology to communicate has increased significantly, a pattern that shows no signs of change since a migration from desktop computers to notebooks can be observed in recent years, of which almost all have a WLAN card preinstalled. User applications have an increasing tendency to require larger bandwidths than it used to. Consequently, amendments to the original standard have been introduced to allow higher data transmission rates (IEEE 802.11b [2] at 11 Mbps, IEEE 802.11a [3] and IEEE 802.11g [4] at 54 Mbps). Quality of Service (QoS) has also been incorporated with the recent publication of IEEE 802.11e standard [5], to provide a means to prioritize traffic sent over a wireless LAN to reduce delay for real-time applications as well as other features to enhance the original protocol. Further needs for higher goodput gave way to amendment IEEE 802.11n [6], which will provide users with at least 100 Mbps wireless connec-

Please use the following format when citing this chapter:

Grote, A., Grote, W., Feick, R., 2007, in IFIP International Federation for Information Processing, Volume 256, Home Networking, Al Agha, K., Carcelle, X., Pujolle, G., (Boston: Springer), pp. 15-28.

tions. These enhancements try to avoid saturation occurrences in wireless networks to provide the connected users with a reliable and fast connection. However, all these enhancements point in the direction of the main focus of this publication: quality assurance for devices operating in IEEE 802.11 wireless networks when operating under different application requirements. The scope of this publication is to be able to establish a set of equations such that an intelligent choice of configuration parameters of standard IEEE.802.11 home devices may improve the performance of the wireless network. Actually, two models are presented and compared, a simple one based on stationary behavior of the network assuming collisions have a negligible effect on network performance, and a second model based on a stationary stochastic model of a network, where devices have a packet ready for transmission at all times. Due to space limitations we will concentrate on ad-hoc networks, but the extension of this analysis to infrastructure network will be quite straightforward.

IEEE 802.11 networks may operate in the ad-hoc mode, where terminals communicate with each other without the need of a centralized access point that is a gateway to a wired backbone network. Random CSMA/CA access is possible by configuring wireless devices of such a network in the DCF (Distributed Coordination Function) mode. DCF employs a backoff mechanism to inhibit transmission once a packet arrives for transmission. The initial value is chosen randomly between 0 and maximum contention window (CW) value. The initial value for the contention window is CW_{min}. This value is increased exponentially by the terminal that is transmitting whenever the transmitted frame collides, thus $CW = 2^{i} \cdot CW_{min}$ where i represents the number of retransmissions. The counter is decreased from the initial value every time that an idle slot time is registered after the successful transmission, followed by a DIFS time. Once the counter reaches zero the terminal transmits. When a successful transmission takes place, all the terminals of the network that are in the transmission range of the terminal that emits the signal learn how long that transmission will take and pause their backoff counters during that time period.

The access mechanisms defined by DCF are basic access (two-way handshake) and RTS/CTS (four-way handshake). The basic access mode consists of sending a data frame and receiving an acknowledgement (ACK) frame from the destination. RTS/CTS involves reserving the shared medium by the source, sending a RTS (Request To Send) to be responded by a CTS (Clear To Send) packet from the destination, if successfully received, after which the data frame is sent, followed by an ACK. A mixed operation is possible defining a threshold that determines the maximum size of a frame that can be transmitted using basic access. If the frame of user data to be sent is larger than this threshold, a RTS packet is issued by the source, instead of sending the user data frame immediately.

Nowadays terminals present in an ad-hoc network may generate different types of traffic, such as web oriented data traffic, massive file exchanges, real-time voice or video. They also may be configured to set parameter values for the RTS Threshold and initial and maximum contention window settings. The challenge is to be able to come up with a model that will make it possible to optimize network performance. We will propose two models aimed to provide solutions for this challenge, based upon recent contributions.

G. Bianchi presents an analytical model to calculate the saturation throughput of a wireless network operating with IEEE 802.11 protocol with a stationary analysis of a stochastic model in [7]. H. Wu et al [8] and Ziouva et al [9] complete the CSMA/CA protocol model of Bianchi, incorporating a maximum number of retransmissions per packet in the backoff algorithm. Y. Xiao [10] improves Ziouva's model by limiting the number of retransmissions and evaluates other performance parameters such as packet drops, packet drop time, throughput limit and saturation delay. The work presented in [11] evaluates the RTS/CTS mechanism comparing it to the basic access mode and presents a method to dynamically modify the contention window to achieve the maximum throughput limit. Y. Xiao et al [12] provide a study of maximum theoretical goodput and delay. J. Jun et al [13] show maximum throughput for IEEE 802.11 networks in absence of errors for different transmission rates and packet sizes.

It is known that voice and video transmission are sensitive to delay and jitter but not so for packet loss as long as losses are less than 5%, [14]. Data packets on the other side are sensitive to packet loss but not so for delays and jitter. In [15] a study is performed to indicate the maximum amount of voice users that an infrastructure network supports for different voice codecs and includes the importance of asymmetric traffic that the access point must transfer, offering a better model than the ones presented in [16-18]. However, these four studies do not consider changing the access priority for the terminals that compose the wireless network. Y. Lin et al [19] develops an analytical model to obtain the saturation throughput for the IEEE 802.11e [5] protocol which is validated by Ns2 [20]. [5] introduces QoS to wireless networks by differentiating traffic packets and based on this assigns minimum contention windows among other amendments. In a simple scenario it is shown that priority packets may reduce the idle DIFS time, thus increasing their probability of successful transmission.

However, none of the above publications address simultaneously the problem of a network dealing with devices that handle different traffic and packet sizes, maximizing performance by setting RTS/CTS Threshold and contention window parameters for each class of stations when employing legacy IEEE 802.11 a/b/g protocols.

2 IEEE 802.11 Throughput Analysis

The IEEE 802.11 standard [1] and its subsequent amendments [2-6] have been characterized by having a high overhead. Throughput obtained on the wireless network is a fraction of the operational transmission rates, e.g. IEEE 802.11b [2] only achieves a maximum 6 Mbps throughput with a transmission rate of 11 Mbps, the exact result depending on the initial contention window size, employing maximum packet size and assuming that no collisions occur to access the channel.

IEEE 802.11a/g show similar behavior even though using higher transmission rates, which may be analyzed as follows.

The maximum available throughput of the IEEE 802.11 standard variations [1]-[4] depend on parameter settings defined by each standard. In Table 1 a summary of parameter values for different standard versions are shown. Some parameters are set to default values in wireless devices, while others may be dependent on the environment where the network is being deployed. For instance, if the wireless network is bridged to an Ethernet, packet size is limited to a maximum of 1500 bytes, as Table 1 shows. Actually, the IEEE 802.11 wireless standards have different values, but for analysis purposes it is advisable to use this value since most wireless networks conforming to this standard are bridged to an Ethernet network. Data rates may vary, depending on channel interference or signal to noise ratio. The contention window settings shown are default values, but may be changed in actual devices and the propagation and processing time may vary depending on the distance among devices.

Table 1. Transmission Parameters IEEE 802.11a/b/g

Parameter	b	a/g	Units
Slot time σ	20	9	μs
SIFS	10	10	μs
DIFS	50	28	μs
ACK	14	14	Bytes
CTS	14	14	Bytes
RTS	20	20	Bytes
MAC header	28	28	Bytes
PLCP header long	192	20	μs
PLCP header short	96	-	μs
Maximum Data Packet Size	1500	1500	Bytes
Header rates R_H	1, 2	6	Mbps
Data rates R_D	1, 2, 5.5, 11	6, 12, 18, 24, 36, 48, 54	Mbps
CW_{min} Minimum Contention Window	32	16	
CW_{max} Maximum Contention Window	1024	1024	
Propagation and Processing Time	1	1	μs

Terminals operating with a DCF CSMA/CA IEEE 802.11 protocol monitor the channel for an idle time, followed by a Distributed Inter-Frame Space (DIFS), and execute the backoff algorithm to send a data frame. The receiver sends an acknowledgement (ACK) after a Short Inter-Frame Space (SIFS) period. After the ACK is received the whole cycle commences again, in which the terminals must wait a DIFS period and a backoff period before transmission.

Goodput is a performance measure that considers the amount of user data transmitted, divided by the time it takes to successfully transmit it. Goodput and throughput are related performance parameters: to obtain throughput from a goodput expression simply divide the latter by the data transmission rate. Since IEEE 802.11 standards can be differentiated by transmission rate, we prefer to use goodput as a performance parameter. Ideal goodput can be calculated as shown in equation (1) not taking into account propagation delay and where L_{data} is the length of data in bits and T_{succ} is the time required to successfully transmit the data frame. T_I is the time the channel remains idle and T_{coll} is the time involved in collisions. When computing ideal goodput, collisions are disregarded ($T_{coll} = 0$) and T_I is equal to the median contention window size times the slot times, expressed in equation (3).

$$S = \frac{L_{data}}{T_I + T_{succ} + T_{coll}}$$
(1)

Equation (2) describes the time required for a successful transmission.

$$T_{succ} = \frac{2 \cdot PCLP + MAC + ACK}{R_H} + \frac{L_{data}}{R_D} + SIFS + DIFS$$
(2)

$$T_I = \frac{(CW_{min} - 1) \cdot \sigma}{2}$$
(3)

Combining equations (1), (2) and (3) and replacing parameter values with the ones specified in the standards (a summary of which have been listed in table 1), it is possible to compute maximum goodput for IEEE 802.11b. For instance, IEEE 802.11b networks that transfer packets of 1500 bytes, assuming $R_H = 1$ Mbps, $R_D = 11$ Mbps, no collisions, results in an effective goodput of 6.4 Mbps. To calculate the goodput for IEEE 802.11a/g the equation must be slightly modified to adjust packet sizes with padding to fit to OFDM (Orthogonal Frequency Division Multiplexing) symbol transmission requirements.

Goodput analysis is normally performed for fixed packet sizes, not having in mind that different applications running on the same network may produce different sizes with different delay requirements. To take into account that the network may be serving different applications equation (1) may be modified. Define a group of d (for data) terminals to transmit data packets of size L_d at a data transmission rate R_d, using an initial contention window CW_{dmin} to access the channel utilizing either basic access mode or RTS/CTS. Another group of v (for voice) terminals to transmit data packets of size L_v at a data transmission rate R_v, using an initial contention window CW_{vmin} to access the channel. To develop an ideal goodput expression, consider that on average all terminals configured with CW_{dmin} access the channel during a transmission cycle once. For arbitrary reasons CW_{vmin} will be equal or less than CW_{dmin}. We will later learn that in order to favor access to real time applications like voice, for instance, this will be a convenient setup. Therefore, in a transmission cycle d transmissions will take place, while, on the other hand, there will be $v \cdot CW_{dmin}/CW_{vmin}$ transmissions of the remaining v terminals. Thus the goodput expression may be written as follows.

$$S = \frac{\left(\dfrac{v \cdot CW_{d\,min}}{d \cdot CW_{v\,min}}\right)L_v + L_d}{\left(\dfrac{v \cdot CW_{d\,min}}{d \cdot CW_{v\,min}}\right) \cdot \left(Tv_I + Tv_{succ}\right) + \left(Td_I + Td_{succ}\right)} \tag{4}$$

Tv_I is the median idle time for the v terminals and Tv_{succ}, and likewise for the d terminals. Thus modifying the value of CW_{min} for the v and d terminals it is possible to grant higher channel access probability to the terminals that require it.

We would like to point out that the idea of separating goodput expressions according to applications is a powerful concept, because it makes it possible to study the effect of configuration parameter settings on terminals running a specific application, not only to on its own group, but also on the other goodput expressions and the total of the network. This is a concept the authors have not seen in the existing literature and may prove to be quite useful for network administrators.

3 IEEE 802.11 Goodput with stochastic model

Similar equations can be developed considering Bianchi's [7] and Wu's [8] approach for stochastic models. Equation (5) shows a generalized formula based on the aforementioned works.

$$S = \frac{L_{data}}{T_I \cdot P_I + T_{succ} \cdot P_{succ} + T_{coll} \cdot P_{coll}} \tag{5}$$

P_I is the probability that the channel remains idle, P_{succ} is the probability that during a contention slot a successful transmission occurs and P_{coll} is the probability that a collision occurs. T_{coll} is the time required to resolve a collision. This model assumes the channel is error free, collisions among ACK and CTS packages are negligible if RTS/CTS is used, no hidden or exposed terminal is present, fixed size packets are transmitted over the network and terminals operate in saturation to ensure the network may achieve the maximum obtainable goodput. The stationary transmission probabilities of a terminal can be readily obtained from references [7] and [8]. These probabilities only depend on the backoff mechanism of the stations.

$$\tau = \begin{cases} if \quad r \le m, \\ \dfrac{2(1-2p)(1-p^{r+1})}{W(1-(2p)^{r+1})(1-p)+(1-2p)(1-p^{r+1})} \\ if \quad r > m, \\ \dfrac{2(1-2p)(1-p^{r+1})}{W(1-(2p)^{m+1})(1-p)+(1-2p)(1-p^{r+1})+W2^m p^{m+1}(1-2p)(1-p^{r-m})} \end{cases} \qquad (6)$$

The probability that a terminal transmits τ, equation (6), depends on the collision probability p, CW_{min} and the maximum contention window CW_{max} and the number of retransmissions r. The protocol defines that at most 4 retransmissions per packet may take place when operating in basic access mode and 7 in RTS/CTS mode. The number of backoff states (m) depends on CW_{min} and CW_{max} given by equation (7).

$$CW_{max} = 2^m \cdot CW_{min} = 2^m \cdot W \qquad (7)$$

The probability that a station collides (p) is given by equation (8).

$$p = P\left(collision \big| one\_terminal\_Tx\right)$$
$$= \left(1-(1-\tau)^{n-1}\right) \qquad (8)$$

It is possible to set up an equation system with the relations developed in (6) to (8), thus obtaining the stationary probabilities that a contention slot may stay idle, a successful transmission takes place or a collision occurs. The probabilities are shown in the following equations and combining these results with (6) it is possible to determine the goodput of the system.

$$P_I = (1-\tau)^n \qquad (9)$$
$$P_{succ} = n\tau(1-\tau)^{n-1} \qquad (10)$$
$$P_{coll} = \left(1-(1-\tau)^n - n \cdot \tau \cdot (1-\tau)^{n-1}\right) \qquad (11)$$

It is possible to extend this to terminals that transmit different types of traffic as described in the previous section. Equation (6) may be written as the sum of goodputs of 2 different traffic types, (12), which has the advantage of being able to individualize contributions of the overall network performance.

$$S_{total} = S_d + S_v \qquad (12)$$

Where

$$S_d = \frac{L_d \cdot Pd_{succ}}{T_I \cdot P_I + T_S + T_{coll}} \tag{13}$$

$$T_S = Td_{succ} \cdot Pd_{succ} + Tv_{succ} \cdot Pv_{succ}$$

$$S_v = \frac{L_v \cdot Pv_{succ}}{T_I \cdot P_I + T_S + T_{coll}} \tag{14}$$

$$T_S = Td_{succ} \cdot Pd_{succ} + Tv_{succ} \cdot Pv_{succ}$$

The probability that a d station suffers a collision when it tries to transmit is one minus the probability that no other terminal in the network transmits, equation (15).

$$p_d = P\left(\text{collision}\middle|\text{d\_terminal\_Tx}\right)$$
$$= \left(1 - (1 - \tau_d)^{d-1}(1 - \tau_v)^v\right) \tag{15}$$

The same expression may be derived for the v terminals replacing the subscript d by v and vice versa. Equation (15) in conjunction with a modified equation (6), where a probability of transmission is described for d and v terminals, creates a set of 5 equations employing equation (7) as well. The probability of an idle slot is given by equation (16).

$$P_I = (1 - \tau_d)^d (1 - \tau_v)^v \tag{16}$$

T_I is equal to a slot time σ. The probability of a successful transmission of a d terminal is given by the probability that only one d terminal transmits in a time slot and that no other d terminals transmit during this time and also that no v terminals transmit. For a v terminal similar equations are shown in (17) and (18). Time associated to a successful transmission of a d or v terminal is similar to equation (2) but the subscript $data$ of L_{data} needs to be replaced by d or v to reflect the appropriate payload.

$$Pd_{succ} = d \cdot \tau_d (1 - \tau_d)^{d-1} (1 - \tau_v)^v \tag{17}$$

$$Pv_{succ} = (1 - \tau_d)^d \cdot v \cdot \tau_v (1 - \tau_v)^{v-1} \tag{18}$$

Collision time is expressed by equation (19), where the collision probability is multiplied by the time it takes to resolve that particular collision Td_{coll} or Tv_{coll} (if it involves two different packet sizes, it will always be the larger packet transmission). These times are identical to a successful transmission times.

$$T_{coll} = \left(1 - (1 - \tau_v)^v\right) \cdot \left(1 - (1 - \tau_d)^d\right) \cdot Td_{coll} +$$
$$+ \left(1 - (1 - \tau_d)^d - d \cdot \tau_d \cdot (1 - \tau_d)^{d-1}\right) \cdot Td_{coll} + \tag{19}$$
$$+ \left(1 - (1 - \tau_v)^v - v \cdot \tau_v \cdot (1 - \tau_v)^{v-1}\right) \cdot Tv_{coll}$$

Combining equations (12)-(19) it is possible to model an ad-hoc network for 2 different kinds of traffic.

4 Saturation Goodput Analysis

Two models that deliver saturation goodput in presence of different traffic types were developed in the previous section. The stochastic model was contrasted to the work done in [19] obtaining identical results. The model developed in section 2 is very simple but provides a quick way to obtain maximum saturation goodput levels.

Employing the parameters from Table 1 for the IEEE 802.11b standard and configuring the maximum transmission speed for the frame payload and headers, basic access mode, long PLCP and two different packet sizes, it is possible to analyze the effect of varying the CW_{min} of the different traffic sources on the saturation goodput of the network. All terminals are in the transmission range of each other and may employ the maximum transmission rate to communicate amongst each other.

A real-time application like voice is transmitted by v terminals. Voice packets should have preferences over data packets transmitted by the d terminals to access the channel. The v terminals will transmit packets of $L_v = 50$ bytes. This packet size is calculated for the G.729A codec, where the voice packet of 10 bytes is encapsulated adding 12 bytes of RTP header, 8 bytes of UDP header and 20 bytes of IPv4 header. Assume data terminals have CWd_{min} set to the default value of 32 and transmit packets of size $L_d = 1500$ bytes. To reduce delay times and delay jitter for voice packet transmissions, let us decrease the value of CW_{min} from the default value of 32 to 16, 8 and 4 for the v terminals. The remaining parameters of all terminals are kept at the default values of the IEEE 802.11b standard. This should have impact on voice, data transmissions and global saturation goodput, Figure 1 shows a scenario where the number of v terminals is increased from 0 to 10, the total being always 10 terminals, evaluated for both models.

Figure 1 shows that indeed reducing delays on voice packets by increasing their transmission probability has an effect over both the aggregate goodput of voice and data terminals. As more voice terminals are incorporated into the network the overall goodput of the network decreases and the aggregate goodput of the voice terminals increases. Diminishing the CWv_{min} grants a higher channel access preference for VoIP packets and this is clearly reflected in both aggregate goodputs of the data terminals and voice terminals. Since smaller VoIP packets have a larger overhead from the MAC IEEE 802.11 layer, their transmission significantly reduces overall goodput of the network. Both figures incorporate a threshold ($S_{Voice\ Minimum}$) curve that represents the minimum aggregate goodput that G.729A codec require to maintain seamless conversations. Thus the aggregate goodput of the v terminals must be over this threshold to support the required goodput.

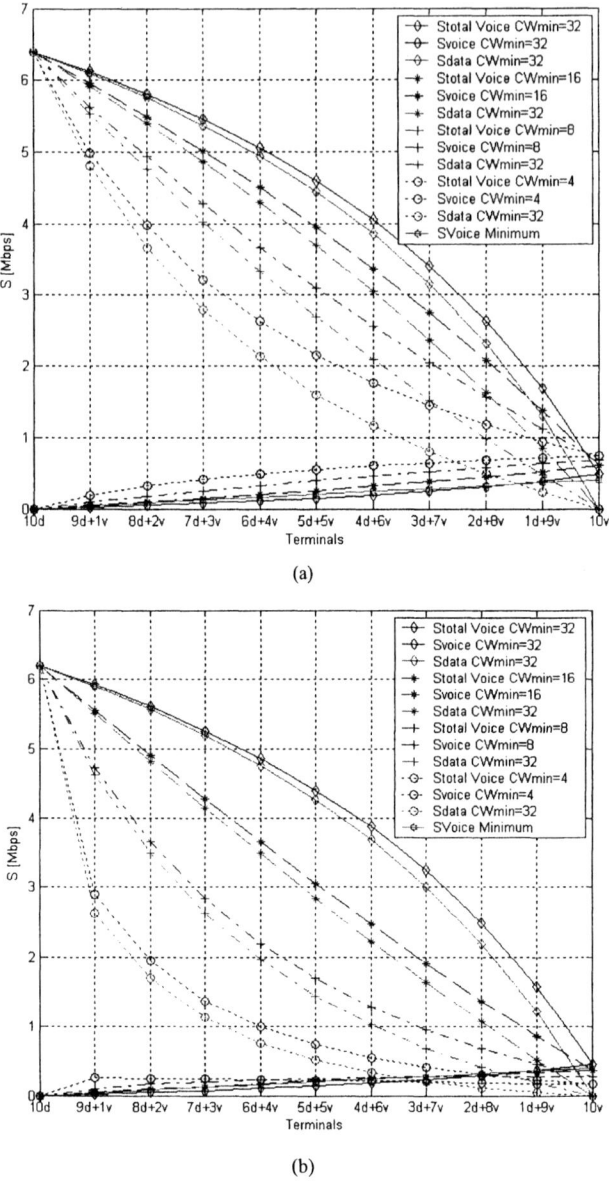

(a)

(b)

Fig. 1. Ad-hoc network with 10 terminals varying the amount of *v* terminal (a) Ideal (Deterministic) model (b) Stochastic model

When CWv_{min} is small, it can be clearly seen that the ideal (deterministic) model does not incorporate collisions and provides an optimistic scenario, when compared to the more accurate stochastic model. However it shows clearly the effect of the contention window parameter setting on goodput when dealing with different traffic types. The accuracy of this model when dealing with small initial contention windows and large number of voice terminals is not good as compared to the more accurate stochastic model. Therefore the deterministic model must be used cautiously when these situations arise since this is a clear case when collisions should start occurring.

The selection of CWv_{min} to improve quality of service for real-time voice station requirements can be done by looking at goodput performance, since higher goodput can be associated to lower delays and delay jitter. Figure 1 shows overall performance, but Table 2 is more accurate than Figure 1, when the decision has to be taken whether the aggregate goodput for voice terminals is sufficient to sustain the minimum required data rate for the vocoder (40 [kbps]). In Table 2 aggregate goodput for voice terminals is shown as calculated by applying both models for certain amounts of voice and data terminals and may be compared to the minimum required aggregate transmission rate, $S_{Voice\ Minimum}$ *(Codec)*. This value for 3 voice terminals is 120 kbps, as Table 2 shows.

Table 2. Goodput values for Voice Terminals from Fig. 1 with different CWv_{min} values

Model	Aggregate Goodput for Voice Terminals, [kbps]		
Number of Terminals	$7d+3v$	$4d+6v$	$d+9v$
$S_{Voice\ Minimum}$ *(Codec)*	120	240	360
Deterministic $CWv_{min} = 32$	77	193	388
Deterministic $CWv_{min} = 16$	144	315	524
Deterministic $CWv_{min} = 8$	254	462	635
Stochastic $CWv_{min} = 32$	74	184	365
Stochastic $CWv_{min} = 16$	133	248	344
Stochastic $CWv_{min} = 8$	208	264	276

Table 2 demonstrates that both models predict that the minimum required aggregate goodput is not met when $CWv_{min} = 32$ and there are less then 7 voice terminals, for the codec used in this example. It can be seen that while the minimum aggregate data rate for 3 voice terminals is 120 [kbps], only less than 80 [kbps] can be provided by the network, as calculated by both models. Similarly, when 6 voice terminals are part of the network, the minimum aggregate data rate should be 240 [kbps], but according to both models, aggregate goodput is less than 200 [kbps]. Under these circumstances, selecting $CWv_{min} = 16$ provides the required minimum data rate transfer for the voice codecs (see Table 2), while not deteriorating data packet goodput significantly (see Figure 1). Clearly, when 9 voice terminals are present, the deterministic model does not predict that the aggregate goodput is not enough to sustain seamless voice connections when $CWv_{min} = 8$ or

16. However it is possible to predict that under default configuration, voice terminals will provide the necessary goodput conditions. This configuration recommendation can only be issued because our approach has been to model both goodputs independently and not as a whole, as most approaches do.

Another interesting aspect is that the configuration recommendations obtained applying the deterministic (collision free) model predict are quite similar to the more precise stochastic model, when the number of voice terminals is not large, although overall goodput values are overestimated. This result has not been reported in the literature, as far as the authors know, and constitutes valuable information for network administrators, since the deterministic model is fairly simple to compute, as compared with the more accurate stochastic model.

5 Conclusions

The migration to technologies that rely on IP networks to transmit media rich content demand assigning priority to applications that cannot accept significant delays. Increasingly, wireless networks intended to provide data terminal connections are being used to transmit other kind of information. Therefore it will be relevant to be able to tune configuration parameters of the network devices to optimize network performance using models like the ones proposed in this publication.

Two goodput performance models were presented and compared, a simple one based on stationary behavior of the network, assuming collisions have a negligible effect on network performance, and a second model based on a stationary stochastic model of a network. These models address the problem of a wireless IEEE 802.11 network with devices that generate different traffic patterns (packet sizes and delay constraints), making it possible to analyze goodput performance either for the total network or a specific group of terminals. Parameter settings of the existing standards, like RTS/CTS Threshold, and initial (and maximum) contention window for classes of stations handling traffic of different nature – voice, video, data, multimedia and web traffic – can be varied, as well as the number of participating stations in each class, to study the effect on goodput performance. The use of the simpler model may provide a quick –but less accurate – approach to determine the saturation goodput of a wireless network for network administrators work to design and deploy a network. A more elaborate model that models the wireless channel access more accurately under similar conditions was also presented.

The fact that our approach consisted in evaluating goodput independently for parameters running different applications, makes it possible to analyze the effect of configuration parameter settings not only on total goodput, but also for individual applications, thus making it possible to tune these parameters for best performance. This is an approach the authors have not detected in prior publications.

Due to space limitations we concentrated our analysis on ad-hoc networks, but the extension of this analysis to infrastructure networks is quite straightforward. The application of these models by network administrators is a good practice, especially if the nature of terminals connected to the network, and their traffic patterns are well known. By elaborating on a simple example, we have shown that not always default values of network parameters will provide satisfactory network performance and it pays off to consider changing them to more convenient settings.

Acknowledgement

This work was supported in part by CONICYT under Grant by project PBCT ACT-11-04 and project UTFSM 23.07.21

References

1. ANSI/IEEE Std 802.11, *Wireless LAN Medium Access Control (MAC) and Physical Layer (PHY) Specifications* (1999 Edition)
2. IEEE Std 802.11b-1999, *Wireless LAN Medium Access Control (MAC) and Physical Layer (PHY) specifications: High-speed Physical Layer in the 2.4 GHZ Band*
3. IEEE Std 802.11a-1999, *Wireless LAN Medium Access Control (MAC) and Physical Layer (PHY) specifications: High-speed Physical Layer in the 5 GHZ Band*
4. IEEE Std 802.11g-2003, *Wireless LAN Medium Access Control (MAC) and Physical Layer (PHY) specifications Amendment 4: Further Higher Data Rate Extension in the 2.4 GHZ Band*
5. IEEE Std. 802.11e, Wireless *medium access control (MAC) and physical layer (PHY) specifications: Medium access control (MAC) enhancements for quality of service (QoS)* (November 2005)
6. IEEE P802.11n Draft 1.0, *Amendment to STANDARD [FOR] Information Technology-Telecommunications and information exchange between systems-Local and Metropolitan networks-Specific requirements-Part 11: Wireless LAN Medium Access Control (MAC) and Physical Layer (PHY) specifications: Enhancements for Higher Throughput*
7. G. Bianchi, Performance Analysis of the IEEE 802.11 Distributed Coordination Function, *IEEE Journal on Selected Areas in Communications*, V.18, No.3 (March 2000)
8. H. Wu, Y. Peng, K. Long, and S. Cheng, A Simple Model of IEEE 802.11 Wireless LAN, *In Proc. IEEE International Conferences on Info-Tech and Info-net (ICII)*, Beijing, Vol. 2, pp. 514-519 (October 2001)
9. E. Ziouva, and T. Antonakopoulos, The Effect of Finite Population on IEEE 802.11 Wireless LAN Throughput/Delay Performance, *In Proc. 11ᵗʰ IEEE Mediterranean Electrotechnical Conference (MELECON)*, Egypt, pp. 95-99 (May 2002)
10. Y. Xiao, Saturation Performance Metrics of the IEEE 802.11 MAC, *In Proc. IEEE Vehicular Technology Conference (VTC) 2003-Fall*, pp. 1453-1457 (October 2003)
11. R. Bruno, M. Conti, and E. Gregori, IEEE 802.11 Optimal Performances: RTS/CTS Mechanism vs. Basic Access, *In Proc. 13th IEEE Symposium on Personal, Personal, Indoor and Mobile Radio Communications (PIMRC)*, Lisboa, Portugal, Vol. 4, pp. 1747-1751 (September 2002)

12. Y. Xiao, and J. Rosdahl, Throughput and Delay Limits of IEEE 802.11, *IEEE Communication Letters*, Vol. 6, No. 8 (August 2002)
13. J. Jun, P. Peddabachagari, and M. Sichitiu, Theoretical Maximum Throughput of IEEE 802.11 and its Applications, *In Proc. of the Second IEEE International Symposium on Network Computing and Applications*, Cambridge, pp. 249-256 (April 2003)
14. R. Onvural, *Asynchronous Transfer Mode Networks: Performance Issues* (2nd Ed, Artech House, 1995).
15. L.X. Cai, X. Shen, J.W. Mark, L. Cai, and Y. Xiao, Voice capacity analysis of WLAN with unbalanced traffic, *IEEE Transactions on Vehicular Technology*, Vol. 55, Issue 3, pp. 752-761 (May 2006)
16. S. Garg, and M. Kappes, An experimental study of throughput for UDP and VoIP traffic in IEEE 802.11b networks, *In Proc. IEEE WCNC*, Vol. 3, pp. 1748–1753 (March 2003)
17. S. Garg, and M. Kappes, Can I add a VoIP call?, *Proc. IEEE ICC*, Vol. 2, pp. 779–783 (May 2003)
18. D. P. Hole, and F. A. Tobagi, Capacity of an IEEE 802.11b wireless LAN supporting VoIP," *In Proc. IEEE ICC*, Vol. 1, pp. 196–201 (June 2004)
19. Y. Lin, and V.W.S Wong, Saturation throughput of IEEE 802.11e EDCA based on mean value analysis, *IEEE Wireless Communications and Networking Conference 2006, WCNC 2006*, Vol. 1, pp. 475 – 480 (April 2006)
20. ns2 Network Simulator; http://www.isi.edu/nsnam/ns/

An efficient trigger to improve intra-WiFi handover performance

Roberta Fracchia, Guillaume Vivier

Motorola Labs, Parc les Algorithmes, Saint-Aubin, 91193 Gif-sur-Yvette, France

Abstract Seamless mobility is now a key requirement for wireless communication systems and users are day after day thirstier of high speed connections. For
indoor communication, WLAN has become the most common technology. In this
paper we introduce a composite trigger for intra-system handover which can take
into account not only signal strength but also access point load and expected
throughput. Simulation results show that the proposed metric provides gains in
term of delays and system overall throughput in various scenarios.

I. INTRODUCTION

Cellular systems are now and from several years fully integrated in the communication landscape. They provide not only wireless connectivity but also seamless mobility: while moving, the users do not experience any interruption in their
service. For that purpose, cellular systems introduced a key feature: handover.
Seamless mobility has become hence a natural feature of any wireless communication system. In parallel, broadband wireless communication in the home, in office, even in public area (airport, railway station, shopping mall, etc...) has been
widely popularized thanks to the WLAN (WiFi). Cheap access points can be easily installed by any individual in its home. Moreover, with the advent of DSL, cable or fiber to the home, customers have access to multiple-play offers, including
broadband access to the internet, voice over IP, IPTV...Thus, the WLAN should
support more and more delay-constrained services (such as voice) providing an
equivalent experience than cellular systems. For that purpose, QoS support has
been introduced in WiFi with the amendment "e" of 802.11 as well as several
ways to mimic handover between various access points. Moreover, more and more
Access Points (AP), mostly offering free of charge services, are becoming available: users could select the less congested or closer AP, thus the AP offering the
best connection performance.

Please use the following format when citing this chapter:

Fracchia, R., Vivier, G., 2007, in IFIP International Federation for Information Processing, Volume 256, Home
Networking, Al Agha, K., Carcelle, X., Pujolle, G., (Boston: Springer), pp. 29-38.

Although numerous works have been done to improve the handover process between 802.11 access points (AP), the trigger to handover is often the same: either a connection loss in the basic scheme or simply the signal to interference and noise ratio. In addition, WiFi handover mechanisms often rely on mobile IP: the mobility is then handled at layer 3 which may lead to too high delay for real-time application.

This paper investigates different triggers, aiming at considering expected data rate or traffic load in the different AP. We propose a simple metric that improves the system capacity as well as individual handover delays. Moreover, we compare L2 and L3 handovers in terms of delay. Section 2 presents related work. Section 3 introduces the new metric and describes a practical implementation for evaluating this metric in the terminal side. Simulation results are provided in section 4 for various typical scenarios.

II. Related Works

Handover is a fundament mechanism to maintain seamless connections during mobility and different works proposing different handover triggers have been published.

Work in [1] proposes to perform a handover when the Received Signal Strength (RSS) on the new cell is higher than that on the old one. Thresholds, hysteresis times and dwell timers are considered.

This mechanism, that lets only to maintain the wireless connection, can be improved, as proposed in [2]: information on speed and mobile user position is used to estimate the time that would be spent in target cell if the handover would be performed. If this time is bigger than a minimum required time, then the handover is triggered. The minimum required time depends on handoff latency, decision latency and on the time necessary to receive, in the target cell, the same amount of data that would have been received in the current cell. However, even if this mechanism takes into account the data rate that could be used, it can not maximize the user performance, since it does not consider the load of each AP.

Conversely, paper [3] utilizes the beacon transmission delay to estimate the available bandwidth towards different APs and decide to hand over, but not the quality of the signal. Similarly, work [4] assumes that every AP broadcast its load, so that each user may decide to hand over considering the load of the new AP. Moreover, neighboring cell lists are broadcasted to facilitate handover. Authors of [5] instead define a 'transition zone' at the border of the cell coverage. When the user enters the transition zone of the current cell, thus leaving its cell, it hands over. When it enters the transition zone of a new cell, it determines if it can achieve a better QoS and, if necessary, it hands over. However this analysis is not periodically performed, thus reducing the gain that can be achieved.

The algorithm we are proposing tries to overcome the limitations of all these works.

III. Handover Trigger

The algorithm we propose combines all the available quality parameters (Signal plus Interference Noise Ratio –SINR-, Packet Error Rate -PER- and network load). In the following, we first describe the proposed trigger and then explain how to derive the metrics used by the trigger.

A. The proposed Triggers

We assume the handover is triggered by a "mobility management" process implemented on the mobile device, which controls continuously the performance of the wireless connection, evaluating the link quality and the channel occupancy, constantly monitored by the 802.11 interface, and triggers the handover toward another AP if needed.

The proposed trigger combines the measured physical layer throughput and the network load in order to maximize MAC layer performance. The metric used to activate the trigger is called "residual throughput" and it is defined as: Data Rate * (1 – PER) * (1 – Channel Occupation). By computing Data Rate * (1 – PER) we deduce the instantaneous PHY layer throughput that reflects the link quality. The word "residual" instead means that a part of network resource is already occupied by other users, and then the handover decision is only based on the remaining bandwidth at the user disposal. The handover trigger is based on a comparison between the estimation of the residual throughput on the current cell (namely, Current_residual_throughput) with the one that could be achieved on another cell (namely, Target_residual_throughput). If the ratio between Target_residual_throughput and Current_residual_throughput is bigger that a threshold,

$$\frac{Target\_residual\_throughput}{Current\_residual\_throughput} > Throughput\_m\arg in$$

then the handover is triggered.

After extensive simulations we decided to set the throughput_margin to 1.1, a value that avoids ping-pong effects and at the same time does not limit the gain that can be achieved with handovers.

B. Monitoring

To derive the Data Rate, the Channel Occupation and the PER, used to compute the residual throughput, the User Terminal (UT) performs measurements in the used cells and on broadcast messages sent by neighbouring APs. Moreover, in order to restrict the number of cells to measure, we assume that the user terminal is supplied with a list of the neighbouring cells, that are the most likely to fulfill the quality requirements at the user terminal location. In this way, measurements are performed only on the cells included in the neighbours list.

To estimate the bandwidth occupancy we consider the WiFi contention-based access mechanism (CSMA/CA): all subscriber stations continuously listen to the channel before competing for channel access. The usage of the channel bandwidth can be approximated as the ratio between the time in which the channel status is busy according to exchanged frames and the considered time interval. The MAC process records the channel busy time, then periodically calculates the channel occupancy percentage and transmits this information to the "mobility management" process.

Moreover, the MAC layer transmits to the "mobility management" process the SINR measured on downlink broadcast packets (Beacon messages) typically sent every 10 to 100ms. The "mobility management" process moreover transforms the measured SINR into the used data rate value, assuming that a SINR based Link Adaptation (LA) algorithm is implemented. A LA mechanism [6] consists in the selection for each packet transmission of the Modulation and Coding Scheme (MCS) most adapted to the instantaneous wireless link quality, and lets to better exploit the channel performance compared to a fixed data rate. Supposing that the best MCS is used for the current SINR, it is possible to know at all times the data rate and the PER (using SINR vs. PER look up tables). The "mobility management", using this information, evaluates the performance of available networks as described in the previous section.

IV. Simulation Results

In this section we present results obtained with simulation, showing the effectiveness of the proposed handover trigger. We consider different scenarios, with one or more UTs.

We evaluate the performance of the proposed algorithm providing simulation results derived with OPNET, by modifying the simulator distribution to implement the considered handover criteria, including the "mobility management" entity, which continuously controls the performance of wireless connection, and triggers the handover if needed.

We consider the 802.11g amendment [7], which operates in the 2.4GHz licensed band and offers coverage of 70-80 meters with a theoretical throughput of 54Mbps. We implemented also the link adaptation mechanism, varying the data rate from 6 Mbps for a SINR of 5.5 dB to 54 Mbps for a SINR of 28.2 dB.

A. Handover latency

In this section we evaluate the handover latency experienced using the residual throughput trigger. We compare the results with the latency of a basic handover trigger, which does not utilize the neighboring cell lists and is triggered by the lost of the connection.

We considered two different deployment scenarios, with layer-2 and layer-3 handover respectively.

A layer-2 handover is performed when the UT hands over between APs controlled by the same gateway. In this case the IP address doesn't change and, as a consequence, the use of Mobile IP to maintain the connection is not necessary.

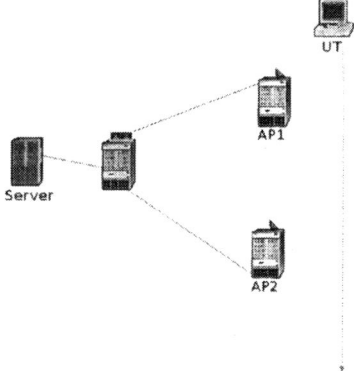

Figure 1. Reference scenario for the evaluation of the trigger without cell congestion

In this context, the handover latency is due to the scanning procedure, the handover decision and the authentication/reassociation phase. Since our simulator does not implement the exchange of signaling messages, the values reported in the figure do not include the authentication/reassociation delay. As reported in several work of measurements in WLANs, that delay usually varies between 5 and 15 ms, depending on the used card. To have a complete overview of the handover latency, these values have to be added to the simulation results.

A layer-3 (plus layer-2) handover is instead performed when the UT hands over between APs controlled by different gateways. In this case, the latency accounts also for the binding updates of the Mobile IP protocol.

The scenario we refer to is represented in Figure 1. Two APs are available and one user terminal, initially connected to AP1 moves away at 5m/s thus entering the coverage of AP2. Different positions of the BSs have been considered: results reported hereafter are averaged over all the performed simulations.

The simulations results are reported in Table 1. We can notice that also in case of layer-2 handover, the latency experienced using the basic trigger is too high to offer seamless mobility. The delay experienced using the residual throughput trigger instead it is equal to zero, since scanning and measurements are done rapidly and periodically on the cells of the neighbouring lists only and no more at the handover time. We have to remember that the signaling delay has to be added to the values reported in the table.

When Mobile IP has to be used to perform a layer-3 handover, the latency dramatically increases, even if the proposed trigger still offers better performance.

	proposed trigger	basic trigger
Layer2 HO	0	0.432 s
Layer2+Layer3 HO	2.7 s	3.6 s

Table 1: Handover latencies

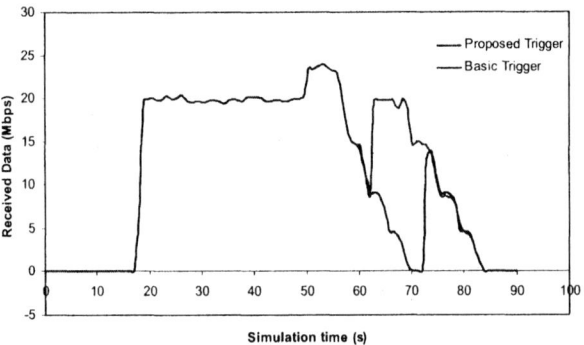

Figure 2. Received data as a function of the simulation time

B. Performance at connectivity's loss

In this section we evaluate the impact of the handover on different applications. We refer to the scenario presented in Figure 1 and we consider long-lived ftp connections generated at the Server node with a rate of 50Mbps.

We report in Figure 2 the amount of received data as a function of the simulation time. We consider again the residual throughput and the basic triggers. As you can see in the figure, the gain achieved with the proposed trigger is not only in terms of latency, but also in terms of achieved throughput: the UT, exploiting information already collected, is able to select the AP that can provide better performance. Without attending the loss of coverage, as soon as the target residual throughput increases the current residual throughput, the handover is performed.

Thus, the handover to another cell allows the use of higher data rates, related to the higher SINR, since an adaptive Modulation and Coding Scheme is adopted.

Finally we consider an interactive application like Voice over IP and we study how the residual throughput trigger impacts on the quality of the communication.

Figure 3 reports the packet delay at the application layer as a function of the simulation time. At the beginning of the communication, which is at 13 s, the UT is in the coverage of AP1 and the delay of the voice packets is about 80 ms. From that moment on, the UT moves in directions of AP2. In the case of the basic trigger, the handover to AP2 is triggered only when the coverage of AP1 is almost lost, that is at 68 s. The poor quality of the communication before the handover and the time necessary to scan all the channels to find the new AP introduce a high delay: you can observe the peak in the delay, that reaches 500 ms. Then the UT continues to move and exits from the coverage of AP2 at 85 s. There are not others APs, so that at 85 s the communication is interrupted. This explains the new arise in the delay between 80 and 85 s.

The behavior of the UT that uses the proposed trigger is the same. The difference in the experienced delay depends only on the handover from AP1 to AP2. Indeed, with the proposed trigger, the handover is performed immediately at 65 s, without degradation in the communication.

This figure clearly shows that the proposed trigger avoids the peaks in the delay due to the interruption of the communication in the classical handover process.

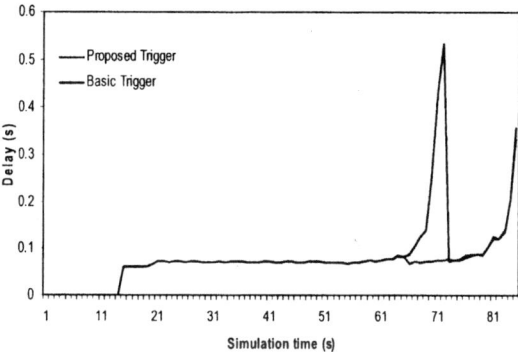

Figure 3. VoIP delay

C.   Performance in Congested Scenarios

In this section we show the performance gain that can be achieved performing handovers triggered by the residual throughput in different load conditions.

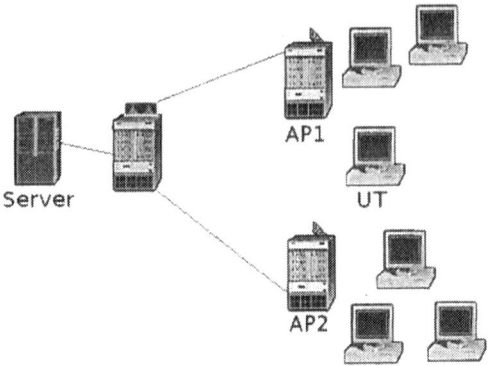

Figure 4. Reference scenario for the evaluation of the trigger with cell congestion

Consider as an example the topology presented in Figure 4. The user terminal UT is under the coverage of both AP1 and AP2 and it is initially connected to AP1. Assume that, due to its placement, the SINR of the radio channel to AP1 perceived by UT is 18.5dB. Then we vary the position of AP2 to achieve SINR in the second cell equal, lower and higher than that in the first cell. Moreover, we assume the other nodes connected to AP1 generate a load of 5 Mbps, while the load of AP2 is varying.

Figure 5 reports the layer 2 throughput achieved by station UT, as a function of the load ratio between the two cells, for different values of the SINR on the target channel (to AP2). The throughput achieved transmitting towards AP1, that is, if no handover is performed, is reported as a reference.

First of all, note that all the handovers result in a throughput gain. The estimation of the residual throughput indeed let the user correctly judge if advantages in performance can be achieved handing over. Moreover, we can gather that when the SINR on the target cell is higher than that one the current cell, the UT can profit of the handover until high values of load of the target cells. Otherwise, if the SINR and thus in the data rate that can be used are lower than that in the current cell, the handover is performed only when the load on the target cell is lower than that on the current cell.

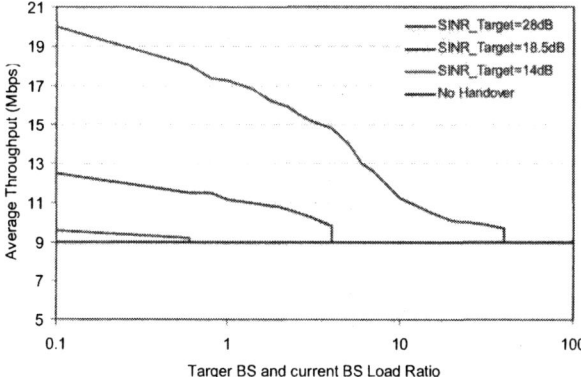

Figure 5. Average throughput of the UT as a function of the load on the target channel for different SINR values

V. Conclusions

In this paper we have simulated the handover between 2 WiFi access points. An efficient but simple metric to trigger the handover has been proposed to take into account user signal quality but also access point load. A practical mean to evaluate the metric was introduced, based on the 802.11 inherent mechanisms. Simulation performance shows that the proposed metric improves handover latency and system throughput, compared to basic handover mechanism.

Although this work concentrates on intra-WLAN handover, the metric can be easily extended to inter-system handover, when for instance WLAN and cellular system are collocated.

Acknowledgments This work has been partially performed in the framework of the IST project IST-4-027756 WINNER II, which is partly funded by the European Union. The authors would like to acknowledge the contributions of their colleagues.

References
[1] G.P. Pollini, Trends in handover design, IEEE Communication Magazine, Mar. 1996
[2] A. Saleh, A location-aided decision algorithm for handoff across heterogeneous wireless overlay networks, Master Thesis. Virginia Polytechnic Institute and State University, 2004
[3] S. Vasudevan, K. Papagiannaki, C. Diot, J. Kurose, and D. Towsley, "Facilitating Access Point Selection in IEEE 802.11 Wireless Networks," in ACM Sigcomm IMC, Oct. 2005.
[4] W. Zhang, J. Jähnert, K. Dolzer, Design and Evaluation of A Handover Decision Strategy for 4th Generation Mobile Networks, IEEE VTC, April 2003, Jeju, Korea.
[5] S. Balasubramaniam and J. Indulska, Vertical handover supporting pervasive computing in future wireless networks, Computer Communications, Volume 27, Issue 8, May 2004

[6] Goldsmith A.J., Chua S.-G., "Adaptive coded modulation for fading channels", IEEE Transactions on Communications, Volume 46, Issue 5, May 1998

[7] IEEE Computer Society, IEEE 802.11 Standard, "Part 11: Wireless LAN Medium Access Control (MAC) and Physical Layer (PHY) specifications", November 2001

Ultra Wide Band over fibre transparent architecture for High Bit-rate Home Networks

Anna Pizzinat, Franck Payoux, Benoit Charbonnier, Sylvain Meyer

France Telecom Research & Development, 2 Av. Pierre Marzin 22307 Lannion, France
Email: name.surname@orange-ftgroup.com

ABSTRACT

Bandwidth hungry services are developing rapidly in home networking and needs for Gigabit Home Networks will appear shortly, following the introduction of Gigabit optical access networks. In addition, ubiquitous wireless connectivity is required by users to connect multiple multimedia devices inside the home. Some wireless standards, such as Ultra Wide Band (UWB), are able to provide Gbit/s data rate but with a limited coverage. In order to extend this coverage, we propose a multipoint to multipoint (MP2MP) radio over fibre (RoF) architecture based on a NxN optical splitter. The UWB MAC layer is able to control the system and no optical MAC layer is required, so that the optical path becomes a "transparent tunnel". Simulations and experimental investigations demonstrate the technical feasibility of this innovative MP2MP RoF architecture.

1. INTRODUCTION

Today two phenomena are driving the increase of the bit rate needed in a home network. The first one is the multiplication of connected devices (i.e. computers, media centers, media renderers etc...) and of services available to the end user (i.e. domestic storage area network, video-phony and video conferencing, TVoIP, ToIP, etc...). The second phenomenon is the evolution of fiber to the home. As a consequence, a well connected home will need an internal network working at speeds of 1 Gbit/s by 2010 [1]. Whereas such a target might not be attained by current wired solutions, the large bandwidth of optical fibers makes them the only solution able to guarantee a long life to the network infrastructure and justify the expense for the installation of a new cable. Moreover, using an optical fiber as a home backbone may be seen as the natural prolongation of the optical access.

Additionally, it has to be noted that users have developed a strong preference for wireless connectivity and will require that future systems evolve to higher data rates while remaining wireless. A solution to this requirement can be found in UWB technology [2], [3]. UWB radio systems operate in the frequency range from 3.1 to 10.6 GHz and offer a wireless connectivity up to 1 Gbit/s, but, as a result, are limited in coverage to a few meters (< 10 m).

In this paper we propose to couple radio UWB systems to an optical fibre backbone as shown in figure 1 so to extend the UWB cell coverage to a few hundred meters, i.e. the typical dimension of an in-building network.

Please use the following format when citing this chapter:

Pizzinat, A., Payoux, F., Charbonnier, B., Meyer, S., 2007, in IFIP International Federation for Information Processing, Volume 256, Home Networking, Al Agha, K., Carcelle, X., Pujolle, G., (Boston: Springer), pp. 39-50.

The radio home networks will then become a multicellular network with the additional potential of transparently distributing, in parallel with the UWB signal mentioned above, other conventional baseband data signals (GbE etc..) or other radio signals throughout the house such as mobile signals (UMTS, 3G etc...), or different standards of WiFi (e.g. IEEE802.11n) [4], [5]. The important point is the mutualisation of the infrastructure that radio over fiber (RoF) achieves.

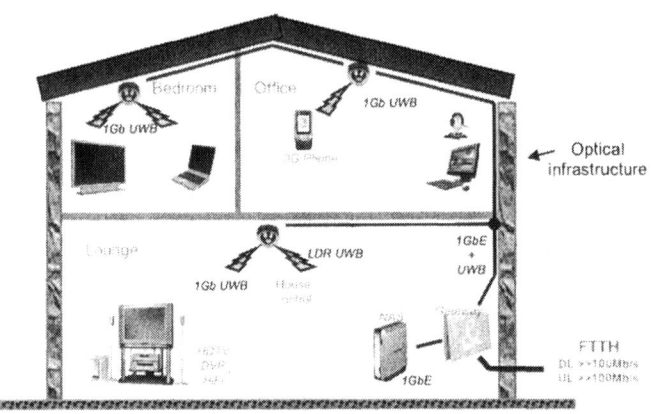

Figure 1: Very High Data Rate Home Area Network supported by an optical infrastructure

In particular, we use the optical fibre as a tunnel that allows enlarging an UWB cell in a completely transparent way, by means of a passive multipoint to multipoint (MP2MP) architecture based on an NxN splitter. This architecture is advantageous because it is equivalent to having all the users in the same room.

RoF has been demonstrated over many types of optical fiber even on legacy multimode fibers [6], but an analysis and experimentation of a complete system keeping into account at the same time for the radio and optical transmission is still lacking. In the following sections we will present the MP2MP architecture and how the RoF system operates. Then, we will introduce the system budget link calculation and compare it with numerical simulations. Finally, we will present the experimental results and come to conclusions.

2. MP2MP ARCHITECTURE

2.1 Physical operation

The proposed architecture is shown in figure 2 and described in [7]. The key point is the NxN optical splitter thanks to which a signal injected at a network input reaches all network outputs. The aim of this optical architecture is to extend the UWB cell coverage, so that it covers a whole apartment or building. Thus, two wireless devices located in two rooms relatively far away from each other can communicate as if they were close to each other. The system operates in the following manner: the signal sent by the first wireless device reaches the RoF transducer. The RoF transducer is mainly composed of one or two antennas, a laser for emission and a photodiode for reception as well as electrical amplifiers to partially compensate for losses induced by propagation in the air. The UWB signal is converted into an electrical signal by the RoF transducer antenna, and this UWB signal directly modulates the laser. The UWB signal in its native format is then carried by the optical physical layer. The signal is transparently propagated through the optical infrastructure. It is in particular broadcasted by the optical splitter to all RoF transducers connected to outputs of the splitter. This can be compared to the diffusion of the radio signal in a room. It has to be noted that the optical splitter is a passive component and does not require any powering. Optical signals are converted into electrical signals by photodiodes in RoF transducers and the original UWB signal is then sent by the antennas in all the other rooms covered by the network. The UWB signal is propagated without any modification at all and it reaches the second wireless device. The entire link is shown in Fig. 3.

As visible in Figure 2, two fibers are used for each transducer, in order to separate propagation directions. One fiber is connected to the laser and the other fiber is connected to the photodiode. The connections of fiber on the optical splitter are done in such a way that every emitted signal is received by all transducers, including itself.

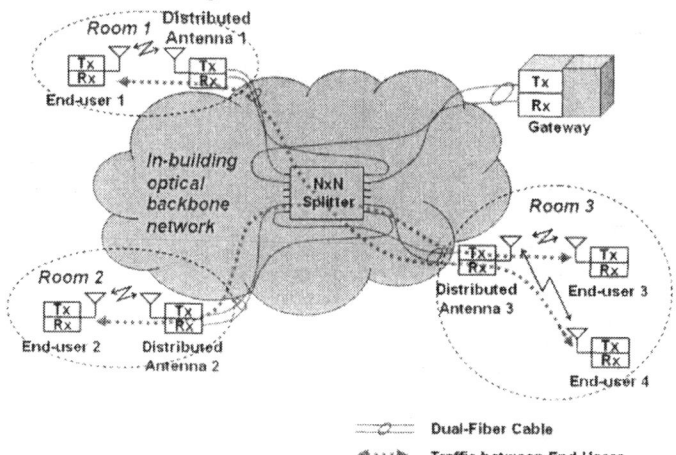

Figure 2: Hybrid Wireless-Optical MP2MP Architecture

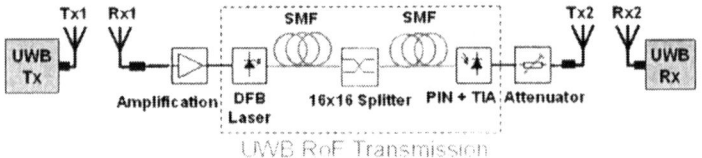

Figure 3: System setup

It has to be noted that the system is independent of the used radio format as far as it respects the laser and photodiode frequency bands. It means that such a system could be used to convey WiFi or 3G signals to extend the coverage of wireless and mobile networks.

2.2 MAC layer operation

With this architecture, the use of different wireless or mobile standards is limited to standards with a MAC layer able to operate with higher reach distances. UWB complies with this requirement and is particularly adequate to this architecture because of the distributed protocol integrated in ECMA 368 MAC layer (DRP: Distributed Reservation Protocol) [3]. There is no Piconet Controller in ECMA 368, each device has the same priority on the network. When a device wants to integrate a network, it first listens to see if grants are available and then it negotiates with all devices of the network to obtain some grants. DRP uses Time Division Multiplexing Access and that enables Quality of Service on the network.

In a classic network solution using two communications technologies (wireless and optical here) there are 2 different MAC layers, in our case, one for the UWB wireless communication, one for the optical communication (Ethernet MAC layer for example). Thanks to radio over fibre technology and to the proposed architecture, the UWB MAC layer alone is sufficient to control communications on the optical and wireless infrastructure. This MAC layer is implemented in end devices and RoF transducers are made of purely physical layer components without any intelligence. This is why the optical infrastructure can be considered as a transparent optical tunnel.

The fact that a device sending a signal receives it because of the connections on the optical splitter is not a problem. This occurs already in a single room with reflections on walls and objects. To avoid the reception of its own signal, the wireless device has an internal switch so that it is either in reception mode or in emission mode but not in both modes in the same time. In addition, in order to eliminate the echo after the end of emission, a guard time is added before switching to reception mode (and vice-versa). In UWB this guard time is 10μs, and during this time a signal can propagate over hundreds of meter of fibre and come back to the device without inducing interference problems. So the distance increase is well supported by the UWB MAC layer.

2.3 System constraints

An important choice concerns the fibre type. Indeed, for cost reasons the use of multi-mode fibre and VCSEL may be preferred, but the perennity of such a home backbone has also an important weight. Thus, we study numerically and experimentally the feasibility of the proposed system in the case of single-mode fibres (SMF). We use DFB lasers carefully controlled to operate in linear region and avoid laser clipping. Considering now only the RoF link between two end users, the link to be dimensioned takes the form shown in figure 3.

The power at the output of the transmitting antenna is fixed to -14 dBm for an OFDM band of 528 MHz (-41.3dBm/MHz is the maximum allowed output power density). The first three UWB bands have been considered.

Electrical amplification is needed before the laser so to partially compensate the free space losses. Optical losses, mainly due to the splitter, are lower than the optical budget given by the laser output power and the PIN photodiode sensitivity. The photoreceiver includes a trans-impedance amplifier that outputs the required electrical power to feed the antenna. The electrical amplification gain and the optical laser output power must be tuned to find a good compromise in terms of link budget and laser linearity, A 16x16 splitter is considered so to simulate 16 access points.

3. ANALYTICAL AND SIMULATION RESULTS

The link shown in figure 3 has been evaluated by means of analytical link budget calculations and extensive simulations using Matlab and VPI Transmission Maker.

Fist of all, the system shown in figure 3 has been analytically characterized in terms of link budget. The gain, noise factor and signal to noise ratio (SNR) at the UWB receiver have been calculated for the global link including radio and optical propagation [8]. The received bit error rate (BER) is also estimated from the SNR [9]. For the radio channel only free space losses have been taken into account as a first order approximation. In spite of being valid only for a linear system, the link budget calculation is of fundamental importance for the system dimensioning, i.e.: the ratio of the NxN coupler and the amplification stage.

For a BER of 10^{-5} without coding (that corresponds to error free propagation with coding), we have found that the dimension of the system can reach 16x16 for a propagation distance on each air link up to 10m.

Besides the system dimensioning, the amplification stage (Figure 3) is also a critical point of the system. This amplification stage is composed of a high gain low noise amplifier (LNA), followed by an electrical variable attenuator and a high power amplifier (HPA). The role of the LNA is to compensate the attenuation of the UWB signal due to the propagation in the first air link. The variable attenuator is used to keep constant the RF power at the laser input independently of the propagation distance on the first air link. Finally, the HPA is used to increase the RF power of the UWB signal at the input of the RoF link, in order to compensate the very weak RF gain of the RoF link (about -32.5dB). At the output of the RoF link, an electrical attenuator is used to ensure that the transmitting power of the Tx2 antenna respects the regulation. The parameters for all the system components are shown in Table 1.

DFB Laser	η_{EO}	$0.08W/A$ @ $I_{Bias} = 80mA$
	Z_{in}	$50\,\Omega$
	RIN	$-140\,dBc/Hz$
SMF	Length	$< 500m$
	Attenuation	$0.2\,dB/km$
	D	$16\,ps/nm/km$
PIN Photodiode	η_{OE}	$0.95\,A/W$
	Z_{out}	$50\,\Omega$
	Z_{TIA}	$500\,\Omega$
	NEP	$11.54\,pA/Hz^{1/2}$
Splitter	Ratio	$16x16$
Optical Loss	15dB (including 12dB optical loss of 16x16 splitter)	
Antenna	$G_{Tx/Rx}$	$7dB$
LNA	G	$56dB$
	NF	$0.6dB$
Var. Atten.	Att. Range	$0dB - 30dB$
HPA	G	$35dB$
	NF	$6dB$
Rx Pre-Amplifier	NF	$2.5dB$

Tab. 1: System parameters

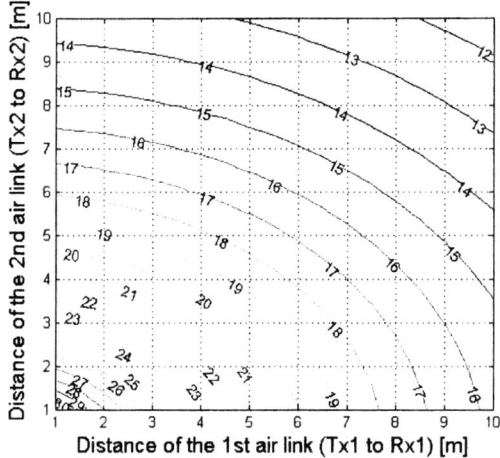

Figure 4 : Estimated SNR (dB) of the first UWB sub-band (3.432GHz) at the system output as a function of the propagation distance on the two air links.

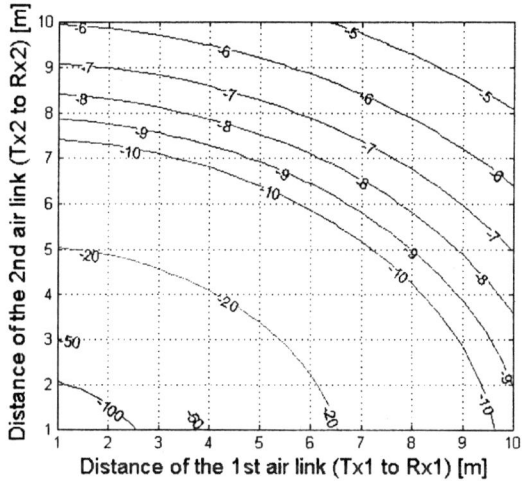

Figure 5: Estimated BER (log10) of the first UWB sub-band as a function of the propagation distance on the two air links.

Two other parameters can also be tuned: the laser input RF power and the laser polarisation current. Their values must be chosen so to avoid laser clipping and third order inter-modulation effects. VPI Transmission Maker simulations and the characterization of a RoF link showed that the RF power injected into the RoF link can be up to +18dBm without strong degradation due to the clipping effect of the laser. Therefore, the RF power injected into the RoF link is adjusted to +15dBm.

Figures 4 and 5 show the evolutions of the SNR and BER of the UWB signal transmitted through the optical - wireless hybrid system (fig. 3) as a function of the propagation distance on the two air links.

The system behavior has been then numerically simulated in Matlab and VPI in order to analyze also nonlinear effects in the electro-optic conversion. For these simulations, we generate a pseudo random bit sequence at 640Mbps for each OFDM sub-band, we apply QPSK modulation and obtain the OFDM signal according to [3] but without coding. Afterwards, we extract the UWB baseband signal and load it into VPI. There, the UWB signal is transposed in frequency to create the OFDM sub-band (at 3.432GHz, 3.960GHz and 4.488GHz). Then, the UWB signal is transmitted through the system (described in fig.3) implemented in VPI. The propagation in each air link is simulated by introducing an attenuation that corresponds to free space propagation losses. At the system output, the UWB signal is brought back to base-band and loaded into Matlab for OFDM demodulation and performance evaluation. Figures 6 and 7 show the temporal and spectral behavior of the UWB signal and the QPSK transmitted and received constellations, respectively.

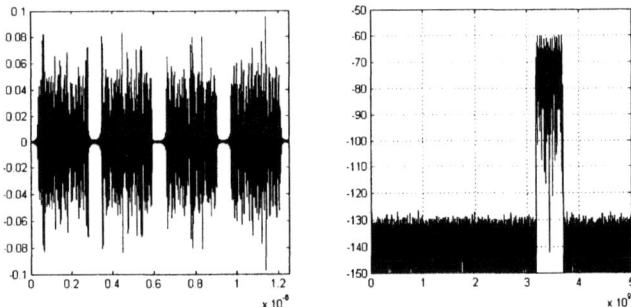

Figure 6: Temporal and spectral representations of the ideal UWB signal (including thermal noise only) in the first OFDM sub-band (3.432GHz).

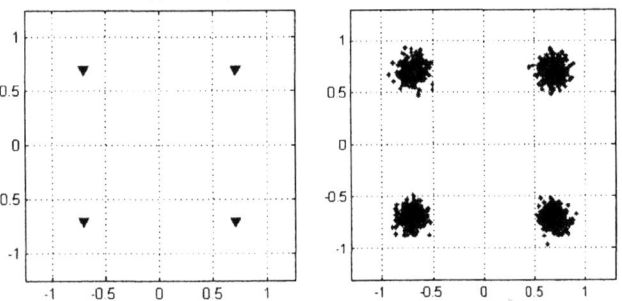

Figure 7: Constellation diagram of DATA sub-carriers: ideal (left) and after transmission (right).

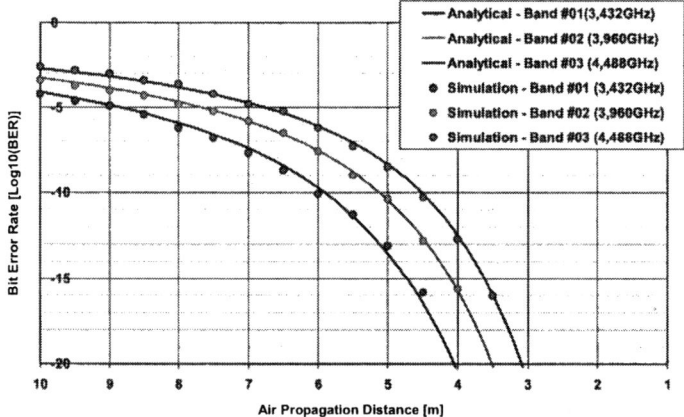

Figure 8: Bit error rate as a function of the transmission distance on the two air links (BER estimated from SNR measurement).

Figure 8 shows the BER as a function of the air propagation distance (supposing equal distances on the two links). A good agreement between link budget calculations and simulation results can be observed.

From this simulation result, we can conclude that the propagation distance on each air link can reach up to 7m for a targeted BER of 10^{-5}.

4. EXPERIMENTAL RESULTS

The feasibility of the system shown in fig. 3 has been then experimentally demonstrated. For the moment, we have tested the transmission of the UWB signal on the optical fibre that is named optical tunnel to underline its transparency. We have introduced RF attenuation in order to simulate free space losses of the first air link. Figure 9 shows the system setup and its composition. It has to be noted that this configuration corresponds to the transmission between a user and the gateway in the architecture of figure 2.

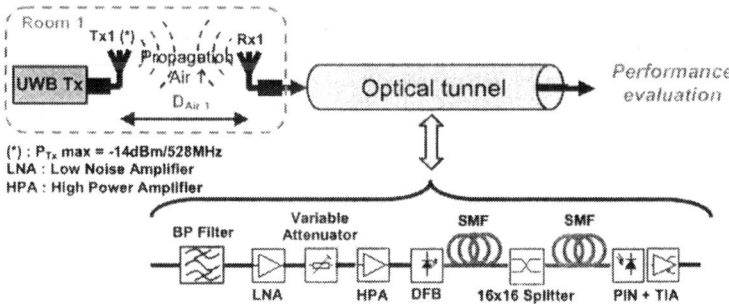

Figure 9: Configuration of the optical tunnel in the MP2MP architecture.

The principle of the experimental characterization is the same as that applied in the case of the numerical simulation. The UWB signal is loaded into an arbitrary waveform generator (AWG) through a LabVIEW interface (figure 10). After an attenuation stage the signal is sent to the optical tunnel for testing. At the tunnel output, the UWB signal is read by the real time oscilloscope and loaded into the computer. Finally, the UWB signal is demodulated and evaluated by Matlab.

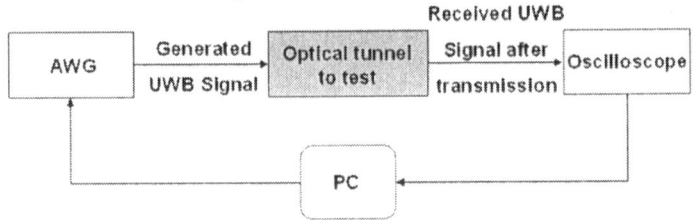

Figure 10: Principle of the experimental test bench (AWG: Arbitrary waveform generator).

The optical tunnel has the parameters given in table 1. To evaluate the performance of the optical tunnel in the same operating condition as in the hybrid optical – wireless system shown in the figure 3, the RF power of the UWB signal at the tunnel input has to be very weak due to the attenuation of the propagation on the first air link. Therefore, the performance of the tunnel is evaluated for an input RF power ranging from -80dBm to -50dBm. The BER of the UWB signal transmitted through the tunnel is reported in figure 11, which includes as well the propagation distance on the first air link corresponding to the input RF power. The reported BER is calculated from SNR measurements according to [9] and corresponds to BER before coding.

From this experimental result, we can conclude that the quality of UWB signal at the output of the optical tunnel is always maintained (BER < 10^{-12}) for the propagation distance lower than 10m on the first air link. As a consequence, if the system does not include the second air link (communication between the end user and the gateway in fig. 2 for example) the RoF system does not introduce significant penalties on the propagation performance on the air link.

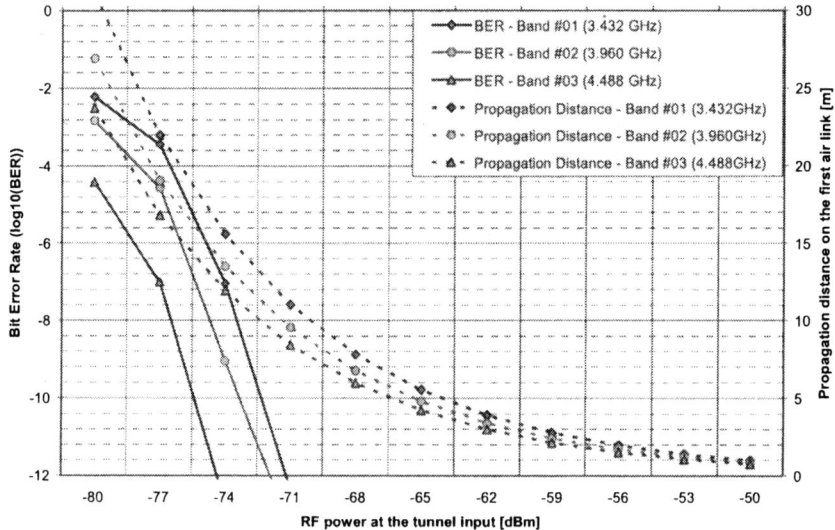

Figure 11: BER of UWB signal transmitted through the optical tunnel as a function of input RF power (BER estimated from SNR measurement).

5. CONCLUSIONS

We have demonstrated the feasibility of using a hybrid optical – RF wireless system based on single mode fiber to transmit UWB radio signals corresponding to first 3 OFDM sub-bands of 528 MHz in 3.1GHz – 4.7GHz frequency range, each carrying 640 Mbps. Such results prove the possibility of deploying very high bitrate, UWB based wireless home networks using multipoint-to-multipoint optical transparent architecture.

6. ACKNOWLEDGEMENTS

This work has been done in the frame of the national project RNRT/BILBAO and of the ePhotonONE+ VDH Network of Excellence.

REFERENCES

1.   M. Bellec, "Home Broadband Home Area Network", Keynote 3, Tuesday 3rd April, European Wireless 2007

2.   FCC, "Rev. Part 15 of the Commission's Rules Regarding UWB Transmission System", ET Docket 98-153, FCC-2-48, 2002.

3.   Standard ECMA-368, Geneva, 1st ed. Dec.2005.

4.   http://www.ieee802.org/15/pub/TG3c.html

5.   Michael J. Crisp et al, "Demonstration of a Radio over Fibre Distributed Antenna Network for Combined In-building WLAN and 3G Coverage", OFC2007, JThA81

6.   Anna Pizzinat et al, "1.92Gbit/s MB-OFDM Ultra Wide Band Radio Transmission over Low Bandwidth Multimode Fiber", OFC2007, OThM6.

7.   P. Guignard et al., "Home network based on CWDM broadcast and select technology", accepted for the presentation at ECOC 2007, Berlin.

8.   C. Carlsson et al, "RF transmission over Multimode Fibers using VCSELs-comparing standard and highbandwidth multimode fibers", IEEE J. Lightwave Technol., pp. 1694-1700, 2004.

9.   V. J. Urick et al., "Wide-band QAM-over-fiber using phase modulation and interferometric demodulation", IEEE Photonics Technol. Letters, vol. 16, pp. 2374-2376, 2004.

Home Networking at 60 GHz: Challenges and Research Issues

Zulkuf Genc, Bao Linh Dang, Jing Wang, Ignas Niemegeers

Wireless and Mobile Communications (WMC) Group Electrical Engineering, Mathematics, Computer Science Faculty Email: {z.genc, l.baodang, jing.wang, i.g.m.m.niemegeersg}@tudelft.nl

Abstract, We highly believe that 60 GHz wireless technology is an ideal candidate to be the future high-speed WLAN standard for home networks thanks to its unique characteristics. In this paper, we review and present the main aspects of the 60 GHz radio regarding future home networks. We introduce the fundamental challenges with the research issues and the considerations on some promising solutions.

Keywords: Home networking, future home networks, 60 GHz, wireless.

1. Introduction

The arrival of broadband communication into homes and the continuing evolution of multimedia and communication devices are increasing user demands for networked homes. The Consumer Electronics Association expects over 50% of U.S. homes will have home networks by 2008. The home network today is typically oriented to sharing of data, internet access and peripherals. The future networks, however, will be dominated by advanced multimedia applications like HDTV, IPTV, multiplayer gaming, and VoIP. The occurrence of currently unpredicted but highly demanding future applications is also quite possible. This kind of applications will bring huge amount of bandwidth and strict QoS requirements into the home networking. For example, the bandwidth required for the raw HDTV signal is about 1.5 Gbps while it is 20 Mbps for MPEG2 compressed signal. In the case of multiple HDTV streams, this need can even go beyond. Additional to bandwidth, mobility will appear as another major factor in future home networks. According to a recent survey, laptops will overtake the domination of PCs all over the world by 2011 [1]. The same

Please use the following format when citing this chapter:

Gene, Z., Linh Dang, B., Wang, J., Niemegeers, I., 2007, in IFIP International Federation for Information Processing, Volume 256, Home Networking, Al Agha, K., Carcelle, X., Pujolle, G., (Boston: Springer), pp. 51-68.

survey also reveals the fact that 88% of laptop users have a wireless network at home. Looking at this picture, it can be expected that homes will mostly be equipped with wireless networks in the future and the expectations from these networks will fairly be high.

This paper basically reviews the 60 GHz wireless technology regarding home networking. It discusses the challenges and the research issues in utilization of this technology for future home networks. The rest of the paper is organized as follows. Section 2 gives the motivation and background for 60 GHz. Section 3 explains a typical use case scenario for a future home network at 60 GHz. Two architectural approaches for home networking at 60 GHz will be presented in Section 4. Section 5 discussed the challenges and research issues. Finally, Section 6 concludes the paper.

2. Motivation and Background

Today's WLAN technologies are not mature enough to support the high expectations for the future home networks. These expectations even do not look like achievable on the roadmaps of existing 802.11x and UWB according to GIT professor Laskar [2]. The IEEE 802.11n, which is still under development as the latest version of 802.11 series, is expected to offer only 100-200 Mbps of actual throughput [3]. On the other hand, specification activities of WirelessHD group towards the next generation wireless digital network interface for consumer electronics and PC products aim to achieve data rates from 2 Gbps to 20 Gbps [4]. SiBeam Inc. recently introduced a new technology for the production of WirelessHD compliant chips for multi-gigabit high definition video and audio distribution in short range [5]. A research group from GIT has already achieved data-transfer rates of 15 Gbps at a distance of 1 meter and 5 Gbps at 5 meters [6]. All these achievements have been made by the utilization of 60 GHz radio. The promising characteristics of 60 GHz radio promote it as the best candidate technology for future gigabit wireless LANs. The most outstanding attribute of 60GHz is 5 GHz continues block of bandwidth in the globally license-free spectrum between 59-64 GHz as seen in Fig. 1. The unique oxygen absorption band at 60GHz also enables the transmission at higher power levels, up to 40 dBm in U.S. and Europe, 10dBm in Japan, than 802.11x and UWB standards. This huge amount of available spectrum and high power levels allow the data transfer at the rate of gigabits per second over indoor distances. The transmission distance, however, is mainly determined by the location of the walls in a typical home. 60 GHz radio signals can not penetrate walls due to heavy attenuation. This characteristic turns each room into a separate cell, in which the use of the whole system capacity is possible. The frequency re-use here helps the network to achieve higher throughput by preventing medium contention and collisions. The naturally isolated cells created by high oxygen absorption and heavy attenuation also form a very secure network environment. Additionally, radios operating at the higher frequencies inherently become more directional and require smaller antennas with narrower beams. These directive antennas can better focus their energy in the transmission direction by minimizing the interference and interception possibility. As for the health concerns, 60 GHz radio does not pose a risk to human health since its signals can not penetrate through human skin into the body [6]. The allowable radiation power limits for 60 GHz are also much lower than the safety levels determined in the studies [7]. Some early critics of 60 GHz technology were generally pointing out its implementation cost. However, recent advances showed that it is possible to produce low-cost CMOS circuits operating at 60 GHz [6, 8]. These advances together with promising features of 60 GHz have leaded the standardization activities. IEEE has formed 802.15.3c study group to develop a millimeter-wave-based alternative physical layer (PHY) for Wireless Personal Area Network (WPAN) [9]. Ecma International has also started to develop an international standard for 60 GHz short range communications to utilize it at bulk data transfer, high-definition multimedia streaming and WPAN applications [10].

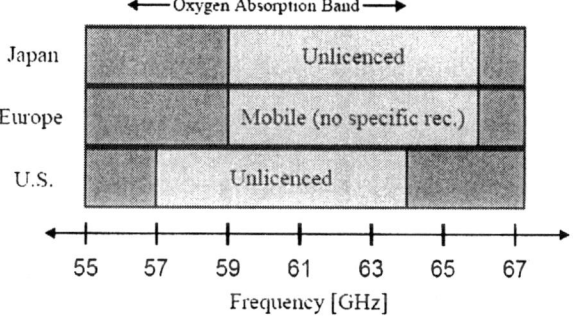

Figure 1: 60 GHz spectrum allocation

3. Use Case Scenario

The High-Definition Television (HDTV) and the Ultra High Definition Video (UHDV) are leading a revolution of home entertainment experience. The trend is being pushed towards such an emergent future home environment, where people are going to be surrounded by high capacity multimedia devices. Those devices can either be the fixed household devices like LCD and DVR or wall-mounted HDTV plasmas, or the personal portable devices such as Laptop, video game consoler and DVD-player for the next generation DVD technologies such as HD-DVD or Blue-Ray. The establishment of multi-gigabit links between these devices will enable the easy and quick delivery of high-definition content without the confusion and unaesthetic view of cables. One example would be a storage device servicing HD video and audio to a HDTV in the vicinity and simultaneously to another one locating in a different room. In the presence of wireless connectivity, people will be free to move around the rooms with their mobile devices by keeping the active multimedia sessions on them without any interruption. The multimedia sessions will also be able to follow a mobile user from one device to the other one in the vicinity of the user. Beside the home networking capabilities, the high-speed wireless connectivity will allow seamless, easy and uninterrupted access to the bandwidth-intensive broadband services as well. People will enjoy these services in the comfort of their homes by ensuring the privacy and security of their home network.

The realization of such a scenario described above will certainly draw more consumers into home networking. In response to this interest, more advanced services and applications can be expected to growingly take place in the market. The key point in this phase will be the availability of a future-proof wireless technology, which will meet the requirements of the desired home network, like enormous bandwidth need (multi-Gbps), simplicity, tight QoS necessities and security. The existence of such a technology can also help overcome the problem of interoperability. We believe that 60 GHz technology can play this role in future home networks once it becomes standardized and gains more maturity.

4. Communication Infrastructures

In order to ensure the full radio coverage at 60GHz within the entire house and the best in-home connectivity between any communication devices, either fixed or mobile, home network communication infrastructure should be designed and be deployed not only to provide high-bandwidth 60GHz radio communication links inside a room, but also to use dedicated equipment and devices to cross walls, connect rooms and reach gateways for connection to access networks. Further taking into account of flexibility and economy in architectural and interior design, the candidate communication infrastructure should at the best eliminate the huge amount of cabling - initial, refitted and extended - in the house, and allow itself being integrated into the user ecosphere in a unobtrusive and aesthetic manner.

We envision two possible infrastructure approaches for home networking by considering the 60GHz radio characteristics. One is to use a mixed wired and wireless infrastructure as shown in Fig. 2.a, i.e. Radio-over-Fiber (ROF) technique [11], which deploys fibers to connect rooms, and put simple antennas at the end of the fiber to emit radio signals to form individual 60GHz radio cells The other approach is to deploy purely wireless infrastructure as in Fig. 2.b, where the network devices are connected in ad hoc manner, with necessary radio relay devices deployed We believe these two candidates are complementary in time frame for market introduction and capabilities.

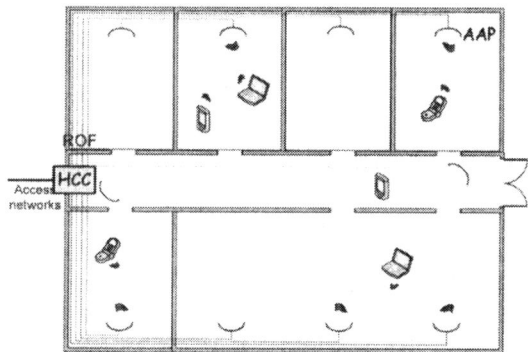

Figure 2.a: Cell-based Home Network Communication Infrastructure

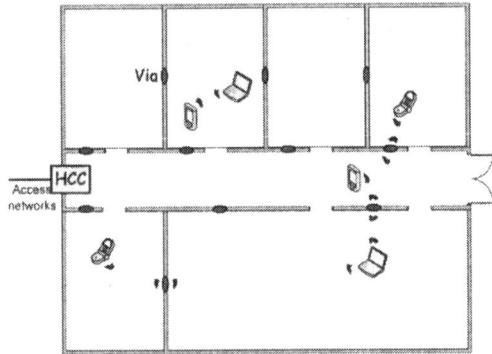

Figure 2.b: Adhoc-based Home Network Communication Infrastructure

4.1 Cell-based Communication Infrastructure

This approach is based on the novel Radio-over-Fiber (RoF) technique, which requires a low-cost plastic optical-fiber infrastructure to be installed in new buildings or retrofitted to existing buildings. Two essential infrastructural elements are:

-    The Home Communications Controller (HCC). The concept evolves from the prevailing residential gateways such as a DSL access gateway or a cable set-top box. Besides the gateway functions of interfacing between home network and the access networks, it should be implemented with the full network stack functionality and additional control and management units as the central intelligence of the network.

-    The Antenna Access Points (AAPs). They are the wall-socket access points, which can be considered as dumb antenna devices only with layer-2 functionality for interfacing the radio signals.

The fiber infrastructure forms a tree with the HCC at the root, and with the AAPs at the tips. In each room at least one AAP is deployed, and thus at least one short-range 60GHz radio cell is formed potentially superimposed to offer 60GHz connectivity. For uplinks 60GHz signal from the source device is picked up by the AAP in the close vicinity, modulated as ROF microwave signals, and guided to the HCC. At the HCC, the incoming signal is converted to the proper optical frequency and routed to the AAP close to the destination device, where the signal is modulated once again into 60GHz radio as the downlink traffic. The inter-room connectivity provided by this infrastructure can thus in principle provide 60GHz radio connectivity cross the entire house.

4.2 Adhoc-based Communication Infrastructure

As an alternative of installing optical fibers, this approach makes use of microwave transponders, or radio relays, pasted on the walls and radiating RF signals across it. The only infrastructural elements required are the HCC and the wall-mounted radio transponders, the so-called Via devices (Via-s). This approach does not require a backbone network to interconnect the room-based cells. It basically forms an in-house ad-hoc network, with a subset dedicated infrastructure nodes, Via-s, which typically have the known fixed locations. In this case, the HCC still serves to connect home network to the access networks, however it is most likely that it won't be the only device implemented with sophisticated control and management units due to the dynamic and distributed nature of ad-hoc networks. Therefore we must seek a solution to distribute network intelligence among, if not all, a subset of network devices.

5. Challenges and Research Issues

Despite the provision of multi-Gb/s data-rates, networking at the 60 GHz band exposes some serious challanges that prevent the adoption of this frequency band in the range of Local Area Networks (LAN). In this section, the challenges of networking at the 60 GHz band and their research issues are discussed.

5.1 Connectivity

As mentioned in previous sections, the propagation of signals at 60 GHz is strongly weakened by surrounding obstacles and walls. Concrete walls can be considered as reliable cell boundaries since they can attenuate signals as much as 40 dB. A person standing in between a line-of-sight connection can also take 20 dB away from the link budget. To further analyze the coverage at 60 GHz band, a simulation study has been carried out using a race-tracing tool called Radio-Wave Propagation Simulator [12]. This simulator has been shown to be accurate in terms of statistical properties [13]. Fig. 3 illustrates the simulated in-home environment containing multiple small rooms (5*8m), a large room (15*8m) and a corridor. Immobile people and objects such as sofas, tables etc. were placed onto the floor. In the first simulation scenario, an omni-directional antenna with 0dBm of transmission power is placed in the center of each room at the height of 3m. The antenna placed in the big room has 3dBm antenna gain. Two others omni-antennas are placed in the corridor. Signal strength is recorded at the height of 1.5m.

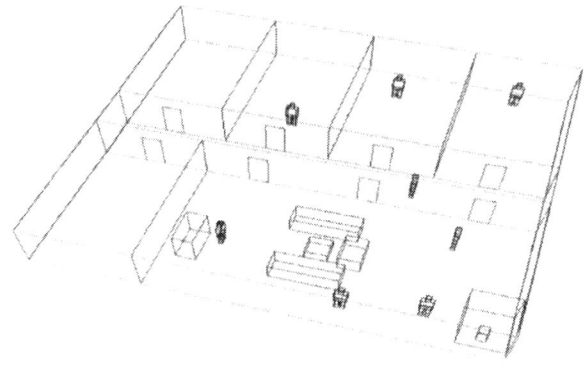

Figure 3: The simulated in-home environment

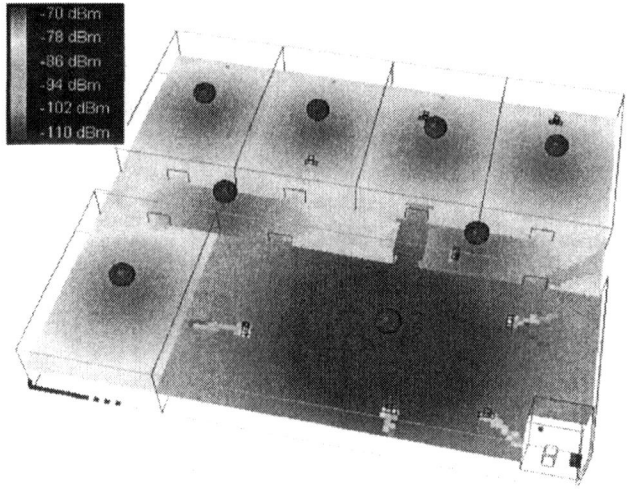

Figure 4: Signal Coverage at the 60 GHz frequency band

Fig. 4 shows the simulated signal coverage of the first scenario. As predicted, the transmission of 60 GHz signals is severely effected by shadowing. Not only can large objects such as trees, furniture etc. cause shadowing, but even a person can completely block the signal. Thus, to achieve the full connectivity in a crowded room is rather challenging by this deployment. Moreover, a number of antennas are required to cover the long corridor.

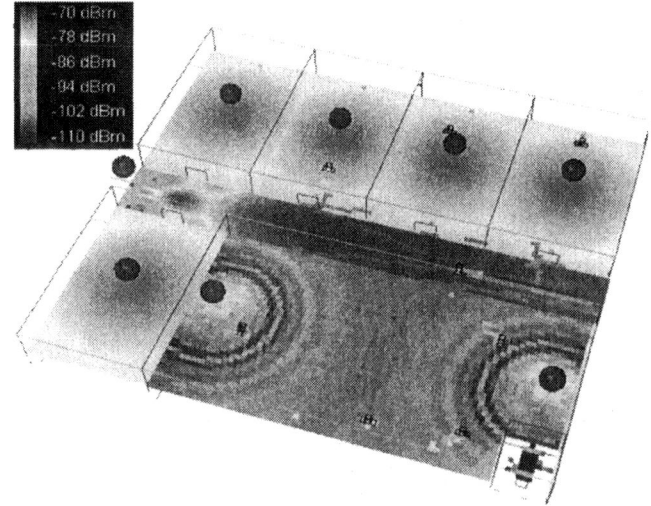

Figure 5: Signal Coverage at the 60 GHz frequency band – Multiple antennas

To improve the signal coverage in the big room, two Dielectric Lens antennas are deployed for the big room in the second scenario (Fig. 5). As a result, the signal coverage is significantly improved. A large part of the shadowed areas behind the people has been removed. In this paper, the use of multiple antennas to improve signal coverage is referred by the term "Antenna Redundancy". Another option to overcome the line-of-sight limitation of 60 GHz propagation is to make use of smart antennas. Since the antenna dimension is inversely proportional to the operating frequency, it is possible to deploy many antennas in a small fixed area. The antenna array formed by these small antennas can intelligently adjust the gain, the transmission power and the beam direction according to the link conditions. For example, if any obstacle blocks the line-of-sight path of the radio wave, a smart antenna array can use the reflections by redirecting the energy onto the reflecting objects [14]. However, these techniques are not enough to create a reliable WLAN covering whole-home since walls are still impassable barriers for 60 GHz radio signals. New methods and devices are required to overcome this problem.

5.2 Mobility

Another problem arose is the directional overlapping areas between cells. As can be seen in Fig.6, overlapping only exists around the opened areas, i.e. opened doors and windows.

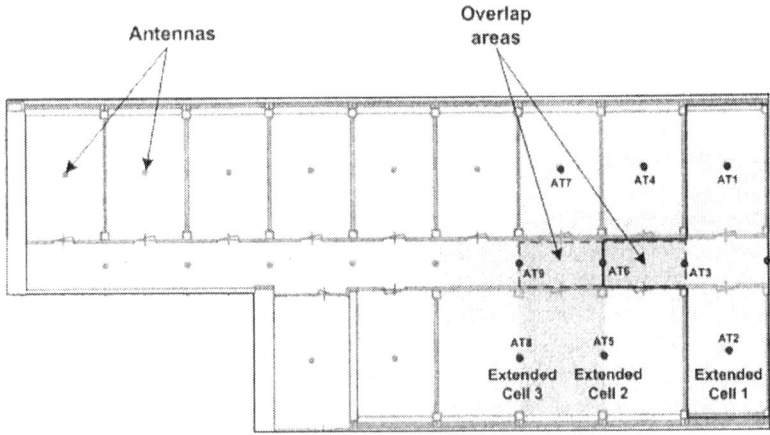

Figure 6: The Extended Cell (EC) Concept

Consequently, overlapping areas are often narrow and directional. In a multi-channel communication system, where handovers (HO) are required when a Mobile Station (MS) roams from one cell to another, these overlapping areas might be too small to allow an MS sufficient time to trigger and complete a handover. In this paper, we use the term "corner effect" to refer to this problem. The directional overlapping poses difficulties on the design of the mobility handling mechanism, since the transition between two cells is too sharp and short to trigger a handover. This problem gets worse as mobile users in an in-home environment are much likely to perform sharp-turns while moving from one room to another. To perform a Radio-Signal-Measurement (RSM) based handover, a good decision has to be made based on the signal strength averaging and hysteresis margin. In order to guarantee a seamless communication environment, it therefore requires a minimum overlapping area between two adjacent cells. In other words, a mobile station must be able to listen to both APs, so it can determine which one is better to connect to. In [15], the relation between the minimum overlapping area and the handover frequency defined by the ratio between a mobile user's velocity and the cell size has been carried out. As calculated in the paper, the minimum overlapping area for an indoor environment is 20% of the cell's diameter (2 meters). It is therefore crucial that large enough overlapping areas are created in the system in order to guarantee a seamless communication environment.

With this target in mind, an infrastructure for broadband in-building networks at millimeter-wave GHz band was presented in [11]. It is proposed to group multiple adjacent antennas into an Extended Cell (EC) and to allow the antennas to transmit the same content over the same frequency channel. Moreover, an EC is designed to cover several adjacent rooms and a part of a transitional area. By doing so, an overlapping area between two ECs can always be created in the transitional zone, and thus seamless communication can be achieved as mobile users always have to pass a transitional area in order to move from one room to another (Fig. 6). Using this concept, the corner effect is mitigated as a mobile user does not have to perform a HO as long as it is still in the EC. The number of HOs will therefore be substantially decreased. Furthermore, a form of spatial diversity can also be achieved with the EC concept since multiple copies of a signal are concurrently sent by all the antennas in an EC. Shadowing is reduced since there is a better chance that a mobile station receives a good signal. To illustrate the effectiveness of the EC concept, simulations have been carried out. The simulation setup was described in [11]. The simulation results in Fig. 7 clearly show the improvement in terms of the average number of drop calls when the EC concept is employed. However, since a call lasts longer, the average number of HOs per call also increases. As a result, a tradeoff should be made between the average EC size and the required quality of service in terms of drop calls.

This EC concept connects well with the Antenna Redundancy ideas and the RoF infrastructure approach presented in Section IV.a. New antennas can be easily connected to the optical infrastructure to improve the signal coverage. Moreover, these new antennas will be included into the existing extended cell.

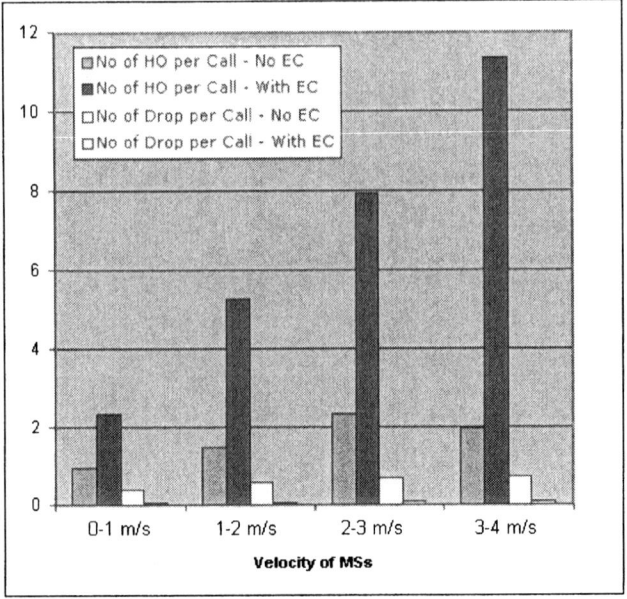

Figure 7: Average number of HOs and Call Drops

5.3 Self-configuration

60GHz radio, while offering great opportunity to prosper versatile bandwidth-demanding home applications, raises greater challenges to realize self-configurable home networking systems. The particular short radio range and vulnerability for line-of-sight obstruction result in frequent changing on link quality and network topology, and thus require a large amount of reconfiguration processes. As the 60GHz radio promises for high data rate and real-time applications, the timeliness of the reconfiguration processes is especially demanded, as it is directly tied to the user perception quality.

Self-configuration is essentially an important issue of network control and management at different connectivity levels (i.e. Physical and Link-, Network- and service level) to enable distributed application entities that spread over the home network components to cooperate for a particular application. While the Network- and service levels self-configuration processes (i.e., addressing, route discovery, service discovery, etc.) have great generality for all radio technologies, the novelty of 60GHz radio calls for special concerns on Physical and Link level self-configuration process. An example with the cell-based communication infrastructure is when the number of users or terminals in a room (e.g., a meeting room) becomes so large that the picocell capacity cannot guarantee the required service quality, the self-configuration process should automatically add extra resources, e.g., establish an extra picocell by turning on an additional wavelength in the fiber to that room, and handing-off part of the load to that new picocell. For Ad-hoc based approach, frequent disturbances of LOS communication links (e.g., people standing in LOS links) require fast resource discovery strategy to re-establish connectivity. Self-configuration is thus required to efficiently organize devices into piconets and scatternets to support multihop connections. Such process must be established for supporting the cooperation between distributed devices, and be tailored for 60GHz radio with respect to the use of directional antenna, LOS links and thus the specialty of the MAC protocol.

Although most current contributions related to self-configuration issue have been focusing on developing and optimizing isolated layer-dependent protocols, we share a vision with the new networking paradigm such as autonomic communications [16], and are seeking a promising way to cooperate different level configurations under a cross-layer optimization strategy, in the sense that the configuration information at different levels may be mutually beneficial. However, as pointed out in [17], cross-layer approach should not only focus on the layer-wise performance enhancement blindly, but rather be guided by the high-level goal required by the applications.

To solve the potential confliction among configuration actions at different layers, a promising way is to employ a general management module to conciliate self-configuration processes in parallel threads, rather than merely increase complexity to achieve local sophistication within individual configuration protocols. Such a self-configuration management module is expected to incorporate three basic functions: (1) information abstraction to aggregate the contextual information from different connectivity levels and to define configuration states of the network; (2) configuration coordination to optimize configuration processes under an overview of the configuration states and under joint consideration and decision of all connectivity levels; and (3) protocol interface to exert the decision from the configuration coordinator to adjust and operate the layer-based configuration protocols. This management module should be implemented in the capable devices in terms of computation, storage and power resources, whilst taking into account the location and mobility. By deploying the cell-based communication infrastructure, as all the traffic goes through the HCC, it should at the best take the role of the self-configuration manager, and forms a centralized management structure. For the ad-hoc based approach, besides the HCC, other capable devices should also be implemented fully or partially the module to provide distributed management. In this way, hierarchical self-configuration management can be organized.

5.4 Cognitive Networking

As the deployment of 60GHz results in a more dynamic and distributed home networking environment, control and management of such networks stringently require the efficiency of the processes. That means on one hand, the timeliness is highly desired for configure and adapt the 60GHz applications to a user desired state. In particular for personal applications, the maximum allowed configuration time is determined by the patience of the user (often of the order of a second). On the other hand, necessity of re-configuration and adaptation processes must be decided on occurrence of the networking state changes, in other words, whether and when a re-configuration process should be triggered. This is critical to achieve a stable networking system, which shields the network dynamics from its users. With further concerns on building home network to be a "self-" capable system, the network should be able to identify its goals centered on its users' need and manage on its own to realize those goals regardless the heterogeneous, distributed and dynamic network environment. This requires new mechanisms to evoke the expert-like intelligence on the network.

One promising solution to tackle such challenge is to incorporate the novel concept of cognitive networking into play. Being specified in [18], a cognitive network has a cognitive process that can perceive current network conditions, and then plan, decide and act on those conditions. The network can learn from these adaptations and use them to make future decisions, all while taking into account the user experience. With the ability to learn from the consequences of the network operations and to accumulate experience on executing such operations effectively and efficiently, the cognitive network is expected to switch network control and management processes from a reactive to a proactive manner. More specifically, the experience can help, for example, to predict when a reconfiguration/adaptation will be needed to start ahead of time. The idea is based on the observation that in-home usage of the network exhibits a lot of patterns over time. An example would be the daily routine of inhabitants of a house, who repeat the same patterns of behavior and, movement from room to room.

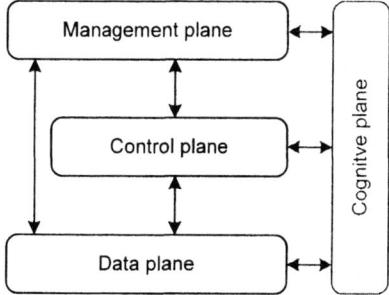

Figure 8: FHN architecture: a view of plane division

Inspired by the idea of constructing a knowledge plane for the Internet [19], the architecture of the cognitive home network is expected to have a Cognitive Plane (CP). In our opinion, the CP is best to be positioned a vertically cross all the other three existing planes (e.g. data-, control- and management planes) as shown in Fig.8. The purpose has two fold. One is to help with sophisticated decision-making for high level instruction. This mainly works for the management plane and control plane to realize network self-management. The other one is for knowledge circulation. Knowledge aggregation and distribution need to be carried out by data plane, while the control and management planes should be responsible for admission of knowledge accessing and provision. Within the CP, four basic functionalities are proposed and will bear further deliberation: (1) a monitoring function perceives environment and collects meta-information from the users, the network, and the environment in which the network operates, from which user patterns and context can be derived; (2) a learning function processes and converts the aggregated information, extracting, adjusting and correcting patterns and deriving context to form the basis for predicting the next services demanded from the network operations; (3) a decision function initiates proactive configuration and reconfiguration, based on learned patterns and context through specific cognitive techniques; (4) an execution function takes decisions made from the decision function and exerts them into actions upon network operation. A key question is how to identify the most applicable cognitive techniques for certain network control and management operation. This should be answered from a joint effort of telecommunication and artificial intelligence expertise. Further we need to identify which information needs to be sensed and what the context consists of. We can build here on work that has been done in context-aware computing and networking [20] and work on ambient intelligence [21]. Although the concept of cognitive networking has illuminated a research direction for realizing network intelligence, the additional cost (e.g. system complexity, power consumption, etc.) by introducing such a new network structure should not be ignored. Introduced in [22], the prices of anarchy, ignorance and control can be considered as further evaluation of the necessity and fitness of adopting cognitive network as the solution for certain problems.

6. Conclusion

In this paper, we review and present the main aspects of the 60 GHz radio regarding future home networks. We also introduce the fundamental challenges with the research issues we are currently working on. With regards to connectivity, antenna redundancy can be a solution for the shadowing caused by immobile and mobile obstacles. This solution is not costly when combined with ROF since the antennas are connected to the existing optical fiber infrastructure and they are very simple. Another promising solution to this problem looks like deployment of smart antennas. To overcome the corner effect and guarantee a seamless communication, the EC concept can be used. For the self-configuration concerns, we consider to employ a general management module operating across the layers. Finally, we investigate the cognitive networking paradigm and its application to the problems of future home networking.

7. Acknowledgement

This research was carried out in the "Future home network" and "Broadband In-home Networks employing Radio over Fiber" projects within IOP GenCom program and Adaptive Ad-Hoc Free Band Wireless Communications project within Freeband program, both funded by the Dutch Ministry of Economic Affairs.

8. References

1. Online BBC article: http://news.bbc.co.uk/1/hi/technology/6474581.stm

2. Interview: http://www.gearlog.com/2007/07/gearlog_interview_joy_laskar_1.php

3. SiBEAM White Paper: The Future of Wireless Technology Achieving Gigabit Data Rates

4. The WirelessHD specification : http://www.wirelesshd.org/company/about.html

5. OmniLink60™ Technology: http://www.sibeam.com/products/omnilink.html

6. GIT News Release: http://www.gatech.edu/news-room/release.php?id=1431

7. Absence of Ocular Effects After Either Single or Repeated Exposure to 10 mW/cm2 from a 60 GHz CW Source, Henry A. Kues, et. al., Bioelectromagnetics, Vol. 20, 1999, pp. 463-473

8. C.H. Doan, S. Emami, A. M. Niknejad, and R. W. Brodersen, "Millimeter-wave CMOS design," IEEE Journal of Solid-States Circuits, vol. 40, no. 1, pp. 144–155, 2005

9. TG3cwebpage: http://www.ieee802.org/15/pub/TG3c.html

10. Ecma International 60 GHz standardization activity:

http://www.ecma-international.org/activities/Communications/ga-2007-015.pdf

11. B. L. Dang, V. Prasad, I. Niemegeers, M. G. Larrode and A. M. J. Koonen, "Toward a seamless communication architecture for in-building networks at the 60 GHz band", In Proceedings of the 31st IEEE Conference on Local Computer Networks (LCN2006), November 2006

12. Radioplan. Radiowave Propagation Simulator. www.radioplan.com.

13. P. Smulders, C. Li, H. Yang, E. Martijn, and M. Herben, "60 ghz indoor radio propagation comparison of simulation and measurement results," in Proc. 11th IEEE Symposium on Communications and Vehicular

14. SiBEAM White Paper: 60 GHz Architecture for Wireless Video Display

15. Marc Emmelmann. "Influence of Velocity on the Handover Delay associated with a Radio-Signal-Measurement-based Handover Decision". In Proc. of IEEE Vehicular Technology Conference (VTC 2005 Fall), Dallas, TX, USA, September 2005

16. S. Dobson et al, "Survey of autonomic communications", ACM Transactions on Autonomous and Adaptive Systems (TAAS), vol. 1, no. 2, pp: 223 – 259, 2006

17. V. Kawadia and P. R. Kumar, "A Cautionary Perspective on Cross-layer Design", IEEE Wireless Communications / IEEE Personal Communications, vol. 12, no. 1, pp. 3-11, February 2005

18. R. W. Thomas, D. H. Friend, L. A. Dasilva, and A. B. Mackenzie, "Cognitive networks: adaptation and learning to achieve end-to-end performance objectives", IEEE Communications Magazine, vol: 44, no: 12, pp: 51-57, December 2006

19. D. Clark, C. Partridge, C. Ramming, and J. Wroclawski, "A Knowledge Plane for the Internet", ACM SIGCOMM 2003, Karlsruhe, August 2003

20. B.N. Schilit, D.M. Hilbert and J. Trevor, "Context-aware Communication", IEEE Wireless Communications, vol. 9, no. 5, pp. 46 -54, October 2002

21. F. Stajano, "Security for Ubiquitous Computing", John Wiley, 2002 Technology in the Benelux, November 2004

22. R. W. Thomas, D. H. Friend, L. A. Dasilva, and A. B. Mackenzie, "Cognitive networks: adaptation and learning to achieve end-to-end performance objectives", IEEE Communications Magazine, vol: 44, no: 12, pp: 51-57, Dec. 2006

Energy Efficiency in Future Home Environments: A Distributed Approach

Helmut Hlavacs, Karin A. Hummel, Roman Weidlich, Amine Houyou, Andreas Berl, and Hermann de Meer

Abstract In this paper, a new architecture for sharing resources amongst home environments is proposed. Our approach goes far beyond traditional systems for distributed virtualization like PlanetLab or Grid computing, since it relies on complete decentralization in a peer-to-peer like manner, and above all, aims at energy efficiency. Energy metrics are defined, which have to be optimized by the system. The system itself uses virtualization to transparently move tasks from one home to another in order to optimally utilize the existing computing power. An overview of our proposed architecture is presented as well as an analytical evaluation of the possible energy savings in a distributed example scenario where computers share downloads.

1 Introduction and Motivation

Modern home environments are envisioned as multimedia homes consisting of a multitude of networked devices presenting and managing multimedia services, like video streaming, IP-telephony (VoIP), video content delivery, and enabling remote access to home services. Examples for platforms supporting these services are OSGI[1] and UPnP.[2]

Although most of the mentioned services are already available today, future home environments are facing new challenges. On the one hand, a shift from multi-service

Helmut Hlavacs, Karin A. Hummel, Roman Weidlich
Institute of Distributed and Multimedia Systems, University of Vienna,
e-mail: helmut.hlavacs, karin.hummel, roman.weidlich@univie.ac.at

Amine Houyou, Andreas Berl, Hermann de Meer
Faculty of Computer Science and Mathematics, University of Passau,
e-mail: houyou, berl, demeer@fmi.uni-passau.de

[1] http://www.osgi.org/
[2] http://www.upnp.org/

Please use the following format when citing this chapter:

Hlavacs, H., Hummel, K. A., Weidlich, R., Houyou, A., Berl, A., de Meer, H., 2007, in IFIP International Federation for Information Processing, Volume 256, Home Networking, Al Agha, K., Carcelle, X., Pujolle, G., (Boston: Springer), pp. 69-84.

networks towards multi-network services is likely to be seen. These services are no longer built by one network provider and a single access network, but rather run on multiple networks supported by several providers. On the other hand, more and more *always-on* services are requested by home users. Always-on services include, for instance, file-sharing or other peer-to-peer (P2P) services, multimedia streaming, or remote home monitoring/control. Furthermore, ubiquitous computing technology [13], like smart artifacts consisting of sensors and actuators, are integrated into future homes to support home automation services. Here, computing is shifted beyond human awareness involving sensing technologies like measuring environmental phenomena (e.g. temperature, humidity, etc.) or motion detection and position recognition (e.g. to support location-based services in the home). Recent research projects investigate the potential of future home environments, like Amigo[3] (Ambient Intelligence for the Networked Home Environment), the Place Lab[4], and Easy Living.[5]

These current and future always-on services rely on home computers running on a 24/7 basis, while most probably being not fully utilized. Always-on computers consume considerable amounts of energy worldwide. For example, a low-cost PC consumes about 100 watts if switched on, a multimedia PC consumes 148 watts, and only a few watts are consumed if the computer is hibernating.[6] In addition to increased CO_2 balance caused by high energy consumption, energy consumption is seen as major cost factor for servers [3] which is becoming true also for home networks.

This paper discusses the current state of the research project Virtual Home Environments (VHE), interconnecting the Universities of Vienna, Passau and Cantabria, and being sponsored by the Network of Excellence Euro-FGI.[7] VHE proposes a distributed approach to assure energy efficiency for future home networks by means of resource sharing, i.e., home services either run locally or they are executed on a remote connected home network. Here, resource sharing allows to shift home services (load) to other under-utilized home networks and, thus, allows to put some computers into hibernate mode. The approach of *distributed energy efficiency* is based on home network virtualization, which supports remote execution in virtual machines, a P2P overlay utilized for distributed management, and a distributed algorithm for deciding where to execute home services most efficiently and which home networks should be contributing resources.

One of the novelties of the approach is the distributed energy saving aspect which has not been addressed so far. The implied reduced CO_2 emission is not quantified but is assumed to result from the new system. The second novelty is the interconnection of home networks in a robust, scalable manner in order to share resources and energy. Our approach is related to other work done in the area of distributed

---

[3] http://www.hitech-projects.com/euprojects/amigo/

[4] http://architecture.mit.edu/house_n/placelab.html

[5] http://research.microsoft.com/easyliving/

[6] Energy Star Europe calculator: http://www.eu-energystar.org/en/en_007c.shtml

[7] http://eurongi.enst.fr/en_accueil.html

resource sharing, as PlanetLab or Grids, which often lack full decentralization, and to energy efficiency research which so far concentrates on local energy saving including data centers (see Section 2). While optimizing for energy efficiency, important system characteristics are considered as well in terms of availability, security, fairness (i.e., contributing and retrieving equal amounts of energy), and QoS in particular necessary for the multimedia and home automation services. We propose distributed monitoring of energy and performance metrics (generation of statistics) and distributed decision making. These functions are implemented in a distributed management component utilizing a P2P overlay. Hereby, virtualization of home networks enables the distributed approach by supporting the shifting of home services (see Section 3). A novel system architecture is proposed and described which details the components necessary for interconnecting home networks (see Section 4). Finally, a discussion of the potential for energy saving in such a distributed environment is provided based on analytical performance evaluation applied to sharing downloads (see Section 5). Section 6 concludes the paper.

2 Related Work

The most comparable platform to the architecture proposed in this paper is PlanetLab [9]. Although PlanetLab represented a similar vision of an open distributed platform for developing large distributed applications [1], it stagnated at the stage where it has become an experimental platform for testing large Internet-based research. This paper proposes an extension to the vision of PlanetLab focused on a distributed home environment and puts energy sharing as a focal point, which would incite users to offer their home PCs for resource sharing.

Similar to server environments [3], energy consumption is becoming a major problem in home networking, as energy costs tend to exceed that of hardware. Koomey [8] mentions that today's energy consumption of volume, mid-range, and high-end servers in the U.S. and worldwide has doubled over the period from 2000 to 2005. The total power demand in 2005 (including associated infrastructure) is equivalent to about five 1000 megawatt power plants for the U.S. and 14 such power plants for the world [8].

Nevertheless, energy efficient computing, is not a new topic. With the need of a longer battery life in laptops, for instance, several techniques such as SpeedStep [6], PowerNow, Cool'nQuiet, or Demand Based Switching [15] have been developed as local power saving measures. These measures enable slowing down the clock speeds (Clock Gating), or powering off parts of the chips (Power Gating), if they are idle [4, 14]. A further power adaptive technique is based on sensing whether the computer has been left idle, based on human-machine interaction input components (e.g. keyboard, mouse, touch-pad, etc). The longer the computer is left idle, the more hardware elements are turned off or suspended, while allowing a turn on mechanism without loss of state or information. This mechanism allows a gradual reduction of power usage. However turning hardware off, doesn't always imply that a computing system is energy efficient. Energy efficiency can be measured in performance per watt [7]. One way to attain a better performance per watt has been achieved through virtualization. Virtualization could be seen as splitting an underlying hardware entity into smaller identical virtual entities which could run isolated from each other. In data centers for instance the rack-mounted servers were configured to run a single workload to guarantee reliability, availability, and scalability of the service. This came at the cost of under-utilized energy expensive machines, which had an average load of about 10% [3]. With virtualization a virtual machine is dedicated to each service, but can run transparently on any available system next to several other virtual machines. This effective consolidation of servers, i.e., running a machine at a higher utilization [7], is usually done by a central management mechanism. A further energy saving method which is currently investigated within the context of data centers [11], consists of turning parts of the machines off while taking cooling cost into account [5, 8].

A similar management type of a virtual environment could be found in Grids, particularly Condor [12]. Condor is a workload management system which allows users to submit their jobs to a single queue. The management system distributes the jobs transparently among the computing Grid. This functionality, however is centralized and does not take energy efficiency into account.

It is such a management mechanism and dynamic behavior which is missing in a platform like PlanetLab. There, virtual environments for users are created centrally, one virtual environment on each PlanetLab machine. However, in PlanetLab [1] shifting load is not trivial, consolidating machines to run at a higher load is not yet possible. Also, there is no automatization in allocating virtual resources to a given user or to a special application. In our architecture, we aim at the automatic allocation of virtual resources in a distributed environment, while consolidating the future home PC and switching those PCs off which run at a light load.

3 Distributed Energy Efficiency

The concept for distributed energy efficiency relies on the concept of interfering characteristics which decide upon where to run home services (where to shift the load to). Hereby, the management algorithm assures fairness, availability, QoS, and security while optimizing for energy saving and energy efficiency. Here, fairness means that each home should consume approximately as much as it contributes to the system. For reasons of robustness and scaling, a distributed solution is proposed considering each of these characteristics. The distributed decision making will utilize other messaging traffic for the exchange of information in order to avoid too much additional network traffic necessary for management. This distributed solution is supported by virtualization techniques.

3.1 Energy Efficiency Optimization and Constraints

In the presented approach, energy consumption should be globally minimized and energy efficiency should be globally maximized. Thus, for a number of N different homes h_i, $1 \leq i \leq N$ the basic energy consumption $E(T)$ over system time T is given as:

$$E(T) = \sum_{i=1}^{N} \int_0^T P_{h_i}(t)\, dt \quad \text{[joule (or kWh)]},$$

where $P_{h_i}(t)$ is the power consumed by a home h_i in watt. In absence of measurement possibilities of homes, the energy consumption of a home might as well be estimated by assigning an energy class level to the home.

To calculate the energy efficiency, the workload introduced by the home network services is related to energy consumption, thus, the work carried out by all homes is defined as:

$$L(T) = \sum_{i=1}^{N} \int_0^T L_{h_i}(t)\, dt,$$

where $L_{h_i}(t)$ describes the work caused by the home services at time t (seen as the work *output* of a home). Similar to [10] we define the overall energy efficiency of the system, which should be maximized, by:

$$\eta(T) = \frac{L(T)}{E(T)}, \tag{1}$$

where it is assumed that $E(T) \neq 0\,\text{kWh}$. If the energy consumption can be reduced by sharing, the energy efficiency will increase.

Additionally, the system assures a certain degree of trust in the non-functional characteristics of home services, thus requiring more computing power, which as a consequence causes additional energy consumption. The addressed characteristics are *availability*, *security*, *fairness*, and *QoS*, which are constraints to the optimization problem to minimize energy consumption and to maximize energy efficiency.

Based on these basic energy formulas, a distributed solution is proposed, where load, i.e., home services, are shifted between homes to optimize $E(T)$ and $\eta(T)$ (to be more precise, a combination of both optimization problems). In absence of a central management, the global behavior emerges based on the local behavior of homes. Each home conducts performance measurements and monitoring of energy consumption as well as a decision algorithm to determine whether to provide resources for home services. In addition to energy consumption, for example, the MTTF (Mean Time To Failure) and the MTTR (Mean Time To Repair) are calculated to describe availability, the mean load caused by home services are monitored for reasons of fairness, and the mean DTR (Data Transfer Rates) for up and down links address QoS constraints. For security reasons, mutual monitoring of past malicious behavior is performed resulting in security levels assigned to homes.

The distributed optimization algorithm for decision taking is based on building groups of homes which exchange performance, security, and energy status information to build partial views of the global state. Based on this information, ideally each home can execute an identical algorithm deciding upon the home's contribution to solving the optimization problems by converging towards the optimal energy saving or energy efficiency while considering the services' requirements.

3.2 Decentralized Virtualization

Mechanisms for resource virtualization have been used in different contexts, aiming at different results. Three examples (Grid computing, server virtualization, and virtualization in PlanetLab) are described to clarify their different targets and to illustrate the next step taken by the architecture which is proposed in this paper.

In Grid and cluster computing (e.g., in Linux clusters) virtualization is used to aggregate a pool of hardware resources. In this context, virtualization aims at hiding the complexity of aggregating several machines in a Grid/cluster from the user.

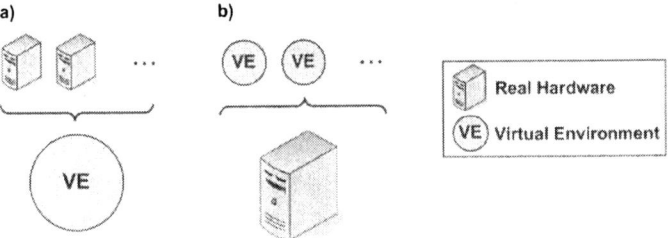

Fig. 1   a) Grid virtualization and b) server virtualization.

The user accesses the aggregated hardware (e.g., high number of CPU's, large amount of memory) as a single virtual environment (e.g., a single Linux shell). This kind of virtualization is shown in Fig. 1a). A number of real machines are aggregated to a single virtual environment (aka *virtual organization*). In contrast to the compositional Grid virtualization, server virtualization uses virtualization methods in a segmenting manner. Server virtualization aims at splitting hardware resources into several smaller virtual environments, enabling more than one virtual environment on a single hardware. Servers are virtualized to achieve load-balancing, to increase resilience, and to save hardware/energy by consolidation, e.g., in data centers. In Fig. 1b) this kind of resource virtualization is shown. A single hardware is split into several virtual environments (aka *virtual machines*).

PlanetLab faces a more complex, distributed scenario of virtualization [1]. Hardware resources are spread all over the planet, interconnected via the Internet, without

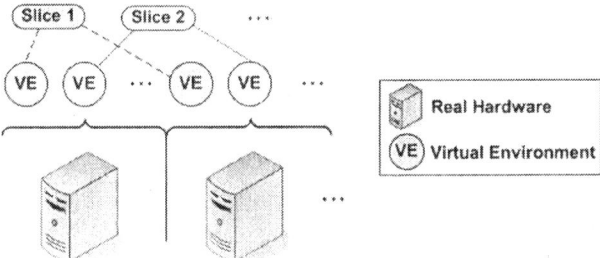

Fig. 2 Virtualization in PlanetLab.

the use of special high-performance links. Within PlanetLab every single machine is split into virtual environments similar to server virtualization. These virtual environments are organized in slices. More precisely, a slice is represented by one single virtual environment per available PlanetLab machine. Thus, a user who has booked a slice receives one Linux-shell per PlanetLab machine. This scenario is illustrated in Fig. 2. It is important to see, that virtual environments in a slice are not aggregated like resources in a Grid. No further abstraction than one shell per machine is provided, leaving users with the problem of dealing with dozens or even hundreds of shells simultaneously.

This paper proposes a distributed virtualization solution that goes one step further than the virtualization in PlanetLab. An architecture is suggested, in which slices are variable in size (number of involved virtual environments) and change their location dynamically. These extended slices are called *flexible slices*. As an example, a flexible slice might consist of 4 virtual environments which are located in the current home network at one time, and consist of 7 virtual environments which are located in other home networks at another time. However, similar to the virtualization used in Grid/cluster computing, this complexity is hidden from the user. The user experiences a single virtual environment (virtual organization) in which the resources of the flexible slice are aggregated.

3.3 Decentralized Management

To take advantage of virtualization, management of the virtualized hardware has to be done. In Grids, available resources have to be adequately allocated. In data centers virtual servers have to be moved, copied, created, and deleted, e.g. for load balancing or consolidation. Similar to the resources of Grids, server hardware is usually located close to each other, e.g. in racks or data centers, and interconnected with high-bandwidth links. Therefore, the management of virtualization in Grids and data centers is mainly implemented in a centralized way, where a central management element allocates resources. The *VMWare Infrastructure 3*[8], for instance, provides such a centralized management element to manage virtual machines in data centers. Although virtualization itself is highly distributed in PlanetLab, the management of hardware and slices is rather centralized. Slices are created, allocated and managed via a central server. Also the user of a slice is a central point of management, having to cope with hundreds of virtual machines.

In the approach proposed in this paper, flexible slices have to be managed in order to provide the envisioned future home environment. Home networks are interconnected by a P2P overlay and share their resources to enable distributed energy efficiency. Always-on services are wrapped into flexible slices (transparent for the users), making them movable within interconnected home environments. Energy saving is achieved by increasing the load on some computers while turning off others. The constraints (fairness, security, availability, and QoS) described in Section 4 in more detail have to be considered within the management decisions. The decision process is based on distributed statistics, which are gathered in the home networks. To achieve a scalable management in a dynamic and vast environment and to avoid single points of failures, the management is decentralized as far as possible. Homes with active computers are involved in the decision process, which concerns all of the interconnected home networks.

4 System Architecture

The proposed architecture for the distributed energy efficient resource sharing approach consists of interconnected homes. Each *home* is an abstraction from a home network consisting of an always-on gateway (or router) which connects the home network to the Internet, one or several computers and displays, connected peripherals, and sensors and actuators. For interconnection, the homes are using a DHT (Distributed Hash Table) based P2P overlay. Fig. 3 shows the proposed architecture. The home network (depicted as a bus system) consists of multi networks, for example wireless networks (like WLAN IEEE 802.11g) and wired networks, like serial line connections or Ethernet (for connecting sensors), and a high-speed up-/down link to the Internet.

Each component of the home, which we refer to as a *node*, (e.g. any computer, sensor, actuator, PDA, etc.) is represented by static (like the processor speed and main memory size) and dynamic (like the utilization and the energy consumption) characteristics. Additionally, each node is in one of the states *active* (online and contributing), *active-blocked* (online but not contributing), or *passive* (in suspended, hibernating, low power mode). The state active-blocked has been introduced to support the user who wants to stay in control of his/her home equipment. For example, if the user wants to join an MMORPG (massively multiplayer online role playing game), bandwidth and computing power should not be contributed for energy

---

[8] http://www.vmware.com/pdf/vi_brochure.pdf

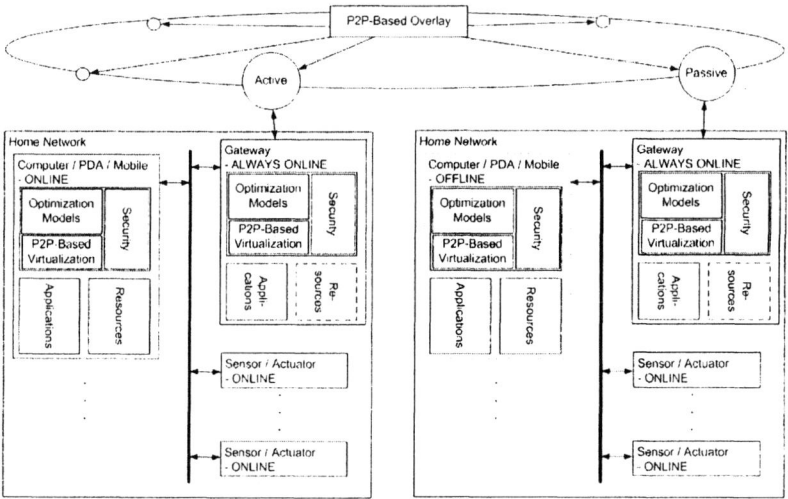

Fig. 3 Distributed energy efficient home network architecture.

efficient resource sharing, because otherwise the gaming experience might be negatively influenced. Similarly, a home is said to be active if it contributes to the system, active-blocked if it is not ready to contribute, and passive, if all possible contributing resources of the home are hibernating.[9] The abstraction of the nodes in terms of their characteristics is aggregated to describe the characteristics of a home.

Virtualization techniques are applied in two ways as described in Section 3. First, the system appears as an abstract *virtual organization* (in compliance with Grid technology) to the service which is executed transparently on participating nodes of the system (residing in homes). Second, load distribution and shifting is implemented by utilizing the technology of *virtual machines*. The management of the load distribution is done in a distributed manner by executing a distributed algorithm on each node. In Fig. 3, the depicted modules Security, Optimization Models, and P2P-Based Virtualization implement the management functionality and are described below in more detail.

Through virtualization, applications can transparently allocate resources like disk space, CPU time, or bandwidth without knowledge about location or configuration of remote computers by logically separating application modules into *frontends* and *backends*. The frontend implements only few functions of the application like the user interfaces, while the backend implements the heavy-loaded business logic. Due to virtualization, many backends could be assigned to the same frontend while the

---

[9] Note, that in case a home is passive or active-blocked, the gateway is still up and the home might consume services like home automation services from the distributed home environment.

distributed execution is hidden. The user only must start his frontend instead of starting the applications on his own computer.

Fig. 3 shows that the intelligence of the distributed management layer is situated in each contributing node, which may be both a full-blown PC with large computational resources (but also large energy consumption), or the home router/gateway, which is assumed to be a simple Linux-based diskless computer with small energy needs. Though this gateway is not able to contribute its own resources to be used by other homes, its computational power should be sufficient to maintain a permanent entry in the system wide DHT for representing its particular home. Since the gateways are assumed to run permanently (as usually all routers/gateways do), the churn as experienced by the P2P system is thus almost zero.

The management layer is based on three major building blocks. The P2P-based virtualization manages the overlay and provides services like identifying other peers, providing a system wide distributed database for storing node statistics persistently (including descriptions of the node resource capabilities, energy class, up-/downlink capacity, resources contributed so far to the system, etc.), or transferring resource requests from one computer to another.

Above it, optimization models implement the true intelligence of the system. They can be roughly divided into the following submodels:

- Energy efficiency. Once a frontend requests to use the resources of a remote computer, depending on the type of request, this submodel tries to identify a set of nodes which should be selected because selecting them would minimize the global energy consumption and maximize global energy efficiency.
- Fairness. This model uses statistics about how much each home has contributed to the system recently. Given a resource request and a set of nodes (from the energy efficiency model), this model identifies those nodes who should be assigned because they have not contributed much recently.
- Availability. This submodel decides how the service should be replicated. For instance, storing data for other computers, or remote home management should be done by using replication in order to increase availability.
- Privacy. This model tries to maximize the degree of privacy that a service is experiencing. Consider for instance the case that a remote home manages resources of other homes. In order to prevent the host computer to find out the identity of the managed home, other homes might function as a proxy chain in between.
- Quality of service. Depending on the application, given a resource request, this model decides whether a particular node is able to host the requested application. For instance, if the user wants to remotely encode video files, the host computer carrying out the work should actually command a large down- and uplink bandwidth and enough free CPU power. These resources, however, would be used only once. A slower computer on the other hand might be sufficient to receive messages from home management services and answer to them. This particular service then would run for a very long time, thus achieving fairness. A third example for QoS decisions is given by the tradeoff between QoS and privacy. Consider again remote home management. When using *long* proxy chains, the degree of privacy is extremely high, whereas the important QoS parameters la-

tency and bandwidth will be much worse. Thus for many applications there is a tradeoff between QoS and privacy.

- Security. This model is part of the P2P layer as well as being part of the optimization models. At the P2P layer it provides services for encryption and key exchange. At the optimization layer it mainly governs the distributed voting process. Voting is necessary because malicious nodes may try to create damage in other homes. Consider once more home management. Shutting down heating might be dangerous and cause damage in winter. Thus, such possibly dangerous applications might rely on a majority voting, where for instance the home gateway acts as a policer, and only commands may pass which have been signed by several other homes, rather than by only one.

5 Analytical Evaluation

In order to investigate the potential energy saving by cooperation we have developed an analytical model for a simple download scenario. In this scenario computers may share downloads with each other. Since we are only interested into the potential energy saving, security and privacy concerns are not included into the model. Downloads are carried out via a conventional file-sharing tool like *KaZaa*, *eMule* or *BitTorrent* from the Internet, i.e., from computers which are not part of the modelled scenario. A computer A may send a download request to another computer B, which will then carry out the download. This way, downloads can be shared and only a small number of computers must be active and thus consume energy. Other computers may sleep, thus not consuming energy at all. Once the download on computer B has finished, B sends back the file to computer A, here waking up A, which will then again consume energy as long as the transfer is going on. As a simplification we assume that computers being active because they download for others, always download their own files.

Furthermore it is assumed that downloads do not use the whole downlink bandwidth B_d as given by the Internet connection. Instead, as is experienced with real life file-sharing tools, the download bandwidth for one single file is limited by some upper limit, but on average uses B_l Kbit/s with $B_l < B_d$. B_l usually depends on the number of seeders and on properties of the used file-sharing tool. The scenario is described by the following parameters. Parameter N denotes the number of computers in the scenario, while $M = \lfloor B_d/B_l \rfloor$ denotes the number of downloads that may be carried out in parallel by each single computer. For instance, if we assume that a computer's raw downlink bandwidth is $B_d = 4$ Mbit/s, and each download on average consumes $B_l = 200$ Kbit/s, then $M = 20$ downloads can be carried out concurrently. Parameter λ denotes the arrival rate of download requests at each single computer, F denotes the average file size, $t_l = F/B_l$ denotes the average time it takes for downloading a file, and thus $\mu = 1/t_l$ denotes the rate at which each download is finished. For instance, if the size of a file on average is $F = 100$ MBytes, and $B_l = 200$ Kbit/s, then $\mu = 1/4000$ downloads finished per second.

In order to make the model analytically tractable, it is assumed that download requests arrive according to a Poisson process, and download times (and thus file sizes) are distributed exponentially. The latter assumption is in conflict to the well known fact that file sizes usually follow a Pareto or lognormal distribution. This will later be accounted for in our future simulations.

We investigate three cases, the local case where no sharing occurs (*local*), the ideal resource sharing case (*ideal*), and the corrected case (*corr*). The two latter cases differ in the way they deal with the actual transfer to the requesting peer: while in the ideal case, this transfer is neglected, in the corrected case, this transfer is included (resulting in additional wake-up time for the requesting computer).

At first, we assume that downloads are carried out on the computer that created the request, i.e., no sharing is going on. Thus, we start by modeling one single computer. The number of downloads carried out by this computer can be modeled by a birth-death process, i.e., the process is in state k if the computer is currently carrying out k downloads. Since M is the upper bound of downloads, the process has exactly $M+1$ states. It is further assumed that if the process is in state M, newly generated downloads are lost. This is done since for the low load investigated here, there is de facto no loss. Otherwise, a much more complicated M/M/M queue would be necessary. The process states and transition rates are shown in Fig. 4.

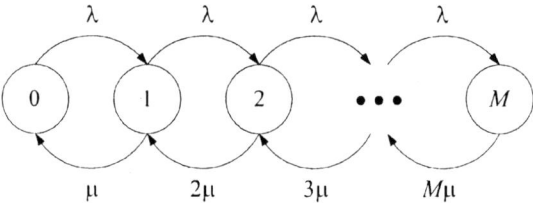

Fig. 4 Birth-death process for local downloads on one single computer.

Simple analysis shows that the probability π_k for being in state k is given by [2]

$$\pi_k = \pi_0 \frac{1}{k!} \left(\frac{\lambda}{\mu} \right)^k, 1 \le k \le M, \text{ with } \pi_0 = \frac{1}{1 + \sum\limits_{k=1}^{M} \frac{1}{k!} \left(\frac{\lambda}{\mu} \right)^k}.$$

Since π_0 denotes the probability that no download is going on, $1 - \pi_0$ denotes the probability that at least one download is going on, i.e., the computer is active. If there are N computers, then the expected number of active computers N_{local} for local downloads only is given by

$$N_{local} = N \left(1 - \frac{1}{1 + \sum\limits_{k=1}^{M} \frac{1}{k!} \left(\frac{\lambda}{\mu} \right)^k} \right). \tag{2}$$

In the next scenario we assume that computers share downloads, i.e., if a computer creates a download request with rate λ, it first searches for an active computer to pass the request to. If there is none, it will start the download itself. Again the scenario is modeled by a birth-death process, this time by modeling the state of all computers. Since there are N computers, and each is able to carry out M downloads in parallel, in total $M \times N$ downloads can simultaneously be carried out, i.e., the process has $M \times N + 1$ states as shown in Fig. 5.

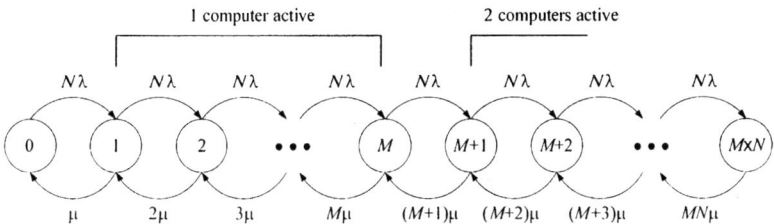

Fig. 5 Birth-death process for simultaneous downloads of N computers.

The solution of this process is similar to the one above, yielding

$$\pi_k = \pi_0 \frac{1}{k!} \left(\frac{N\lambda}{\mu} \right)^k, 1 \leq k \leq NM, \text{ with } \pi_0 = \frac{1}{1 + \sum\limits_{k=1}^{NM} \frac{1}{k!} \left(\frac{N\lambda}{\mu} \right)^k}.$$

When assuming zero communication overhead, and not taking into account sending back the download results (*ideal* situation), then the number of active computers necessary to carry out k downloads is $a = \lceil k/M \rceil$. In other words, no computer must be active in state zero, $a = 1$ computer must be active in the states 1 to M, $a = 2$ for the states $M + 1$ to $2M$, and so on. The probability for needing exactly one active computer is thus given by the sum of the $\pi_k, 1 \leq k \leq M$, and in general the probability for needing exactly a active computers is therefore the sum of the $\pi_k, (a - 1)M + 1 \leq k \leq aM$. For computing the expectation N_{ideal} of a, we derive

$$N_{ideal} = \sum_{a=1}^{N} a \sum_{k=(a-1)M+1}^{aM} \pi_k. \tag{3}$$

In order to catch the effect of additional transfer to computer A, after the download has finished on computer B, the system is observed for a long time T. Then the

total time that computers are active within T is given by $N_{ideal}T$, and the time that
the system was in state k is given by $\pi_k T$. From this it follows that the number of
finished downloads while being in state k is given by $\pi_k T k\mu$. Since all N computers contribute equally to the system load, i.e., all create download requests with the
same λ, the origins of download requests are distributed evenly amongst all computers, but only $\lceil k/M \rceil$ of them are active. It follows that on average the number
of downloads finished in state k, which were carried out for a *currently sleeping*
computer is given by

$$\pi_k T k\mu \frac{N - \lceil k/M \rceil}{N}.$$

The time for sending back the result to the initiating computer is given by $t_u = F/B_u$,
here taking the full raw uplink bandwidth B_u given by the Internet connection (e.g.,
$B_u = 1$ Mbit/s), which is considered to be much faster than the average download
bandwidth B_l limited by the file-sharing tool. Thus, when sending back a finished
download to a computer that was sleeping previously, the sleeping computer must be
woken up, and must be active for at least t_u seconds. It follows that when observing
the system for T seconds, the additional active time T_{corr} for sending back finished
downloads to computers which have been sleeping previously, is given by

$$T_{corr} = t_u \sum_{k=1}^{MN} T \pi_k k\mu \frac{N - \lceil k/M \rceil}{N}.$$

The total time of active computers observed over the time T is thus $T_t = N_{ideal}T + T_{corr}$, the *corrected* average number N_{corr} of active computers observed is derived
by dividing T_t by T. When considering additionally that $t_u = F/B_u$ and $\mu = B_l/F$,
N_{corr} takes the form

$$N_{corr} = N_{ideal} + \frac{B_l}{B_u} \sum_{k=1}^{MN} k \pi_k \frac{N - \lceil k/M \rceil}{N}. \tag{4}$$

Equ. (4) is in accordance with the simple intuition that active time is likely to be
saved only if the download bandwidth B_l is smaller than the raw uplink bandwidth B_u. Fig. 6 shows results for $N = 1000, F = 100$ MByte, $B_d = 4$ Mbit/s,
$B_l = 200$ Kbit/s, and $B_u = 1$ Mbit/s. Each single computer generates a certain number of download requests per week, shown at the x-axis. The possible saving of
computer energy is reflected by the difference between the number of active computers in the local case (2) and the corrected case (4). It can be seen that even when
taking into account the distribution overhead, i.e., sending back the files to the requesting computers, the shared scenario (Corr) can save a substantial amount of
energy. For instance, when assuming that each computer consumes 100 W and creates 35 download requests every week, without cooperation, 1000 non-cooperative
computers would *constantly* consume more than 20 kW on average just for downloading files, while cooperating computers would only consume about 5.7 kW for
the same task. However, the distribution overhead, i.e., sending files back to the requesting computer, clearly dominates the shared scenario, which can be seen by the

difference between the ideal and the corrected case, and which is mainly determined by the relation between B_l and B_u. Note that changing B_l alone does not have a large effect in (4), since B_l also determines M, and a smaller B_l will result in a larger M, enabling a larger degree of sharing. On the other hand, increasing B_u does have a dramatic effect and yields much better energy efficiency.

The energy efficiency η given by (1), here in downloads per kWh, is shown in Fig. 7. The energy efficiency of the sharing scenario (Corr) is clearly much better than the one for the scenario without cooperation (Local). It can be seen that if the load is too small then downloads are usually carried out sequentially, and even the ideal case cannot save energy by clustering the downloads. For increasing load, the energy efficiency approaches a system-specific upper limit.

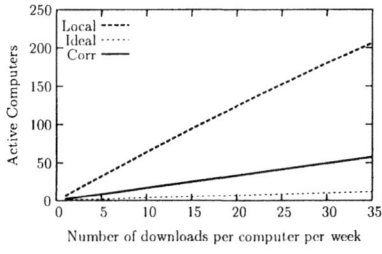

Fig. 6 Number of active computers.

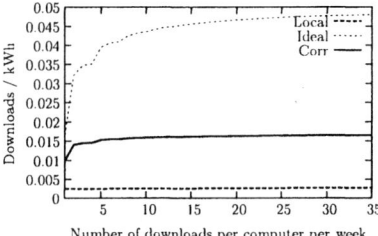

Fig. 7 Energy efficiency η.

It must be noted that the corrected model does not take into account several details, such as representative file size distribution and protocol overhead. In order to include all the above mentioned issues, currently a discrete event simulator is developed, to evaluate the energy consumption for various applications and sharing patterns.

6 Conclusion

In this paper, as a first result of the research project Virtual Home Environments, a novel architecture for virtualizing and sharing hardware resources in future home environments is presented. The architecture aims at utilizing existing home re-sources in such a way that the consumed energy is minimized and the energy is efficiently used. A fully decentralized management system is proposed, intercon-necting possibly thousands of homes in a peer-to-peer like manner. Energy opti-mization is done in a decentralized way by converging to a global energy optimum based on energy and performance metrics which have been defined. For the example scenario *file download* an analytical model has been developed which demonstrates the possible amount of energy that can be saved if computers cooperate and share file downloads, rather than if each computer downloads its own files. The future work will include the further development of shared applications and sharing patterns for a simulation environment. We aim at identifying thresholds which help to distinguish useful sharing from sharing that actually consumes more energy than it saves while considering the introduced constraints.

Acknowledgements This project was partly funded by the German Research Foundation (Deutsche Forschungsgemeinschaft - DFG), contract number ME 1703/4-1 and by the EURO-FGI - Network of Excellence, European Commission grant IST 028022.

References

1. T. Anderson and T. Roscoe. Learning from PlanetLab. *Proceedings of the 3rd WORLDS*, 2006.
2. G. Bolch, S. Greiner, H. de Meer, and K.S. Trivedi. *Queueing Networks and Markov Chains*. Wiley & Sons, 2nd edition, 2006.
3. IBM Virtualizatin View. Virtualization Can Help Power Efficiency. http://www-03.ibm.com/systems/virtualization/view/011607.html, January 2007.
4. Intel. Energy Star* System Implementation. www.intel.com/cd/channel/reseller /asmo-na/eng/339085.htm, 2007.
5. Intel. Increasing Data Center Density while Driving down Power and Cooling Costs, June 2006.
6. Intel white paper 30057701. Wireless Intel SpeedStep Power Manager: Optimizing Power Consumption for the Intel PXA27x Processor Family. http://sunsite.rediris.es /pub/mirror/intel/pca/applicationsprocessors/whitepapers/30057701.pdf, 2004.
7. J.G. Koomey, editor. *Energystar, Server Energy Measurement Protocol, Version 1.0*, Following Energy Efficiency Server Benchmark Technical Workshop, Santa Clara, CA, March 2006.
8. J.G. Koomey. Estimating Total Power Consumption by Servers in the US and the World. Technical report, Lawrence Berkeley National Laboratory and Stanford University, 2007.
9. L. Peterson and T. Roscoe. The Design Principles of PlanetLab. *ACM SIGOPS Operating Systems Review*, Vol 40(Issue 1):11–16, 2006.
10. Suzanne Rivoire, Mehul Shah, Parthasarathy Ranganathan, and Christos Kozyrakis. JouleSort: A Balanced Energy-Efficiency Benchmark. In *Proceedings of the 2007 ACM SIGMOD International Conference on Management of Data (SIGMOD)*, June 2007.
11. J. Stokes. Power Plays: How power Consumption Will Shape the Future of Computing. *online Article: Ars Technica*, June 28 2007.
12. D. Thain, T. Tannenbaum, and M. Livny. Condor and the Grid. *Grid Computing: Making the Global Infrastructure a Reality, John Wiley & Sons Inc.*, March 2002.
13. M. Weiser. The Computer for the 21st Century. *ACM SIGMOBILE Mobile Computing and Communications Review: Special issue dedicated to Mark Weiser*, Vol 3(Issue 3):Pages 3 – 11, July 1999.
14. C. Windeck. Energy Star 4.0. *C't German Magazine for Computer Techniques*, Vol 14:Pages 52–53, 2007.
15. Christof Windeck. Spar-o-matic. *C't German Magazine for Computer Techniques*, Vol 15:Pages 200–207, 2007.

Avoiding energy-compromised hotspots in resource-limited wireless networks

Joseph Rahmé[1], Aline Carneiro Viana[2], Khaldoun Al Agha[1]

Abstract The vast literature on the wireless sensor research community contains many valuable proposals for managing energy consumption, the most important factor that determines sensors lifetime. Interesting researches have been facing this requirement by focusing on the extension of the entire network lifetime: either by switching between node states (active, sleep), or by using energy efficient routing. We argue that a better extension of the network lifetime can be obtained if an efficient combination of management mechanisms can be performed at the energy of each single sensor and at the load distribution over the network. Considering these two accuracy levels (*i.e.*, node and network), this paper presents a new approach that uses cost functions to choose energy efficient routes. In particular, by making different energy considerations at a node level, our approach distributes routing load, avoiding thus, energy-compromised hotspots that may cause network disconnections. The proposed cost functions have completely decentralized and adaptive behavior and take into consideration: the end-to-end energy consumption, the remaining energy of nodes, and the number of transmissions a node can make before its energy depletion. Our simulation results show that, though slightly increasing path lengths from sensor to sink nodes, the proposed scheme (1) improves significantly the network lifetime for different neighborhood densities degrees, while (2) preserves network connectivity for a longer period of time.

1 Introduction

Context. Self-configuring wireless sensors are revolutionizing the way to integrate computing in our daily environment. This is mainly due the fact that they make possible to gather and to process information in ways not previously possible [7]. Beside this feature, they include data accuracy, flexibility, cost effectiveness, and ease

---

[1] LRI, Université Paris-SUD XI – Paris, France. Contact email: {rahme, alagha}@lri.fr
[2] ASAP, INRIA Saclay - Ile de France sud, France

Please use the following format when citing this chapter:

Rahmé, J., Viana, A. C., Al Agha, K., 2007, in IFIP International Federation for Information Processing, Volume 256, Home Networking, Al Agha, K., Carcelle, X., Pujolle, G., (Boston: Springer), pp. 85-100.

of deployment characteristics. As a consequence, sensor-based networks play an important role in the design of applications whose aim is surveillance, data-gathering, or monitoring. It consists in deploying a large number of sensors to execute a determined task in a specified geographic area. The task can be the monitoring of specific events or the tracking of targets within the area of interest. Sensor-based networks have thus, attracted the attention of civil, medical, and military domains, justifying the numerous research in the wireless sensor area.

It is usual to consider application scenarios where sensors are deployed in regions of difficult access, and/or human intervention is not feasible. In this scenarios, self-organization is a particularly important attribute for the autonomy dimension of the network. This requires the network to be able to organize/configure by its own self in order to solve problems such as routing, load balancing, or energy consumption.

Motivation. Despite the recent advances in electronics, numerous constraints are still imposed on sensors devices and especially on their energy. This fact makes the proposal of energy optimization mechanisms an important requirement. In this context, an important question raises: *how energy consumption can be managed in order to increase network lifetime?* This is the topic addressed in the paper.

The vast literature on the wireless sensor research community contains many valuable proposals for managing energy consumption. Recently, interesting researches have been facing this requirement by focusing on the extension of the entire network lifetime. In a global point of view, these researches :

- switch nodes' energy level between sleep and awake states [4, 2, 6, 15, 11] or
- by keeping nodes in the active state, perform power control [9, 3, 1] or energy-aware routing [10, 13, 8, 5, 14, 16].

Despite having clearly defined outlines and presented good solutions, those works deal with the network lifetime's extension problem (*1*) by reducing the energy consumption at each single sensor (*i.e.*, at a node accuracy level) **or** (*2*) by assuring a homogeneous load distribution over the network (*i.e.*, at a network accuracy level). Section 2 gives a detailed review of these works.

Contributions. Instead, our approach takes into account both: the overall energy consumption and the load distribution over the network. By considering those two accuracy levels (*i.e.*, at the node and at the network scope), this paper presents a new approach that uses cost functions to determine energy efficient routes. By making different energy considerations at a node level, our approach distributes routing load, avoiding thus, energy-compromised hotspots that may cause network disconnections. In addition, the end-to-end energy consumed when sending a packet is minimized. So, different from the previous approaches, cost functions group what is needed to increase network lifetime.

In summary, the contributions of this paper are twofold:

- an intelligent method allowing to (*i*) determine energy efficient paths between nodes in the network, (*ii*) distribute routing load over the network, and (*iii*) avoid energy-compromised hotspots nodes;

- a set of self-configuring cost functions used to determine energy efficient routes and to optimize energy consumption.

The proposed cost functions have completely decentralized and adaptive behaviors and take into consideration: the end-to-end energy consumption, the remaining energy of nodes, and the number of transmissions a node can make before its energy depletion. Our simulation results show that, though slightly increasing path lengths from sensor to sink nodes, the proposed scheme (1) improves significantly the network lifetime for different neighborhood densities degrees, while (2) preserves network connectivity for a longer period of time.

Outline. The paper is organized as follows. In Section 2, we present a review of the main related works by providing a general classification of existent approaches. After introducing our system model in Section 3, we present our proposal by introducing the cost functions in Section 4. Performance results are presented in Section 5. Finally, Section 6 concludes this paper and discusses future works.

2 Related Work

This section discusses the works in the literature related to the energy management in wireless sensor networks. Moreover, at the following sub-sections, we provide a general classification of these works into three different categories. These categories are the following: energy efficient routing, power control, and the management of nodes activity by state switching.

2.1 Energy efficient routing

We discuss here the works that, in order to increase the network lifetime, proposes to perform routing by considering the energy consumed by nodes in the network. In particular, they intend to determine paths that optimize this energy.

In [10], Kwon *et al.* propose a routing protocol to find a route that minimizes the energy consumption of a flow. They thus calculate, for each link in the network, the increment ΔE in energy dissipation resulting from the routing of a flow. A route between two nodes is calculated using a shortest path algorithm with the increment ΔE as the weight of the links. This proposal, however, does not guarantee an end-to-end energy optimization, as one of our cost functions do (presented in Section 4.2.1), and does not take into account the remaining energy of nodes (described in Section 4.2.2).

Authors in [13, 5], propose a reactive and multi-routing protocol that uses the remaining energy in the node to improve network lifetime. In [13], routes are selected using a *cost* that depends on the remaining energy of intermediate nodes. The probability of using a route for a flow is inversely proportional to its cost. Thus, contrarily to our approach, authors do not take into account the energy dissipated by interferences, which makes it not realistic. In [5], each node constructs a vector containing the remaining energy of every intermediate node, being a route considered shorter than another if it contains a node with minimal remaining energy. An energy efficient route is the longest route that avoids using nodes with low energy. This method requires, however, a centralized management in order to be properly implemented, which is not always feasible in wireless sensor networks.

In [16], authors introduce a query-based protocol that searches for the route with nodes having maximal remaining energy. Therefore, a source node sends a route request with an energy threshold, all intermediate nodes with higher energy reply to this request. If no route is found, the threshold is decreased and the same procedure is repeated until a route is found. This protocol presents a problem when the threshold is not properly chosen, which consequently generates multiple flooding.

2.2 Power control

Some approaches deal with the problem of increasing the network lifetime by changing each node transmission power. They then look for the decrease of the consumed energy in data transmission, while assuring network connectivity.

In [9], authors show that reducing the transmission power of nodes will not necessarily minimize the energy consumption, since it will increase the number of hops. They proved that at a certain radius range, the energy consumed for communication is minimal. Nevertheless, the optimal radius for global diffusion differs from the optimal radius for point to point communications. Changing the radius for each communication type makes this solution difficult to implement.

In [3] the paper presents an algorithm to obtain a strongly connected topology by adjusting the transmission power of every node in the network. The Hitch-Hiking mechanism is used for that. This approach enables every node to locally choose its transmission power by using the available information about its 1- and 2-hop neighbors.

In [1] the authors use a closed loop for power control. For this, the destination node embeds in each answer (CTS for RTS or Acks for DATA) the reception power and the minimal threshold required for a good reception. The source receiving the response can then adjust its energy. This approach presents a problem when the MAC layer does not receive a response for a CTS or Ack due to an interference: the transmission power of the source will be incremented without any real need.

2.3 Management of nodes activity by state switching

The approaches in this category propose to alternate the activity level of nodes into sleep or awake modes.

In [2], the approach divides the network into disjoint set of sensors such that every set covers all the monitored targets. These sets are activated successively such that at any instant, one set is active and all the other sets are in the sleep mode. Although to significantly improve network's lifetime, it requires a centralized management.

In [4] the authors use a localized method to switch the nodes state between active and sleep. For this, the proposed method chooses a dominant set of nodes that are not energy constrained to stay active and all the other nodes are in the sleep state. This set must keep the network connected and the surveillance zone covered. The periodic execution of the algorithm makes the dominant set dynamic and avoids that certain nodes loose their energy early. This methods requires a good knowledge of the overall network. In a similar way, authors in [11] propose to switch nodes energy state into sleep, forwarding, or sensing-only. The proposed method relies on a distributed probing approach and on the redundancy resolution of sensors for getting energy optimizations. Contrarily to [4], this method does not require any global network knowledge, but, for some particular cases, it fails to guarantee network connectivity.

In [12] every node detecting that two of his neighbors cannot communicate using an active node, becomes active. The duration of the active state is subject to the remaining energy of the node and the number of nodes it can connect together. This rule permits the node to switch between the active and the sleep state and optimizes the energy consumption. This method requires nodes to change their neighborhood lists in order to correctly activate nodes.

In [15] the network is divided into virtual grids using node positions given by a GPS. All nodes in a grid are equivalent in terms of routing and packet forwarding. A node in the active or discovery state becomes inactive when it determines that another node in the same grid can do the routing. The lifetime of the network is optimized by activating one node in each grid. The choice of this node is based on its remaining energy. This method requires a GPS embedded in every node which is unfeasible in large scale networks.

3 System Model

We will target a general application scenario where the n sensor nodes are randomly deployed in a zone of interest difficult to access and/or where human intervention is not feasible. The considered scenario has then, a finite set of n nodes, each uniquely identified. We consider that sensors form at the begging, a connected network.

Nodes are all *equal*, in the sense that they have the same attributes, *i.e.* computational, memory, and communication capabilities. We do not consider Byzantine failures, so nodes may only go out of the system when their battery goes off. Regarding energy, a node may only be in the active state. That is all the nodes in the network are active until their depletion and they all have the same energy when they are deployed.

Each node has the same radio communication range r that allows it to communicate by broadcasting messages. Thus, a node i is able to directly communicate wirelessly with a subset of nodes that are located in the transmission range r_i, and no obstacles interfere with the communication – we refer to that subset as the *neighbors* of the node i. We assume *bidirectional* communications: for any nodes i and j, if i can communicate with j, then j can communicate with i. We consider that sensing and communication ranges are equal. No synchronization is required.

Table 1 Parameters summary.

Parameter	Description
E_{TX}	Energy consumed at a packet's transmission by source nodes.
E_{RX}	Energy consumed at a packet's reception by 1-hop neighbors.
E_I	Energy consumed due the interference caused by a 2-hop neighbor transmission.
$E_r(i)$	Remaining energy at the node i.

Our energy model uses the parameters described at the Table 1. In particular, we consider a 2-hop interference model. When a node i transmits a packet, it consumes an energy E_{TX} to code and transmit the packet. All the nodes existing 1-hop away from the emitting node i, *i.e. neighbors$_i$*, receive the packet and decode it. The nodes in *neighbors$_i$* that are not the destination, receive the packet, consume E_{RX} energy to decode it, and then, discard the packet. The 2-hop neighbors of the transmitting node, receive an non-intelligible signal. This reception makes these nodes to consumes E_I energy.

4 Our proposal

In sensor network, the nodes use batteries with limited energy as their source of energy. In large-scale sensor networks, nodes are often deployed in hostile environment. If nodes batteries deplete, the possibility of their replacement is almost impossible. Moreover, in case the nodes are accessible, replacing their battery is not always feasible if large networks are considered. In this case, the optimization of nodes' energy consumption is essential to extend network's lifetime. To change nodes states between active and sleep seems interesting but presents a major challenge in decentralized systems like WSNs, in other words: *how to determine the duty cycle of nodes and still guarantee connectivity without requiring a global knowledge of the network?*

Instead, our proposal considers that nodes are always in the active state. In addition, to optimize the energy consumption in the network, our proposal implements an energy efficient routing that chooses routes based on energy-related weight associated to links. At the following, we briefly describe this routing mechanism and then provide a detailed description of how links are associated to energy-related weight.

4.1 Energy efficient routing

The proposed routing algorithm is in fact, a modified shortest path algorithm, being energy efficiency gotten through *energy-based cost functions*. The values given by these functions represent the weight of the link between a node and his 1-hop neighbors. Thus, once weight of links are computed, routing is performed by following the routes that minimizes the total energy consumed to send a packet from the source to the destination.

The next sections introduce three different cost functions to associate weights to links. Each of them considers distinct but dependent nodes' energy-related parameters. Since the links' weights are updated each time a transmission is performed, routing load is distributed among links that present better energy levels. In addition, energy-compromised hot spots are detected and consequently avoided, before packet transmissions.

4.2 Energy-based cost functions

This section presents and discusses the three proposed cost functions, named:

- $E_{\theta_1}(i)$: considers the amount of energy consumed by a emitting node i and its 1- and 2-hop neighbors, when i performs a packet's transmission.
- $E_{\theta_2}(i)$: considers the remaining energy of node i and its 1- and 2-hop neighbors.
- $\omega(i)$: considers the maximal number of transmissions that node i can perform before node i, or one of its 1- or 2-hop neighbors dies.

4.2.1 Considering consumed energy – 1st cost function:

When a node transmits, all its 1-hop neighbors will consume energy to decode the packet. Therefore, energy consumption for a transmission is proportional to the number of neighbors. Having this in mind, we introduces cost function E_{θ_1} which avoids the participation of nodes with a lot of neighbors in the routing process. This is due the fact that their energy consumption after a transmission, may represent a significant amount for the network lifetime. thus, This E_{θ_1} is used to assign weights between a node and his 1-hop neighbors: the weight of the link (i, j) between i and any 1-hop neighbor j is equal to E_{θ_1} of node i. E_{θ_1} is thus, defined as:

$$E_{\theta_1}(i) = E_{TX} + \sum_{n_1 \in N_1(i)} E_{RX} + \sum_{n_2 \in N_2(i)} E_I \tag{1}$$

, where

- $N_1(i)$ is the set of 1-hop neighbors of node i;
- $N_2(i)$ is the set of 2-hop neighbors of node i;
- and E_{TX}, E_{RX}, and E_I are described at the Table 1.

In fact, cost function E_{θ_1} calculates the impact a node's transmission will have on the energy of the network, *i.e.,* the amount of energy consumed by the emitting node and his 1- and 2-hop neighbors.

One important point to remark here is that the total energy consumed for routing a packet p from a source to a final destination is additive, representing the amount of energy consumed by the network to route the packet p. Thus, since E_{θ_1} is the energy consumed for a packet's transmission, the whole energy consumed to route the packet to its final destination is the sum of the link weights (E_{θ_1}) forming the route. Therefore, a simple shortest path algorithm using E_{θ_1} as a metric, can easily find an energy efficient route. The weight of a route between two nodes exchanging packets is the sum of intermediate links weight forming this route. The route having a minimal sum of weights is then, the optimal route given by the modified shortest path algorithm.

Moreover, E_{θ_1} enables the shortest path algorithm to avoid nodes that, if used for routing, will waste a lot of energy in the network. Looking at the formula of E_{θ_1}, it is evident that E_{θ_1} gives a high weight for the nodes with a lot of neighbors, which can be seen in the following part of the formula: $\sum_{n_1 \in N_1(i)} E_{RX}$ and $\sum_{n_2 \in N_2(i)} E_I$. In a dense area, the weight of these two factors will be high and the routing protocol *will not* route through nodes with high neighbors' density. In this situation, the routing is biased toward using nodes deployed at the borders because they possess a minimal number of neighbors which reduces energy consumption in the network.

Despite having the interesting property of minimizing network disconnections, the presented cost function does not consider the remaining energy of nodes. In particular, E_{θ_1} only considers the energy consumed for transmission E_{TX}. This means that a node with a remaining energy that is insufficient for performing one packet's transmission can still be selected as next-hop.

To deal with this problem, we use the *remaining energy* of the 1-hop neighbors and E_{θ_1} of the source node to calculate the weight of a link. Thus, our new approach to assign weights for links is the following: the weight of a link (i, j) is equal to $c_f \times \frac{E_{\theta_1}(i)}{E_r(j)}$ where c_f is a weighting factor and $E_r(j)$ is the remaining energy of the 1-hop neighbor j. This approach permits the routing protocol to distinguish between two neighbors of i having different energy remaining: the neighbor with greater energy remaining will form the link with i. The new approach let the routing protocol avoids the nodes with low neighbors density (*i.e. small* E_{θ_1})and remaining energy.

Next section presents the second cost function E_{θ_2}, which explicitly considers the reaming energy in the cost function.

4.2.2 Considering remaining energy – 2nd cost function:

The second cost function E_{θ_2} takes into account the remaining energy of a node and of its 1- and 2-hop neighbors. The cost function E_{θ_2} is as follows:

$$E_{\theta_2}(i) = \min\{(E_r(i) - E_{TX}),$$
$$\min_{n_1 \in N_1(i)}(E_r(n_1) - E_{RX}) \quad\quad (2)$$
$$\min_{n_2 \in N_2(i)}(E_r(n_2) - E_I)\}$$

, where

- $E_r(i)$ is the remaining energy of the node i emitting the packet;
- $E_r(n_1)$, $E_r(n_2)$ are the remaining energy of the 1-hop and 2-hop neighbors affected by the transmission of node i;
- E_{TX}, E_{RX}, and E_I are the consumed energy as described at the Table 1.

As for the 1st cost function, the function E_{θ_2} is used to calculate links' weights between a node and his 1-hop neighbors, thus, for a link (i, j) where j can represent any 1-hop neighbor of i, the weight is equal to $E_{\theta_2}(i)$. By considering the emitting node's remaining energy after a transmission, *i.e.*, $(E_r(i) - E_{TX})$, we avoid the case where a node with a minimum remaining energy participates in the routing of a packet. By consequence, only links with the highest weights (*i.e.*, nodes with highest level of remaining energy) will compose the determined route. The others factors of the cost function (2) gives the minimum remaining energy at $1-$ and $2-hop$ neighbors after a transmission.

In summary, the use of E_{θ_2} to assign a weight for a link between two nodes, allows us to find a route that uses nodes with a high level remaining energy. This insures an homogeneous consumption of nodes energy, preventing the case where some nodes deplete their batteries before others. Nevertheless, E_{θ_2} does not consider neither the overall energy consumption of the route selected by the algorithm nor the number of hops. As a consequence, it may result in longer routes, consuming by consequence, a high level of energy for the routing of a packet.

Since the remaining energy is not an additive metric, routes that maximizes the sum of the weights resulted from E_{θ_2} can not be considered at the energy efficient route's computation. Therefore, a shortest-widest route algorithm (widest in term of remaining energy) is used.

The optimal route between two nodes is the route where the minimum remaining energy among intermediate nodes is maximal. To find the optimal route, a modified shortest-widest route algorithm is used. The shortest widest algorithm chooses among all the routes between a source and a destination, the one where the minimum remaining energies of intermediate nodes is maximal. More specifically, the weight of a route is the minimum weight among intermediate links connecting the source to the destination and the shortest-widest route is the route with the maximum weight. If multiple routes have the same maximum weight, the shortest-widest route algorithm chooses the one with the minimum number of hops. In this way, the algorithm tries to minimize the number of hops from the source to the destination and still keeps a maximal gain in remaining energy.

Despite this, the number of hops is not considered at the weight computation of E_{θ_2}. This imposes long routes to the shortest-widest route algorithm. Longer routes result in more transmissions in the network which increase the energy consumption and consume the remaining energy of nodes.

The next section introduces a third cost function that tries to solve this problem.

4.2.3 Considering number of transmissions – 3rd cost function:

Despite to also consider the remaining energy of nodes, the third cost function $\omega(i)$ uses a strategy different from the previous functions. $\omega(i)$ calculates the weight of a link (i, j) between two nodes as following:

$$\omega(i) = \min\{\frac{E_r(i)}{E_{TX}},$$
$$min_{n_1 \in N_1(i)} \frac{E_r(n_1)}{E_{RX}} \tag{3}$$
$$min_{n_2 \in N_2(i)} \frac{E_r(n_2)}{E_I}\}$$

, where $E_r(x)$, E_{TX}, E_{RX}, and E_I represent the energy level as previously explained for the Equation 2.

$\omega(i)$ uses the ratio $\frac{E_r(i)}{E_{TX}}$ to determine the remaining energy level of a node. Thus, besides indicating the energy of the node, the ratio $\frac{E_r(i)}{E_{TX}}$ also represents the maximal number of transmissions that the node can perform. For example, a ratio equal to n means that the node remaining energy is $n \times E_{TX}$ and that it can still transmit n packets before having its battery off. In the same way, the ratio $\frac{E_r(n_1)}{E_{RX}}$ indicates the number of packets a node can receive before its depletion . And finally, the ratio $\frac{E_r(i)}{E_I}$ determines the number of non-intelligible packets a node can receive before depleting all his energy.

Combining these three ratios and computing their minimum will give the $\omega(i)$ metric. The final result of this cost function is then, to give the minimum number of transmissions a node can execute before it or a node in its 1- or 2-hop neighborhood looses all their energy.

The weight of a route between two nodes is thus, the minimum weight among intermediate nodes forming this route. As described in Section 4.2.2, to find an energy efficient route between a source and a destination, we use the modified shortest-widest route algorithm with $\omega(i)$ as the cost function. The use of $\omega(i)$ allows an homogeneous load distribution over the network by avoiding nodes with low remaining energy.

Nevertheless, $\omega(i)$ does not consider the energy consumed to route a packet. It only insures an homogeneous energy consumption in order to prevent the depletion of some nodes' batteries before others. Thus, like the previous cost function E_{θ_2}, $\omega(i)$ will give routes with a significant remaining energy but will not take into consideration the energy consumption for routing packets from the source to the destination.

5 Performance evaluation

We have performed some experiments by simulation in order to better evaluate the proposed cost functions. In our experiments, we use a homemade C++ simulator. Our simulator takes into consideration the energy consumed by a node due to interferences, in particular, the energy consumed by the 2-hop neighbors of an emitting node. For every experiment, the network is composed of 20, 50, 70, 100, 200, 300 and 400 fixed nodes randomly distributed over a square area of 100 meters on a side. The detection range of a node is 20 meters and all nodes possess the same initial power. We consider that at any time only one event can occur in the network. The model of interference is the one described in Section 3.

Our simulator, is a discrete time-based engine in which the network lifetime is considered as a series of rounds. A round represents the arrival of an event in the network which is implemented by the routing of the packet generated by a source to a destination. We consider that all nodes have the same initial remaining energy estimated to 5000 unities (u). The power consumption for each node state is shown in Table 2. A single event is generated per round of simulation over the network and no wireless routing protocol is implemented. To evaluate the connectivity of the network, we choose arbitrarily a source and a destination and try to find a route between these two nodes. The energy of the nodes in the network is updated after the routing of each packet. The simulation stops when the first node in the network depletes its energy.

Table 2 Energy consumption

Node state	Energy consumption
Transmission	$1.3u$
Reception	$0.9u$
Interference	$0.4u$

Figure 1 compares the different cost functions with Dijkstra's algorithm. The figure shows for different network sizes, the number of round a network can support before the depletion of the first node. We vary the number of nodes in the network between $20, 50, 70, 100, 200, 300, 400$, which represents different nodes densities.

The results show that for all node densities, the shortest path algorithm gives low performance compared to the results obtained with E_{θ_1}. This is expected because E_{θ_1} finds the route that consumes the minimum energy in contradiction with Dijkstra which minimizes the number of hops. Since Dijkstra's algorithm uses the minimal number of hops to attend a destination, it tends to put the major load on the nodes situated in the center of the network. Consequently, this depletes the energy of nodes located in dense regions, violating the homogeneous distribution of the energy consumption and increasing the probability of network partition. Instead, E_{θ_1} increases the lifetime of the network by:

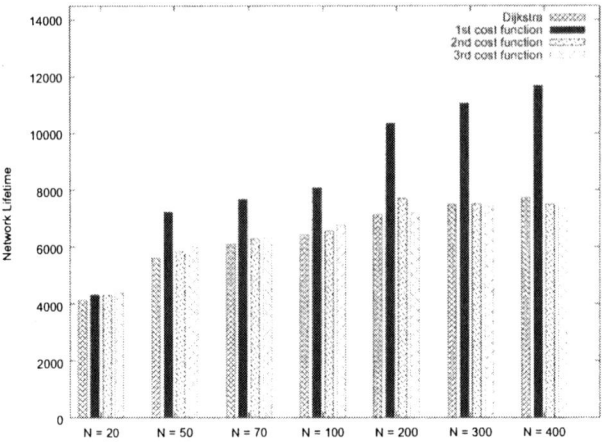

Fig. 1 Network lifetime with different cost functions and node densities.

- avoiding nodes that make the network consumes a lot of energy (nodes with large number of neighbors);
- minimizing the sum of the energy used to route the packet from source to destination.

For low node density ($N = 20, 50, 70, 100, 200$), it can also be observed that E_{θ_2} and $\omega(i)$ slightly increase the lifetime of the network when compared to Dijkstra. In addition, for a very low node density (*i.e.,* for $N = 20$), E_{θ_2} and $\omega(i)$ surpass E_{θ_1}.

Since E_{θ_2} and $\omega(i)$ use the remaining energy in the calculation of links' weights, the network load is distributed over nodes with high remaining energies. This only increases the lifetime in low dense networks because the extend in routes length is not significant. For high node density (*i.e.,* for $N = 100, 200, 300, 400$) the route length increases dramatically (as shown in Figure 2), which impacts the energy consumption in the network and decreases its lifetime.

Figures 2 and 3 show the average number of hops and the average consumed energy per route for different nodes densities. The figures show high values (*hop, energyconsum* E_{θ_2} and $\omega(i)$ when the network size increases. This explains why they have a lifetime close to Dijkstra, as shows Figure 1.

More specifically, in Figure 2, for $N = 400$, the number of hops for E_{θ_2} and $\omega(i)$ is very high compared to Dijkstra, which by consequence, explains the high consumed energy showed in Figure 3 and decreases the lifetime of the network. Therefore, it can be concluded that these two cost functions are better adapted for networks with a small number of nodes. We have, however, verified that contrarily to Dijkstra where the first node to die is in the center of the network (consequently, in a dense region), for these two cost functions, the first node is closer to the border

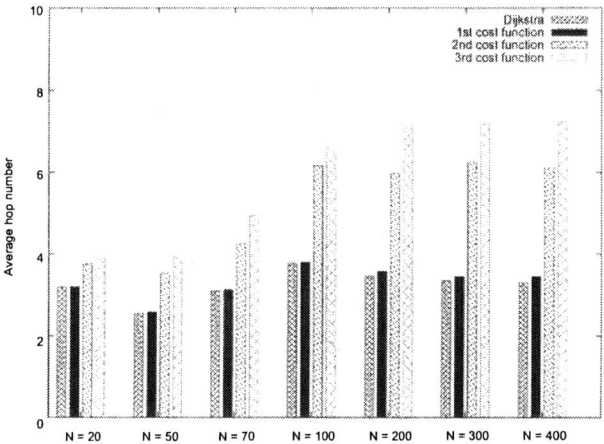

Fig. 2 Average hop number per route for different cost functions and node densities.

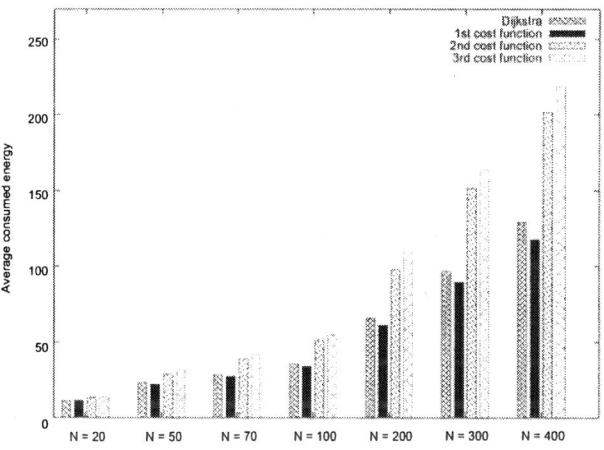

Fig. 3 Average energy consumed per route for different cost functions and node densities.

or on the border of the network. This is an interesting property to be considered, specially in cases where network lifetime is considered as *the maximum operational time of the network before the first disconnection with any sink node happens.*

All these analysis lead us to the following conclusion: E_{θ_1} gives good results but does not explicitly take into account the remaining energy of the nodes. Adding the remaining energy of the node in the cost function avoids nodes depletion. Nevertheless, cost function E_{θ_2} gives poor performance in terms of network lifetime compared to the shortest path algorithm. Moreover, since the cost functions E_{θ_2} and $\omega(i)$ use the shortest-widest algorithm to calculate the route between a source and a destination, it results in long routes that dramatically increase the energy consumption.

The results given by the cost function $\omega(i)$ prove that despite preventing the depletion of nodes, the network lifetime is increased slightly and only for certain node densities compared to the network using Dijkstra's algorithm. $\omega(i)$ takes into consideration:

- The remaining energy of a node by using the ratio of the residual energy and the one needed for a transmission
- The remaining energy of a 1-hop neighbor by using the ratio of the energy of 1-hop neighbors divided by the energy needed for a good reception.
- The remaining energy of a 2-hop neighbor by using the ratio of the energy of 2-hop neighbors divided by the energy needed for decoding a non-intelligible signal

, and chooses the minimum among them. This efficiently prevents node depletion.

Nevertheless, the results in Figure 3 indicate that a limit must be introduced on the amount of energy consumed when choosing a route. We can notice this for $N = 400$, where the energy consumption per route is very high when compared to Dijkstra's algorithm. The function $\omega(i)$ presents the same disadvantage as the 2nd cost function because they both use the shortest-widest algorithm to find a route. In order to choose the route with the maximum of the minimum $\omega(i)$ among all paths, this algorithm tends to choose longer routes consuming more energy.

By benefiting from the results given by our simulations, we can see that insuring a minimal number of hops per route is crucial for extending the lifetime of the network. Therefore, we will intend to calculate the route between the source and the destination using multiple constraints. *A good improvement would be to combine E_{θ_1} with the minimization of the number of hops in the calculation of routes.*

6 Conclusion and future work

This paper presented an approach to distribute the routing loads in the network, avoiding thus, the use of energy-compromised hotspots that may cause network disconnections. A modified shortest path algorithm is proposed, where energy efficiency is gotten through *energy-based cost functions* that assigns energy-related weights to links in the network. Three cost functions were presented and evaluated by simulations. Simulation results helped us to better understand the behavior of each proposed function, and by consequence, to find future directions.

Our future work is based on the results of our simulations. The first cost function reduces the energy consumption considerably and increases network lifetime. Therefore, we will use this cost function combined with another constraint on the number of hops that seems very crucial to extend network lifetime. In particular, we will use the cost function E_{θ_1} to calculate the weight of the link of a route, while minimizing at the same time the number of hops of this route. This will preserve at the same time the residual energy without using long route that consumes a lot of energy.

We will also implement a method using three constraints. Thus, in future work, we intend to solve the following problem: to minimize the energy consumption to route a packet from the source to the destination while at the same time (1) to reduce the number of hops between the source and the destination and (2) to maximize the residual energy of intermediate nodes.

References

1. Agarwal, S., Krishnamurthy, S., Katz, R., Dao, S.: Distributed power control in ad-hoc wireless networks. Proceedings of PIMRC (2001)
2. Cardei, M., Du, D.: Improving wireless sensor network lifetime through power aware organization. ACM Journal of Wireless Networks (2005)
3. Cardei, M., Wu, J., Yang, S.: Topology control in ad hoc wireless networks with hitch-hiking. The First IEEE International Conference on Sensor and Ad hoc Communications and Networks (SECON04 (2004)
4. Carle, J., Simplot-Ryl, D.: Energy-efficient area monitoring for sensor networks. Computer **37, no.2**, 40–46 (2004)
5. Chang, J., Tassiulas, L.: Energy conserving routing in wireless ad-hoc nertworks. IEEE INFOCOM 2000, Tel Aviv, Israel (2000)
6. Chen, B., Jamieson, K., Balakrishnan, H., Morris, R.: Span: An energy-efficient coordination algorithm for topology maintenance in ad hoc wireless networs. Wireless networks **Vol.8 Issue 5** (2002)
7. Culler, D., Estrin, D., Srivastava, M.: Overview of sensor networks. IEEE Computer Society pp. 41–49 (2004)
8. Hassanein, H., Luo, J.: Reliable energy aware routing in wireless sensor networks. Second IEEE Workshop on Dependability and Security in Sensor Networks and Systems DSSNS (2006)
9. Ingelrest, F., Simplot-Ryl, D., Stojmenovic, I.: Optimal transmission radius for energy efficient broadcasting protocols in ad hoc networks. IEEE Transactions on Parallel and Distributed Systems (2006)
10. Kwon, S., Shroff, N.B.: Energy-efficient interference-based routing for multi-hop wireless networks. IEEE INFOCOM 06, Barcelona, Spain (2006)
11. Merrer, E.L., V. Gramoli, A.C.V., Bertier, M., Kermarre, A.M.: Energy aware self-organizing density management in wireless sensor networks. In: ACM MobiShare. Los Angeles, CA (2006)
12. Mirza, D., Owrang, M., Shrugers, C.: Energy-efficient wakeup scheduling for maximizing lifetime of ieee 802.15.4 networks. International Conference on Wireless Internet (WICON'05), Budapest, Hungary (2005)

13. Shah, R., Rabaey, J.: Energy aware routing for low energy ad hoc sensor networks. Proceedings of IEEE Wireless Communications and Networking conference (WCNC) 1, 17–21 (2002)
14. Shresta, N.: Reception awarness for energy conservation in ad hoc networks. PhD, Macquarie University Sydney, Australia (2006)
15. Xu, Y., Heidemann, J., Estrin, D.: Geography-informed energy conservation for ad hoc routing. Proceedings of the 7th annual international conference on Mobile computing and networking, Rome, Italy (2001)
16. Zhang, B., Mouftah, H.: Energy-aware on-demand routing protocols for wireless ad hoc networks. Wireless Networks **12 Issue 4** (2006)

QOS MANAGEMENT IN AUTONOMIC HOME NETWORKS

Kaouthar Sethom, Nassim Laga, Guy Pujolle

LIP6, university of Paris 6, France

Firstname.lastname@lip6.fr

ABSTRACT

Ambient intelligence is the driving force of the new digital world. The trend is to equip everyday life objects even inside home environment with intelligence, which will make our lives easier and more productive. Wireless mesh networking (WMN) has emerged as a promising concept to meet such challenges. This paper considers the problem of achieving QoS inside home networks relying on a wireless mesh networks.

Keywords: Home networking, mesh networks, routing

1. INTRODUCTION

Wireless mesh networks (WMNs) have emerged as a key technology for next-generation wireless networking. Because of their advantages over other wireless networks, WMNs are undergoing rapid progress and inspiring numerous applications. One example of such applications is "home networking". WMN is a self configuring and a self organizing network, which makes it a very suitable option for home networks. Communication within home can then be realized through mesh networking without going back to the access hub all the time. Thus, network congestion due to backhaul access can be avoided. Wireless mesh networking in the home could link desktop PCs, notebook and handheld computers, High-Definition TVs, DVD players, game consoles,

Please use the following format when citing this chapter:

Sethom, K., Laga, N., Pujolle, G., 2007, in IFIP International Federation for Information Processing, Volume 256, Home Networking, Al Agha, K., Carcelle, X., Pujolle, G., (Boston: Springer), pp. 101-110.

camcorders, and other consumer electronic devices, without the need to pull cables, install network jacks or configure devices.

Traffics generated by this variety of applications, ranging from Internet browsing, data backup, and telephony, to entertainment and gaming have different requirements. A new Qos based routing protocol is thus needed for best management inside home.

Despite the availability of several routing protocols for ad hoc networks, the design of routing protocols for WMNs is still an active research area. In this paper, we present a novel routing protocol, named Wireless Mesh Protocol for QoS routing (WMP_QoS) inside home networks. The rest of the paper is organized in the following way. An analysis of routing metrics in mesh networks is presented in Section 2. In Section 3 we introduce our WMP_QoS protocol. Simulation results obtained using NS-2 are presented in Section 4. Section 5 concludes the paper.

2. ROUTING IN WIRELESS MESH NETWORKS

Wireless mesh networks (WMN) seem to be the best architecture for home networks for the following reasons:

- In a home, we can find nodes with high mobility (such as laptops, cameras, and mobile phones), and low mobility (such as PCs, and TV).
- The user is not an expert in the domain, so auto-configuration and auto-organisation are required functionalities. WMN have these properties.
- The components must be connected to the internet, so a pure ad-hoc network is not an optimal architecture.

Since WMNs share common features with ad hoc networks, the routing protocols developed for ad hoc networks were applied to WMNs. For example, Firetide Networks [1] are based on the TBRPF protocol [2], Another example is dynamic source routing (DSR) [3,4]: This protocol is divided into two parts: route discovery and route management. The first part discovers a path between a source and a destination, whereas the second one manages this route and notifies the source if there was a problem in the path (link failure). Source routing makes the protocol much more reactive and prevents loops. Moreover, the IEEE 802.11s standard [5] for wireless mesh networks defines a default mandatory routing protocol (Hybrid Wireless Mesh Protocol, or HWMP) that is inspired by a combination of AODV [6] and tree-based routing. However, Ad Hoc Networks like AODV and DSR decides the route on the basis of number of hops. However it is been proved by Woo et al.[7] that these minimum hop count paths degrades the performance of the network.

Selecting a good path is considerably harder in wireless networks than in traditional wired networks (where the routing problem is usually solved by running a distributed shortest-path algorithm on a graph) because the notion of a "link" between nodes is not well-defined. The properties of the radio channel between any pair of nodes vary with time, and radio communication range is often unpredictable. The communication quality of a radio channel depends on background noise, obstacles, and channel fading, as well as on other transmissions occurring simultaneously in the network.

To ensure good performance, routing metrics must satisfy four requirements. First, the routing metrics must not cause frequent route changes to ensure the stability of the network. Second, the routing metrics must capture the characteristics of mesh networks to ensure that minimum weight paths have good performance. Third, the routing metrics must ensure that minimum weight paths can be found by efficient algorithms with polynomial complexity. Finally, the routing metrics must ensure that forwarding loops are not formed by routing protocols.

There are some promising approaches for improving routing in wireless mesh networks. In this section, we will analyze the performance of four existing routing metrics for mesh networks: RTT [8], ETX [9], ETT [8], WCETT [10].

2.1. Per-hop Round Trip Time (RTT)

This metric is based on RTT measurement between a node and its neighbours. It was introduced by Adya and Al [3]. It is computed as follow:

- Every node sends a prob packet every 500ms; this packet contains the send time.

-Every node which receives this packet sends an acknowledgement which contains the send time retrieved in the received packet. This allows the source to compute the RTT.

-To avoid oscillations, the sending node keeps an exponentially weighted moving average of the RTT samples to each of its neighbours.

2.2. Expected Transmission Count (ETX)

ETX is defined as the expected number of MAC layer transmissions that is needed for successfully delivering a packet through a wireless link. The drawbacks of ETX is that it does not consider interference or the fact that different links may have different transmission rates.

2.3. Expected Transmission Time (ETT)

This metrics traduces the number of required MAC retransmissions to reach a destination. To compute ETX, the implemented method works under 802.11 environment. This method will not work under other environment since it is based on the fact that 802.11 does not retransmit broadcast packets. To compute ETX we:
-Send probe packets every second to all neighbours.
-Every 10 seconds, report the number of received packet to the sending node.
The ETT metric captures the impact of link capacity on the performance of the path. However, the remaining drawback of ETT is that it still does not fully capture the intra-flow and inter-flow interference in the network [11].

2.4. Weighted Cumulative ETT (WCETT)

A routing protocol named (MR-LQSR) is proposed in [11] for multi-radio WMNs. A new performance metric, called the weighted cumulative expected transmission time (WCETT) is proposed for the routing protocol. WCETT have fixed some constraints:
-The routing protocol metric must reflect the loss rate and the bandwidth of the path.
-The metric must be increasing according to the path length.
-The metric must care of interference and the channel diversity.

3. THE WMP_QoS PROTOCOL

The goal of WMP_QoS is to build a WMN routing protocol that provides QoS guarantees to applications. This means that the service level and the network level cannot work as separated universes, each towards its own goals. Rather, the routes discovered by our routing protocol will feet to application requests for desired bandwidth and delay bounds for the flow, or deliver an end-to-end flow that satisfies those performance bounds at the time of the request. If and when the route is disrupted by node or link failure, the protocol automatically detects the route breakages, and re-discovers alternate routes if they exist. WMP_QoS is a reactive protocol that discovers routes on-demand.

3.1. Service classes and QoS algorithm

The objective of WMP_QoS is selecting network paths that have sufficient resources to satisfy the QoS requirements of the admitted connections. Many paths between the source and the destination may be available. Because there is no available centralized controller that knows the whole picture of the network resources, WMP_QoS calculates link weights hop by hop, and then combines them into a path metric. WMP_QoS is a source-routed protocol derived from AODV. Route discovery and metric calculation is based on Route request and route response.

3.1.1 Assumptions

We begin by listing the assumptions we made about the networks in which WMP_QoS is supposed to operate. These assumptions are not necessary for the correct operation of our protocol; they only simplify the case study.

First, we suppose that the home network is only composed by three technologies: WiFi, Bluetooth and Ethernet. We assume that each service flow will provide the following QoS parameters: the minimum required bandwidth B_{min} , the maximum end-to-end delay from the source to the destination, T_{max} and the minimum required security level S_{level}.

Instead of shortest-path, WMP_QoS uses a combination of WCETT, available bandwidth B_{avai}, end-to-end delay T_{max}, link energy E_i and link security level S_i as metrics.

The conceptual architecture of autonomic communications requires a knowledge plane to facilitate effective, transparent and high level self-management capabilities. We assume that each node can get its available bandwidth B_{avai} and WCETTi on the current link i by simply asking the knowledge plane.

3.1.2 Route selection algorithm

Our routing algorithm is implemented in the following four-step on-demand hop-by-hop route discovery procedure:

Step 1: Route Exploration: Nodes along possible routes are explored by the route request packets from the source. These packets travel through each node along the candidate routes to obtain bandwidth availability, link energy E_i and link security level S_i as well as gather the end-to-end delay information of the route.

Step 2: Route Registration: Bandwidth B_{min} is registered at each node along the reverse routes explored, by the route reply packets from the destination.

Path security level and Enery consumption on a particular route are then obtained from (1) and (2):

$$S = min\ Si \hspace{10em} (1)$$

$$E = sum\ Ei/\ number\ of\ hops \hspace{6em} (2)$$

Step 3: Route selection:

> - *Case : application = voice*
>
> $P= \{Paths\ /\ delay =< T_{max}\ \&\ Security\ S >= S_{level}\ \}_{min\ E}$
>
> - *Case : application = client/server (email, telnet ...)*
>
> $P= \{Paths\ /\ S >= S_{level}\}_{min\ (WCETT,\ E)}$
>
> - *Case : application =file transfer*
>
> $Path= \{Paths\ /\ B_{avai} >= B_{min}\ and\ S>=S_{level}\}_{min\ E}$
>
> - *Case: application =video conferencing, multicasting*
>
> $P= \{Paths\ /\ B_{avai} >= B_{min}\ and\ S>=S_{level}\}_{min\ (WCETT,E)}$

We denote P as the selected path. Our algorithm adopts different selection criteria based on the application's flow type (voice, video…). For example, for voice the selected route will be the path that minimises energy while having an end-to-end delay least or equal to the max tolerated application delay T_{max} and a security level superior or equal to the S_{level} required by the application.

Step 4: Route Activation: The route is activated by the data transmission of the actual traffic flow, and bandwidth reservation will take effect.

The choice of radio technology influences the performance of the network and thus the routing protocol needs to be aware of it, and cannot operate in the same way as wired networks which are agnostic about the underlying medium. For better path selection process, we introduce technologies specificities and preferences in the routing algorithm through the value that we attribute to the link energy consumption parameter E_i and link security level parameter S_i. for example: S_i is high for an Ethernet link and low for an insecure WiFi link. Respectively, E_i is high for wireless connections and low for an Ethernet link.

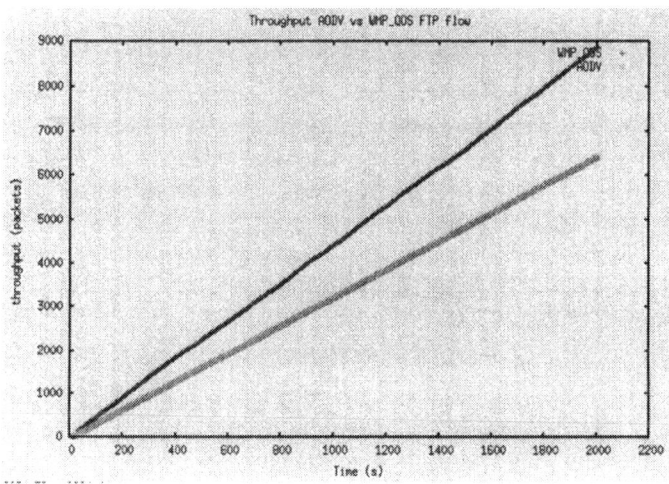

Figure-1: WMP_QoS versus AODV under FTP Flow

3.2 Performance results

We evaluate the performance of WMP_QoS under using the *ns-2* network simulator [12]. Mainly two types of traffic sources are used (FTP and voice). The source-destination pairs are spread randomly over the network. First, an attempt was made to compare WMP_QoS to the basic AODV standard under the same application flow.

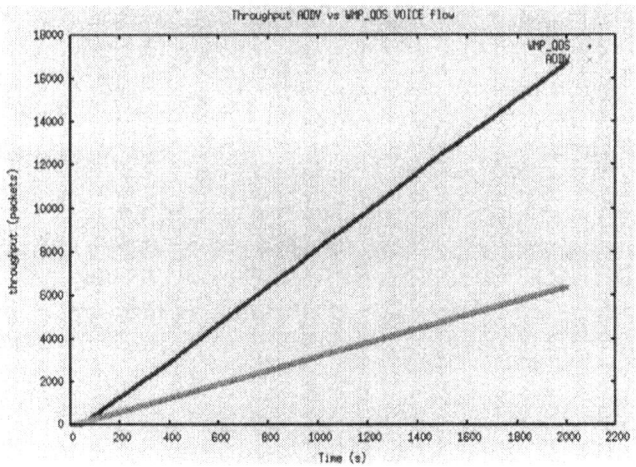

Figure-2: WMP_QoS versus AODV under voice Flow

Figure 1-2 shows that WMP_QoS outperforms AODV under the two types of applications flows. To confirm that WMP_QoS offers a differentiated routing service per application type, we have compared in Figure 3 the end-to-end delay under WMP_QoS for an FTP and voice traffic. The same source and destination nodes where used in both scenarios. You can see that the average end-to-end delay of packet delivery was higher in FTP as compared to voice flow. This means that WMP_QoS choose a different path for FTP and voice flow, while trying to minimize the delay for voice because it's a time sensitive application.

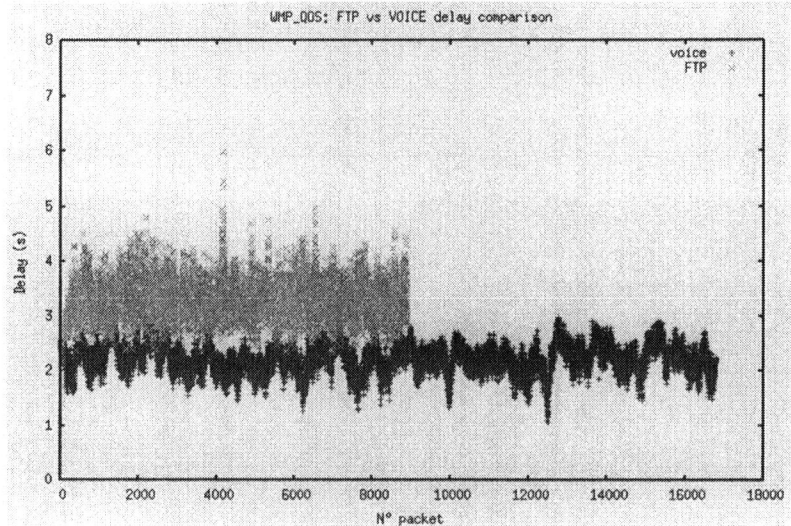

Figure-3: end to end delay FTP vs voice under WMP_QoS

4. CONCLUSION

Based on an analysis of existing routing metrics in wireless mesh networks, we have presented in this paper a QoS routing protocol called WMP_QoS for multi-hop home networks. Our goal is to maintain a stable route which provides per flow guarantee quality of service while taking advantage of heterogeneous link layer characteristics. We have shown through simulations the viability of our protocol.

References

[1]. Firetide Networks. www.firetide.com

[2]. R. Ogier, F. Templin, M. Lewis, Topology dissemination based on reverse-path forwarding (TBRPF), IETF RFC 3684, February 2004.

[3]. Microsoft Mesh Networks:http:// research.microsoft.com/mesh

[4]. D.B. Johnson, D.A. Maltz, Y.-C. Hu, The dynamic source routing protocol for mobile ad hoc networks (DSR), IETF Internet-Draft: work in progress, July 2004.

[5]. 802.11s draft :www.ieee802.org/11/Reports/tgs_update.htm

[6]. C. Perkins, E. Belding-Royer, S. Das, Ad hoc on-demand distance vector (AODV) routing, IETF RFC 3561, July 2003.

[7]. Woo, T. Tong, and D. Culler. Taming the underlying challenges of reliable multihop routing in sensor networks. In *SenSys*, 2003.

[8]. Richard Draves, Jitendra Padhye, and Brian Zill, Comparison of routing metrics for static multi-hop wireless networks. Proceedings of the 2004 conference on Applications, technologies, architectures, and protocols for computer communications, August 2004.

[9]. D.S.J. De Couto, D. Aguayo, J. Bicket, R. Morris, A high-throughput path metric for multi-hop wireless routing, in: ACM Annual International Conference on Mobile Computing and Networking (MOBICOM), 2003, pp. 134–146

[10]. WCETT: R. Draves, J. Padhye, B. Zill, Routing in multi-radio, multi-hop wireless mesh networks, in: ACM Annual International Conference on Mobile Computing and Networking (MOBICOM), 2004, pp. 114–128.

[11]. Akyildiz, I.F., Wang, X. and Wang, W., Wireless Mesh Networks: A Survey, Computer Networks Journal (Elsevier), March 2005.

[12]. NS-2 simulator, www.isi.edu/nsnam/ns/

Managing collaboration and competition of multiple WAN services in a residential network

Wouter Haerick, Nico Goeminne, Jan Coppens, Filip De Turck and Bart Dhoedt

Abstract Open service platforms like the OSGi-platform offer a standard, scalable way for service providers to remotely deploy their services inside many residential networks. However, the lack of control by WAN service providers on the home environment together with too complex end-user policy configuration hinder widespread e-deployment of services into the home. Several architectures have been presented for next generation home networks, coping with the deployment, discovery and run-time control of residential services in order to enforce service levels. However, to evolve towards true collaboration scenarios where a service from one service provider can interact with a service from another service provider without configuration inconvenience, or where a service from one service provider can co-exist with an identical service from another provider on the same device, proper security and policy configuration needs to be addressed. This paper contributes therefore to the already presented architectures by discussing secure remote policy configuration in a multi service provider environment. A security framework is proposed based on the OSGi specification that limits not-trusted service providers in their control on other services. The strength of the framework lies in its generic XACML-compliant policy configuration module and its compatibility with existing services. This makes the framework easy to adopt for remote configuration providers, which allows service providers to delegate configuration support to a service aggregation provider.

1 Introduction

The past three years increased effort has been spent by the academic world, industry and standardization bodies to lower the barriers to integrate wired and wireless

Wouter Haerick, Nico Goeminne, Filip De Turck, Bart Dhoedt
University of Ghent, Gent, Belgium, e-mail: wouter.haerick@intec.ugent.be

Jan Coppens
Alcatel-Lucent, Antwerp, Belgium e-mail: jan.jc.coppens@alcatel-lucent.com

Please use the following format when citing this chapter:

Haerick, W., Goeminne, N., Coppens, J., De Turck, F., Dhoedt, B., 2007, in IFIP International Federation for Information Processing, Volume 256, Home Networking, Al Agha, K., Carcelle, X., Pujolle, G., (Boston: Springer), pp. 111-128.

home devices in a vendor-neutral way and turn a house into a smart home. Organisations like DLNA and UPnP Forum have succeeded to specify interoperable middleware blocks to share local media services with compliant output devices spread over the home. These efforts have enabled a new way of digital entertainment allowing seamless sharing of music, video and pictures using customer equipment from different vendors. Both organizations have their main focus today on discoverable media services running inside the LAN environment. As a result these services have an inside view of the home network and hence can use the local network information in their auto-configuration and or self-healing processes. In contrast to DLNA and the UPnP Forum, the DSLForum - which also represents the telecommunication industry and service providers, apart from the customer electronics industry - is concerned on how service providers can get a view on the individual home network in order to offer predictable QoS like the locally running services can do, and thus to enable WAN service providers to compete with locally running plug-and-play media servers. The question rises here which WAN service should be allowed to discover which other WAN or LAN services, and more in particular which service should be able to reconfigure or interact with which other services. This paper therefore deals with the problem of how to remotely enforce unidirectional use of a service by another service with no or limited configuration by the end-user, and how to deal with overwritten or conflicting configurations that could possibly degrade the service level from other services in a multi service provider environment.

In the remainder of this paper, we will consider a service provider to be a third party provider which offers a client-server service to a residential network as depicted in Figure 1. The server part could run on the WAN network or could be remotely deployed into the residential network. In both cases, the service provider has interest in knowing which other services are present in the home network, and how the LAN network is behaving, in order to offer predictable QoS. In a multi service provider environment, where multiple WAN service providers offer IP services to a single home network, it gets more complex as configuration requests from one service provider could conflict with previous configuration requests.

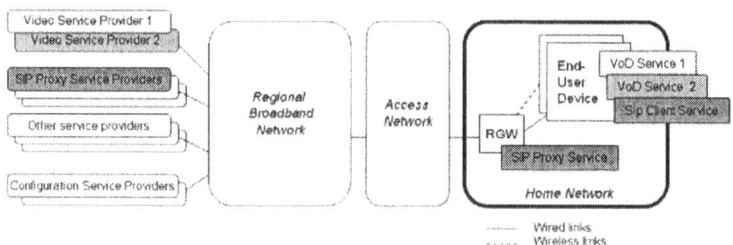

Fig. 1 End-to-end residential service architecture in a multi service provider environment with a single internet access provider

In any case we would like to avoid that service providers start competing for example for shared bandwidth and therefore continuously change each other settings. In a more general case, we would like to take a look at the concept of a "configuration service provider" that is in charge of the service configuration of many other service providers. This type of service provider is also introduced in DSL TR-069 WAN CPE Protocol specifications. We contribute to this concept by defining a secure framework to delegate the configuration from a service provider to a configuration service provider. Internet service providers could take up the role of a configuration service provider for all the services that are offered through their internet service and access gateways.

In the margin of the standardization organisations, a short note can be made on "the battle of end-user devices". When looking at the MP3 player market dominated by Apple's iPod player, and at the rivaling Microsoft Zune player, it becomes clear that the battle on the end-user device is not purely about selling more devices, but about installing marketshare for their respective music service providers iTunes and Zune.net. The same battle is ongoing between Skype certified devices (Skype protocol) and MSN Live compatible devices. These devices contain software that acts as (1) device management software, (2) client software to the WAN service provider and (3) as local media player. The inherent configuration issues of multiple service provider environments are however today often avoided by offering devices, pre-configured by the manufacturer, to work only with a single service provider.

However, the general purpose terminals are evolving to support multiple services, and thus different service providers become able to provide each a set of services on one single device. This leads to a situation were different parties are involved in the management and configuration of home network resources, as well as in the service deployment. Hence, one should be aware that:

- Subscribing to different services from different service providers often requires a complex re-configuration of the terminal or the home gateway. While reconfiguring a device, the integrity of the local network and other running services must be guaranteed to ensure that installed services will not degrade or stop working.
- Configuration conflicts can arise as a result of applications which are able to provide themselves a certain configuration without intervention of a configuration provider or a local user. Also, configurations made by the end user can conflict with previous settings executed by service providers.

The next section of this paper describes related work on home network architectures and remote configuration. Then, an OSGi-based security architecture is proposed. First, the generic XACML-compliant policy enforcement components are introduced. These components comply with the ISO security model on authentication and authorization. Afterwards, two architectural options are described to deal with multi-service provider security using the underlying XACML components. In a next section, a remote security interface is proposed that follows the TR-069 requirements on WAN CPE remote configuration. The complete architecture is illustrated with a proof-of-concept implementation in the following section. For two WAN service providers, one offering a video service and the other offering a SIP proxy service, the usage of the security framework is discussed. A last section contains the conclusions.

2 Related work

Several architectures have been presented for next-generation residential gateways [2],[3],[4] as core component of the smart home. While each of these architectures use their own naming for the subcomponents, the different components can be mapped to one of following three layers: a driver layer, a common access layer and a service layer. The common access layer consists of both hardware and native software and provides access to hardware devices inside the LAN or WAN. The native software could for example provide functionality to guarantee QoS. The driver layer acts as a translator between the common access layer and the higher level service layer. The service layer consists of hardware independent services that can remotely be deployed by a service provider. These architectures however do not detail an additional layer to protect the local services from non-trustworthy service providers.

With respect to security, specifications are discussed in the UPnP Forum [8], the Home Gateway Initiative [5] and also in the latest OSGi release 4 specifications [6]. The DSLForum specifications for remote CPE management [7] refer to SSL, IPsec and WS-Security as security mechanisms. Although final documents are available for UPnP security and OSGi security, it lacks of practical implementations. A main reason could be that the configuration of security settings did not get the focus it possibly needs to make it convenient to use. With our work, which includes a proof-of-concept implementation, we aim to contribute with convenient security configuration components. To increase the convenience, it is described how the security settings can be delegated from local end-users or service providers to configuration providers. In addition, we focus on multi-provider environments, where WAN service providers can possibly overwrite configuration settings that could degrade other services. With respect to multi-service broadband architectures we would like to refer also TR-101 from DSLForum that provides a standardized approach to an Ethernet-centric multi-service broadband architecture as well as a QoS and multicast blueprint.

3 Secure multi-provider architecture

We consider an end-to-end network with multiple WAN service providers offering an IP-based service to one ore more wired or wireless devices in the home. Two alternative architectures will be explained that limit service providers in the actions that can be performed from a remote WAN-location. The first architecture combines an XACML-based policy framework with multi-service-provider security enforcement to hide certain services from certain service providers. In fact, the framework does not restrict the visibility towards the locally running services but enforces very stringent rules so that unauthorized service providers will never be able to make configuration changes to other services. A second architecture is proposed that indeed changes the visibility, and also protects the life-cycle actions to avoid that any service can start, stop or uninstall a service with too stringent security restrictions. Before discussing the two alternative architectures to deal with the multi-service provider issues, the underlying XACML policy components are discussed.

3.1 XACML-based security components

We adopt the ISO security model for authorization and authentication (Figure 2) and apply it to a service-oriented home architecture that is built upon the OSGi framework.

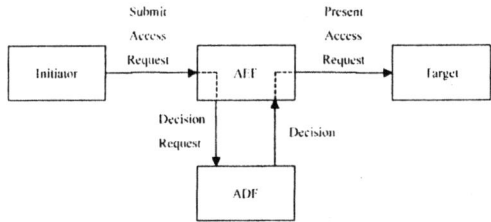

Fig. 2 ISO 10181-3 Access Control Framework

In the ISO model, the Access Control Enforcement Functions (AEFs) mediate access requests and submit decision requests to Access Control Decision Functions (ADFs). The ADFs make the final decision to allow or deny the access of the target by the initiator. The AEF requires Access Control Information. This information typically includes (1) Initiator information, (2) Request information and (3) Target information.

In order to take a decision, the ADF should first authenticate the initiator. If the authentication is successful, the ADP should enrich the Access Control Information with contextual Access Decision Information. With this information, the ADF can police based on predefined policy rules.

The decoupling of the AEF and ADF allows representing policies in a generic format while the access control enforcement remains target specific. This way an AEF for OSGi services and another AEF for Internet access can both share common, generic policies that use the same policy language.

To control the access to the WAN, to locally running OSGi services and even to local non-OSGi services, distributed enforcement is needed at the firewall, OSGi service registry and at other services (eg a print server). Although the enforcement points are distributed, a central policy repository makes the administration a lot easier, and allows for more consistent reasoning about possible policy conflicts. For such a central policy repository, it is important to adopt a standard policy language. Only then the policies can be interpreted and shared by different applications in the home. With respect to access control, this leads to the standardized specifications of XACML. XACML is standardized by the Organization for the Advancement of Structured Information Standards (OASIS) and describes both a policy language and an access control decision request/response language (both written in XML). The policy language is used to describe general access control requirements, and has standard extension points for defining new functions, data types, combining logic, etc. The request/response language lets you form a query to ask whether or not a given action should be allowed, and interpret the result. The response always includes an answer about whether the request should be allowed using one of four values: Permit, Deny, Indeterminate (an error occurred or some required value was missing, so a decision cannot be made) or Not Applicable (the request can't be answered by this service). The power of XACML lies in its generic and powerful format to describe access policies for any application. Each policy corresponds with a single access control policy and is expressed using multiple rules. Policies can be stored in different files, stored locally or distributed, or can be bundled inside a PolicySet document.

The diagram below shows a total view of the end-to-end security architecture for secure service delivery in OSGi-based home environments. The OSGi-based security bundles, which run on the residential gateway, consist of 3 sub-components: (1) A TR-069 Security Management Agent (MA), (2) an Access Control Service and (3) a Security Configuration Service.

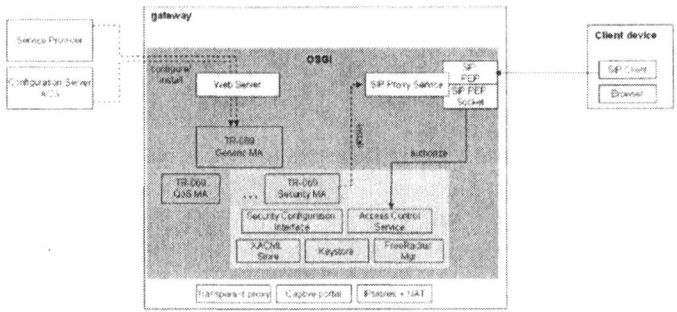

Fig. 3 XACML-based security component architecture with central gateway running OSGi

3.1.1 TR-069 Security Management Agent

For each bundle that gets installed via the TR-069 security management agent, the integrity of the bundle is verified by checking the signed jar file. If the key used for the signature is known to the security framework, this means it is stored in the key store, then the bundle gets access to all methods offered by the Security Configuration Service. These access rights are stored using the XACML syntax. If required, these settings can be overwritten in a way that only a subset of protected methods is accessible by the installed bundle. This fine grained access control mechanism thus allows to block service request on a method-level instead of on the service-level. This bundle depends on a java TR-069 library and introduces a new new TR-069 security object "Device.Services.Management.ServiceProviders". This object is an extension of a BundleManager object tracking the different services/bundles of each service provider. The new TR-069 object allows already trusted service providers to add/remove their certificates and install/uninstall/share/unshare their services with services of other service providers, increasing the configuration convenience for the end-user. The TR-069 ServiceProviders object could also act as a TR-069 object proxy for any TR-069 configuration request. In that case the proxy needs to extract the additional security parameters (retrieved by the SOAP header or SSL certificate) enabling the TR-069 ServiceProviders object to identify the origin of the request. Based on the origin parameters, the TR-069 ServiceProviders object from the proxy can select the corresponding TR-069 configuration object. Based on the origin, the TR-069 ServiceProviders object decides if the requested configuration to that specific TR-069 target object is permitted. The communication is typically allowed if the origin of the request is also the owner of the targeted object.

3.1.2 Access Control Service

The access control service provides a generic access interface to any OSGi service that is protected with a Policy Enforcement Points (PEP). Note that a PEP from the XACML specifications corresponds with AEF from the ISO security model. Bundles that do not have such a PEP can be automatically modified using an access control adder script. The latter creates a new service interface that adds authorization to each method, updates the Activator class-file to register the new service interface into OSGi and adapts the meta-inf file to include the necessary java packages for XACML support. The access control service has only one method in its interface:

```
public boolean requestAccess(Subject s, String obj, String action, List args)
throws AccessDeniedException;
```

By supplying the proper information of the Subject - for example the symbolic name of a BundleSubject or the SIP-id of a SIPSubject in case of a SIP proxy service - and the information on the target service including the action to perform, the access control service makes a decision whether or not to allow access to the Subject. Therefore, an XACML access request is constructed and matched against the XACML policies in the local policy store. For the implementation we considered the following requirements:

- Policy Initialisation: Initial policies of trused services should automatically be added to the policy store the first time a service starts up in the OSGi framework. These initial configuratons are of utmost importance to achieve a high convenience. At any time modifications to the policies can be performed by the local user or by the remote configuration server.
- Highly flexible policies: A (modified) policy can be made up of simple predefined functions like string equations or regular expressions or custom made functions. These custom made functions can refer to methods exposed by other OSGi services. Using custom functions one can easily construct accounting policies for billing services.

The Access Control bundle depends on the com.sun.xml library, the javax security auth library, the Policy Access Point bundle, the Policy Authentication Point bundle and the credential bundle.

3.1.3 Security Configuration Service

The Security Configuration Service offers the interface to all underlying security mechanisms like the XACML policy store, the key store, the RADIUS database and the IPtables firewall. This interface is protected with a PEP which makes it only accessible for trusted, signed bundles that have access rights for the individual methods.

3.2 Architectural option 1: TR-069 Management Agent with multi-service-provider security enforcement

Service providers can control services that run on a home gateway using the TR-069 protocol, sending messages over SOAP/HTTP. In order to enforce strict security rules, each service provider participating in the security framework should authenticate itself to the TR-069 management agent. Three different options are possible:

- two-way SSL is used between the service provider and the home gateway; during the SSL handshake the certificate of the service provider is stored by the Management for later use;
- WS-Security is applied to the SOAP messages including the service provider certificate; the security information is stripped from the SOAP header by the Management Agent and stored for later use;

• the certificate is sent to the Management Agent as one of the TR-069 datafields. These data is securely sent (at least using a signature to verify that the message has not been modified by an untrusted party) and forewarded to the service management bundle.

No matter which option is used by the Management Agent to retrieve the origin of the service provider that sends configuration requests, the MA should forward the security information (or a link to the place where this information is stored) to the service management bundle. The latter component will then verify if the security information corresponds with a trusted party by looking up the certificate in the key store. If the service provider is trusted then the Multi Provider policy is evaluated to verify if the service provider is allowed to change the policies/configuration of the target object included in the configuration request. The multi provider security file should include the following information, which expresses for each service which service provider is allowed to change the (XACML) configuration.

Service	Symbolic Name	Location	Service Provider	Hash of the certificate
VideoService	VideoService	http //video.com	VideoProvider	er4rfg vldf34df44
VideoService	VideoService	http //video com	ConfigProvider	chfkkgf4ld3g4dffk

Fig. 4 A proposal for a multi provider policy format

Figure 4 depicts a video service that not only can be configured by its owner but also by the configuration provider. This multi provider policy file can only be updated by the service owner, or by the local administrator (through a confirmation pop-up).

Figure 5 shows how we extend the XACML-based archicture from the previous section with a modified Service Management Bundle to allow interaction with the multi provider policy file.

A service provider that wants to configure a service on the home gateway now only has visibility on those services for which it has the grants (as stated in the multi provider configuration file). The actual access to the individual service methods is further controlled by the XACML policies. The result is fine-grained access control used in favor of multi provider security.

Figure 6 shows how the multi service provider security components filter the view a service provider has on the home gateway. Service Provider A is a trusted service provider and has the grants to configure its own videoService but also to modify the Resource Sharing Framework [1] configuration to make resource reservations in case additional CPU is required to display a videostream. Apart from those two services it can also see the untrusted services "X10" and "back-up". Service Provider B can only configure its SIP service and the two untrusted services. While this configuration restricts the use of a service by another service bundle, it does not restrict the visibility of the services offered by the video service or any other local bundles.

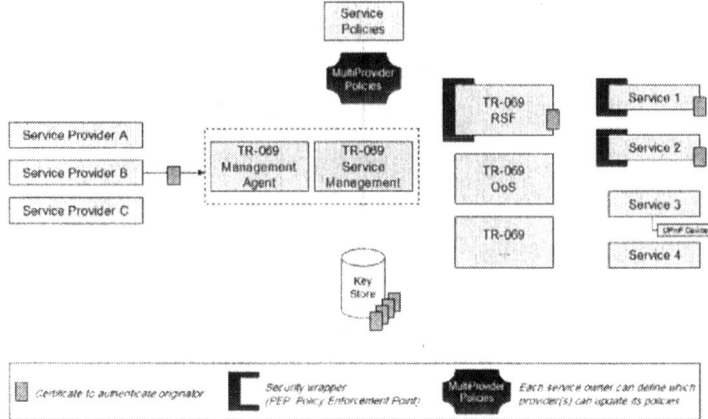

Fig. 5 Architectural option 1: Secured Management Agent to support multi provider configuration

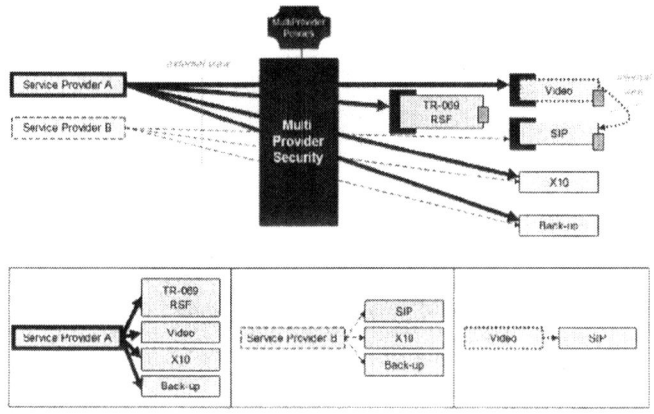

Fig. 6 Restricted external and internal visibility

3.3 Architectural option 2: Modification of the core OSGi framework to add bundelContext security

An alternative solution to obtain multi provider security is explained in this section but requires changes to the core OSGi framework. This security solution can thus not be added as a separate bundle by a remote configuration server. It must be included in the OSGi framework jar-file and therefore should replace the existing OSGi framework. As a direct consequence of the integration into the framework, it has the advantage that the security solution can not be replaced easily by another bundle at runtime. The alternative solution we propose will prevent that a trusted bundle will be replaced with a malicious bundle because it is intertwined with the core OSGi objects BundleContext and Bundle. Therefore, it will no longer be possible for a random bundle to stop, update or uninstall another bundle.

The BundleContext object has the global overview on the OSGi registry and thus on all the locally registered bundles and listeners (see code listing 1 below). The actual life-cycle controlling methods are defined by the Bundle interface (see code listing 2 below). By modifying the BundleContextImplementation and BundleImplementation each of these methods can be linked to the XACML compliant security framework in order to evaluate if the calling party has the permissions to perform the life-cycle method.

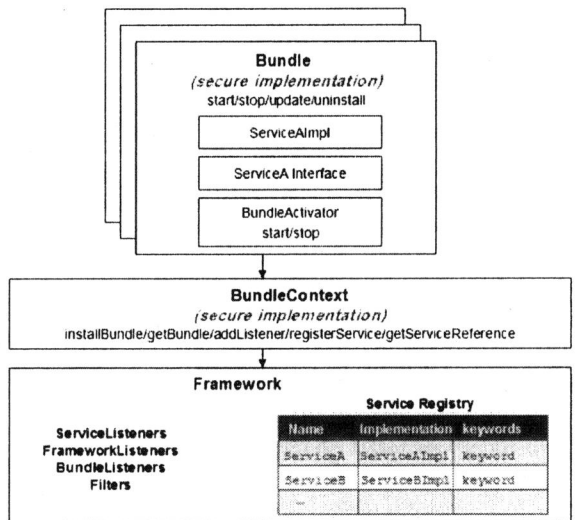

Fig. 7 Architectural option 2: Modifications to the core OSGi framework for multi provider security

In the implementation of the BundleContext object and the Bundle object, each of the sensitive operations (installation of a bundle, get Service References) should be extended with a condition that first evaluates the permissions of the calling bundle. Compliant with release 4 of the OSGi specifications, the origin of the calling bundle can be verified against the bundlename or the bundlelocation.

The XACML compliant service policies define which actions should be made accessible to which other bundles. For OSGi frameworks that are compliant with OSGi release 4, the implementation of the bundle interface method "hasPermission" could be linked to the Service Management bundle of the security framework to evaluate the request for permission.

Code listing 1 - An extract from the BundleContext Interface

```
public interface BundleContext {
public abstract String getProperty(String s);
public abstract Bundle getBundle();
public abstract Bundle installBundle(String s) ...;
public abstract Bundle installBundle(String s, InputStream is) ...;
public abstract Bundle getBundle(long l);
public abstract Bundle[] getBundles();
public abstract void addServiceListener(ServiceListener sl, String s) ...;
public abstract void addServiceListener(ServiceListener sl);
public abstract void removeServiceListener(ServiceListener sl);
public abstract void addBundleListener(BundleListener bl);
public abstract void removeBundleListener(BundleListener bl);
public abstract void addFrameworkListener(FrameworkListener fl);
public abstract void removeFrameworkListener(FrameworkListener fl);
public abstract ServiceRegistration registerService(...);

public abstract File getDataFile(String s);
public abstract Filter createFilter(String s) ...; }
```

Code listing 2 - An extract from the Bundle Interface

```
public interface Bundle {
public abstract int getState();
public abstract void start() throws BundleException;
public abstract void stop() throws BundleException;
public abstract void update() throws BundleException;
public abstract void update(InputStream inputstream) ...;
public abstract void uninstall() throws BundleException;
public abstract Dictionary getHeaders();
public abstract long getBundleId();
..
public abstract boolean hasPermission(Object obj); ..
}
```

4 Remote configuration interface

The security settings offered by the OSGi java security bundles can be exposed to a remote management server in a generic way adhering to the TR-069 protocol. The goal of the security interface is different for the configuration service provider, service providers and home user.

The benefits for the configuration service provider of a secure remote interface should include:

- centralized set-up of trust relations by the configuration service provider;
- centralized policy management by the configuration service provider;
- provide a generic interface to update policies.

Service/Bundle providers should benefit from centralized trust relations and be able to delegate policies and their management to a central policy store owner. Home users should benefit from new trusted services without any additional security configuration.

The security interface we propose is transparent for the TR-069 Management Agent (MA) (Figure 8. Hence, this MA has no knowledge about the security data model but is only involved in translating TR-069 messages in generic java calls. In particular for security configuration, a security data model has been defined that allows configuration of (1) physical credential/policy stores, (2) add credentials (certificates, passwords, etc.), (3) add policies and (4) configure visibility.

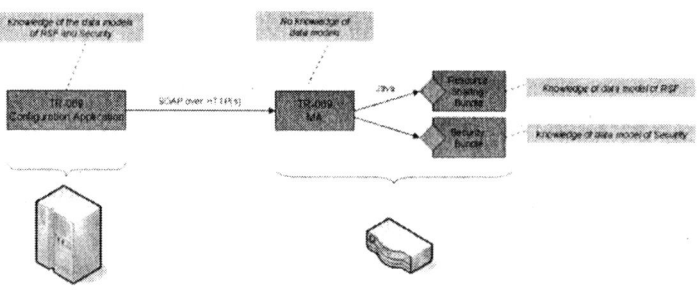

Fig. 8 Transparent TR-069 Management Agent.

Each TR-069 configurable entity is required to expose its functionality through the generic TR-069 java interface (orange diamonds in Figure 8. However, the implementation of the interface is different for each of these entities. The following three methods should be supported:

```
setParameterValues(TR09Object[] args) returns TR69Result[]
    getParameterValues(String[] keys) returns TR69Object[]
getParameterNames(String parameterPath, boolean nextLevel) returns
                    TR69Parameter[]
```

The first function, setParameterValues, sets the parameters, given by their name (full path), to a certain value. This function can be used to adjust a policy, a credential or a visibility. The argument is an object that combines a key (parameter name) with a certain value.

The second function, getParameterValues, retrieves the values of the listed parameters, given by their names (full path). The agument is an array of strings containing parameter names with their full path.

The third and last function of the TR-069 interface, getParameterNames, returns a list of all parameters with their name (with full path) and an indicator which indicates whether or not the parameter can be changed. The boolean argument of this function indicates if the parameters of the next branch(es)/level also need to be included in the result.

5 Proof-of-concept implementation

The targeted setup of the demo is shown in figure 9. The setup contains a home net-work, representing a home environment of a potential customer, and a broadband network representing the real internet with numerous service providers. The home network has a desktop PC with a softphone, a browser and an OSGi framework in-stalled on it and the gateway runs a captive portal, web server, authentication server and another OSGi framework. The goal is to illustrate how a video service can be configured by its service provider - or a configuration provider - to be paused by a trusted VoIP/SIP proxy as soon as a valid phone call is received.

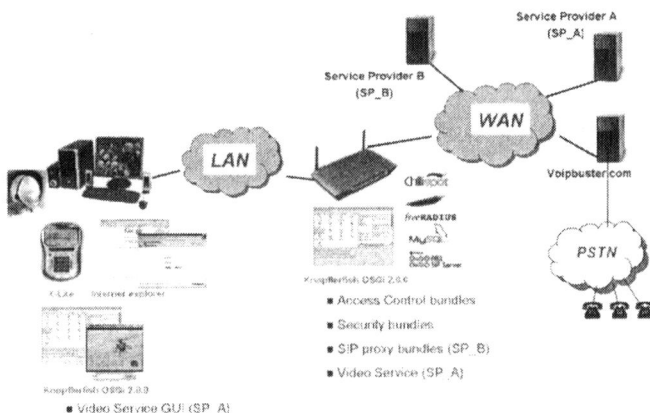

Fig. 9 Collaboration scenario: Configuration of a remote video service to be interrupted in case of incoming VoIP/SIP calls.

Two service providers are part of the proof-of-concept: service provider IBCN-Ugent and service provider RnD.

A standard non-protected video service from provider IBCN is parsed by two scripts two add the required security support. The first script, named the Access-Control-Adder tool, adds fine-grained access control to the video service to allow security enforcement on method level. The second script adds a signature of the ser-vice provider to the jar-file, together with an XACML default policy file. The video service is implemented as a UPnP controlpoint for the UPnP video player provided by VideoServiceGUI.jar. The controlpoint exports this (Access Controlled) service to the OSGi framework and so enables other bundles to control the UPnP video player. The use of these actions is controlled by the XACML based security frame-work.

Service provider RnD offers two services that would like to interact with the video player from service provider IBCN. The two services are VCRRemote and a SIP Proxy service.

Using the TR 069 "Device.Services.Management.ServiceProviders" object, the service providers can add/remove their certificates and install/uninstall/share/unshare their services with services of other service providers. We have opted for architectural option 1 to have a security framework that is decoupled from the OSGi implementation version. We used the Knopflerfish implementation of OSGi.

First, the certificates of the trusted service providers need to be added to the central certificate store. When a service provider wants to add his certificate, a pop-up is shown asking to approve the addition of the certificate to your keystore (Figure 10). Once accepted, one can start installing services from the corresponding service provider on your gateway.

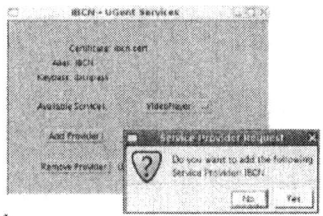 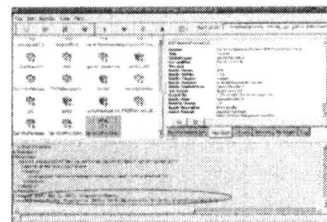

Fig. 10 After user approval (one click) the PEP from the Security Configuration Service permits the installation of a trusted certificate.

When installing a service of a known service provider, the Security Framework will ask to confirm the installation of the new service/bundle. Attempts of unknown service providers to install services are ignored. When a (signed) service is installed, it can also make use of the Security Framework. This makes it possible to create own policy and/or credential stores containing service dependant data. In the demo scenario, first the certificates of the two service providers IBCN and RnD are added to the local keystore. Afterwards a VideoService from IBCN and a VCRRemote from RnD are installed. The installed services are signed and thus have access to the Security interface. When the VideoService starts, it will create a new policystore and write the default access policies to it (Figure 11). A SIP-Proxy service, installed on the gateway by provider RnD, could now request the VideoService to pause the video player when detecting an incoming phone call.

The default policies however make the VideoService initially only accessible for the VideoRemote service of IBCN. Consequently, attempts of the VCRRemote or SIP-Proxy service to use the VideoService will fail (figure 12).

The policies of the VideoService will now be remotely updated according to an offline agreement between IBCN and RnD to share their services in a collaboration scenario. Upon agreement, service provider IBCN can configure its services to become shared with RnD . From now on, noth the VCRRemote and the SIP proxy service of service provider RnD can use the pauze function of the VideoService, provided by IBCN. Figure 13 illustrates the XACML permit-decision message.

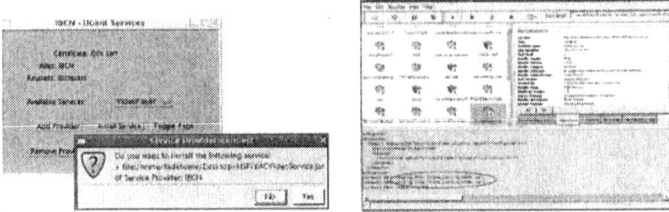

Fig. 11 At initial start of the trusted video service, all default policy settings are added to a central repository made available to a configuration provider via the TR-069 interface.

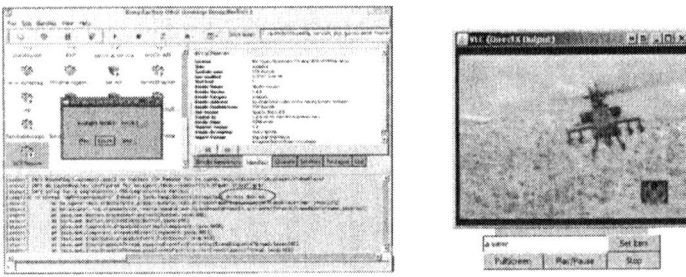

Fig. 12 The default configuration does not allow the VCR Remote service to access the video service

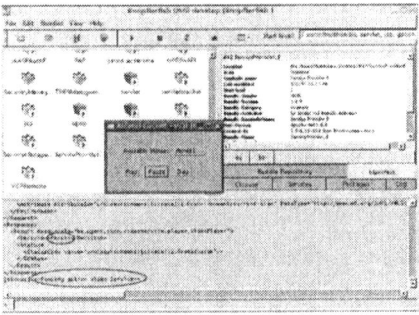

Fig. 13 VCR Remote from service provider RnD is granted to pause the video service. The XACML permit-decision message is shown.

When the agreement comes to an end, IBCN can again unshare its services for RnD as illustrated in Figure 14.

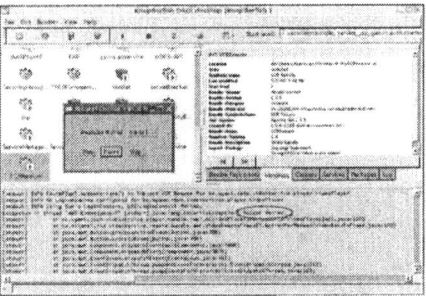

Fig. 14 The video service is no longer accessible for services from provider RnD (Access Denied).

6 Conclusions

WAN Service providers need (at least limited) control on the residential network and the locally running services, to be able to offer end-to-end predictable service levels. Only then they are able to compete with local plug-and-play services which usually have a full view on the local network and its resource usage. In order to limit the view of WAN service providers on the residential network, a security framework is needed. This paper has discussed n XACML-based security framework, with two architectural options to extend the framework for multi-service provider environments. It was the aim of the security framework to allow convenient remote configuration of any service by a remote configuration provider, and to avoid conflicting service provider configuration. With a proof-of-concept implementation it is illustrated that the framework not only eases configuration of a single service, but also allows to configure in a generic and secure way collaboration scenarios between service providers. The latter implies that the security framework also allows to deny untrusted service providers to extend their view on the home network beyond the view on their own service. The framework has the additional advantage that it remains compatible with existing OSGi services by simply extending these services with a 100% automated script to add a signature and access control extensions. These scripts aim to further ease adoption of the proposed security approach by WAN service providers.

Acknowledgements This work has been funded by the Institute for the Promotion of Innovation through Science and Technology in Flanders (Belgium) within the scope of the FADE-Home project.

References

1. Haerick W., Goeminne N., Cauwel K., De Jans G., De Turck F., Dhoedt B., Demeester P., Bracke S., Acke W., Bouchat C., *Success in home service deployment: zero-touch or chaos?* Proceedings of the 44th FITCE Congress 2005, Vienna, Austria, 1-3 September 2005, pp. 36-44
2. Corcoran, P. M., *Mapping home-network appliances to TCP/IP sockets using a three-tiered home gateway architecture.* IEEE Transactions on Consumer Electronics, Aug. 1998, 44(3), pp. 729736.
3. Valtchev, D., et al., *Service Gateway Architecture for a smart home.* IEEE Communications Magazine, Apr 2002.
4. Nguyen T., Bouwen J., *The Next-Generation Residential Gateway.* The Journal of the Institution of British Telecommunications Engineers, JulySeptember 2001, 2(3), pp. 134138.
5. Home Gateway Initiative, *Home Gateway Technical Requirements: Release 1.* The http://www.homegatewayinitiative.org/publis/HGI_V1.0.pdf, July 2006.
6. OSGi Alliance *OSGi Server Platform Release 4,* October 2005
7. DSLHome Technical Workgroup *CPE WAN Management Protocol. TR-069,* May 2004
8. Universal Plug and Play Forum *UPnP Device Architecture v1.0 2002,* http://www.upnp.org

Coherence Bandwidth and its Relationship with the RMS delay spread for PLC channels using Measurements up to 100 MHz

Mohamed Tlich[1], Gautier Avril[2], Ahmed Zeddam[2]
[1]Teamlog, [2]France Télécom division R&D
2, Av. Pierre Marzin – 22303 Lannion, France
Mohamed.tlich@wanadoo.fr

Abstract— Estimations of coherence bandwidth from wideband channel sounding measurements made in the 30KHz–100MHz band in several indoor environments are described. Results are intended for applications in high-capacity indoor powerline networks. The coherence bandwidth and the RMS delay spread parameters are estimated from measurements of the complex transfer function of the Powerline Communications (PLC) channel. The 90th percentile of the estimated coherence bandwidth at 0.9 correlation level is above 65.5 KHz and 90% of estimated values of $B_{0.9}$ are below 691.5 KHz. $B_{0.9}$ was observed to have a minimum value of 32.5 KHz. The RMS delay spread describes the dispersion in the time domain due to multipath transmission. 80 % of the channels exhibit an RMS delay spread between 0.06µs and 0.78µs. Its mean value was equal to 0.413µs. The paper studies the variability of the coherence bandwidth and time-delay spread parameters with the channel class [9], and thus with the location of the receiver with respect to the transmitter. And finally relates the RMS delay spread to the coherence bandwidth, which in turn, affects the powerline channel capacity.

Keywords— Powerline Communications (PLC), Coherence bandwidth, RMS delay spread.

– Introduction

P owerline Communications (PLC) appointed for future wideband wireline services in the 2-30 MHz frequency band envisage data transmission rates up to 200 Mbits/s [1]. Generally, Effective data rates do not exceed 70 Mbits/s [2]. In order to increase much more the data rates, the PLC equipment suppliers are studying the possibility of extending the PLC frequency band up to 100 MHz. The successful implementation of this solution requires a detailed knowledge of signal propagation modes inside this enlarged band.

Please use the following format when citing this chapter:

Tlich, M., Avril, G., Zeddam, A., 2007, in IFIP International Federation for Information Processing, Volume 256, Home Networking, Al Agha, K., Carcelle, X., Pujolle, G., (Boston: Springer), pp. 129-142.

Extensive characterizations of powerline channels have been reported in [5, 6, 7, and 8]. However, these studies are mainly focused on frequencies up to 30 MHz.

The coherence bandwidth is a key parameter whose value relative to the bandwidth of the transmitted signal, subsequently determines the need for employing channel protection techniques, e.g. equalisation or coding to overcome the dispersive effects of multipath [3, 4]. The impulse response of transmission channels can be characterised by various parameters. The average delay is derived from the first moment of the delay power spectrum and is a measure of the mean delay of signals. The RMS delay spread is derived from the second moment of the delay power spectrum and describes the dispersion in the time domain due to multipath transmission.

For PLC channels, and for the 1-30 MHz frequency band, thorough studies were undertaken in [5, 6]. It was observed that 99% of the studied channels have an RMS delay spread below 0.5µs. In [5], $B_{0.9}$ was observed to have an average value of 1 MHz.

Also, in [7], it was indicated that for signals in the 0.5-15 MHz frequency band, the maximum excess delay was below 3µs, and the minimum estimated value of $B_{0.9}$ was 25 KHz.

In [8] and for the frequency range up to 30 MHz, it has been found that, for 95 % of the channels the mean-delay spread is between 160ns and 3.2µs. And 95 % of the channels exhibit an RMS delay spread between 240ns and 2.5µs.

In this paper, coherence bandwidth and delay spread parameters studies are extended until the 100 MHz frequency band. For this purpose wideband propagation measurements were undertaken in the 30 KHz – 100 MHz band in various indoor channel environments (country and urban, new and old, apartments and houses) as demonstrated Table 1.

The measurements taken using a swept frequency channel sounder yielded sufficient statistical data from which frequency correlation functions were derived. These results were used to obtain the coherence bandwidth of the PLC channels investigated and their impulse responses, obtained by applying the inverse Fourier transform to the estimated frequency response [4].

The PLC transfer functions study presented hereby relates to seven measurement sites and a total of 144 transfer functions. For each site, the transfer function is measured between a principal outlet (most probable to receive a PLC module) and the whole other outlets (except improbable outlets such as refrigerator outlets...). The distribution of the transfer functions by site and the characteristics of each site are given in the table 1.

TABLE 1
DISTRIBUTION OF TRANSFER FUNCTIONS BY SITE

Site number	Site information	Number of transfer functions
1	House - Urban	19
2	New house - Urban	13

Coherence Bandwidth and its Relationship with the RMS delay spread for PLC
channels using Measurements up to 100 MHz
131

3	Recently restored apartment – Urban	12
4	Recent house – Urban	28
5	Recent house – Urban	34
6	Recent house – country	22
7	Old House - country	16

Because calculating distances separating transmitters from receivers was impossible, the PLC channels were classified into 9 classes per ascending order of
their capacities (according to the Shannon's capacity formula and for a same reference noise and PSD emission mask). In [9] and as shows Fig.1, we have demonstrated that the channels of each class had a transfer functions with a same average
magnitude.

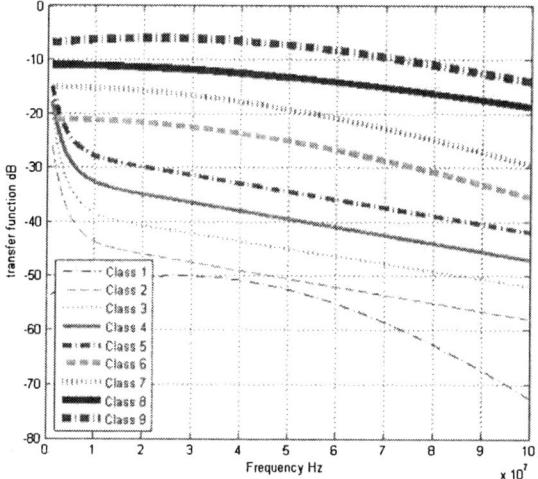

Fig. 1. Average transfer function magnitude by class.

Thus, a class 9 channel will, for example, be supposed to have a shorter trans-
mitter-receiver distance than a class 2-8 channel, and so on.

– Channel Sounder Hardware

This section outlines the swept frequency channel sounder design, its calibra-
tion and the devices used in the measurements. Transfer function measurements
were carried out in the frequency domain, by means of a vectorial network analyser, as show the block diagram of the Fig. 2.

The coupler box plugging into the AC wall outlet behaves like a high-pass filter, with the 3 dB cutoff at 30 KHz. The probing signal passes through the coupler

and the AC power line network and exits through a similar coupler plugged in a different outlet. A direct coupler to coupler connection is used to calibrate the test setup.

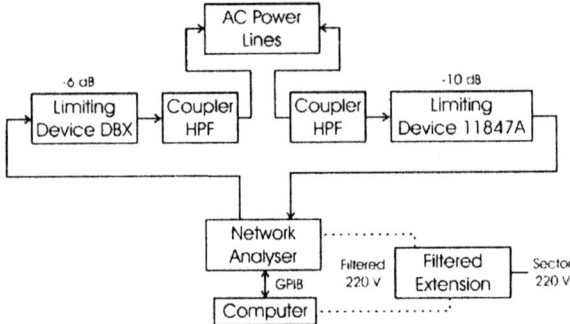

Fig. 2. Power line channel measurement system.

Two over-voltage limiting devices with a -10 dB and -6 dB losses, respectively, are used in front of the entry port of the vectorial network analyser 8753ES and its exit port, which can serve as an entry port, to protect it from over-voltages produced by the impulse noises of the AC power line.

A computer is connected to the network analyzer through a GPIB bus. This allows it to record data and control the network analyser by the INTUILINK software.

The network analyzer and the computer are isolated from the Powerline network using a filtered extension. This extension is systematically connected to an outlet nonlikely to be connected to a PLC modem, such as washing machine outlet. These precautions are taken in order to minimize the influence of the measurement devices on the measured transfer functions.

−   Wideband Propagation Parameters

Characterisation of wideband channel performance subject to multipath can be usefully described using the coherence bandwidth and delay spread parameters.

Coherence Bandwidth

The frequency-selective behaviour of the channel can be described in terms of the auto-correlation function for a wide sense stationary uncorrelated scattering (WSSUS) channel. Equation (1) gives $R(\Delta f)$, the frequency correlation function (FCF):

$$R(\Delta f) = \int\limits_{-\infty}^{+\infty} H(f)H^{*}(f + \Delta f)df \qquad (1)$$

Where $H(f)$ is the complex transfer function of the channel, Δf is the frequency shift and $*$ denotes the complex conjugate. $R(\Delta f)$ is a measure of the magnitude of correlation between the channel response at two spaced frequencies. The coherence bandwidth is a statistical measure of the range of frequencies over which the FCF can be considered 'flat' (i.e. a channel passes all spectral components with approximately equal gain and linear phase).

In other words, coherence bandwidth is the range of frequencies over which two frequency components have a strong potential for amplitude correlation. It is a frequency-domain parameter that is useful for assessing the performances of various modulation techniques [10]. No single definitive value of correlation has emerged for the specification of coherence bandwidth. Hence, coherence bandwidths for generally accepted values of correlations coefficient equal to 0.5, 0.7 and 0.9 were evaluated from each FCF, and these are referred to as $B_{0.5}$, $B_{0.7}$ and $B_{0.9}$, respectively.

RMS Delay Spread

Random and complicated PLC propagation channels can be characterized using the impulse response approach. Here, the channel is a linear filter with impulse response $h(t)$. The power-delay profile provides an indication of the dispersion or distribution of transmitted power over various paths in a multipath model for propagation. The power-delay profile of the channel is calculated by taking the spatial average of $|h(t)|^2$. It can be thought of as a density function, of the form:

$$P(\tau) = \frac{|h(t)|^2}{\int\limits_{-\infty}^{+\infty} |h(t)|^2 \, dt} \qquad (2)$$

The RMS delay spread is the square root of the second central moment of a power-delay profile. It is the standard deviation about the mean excess delay, and is expressed as:

$$\tau_{RMS} = \left[\int \left(\tau - \tau_e - \tau_A \right)^2 P(\tau) d\tau \right]^{1/2} \qquad (3)$$

Where τ_A is the first-arrival delay, a time delay corresponding to the arrival of the first transmitted signal at the receiver; and τ_e is the mean excess delay, the first moment of the power-delay profile with respect to the first arrival delay:

$$\tau_e = \int \left(\tau - \tau_A \right) P(\tau) d\tau \qquad (4)$$

The RMS delay spread is a good measure of the multipath spread. It gives an indication of the nature of the inter-symbol interference (ISI). Strong echoes (relative to the shortest path) with long delays contribute significantly to τ_{RMS}.

A typical plot of the time delay parameters is shown in Fig. 3.

– **Analysis of Results**

In this section, an analysis of the measured results, estimation of coherence bandwidth, its variability and interrelationship with RMS delay spread are outlined.

Coherence Bandwidth Results

Fig. 4 shows the frequency correlation functions obtained for three transmitter receiver scenarios; a class 9 channel (curve (i)), which can be assumed to have the least multipath contributions. Curves (ii) and (iii) correspond to the FCFs obtained from a class 6 and class 3 channels, respectively.

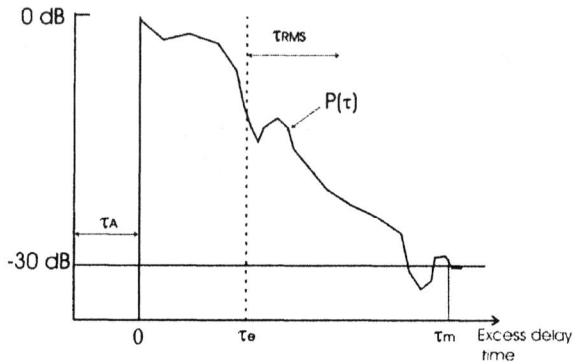

Fig. 3. An illustration of a typical power-delay profile and the definition of the delay parameters

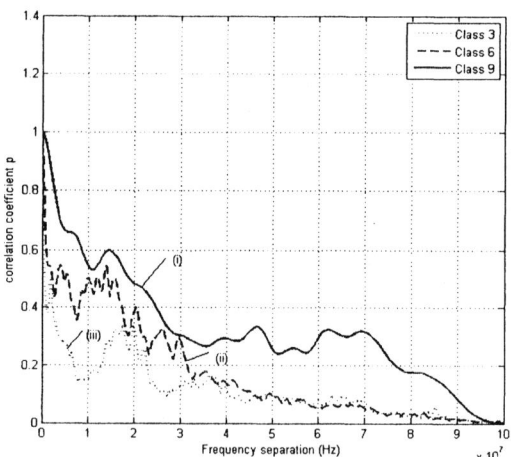

Fig. 4. Frequency correlation functions of the measured channels.
(i) class 9; (ii) class 6; (iii) class 3

The degradation of the frequency correlation functions corresponding to class 6 and class 3 channels with respect to the class 9 channel can be seen in Fig. 4. Rapid decrease of the frequency correlation function with respect to the frequency separation and also as the class number decreases can be observed. The decrease in frequency correlation function is not monotonic, and this is due to the presence of multipath echoes in the PLC channel.

Coherence bandwidth values for 0.5, 0.7 and 0.9 correlation levels for the curves of Fig. 4 are given in Table 2, and statistics of the coherence bandwidth function for 0.5, 0.7 and 0.9 correlation levels for all channel measurements are shown in Table 3. In general, the smallest frequency separation value is normally chosen to estimate the coherence bandwidth.

For the 0.9 coherence level, the coherence bandwidth was observed to have a mean of 291.97 KHz, minimum coherence bandwidth of 32.5 KHz, and 334.36 KHz standard deviation (Std). For 90% of the time, the value of $B_{0.9}$ obtained was below 691.5 KHz and above 65.5 KHz. For the 0.7 coherence level, a mean coherence bandwidth of 833.9 KHz was obtained. Here, the minimum value emerged as 98.5 KHz and the standard deviation as 1.06 MHz. In the 0.5 coherence level, 80% of the channel measurements have a $B_{0.5}$ values below 13.376 MHz and above 423.5 KHz.

TABLE 2

COHERENCE BANDWIDTH VALUES FOR 0.5, 0.7 AND 0.9 CORRELATION LEVEL FOR THE CURVES OF
FIG. 4.

Curve	Coherence bandwidth KHz		
	$B_{0.5}$	$B_{0.7}$	$B_{0.9}$
(i)	18 819.5	3 852.5	1 586.5
(ii)	2 171.5	586.5	249.5
(iii)	909.5	347.5	50.5

TABLE 3

STATISTICS OF THE COHERENCE BANDWIDTH FUNCTION FOR 0.5, 0.7, AND 0.9 CORRELATION
LEVELS

	Min	Max	Mean	Std	90% above	90% below
$B_{0.5}$ (KHz)	2 30	33 850.5	4 539.3	6 544.7	4 23.5	13 376
$B_{0.7}$ (KHz)	9 8.5	8 054.5	833 .9	1 063.2	1 81.5	1 774.5
$B_{0.9}$ (KHz)	3 2.5	1 859.5	291 .97	334.3 6	6 5.5	691. 5

Coherence Bandwidth versus Channel Class

The min, max, and mean values of coherence bandwidth function for 0.9 correlation level as a function of the channel class is given in Fig. 5. It can be observed
that the coherence bandwidth is highly variable with the location of the receiver
with respect to the transmitter.

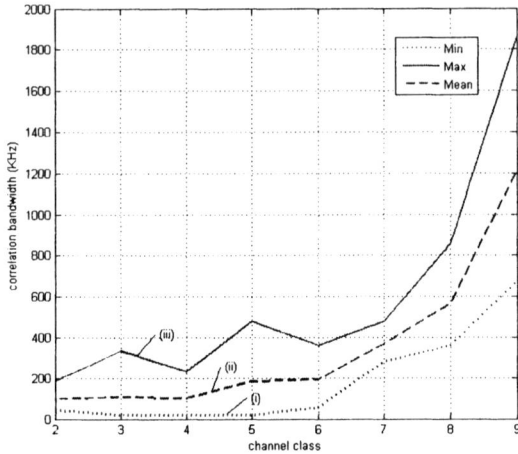

Fig. 5. Coherence bandwidth for 0.9 correlation level as a function of channel class. (i) Min; (ii)
Mean; (iii) Max

To investigate the reasons for the fluctuations of the values of coherence bandwidth, magnitude curves of the complex frequency responses are shown. Fig. 6
represents the channel frequency response for the case where the coherence bandwidth was estimated at 1.859 MHz. This is the dominant peak value that appears
in the curve (iii) of Fig. 5. Fig. 6 clearly shows that the channel frequency response presents few notches, large peaks, and is relatively flat over the 100 MHz
bandwidth. Not surprisingly therefore, the coherence bandwidth assumed a relatively high value.

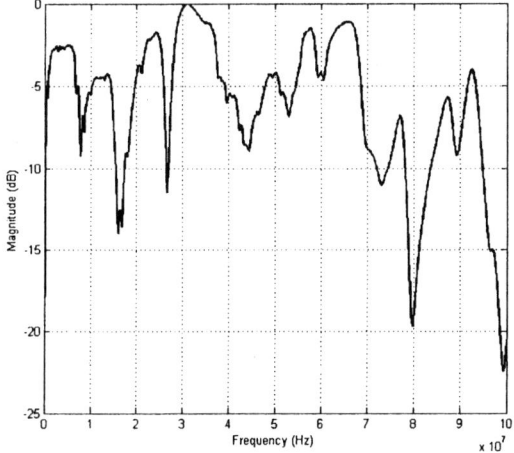

Fig. 6. Measured transfer function envelope of the maximum $B_{0.9}$ value

Next, the least value of the coherence bandwidth (32.5 KHz) was investigated.
Fig. 7 shows the magnitude response in this case which shows significant frequency selective fading of the channel, resulting in deep fades at several frequencies and narrow peaks. The presence of this significant frequency selective fading
explains the relatively small value of coherence bandwidth observed. Both of
these cases demonstrate that the PLC indoor channel is considerably affected by
multipath, and that the coherence bandwidth value decreases with frequency selective fading.

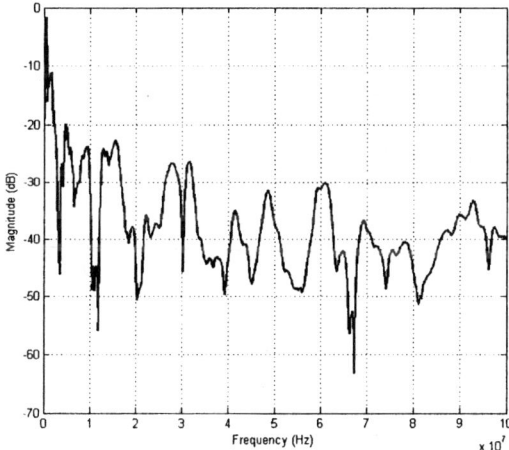

Fig. 7. Measured transfer function envelope of the minimum $B_{0.9}$ value

From an implementation point of view, the highly fluctuating coherence bandwidth means that the system designer can rely only on the lowest value of this parameter in such an environment. From Fig. 5, this is 32.5 KHz.

The coherence bandwidth, determined from (1) is calculated from the complex frequency response of the channel, in which the phase changes instantaneously and significantly over any change on the state of an electrical device. The coherence bandwidth thus determined is more appropriately termed the instantaneous coherence bandwidth. To study the time dispersive nature of the PLC channel, it's more suitable to focus on the RMS delay spread parameter.

Delay Spread Results

By means of an inverse Fourier transform the impulsive response $h(t)$ can be derived from absolute value and phase of a measured transfer function. The amplitudes of the impulse responses of the channels of Fig. 6 and Fig. 7 are depicted in Fig. 8 and Fig. 9, respectively.

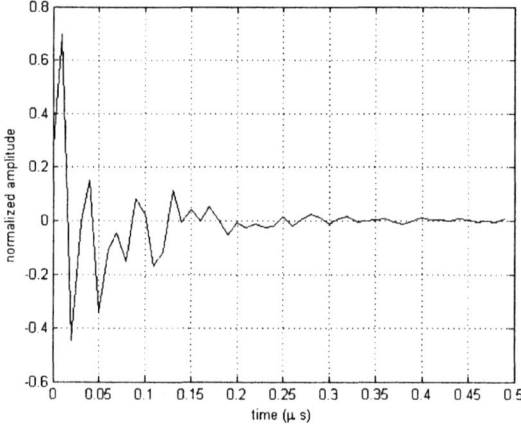

Fig. 8. Impulse response of the channel of Fig. 6.

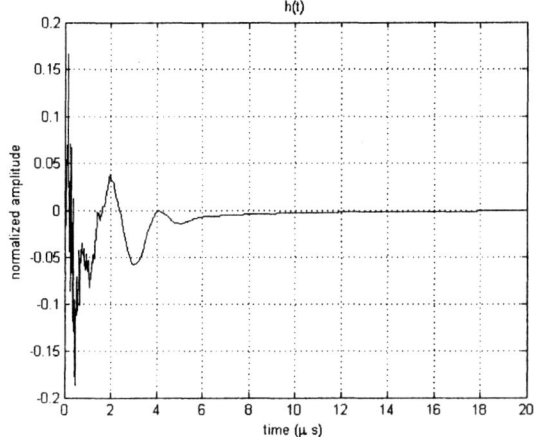

Fig. 9. Impulse response of the channel of Fig. 7.

The impulse responses of Fig. 8 and Fig. 9 show some peaks which confirm the multipath characteristics of PLC channels. The impulse response of Fig. 8 exhibits a maximum peak at a delay $\tau_A = 0.01\mu s$ and an RMS delay spread $\tau_{RMS} = 0.0368\mu s$. The same parameters of the impulse response of Fig. 9 are $\tau_A = 0.32\mu s$ and $\tau_{RMS} = 1.3674\mu s$. This is quite foreseeable as the impulse response of Fig. 8 is associated to a shorter PLC channel and much less affected by multipath.

Statistics of First arrival delay and RMS delay spread for all measured PLC channels are given in Table 4. The first-arrival delay (τ_A) was observed to have a mean of 0.175µs, minimum of 0.01µs, and 0.11µs standard deviation. 80 % of the channels exhibit an RMS delay spread between 0.06µs and 0.78µs. The mean value of the RMS delay spread was 0.413µs.

TABLE 4

STATISTICS OF TIME-DELAY SPREAD PARAMETERS

	Min	Max	Mean	Std	90 % above	90 % below
τ_A (μs)	0.01	0.55	0.1751	0.1134	0.05	0.31
τ_{RMS} (μs)	0.027	1.367	0.413	0.294	0.066	0.784

Delay spread versus Channel Class

The mean values of first-arrival delay and RMS-delay spread as a function of the channel class are given in Fig. 10. It can be observed that these parameters are highly variable with the class number.

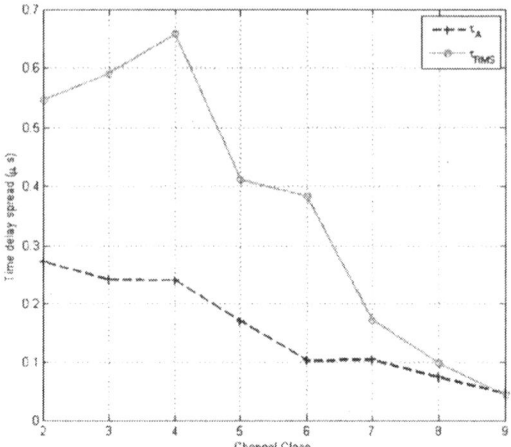

Fig. 10. Time-delay spread parameters as a function of the channel class

Generally speaking, the first arrival delay and RMS delay spread parameters decrease with the class number. In fact, the highly numbered classes are those whose channels are shorter and less affected by multipath. The transmitted signal arrives to its destination more quickly; furthermore, the number of echoes and their delay excess are less than those of low numbered classes.

An important fact is that the average value of the RMS delay spread of the class 4 channels is higher than that of classes 2 and 3. Indeed, the relatively small number of measurements made that class 4 channels, although with higher average magnitude than those of the classes 2 and 3 channels, have many low valued coherence bandwidth channels (the $B_{0.9}$ 32.5KHz min value pertains to the class 4) and thus many RMS delay spread values relatively large.

Coherence Bandwidth versus RMS Delay Spread

Fig. 11 shows a scatter plot of the RMS delay spread against the coherence bandwidth of the PLC channel measures. The scatter plot shows a high concentration of points in the range 0.1μs-0.9μs at which the coherence bandwidth is almost under 500 KHz and over 50 KHz. Higher values of coherence bandwidth are observed for RMS delay spread values less than 0.1μs. In system design terms, higher coherence bandwidth translates to faster symbol transmission rates [10].

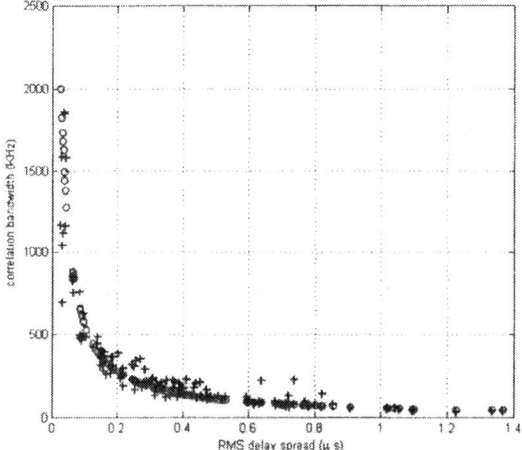

Fig. 11. Scatter plot of coherence bandwidth against RMS delay spread.

Fig. 11 depicts a clear relation between the values of $B_{0.9}$ and τ_{RMS} estimated in the overall set of measured channels, and which can be approximated by:

$$\tau_{RMS}(\mu s) = \frac{55}{B_{0.9}(KHz)} \qquad (5)$$

On Fig. 11, the relation (5) is represented by the red circles curve.

– Conclusion

Based on a multitude of measurements in different environments, the paper includes analysis of both coherence bandwidth and RMS delay spread parameters for in-house powerline channels in the frequency range up to 100 MHz.

Rapid decrease of the frequency correlation function with respect to frequency separation and also as the channel class increases was observed.

The 90th percentile of the estimated coherence bandwidth $B_{0.9}$ at 0.9 correlation level stayed above 65.5 KHz. Also, 90% of estimated values of $B_{0.9}$ were below 691.5 KHz. $B_{0.9}$ was observed to have a minimum value of 32.5 KHz.

The RMS delay spread results show that 80 % of the channels exhibit values between 0.06μs and 0.78μs. Its mean value was equal to 0.413μs.

Additionally, a relationship between the RMS delay spread and the coherence bandwidth was determined.

These results are intended for applications in high-capacity indoor powerline networks whose frequency band is up to 100MHz.

REFERENCES

[1] Homeplag Powerline Alliance, "HomePlug AV Specification, Version 1.0.05", October 2006.

[2] Sherman Gavette, Sharp Labs, "HomePlugAV – Detailed Architecture", homeplug executive seminar, November 2005.

[3] Bultitude R., Mahmoud S., and Sullivan W., "A comparison of indoor radio propagation characteristics at 910MHz and 1.75 GHz", IEEE J. Sel. Areus Commun., January 1989, 7, (1), pp. 20-30.

[4] Bultitude R., Hahn R., and Davies R., "Propagation considerations for the design of indoor broadband communications system at EHF", IEEE Trans. Veh. Technol., February IYY8,47, (1), , pp. 20-30.

[5] V. Degardin, M. Lienard, A. Zeddam, F. Gauthier, and P. Degauque, "Classification and characterization of impulsive noise on indoor power lines used for data communications". IEEE Transactions on Consumer Electronics, Vol. 48, November 2002.

[6] T. Esmailian, F. R. Kschischang, and P. Glenn Gulak, "In-building power lines as high-speed communication channels: channel characterization and a test channel ensemble", Int. J. Comm. Sys. 2003.

[7] T. V. Prasad, S. Srikanth, C. N. Krishnan, and P. V. Ramakrishna, "Wideband Characterization of Low Voltage outdoor Powerline Communication Channels in India", International Symposium on Power-Line Communications and its Applications (ISPLC'2001), Sweden, April 2001.

[8] Holger Philipps, "Development of a Statistical Model for Powerline Communication Channels", Proceedings of ISPLC 2000, pp.153-162

[9] M. Tlich, A. Zeddam, F. Moulin, F. Gauthier, and G. Avril, " A Broadband Powerline Channel Generator", Proceedings of ISPLC 2007, pp. 505-510, 26-28 March 2007.

[10] Lutz H.-J. Lampe and Johannes B. Huber, "Bandwidth Efficient Power Line Communications Based on OFDM"

Time/Frequency Analysis of Impulsive Noise on Powerline Channels

Gautier Avril[1], Mohamed Tlich[2], Fabienne Moulin[1], Ahmed Zeddam[1], Fabienne Nouvel[3]

[1] Orange Labs - 2 Av. Pierre Marzin - 22307 Lannion, France
[2] Teamlog France
[3] IETR – 20, av. des buttes de Coësmes, 35000 Rennes
gautier.avril@orange-ftgroup.com

Abstract — Powerline communication systems are used to transmit audio and video transmissions with delay, datarate and QoS requirements. However, the Powerline medium is shared with other devices connected to any socket. When switching, and even during normal operation, these devices can generate some noises (stationary, cyclo-stationary & impulsive). A good knowledge of these noises is essential to counter them and to ensure a fair quality of service. This study describes an new method to monitor impulsive noise, which tries to be very close to the mechanism of Powerline modems, so the impact of these noises is better evaluated

Keywords—Powerline, Impulsive noise, Time/Frequency Analysis, Spectrogram

– Introduction

Powerline Systems are one of the main technologies to build a Home Network. These technologies are low cost, easy to use and offer the possibility to transmit high data rate with associated services (internet, high definition video, video on demand...). Some of these services, especially video and audio services, require a sufficient quality of service. However, the powerline medium used by powerline modem is shared with a lot a devices which may generate noises (stationary, cyclo-stationnary & impulsive noise). Impulsive Noise (IN) is one of the main sources of interference which causes bit errors in power line communication (PLC) systems. Sources of these impulses are multiple: commutation of switches, power supplies... Some studies tried to classify their length, the bandwidth they use and interarrival time into different classes [ZIM00], [DEG03], [BAL03].

To counter these noises, Error Correction Codes (ECC) associated with interleaving and Automatic Repeat reQuest (ARQ) are generally used. Indeed, the power of these impulses makes it difficult to estimate impacted data. Different studies proved that impulsive noise varies from some µs to some ms and that in-

Please use the following format when citing this chapter:

Avril, G., Tlich, M., Moulin, F., Zeddam, A., Nouvel, F., 2007, in IFIP International Federation for Information Processing, Volume 256, Home Networking, Al Agha, K., Carcelle, X., Pujolle, G., (Boston: Springer), pp. 143-150.

terarrival time can go up to a few seconds. So ECC length, interleaving and ARQ scheme are designed to neutralize these kinds of noises.

However, time, frequency and amplitude characteristics of impulsive noise can't be treated separately. Indeed, a long noise with very high amplitude may have a Power Spectral Density (PSD) concentrated on a small number of frequencies so the perturbation may be insignificant. On the contrary, a very short noise may affect a whole OFDM symbol... Moreover, PSD of the impulse may often vary between the beginning and the end of the impulse. To get a better estimation of the impact of impulsive noise, we bring together frequency and time, leading to a Time/Frequency analyzer for impulsive noise.

To have sufficient data for this analyzer, about 17 houses in France were monitored which provide us about 55000 noise acquisitions!

–   Experimental Hardware Configuration

Measurements of impulsive noise are carried out, in time domain, by means of a numerical scope, as shows Figure 1.

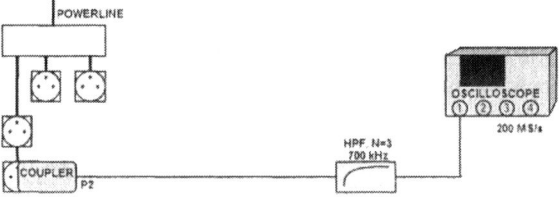

Fig. 1. Impulsive noise measurement hardware.

On each site, the acquisition of the impulsive noises is carried over 24 to 48 hours duration. An impulsive noise is recorded over a 48ms duration when its amplitude exceeds the trigger level. This level depends on the stationary noise present on the line and can thus vary from one site to another. For the majority of sites, the trigger level is fixed to 50mV.

The noise is recorded on several scope channels with different sensitivities. This makes it possible to have at the same time a good sensitivity for the low-amplitude noises and not to clip the strong-amplitude noises.

Let's note, finally, that the sampling rate was fixed to 250MHz.

–   General Observation

The observation of the measured impulsive noises highlighted two principal noise categories:

- Asynchronous impulsive noises, for which the duration varies from few microseconds to few milliseconds and whose frequency of appearance is random.
- Pseudo-stationary periodic impulsive noises synchronous with the sector frequency. Their repetition rate is thus of 50Hz or 100Hz.

These two categories are part of the five noise categories (stationary noise included/understood) established by Zimmermann and Dostert in [ZIM00]. Impulsive and pseudo_stationnary noise can be seen on Figure 1.

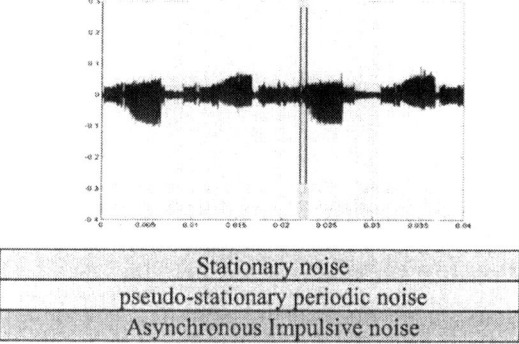

Stationary noise
pseudo-stationary periodic noise
Asynchronous Impulsive noise

Fig. 2. Temporal observation of PLC noise.

In order to illustrate the importance of characterizing the impulsive noises by a system approach, we consider the example of an asynchronous impulsive noise generated by a computer screen. This noise, shown in Figure 3 in time domain and in Figure 4 in frequency one, lasts almost 50ms and its energy is mainly concentrated in low frequencies.

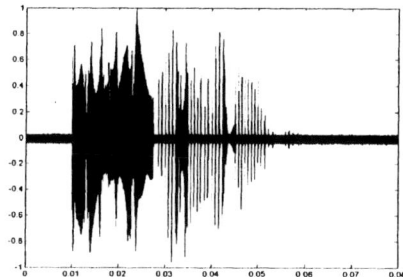

Fig. 3. Impulsive noise generated by a computer screen (time domain).

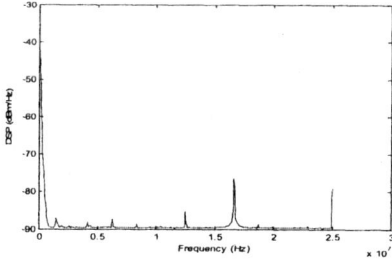

Fig. 4. Impulsive noise generated by a computer screen (frequency domain).

As Figure 5 shows, when this noise is treated according to the system approach, i.e. cut out in PLC OFDM symbols for which the FFT is applied, we observe that the noise PSD differs from its PSD calculated over its total duration, and also varies from an OFDM symbol to another.

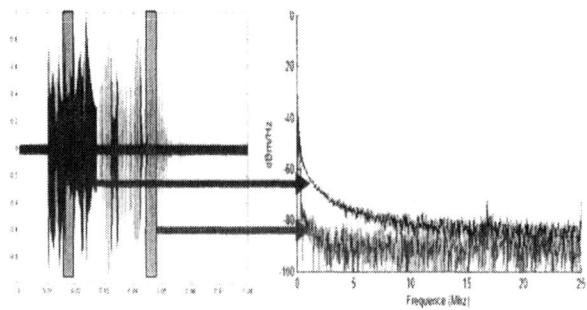

Fig. 5. PSD of an impulse at 2 different points

– Spectrogram Representation

This observation brought us to think about a spectrogram representation of the impulsive noises. This representation makes it possible to observe the noise in time and in frequency as it is really perceived by a communication system.

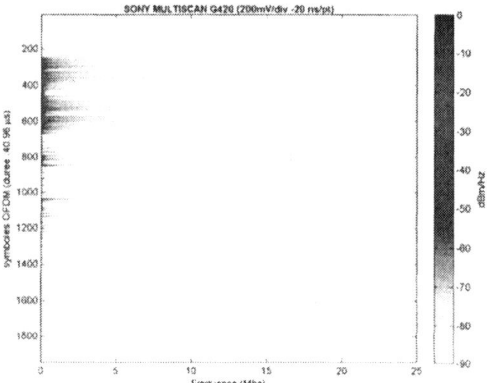

Fig. 6. Time/frequency spectrogram of the impulse

Figure 6 gives the time/frequency spectrogram of the same impulsive noise generated by a computer screen. For each OFDM symbol whose duration is equal to 40.96μs, its PSD is calculated and its noise strength is represented by suitable colour darkness.

This representation has the advantage of determining:
- The number of symbols really affected by the impulsive noise.
- The OFDM carriers affected by the impulsive noise.

Such kind of representation makes it possible to identify the signatures of various disturbers.

In particular, this analysis was also performed on pseudo-stationary periodic noise synchronous with the 50Hz frequency, which strongly affects powerline systems ([CAI05] [KAT06]).

In Figure 7 is reported the impulsive noise spectrogram generated by a low consumption lamp, while Figure 8 shows the PSD of this noise calculated on two time-distant OFDM symbols. We can easily distinguish a 4ms duration pulse, which repeats every 10ms.

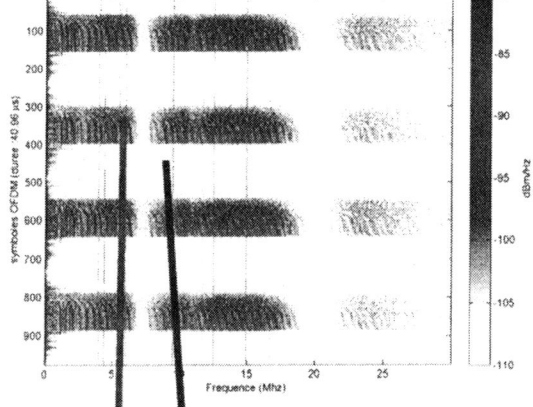

Fig. 7. Impulsive noise spectrogram generated by a low-consumption lamp.

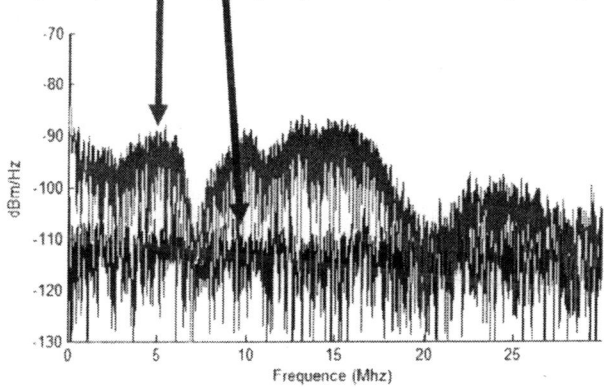

Fig. 8. PSD of the Fig. 7 noise on two time-distant OFDM symbols.

Impact on Powerline Systems

It is very difficult to determine the impact of asynchronous impulsive noise on powerline systems. Indeed, Automatic Repeat reQuest (ARQ) is used on these systems and is very efficient to fight most of powerline noises.

To limit the effect of Automatic Repeat reQuest, we send a fixed 12 Mb/s HDTV UDP stream on a given powerline link which allows up to 13- 14 Mb/s datarate. This approach is useful because HomePlug AV (HPAV) modems use ARQ even for UDP stream.

With only a 1 or 2 Mb/s datarate margin, it becomes more difficult for Home-Plug modems to reemit impacted data.

Some of previously recorded noises were injected with an Arbitrary Waveform Generator (AWG) as shown on Fig. 9.

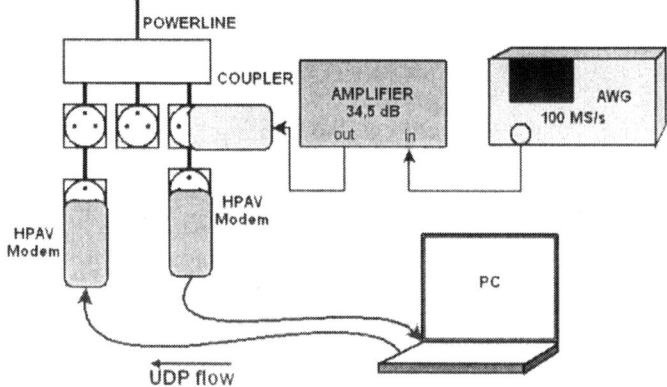

Fig. 9. Injection of recorded noises.

Table I presents the impact of some noises on the UDP transfer.

TABLE I

MEASURED PERIODIC NOISES IN 5 SITES

Noise Recording	Impulse length (μs)	Affected points	UDP Packet loss
1	< 41	125	0
2	< 41	2068	0
3	82	1568	0
4	4915	765	1920
5	28795	79802	19862
6	36740	$7,7e^7$	22056
7	37068	$4,1e^6$	25432

We see that the impact on UDP transfer is more linked with the length of the impulse than with the number of affected points. However, this only proves that ARQ is dependant of the length of the impulse. Our approach may however be used to evaluate error correction codes algorithms.

The impact of pseudo stationary impulsive and pseudo-stationary periodic noise synchronous with the 50Hz was also studied.

For every device which produces impulsive noise, we make statistics on each point (one frequency for one OFDM symbol) affected by impulsive noise per 50Hz cycle. These results are put together with the datarate obtained with a Homeplug 85 Mbits/s modem.

Table II presents an example of some of these results.

TABLE II

MEASURED PERIODIC NOISES IN 5 SITES

Device	impulse length per 20 ms (μs)	Amplitude (V)	Affected points	HomePlug Datarate loss
1	120	2,3	682	- 9%
2	1000	6,0	3286	- 11 %
3	1000	3,3	11535	- 24 %
4	1500	1,1	14488	-23 %
5	120	0,5	58	-
6	1000	0,9	568	-7 %
7	4000	4,1	45454	- 73 %
8	7000	1,3	42023	-56 %
9	1200	3,3	17045	-28%
10	9000	5,1	32010	-72 %
11	160	1,7	470	-8%

This table shows that more than impulse length, amplitude or PSD, the knowledge of the number of affected points may be used to predict the impact of noise on a PLC modem.

By looking at the worst recorded impulse, we can imagine new techniques to improve the next generation of Powerline modems.

– Conclusion

This system-based analysis of the impulsive noise is very useful to evaluate the impact of impulses on powerline modem as it processes the data as the modems do. Here, the impulses are divided into segments whose durations are equal to the Homeplug AV symbol duration. The spectrogram representation, selected for this approach, makes it possible to visualize the impact which the noise would have on the transmission (visualization of the symbols and OFDM carriers potentially affected by the impulsive noise).

Moreover, general statistics are obtained and allow us to propose new algorithms to better fight impulsive noise for the next generation of PLC.

– References

[HPAV] HomePlugAV Specification.

[ZIM00] An Analysis of the Broadband Noise Scenario in Power-Line Networks, L. Zimmermann, K. Dostert, ISPLC 2000.

[BAL03] Potential Limits on Power-Line Communication over Impulsive Noise Channels V.B. Balakirsky, A.J.H. Vinck , ISPLC 2003.

[CAI05] Fundamentals of the Cyclic Short-Time Variation of Indoor Powerline Channels, F.J Caiiete, L. Diez, J.A. Cortes, J.T. Entrambasaguas, J.L. Carmona, ISPLC 2005.

[KAT06] Channel Adaptation based on Cyclo-Stationary Noise Characteristics in PLC Systems. S. Katar, B. Mashburn, K. Afkhamie, H. Latchman, R. Newman. ISPLC 2006.

[DEG03] Impulsive Noise on Indoor Power lines : Characterization and Mitigation of its Effect on PLC Systems V. Degardin, M. Lienard, P. Degauque, A. Zeddam, F. Gauthier, EMC 2003.

New architecture for an Ultra Broadband Home Area Network with spread connectivity and autonomic functions.

Pierre Jaffré[1], Romain Insler[1], Vasilis Freiderikos[1], Sylvain Meyer[1] and Martial Bellec[2]

[1] France Telecom Research & Development, 2 Av. Pierre Marzin 22307 Lannion, France

[2] France Telecom Research & Development, 4 rue du Clos Courtel 35512 Cesson Sevigne, France

Email: name.surname@orange-ftgroup.com

Abstract. Operating Local Area Networks, in the home of their customers, has recently become a new business for Network Operators. On the other hand, Gigabit optical technologies are introduced in the operators' access network and new digital terminals appear in the customer premises, such as HDTV videos, PCs and home servers, requiring more and more a high speed data transfer inside the apartment. These evolutions will appeal for the emergence of an Ultra Broadband Home Area Network (UBB-HAN) with advanced connectivity capabilities that will combine many technologies. We introduce a new architecture for this future UBB-HAN which includes some foreseeable autonomic functions to cope with the management and the increased complexity of such a heterogeneous HAN.

1 CONTEXT

1.1 The Home Area Network is a new business for Network Operators

In 2004, France Telecom started the commercialization of a Home Gateway named "Live Box". After three years, about 5 Millions of these Customer Premise Equipments (CPE) are in operation in European countries. Services such as TV programs or Video on Demand over xDSL [1] are already a commercial success. But beside the quadruple play services that this box provides, customers use it as a Home Networking tool.

1.2 Emergence of Gigabit optical technologies in the Access Network

In 2006, France Telecom introduced GPON systems in its access network within the framework of a "Very High Speed" program for a

Please use the following format when citing this chapter:

Jaffré, P., Insler, R., Friederikos, V., Meyer, S., Bellec, S., 2007, in IFIP International Federation for Information Processing, Volume 256, Home Networking, Al Agha, K., Carcelle, X., Pujolle, G., (Boston: Springer), pp. 151-162.

FTTH offer [2]. FTTH is today widely deployed in countries like Japan and Korea, while in Europe and in the US several companies are developing detailed commercial plans for a mass deployment. It is thus possible to envision in the near future a scenario in which a large amount of users will be offered a very high performance connection up to the "main door" of their apartment. Several hundreds of Mbps are reasonably reachable in the coming future, backed up by emerging standards such as GPON 2.4 G.984 [3]. A Dynamic Band Assignment mechanism allows the system to dedicate several hundreds of Mbps to a single user for a short time period, when bandwidth is available.

1.3 Requirement of Gigabit Data Rates in the Home Area Network

Digital Mass storage devices gain more success to the home every day. These devices, whose standardization is ongoing by e.g. within DLNA [4] or HGI [5] fora, offer not only demodulation of digital broadcast programs, access to remote operator services but also high connectivity to end devices such as TVs, home cinema or PCs. To enable the use of these devices, the trend is that it shall be possible to use them everywhere at home with high data rate connectivity to transfer content either from remote servers or between end devices sparsely distributed everywhere at home. Moreover, end user devices are fitted with high speed interfaces to easily transfer all types of multimedia supports. In the coming future these trends will certainly make the UBB-HAN a convergence arena where these devices and services will have to interoperate at home and in continuity with the operator's network. A well connected home will need an internal network operating at data rates around 1 Gbit/s by 2010 [6].

1.4 Necessity for a new architecture for Ultra Broadband Home Area Networks

Until now, with DSL technology in the access network, customers connected their box to a telephone set, locating the Access Point of their Home Network in the central part of their living space. With the optical technology at the access, a very high performance connection will be available in front of the Optical Network Termination (ONT) that is located near the "main door" of their apartment. It is anticipated that some of the gateway functions enabling connection to the service platforms through the network will be integrated to the ONT. On the other hand, a Gigabit coverage of the living space will require more than one AP, with probably several technologies involved. To guarantee the coverage, we anticipate the necessity to hybridize many connectivity technologies that can be divided in 3 types:

- Wireless, like radio or Free Space Optics,
- Wired, but without installation of a new wire, like Power Line Communication or over phone lines, like HomePNA or MoCA…

- Wired, with installation of a copper or optical physical media required

From the operator's point of view, it is essential to guarantee the Quality of Service of his own services transported over this complex Home Network. In particular, the quality evaluation of links using different technologies has to be homogeneous. Congestions have to be managed, with eventually reconfiguration of the network. Finally, it is essential for an operator to protect his own flows from local flows that can require resources on the same Home Network.

2 New architecture for an Ultra Broadband Home Area Network

2.1 The concepts of bridge and backbone in the UBB-HAN

A UBB-HAN requires new functionalities to improve its coverage and performance. A potential solution would implicate the distribution of numerous access points supporting different connectivity technologies. We present hereafter a new architecture answering these requirements (figure 1). Its main components are:

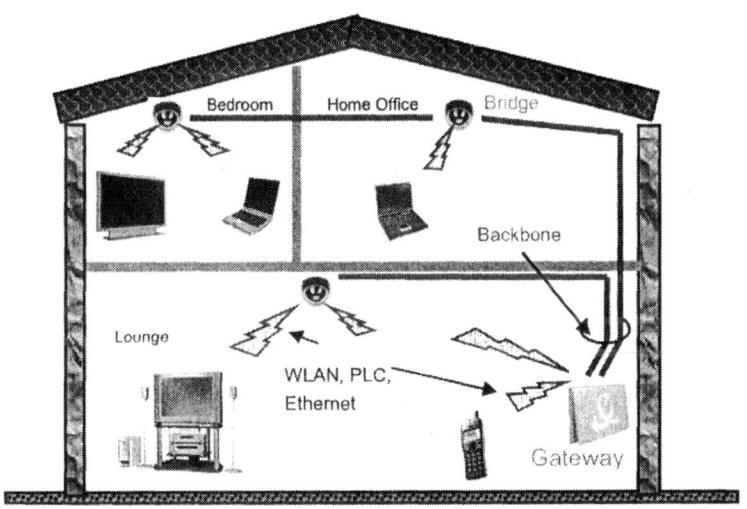

Figure 1: Outline of the Ultra Broadband – Home Area Network Architecture

- **Home Gateway:** interface between the access and the home network. The gateway may be just an interface without any other functions or even a more complex device with advanced functionalities.

- **Bridge:** node of the home network. This new device spreads the connectivity and improves home network coverage and performance. The bridge answers specific requirements newly identified within the UBB-HAN (availability of very high bandwidth, differentiated QoS, alternative route in case of congestion or link failure)

- **Backbone:** a very high data rate core constituted by the various bridges and the gateway. It may involve any high performance connectivity technology. The backbone network must provide a back-up solution in case of link congestion or failure.

2.2 Innovative techniques for the UBB-HAN architecture

The Ultra Broadband - Home Area Network (UBB-HAN) can be presented as a set of segments made up each one by a technology of connectivity (plastic or silica optical fibre, radio over fibre, free space optics, UWB, WiFi, PLT, Ethernet cabling...). Each segment carries several terminals, and the various segments are inter-connected by the Home Gateway and the bridges. This architecture represents a new situation where several paths and connectivity modes can be chosen to interconnect the various devices of the LAN. (example of figure 2 where a dual-mode terminal WiFi/UWB is connected to another PLT terminal either through the Home Gateway or through the bridge).

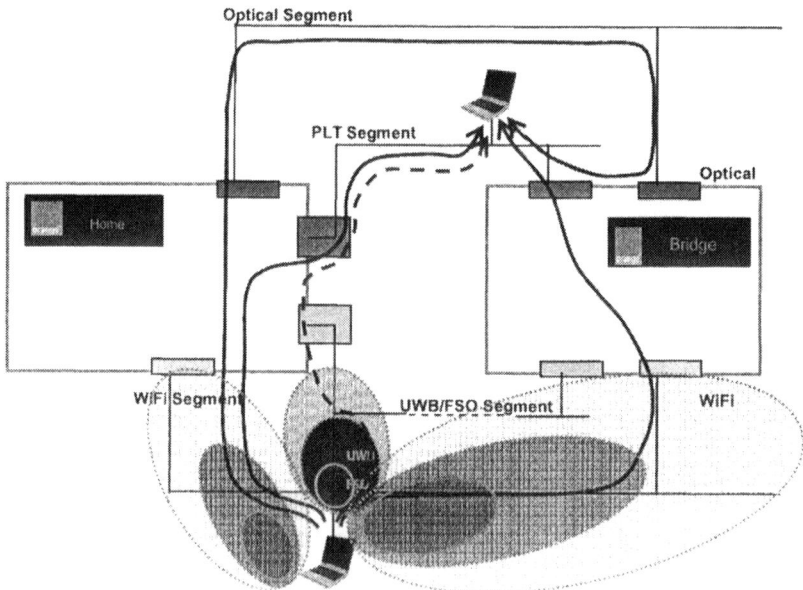

Figure 2: Illustration of path & connectivity selection functions in the UBB-HAN

According to whether this function of path selection is concentrated on the level of the Home Gateway or distributed between the Home Gateway and the bridges, one makes the distinction between centralized architecture (around the Home Gateway) and distributed architecture.

In the centralized approach, the network can be organized either in a tree or star structure around the Home Gateway (HGW) which will act as the main home manager, whereas the bridges act as relays. The role of the bridges is twofold, firstly, to extend the coverage to the whole home and secondly to update the HGW with the information on link status. Therefore, the network topology management is performed in a centralized way by the HGW: the forwarding function is coordinated by the HGW.

As illustrated in figure 3, the traffic is handled by disseminating the routing policies from the HGW to the network elements which will enforce them. Indeed, the HGW makes a centralized decision of a path, and then it establishes the path by informing all the bridges of the relevant path information. Note that in some specific scenarios the whole traffic may go through the HGW to perform specific processing (authentication,...). As a matter of fact, this approach should be simpler than the distributed one, but it could raise point of failure and bottleneck issues inside the HGW.

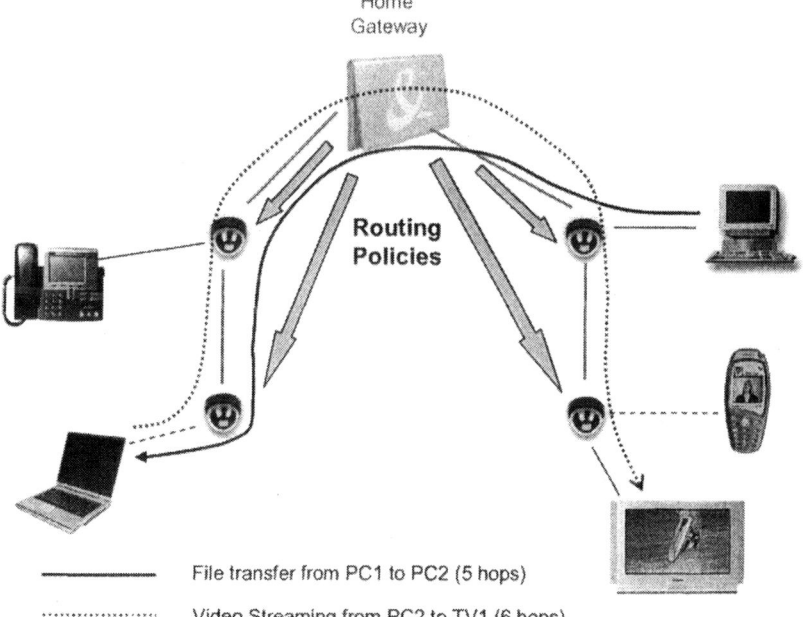

Home
Gateway

Routing
Policies

———————   File transfer from PC1 to PC2 (5 hops)

·················   Video Streaming from PC2 to TV1 (6 hops)

Figure 3: Centralized approach in the UBB-HAN

In contrast with the centralized approach, in the distributed approach, the topology management (path selection and establishment decisions) is performed in a distributed manner between the bridges and the HGW in using mesh network principles. Indeed, the HGW and the bridges are interconnected without any predefined constraint forming therefore a mesh network. This approach implies that either proactive or reactive ad hoc forwarding protocols can be applied at each bridge for path computation and establishment.

For the deployment matter, the distributed model seems to be more upgradeable and more flexible. However, the distributed character of the solution bringing more reliability and scalability by avoiding the gateway-centric routing effects, generate on the other hand some potential issues related in particular to the QoS insurance like resource reservation, scheduling and routing decision that requires nevertheless more efficient policies.

The Figure 4 illustrates how the forwarding of flows is performed in the case of fully distributed approach.

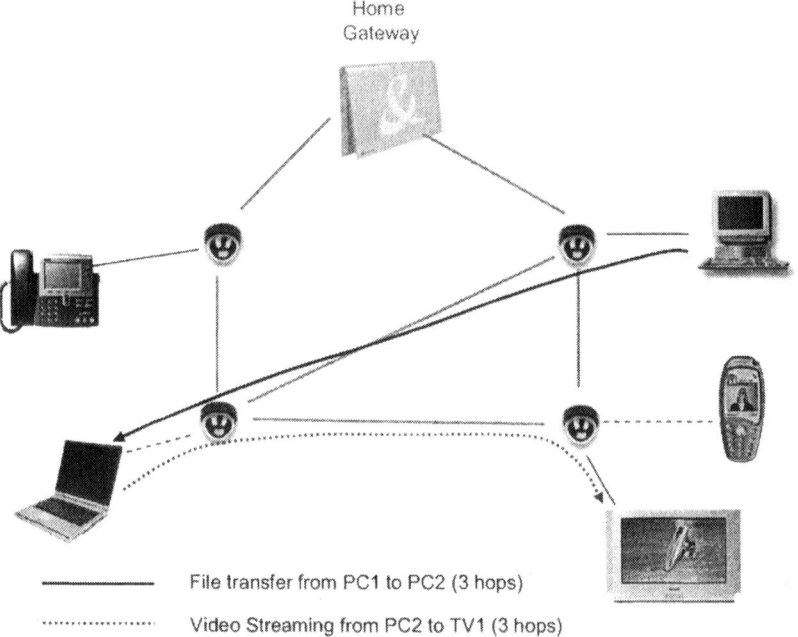

Home
Gateway

——————— File transfer from PC1 to PC2 (3 hops)

·················· Video Streaming from PC2 to TV1 (3 hops)

Figure 4: Distributed approach in the UBB-HAN

On the example of figure 4, one sees that the implementation of a mesh structure makes it possible to optimize the forwarding of flows regarding a criterion of a number of hops between source and destination. Some other metrics appear relevant for the choice of the path used for a given flow : for example, one may choose the path presenting the best signal to noise ratio, or the path ensuring the best distribution of the traffic, with respect to the QoS aims of the system (packets error rate, latency, jitter).

Thus, the UBB-HAN seems to be a mesh structure mixing technologies, from where the idea to transpose radio mesh techniques to the context of a network based on heterogeneous technologies, cascading wired and wireless media.

Another innovating feature is related to the definition of a convergence layer making possible the cohabitation of very heterogeneous technologies of the UBB-HAN, in the context of the work initialized by authorities of standardization and various organizations of research (examples of the forum IEEE 802.21 [7] and of the Berkeley Wireless Research Center [8]). According to the context, this layer of convergence can actually address very different concepts, from the continuity between networks (in the IEEE 802.21) up to the interactivity between the services. In our case, associated to the function of path selection (and connectivity selection), it appears in a first step like a function ensuring the consistency of information collected at the level of the MAC layers of various technologies, or function of InterMAC co-operation. In a second step, it will be able to take into account the mechanisms ensuring the continuity of the UBB-HAN with the access.

By its highly interactive character, the UBB-HAN has a sensitivity particular to the concerns of configuration, safety, maintenance and management of the Quality of Service. In order to face up to them, the prospects for transposition to the UBB-HAN of the autonomic techniques imagined for the large networks can be taken into consideration. These techniques are indeed suitable to provide the networks with the capacity to react in an autonomous way to a situation of new configuration (example the customer modifies its installation), with a problem of safety, a local degradation of the conditions of transmission, or with an evolution of the distribution of the traffic, and that without external intervention of the customer or the information system of the operator, which is particularly critical in the situation of complexity of the UBB-HAN. This topic is addressed in the section 3.

3 Autonomic functions

3.1 Autonomic technologies

Autonomic technologies represent a recent and ongoing effort to cope with the ever increasing complexity and heterogeneity of IT and communication systems. It's all about systems that are particularly designed in order to be able to manage themselves without any human intervention. They introduce a plethora of so-called self-* properties, such as self-healing, self-configuration, self-protection, self-optimization [9].

In the world of communication networks, an autonomic architecture should consist of network elements that are able to sense their environment, collect information about its operational state, analyze these data, make decisions and plan future configurations and finally reconfigure themselves. In a more synergic scenario, these network elements should be capable of communicating with each other, and sharing their resources in order to control the system's global behavior.

3.2 Knowledge plane and 4-plane architecture.

In the "Authone" Project [10] a 4-plane architecture is proposed in order to "inject" the intelligence of an autonomic system in the home area network. We will use a similar model to describe the autonomic behavior and expectations of our UBB-HAN. This architecture involves the following planes:

- The data plane which includes all the functions, operations and services related to layers 1-4 of traditional networks.
- The knowledge plane which is responsible to collect any significant information for the state of the network produced by the data plane, in order to ensure optimal resource management, QoS, traceability and mobility.
- The governance plane which processes the data of the knowledge plane, in order to make decisions concerning the reconfiguration of the system.
- The control plane, which contains reactive agents that act on the controlled elements to achieve the goals imposed by the governance plane.

3.3 Autonomic functions for a UBB-LAN.

Back to our architectural model, one can imagine the data plane like the source of operational information for the "gateway" and the various "bridges" (and possibly of certain terminals) which feeds the knowledge plane. This one can be thought of as a database system which provides the governance plane with an almost complete image of these network elements' state. The governance plane has the role of the system's "brain"; it could be an intelligent agent which exploits the information of the knowledge plane and based on decision algorithms plans, when it is necessary, the reconfiguration of the system. These algorithms can be as well simplistic (preset rules in collaboration with a policy-based management system), as well as more sophisticated, such as self-learning systems that use their experience in order to improve their performance (e.g.: neural networks). Last in the chain of interaction, is the control plane, a kind of "actuator" agent, which applies the new configuration to the concerned network elements.

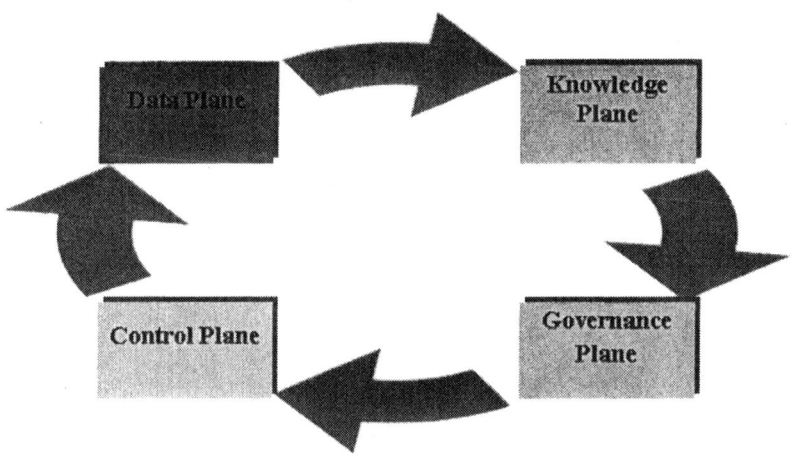

Figure 5: Plane interaction model

Given the home network environment such as it is described earlier (Par.2), we can consider various application scenarios for the autonomic technologies, all aiming at making the HAN intelligent and self-managed. The following figure (fig.6) represents the UBB-HAN as a mesh network structure, but this time extended by a knowledge and a control plane on each element of the residential backbone. Each node of the backbone has a situated view of the network, which means that it is conscious of the current state of network links and nodes in its neighborhood (ex.: 1 hop). This information can be shared on request with the knowledge plane of neighbor nodes, so that they can make decisions aligned with a global network configuration goal. The area covered by the situated view is a very important factor for the operation of this architecture. A large area produces more information to be exploited by the knowledge plane but also a more important "secondary" traffic dedicated to network management. An acceptable compromise must be chosen.

Combined procedure of path and connectivity selection: Traditional approaches for the resolution of this type of problems, often similar to routing algorithms, are likely to prove insufficient. A group of autonomous and interactive agents, able to feel the state of the links and other network elements and build a distributed knowledge plane, could possibly offer more adequate solutions. Moreover, a multi-agent system which functions independently of the network, can act in a proactive way in order to improve the performance of the transition in terms of time. In this case, the knowledge plane will comprise information such as link state, packet delay and transmission time between different nodes, available resources and quality of radio signals (SNR).

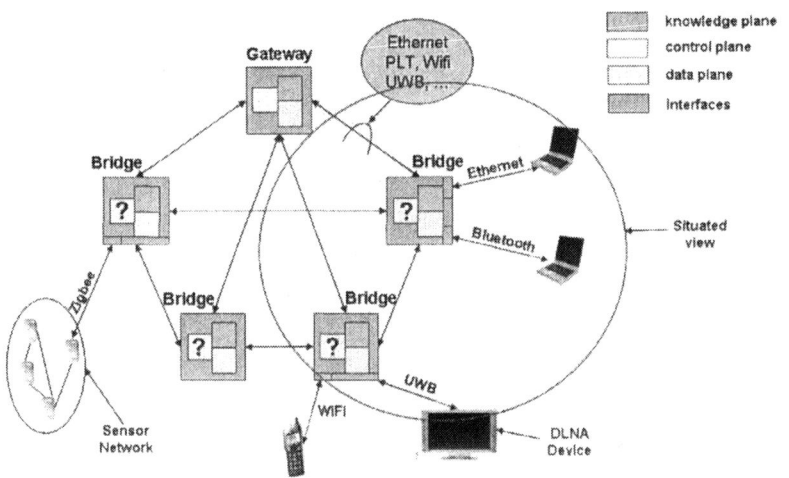

Figure 6: UBB HAN with Autonomic Functionalities.

UBB-LAN maintenance: In the same spirit as above, a distributed operational database could assist with the maintenance and the automated troubleshooting of the residential network. It is an essential functionality for the operator and his centralized management platforms which would have a heavy or even impossible mission to accomplish in a network of tens of million gateways and bridges. However, even we choose this distributed management structure for the knowledge plane, we can always keep in the gateway a summary of the different knowledge planes located on the bridges, for further processing by the operator's information systems.

Security: Security in a residential network imposes a minimum of feedback and handling by the end user, especially when it concerns authentication aspects. Thus, one could easily say that there is not much space for the deployment of autonomic technologies. However, they can be used to face other threats of security such as intrusions or "Denial of Service" attacks. For example, a system of intelligent agents in collaboration with a knowledge plane, able to analyze the traffic in any moment and discover abnormal flows, could answer these situations and ensure a transparent experience for the home user.

Fault diagnosis and troubleshooting: Automatic fault diagnosis and troubleshooting will be critical for the operation of an autonomic UBB-HAN. L.Qiu and al. presented a simulation-based fault detection system for wireless mesh networks [11]. Inspired by their approach, we can consider a diagnostic system adapted to the autonomic principles. This system would be composed of two distinct software modules. An agent that will run on every node of the residential backbone, gathering information about various protocol layers and a manager that will be fed with the agent's data in order to analyze them and act in a suitable way. With respect to our main UBB-HAN architecture, we can choose between a manager that runs on a single node (centralized architecture), or in a set of nodes (distributed architecture). In a first step, agents gather and exchange their situated view of the network's operation. Then, the manager, using the experience of a knowledge plane properly built to describe the operational points of our network, decides if the observed result is normal for the given configuration and traffic model. A fault is detected when the expected performance is far from the observed performance. Root cause analysis is done by finding the set of faults which minimizes this difference. It remains to us to specify the exact mechanism of data analysis. A neural network well-trained in various operation conditions could produce reliable results.

Quality of Service Management (QoS): The wide diversity of coexisting services in the UBB-HAN forces us to invent new methods to protect flows coming from the operator's specific services with respect to flows generated locally in the residence. Moreover, it is important that we propose new congestion avoidance mechanisms to manage efficiently and automatically the various considered flows among devices with different characteristics and processing capacities:

- WAN → LAN (VoD, Broadcast TV, VoIP, Internet,...)
- LAN → WAN (Zapping for Broadcast TV, VoIP,...)
- LAN → LAN (File transfer PC to PC,...)

Lastly, one should conceive a new admission control and flow classification system adapted to the needs of a UBB-HAN. An autonomic system could assist with keeping the QoS contract in such a dynamic environment. Based on network state information, provided by the knowledge plane, it could improve the reaction performance of existing control algorithms, in cases such as bridge congestion or broken radio channel.

4 Conclusions

The penetration of bandwidth hungry services inside the home and the arrival of very high performance optic connection up to the "main door" will push the deployment of Ultra Broadband Home Networks. For a good coverage, these networks will combine many connectivity technologies, with Access Points spread over the home. This deployment will call for a more complex architecture for the Home Network and a new repartition of the functions in the network as a whole. Some autonomic functions could be helpful to hide this complexity to the user and for keeping the management of the home network simple.

References

1. MaLigneTV. Digital TV on ADSL; http://www.malignetv.fr/
2. Very High Speed pilot program ("Fiber To The Home"); http://www.francetelecom.com/en/financials/journalists/press_releases/CP_old/cp060117.html
3. GPON 2.4 G; http://www.itu.int/newsarchive/press_releases/2003/04.html
4. Digital Living Network Alliance; http://www.dlna.org/home
5. Home Gateway Initiative; http://www.homegatewayinitiative.org/
6. M. Bellec, Home Broadband Home Area Network, Keynote 3, Tuesday 3rd April, European Wireless 2007
7. http://www.ieee802.org/802_tutorials/july06/802%2021-IEEE-Tutorial.ppt
8. http://bwrc.eecs.berkeley.edu/Publications/2006/Presentations/Conference_42.pdf
9. J. Kephart and D. Chess, The vision of Autonomic Computing, *IEEE Computer* 36(1): 41-50, 2003.
10. "AUTHONE" IST Celtic Project Proposal, H. Zimmermann et al., 2007; http://www.celtic-initiative.org/Projects/AUTHONE/.
11. L. Qiu, P. Bahl, A. Rao and L. Zhou. Troubleshooting wireless mesh networks. *Computer Communication Review* 36(5): 17-28 (2006)

Group Source Routing Protocol with Selective Forwarding for Mobile Ad Hoc Networks

Hoon Oh[1] and Do Minh Ngoc[2]

Abstract. In this paper, we have proposed a group dynamic source routing protocol, GDSR, for mobile ad hoc networks with high mobility. We focus on pursuing routing stability and making a fast recovery of link failure. Nodes in a network are divided into clusters, each being assigned a unique cluster label. A routing path is represented by a source route including a sequence of cluster labels, and the nodes having an identical cluster label are responsible for delivering packets cooperatively to the cluster whose label is the next one in the source route. We have also employed a distributed self-pruning algorithm DSP to prevent intermediate nodes from relaying RREQ unnecessarily, thus reducing considerable overhead. We compared our protocol with some existing ones and the result is proven to be highly dependable.

1 Introduction

In recent years, there has been an increasing interest in Mobile Ad Hoc Networks (MANETs). Many routing protocols have been proposed for MANETs. Basically, these protocols fall among three kinds based on their mode of operation: proactive, reactive and hybrid routing.

Proactive routing protocols such as DSDV [6] and OLSR [4] maintain fresh lists of destinations and their routes by distributing routing tables in the network periodically. Therefore, a source host can get routing path immediately if it needs one. The main disadvantages of such algorithms are bandwidth wastage in transmitting routing table and useless overhead in maintaining routes that are never going to be used in future.

Reactive routing protocols find routing path on demand by initiating a route discovery. That is, routing paths are searched only when needed. Reactive protocols have less control overhead and better scalability than proactive routing protocols,

---

[1] He is an assistant professor at the Department of Computer Engineering and Information Technology, University of Ulsan, Korea (hoonoh@ulsan.ac.kr).

[2] He is a graduate student at the same department (ngocdm@mail.ulsan.ac.kr).

Please use the following format when citing this chapter:

Oh, H., Ngoc, D. M., 2007, in IFIP International Federation for Information Processing, Volume 256, Home Networking, Al Agha, K., Carcelle, X., Pujolle, G., (Boston: Springer), pp. 163-177.

but suffer from long delay due to route searching. DSR [2] and AODV [7] are examples of reactive routing protocols.

An approach providing a better trade-off between proactive routing and reactive routing is hybrid routing protocols that are designed to increase scalability by allowing nodes to work together as a zone or cluster. These protocols proactively maintain routes to nearby nodes while determining routes to distant nodes using on-demand route discovery strategy. Some protocols belonging to this kind of routing such as CBRP [3] and ZRP [1] have been proposed during the recently years.

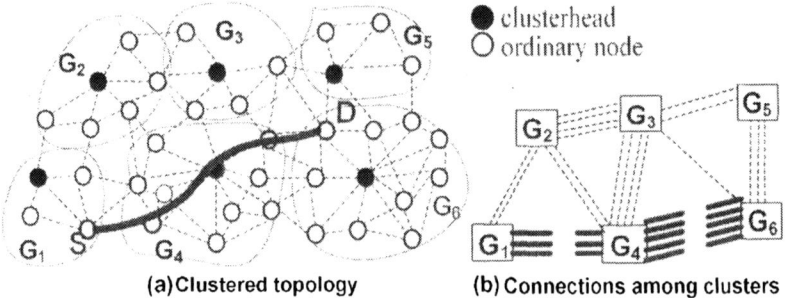

(a) Clustered topology   (b) Connections among clusters

Fig. 1 GDSR's routing mechanism.

In this paper, we investigate a group dynamic source routing protocol (shortly GDSR) in which a group of nodes cooperates to deliver packets from one cluster to its neighbor cluster in the clustered network topology. In order to form and maintain the clustering of networked nodes, we employ the clustering algorithm proposed in our previous work [5]. Although DSR has low control overhead, its performance is not high in unstable networks because a source route including a sequences of node addresses represents only one path and becomes invalid when the path is broken. GDSR overcomes this shortcoming by dividing the network into clusters, each being assigned a unique cluster label. In GDSR, a source route representing routing path consists of a sequence of cluster labels instead of a list of node addresses as in DSR. Because of a high intra-cluster and inter-cluster connectivity in mesh networks, a source route may represent multiple paths from the source node to the destination and be still valid even when one path is broken, thus enabling a quick route recovery. Let us take a look at Fig. 1-(a) where the network is grouped into six clusters labeled with G_1, G_2, ..., G_6. Suppose that S in G_1 wants to communicate with D in G_6. Then, the source route becomes (G_1, G_4, G_6) that represents 15 paths (3 x 5). The abstract representation of multiple paths in this network is given in Fig. 1-(b). The nodes in the G_1 cooperate to deliver packets to the G_2 that in turn does to G_6. Thus, note that if links between a pair of neighbor clusters are not completely broken, there always exist alternative paths. GDSR can therefore provide the excellent route stability and the high delivery ratio compared with DSR, especially in high mobility networks.

Moreover, we employ and modify a distributed self-pruning algorithm, DSP, from our previous work [8] by which only selective intermediate nodes forward route request message. About 50% to 70% of nodes are blocked from forwarding the route request message, which reduces considerably overhead as well as collision. The rest of this paper is organized as follows. Section 2 assesses some related works. Section 3 and Section 4 demonstrate the employed clustering algorithm with some improvement and our proposed routing protocol, respectively. Section 5 presents the DSP algorithm, and is followed by performance evaluation in Section 6. Finally, we summarize our contributions in Section 7.

2 Related Works

In this section, we briefly overview some previous protocols closely related to our approach for their key concepts and weak points.

In the DSR protocol [2], when a node wants to send a packet, it initiates a route discovery by flooding a route request (RREQ). Upon receiving a route request, a node checks if it knows a route to the destination or itself is the destination. In both cases, the complete route (represented as a sequence of nodes) from the source node to the destination is replied to the source node by using RREP. Otherwise, the node appends its address and rebroadcasts the request if it has not received the same request before. The source node attaches the found source route in the packet. All the intermediate nodes forward the packet to their next hop based on the source route. If a node in the route finds out that it can not forward the packets to the next hop, it immediately sends a route error to the source node. The source node therefore is able to quickly detect an invalid route and stop using it any longer. Since DSR does not use any periodic control message like HELLO, it has a low overhead. However, the DSR protocol is not dependable in high speed networks since a source route representing only one path becomes invalid when the path is broken. Furthermore, the protocol's performance largely depends on the cached routes that are determined to be fresh. However, in high speed networks, intermediate nodes might reply with a staled route frequently that was determined to be fresh.

AODV [7] shares the same on-demand characteristics as DSR but owns a different mechanism to maintain routing information. Each node maintains a routing table. Each entry in the table corresponding to a destination records next hop and the number of hops to reach to the destination. AODV discovers a route through broadcasting RREQ. When an intermediate node forwards RREQ, it records in its table the previous node from which the RREQ came to construct reverse path for RREP. A RREP sent by the destination contains the total hop count of the route. As the RREP travels back, each intermediate node sets up the forward link as a route entry. In AODV, HELLO messages can be optionally used to discover neighbors. An invalid link can be detected through MAC layer or by periodic HELLOs. Whenever a link in use is no longer valid, the upstream node of that link immediately notifies active neighbors of the link which, in turn, notify their active neighbors for the route and so on until the source nodes using that link are reached. AODV works efficiently in the networks that requires low end to end delay but it does not has good performance as well as generate high routing overhead.

CBRP [3] is a routing protocol in clustered ad hoc networks. Every node maintains 2-hop topology information and a cluster adjacency table that stores the addresses of the neighboring cluster heads and the gateway through which the corresponding cluster head can be reached, by periodically broadcasting HELLO message. HELLO contains the sender's neighbors and cluster adjacency table. A node that needs a route to a destination broadcasts a RREQ to its cluster head. Subsequently, the request is flooded to the neighboring cluster heads through the gateway nodes, and so on until it reaches the cluster head of the destination which forwards the request to the destination. The RREQ only records the cluster heads it has passed. The actual route can be shortened during the returning of the route reply. A node can do local route repair based on 2-hop topology. However, CBRP suffers from three things. HELLO message size is relatively big. A cluster head broadcasts RREQ and for each neighbor cluster head, only one appointed gateway is allowed to forward it: If the gateway moves away, the RREQ delivery to the neighboring cluster head fails. Lastly, recovery for a broken link is made only when there does exist an alternative 2-hop path.

3 Backbone Constructions

In our previous work [5], nodes are grouped into clusters based on the lowest-ID, each being assigned a unique label, simply called *cluster label*. Cluster labels themselves create the network backbone. Fig. 2 shows an example topology including four clusters with labels 0.1, 1.1, 4.1 and 9.1.

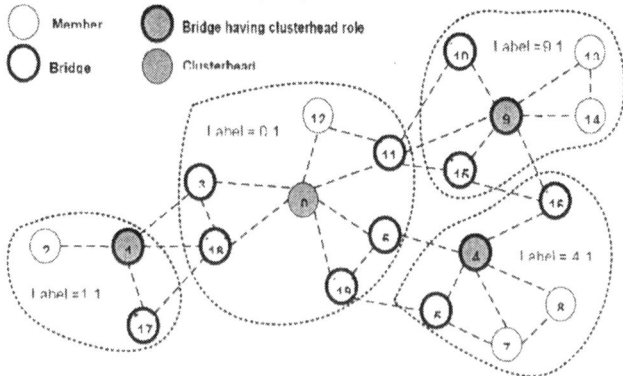

Fig. 2 The lowest-ID based clustering with labeling.

Every node periodically broadcasts HELLO message that contains the sender's address, state, cluster label and some information described later. It is assumed that if HELLO messages from a neighbor are missing for twice the hello-interval, the corresponding link is broken. A node is in either cluster head or member state if it joins in a cluster. Otherwise, it is in the orphan state. A node that has at least one neighbor belonging to another cluster is called bridge. A cluster label created by a cluster head includes the cluster head ID when the cluster is formed and the counter number that is initially set to one, two numbers being separated with a dot. If a cluster head disconnects from all the bridges that connect to one of its neighboring clusters, and finds a member in the same cluster to replace its role, it can form a new cluster as a cluster head. In this case, the counter number of the new label increases by one. More details about the clustering algorithm are presented in [5].

We modify the backbone maintenance mechanism in [5] to achieve the better cluster stability. A cluster head, when detecting a disconnection to its neighboring cluster, tries to find a member in the same cluster to replace its role based on criteria in a prioritized order as follows:

1. Select a node that provides as many connections to neighbor clusters as possible. Of course, the selected node should have more connections to neighboring clusters than the current cluster head.
2. Select a node that would have as many cluster members as possible if it were selected.

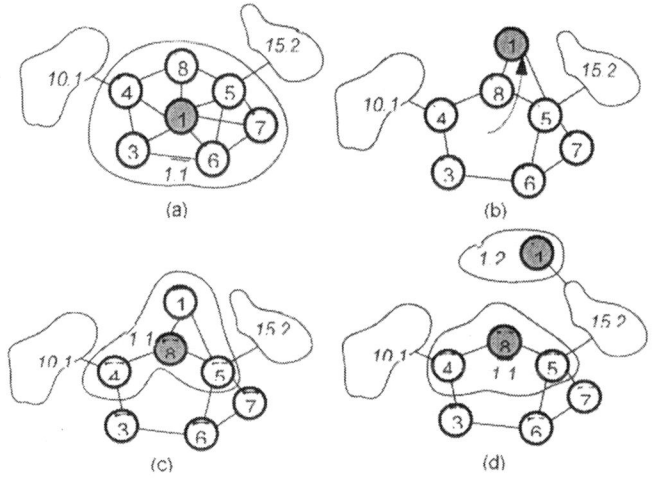

(a)   (b)

(c)   (d)

Fig. 3 An example of a new cluster head selection.

Consider an example in Fig. 3. Fig. 3(a) illustrates the network at the beginning. When node 1 moves away as shown in Fig. 3(b) and detects a complete disconnection from the only bridge 4 connecting to its neighboring cluster with label

10.1, it broadcasts an UpdateState message. Among the receiving nodes 5 and 8, node 8 is selected to replace the role of node 1 according to criterion 1 (such a choice enables routes from 10.1 to 15.2 and vice versus). Then, node 1 becomes a member immediately upon receiving UpdateState message from the new cluster head 8 as shown in Fig. 3(c). If node 1 continues to move away as shown in Fig. 3(d), it does not belong to cluster 1.1 and forms a new cluster, and its cluster label becomes 1.2, but not 1.1.

4 GDSR Algorithm

To route packets, every node maintains its *Connecting Cluster List* (CCL) that lists the cluster labels of the clusters it bridges, and *Bridge List* (BL) that consists of all neighboring labels and for each neighboring label, a set of bridges that directly connect to the cluster having the label. HELLO messages need to contain the sender's CCL. Neighbors of a bridge receive HELLO messages from the bridge and update their BL using CCL in the received HELLO message. For example, in Fig. 2, there are bridges with CCL as follows: $CCL_0 = \{\}$, $CCL_1 = \{0.1\}$, $CCL_3 = \{1.1\}$, $CCL_4 = \{0.1\}$, $CLL_5 = \{0.1\}$, $CCL_6 = \{4.1\}$, $CCL_9 = \{0.1, 4.1\}$ and so on. Every node has its BL as follows: $BL_0 = \{(1.1, \{3, 18\}), (9.1, \{11\}), (4.1, \{6.1, 19\})\}$, $BL_1 = \{(0.1, \{3, 18, 17\})\}$, $BL_2 = \{(0.1, \{1\})\}$ and so on.

A. Route Discovery

A node that has data to send initiates a route discovery by broadcasting a RREQ = (*destAddr, srcAddr, seqNum, ll*) where the *destAddr* is the address of the destination, the *srcAddr* is the address of the source node, the *seqNum* is incremented with every new RREQ the node initiates, and the *ll* is a label list to which a node receiving the RREQ appends its cluster label, only if its label has not been appended previously. Every node detects duplicate reception of the identical RREQ based on the seqNum and srcAddr fields. When a node receives a RREQ, it processes the request according to the following rules:

- *Discard rule*: If either the same RREQ was received previously, or the label of this node appears before at least one other label in ll, or this node is not a cluster head or a bridge, the RREQ is discarded.
- *Reply rule*: If this node is the destination, it creates a reply, RREP including a copy of ll and sends it toward the source node along the reverse path in ll. The way the RREP reaches the source node is similar to the one a packet data does (*Section B*).
- *Relay rule*: If this node does not satisfy both the discard and the reply rule, it appends its label to the ll of the RREQ, and then broadcasts RREQ.

B. Data Transmission

Every packet carries a source route with it. Since the source route tells only the sequence of groups identified by their respective labels, every node has to find a particular node (*bridge*) to forward. A node makes a routing decision by looking up both its BL and the source route in the packet. A node having a packet first takes the next label that comes right after its own cluster label in the source route. If this node is a cluster head, it finds a neighboring bridge that connects to the cluster with the next label of the source route by looking up its BL. If there does exist one, it forwards the packet to the selected bridge. Otherwise, the cluster head sends an error message, RERR to the source node. In case of a member having a packet, it finds a neighboring bridge that connects to the cluster with the next label of the label route by looking up its BL. If there does exist such a bridge, the node forwards a packet to the bridge. Otherwise, it forwards the packet to its cluster head. The same process continues until the packet reaches the destination.

C. Route Maintenance

In our implementation, each node that transmits a packet is confirmed for a successful data delivery over the corresponding link by exploiting the IEEE 802.11 ACK mechanism. A node that has sent a packet to the next hop without receiving ACK concludes that the link is broken. The node then selects one more link, if any, by looking up the BL. If there is no alternative link, the node initiates a route error RERR toward the source node. The source node then should explore another route to the destination.

5 Distributed Self-Pruning Algorithm

Recall that a RREQ is initiated by a source node to explore a route to destination. Following the rules in Section 4 may cause high overhead. In Fig. 4, all nodes except node 6 participate in relaying RREQ if the rules are applied. We therefore modify a distributed self-pruning algorithm named DSP from our previous work [8] to prevent intermediate nodes from relaying RREQ unnecessarily.

In DSP, every node maintains a data structure called *coverableSet* that stores labels of clusters to which the node connects and belongs, and distance in number of hops to the corresponding cluster heads. Note that the distance of a cluster head to itself is given 0 to make sure that a cluster head always has to broadcast. A RREQ carries the *coverableSet* of the sender that becomes *coveredSet* in view of the receiving nodes. Fig. 4 depicts in detail all of the nodes' *coverableSets*.

Let us explain how the DSP algorithm works. In Fig. 5, a node that receives a RREQ puts it into a queue with a calculated timeout according to Eq. (3). When the timer expires, the node decides to relay RREQ if one of the following conditions is satisfied:

1. There is at least one cluster that is covered by this node but not covered by any neighboring node from which the RREQ was received.
2. There is at least one element in coverableSet such that its distance is smaller than that of any element having the same label in the union of coveredSets of the RREQs received along different routes.

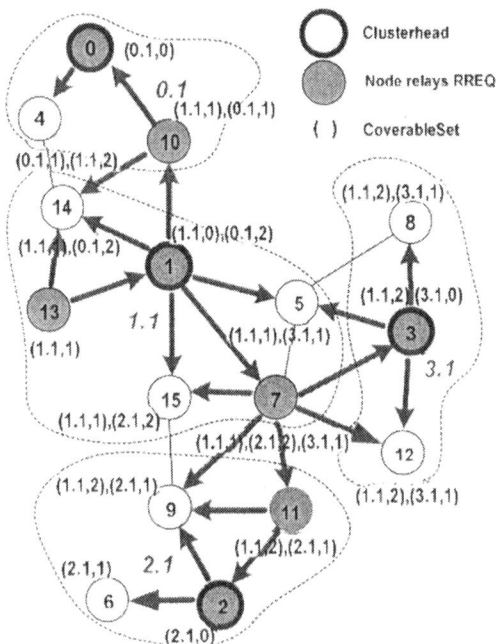

Fig. 5 The DSP algorithm (node 13 initiates a RREQ to find a route to node 6).

In DSP, if multiple nodes receive the same RREQ, which node relays the received RREQ first is extremely important. The equation that determines node's relay delay time is derived based on the following rules:

1. Cluster head always has to relay RREQ and should be earlier than the others because it may have some members that can not be reached by the RREQs from any other nodes.
2. The more clusters a node covers, the sooner the node relays.
3. Collision because of multiple initiations of RREQ should be prevented if possible.

From rules (1) and (2), Eq. (1) and Eq. (2) in Fig. 5 are derived, respectively. From (3), we include the term random(t) in Eq. (3), where t is given $\alpha \times$ fixedTime, $0 < \alpha \le 1$. Basically, α has to be chosen such that Ratio $\times$ fixedTime is dominant over random(t).

```
// RREQ = (destAddr, srcAddr, seqNum, ll, coveredSet)
o Node k that receives RREQ:
  if node k is ORPHAN then
    Free RREQ;
  else
    if node k is DESTINATION then
      Send RREP;
    else          // I decide to relay or drop
      if <srcAddr, seqNum> has been seen already then
        Free RREQ;
      else
        if node k is CLUSTER HEAD then
          Ratio = 0;                                          (1)
        else
```
$$Ratio = \frac{| \ RREQ.coveredSet \ |}{| \ coverableSet_k \ |} ; \qquad (2)$$
```
        endif;
        // random(t) gives a random value from 0 to t
        t = α×fixedTime;          // 0<α≤1
        Delay = random(t) + Ratio×fixedTime;                  (3)
        Put RREQ into the queue with timeout = Delay;
      endif;
    endif;
o Node k whose timer expries:
  if <srcAddr, seqNum> does not exist in seenList then
    S = coverableSet_k;
    for each RREQ the queue do
      Get element (l,d) from S;      //l: label, d: distance
      if ( ∃(l,e) ∈ RREQ.coveredSet) such that  (x ≤ d)
        S = S - {(l,d)};
      endif;
    endfor;
    if (S != ∅) then
      Relay RREQ;
    endif;
    Add <srcAddr, seqNum> to seenList;
    Remove all RREQ from the queue;
  endif;
```

Fig. 6 Steps in GDSR using DSP.

For an example, let α and fixedTime be 1/6 and 30 ms, respectively. In Fig. 4, node 1 broadcasts the RREQ initiated by node 13 since it is cluster head. Nodes 5, 7 and 15 receive the RREQ from node 1, and then put it into their queues with timeout calculated by equations in Fig. 3. Delays of nodes 5, 7 and 15 are given 1

+ (2/2)×30 = 31, 5 + (2/3)×30 = 25, and 0 + (2/2)×30 = 30, respectively, where values 1, 5 and 0 all come from random(t). Node 7, although it has random(t) higher than any of the other nodes, has the smallest delay. So, it relays the RREQ before the other ones. Nodes 5 and 15 decide not to relay the RREQ after receiving the RREQ from node 7 since clusters to which they connect are covered by node 7. In case of nodes 9 and 11 that receive the RREQ from node 7, their delay times solely depends on random(t) because they have the same coverableSet size. For nodes 2 and 9, cluster head 2 always relays RREQ before node 9 although node 9 covers more clusters. Finally, in Fig. 4 only 8 nodes participate in relaying RREQ when DSP is applied to GDSR.

6 Performance Evaluation and Discussion

Our approach, GDSR, based on both cluster label and DSR was implemented on the ns2 simulator to compare with its ancestor - DSR, the cluster-based routing protocol - CBRP, and AODV. Furthermore, DSP's efficiency is also examined by simulation. Note that in figures, the notation GDSR_NO_DSP refers to the GDSR protocol without using the DSP algorithm while GDSR corresponds to GDSR using DSP.

In simulations, the IEEE 802.11standard was used as the MAC layer to avoid collision. Mobile nodes used a shared media radio with normal bit rate of 2Mb/sec. Traffic sources were Continuous Bit Rate, CBR. Pairs of source and destination were randomly chosen over the network. We used Random Waypoint Model for node mobility. Each node started moving from a random location with a randomly chosen speed. Each experiment ran ten times with the same traffic but different randomly generated mobility scenarios, and we present the average result for each metric.

Four important metrics evaluated in our experiments are:

- *Delivery ratio*: the ratio of data packets delivered to destinations to those generated by CBR sources
- *Normalized routing overhead*: the number of routing packets transmitted per data packets delivered at the destination.
- *End-to-end delay*: the sum of all possible delays caused by buffering during route discovery, propagation…
- *Average jitter*: measured as the average variance of the inter-arrival times of packets at destinations.

The first simulation with parameters listed in Table. 1 was performed with the variation of mobility speed as 0, 5, 10, 15, 20 and 25 m/s.

Fig. 6 shows that GDSR significantly outperforms the other protocols in terms of delivery ratio, especially in high mobility because of the existence of multi-paths between pairs of source and destination in mesh networks. When nodes move fast,

the gap of the ratio between GDSR and its ancestor, DSR, is about 20% while in
most cases, AODV has difficulty with the ratio less than 50%.

Simulation time	500 secs
Dimension area	1500x1500 m^2
Transmission range	250 m
CBR sessions	50 sessions with 2 pkts/sec
Packet size	400 bytes
Number of nodes	100
Pause time	30 secs

Table 1 Parameters of simulation 1.

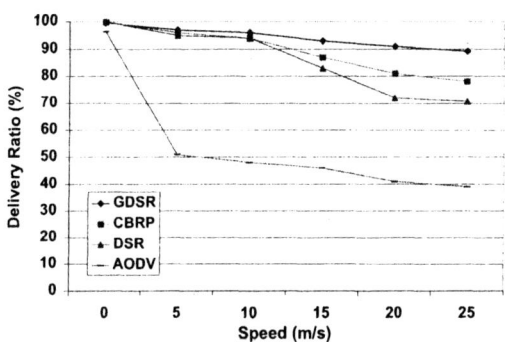

Fig. 6 Delivery ratio.

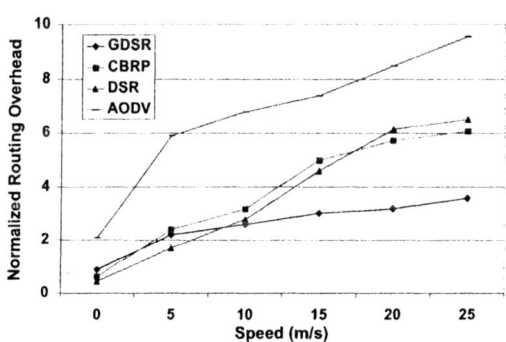

Fig. 7 Normalized routing overhead.

Referring to Fig. 7, when nodes move relatively slow, DSR that does not use any
periodic Hello message generates the least overhead of them. AODV shows the
highest overhead because it executes frequent route discoveries, each of which in-

volves network-wide broadcasting. As node speed increases, overhead of CBRP and GDSR become less than that of DSR because they do not flood RREQ. Especially, GDSR shows the lowest overhead overall because it not only does less route discovery by maintaining multiple paths but also reduces the number of relayed RREQs greatly by employing the DSP algorithm (refer to Fig. 10 and Fig. 11). Consequently, we can tell that GDSR is very stable with variation of node speed compared to the other protocols.

According to Fig. 8, it is shown that CBRP has the highest end-to-end delay. In case of CBRP, a node that fails to send packet to next hop saves the packet and tries to fix the route locally by finding another next hop based on 2-hop topology information. Furthermore, error is reported to source node, and a new route discovery is performed to maintain the shortest path, even though the route is fixed locally. Because of these behaviors, CBRP suffers from the high end-to-end delay. DSR shows slightly lower end-to-end delay than GDSR since DSR always tries to establish the shortest path and does not salvage a packet frequently. On the other hand, AODV has the shortest end-to-end delay, but fails to deliver a lot of packets to destinations. However, the lost packets may increase end-to-to-end delay if they are salvaged and delivered successfully along a repaired path.

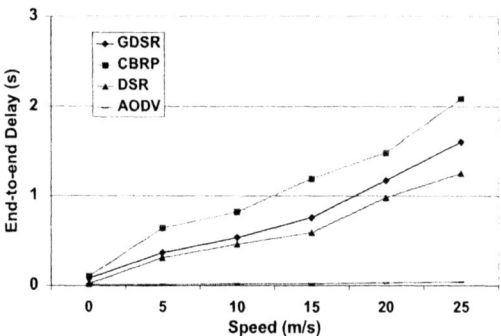

Fig. 8 End-to-end delay.

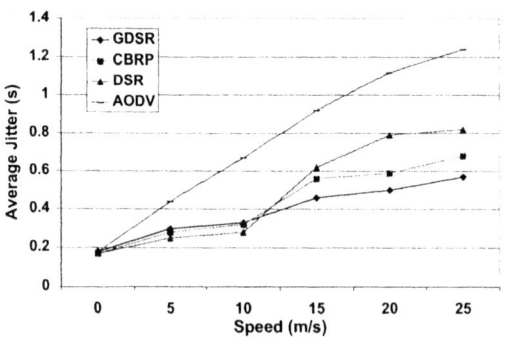

Fig. 9 Average jitter.

Fig. 9 compares the average jitter. GDSR shows slightly higher jitter than both CBRP and DSR. However, as node speed increases, it shows a competitive value in the jitter even though it maintains the high delivery ratio. AODV has the highest jitter overall since it loses lot packets.

Simulation time	500 secs
Dimension area	1000x1000 m^2
Transmission range	250 m
CBR sessions	30 sessions with 4 pkts/sec
Packet size	400 bytes
Speed	10 m/s
Pause time	30 secs

Table 2 Parameters for simulation 2.

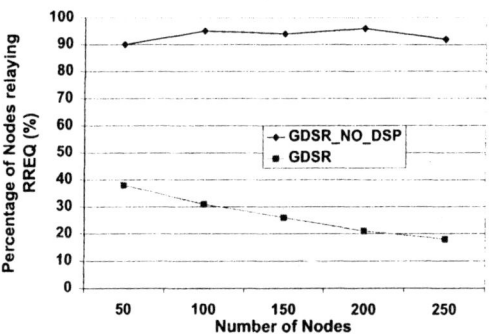

Fig. 10 Percentage of nodes that relay RREQ.

We examined the effect of the DSP algorithm applied to GDSR by comparing the percentage of nodes that relay RREQ and generated routing overhead through the second simulation with parameters listed below.

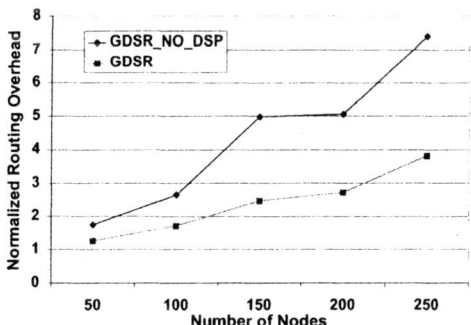

Fig. 11 Normalized control overhead.

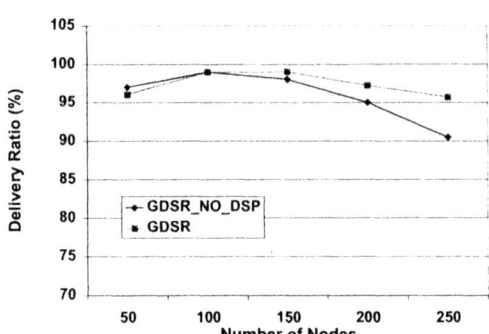

Fig. 12 Delivery ratio.

Take a look at Fig 10. In the terrain of 1000x1000 m^2, among 50 nodes, only 20 nodes (40%) relay receiving RREQs if DSP is used with GDSR while up to 45 nodes (90%) do this if GDSR works alone. In the same terrain, only 50 (18%) of 250 nodes relay RREQ, compared with 225 nodes (90%) if DSP is not applied. Obviously, when GDSR works together with DSP and the simulation terrain size is kept unchanged, the higher the density of nodes is, the smaller the percentage of nodes participating in relaying RREQ is. Fig. 11 depicts how much generated control overhead is reduced in GDSR using DSP.

Fig. 12 depicts the difference of delivery ratios between GDSR using and without using DSP. About 5% is the gap of these ratios when there are 250 nodes in the square of 1000x1000m^2. When the density of nodes increases, the collision caused by HELLO transmissions and control messages as well as data packets becomes higher. By using DSP, GDSR lessens the number of broadcasted RREQs, which leads to reduce the collision and increase delivery ratio.

7 Conclusions

We proposed a novel reactive and source routing protocol, GDSR, based on the clustering technique [5] and DSR [2]. Our protocol improves routing stability significantly over DSR by allowing a group of nodes to collaborate in delivering packets toward destination. The source label route is highly stable because it represents multiple paths between source and destination by a list of cluster labels. Actually, an effective route recovery mechanism is naturally constructed in its label route. Therefore, the control overhead caused by route rediscovery is decreased and delivery ratio is significantly improved. Data transmission does not fully depend on cluster heads; it only uses cluster head as the last resort if any other path is not available, preventing cluster heads from being congested. In addition, we proved GDSR that employs the proposed DSP algorithm improves overhead as well as reduces collision significantly.

Acknowledgments

This research was supported by the MIC (Ministry of Information and Communication), Korea, under the ITRC (Information Technology Research Center) support program supervised by the IITA (Institute of Information Technology Assessment) (IITA-2007_C1090-0701-0039)). This work was also supported by the Korea Research Foundation Grant Funded by the Korea Government (MOEHRD)" (KRF-2006-211-D00101).

References

1. Z. Haas, M. Pearlman, and P. Samar, "Zone routing protocol (ZRP)", IETF Internet Draft, draft-ietf-manet-zrp-04.txt, July 2002.
2. D. Johnson, D. Maltz, Y Hu and J Jetcheva, "The dynamic source routing protocol for mobile ad hoc networks," IETF MANET Internet Draft, Feb 2002.
3. M. Jiang, J. Li, and Y. C. Tay, "Cluster based routing protocol (CBRP) functional specification", IETF Internet Draft,draft-ietf-manet-cbrp-spec-01.txt, July 1999.
4. P. Jacquet, P. Muhlethaler and A. Qayyam, "Optimized link-state routing protocol," IETF MANET Internet Draft, Mar 2002 (work in progress).
5. V. Li, H. S. Park and H. Oh, "A cluster-label based mechanism for backbones on mobile ad hoc networks," Springer Verlag, LNCS 3970, pp. 26-36, May, 2006.
6. C. Perkins and P. Bhagwat, "Highly dynamic destination sequenced distance vector routing for mobile computers," In Proceedings of ACM SIGCOMM, 24(4), Oct 1994.
7. E. M. Royer and C. E. Perkins, "Ad-hoc on-demand distance vector routing," In 2nd IEEE Workshop on Mobile Computing Systems and Applications, pages 90-100, Feb 1999.
8. H. Oh and S. Y. Yun, "Distributed Self-Pruning (DSP) Algorithm for Bridges in Clustered Ad Hoc Networks", ICESS 2007: 699-707, May 2007.

Intelligent Routing Scheme in Home Networks

Gérard Nguengang, Lionel Molinier, Julien Boite, Dominique Gaïti, and Guy Pujolle

Abstract Apart from ethernet, both wired and wireless technologies involved in home networking are prone to bandwidth fluctuations mostly due to interferences with others home devices or appliances. Channels characteristics are time variant and environment sensitive. Mobility and end devices density in a wireless cell may collapse available network resources. Therefore, quality of service provision for delay sensitive multimedia applications in such an unstable and dynamic network environment is important since there is no way to ensure that a reserved resource will maintain the required level of service over time. This paper presents an intelligent routing scheme based on the multi-agent system technology. Agents are embedded in nodes and cooperate to build alternatives routes. These routes are used as backup routes when those defined by the routing protocol become inadequate.

Gérard Nguengang
Ginkgo Networks, Paris, France e-mail: gerard.nguengang@ginkgo-networks.com
University of Paris 6, France e-mail: gerard.nguengang-fanmegne@lip6.fr

Lionel Molinier
Ginkgo Networks, Paris, France e-mail: lionel.molinier@ginkgo-networks.com
University of Paris 6, France e-mail: lionel.molinier@lip6.fr

Julien Boite
Ginkgo Networks, Paris, France e-mail: julien.boite@ginkgo-networks.com

Dominique Gaïti
University of Technology of Troyes, France e-mail: dominique.gaiti@utt.fr

Guy Pujolle
University of Paris 6, France e-mail: guy.pujolle@lip6.fr

Please use the following format when citing this chapter:

Nguengang, G., Molinier, L., Boite, J., Gaïti, D., Pujolle, G., 2007, in IFIP International Federation for Information Processing, Volume 256, Home Networking, Al Agha, K., Carcelle, X., Pujolle, G., (Boston: Springer), pp. 179-196.

Introduction

Not so long ago, most homes used a single PC to access the Internet and share files. Nowadays, the situation is different. A myriad of disparate electronics ecosystems populate the average household, including:

- PC centric ecosystems composed of modems, scanners, digital cameras, and printers connected to a localized network
- Multimedia ecosystems consisting of set-top boxes, digital TV, digital video recorders, stereos, and DVD players
- Wireless centric ecosystems that comprise personal digital assistants (PDAs) and mobile phone sets

The home networking challenge is to enable a transparent communication among these ecosystems and also home devices connection to the broadband Internet. Indeed, customers want their devices to work together everywhere and at any time. With the emergence of advanced networking technologies such as PLC (Power Line Communication), MoCA (Multimedia over Cable Alliance), HomePNA (Home Phoneline Networking Alliance) and various wireless communication technologies, home networking has become a reality. However, these home dominant networking technologies suffer from several shortcomings. Their channels characteristics are environment sensitive and often fluctuate over time. The provided bandwidth can collapse rapidly if any interference occurs. For instance, a washing machine turning on can degrade considerably the power line network performance and affect the overall quality of service. Since such a situation is unpredictable, the use of a bandwidth reservation mechanism to ensure QoS to multimedia applications does not guaranty network resources availability over time. A resilient mechanism is required to ensure route maintenance during a multimedia content delivery.

In this paper, a distributed knowledge plane over a mesh home network architecture is proposed. Based on a lightweight multi-agent system, it enables an efficient piloting of the routing process. The knowledge plane is built in overlay of the routing protocol and contains a set of alternatives relevant routes to nodes' routing table destinations. These routes are activated each time a problem occurs.

The paper is organized as follows. Section 1 introduces our home network architecture. Section 2 describes the distributed knowledge plane that enables intelligent routing. Then, sections 3 and 4 respectively provide a testbed environment presentation and some simulated cases. Finally, results are analyzed in section 5 and future works are outlined in section 6.

1 Home Network Architecture

The main purpose of the home network is to allow users to connect various devices such as desktop computers, laptops, games consoles, and cameras to the Internet and to each other. For instance, end users must be able to watch a movie stored on digital video recorder (DVR) located in the living room on a TV located in the bedroom. Until now, there is no common accepted architecture for home networks. Two organizations with different approaches are working actively on the home networking definition.

The first regroups telcos in the HGI (Home Gateway Initiative) consortium. The HGI approach consists of building home networks around a single device: the home gateway which acts as a central point for distributing both LAN-initiated and WAN-initiated services [1]. The second, DLNA (Digital Living Network Alliance), is composed of consumer's electronics manufacturers and proposes a device centric home network architecture where each device can communicate directly with others through wired or wireless connectivity [2].

Both network set-ups have some weaknesses. The HGI architecture provides a better management of communications and facilitates the provision of QoS since the home gateway has a global vision of the network. However, the whole network depends on the gateway operation. This approach is not fault-tolerant. DLNA prone a fully distributed network architecture (scalability, availability, robustness) but does not define how the network should be implemented.

1.1 Home network basic requirements

A home network must satisfy the following requirements:

- **The whole house coverage**: home devices should be connected everywhere and at all times. That is why the network must cover the whole house.
- **Resiliency**: the home network is not at the shelter of breakdowns. The network architecture must ensure as much as possible that a link breakdown or a device outage will not affect the global network availability.
- **No new wire installation**: the deployment of a home network must not require a large scale installation of new wiring in the home.
- **Efficient use of technologies' diversity**: the home network architecture should ensure that applications take advantage of the networking technologies diversity for the QoS provision.

1.2 The proposed architecture

To achieve these requirements, we propose to build the home network around a set of dedicated devices.(figure 1). These devices form the network core and are connected to each other at least with one the networking technologies. They act as access points for end devices. The network is thus composed of:

- **mesh access point routers** (MAPs) disseminated in the house so that each home device has at least one network access. A MAP has multiple interfaces, one for each networking technology. It combines routing and bridging functions. MAPs form an hybrid mesh network.

- **end devices** that can access the network with a wireless technology through a MAP or directly with PLC or MoCA technology. However, mobile end devices do not have a wired connection.

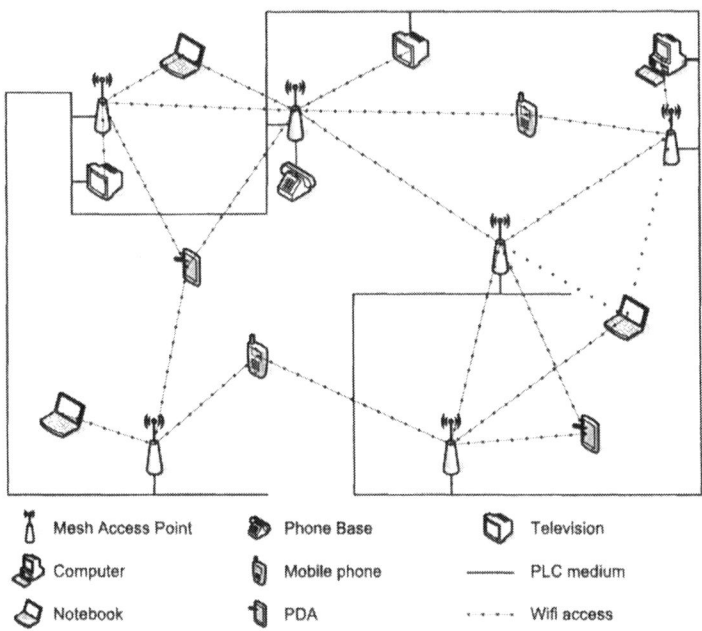

Fig. 1 Home Network architecture

2 A distributed knowledge plane for intelligent routing

The home network architecture described previously lies mainly on in-house telephone wiring, TV coaxial cable, existing power line, or radio frequency for wireless. These mediums are sensitive to electromagnetic noise, fading and interferences which introduce bandwidth fluctuations over time and make the QoS provision difficult to implement. We propose the use of a knowledge plane to overcome the aforementioned problem. This section briefly presents the knowledge plane concept and its implementation in the home context.

2.1 Why a knowledge plane?

The concept of knowledge plane in network was first introduced by David Clark [9, 10]. It was defined as a distributed and decentralized construct within the network that gathers, aggregates, and manages information about network behavior and operation. Clark's vision was to integrate self capabilities to the networks. Thus, the knowledge plane allows autonomic piloting of the standard control plane algorithms.

In the home context, the network should be aware of its resources state to provide an efficient routing and maintain the required QoS for critical flows. A knowledge plane is therefore necessary to enable a self adjustment of routing based on the ongoing application's requirements and available network resources.

To achieve this, we have designed a knowledge plane based on a multi-agent system, which provides a decentralized approach to solve problems in complex environments [16, 23]. One of the main ideas of multi-agent systems is to generate approximate solutions to complicated problems by distributing them to autonomous rational problem solvers called agents that have local problem solving capacities. So, the global issue comes from the cooperation between agents [13].

2.2 The knowledge plane framework description

Each network element (end device/MAP) has an embedded agent whose architecture is outlined in figure 2.

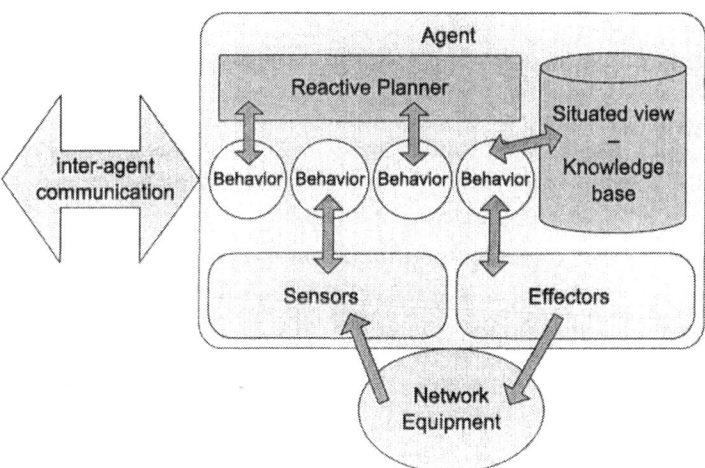

Fig. 2 Agent architecture

Each agent obtains and maintains a network view:

- directly from the network element
- indirectly via cooperative communication with other agents

Each agent thus has an updated knowledge of its close environment, essentially focused on its neighborhood. This knowledge base is called the *situated view* [7,18]. The agent's capabilities are defined as a set of behaviors. Behaviors are specialized functions used to perform agent's internal and external actions. They have access to the situated view which operates internally as a common blackboard. The agent's Reactive Planner triggers and dynamically schedules behaviors.

2.3 Knowledge plane based intelligent routing scheme

The routing process in home networks has to be reactive and adaptive to avoid service disruption for bandwidth sensitive applications such as video streaming and voice over IP. For each new flow created, the routing protocol will reserve the required resource all along the path. Once a route is established, agents of the knowledge plane cooperate to build an alternative solution in order to prevent any performance degradation.

2.3.1 Building the agent's situated view

The agent's situated view contains useful knowledge for the decision-making process. To accomplish its route restoration mission, the agent has to be aware of alternative routes to a destination that provide at least the same level of service as the current active one.

To gather this knowledge, agents exchange their node's routing table with peers from their situated view, limited to the one hop neighborhood. Based on received informations, each agent computes its alternative routing table (ART) that is made up of the best (in terms of available resources) alternative next hop. Those exchanges are made periodically in order to take into account recent routing table updates. Figure 3 outlines the ART derivation process.

2.3.2 Agent decision making process

The ART represents the agent's knowledge. Each time the required bandwidth is no longer available, the agent precedes the routing protocol to interrupt the signalization process. Instead of stopping flows as the routing protocol would have done, the agent replaces the faulty route with the alternative one provided by the ART. If this route does not exist, the routing protocol is resumed.

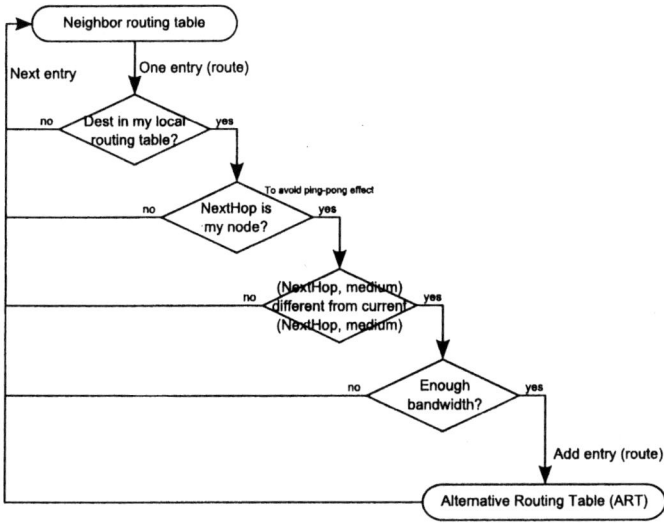

Fig. 3 ART derivation process

3 Testbed environment

3.1 Simulation

Sections 1 and 2 have presented the home network problematic and our proposal. A simulator has been implemented to evaluate our approach's relevance. A real testbed was not appropriate at this stage because we needed to focus on the problem's core complexity.

So far, we have been concentrating our efforts on two networking technologies: CPL and WiFi. Other wireless technologies can be added but this choice was made to simplify the simulation. However, these two dominant technologies raises most of common problems.

Our aim was to evaluate agents' efficiency facing the resource fluctuation problem and its ability to maintain QoS. We have chosen to implement a QoS-aware version of AODV (see [19, 20]), since we needed a functional network with a routing protocol in charge of building routes.

3.2 AODV implementation

The choice of AODV is justified as follows. In home networks, traffic can be approximated with flows: a user is downloading a file, is watching TV, is calling via it's VoIP phone... A reactive protocol, like AODV, is slower than a proactive one to open a flow because the route needs to be created before the first packet can be sent. Otherwise, flows in home networks are much longer than this initial phase duration. OLSR [11] could also be a pertinent choice, but we have preferred AODV, for industrial implementation reasons.

When a route has been computed, it is difficult to maintain it in a highly variable environment. This observation was made by [5] using a real testbed: *unstable* link causes poor AODV performance.

Otherwise, [12] compares AODV and DSR [17] and states that AODV outperforms DSR in a heavy load network, which is the case of home networks that must support high bandwidth flows from various sources (phone, TV, laptop, desktop, ...).

To support QoS in AODV, we have implemented [20] which is named AODV+ in the following. The purpose of this version is to mix RSVP [6] and AODV to create routes with a defined bandwidth (or delay). Until now, we have only considered QoS in terms of bandwidth, since this is the main criteria to ensure.

In the simulator, our aim was not to implement routing message exchanges, but to build the same routing tables as AODV+ would have done. Nevertheless we were interested in the route maintenance process, so we paid special attention to the implementation of this aspect.

3.3 Our simulator's capabilities

We have developed a simulator which allows us to represent a home network topology and to implement routing protocols and our knowledge plane, in order to evaluate our proposal's relevance. This simulator has been developed in Java 1.5 [3], in a modular way so that we can easily implement many specific environments. Nowadays, this includes a Graphical User Interface (GUI) which allows us to see information about:

- topology changes (mobile hosts can move, medium can suffer from interferences)
- existing flows
- nodes' routing tables, alternative routing tables
- routes creation, changes, ...

We can also prepare and execute precise scenarios, using Jython [4], including control of hosts's moves and mediums perturbations.

In this environment, we have represented the home network topology shown in figure 1 and executed a scenario which led to the following simulation cases.

4 Simulated cases

In this section, we are going to explain how the knowledge plane is built and how agents improve home networks reactivity when problems due to mobility or medium perturbations occur, and so, how agents pilot routing to ensure QoS.

We have seen that using a routing protocol alone is not always efficient in home networks. Indeed, AODV+ is not suitable to react quickly when a host is moving away from a MAP, or when interferences alter mediums quality.

By associating agents embedded in the network's nodes to AODV+, we managed to improve routing efficiency in some situations. Seeing that, an agent needs to know a few pieces of information:

- its parent's node routing table
- its neighbors' node routing tables

With those, an agent can find a suitable alternative route to reach each destination of its node's routing table. When a problem raises, the agent switches on this alternative route. We are now going to illustrate how it works with situations we have simulated.

4.1 First situation - Loss of access

The home network is made up of MAPs covering all the environment in which hosts, mobile or not, can be set.

An application generates a symmetric flow of 1 Mb/s between two hosts of the home network:

- the first one is not mobile, we call it *computer*
- the second one is mobile, we call it *mobile host*.

During the simulation, the application requests AODV+ to establish a route of 1 Mb/s between these two hosts. As shown in dotted line on figure 4, AODV+ creates this route, through two MAPs, B4 and B5. This route (going through B4 to reach the computer) is in the *mobile host*'s routing table, and the reverse one (going through B5 to reach the mobile host) is added in the *computer*'s routing table.

Among all flows, we can see one in figure 4 (pointed line) going from H9 to the computer through B1. So, this flow has added a route to the *computer* in B1's routing table.

The mobile host is moving away from B4 and heading toward B1. We are now going to explain how agents manage to keep the application running whereas the mobile host is going to lose its access to B4.

Every 10 seconds, the agent on each node updates its list of neighbors and sends them its current routing table.

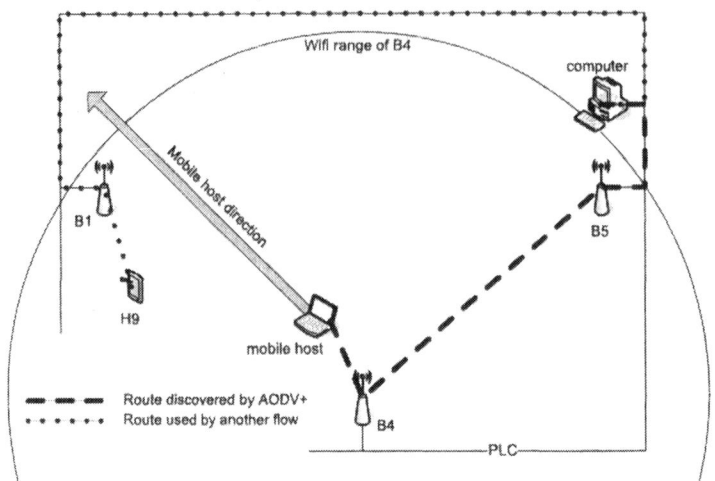

Fig. 4 Route discovered by AODV+

In our example, we focus on the *mobile host* which has two neighbors (B1 and B4) and so receives their routing tables shown in tables 1 and 2[1].

Dest	NextHop	Interface	Bandwidth
computer	computer	PLC	85 Mb/s
H9	H9	B1-wifi	23 Mb/s

Table 1 B1's routing table

Dest	NextHop	Interface	Bandwidth
mobileHost	mobileHost	B4-wifi	4 Mb/s
computer	B5	B4-wifi	16 Mb/s

Table 2 B4's routing table

The agent stores each received route into a local database called Neighbor Routing Info Base (NRIB), as illustrated in table 3.

Then, the agent scans its NRIB and, for each active route, it searches for an alternative one applying the ART derivation process illustrated in figure 3. According to the *mobile host*'s routing table shown in table 4, the agent has to find an alternative route to the *computer*.

---

[1] Only interesting routes are mentioned in tables.

SenderAgent	Dest	NextHop	Interface	Bandwidth
B1	computer	computer	PLC	85 Mb/s
B1	H9	H9	B1-wifi	23 Mb/s
B4	mobileHost	mobileHost	B4-wifi	4 Mb/s
B4	computer	B5	B4-wifi	16 Mb/s

Table 3 Mobile host's Neighbor Routing Info Base

Dest	NextHop	Interface	Bandwidth
computer	B4	B4-wifi	4 Mb/s

Table 4 Mobile host's routing table

While scanning its NRIB, the agent notices that both B1 and B4 have a route to the *computer*, but it excludes routes going through B4 because the current one already goes through this MAP. Finally, the agent deduces that going through B1 could be a good solution to reach the *computer* and, since the capacity is larger than the current one[2], it stores this route in its Alternative Routing Table (ART), shown in table 5.

Dest	NextHop	Interface	Bandwidth
computer	B1	B1-wifi	26 Mb/s

Table 5 Mobile host's Alternative Routing Table

In this way, when the *mobile host* loses its access to B4, the embedded agent looks up its ART to find an alternative route which is settled as the new active route, as indicated in figure 5. Thus, the application is not altered by this loss of access.

This process also works when a link does not offer the appropriate QoS anymore (because of an increasing distance between a host and its access point) or when mediums suffer interferences, as explained in the next part.

4.2 Second situation - Medium perturbation

We are now considering an application which needs a constant transfer rate of 10 Mb/s between the *computer* and the *mobile host*.

As shown in figure 6, a route (dotted line) that uses PLC has been established between these hosts. Another flow (pointed line) creates an entry to reach the *mobile host* in B4's routing table.

---

[2] At the moment, it is a required condition to add a route in the ART. This is subject to modification (see 6.1).

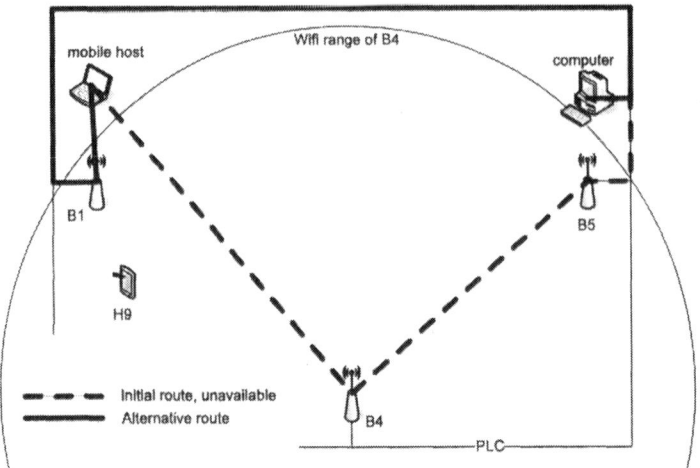

Fig. 5 Alternative route found thanks to agents

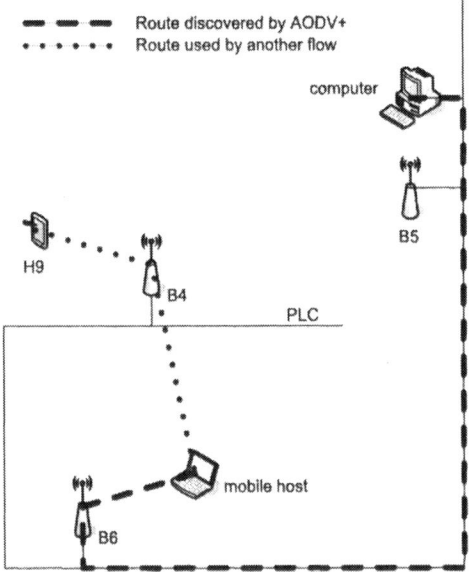

Fig. 6 Route discovered by AODV+

We are now going to simulate an interference on this PLC medium so that the available bandwidth on the route will no longer be sufficient for the 10 Mb/s flow.

Let's focus on the *computer*: we have said previously that B4 knows how to reach the *mobile host*. While receiving B4's routing table, the *computer*'s agent saves this route to the *mobile host* in its NRIB and later decides to store it into its ART.

When the PLC interference occurs, the current route can not satisfy the QoS anymore and the alternative route is settled in the *computer*'s routing table as shown in figure 7. Once more, our knowledge plane maintain the QoS, and the application is not perturbed.

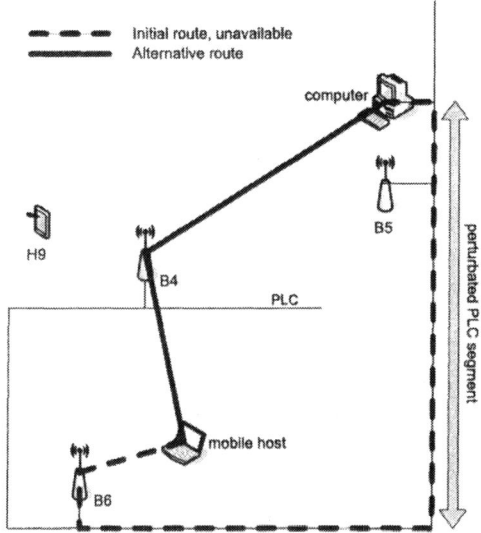

Fig. 7 Alternative route found thanks to agents

5 Results analysis

The previous section has explained how our routing scheme can improve AODV+ performance. This piloting system formed by agents is the first step of our implementation. With our simulator, we have noticed some deficiencies in AODV+. An enhanced knowledge plane will allow us to solve most of these problems.

During our simulation, we noticed two major problems. The first one, and probably the most complex is the bandwidth fluctuation in the reserved path. It is detailed in subsection 5.1. The second one concerns the way of handling path disruption, see subsection 5.2.

5.1 Bandwidth update problem

When AODV+ is building a route, the available bandwidth is set as the minimal value along the path. In a perturbation sensitive network, the bandwidth is constantly changing and there is no way to update it.

This point is tricky in the home network context, because of bandwidths unstability. An electromagnetic interference may temporarily alter both wireless and PLC links, and the QoS may no be longer satisfied. In this case, AODV+ specifies that the router sends an ICMP_QOS_LOST[3] packet to each source node which has to request a new route. If the bandwidth is increasing and decreasing quite fast, this may lead to an unstable convergence of AODV+, an important overhead and poor end-user performances.

The problem of QoS-aware routing in interference sensitive networks is complex and concerns other routing protocols as well as AODV+. There are many papers that mainly focus on bandwidth correlation: when a link is used, neighbors' ones are perturbed. This is an NP complex problem as concluded [8, 15, 24]. Apart from this problem, there are bandwidth fluctuations on links that may lead to unsatisfying QoS. Our routing scheme has to face this problem.

This problem has been eluded in our first simulations. Now that we have a functional testbed, we can take a closer look at this. We think that only agents can handle such a complexity and may be able to approximate the optimal solution. In routing protocols, there is a limited information exchanged between nodes. This can be improved with our knowledge plane, and the correct use of the situated view can handle more information. This is discussed in further details in section 6.

5.2 Route disruption

Beyond the QoS guarantee problem, there is a suboptimal mechanism in AODV+ due to its AODV's inheritance. When a link is no longer satisfying the reserved bandwidth, it specifies that each source of each route using it is notified by an ICMP_QOS_LOST message. This causes sources to reopen a new route (after a short disruption for the end-user).

It is harmful for overall performances to perturb each flow, whereas rerouting only one flow could solve the problem. For example, if there are 3 flows of respectively 5 Mb/s, 3 Mb/s and 1 Mb/s, the route is initially set to support 9 Mb/s. Due to an external event, the bandwidth falls down to 8 Mb/s. AODV+ is disrupting the 3 flows, whereas an *intelligent* action would have been to reroute the 1 Mb/s flow (admitting that this last flow is not more important than the others). In AODV+, there is no way to set priority, so the selection can only be done randomly (which can be disastrous for the overall performance).

---

[3] Defined in [20] as to inform sources that the route no longer satisfies the initial QoS agreement

An approach *DiffServ*-like might help us in this case, as mentioned by [21] but we don't think it is directly usable in home networks. The need for an *ingress node*, in charge of classifying flows, is in contradiction with our decentralized view of the home network. In [22], the FQMM architecture is proposed, but the source node has to request for QoS, which means a deep modification of end devices. We would rather keep our architecture and investigate a solution based on our agents.

Agents can *learn* about flow types[4], regarding to source, destination, duration, bandwidth, ... Fuzzy logic may help agents to mix several criteria and select the best flow to be rerouted.

6 Future works

In the previous section, we mentioned some limitations inherent to QoS routing in perturbation sensitive environments. We think that our knowledge plane can considerably improve routing performance at a reasonable cost. Up to now, our implementation is quite simple, but already useful as explained in section 4.

However, there are several points to be enhanced. Initially, agents were designed to compute a better route than the current one. This point is now outdated as explained in subsection 6.1. Subsections 6.2 and 6.3 are purposes to enlarge information known by agents and can be used to improve decision algorithms.

6.1 Alternative route selection

So far, agents are selecting an alternative route when it is better than the current one. This may lead to an empty ART, which means that there is no alternative routes. If an interference occurs, agents are unable to find a quick solution, and so there is a flow disruption.

While writing agents' specifications, our aim was to improve AODV+ routing. However, we found out that in most cases the routing is sufficient. Problems arise with interferences, which means a fast modification of route's quality. The objective criterion of the *best* route is meaningless in those cases. That is why we are now focusing on building alternative routes as often as possible, even if the current one is better. This new approach corroborate AODV performance analysis of [5, 12].

---

[4] Basically, a flow between the Internet gateway and a VoIP phone is more important than a file transfer between PCs.

6.2 AODV+ stressing

For now, the alternative routes derivation process, illustrated on figure 3, is based on node's routing table. AODV is a reactive protocol, which means that routes are built on-demand. In a low-loaded network, there are only a few entries in the routing table, therefore agents know few alternative routes. In case of interferences, they are unable to rescue the routing protocol. This correlation between load and agent's performance is not satisfying.

Our solution is to stress AODV to build routes which can be done easily by generating regularly fake packets between agents. This action should be done only when the network is idling, and only for regions[5] with an obvious lack of alternative routes. This task can be fulfilled by our knowledge plane.

6.3 Mobility prediction

Situated views can solve yet another problem. We have concluded in section 5.2 that QoS in home networks is such a difficult problem that a protocol cannot solve by itself.

Our point is to manage this complexity with the knowledge plane, therefore we need to add information into agents to enable them to make complex decisions. A piece of information can be used for handover[6] prediction. [14] presents generic models for mobility prediction in wireless networks. Home networking is more specific because there are few access points and end devices as well as few handovers. A simple mechanism can be implemented into agents to *learn* about mobile hosts, and to anticipate disruptions.

Conclusion

To conclude, we can say that these first results are quite promising. Indeed, our first simulations have shown that our approach is realistic. There are, of course, some points to be improved. Nonetheless, our simulation enabled testing several routing protocols. AODV+ was the first protocol chosen, and we have pointed out some deficiencies 5.

We have concluded that these problems are far from being specific to AODV+, and that our knowledge plane is able to handle them. Indeed, agents can collect and manage more information than a routing protocol in order to extract useful

---

[5] The concept of region is still to be defined, but we can reasonably established situated views on regions as a first approximation.

[6] The fact to change from on bridge to another

knowledge. So, this distributed *intelligence* may be able to approximate optimal solutions.

Our simulator grants us a complete control of the testbed, which will allow us to take a closer look on proposed improvements mentioned in 6.

References

1. Home gateway technical requirements: Release 1. Tech. rep., Home Gateway Initiative (2006). URL http://www.homegatewayinitiative.org
2. Dlna overview and vision whitepaper. Tech. rep., Digital Living Network Alliance (2007). URL http://www.dlna.org
3. Java 1.5 by sun microsystems (2007). URL http://www.java.com/
4. The jython project (2007). URL http://www.jython.org/
5. Borgia E., Delmastro F.: Effects of unstable links on aodv performance in real testbeds. EURASIP Journal on Wireless Communications and Networking **2007**, Article ID 19,375, 14 pages (2007). Doi:10.1155/2007/19375
6. Braden R., Zhang L., Berson S., Herzog S., Jamin S.: Resource reservation protocol (rsvp) – version 1 functional specification. RFC 2205 (Proposed Standard) (1997). URL http://www.ietf.org/rfc/rfc2205.txt. Updated by RFCs 2750, 3936, 4495
7. Bullot T., Khatoun R., Hugues L., Gaïti D., Merghem-Boulahia. L.: A situatedness based knowledge plane for autonomic networking. International Journal of Network Management (2008). To appear
8. Chiu C.Y., Kuo Y.L., Wu H.K., Chen G.H.: Bandwidth constrained routing problem in multi-hop wireless networks. In: MSWiM '06: Proceedings of the 9th ACM international symposium on Modeling analysis and simulation of wireless and mobile systems, pp. 365–369. ACM Press, New York, NY, USA (2006). DOI http://doi.acm.org/10.1145/1164717.1164779
9. Clark D.: A new vision for network architecture (2002). URL http://www.isi.edu/know-plane/DOCS/DDC_knowledgePlane_3.pdf
10. Clark D.D., Partridge C., Ramming C.J., Wroclawski J.T.: A knowledge plane for the internet. In: SIGCOMM '03: Proceedings of the 2003 conference on Applications, technologies, architectures, and protocols for computer communications, pp. 3–10. ACM Press, New York, NY, USA (2003). DOI 10.1145/863955.863957. URL http://portal.acm.org/citation.cfm?id=863957
11. Clausen T., Jacquet P.: Optimized link state routing protocol (olsr). RFC 3626 (Experimental) (2003). URL http://www.ietf.org/rfc/rfc3626.txt
12. Das S.R., Perkins C.E., Royer E.E.: Performance comparison of two on-demand routing protocols for ad hoc networks. In: INFOCOM (1), pp. 3–12 (2000)
13. Fischer K., Ruß C., Vierke G.: Decision theory and coordination in multiagent systems. Tech. Rep. RR-98-02, Deutsches Forschungszentrum für Künstliche Intelligenz GmbH, Erwin-Schrödinger Strasse, Postfach 2080, 67608 Kaiserslautern Germany (1998). URL http://citeseer.ist.psu.edu/fischer98decision.html
14. Francois J.M., Leduc G., Martin S.: Learning movement patterns in mobile networks: A generic method. (2004)
15. Georgiadis L., Jacquet P., Mans B.: Bandwidth reservation in multihop wireless networks: Complexity and mechanisms. In: ICDCSW '04: Proceedings of the 24th International Conference on Distributed Computing Systems Workshops - W7: EC (ICDCSW'04), pp. 762–767. IEEE Computer Society, Washington, DC, USA (2004)
16. Jennings N.R., Sycara K., Wooldridge M.: A roadmap of agent research and development. Journal of Autonomous Agents and Multi-Agent Systems 1(1), 7–38 (1998). URL http://citeseer.ist.psu.edu/article/jennings98roadmap.html

17. Johnson D., Hu Y., Maltz D.: The dynamic source routing protocol (dsr) for mobile ad hoc networks for ipv4. RFC 4728 (Experimental) (2007). URL http://www.ietf.org/rfc/rfc4728.txt
18. Nguengang G., Bullot T., Gaïti D., Hugues L., Pujolle G.: Autonomic resource regulation in ip military networks: A situatedness based knowledge plane. Special Issue of the WT Series dedicated to Advanced Autonomic Networking and Communication (2007). To appear
19. Perkins C., Belding-Royer E., Das S.: Ad hoc on-demand distance vector (aodv) routing. RFC 3561 (Experimental) (2003). URL http://www.ietf.org/rfc/rfc3561.txt
20. Perkins C., Royer E.: Quality of service in ad hoc on-demand distance vector routing (2001)
21. To V.S.Y., Bensaou B., Chau S.M.K.: Quality of service framework in MANETs using differentiated services. In: Vehicular Technology Conference, 2003. VTC 2003-Fall. 2003 IEEE 58th, vol. 5, pp. 3463–3467 (2003). DOI 10.1109/VETECF.2003.1286358
22. Wang X., Zhang Y., Liu J., Li H.: A flexible quality of service management model in distributed multimedia systems. In: Intelligent Processing Systems, 1997. ICIPS '97. 1997 IEEE International Conference (1997)
23. Wooldridge M.: An Introduction to Multi-Agent Systems. John Wiley & Sons, Inc., New York, NY, USA (2001)
24. Zhu C., Corson M.: Qos routing for mobile ad hoc networks (2001)

Openpattern project: a comprehensive modular routing platform

Florian Fainelli[1], Xavier Carcelle[2], Etienne Flesch[3], Gwenaël Saint-Genest[4], Hossam Afifi[5]

[1] Florian Fainelli, Institut National des Télécommunications (INT), Paris, France, florian.fainelli@telecomint.eu

[2] Xavier Carcelle, Open Pattern Foundation, xavier.carcelle@openpattern.org

[3] Etienne Flesch, Open Pattern Foundation, etienne.flesch@openpattern.org

[4] Gwenaël Saint-Genest, Open Pattern Foundation, gwenael.saint-genest@openpattern.org

[5] Hossam Afifi, Institut National des Télécommunications (INT), Paris, France, hossam.afifi@int-edu.eu

Abstract. The last developments of the home gateways, DSL-boxes, off-the-shelf wireless routers, wireless communities initiatives have brought a great number of network hardware to the home. These different developments have been followed by different initiatives of "hacking the box" to be able to flash this specific hardware with open-source firmware resulting from the contribution of several open-source developers (OpenWrt, Freifunk...). Due to the lack of "open hardware" off-the-shelf available to adjust the platform to the home-networking (and networking) applications, OpenPattern is a project to develop such a hardware based on the inputs from the past initiatives and bringing a box based on an open hardware (i.e. open specifications of the targeted hardware), using a motherboard and able to receive daughterboard to expand the functionalities in conjunction with the current open source project to be using the box once this one is ready to be shipped.

Keywords: Wireless, Home Networking, open hardware, electronic, boards, routing, open source, network interfaces.

Please use the following format when citing this chapter:

Fainelli, F., Carcelle, X., Flesch, E., Saint-Genest, G., Afifi, H., 2007, in IFIP International Federation for Information Processing, Volume 256, Home Networking, Al Agha, K., Carcelle, X., Pujolle, G., (Boston: Springer), pp. 197-214.

1. Introduction

This paper introduces the OpenPattern modular routing platform (OMRP). We will explain what current problems this platform ad-dresses, as well as its innovative characteristics to explain the architectural choices we have made accordingly. Finally we will explain the set of modules and various interfaces that will be shipped within the base board.

OpenPattern is a modular routing platform, composed of a powerful single board computer, on top of which you plug network interface modules. The software running on this board is fully open source from the kernel and user-space applications on the CPU to the bit stream of the FPGA. You also benefit from the mailing-lists and code repository to contribute and talk with people interested in the project.

The SBC supports a wide variety of network interfaces such as Wi-Fi 802.11n, WiMAX, Bluetooth 2.0, ZiBee and WiBree, as well as ADSL2+ and PLC. The modularity of the motherboard will allow any new network interfaces to be adapted to become a daughter-board for the OMRP. The first chapter will address a state of art of the past and current concept of "free electronic", the second part will explain the objectives of the OpenPattern project and finally the third part will go deeper into the targeted architecture of the OMRP (hardware and software).

2. The context of "free electronic" and state of the art

The concept of "Free electronic" is vast and had been in the past a hot topic within the open source (software mainly) community worldwide. This concept is trying to extend the notion of open source of code (along with the right licensing of the work done such as the GPL license) to the development of hardware platform but this extension is harder than simply opening a work done on a software project to the public by the fact that hardware means third and fourth parties such as manufacturers and OEMs. Having said that the concept of "free electronic" is more and more important nowadays to allow people to be able to develop their own applications (with open source) based on open specifications of the hardware platform. In this part we will describe the current situation of such project and the relations between major open source projects and their implementations on "to-soon-open" hardware platform.

2.1 Open and closed electronic components

A hardware platform such as a cell-phone, a routing board or a home gateway is composed of an electronic board and several key components along with discreet components to fine-tune the impedance, current and voltage levels needed for the components to remain in their manufacturer specifications.

In the past years, several open source communities have developed such projects targeting several applications where the hardware had been "closed" for several months along with a huge development of radio communications and home networking applications. Table I gives a list of several "open hardware" projects that aim to open up the platform, the drivers and the applications source code.

TABLE I
DIFFERENT "OPEN HARDWARE" PROJECTS

Project	Field of interest
OpenMoko	Cellphones (closed GSM stack)
OpenWrt	Wireless Routers
Gecko3	Fully open FPGA
GnuRadio	Radio communications
GSM Cracking project	Open GSM receivers
OpenGraphics	Graphic adapters
OpenSPARC	SPARC arhictecture
Atheros Driver / Linux kernel	Atheros Wi-Fi chipsets
Leox	System on Chip core and busses

One of the most known project nowadays is *OpenMoko* aiming (with the support of certain hardware manufacturers), at developing an "open cell phone" with several radio interfaces (GSM, Wi-Fi...) allowing the end-users to develop their own applications on top of the hardware. The GSM stack is not yet open as the GSM Telcos are not prone to open up the GSM stack for now.

2.2 Home gateways boards

With the huge development of triple and quadruple play offers from the world-wide ISPs (IP-browsing, VoIP, IPTV, IP-phone), end-users are now using on a daily basis home gateways embedded in proprietary hardware from the different manufacturers. For instance, French ISPs are now delivering so-called *Internet-box* (Livebox, Freebox, 9box ...) which are hardware platforms able to implement Linux for routing, VLC client [1], video decoding, web-GUI, SIP-client, file-sharing server. This home gateway boards may be in a near future generic hardware with open source applications and proprietary software stack for the identification on the ISP network for secure connexions. Moreover, end-users are now holding others embedded boxes for their home-networking applications such as wireless LAN, PLC (Power Line Communications) interfaces or file sharing based on proprietary hardware that may be open too in a close future.

2.3 Routing boards and platforms

From a software point of view, several open source projects have been active nowadays based on the famous Linksys WRT serie (WRT54G and others) router board trying to find the most appropriate implementation of open source firmware. These implementations have been using the hardware specifications that Linksys had been giving to the public.

Among these firmwares, OpenWrt is one of most widespread and had been used even natively in certain commercial applications available.Here is a list of certain boards running OpenWrt natively:

- Neuf/Cegetel EasyGate
- Mindspeed Comcerto
- Meraki Mini
- Fon La Fonera
- Ubiquity LiteStations
- Infineon Amazon

This list shows that open source firmwares have now reached a level of quality (along with the right implementations based on the targeted hardware) enough for wide commercial applications.

2.4 Wireless communities boards

Another big area of development of open hardware and software have been the different wireless communities around the world implementing different firmwares based on the IETF and IEEE standards around the Wi-Fi (802.11 flavors, IP-mesh standards such as OLSR). Table II is giving a non-exhaustive list of the different boards and firmwares used by these communities.

TABLE II
WIRELESS COMMUNITIES BOARDS

Community	Boards	Firmware
Freifunk	Meshcube / WRT54G	Nylon / OpenWrt
France-Wireless	WRT54G / Fonera	OpenWrt / OpenWrt
Meraki	Meraki	OpenWrt
Fon	La Fonera	OpenWrt
Seattle-Wireless	Various	Original firmwares
TIER Project (UC Berkeley)	Gateworks Avila 2348	Custom linux

For instance, the Freifunk wireless community in Berlin and Leipzig (Germany) are using two different hardwares (Meshcube and Linksys WRT) to implement very large ad-hoc networks. These networks are based on 802.11 MAC layer along with an OLSR-based IP-layer embedded in the OpenWrt firmware. This implementation allows anyone in the world aiming at launching a new wireless community to do the same by getting some Linksys boards and flashing the hardware with the Freifunk flavor. So far several Freifunk wireless implementation had been done and the Berlin network is now reaching several hundreds OLSR nodes (up-to 5 hops from the wired IP feed) to allow shared wireless Internet access. The TIER project from UC Berkeley is also aiming at developing wireless network in developing countries by using standard hardware with a custom Linux distribution to implement long distance wireless based on a modified 802.11 MAC layer with TDMA medium access for a better QoS (Quality of Service).

3. Project motivations and objectives

3.1 Is Free as in free software electronics possible?

Nowadays, the core of electronics and microelectronics is what is called an Intellectual Property block (IP-block). This block is nothing more than a piece of code, written in a Hardware Description Language (HDL), which describes common electronics subsystems: processors, memory controllers, Ethernet controllers and more as the layout that a bunch of programmable transistors should have. This small piece of code is part of a library, in which electronic component designers pick their items to design a subsystem and then put this together to finally produce an electronic component.

Ten years ago, some electronic engineers realized that every time they developed a new dedicated electronic component such as processor or a microcontroller, they were reinventing the wheel, even for the smallest part of the system like doing a logical and between two bits. The goal of the *OpenCores* project was to offer to electronic designers a common place to share, improve and discuss Intellectual Property blocks, and reduce the time to test and market. Though this project has been hosting a wide range of IP-block of a good quality, there is another problem which is the software used in simulating, testing and designing electronic components.

Most FPGA vendors also supply a development tool, which allows electronic designers to place analyze, change their IP-blocks, to design the whole electronic component. This tool is also in charge of doing the routing and placement of the different IP blocks on the FPGA, and finally produces the "bitstream" and netlist that will be sent to the FPGA to make it be the component freshly designed. These tools are not released under a Free Software compatible license, but can are available freely online. There is an ongoing effort to release open source tools that will be able to generate a bitstream. The good point of these tools is that they can run on a GNU/Linux system and therefore you can use them in combination of proprietary software running on open source software.

Since we cannot have free software to develop freely available IP-blocks, can we really do *Free Electronic* as in Free Software? Well, the answer is yes we can, as long as we keep the whole process open in terms of tools being used, documents and schematics produced as well as the project management and the capability for people to produce their own board based on that design. The project remains free because everything that has been produced or discussed is freely available under licenses that will protect the materials, but not prevent people from contributing. We can see this as the logical extension of free software concepts being applied to software programmable components including the "make it yourself" part of it that hardly exists with hardware developments.

By offering schematics, source code and tips to produce their own Printed Circuit Boards (PCB), people will really be able to produce their own cards and implement their own applications on-top of it.

3.2 Who would use this design?

Since the design is completely open, quite a lot of people can be interested in using it, especially:

- academic researchers
- industrial researchers
- consumer electrics companies
- wireless communities
- core routers for emerging countries

Academic and industrial researchers really need to have an open design to work on because otherwise they will spend their time in getting information they can possibly never have from the manufacturers or distributors because they prefer to keep it secret for commercial reasons. Since designing hardware from scratch is risky and time-consuming, we provide a working hardware platform so researchers can focus on developing code or making the existing project evolve instead of dealing with a new design every time they want to test something.

The *OpenPattern* platform is also ideal for anyone needing a board that can host a wide range of network interfaces, would it be for rapid deployment, development or testing. Since we have been designing and validating the most complex parts of the system, such as the memory and the DMA controller, people can use the design to even validate their own hardware.

Quite a lot of people in the world are looking for ready-to- use devices they can deploy in a meshed network, which is what devices like the Linksys WRT54G currently do. More and more countries will use cheap wireless equipments to build mesh networks for their cities, and therefore the *OpenPattern* board can be ideal because it can act as gateway for multiple network interfaces, mainly Wi-Fi and WiMAX. As it was described, getting decent open source support, for a given hardware, takes from one month to several years after the hardware public relase depending on the Board Support Package that was shipped with.

3.3 Where is the innovation?

The *OpenPattern* project can be seen as innovative in several manners including: project management, consumer electrics design process, hardware and software features. Regarding the problems explained before, it was clear that a modular platform was needed, open and upgradeable hardware to help on-going efforts to focus their energy on developing or designing software instead of hardware.

This project aims to have contributions from the beginning unlike some open source related projects that were first developed and then open up to the public. The *OpenPattern* project aims at sharing the information to allow the maximum of contributions such as the design of new modules, new applications and better drivers for the open hardware. Finally it seems important that end-users can be able to use the PCB to build their own boards or even add modifications and add-ons to the original PCB.

4. Hardware and software architecture

The *OpenPattern* architecture has been designed to provide an effective software and hardware architecture. Since modularity is important and the lifetime of this product chosen is a combination of dedicated hardware providing good performances, and modular hardware to host future modules.

From a software point of view, it had been providing *paravirtualisation* for this embedded system with the same usage as desktop or server *paravirtualisation* software.

4.1 Hardware architecture

Embedded devices are designed around a central and dedicated component (ASIC) which is called a System-on-chip (SoC) in which functional subsystems such as a CPU, memory controller and Ethernet controller was put in with a high rate of integration and cost reduction. The main problem with this approach is that there is a dedicated SoC every time a new device is marketed, cheap with a high level of integration. Also, the SoC takes place in a specific design method called, co-design, where both the system features and software programming is done to reduce the time to market. This approach fits very well to a mass-market production and selling but is unaffordable for custom designs.

This kind of System-on-Chip is widely used to reduce the cost and physical space required by the equivalent and standalone chips. For instance, most hardware manufacturers integrate a CPU, memory controller, Ethernet controller and Wi-Fi MAC processor inside the SoC for a occupied space of less than 5 square centimeter. The SoC manufacturing cost can be reduce up to few dollars for a million pieces.

Taking that into account, the design is done by thinking of a chip that is capable of evolving simply by making software upgrades on a programmable flash, and which could be powerful enough to even replace a SoC in later design revisions. Such functionality is achieved by a Field Programmable Gate Array (FPGA) while storing its bitstream code is done in a programmable Flash.

FIGURE 1
HARDWARE ORGANIZATION OF THE OMRP

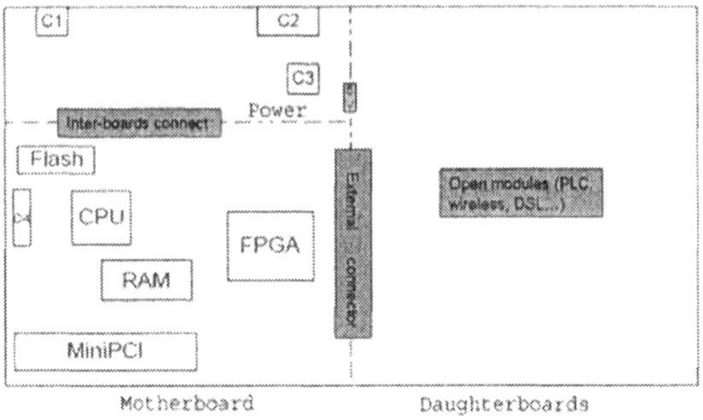

The figure 1 is showing the hardware organization targeted on the board with the motherboard on one side and the place for the modules (daughterboards) on the other side. Table II shows the targeted hardware component to be used for the OMRP.

TABLE III
OMRP HARDWARE FEATURES

CPU	400 Mhz ARM
FPGA	Xilinx Spartan-3 family
CPU Flash	16 Mo NAND
RAM	128 Mo SDRAM

Unlike SoC that does everything needed, the FPGA allows the designer to choose a SoC with less features (cheaper and smaller), and do the rest in the software running on the FPGA. Combining this architecture design with a good placement and interconnection with the network interfaces will lead to a fully modular design.

These arguments gave the reason to place the FPGA as an intermediate component for the microcontroller to access hardware such as Wireless and Ethernet interfaces. The FPGA placement and feature can be compared to what is done on the PC architecture with the so-called "chipsets" which are basically allowing the

CPU to access hardware resources without the need to have specific analog/digital front-end circuitry. The advantages of this architecture are very clear:

- The FPGA is more tolerant to electric surges and temporary designs than the CPU
- The CPU is not loaded with the hardware interruption handling the FPGA does this
- There is a clear separation between the hardware accesses and the software, allowing virtualization techniques
- The FPGA bitstream can be easily changed to handle different network interfaces
- Reduction of the front-end components doing hardware interfacing.

Since the SoC has fewer features, it gets smaller and cheaper, as well as the FPGA, because there is no need for either highly integrated and/or powerful components to handle the same functionalities. The cost of the two components makes less than either a powerful FPGA or a full-featured SoC.

The figure II shows the organization of the components on the OMRP and the data-bus connections between the two core components (SoC and FPGA), the different network interfaces and the memory chips.

FIGURE II
ORGANIZATION OF THE COMPONENTS

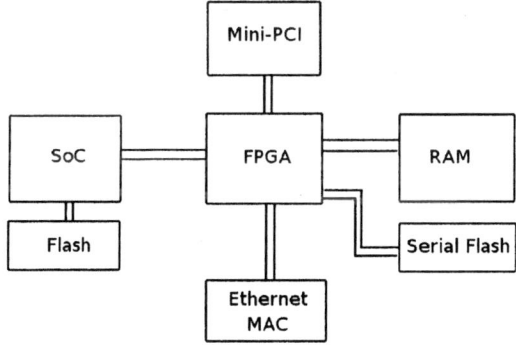

Because of its central role in the hardware interfacing with the CPU, the FPGA implements the following IP-blocks:

- RAM memory controller for the CPU
- memory segmentation and/or paging
- Direct Memory Access controller
- Layer-2 and/or Layer-3 networking
- hypervisor for paravirtualization

To fully benefit from modularity, it has been left intentionally unpopulated pins so that one can either plug a custom daughterboard or a networking module for instance.

Since the design had been thought to be modular, the hardware will use several connectors that can host a wide range of network interfaces. The default layout features are:

- 2 x Ethernet MAC, 1x Ethernet PHY
- 2 x Mini-PCI connectors
- 2 x USB host 2.0 connectors
- SPI and GPIO connectors
- 1 x UTOPIA2 connector

One Ethernet MAC controller is not connected to any PHY controller because one can choose to plug a Power Line Communication PHY module. This PLC module can be designed using either a HomePlug-based chip or a Opera-based chip, or any other standard. Mini-PCI is the standard for connecting Wi-Fi and WiMAX cards when not built in a System-on-Chip. Having two MiniPCI slots allows one to setup the board as a WiMAX/Wi-Fi router for instance. Finally, one can plug a xDSL module on the UTOPIA2 high-speed digital bus to be used by any ISP along with the proprietary radius stack.

It has been clear that using a CPU coupled to a FPGA will improve the overall performance of the system because the CPU will not be loaded with all the interrupt handling routines while scheduling for over tasks. This design is very near to what has been done recently by some hardware manufacturers while marketing "Network processors.

It can be found two fairly closed designs to the OMRP design. The first one is the *Realtek* RTL8651B design [1], which integrates the *Realtek* RE856x network processor, capable of doing up to Layer-4 networking (NAT, IPsec, VPN...) and hardware cryptography. This solution is fully open source but lacks decent support in the Linux kernel. Also, the network chip is an ASIC, which is partly software controlled, thus making it hard-to-change or hard-to-optimize for different task. Another design having similar capabilities is the *Ikanos Fusiv* DSL platform [2], which includes a routing processor to which the Linux kernel directly passes its routing table. This approach is very interesting because the chip handles up to Layer-3 networking based on a formatted routing table. The main problem with this platform is that it is currently only available to integrators and therefore only under Non Disclosure Agreements. Both lack decent Open Source support and were designed for two particular targets: SOHO routers for *Realtek*, and DSL CPE for *Ikanos*, which does not make them suitable for evolving networking applications.

4.2 Software architecture

Nowadays, most research and industrial funding on embedded system target virtualization features, comparable to what is done for servers and desktops. Virtualization has been for years, the key to delivering fast, flexible and secure to deploy systems in most internet hosting companies and service providers. Virtualization intends to separate an operating system from the hardware or another operating system by putting it in a software jail and by defining traps mechanism to access the hardware when required. This task is done by a computer program which is responsible for securing every operating system instance and hardware accesses.

FIGURE 1II
SOFTWARE ORGANIZATION OF THE OMRP

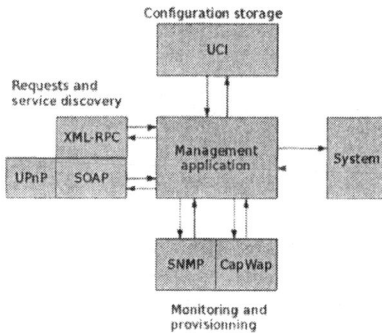

The figure III indicates an example of targeted software architecture for the OMRP for network applications.

Since the operating system is responsible for isolating and providing mechanism to programs to access the hardware, it runs in a privileged space so-called kernel space, while programs run in a less privileged space, the user space. This isolation is very important because otherwise, either we should be running only one application, then quickly becoming a kernel by itself, or programs should have mutual exclusions and protection mechanism, which makes them non standard and compatible. All processor architectures include at least two protection mechanisms (privileged and unprivileged modes) to allow such memory and resources separation. Some architecture like the Intel x86, allows more levels of protection, which are called rings, up to four.

4.3 Virtualization

Virtualization techniques use this hardware and operating system architecture to provide memory boundaries and isolation between either user-space programs or different instances of the kernel. The main problem is that different techniques require more or less modification of the existing operating system to be virtualized, and sometimes with a lot of performance cost.

One can make the distinction between **5 kinds of virtualization techniques**. The first one is what we call an **isolator**, which is a piece of software interfacing an existing and unmodified operating system with a user-space application (Linux VServer [3], OpenVZ [4]). The second one is **user-space kernel**, which an operating system running in user-space, then running programs in user-space. This solution is one of the least effective solutions, but is very convenient for kernel development (User-mode Linux [5], Cooperative Linux [6]). The third one is a **virtual machine** running on top of an existing kernel and providing hardware resources and access. The main advantage of this solution is that the guest operating system, running in the virtual machine "sees" the hardware like if it was the real operating system, but with a huge performance cost (VMWare [7], Qemu [8], and Parallels [9]). The fourth requires the use and design of a **paravirtualizer or hypervisor**, which interfaces the hardware with a domain 0 kernel. Most of the time, the domain 0 kernel must be modified to run on-top of the operating system. The domain 0 kernel then can start guest OS on top of it, but they will interact with the hypervisor so that the domain 0 kernel is only here for control. This solution is a good compromise between low-level development which is architecture specific and performance. Recent works now allow hypervisor to use the hardware virtualization instructions provided by some processors like *Xen* [10] or the jails in FreeBSD [11]. The last one is **hardware virtualization**, which more or less uses the same design as the paravirtualization with a hypervisor, except that the hypervisor is a dedicated component or even part of the processor. This solution is widely used in the business class servers such as AIX or Sun servers, and more recently for desktops with *Intel Vanderpool* [11] and *AMD Pacifica* [12] technologies.

Virtualization, as most industrial actors want to use it for embedded targets, should bring a secure way to make online payments handled by an application running on its own operating system copy, while other applications such as messaging, internet browsing would run in a separate operating system copy. The main drawback with this approach is that it will only bring virtualization features to a mass-marketed business, exclusively for security reasons while other features are available. Most of the works on embedded targets focus on using paravirtualization instead of hardware virtualization because it allows software upgrades to gain virtualization whereas a hardware solution would require a lot of changes.

Most embedded systems, especially in networking environnement run with no or few management and software upgrades, because of a high availability needed. Virtualization can help in reducing the downtime while upgrading the software. Since the hypervisor will hardly be changed, it can easily start another operating instance, because there is no need to reinitialize all the hardware and go to any recovery procedure or such. This is also very useful because you might want to test development versions of your operating system, while keeping a production instance of it running. It becomes convenient to decide when to switch from a production release to another with a minimum downtime as allowed by the hypervisor. By promoting *Free Electronic*, *OpenPattern* promotes free software running on open designs by using standard and carrier-class operating systems such as Linux or *BSD. The software stack that will be running on the OpenPattern design is shown above. The figure IV show an example of software layers in the case of virtualization on top of the OMRP.

FIGURE IV
SOFTWARE LAYERS OF THE OMRP

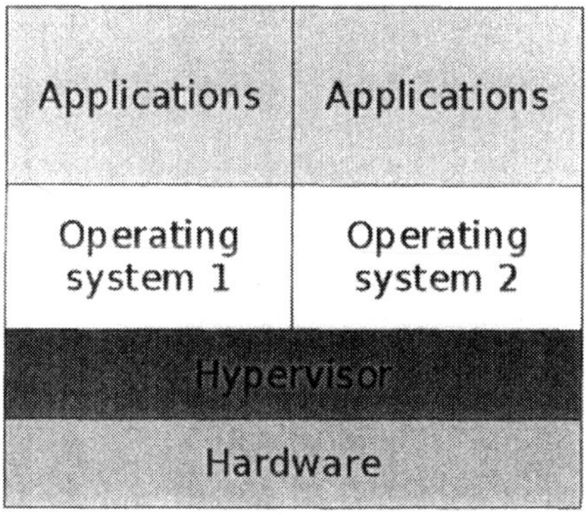

The great advantage of the FPGA handling RAM accesses, is that the FPGA can provide a hardware separation of the memory for the processor, and even doing context switching for it when it needs to run either one instance of the operating system of the other. Starting an architecture and design from scratch allows this project to benefit from the development done on the *Xen* hypervisor and on the recent version of jails in the FreeBSD environment, while preventing too much software work by having hardware mechanisms. This also allows unmodified kernels to run on the *OpenPattern* design, while porting the *Xen* hypervisor to the ARM architecture would require a lot of changes [13].

4.4 Managing the board

Most network and system administrators, whether they work for large scale or community networks face the same problem with an increasing rate of heterogeneous equipments being part of the system to manage. Nowadays, most network equipment manufacturers will ship their custom software solution based on the SNMP protocol [14]. These systems can manage other manufacturer's networks because of the SNMP design which uses a Management Information Base. You just need to provide a per-equipment MIB [15] and a SNMP program to read and set values for the system.

This solution has been accepted as *de-facto* standard for managing network equipments and server, brought together on a central administration console. Another standard that is being worked by the IEEE is the CapWap [16], which is mainly targeted to managing wireless access points. Though a lot of work has been done to get it mature, there seems to be few implementations of it, except OpenCapWap [17. Using CapWap for wireless home gateways makes a lot of sense, CapWap can be a great software implementation on top of the OMRP.

5. Conclusion and perspectives

OpenPattern aims not to be "yet another open source project" but to gather hardware and software people around an open platform able to be duplicate, modified, improved. Hardware is now a key point for the home gateways as well as for the wireless communities (in developed and developing countries as it has been described earlier) and giving it fully open will allow people to choose between designing their own hardware with the public PCBs, getting a standard OMRP or buying a proprietary hardware from an OEMs. Certainly the latest success of the *OpenMoko* project and the achievement of the *"One Laptop-Per-Child"* (OLPC) initiative had show that opening the hardware is now possible. Ideally the OMRP can be seen as a cheap, upgradeable and open routing board for wireless networks in developing along with open hardware for the end-users such as *OpenMoko* phones or OLPC computers making a telecommunications infrastructure fully open from the PCB of the board to the software implemented in the core of the network to the user interface.

References

[1] http://www.videolan.org/vlc/

[2] http://www.realtek.com.tw/products/productsView.aspx?Langid=1&PFid=11&Level=4&Conn=3&ProdID=70

[3] http://www.ikanos.com/solutions/security/index.cfm

[4] http://linux-vserver.org/Welcome_to_Linux-VServer.org

[5] http://openvz.org/

[6] http://user-mode-linux.sourceforge.net/

[7] http://www.colinux.org/

[8] http://www.vmware.com/fr/

[9] http://fabrice.bellard.free.fr/qemu/

[10] http://www.parallels.com/

[11] http://www.xensource.com/Pages/default.aspx

[12] "Jails in FreeBSD", Isaac Levy, EuroBSD Conference September 2007, Copenhagen, Denmark.

[13] http://www.intel.com/technology/platform-technology/virtualization/index.htm

[14] http://enterprise.amd.com/us-en/AMD-Business/Business-Solutions/Consolidation/Virtualization.aspx

[15] http://www.cs.uiuc.edu/class/sp06/cs523/lectures/26/XenARM-Final.ppt

[16] http://tools.ietf.org/html/rfc1157

[17] http://tools.ietf.org/html/rfc1156

[18] http://www.ietf.org/html.charters/capwap-charter.html

[19] http://opencapwap.org/

A Design of Context aware Smart Home Safety Management using by Networked RFID and Sensor

Byunggil Lee and Howon Kim,

Electronics and Telecommunications Research Institute, Korea

Abstract   Recently home intelligent service is extended to context aware and situation aware automation service by using ubiquitous technology. In this paper, we focused on user's context based intelligent security management for home safety application using RFID and WSN(Wireless Sensor Network). We propose a context aware home safety application model. The proposed context service support security and privacy control by using user's situation aware security management. It will be a practical application of RFID and sensor network for ubiquitous home safety environment. The proposed system has lots of advantages in user safety and energy efficiency.

1. System Architecture

Home intelligent services may be generally defined with home network service, home automation service, home theater service, and internet service to interwork other device or networks in inside and outside of home. Recently home intelligent service is extended to context aware and situation aware automation service by using ubiquitous technology. Ubiquitous services will be available to support the user identification and situation awareness with interconnected various sensors and user with RFID tags.

As an ubiquitous technology, radio frequency identification(RFID) has proven to be a powerful solution for not only supply chain management (SCM), inventory management and businesses process improvement [1], [2] but also access control and safety. The RFID is an automatic identification technology whereby digital data encoded in an RFID tag is captured by reader using RF signal. It is different

Please use the following format when citing this chapter:

Lee, B., Kim, H., 2007, in IFIP International Federation for Information Processing, Volume 256, Home Networking, Al Agha, K., Carcelle, X., Pujolle, G., (Boston: Springer), pp. 215-224.

from bar code in usage of tag memory, identity multi-items, writing of new data, interfacing with sensor and digital data source.

Using RFID and sensor network, we can store all information about the reading item in a networked information server with backend database, and ensure reliable and timely update context information based on physical user's location at home.

RFID systems are increasingly being used in high security applications, such as access systems for making payments or issuing tickets. However, the use of RFID and sensor network in these applications necessitates the use of security measures to protect against attempted attacks, in which people try to trick the RFID and sensor related system in order to gain unauthorized access to home network.

On the other hand, home network has various threats, include cyber attacks of Internet, security homes against hacking, malicious codes, worms, viruses, DoS attacks, and eavesdropping, since it is connected to the access network.

In this paper, RFID and sensor technology is applied surveillance and detection of intrusion in home security systems. Using these kinds of management systems, an innovative business process can be constructed and various convenient services can be realized [3]. However, unless these security systems are situation based designed and context based constructed, they can cause severe problem to home user when user be in trouble or have an accident by same security rule [4].

So, we proposed a context aware RFID system which has been integrated to identification RFID Tag and sensor network for acquisition time and location of context. Context aware based RFID means that equipment is able to take actions automatically on capturing event time and location of user Tag. The proposed context aware RFID system is capable of recognizing such a situation and determining the use of the resource based on the recognized location and time situation information. The primary purpose of this paper is to design of context aware RFID system and sensor network. The secondary purpose of this paper is to analyze about the access control and security management for home networking application. The remainder of this paper is organized as follows, Section 2 gives a brief description of intelligent home safety service architecture. Section 3 delineates a model of context based home security management service by using RFID and sensor network. Finally, conclusions and a discussion of advantages are presented in Section 4.

2. RFID and Sensor Network based Ambient Home Service Architecture

Many companies and organizations, including EPC Global Network[5], have developed RFID systems and international standardization is ongoing. The basic architecture of an RFID system is shown in Fig. 1.

For user's specific location based RFID service, we also include a mobile terminal with RFID reader which is read simply RFID tag for identify the objects. Users get information of objects by reading RFID tag and resolve it by inquiring to a network through mobile network. In the platform, WIPI(A kind of Korea's mobile standard platform. It is based on Java platform) is used as a RFID platform.

Typical applications will be a B2C model such as after sale service in home appliance or authentication service of a stuff(pearl, portrait) or guide to a demo video download and advance booking triggered by a mobile phone's menu after read RFID code from tag attached movie poster.

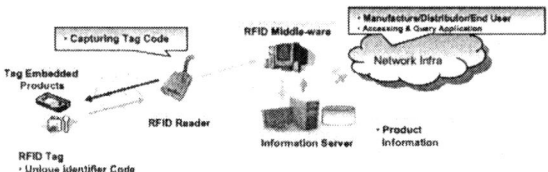

Figure 1. The basic architecture of RFID system.

As shown in Figure 1, quite briefly, RFID systems consist of RFID tag embedded product, Reader, RFID middle-ware, ONS (Object Name Service) for IS lookup, IS(Information Server) for product business data with code and the accessing application[5].

The context based RFID and sensor network is suitable for the coming ubiquitous environment, and situation information for the sensors and RFID identification Tag[7][8].

In the near future, Tag component of RFID and sensor will be integrated to sensing Tag. Home intelligent systems provide automatic home device control of the conditions of indoor environments by context based control service[10].

In this paper, however, we focus on the automated processing of user's context related safety and control functions, such as gate control, parking-gate control, room light control, room temperate control and device control such as TV, audio, window, curtain and safety level in home security system when user fall asleep or absent.

In our system, called "u-IHS(Ubiquitous computing based Intelligent Home Safety management service)", we use the RFID technology for context based identifying the user, here, an RFID tag is attached in home user's ID.

As shown in Figure 3, proposed service architecture is consist of RFID system and wireless sensor network for home user identification and context sensing.

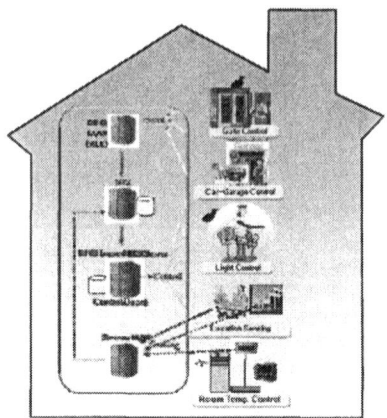

Figure 3. The service architecture of u-IHS system.

Our system for intelligent home networking management service[6] is consists of following elements.

- RFID Tag, IP based Sensor and Sensor networks
  .   . Capturing : Home User, Car, etc.
  . Sensing : User's motion, Location, Temperature, Humidity, Luminance, etc
- RFID Home Reader,
- mobile phone with RFID Reader
- RFID Home Middleware
- Sensor Home Middleware
- Secure IS server for RFID and sensor
- Context aware IHS Server
- Security and Privacy management by dynamic context policy

. Real-time SMS Notification : Safety situation to user

. Controlling : Heating Device, Air conditioning

- Device, Lightings, Locking Device of Door, Gate of cargo, TV, window, curtain and safety level in home security system etc.

3. Context aware dynamic reconfiguration of privacy and security for u-IHS service

We considered a smart home scenario in which appliances in the kitchen can only be activated in the presence of an adult. And if the temperature at the stove is getting higher or the smoke alarm detects some amount of smoke, heat from the stove can be automatically turned off. Hence, instead of fixed security levels or security action, it is possible to map home user's context to security action, safety levels and safety related actions such as Figure 3.

Figure 3 depicts the classified context based RFID and WSN service architecture which is based on functions for supporting user's situation awareness concept and related operations. There are the two sides from the home service access view points. One is the local service access at inside home or home area network. The other is the outside of home. It will be remote service access from the customer attached to the BcN networks

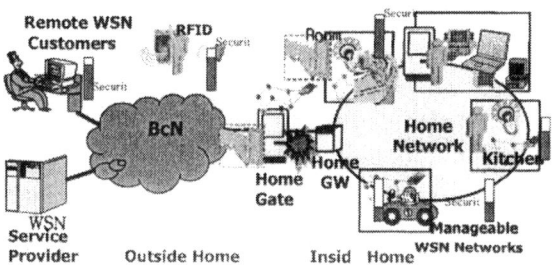

Figure 3. Dynamic Security Management with context aware mechanism

The default privacy protection level is determined based on the privacy impact assessment result undertaken by the government and the default privacy protection level is stored as the default policy of the tag and the home server. And user also can manage the privacy level by subscription and modification, after he purchases the product.

We begin by describe the network configuration and system features for u-IHS in this section. A context based processing system is designed to safe home environment, and it is described in Figure 4.

Figure 4. The block Structure of a context aware safety Management

In this model, the home user holding the RFID tagged identification card create capturing event and location event by reader and location sensor in door, kitchen or room and the event data and sensing data is transfer to back-end information server via middle-ware. The information server subsequently finds the matching context rule ID and selects context service server. Specifically, we consider a safety and context aware scenario in u-IHS system where. The secure information server sends the received RFID event and sensor data and parameters to IHS system. Then, IHS verifies the family or personal context policy for authorization and transform into each control board or control system for context based identity or safety and sophisticated control.

In view of information security protection, a serious problem for the RFID and sensor network service is a threat to DoS and information hacking. Here, the safety issue involves the risk of exposing information stored in IHS or other server and the leakage of information including personal moved data related to the user's home. Verification in IHS is for checking the user's context based safety level and user's context based privacy policy. Whenever RFID events and continuous sensing context value is received in secure IS server, it is transfer to meaningful context data and events, the IHS server checks the filtered and selected information and authorize user's context based safety level.

Our model of context based home networking safety and system in this regard, ID and parameter encryption and access control are used for prevention of service hacking or DoS attack in data transportation[6]. Integrating security function and intelligent context based safety and control mechanism in home network is particularly challenging due to the high demands made on their dependability[10][11].

The IHS server control machines and equipments in room automatically by event. The typical equipments of home are gate, parking garage, air conditioner,

heater, TV, audio, window, curtain and all other home device for user's convenience by notified web service.

4. System Design of Combined System with Context aware and Dynamic Security mechanism

In this section we discuss the functions and block diagram for the RFID sensor
network based context aware system, which provides a automatic and secure
controlling service by capturing the tag(sensor) and get out of the user's information.

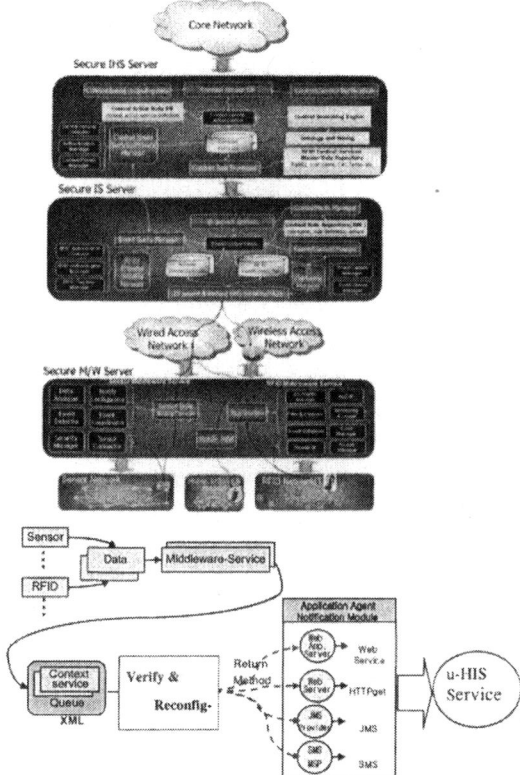

Figure 5. The proposed system design for context-aware home safety and
managed security control service

First, our IS server architecture is context driven in nature, defined context events are connected to specific service as a continuous tree topology, as shown in Figure 5. The Secure IS Server in Figure 5 represents the information server and context processing point, event data flow context filter and mapped by context rules in a continuous event unit. Data processing which needs continuous monitoring can be performed. The processed result is collected in result queue for interworking with application. These results are connected to proper application system by return methods. The return methods are Web service, HTTPget, JMS and mobile phone SMS for user's urgent event. This approach is desirable when home intelligent system, such as IHS need to be connected IS server with different way and different control network system. A variety of Web servers for context aware service and control are available. The main advantage of this approach is the secure connection and context policy based home device control and safety management. In particular, WS security and AS2 binding is used for secure transmission between servers. The IHS server is connected to IS server for family or personal context based service, covered in[7]. For context processing, the IHS server stored user's context policy data. Protocol and context rule and language like XML based GPDL(Generalized Policy Definition Language) are designed for context policy management. Each policy contains a subject role(the subject on which the policy is to apply), and object role(the object to which the policy applies) and action(on the object), an environment role(the context of the action) and the permissions(whether the action is to be permitted or not).

Context policy based detailed safety and access control mechanism is desired, since someone request and receive the context information of specified person without approval. Figure 3 describes the context based flow diagram for supporting user's situation awareness concept and related security operations.

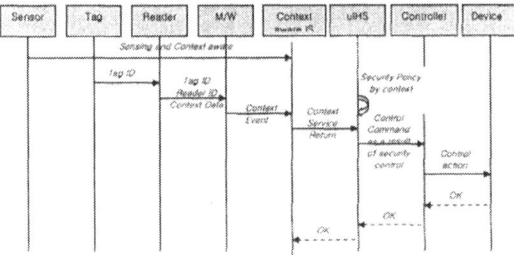

Figure 5. The proposed flow design of context-aware security control

The security level of context data defines different level for user's situation and context. And he wants to make the decision whether provide or not. The Information server stores the context result data and event logs by context policy and transfers them to the IHS server. The user can also re-configure the context action preference in IHS. From this point of view, we define access control features as following way.

. Access control of the context result data of an RFID/sensor

. Access control of the source data of an RFID/sensor

. Access right of a specified log data

. Mode of operator

(General Administer/Part administer/User etc)

The Secure M/W Server is consists of two part, one is for wireless sensor network and the other is for RFID middle-ware service. In this section, we discuss the IHS application server aspects of our system. For automatic control service, we designed IHS server, device control board and control software. The advantages of this system are as follows: first, we provide context based security management in home safety management aspects. Second, energy efficiency in home maintenance can be achieved. Third, advanced automatic home conditions are supported by utilizing the identity and context awareness in u-IHS system.

5. Conclusion

In this paper, we considered intelligent home safety management service by using context aware u-IHS system.

We designed the secure and automatic control service using RFID tagged ID card and context based light and temperature management using sensor and RFID tag. And we also describe the automatic parking garage control service using RFID tagged car. In the proposed u-IHS system, we presented in terms of context policy whereas we introduced a context based action scheme using configured context authorization in IHS. By doing so, context based dynamic security/privacy management and also intelligent home safety can be realized.

In this regard, the suggested u-IHS system is an effective solution for context-aware home safety management service using RFID and Sensor network.

6. Acknowledgements

This work was supported by the IT R&D program of MIC/IITA. [2005-S088-03, Development of Security technology for Secure RFID/USN Service].

References

[1] Siio, I., Hayasaka, T., "Putting information to things : RFID tags and their application", *IPSJ Magazine,* Vol. 40, No.8, pp. 846-850, Aug. 1999.

[2] EPCglobal. "The EPCglobal Network:Overview of Design, Benefits and Security", *http://www.epcglobalinc.org/* Sep. 2004.

[3] G. Avoine and Ph. Oechslin, "A scalable and provable secure hash based RFID protocol", International Workshop on Pervasive Computing and Comunications Security", *PerSec 2005,* pp. 110-114. IEEE, 2005.

[4] Sanjay E. Sarma, et al., "RFID Systems and Security and Privacy Implications", CHES 2002, *Lecture Notes in Computer Science* 2523, pp. 454–469. 2002.

[5] EPCglobla Inc. *http://www.epcglobalinc.org/.*

[6] B.G. Lee, H.W. Kim, "A Design of Privacy Conscious RFID System Using Customizing Privacy Policy Based Access Control", *Lecture Notes in Computer Science* Vol. 3823, pp. 673-682, Nov. 2005.

[7] G.D. Abowd, M. Ebling, G. Hunt, H. Lei, and H.W. Gellersen, "Context-Aware Computing," *PERVASIVE computing.* JULY–SEPTEMBER 2002, pp. 22–23.

[8] Chemishkian, S., "Building smart services for smart home", Networked Appliances, p.p 215-224, January 2002

[9] Jiang, L., Liu, D., Yang, B., "SMART HOME RESEARCH", Machine Learning and Cybernetics, p.p 659-663 vol. 2, August 2004

[10] Mostefaoui, G.K.., "Context-Aware Computing: A Guide for the Pervasive Computing Community", Pervasive Services, p.p 39-48, July 2004

[11] Wullems, C., Looi, M., Clark, A., "Towards context-aware security: an authorization architecture for intranet environments", Pervasive Computing and Communications, p.p 132-137, March 2004.

[12] Covington, M. J., Fogia, P., Zhiyuan, Z., Ahamad, M., "A Context-Aware Security Architecture for Emerging Applications", Annual Computer Security Applications Conference, p.p 249-258, December 2002.

Embedded Script-Driven Home-Automation with Sensor Networks

T. Haenselmann, T. King, M. Busse, W. Effelsberg and M. Fuchs

Abstract Today, proprietary home automation targets very specific applications which operate mostly on a cable based infrastructure. In contrast to that, our implementation builds a wireless ad-hoc multi-hop network based on the ESB sensor node platform from the FU-Berlin. The nodes gather sensor readings in a home and transmit them to a central automation server. There, the readings are matched against a list of script statements. In case of a match, a specific action is performed. In this work we will show how the user can implement complex home automation applications optimized for his specific needs by defining very simple script statements. An important property of the system is also that the control of all home appliances is done by means of IR communication and Ethernet enabled multiple plugs. This way, the cooperation between manufacturers is no necessity in order to connect devices to the home automation network.

Key words: home automation, building automation, sensor networks

1 Introduction

While the field of RFID technology constantly produces new applications and solutions for real world problems, research on sensor networks tends to be a mostly academic topic in which strong commercial applications are still rare [16, 11]. For this reason we want to describe a home automation project with sensor networks we have done in conjunction with Siemens Corporate Technology CT/SE2.

Home automation offers a not yet exploited degree of convenience, both for the private home and the office. Although the idea has been around for many years, the

Haenselmann, King, Busse, Effelsberg
University of Mannheim, e-mail: haenselmann,king,busse,effelsberg@
informatik.uni-mannheim.de

Fuchs
Daimler, e-mail: Foox@gmx.de

Please use the following format when citing this chapter:

Haenselmann, T., King, T., Busse, M., Effelsberg, W., Fuchs, M., 2007, in IFIP International Federation for Information Processing, Volume 256, Home Networking, Al Agha, K., Carcelle, X., Pujolle, G., (Boston: Springer), pp. 225-238.

market can still be considered to be in its infancy. Today's home automation solutions are mostly proprietary. They usually target a small number of problems, such as satisfying security needs or the control of a limited number of devices, typically all from the same manufacturer. They operate based on a particular infrastructure, which requires extra cabling. So they are best suited for new buildings. They are limited to the applications a manufacturer offers.

The future proliferation of home automation will depend on its ease of installation. That is why we argue for wireless home automation. In addition, this might be the only solution for ex post installations and historic buildings which must not be remodeled. At the same time, we believe that an even more important aspect to making the smart home a success will be to offer more freedom for a user to customize home automation application to his specific needs.

In short, the idea of our prototype is to gather all kinds of sensor readings in a home and forward them hop-by-hop to an embedded system to which we refer as the home automation server. Each time a new event is detected, the server runs over a list of script statements which can be defined by the user. In case of a match between the received event and the matching part of a statement, one or more actions are performed which can either be executed by the sensor nodes themselves or by multiple plugs which can be controlled via an Ethernet connection by the embedded home automation server itself.

The strength and contribution of our application lies in the combination of a larger number of sensor readings which allows to derive higher level semantics as compared to reacting on single sensor readings only.

In the following Section 2, we analyze todays existing standards in the field of home automation. In Section 3, we describe all technical aspects of our system and how to exploit multiple readings for concluding deeper semantics as compared to using single sensor readings, only. Section 4 concludes with an analysis of strengths and weaknesses of the system.

2 Related Work

Since the beginning of electrification, switching electrical devices has been done by means of connecting or disconnecting them to the power grid. In recent years, physically disconnecting a device from its energy source has become less popular. Instead, switching is done electronically. This means, that the inner device is separated from the switching circuit. As a consequence, the device can be powered on or off by a remote control. Some computer main boards even allow to react on network events. However, the downside is that the switching unit keeps consuming energy as long as it stays alert.

The changing paradigm in home automation is also that a device is no longer disconnected from the power grid. The function of the switch on the wall or even in the device in taken over by a network which is solely signaling events. The network which controls devices by transmitting datagrams is powered with a much lower current. The earliest instance of a pure datagram based network standard for building automation is the EIB standard implemented in 1992.

Even earlier home automation systems like the X10 system, combined the signaling network with the power grid. This technology denoted as *power-line* based has regained popularity recently as an alternative to DSL technology which requires dedicated signaling cables like telephone lines. On the other hand, power-line based systems have inherent problems like radio interference, security flaws and reliability issues which have never been solved completely.

2.1 Powerline-based home automation protocol X10

X10 is a power-line based building automation protocol. It is used to transmit the control signals via existing power lines without the need of dedicated signaling cables. X10 is used to trigger simple control events. However, it never gained a strong foothold for mission critical applications because no feedback channel is provided and the effective data rates are only about 20 bit/s. The bits of a message are modulated on a 120 kHz signal. In oder to be more error resilient, only the zero-crossings of the alternating current are used. In addition to the power-line based approach, X10 provides remote controls and switches based on radio communication, as well [15].

The X10 protocol was developed by the Irish company Mico Electronics in the 70ies. Due to its adoption and promotion by General Electric is became very successful in the United States. In Europe, a modified standard was sold which did not have to same success as compared to the one overseas. Due to different regulations, the signal strength had been reduced significantly thus rendering the solution less useful for many applications. As a consequence, the technically more advanced EIB protocol became dominant in Europe.

2.2 European Installation Bus (EIB)

As early as in the mid-80ies, different companies though about using bus-topologies for home- and building-automation. Even at that time it was obvious that proprietary home automation solutions would hinder the proliferation of home automation. Leading manufacturers of electrical installation technology among them Siemens, Jung, Merten et al. founded the *European Installation Bus Association (EIBA)* in 1990 which became the *Konnex* association later. Their aim was to establish a joint standard for home automation [4, 12, 14]. This standard guarantees the interoperability of various devices and of systems like home appliances, air conditioning etc. from different manufacturers. In 1991, the first products were manufactured according to the standard. Today, there are as much as 4000 groups consisting of products manufactured by more than 100 companies. These products are compliant to the

EIB/KNX specification which is the first globally agreed standard for home- and building automation. The standardization by the ISO committee is currently on its way.

2.3 KNX

KNX can be considered the international successor of the EIB standard. KNX is downward compatible to EIB and it has been acknowledged by more than 100 companies.

3 Scriptable sensor network based home automation

Our system consists of the ESB [9] sensor nodes describes in the next section. They transmit messages hop-by-hop over a tree topology which has to be initialized by the user semi-manually in advance. The root node is connected via its serial interface to the embedded home automation server described in Section 3.1.2. The embedded board runs a striped down version of Linux and a minimal web server to allow the user to configure the system remotely.

The nodes not only act as sensors but also as actuators which can control basically all devices which come with an IR remote control. Therefor, we have extended the ESB's firmware to be compatible with the three de-facto standards for remote controls by Philips, Panasonic and Sony. In addition, the buzzer and the LED lights can be used as actuators in some cases. More important is the multiple power plug with an Ethernet interface. It allows to switch all devices switch can be turned on and off only and which can not be controlled elsewhere.

In the beginning, the nodes have to be distributed in the house according to the requirements of the considered applications. In the distribution process, the user is given hints by the system on where to place intermediate nodes for the purpose of communication.

In the operational phase, events are forwarded by the network to the root node and eventually to the home automation server in a tree-like fashion like it has been proposed e.g., by [10] in the context of the *TAG*-approach and may others [1, 13]. There, they are matched against so-called script statements which have been configured by the user via a web-interface as described in Section 3.4. In case of a matching statement, a defined action is executed which implements one particular home automation application resp. which serves one particular purpose like e.g., baby surveillance. In this case, the executed action could be as simple as signaling the user with the buzzer or by sending him some information over the web by the embedded server, e.g., to submit an SMS via an external service.

3.1 Hardware used

3.1.1 The electronic sensor board

Due to its rich instrumentation with various sensors we chose the ESB sensor node shown in Figure 1 developed by the FU-Berlin.

The ESB is equipped with the MSP430 [3], an embedded system on a chip from Texas Instruments. It runs at 8MHz and contains 64kB of memory in the version of the chip used here. The MSP430 is designed as a general purpose embedded system with a 12-Bit AD/DA (analog <-> digital) converter. The energy consumption is in the order of magnitude of 1mA at a current of 3V if the MSP430 if fully operational. In sleep mode which can be adjourned by external events, the power consumption is again about 1000 times lower which is roughly equal to the self-discharge of the batteries.

Most of the 64kB are implemented as flash memory which will contain the software and all constant data. The RAM occupies only 2048 bytes within the whole memory map which is a fairly limited amount of space for dynamic data. The situation is mitigated to a degree by the fact that the flash memory can also be written in chunks of 128 bytes during operation if the state of the battery allows for this energy consuming operation.

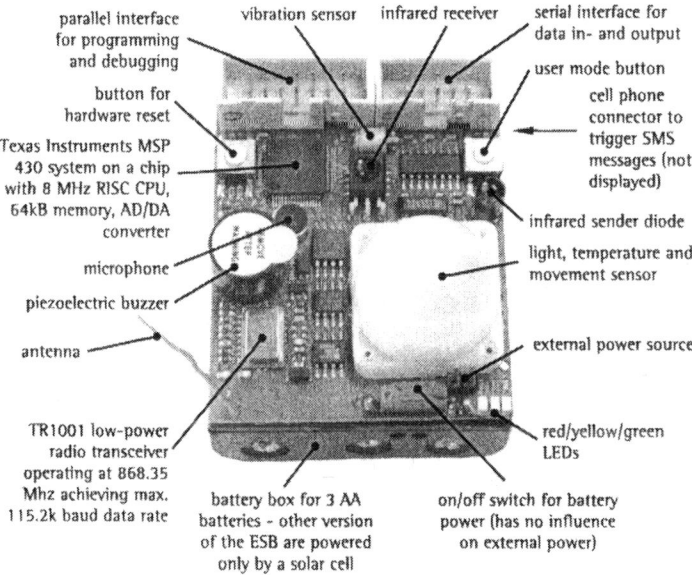

Fig. 1: Overview of the components of the Embedded Sensor Board (ESB) from the FU-Berlin.

Under the ESB's white hemisphere are is a temperature and PIR (passive infrared) sensor hidden. The PIR sensor can be used for monitoring the space around the ESB up to a distance of 8 meters to detect moving objects like it is used for alarm systems.

There are two other IR (infra red) diodes on the circuit board for sending and receiving e. g., RC-5 codes that are used by remote controls for consumer electronics. The IR-communication is particularly important because it allows the nodes to serve as actuators which can influence their environment by interacting with many home appliances like air conditions, home entertainment devices etc. At the same time the IR communication provides another way to influence nodes with consumer remote controls. They are treated like any other sensor event, sent to the embedded board and matched against a user-defines script statements.

Furthermore, the ESB is equipped with a vibration sensor that can sense slight vibrations of the device. Last not least, the ESB is equipped with a microphone and a piezo-electric buzzer. The buzzer is another simple actuator used to signal the user acoustically. By its design, it can only produce a single frequency, however, by switching it on and off rapidly, the firmware can also simulated other frequencies. There is also a microphone attached to the ESB. It can be used to measure the loudness of noises in the node's proximity. A very simple application would be to implement a baby-phone by signaling the owner in case of noise in the nursery.

The red, yellow and green LEDs are useful for signaling simple events. We use it in the deployment phase described in Section 3.5.

3.1.2 PowerPC-603 based embedded board

As what we refer to as a *home automation center*, we used the embedded board EP5200 from Embedded Planet[1]. It is a complete system on a single motherboard. Though there is an IDE connector for a hard drive, we used the on-board 16MB flash memory for installing a minimal Linux installation based on the Linux distribution *Gentoo*[2]. The flash memory can be accessed like a hard-drive using the *jffs2*[3] file system.

Besides the need to cross-compile the kernel and to replace the hard drive by the flash memory, there is no different to using an IBM PC-compatible system. However, it is important to delete all files not needed in the boot process to achieve a memory footprint which fits into the bounds of the 16MB flash memory. In the development process we attached a simple USB stick to the USB port to host the GNU tool chain and other essentials.

We believe that an embedded system is suitable for its small form factor, price and stability. It has no moving parts, needs no ventilation and is certified for continuous operating in an environment of between -40 to 80 degrees Celsius.

---

[1] http://www.embeddedplanet.com/

[2] http://www.gentoo.org

[3] http://sources.redhat.com/jffs2/

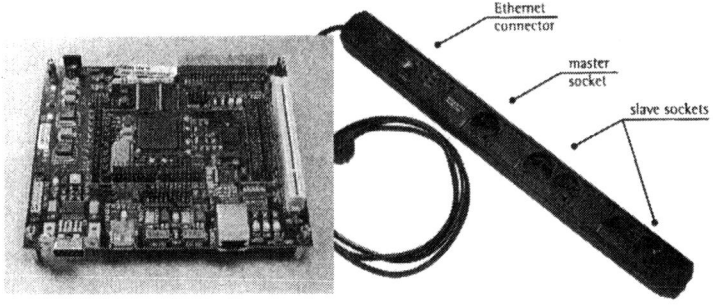

Fig. 2: Left: The EP5200 board is based on an PowerPC-603 processor. It has no moving parts. The flash memory can be used to host the root file-system. Right: The Ethernet-capable multiple plug is an important actuator for controlling all kinds of devices which can be switched on and off only.

3.1.3 Ethernet-enabled multiple plug

An important actuator is the ethernet-enabled multiple plug shown in Figure 2. It can be used to switch all electric equipment which has an on/off switch only like e.g., lamps. From a user's perspective, the multiple plug can be controlled via a web-interface. In our implementation, the home automation center sends simple http-requests to the socket in order to switch one of the two relays on or off.

The downside of the solution is so far, that the multiple plug needs to be connected to a cable-based LAN. However, we expect similar wireless devices to be available soon as well. As an intermediate solution we connected an Ethernet bridge to the plug in order to become independent of the LAN-cable.

The master socket can be used to switch one or the two slave sockets on if the attached master device consumes energy. At the moment, we control the slave sockets via Ethernet only.

3.2 New home automation paradigm

Traditional home automation solutions target isolated problem. They may e.g., close the window's roller blinds at night, control the central heating and air conditioning or they may serve security needs.

Some solutions are helpful for handicapped people. If the doorbell or the telephone can not be heard, sensors capture the acoustic signals and trigger actuator like spot lights or vibrating haptic devices which wake or signal the hearing impaired owner.

In recent years, even solutions for pet owners have emerged. A cat's collar is equipped with a passive RFID transponder. At the cat door, a reader reads the passive tag within a range of about 30cm. Once the cat approaches the reader and the tag is authenticated, the door is unlocked by a simple mechanism. This way, alien cat, rats or other small animals can be prevented entry from the house.

All those solutions have in common, that they target a very specific application only. Especially those for disabled people can be very costly and may not always solve all individual needs. So we propose a new paradigm which enables the user himself to devise customized solutions by means of simple script statements.

3.3 User-define home automation scripts

In the home automation center, all sensor readings are gathered. The user defines script statements like the following one which are matched against the incoming sensor readings.

```
IF movement_detected(sensor-5) == true THEN
    switch_power(multi_plug-5, on),
    switch_power(multi_plug-6, on)
```

Every script has a *matching part* and an *actuator part*. The server software on the home automation center iterates over all script statements each time an event is received. In case of a match, the actuator part is executed.

The above example switches on two lamps connected to a multiple plug outlet each time a room is entered by a person. Besides these trivial statements, the strength of the approach lies in the combination of more than one sensor readings. The more readings are combined, the higher the semantics that can be derived.

The example above could be extended by the time of day to differentiate between various situations. E.g., switching on the light is not necessary at any time but only at dusk or at night. So we add a light reading on the matching side:

```
IF movement_detected(sensor-5) == true AND
    lightness(sensor-5) < 800 THEN
    switch_power(multi_plug-5, on),
    switch_power(multi_plug-6, on)
```

Not all events have to be triggered by sensors. Another independent event can be the daytime.

```
IF time_within(05:00,23:00) == true AND
    movement_detected(sensor-5) == true AND
    lightness(sensor-5) < 800 THEN
    switch_power(multi_plug-5, on),
    switch_power(multi_plug-6, on)

IF time_within(23:00,05:00) == true AND
    movement_detected(sensor-5) == true THEN
    switch_buzzer(senor-7, on)
```

In the first line, a movement at daytime causes a light configuration to be switched on. In the second line, the same movement will trigger an alarm if it occurs while the owner sleeps at night.

Another example for deriving higher level semantics from sensor readings is shown in our demo-video[4]. One of the ESB sensor nodes is attached to a door facing the inside. Two different readings are transmitted by the sensor, one originating from a passive infrared movement sensor that detects movement in a proximity of about 8 meters. The other reading comes from a vibration sensor which detects if the sensor itself is shaking. The two sensor readings can be used to differentiate between a door being opened from the inside or outside. To be more precise, the order of occurrence determines the case.

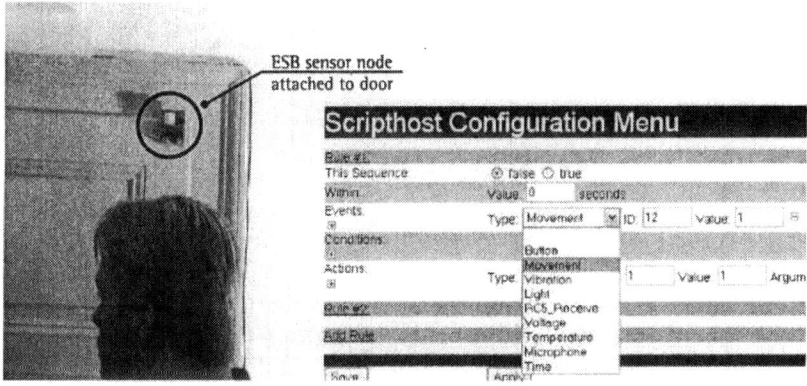

Fig. 3: Left: Extract from our demo video: Two sensor readings are used to distinguish whether the door is approached from the inside or the outside. Right: Browser-based configuration.

Door being opened from the inside: Here, a person approaches the door resp. the attached sensor node. The passive infrared sensor will trigger an event which is sent to the embedded home automation center. Then, the person will open the door which triggers the vibration sensor in addition because the entire node is moving together with the door.

Door being opened from the outside: A person approaches the door from the outside. No sensor readings are triggered so far because the sensor is attached to the opposite side. Once the door is opened, both sensors react at the same time. The vibration sensor because it is moving together with the door and the passive infrared sensor because it is rotated by the opening door. Move precisely, from its perspective, the environment rotates around the node. So both events occur more or less simultaneously.

But not only taking multiple sensor readings into account at a time can help to derive higher level semantics. Historic events can help as well.

---

[4] See http://www.informatik.uni-mannheim.de/~haensel/sn_homeautomation.avi

Example: We assume that a house is empty in an initial state and no door has been opened so far. If movement occurs in a room, someone may have entered though a window. If there was prior movement in the hall or the door has been opened it may be an inhabitant. Historic events are modeled by conditions which are described in the next section.

The examples above should only provide a first impression of the possibilities which emerge if many sensor reading are gathered and matched in order to draw conclusions. These conclusions can be far more valuable than those which are derived from single sensor readings as done in many isolated home automation applications. In this work we only want to sketch the idea of customized home automation and prove its feasibility by means of the implementation. As is true e.g., for the World Wide Web as well, the most interesting applications will likely come from creative practitioners and not from academia.

3.4 Web configuration of rules

Figure 3 shows the browser based configuration. The user can define an arbitrary number of rules each of which appears as a single line that can be unfolded to a dialog for later editing.

A rule consists of three elements whereas the triggering event and the action to be performed are the two compulsory elements. Whenever an event like a sensor reading occurs, it is compared with all rules. If the event matches a rule, the according action is performed.

Whether an action is performed must not always depend on an event only but also on a condition which, unlike the event, persists over some time and does not occur at a single moment only. So a rule can have an arbitrary number of conditions which have to be met in addition to an occurring event. A condition can e.g., be a specific time of the day or a prior sensor reading like light or temperature. Multiple events, conditions and even actions can be defined within a single rule by the user. This way, the above mentioned deeper semantics can be accomplished.

Technically, the page is generated by a php-script on the server side and the rules are stored in a single XML file.

3.5 Deployment phase

Prior to the operational phase of the home automation network, the sensor nodes have to be deployed. In the beginning, the root node and the leave nodes have to be installed. The root node has to be connected to the embedded board which should have access to the home's LAN. The LAN connection is mainly used to control the Ethernet enabled multiple plug that is used to switch simple electronic devices on and off.

The location of the leave nodes is determined by the purpose of the application. If the audio-sensor should e.g., be used as a baby-phone, a sensor node has to be positioned in the nursery. The root node and the leave nodes are considered as *active nodes* in our implementation because they server a specific purpose. Especially in an indoor environment, the range of the sensor nodes can be limited, particularly if neighboring nodes are separated by walls. So direct communication between leave nodes and the root can not be assumed in general. This is why the user has to bridge the gaps between the root and the leaves by positioning intermediate *passive nodes* which server as packet forwarders only.

All nodes connected to the root directly or indirectly are considered to belong to the *active partition*. The task of the user is now to connect the active partition to all leave nodes which are unconnected. In the deployment process he picks up initialized nodes and carries them away from the active partition into the direction of a leave nodes. While being close enough to a connected node of the active partition, the green LED is blinking to indicate a good connection. It is considered to be good as long as three consecutive ping packets return from the root node. Less than three packets result in a yellow indicator and no arriving ping packets are signaled red. The relatively small number of test packets has been used because each of them takes about 300ms to be transmitted. A latency of about 1s is still small enough as feedback for the user.

So he will start at the active partition and walk towards a yet unconnected leave node. As soon as the quality of the connection decreases, he has to step back and position the nodes permanently. In the end, the node is put into its operational mode by pressing the user definable button. The leave node will also try to reach the active partition by sending broadcast ping packets. As soon as there is a good connection it will start to blink green as well and can be set into the operational mode in the same way as the nodes carried around.

The user has to continue this process until all leave nodes are connected. Note that in some cases, active nodes can and will serve as forwarders also if they are connected to the active partition themselves.

The routing of the packets among the nodes is done according to the tree which is generated by the user implicitly by deploying the nodes. As a consequence, each node forwards information only to its direct father via static routes. Gathering the sensor readings was also easy to implement on the side of the nodes as the firmware readily supports sending events in regular intervals and based on thresholds.

4 Evaluation

In the evaluation, we mainly focused on a qualitative analysis of our implementation since there were not prior wireless home automation systems available to us.

4.1 Energy supply

Even though the use of sensor nodes eliminates the need for cables, it creates the new problem of supplying the nodes with energy. Even under optimal conditions, our ESB notes will not operator more than a couple of months on a single set of batteries. Having 20 or more nodes installed, this would mean for the user to change some batteries once in a week on average.

The ESB nodes come in different versions. One of them replaces the battery box by a photo diode which charges a capacitor. Depending on the light conditions, the energy stored this way is enough to operate for a few seconds. Though this does not seem to be much, for many applications it suffices for making some measurements and sending them over the network. Often, this does not require more than several hundred milliseconds. A useful property for the ESB platform is in this context that sensor readings can be used to wake the node from its power saving mode without using the processor. Waking up a node means to raise the clock rate of the processor which can e.g., be triggered by defining a threshold for a sensor. Though the threshold is a simple means of measurement it is useful for saving energy in times of inactivity.

At a first glance, intermediate nodes must not sleep since they may have to forward packets from their neighbors at any time. However, a number of MAC schemes like *WiseMAC* have been developed in recent years which keep a network alert while almost completely reducing idle times [8, 7].

4.2 Security problems

Wireless transmission is know to be error-prone in general and in particular in case of many sensor nodes. We exemplary evaluated the transmission characteristics of our sensor platform [6]. One outcome of the studies was that there is a very strong variance both in transmission and reception characteristics among different nodes of the same type [5]. Furthermore, the quality of a directed link between two nodes can deviate significantly from the inverse direction.

Another problem which is inherent to all wireless networks is that it can be sabotaged easily by jamming the frequency band used. So the wireless channel is more useful for less mission-critical applications. In case of an alarm system, a beacon based approach might be adopted. The alarm could be triggered by missing beacons so that distorting the channel would not prevent the alarm. Though less critical, an attacker could still trigger false alarms.

On the other hand, the use of wireless communication is more and more debated, e.g., for industry automation [17] and even for communication within airplanes. The later one is referred to as *fly-by-wire*. First prototypes have been build based on unmanned planes [2].

5 Conclusion and outlook

In this work we described a wireless home automation system based on sensor networks. The ESB platform we chose allows for easy installation and extension of the system.

Other than commercial home automation solutions available today, we propose to let the user come up with customized solutions for his individual requirements by formulating script statements. These statements which are entered via a web interface react on a combination of events and can trigger a list of actions in case of an occurring match. Furthermore, the execution of the actions can be made dependent on an arbitrary number of conditions which have to be met.

The nodes do not only act as sensors but as actuators as well. By sending infrared RC5 codes, almost all electronic equipment using a remote control can be switched. Simple devices are switch by means of a multiple plug with an Ethernet connection.

Though an increasing number of home appliances are controllable by IR remote controls today, we plan to connect to the European Installation Bus in addition. In this context it will make sense to adopt the EIB protocol for the wireless communication as well, at least on the application level. The extension of EIB to a wireless implementation could work in the style know from the Bluetooth standard. There, the layer two serial line connection is emulated by an underlying wireless connection. The actual application level communication does not have to be changed. In our case we aim at running the EIB protocol on top of the wireless connection in the next version of our prototype.

References

[1] Abramson N (1970) Power-aware routing in mobile ad hoc networks. In: Proceedings of the Fall 1970 AFIPS Computer Conference
[2] Afonso JA, Coelho ET, Macedo R, Carvalhal P, Silva LF, Almeida H, Santos C, Ferreira MJ (2006) A fly-by-wireless platform based on a flexible and distributed system architecture. In: IEEE International conference on industrial technology, Mumbay, India
[3] Bierl L (2004) Das große MSP430 Praxisbuch. Franzis Verlag GmbH
[4] Bruegge B, Pfleghar R, Reicher T (1999) Owl: An object-oriented framework for intelligent home and office applications. In: Proceedings of the Second International Workshop on Cooperative Buildings (CoBuild99)
[5] Busse M, Haenselmann T, Effelsberg W (2006) The Impact of Resync on Wireless Sensor Network Performance. In: Proc. of Performance Control in Wireless Sensor Networks (PWSN'06), Coimbra, Portugal
[6] Busse M, Haenselmann T, King T, Effelsberg W (2006) The Impact of Forward Error Correction on Wireless Sensor Network Performance. In: Proc. of ACM Workshop on Real-World Wireless Sensor Networks (RealWSN'06), Uppsala, Sweden

[7] van Dam T, Langendoen K (2003) An adaptive energy-efficient mac protocol for wireless sensor networks. In: Proceedings of the 1st international conference on Embedded networked sensor systems, Los Angeles (CA), USA, pp 171–180

[8] El-Hoiydi A, Decotignie JD, Enz C, Roux EL (2003) Wisemac, an ultra low power mac protocol for the wisenet wireless sensor network. In: Proceedings of the 1st international conference on Embedded networked sensor systems, Los Angeles (CA), USA, pp 302–303

[9] Kappe E, Liers A, Ritter H, Schiller J (2004) Low-power image transmission in wireless sensor networks using scatterweb technologies. In: Workshop on Broadband Advanced Sensor Networks, San Jose (CA), USA

[10] Madden S, Franklin M, Hellerstein J, Hong W (2002) Tag: a tiny aggregation service for ad-hoc sensor networks. In: Proceedings of the OSDI'02 Symposium, Boston (MA), USA

[11] Orr R, Abowd G (2000) The smart floor: A mechanism for natural user identification and tracking

[12] Pitzek S, Elmenreich W (2003) Configuration and management of a real-time smart transducer network

[13] Singh S, Woo M, Raghavendra CS (1998) Power-aware routing in mobile ad hoc networks. In: ACM SIGCOMM Computer Communication Review archive, vol 28 (3), pp 5–26

[14] Spinellis D (2002) The information furnace: User-friendly home control. In: In Proceedings of the 3rd International System Administration and Networking Conference SANE 2002, pp 145–174

[15] Wang Y, Russell W, Arora A, Jagannathan RK, Xu J (2000) Towards dependable home networking: An experience report. In: International Conference on Dependable Systems and Networks (DSN 2000), p 44 ff

[16] Want R, Fishkin KP, Gujar A, Harrison BL (1999) Bridging physical and virtual worlds with electronic tags. In: CHI, pp 370–377

[17] Wiberg PA, Bilstrup W (2001) Wireless technology in industry-applications and user scenarios. In: 8th IEEE International Conference on Emerging Technologies and Factory Automation, Antibes-Juan les Pins, France, vol 1, pp 123–131

Next WSN applications using ZigBee

Xavier Carcelle[1], Bob Heile[2], Christian Chatellier[3], Patrick Pailler[4]

[1] Xavier Carcelle, IEEE Member, xavier.carcelle@ieee.org

[2] Bob Heile, ZigBee Alliance Chairman, bheile@ieee.org

[3] Christian Chatellier, University of Poitiers, France, chatellier@sic.sp2mi.univ-poitiers.fr

[4] Patrick Pailler, University of Poitiers, France, Patrick.pailler@etu.univ-poitiers.fr

Abstract. Among the latest events of the wireless revolution, the fast-growing of ZigBee as a standard for WSN (Wireless Sensors Networks) is certainly one of these. ZigBee and 802.15.4 had been proving in the last years that they can achieve the results that Wi-Fi had achieved for high bit-rate wireless LANs and some large reliable deployments are now in place implementing ad-hoc WSN in critical applications. Therefore this paper will emphasize on the past, present and future features for ZigBee, taking a look on the feedback from previous implementations to finally design the next generations of WSN based on ZigBee.

Keywords: Wireless, Home Networking, Wireless Sensor Networks, ZigBee, IEEE 802.15.4.

Please use the following format when citing this chapter:

Carcelle, X., Heile, B., Chatellier, C., Pailler, P., 2007, in IFIP International Federation for Information Processing, Volume 256, Home Networking, Al Agha, K., Carcelle, X., Pujolle, G., (Boston: Springer), pp. 239-254.

1. Introduction

One of this paper's aims is to give an up-to-date state-of-the-art concerning the WSN and their applications from a HAN (Home Area Network) point of view. WSN has been a hot topic lately with the development of embedded systems and the optimization of ad-hoc networks versus battery-friendly nodes. ZigBee has been definitely the most dominant wireless standard with the support of the IEEE 802.15.4 working group since the version 1.0 in 2004 to the adoption of the protocol by some major industrial actors in 2007. WSN are requiring reliable, battery-friendly, secure, auto-configurable ad-hoc protocols and the second part of this article will give a view on the feedbacks of the first deployments using ZigBee. Then the article will emphasize on the use of ZigBee in the HAN applications showing possible cases for the positioning of ZigBee nodes. Finally the article will present an ideal plate-form based on several protocols and medium to get the best transmission for WSN using wired and wireless networks.

2.   ZigBee past, present and next features

ZigBee is now a well-known wireless standard within the landscape of IEEE since several years. The first proposal to IEEE was in late 2000 and the first specifications came out in 2003 for the MAC and PHY layer (from the IEEE 802.15.4) and in 2004 for the Network layer and remaining upper layers (from the ZigBee Alliance). 802.15.4 was revised in 2006 as were elements of the ZigBee to improve the functionalities, features and coexistence in the loaded 2.4 ISM band. Frequency Agility, network layer enhancements and added support for very large networks were added in 2007.

The figure 1 overviews the milestones of the development for the MAC and Network layer since the first initial MRD in 1999.

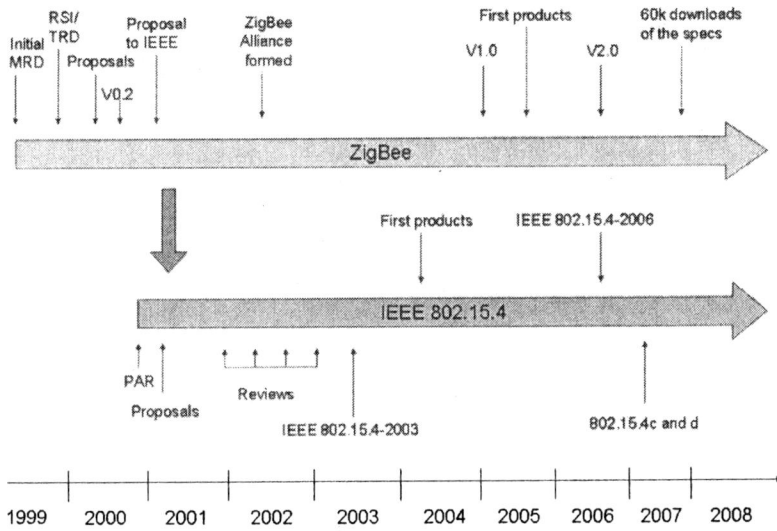

Figure 1: Milestones in the ZigBee history

Since the first products came out after the 1.0 version of the specifications of the ZigBee network stack, lots of ZigBee networks are now implemented worldwide in the WSN area such as the 4k nodes network in Korea, networks in Scandinavian sugar mills and North American hotels with ZigBee planned for deployment in 200K electric meters in Gotenberg, Sweden. The past and current implementations are using extensively the ad-hoc features from the MAC (Medium Access Control) and network layer with the three types of nodes with such a network (ROUT for router, COORD for coordinator and END for end-device with reduced functionalities).

Concerning the PHY (PHYsical) layer, ZigBee is based so far on two implementations: the "short-distance" one based on the ISM 2.4GHz band and the "long-distance" one based on the ISM 868/915MHz band. The specifications of these two bands are detailed in the table 1. 15.4-2006 adds higher data rate modulations schemes to the sub 1 GHz bands as well.

PHY (MHz)	Frequency Band (MHz)	Spreading parameters		Data parameters		
		Chip rate (kchip/s)	Modulation	Bit rate (Kbits/s)	Symbol rate (KSymb/s)	Symbols
868/915	868-868.6	300	BPSK	20	20	Binary
	902-928	600	BPSK	40	40	Binary
2450	2400-2483.5	2000	O-QPSK	250	62.5	16-ary Orthogonal

Table 1: Frequency bands for ZigBee

In the past and current implementations, most of the chips available are based on the 2.4GHz bands due to the fact that this band allows devices to be sold anywhere in the world. For fixed equipment regional markets like outdoor metering networks, the sub 1GHz bands should start finding more interest. The IEEE 802.15.4 is currently releasing two new flavours available at the PHY layer: 802.15.4c for China 780MHz band and 802.15.4d for Japan 950MHz RFID band. These two new bands available for "long-distance" ZigBee will extend the possibilities of applications for outdoor implementations namely in those markets. The ZigBee eco-system is implement on top of the 802.15.4 MAC layer and the ZDO (ZigBee Device Object) allows the implementations of several ZigBee profiles targeting the appropriate applications (in-building automation, sensitive applications, mobile WSN...). The architecture is presented in the Figure 2.

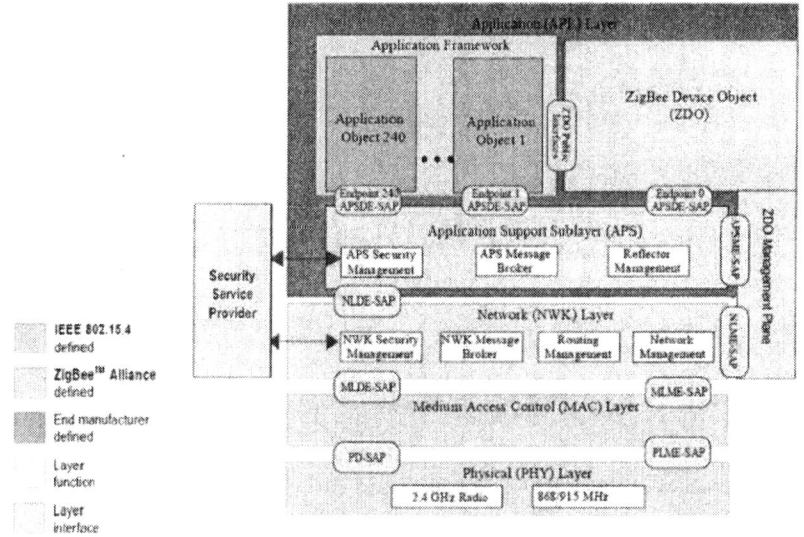

Figure 2: Architecture of the ZigBee stack

The ZigBee solution has been seen as a battery-friendly wireless standard for low-bit-rate, self-healing, mesh networks using its main strong features:
_IEEE 64-bit or 16-bit network addresses for large WSNs
_Flexibility of the configuration targeting the application (retransmission frequency, functions of each node on the net…)
_Good implementation of the current ad-hoc functionalities
_Flexible implementation of gateways to the outside world
The table 2 sums up the features of ZigBee as they can be seen from a timeline prospective

	Past	Present	Future
ZigBee Features	*868/916MHz possible usage *Star topology preferred *Fixed and small WSN *Development kits	*2.4GHz preferred for indoor apps *Small mobile WSN *Large ad-hoc fixed MSN *Long distance ZB *Wi-Fi / ZB cohabitation and gateways *US Laws enforcement to recognize ZB as a WSN standard	*Multiple homogeneous gateways to others protocols *Channel auto-adaptation with the new version *Chinese/Japanese ZB *Embedded ZB applications *ZB pro version

Table 2: ZigBee past, present and future features

3. Feedbacks on existing ZB applications

Based on the existing WSNs deployed using ZigBee, there is a certain number of feedbacks available publicly on the performances and drawbacks of the current features. One of the issues in terms of design for ZigBee networks were the interference problems in the "busy" 2.4GHz frequency bands regarding the others technologies in the same ISM band. The 802.15.4 standard had been designed to keep some "immune" channels at the very edge of the 2.4 ISM band.

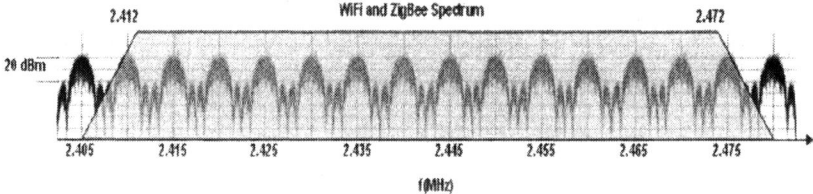

Figure 3: Wi-Fi and ZigBee spectrum

The figure 3 shows both the 802.11(b/g) spectrum and the 802.15.4 16 channels and as we can see the channels 1 and 16 are actually out of the scope of the Wi-Fi spectrum. This is the same consideration for the 802.15.1 (BlueTooth at the network layer) interferences which remains in a narrower band than the 1 and 16 channels of ZigBee. Finally concerning the potential interferences coming from 2.4GHz microwaves, the duty cycle of the ovens keep a certain sufficient timeslot for the 802.15.4 to be transmitted properly with not too many re-SYN packets. Measured ZigBee network performance in the presence of heavily loaded 802.11 networks has been very good as has been the performance for products implementing both technologies in the same box. This is true even for channels withing the 802.11 channel assignments.

Secondly the ZigBee had been seen also as wireless standard adjustable for the applications namely in the automation world. For instance the latency and the transmission frequency are not always depending on the applications. Therefore one can enable a certain number of options while deploying:

- **Sleep and wake-up sensors for better battery life** can be implemented with short duty timeslot as seen in figure 4

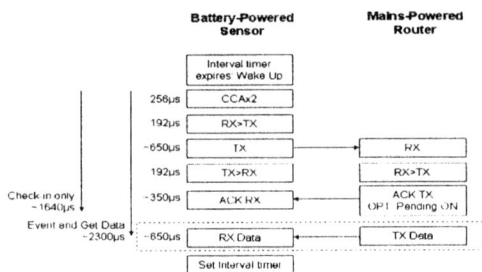

Figure 4: Sensor timing application (copyright ZigBee Alliance)

- **Beacon-enabled or not ZigBee networking** depending on the QoS (Quality of Service) requested on the deployed WSN. The figure 5 shows the communication to and from the COORD in the two cases and therefore the ACK (acknowledgment) can be optional.

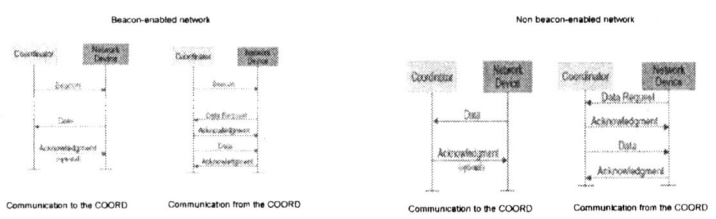

Figure 5: Transmission with the COORD with beacon frames enabled and not

- **Long distance ZigBee for outdoor net-to-net uplinks.** As shown in the figure 6, some situations imply the deployment of WSN over several buildings while trying to have only large network (easier implementation, better monitoring, same on-top applications...). This can be achieved, for instance, by using ZigBee COORD nodes with an amplified RF inter-faces (several 100mW instead of the standardized few mW of the ZigBee specifications), this allowing reliable radio transmission over several hundreds meters outdoor up to one kilometer with a Line Of Sight con-figuration. The figure 6 presents an example of a unique WSN over a two-buildings topology.

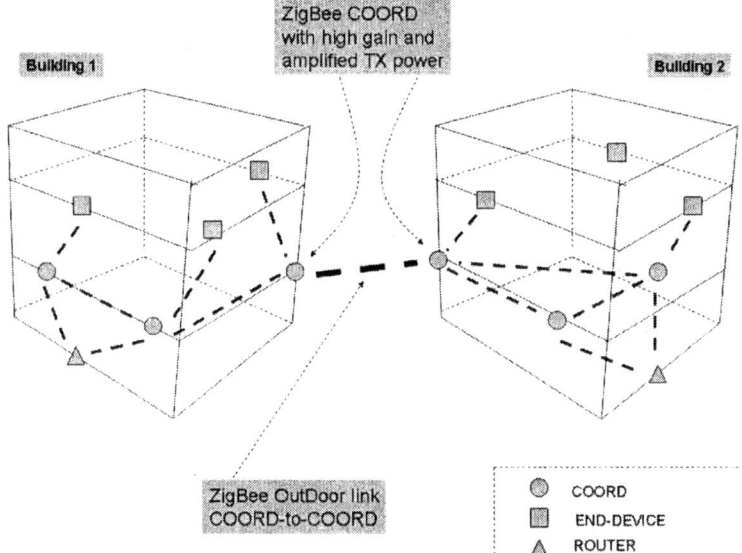

Figure 6: OutDoor two-buildings ZigBee applications

- **Optimization of the data frame** based on the targeted application. The figure 7 shows the IEEE 802.15.4 data frame (maximum size of 127o).

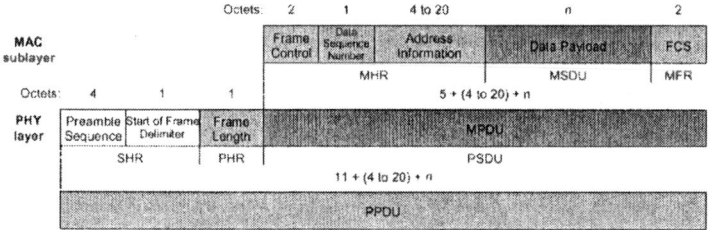

Figure 7 : Data frame format in IEEE 802.15.4

4. ZB, the best configurations for a HAN application

4.1 Positions of ROUTERS, COORD, ZED in the HAN

At the MAC layer, the IEEE 802.15.4 standard specifies two types of devices (FFD for Full Function Device and RFD for Reduced Function Device) and at the network layer three type of devices (COORDINATORS, ROUTERS, and Zig-BeeEndDevices) are defined by the ZigBee specifications. A Coordinator device is the same as a Router device except for its role in the network. Basically it is a Router that has acted as the leader in network formation. Each network has one Coordinator. A Router is able to forward packets and participate in the mesh network. A ZED can only send a receive packets intended for it. Ideally all powered devices should be Router devices allowing the device to be a node of the ad-hoc network. In a real case it should be appropriate to have ZEDs for battery powered devices anywhere in the network and the remote sensor nodes at the network edges (such as upper floors, corners, hidden parts, ceiling…) and relay through Router devices placed in several central positions in-house. As long as there are a reasonable number of Router devices distributed around the building in powered applications like load controllers and lights, ZEDs can be anywhere in the network. For "thin" networks it is better to have then near the edges.

4.2 The Smart-House case

The figure 8 presents the illustration of a large house equipped with a high number of sensors allowing several applications based on those. This smart house is equipped with different type of sensors (temperature, heat alarms, gas, time controls, pressure, HVAC controls…) spread out all over the different floors, indoor and outdoor.

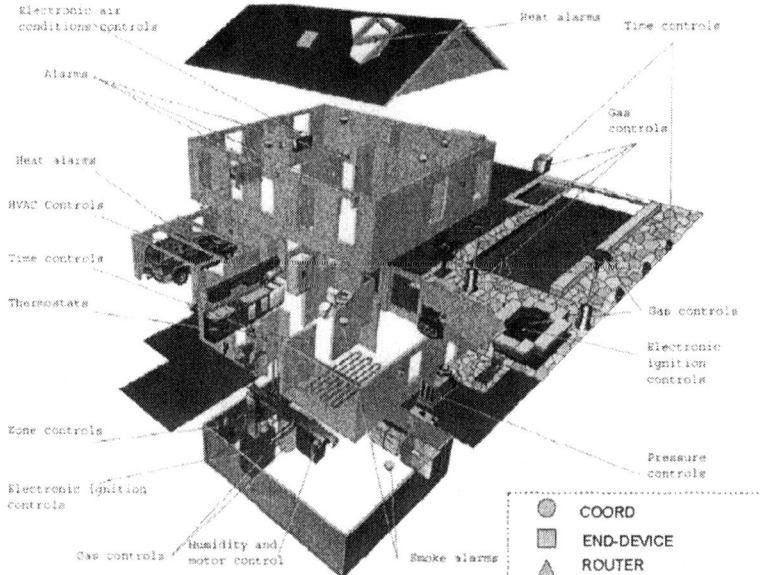

Figure 8: The ZB smart house

Based on the design of this smart house, each ZigBee device should be place at the best position, with the best functionalities to improve the all WSN and allow battery-friendly applications to retrieve the data from each sensor with a reliable wireless link. The figure 9 represents the same design of smart house with the frames of each floor allowing a better identification of the best position for each node.

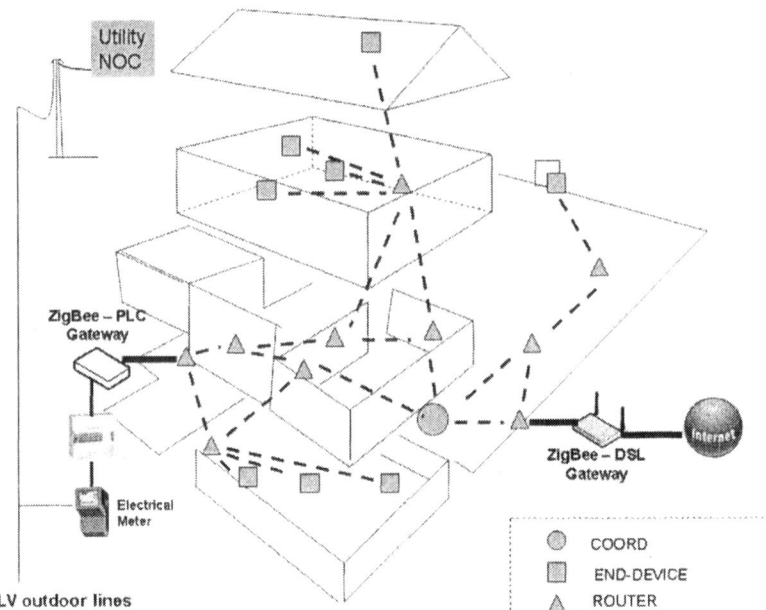

Figure 9: ZB Smart-House - Positions of the devices

Most of the remote nodes (high floors, far-end of the garden, basement, ceiling…) can be implemented as ZEDs allowing a better battery life and no routing functionalities. The ZEDs connect to a nearby Router in a star topology. Then the central nodes (mid-floors, central rooms…) should be implemented where possible as Routers to allow a mesh network relaying the data from the ZEDs to the end of the network. The different Router devices form a mesh topology where each node relay the data and update its routing table based on the IETF-certified protocol AODV. Finally, the Router devices are connected to one or several ROUT devices that are part of the gateways. In this example, two gateways are shown:

- **A ZigBee-to-DSL gateway.** This gateway allows the connexion of the WSN to Internet, therefore to the online applications to retrieve, monitor and control the sensors offsite.
- **A ZigBee-to-PLC gateway.** In this example, we consider that the electrical utility has implemented a PLC access network enabling the IP connexion from each house (each meter in each house) the backhaul of the utility and to the NOC (Network Operation Center).

4.3 Battery considerations

During the design and deployment of a WSN, the questions of battery are very important and should be addressed by using the best features from the wireless technology selected. The table 3 shows a comparison between two PAN (Personal Area Network) technologies in the IEEE 802.15 working group. The ZigBee standard has been designed to prevent the problem of heavy power cycle based on the best RF transmission modulation technique, the optimization of the SYN/ACK methods and the low data rate allowing the transmission of small PPDU.

Standard	Modulation	Max data rate	Sensitivity of the interface	Duty cycle
ZigBee	OQPSK with shaping	128Kbits/s	-90dBm / 40ppm xtal	Extremely low
Bluetooth	FSK	720Kbits/s	-85dBm / 20ppm xtal	Cycled power applications (handsets, cellphones...)

Table 3: Battery considerations with a comparison between ZigBee and BlueTooth

This considerations lead to think the positioning of each node in a smart house as for example:

- ZigBee ZED nodes: sensors with long-battery life, specific wake-up-on-beacon activation enable and long retransmission period (based on the needs of retransmitting the data of the sensors)
- ZigBee COOR/ROUTER nodes: central sensors (positioned centrally in the house) with mesh-routing enable and powered directly to the power-line of the house.
- ZigBee Gateways: positioned next to an external network connection (connecting the WSN to the outside world) such as a DSL/Cable/WiMAX Internet-box or next to the circuit breakers box. In a large network, it may be necessary to have more than one gateway. These should be distributed around the network.

5. A potential ideal platform for HAN

The different considerations developed here in this article lead to think the next-generation of WSN as a ZigBee large network coupled with different others protocols to allow a better radio transmission and a pervasive connectivity. The recent co-developments of ZigBee with different others network protocols imply in a close-future all-in-one gateways from ZigBee to others standard protocols for WSN or for Ethernet-based network.

5.1 Embedding ZigBee

The next generation of products based on ZigBee will help to build embedded ZigBee systems. These embedded systems will allow an easier design of a WSN with the possibility of using cheaper and standard OS (Operating System) with access to the ZigBee/802.15.4 stack. Lately the next generation of ZigBee products had been based on:

- New Soc (Systems on Chip)
- PCMCIA/USB pccards
- ZigBee female power plugs
- OEM ZigBee set-top-boxes

5.2 Gateways to the wired standard protocols

In the scope of the WSN protocols, the wired protocols are still seen as more reliable, stable and easy to connect to the standard networks media (Ethernet, FTP cable, coax, twisted pairs, powerline cables...). Therefore the ZigBee had been developing better interfaces between the ZigBee stack (and the 802.15.4 frames) and different others Home Automation protocols

Standards	Functionalities
ZigBee and BACNet	Building Automation and Control Networks based on the ISO-16484-5 with messages-based protocols. Classes of applications services for Home Automation and Object Access Services. Ethernet LAN options. "BACNet/IP"-like encapsulation of BACNet messages in 802.15.4 frames.
ZigBee and DALI	Digital Addressable Lighting Interface based on the IEC 62386 lighting control systems. Uses ballasts, transformers, actuators from multiple manufacturers in the one installation. Up to 64 DALI light sources. Cabling consists of a simple two wire cable
ZigBee and Lonworks	The LonWorks protocol can be implemented over ba-

	sically any medium, including <u>power line</u>, twisted pair, radio frequency (RF), infrared (IR), coaxial cable and fiber optics. Therefore a LonWorks encapsulated into a ZigBee network can be designed as well as a ZigBee large WSN including <u>LonWorks-to-ZB</u> sensor nodes.
ZigBee and HomePlug	HomePlug is from a market point of view the PLC worldwide standard allowing the design of Ethernet network over the electrical wiring of a building. Therefore ZigBee nodes can be connected to the wireless eco-system but also to PLC gateways allowing the 802.15.4 frames to be encapsulated into Ethernet frames (802.3). Finally this network then can be seen as a ZigBee network using a PLC backhaul.

Table 4: ZigBee to other gateways functionalities

5.3 Up-grading to the newer version

The different ZB nodes of the WSN are now based on different vendors SoC implementing the specifications from the ZigBee Alliance and from the IEEE 802.15.4 working group. These Soc are then based on the features from the ZB specifications such as remote commands at the MAC Layer. Therefore the ZB chip can be upgraded on-the-fly from a central point of the network without loosing the applications layer and the services on top of that. The next generation of WSN will allow a complete pervasive topology where from any IP network address, all nodes from the WSN will addressed and then flashable with the latest specifications and optimization.

6. Conclusion

The next generation of WSN will enjoy the coming features of standardized wireless protocols like ZigBee which seams to be seen as the "Wi-Fi of the sensors". ZigBee is a battery-friendly protocol, able to implement a mesh network for up-to 2000 nodes as seen in different industrial applications. Moreover the next ZigBee specifications are covering the interfaces with different other Home Automation protocols to design a complete WSN using wireless and wired interfaces. The last deployment using ZigBee had been proving reliability sufficient to be applied for sensitive applications by implementing the correct retransmission process, error correction algorithm and radio link quality estimation.

The next generation WSN can be seen as a hybrid network (wired/wireless, IP-to-ZigBee encapsulation, multiple gateways...) with different connexions to the outside world of IP, different levels of services, different ways of monitoring (push from the public network, get from the end-users, alarms-based messages sending, online HTTP interfaces...) where the IP networking is prolonged to the last nodes of the WSN.

References

[1] J.Y. Chen, X.P. Zhou, "ZigBee Wireless Communication Technology in Industrial Controls," Radio Engineering of China, Vol. 36, No. 6, pp. 61-64, 2006.

[2] G. Pekhteryev, Z. Sahinoglu☐P. Orlik, G. Bhatti, « Image transmission over IEEE 802.15.4 and ZigBee networks " Proceedings of ISCAS 2005. Japan: Kobe☐2005, pp. 3539-3542.

[3] W.Y. Zhang, L. Feng, Z.C. Wei, "Research on home networking with ZigBee," Journal of Hefei University of Technology(Natural Science), Vol. 28, No. 7, pp. 755-799, July 2005.

[4] P.G. Feng, L. Feng, Z.C. Wei, "An Application Model in Home Network Based on Zigbee," Journal of Henan University of Science & Techn

[5] R. Yang, T. Yang, "Wireless Sensor Network Based on ZigBee with Applications for Smart Building," Agricultural mechanization of China, Vol. 5, pp. 76-79, May 2005.

[6] P Baronti, P Pillai, Vince W.C. Chook, S Chessa, AGotta, Y. Fun Hu, Wireless sensor networks: A survey on the state of the art and the 802.15.4 and ZigBee standards, Computer Communications 30 (2007) 1655–1695

[7] I F Akyildiz, X Wang, W Wang, "Wireless mesh networks: a survey", Computer Networks 47 (2005) 445–487

Adding functionality to X10 networks with 802.15.4.
Using 802.15.4 to communicate and add functionality to X10 wired networks.

William Wallace, Jose I. Moreno, Ruben Hidalgo

Universidad Carlos III de Madrid, Dpto. Ing. Telemática
Avda. Universidad 30,
28911 Leganés, Madrid, Spain
{williamdaniel.wallace, joseignacio.moreno, ruben.hidalgo}@uc3m.es

Abstract. Although several newer technologies exist in the domotics market, one of the oldest remains extremely popular. Despite of its very limited functionality and performance, X10 is still a very common technology to manage simple Home Networks. Even if other wired solutions such as KNX/EIB or LonWorks out perform X10 in every single aspect, they might still be a bit of an overkill when addressing simple needs in a modest Home Network. However, X10 lacks support for wireless networks that could add a lot of functionality to its wired network. A good example would be how sensor networks could communicate with already existing X10 modules to allow full home automation in, for example, light and shutter control.

This paper will focus on the use of 802.15.4 to add functionality to simple X10 networks, in particular how 802.15.4 could allow the use of remote controls (or switches) acting over regular X10 modules, and how X10 switches can act over wireless modules using 802.15.4 as the transport layer. We will also see how 802.15.4 doesn't add complexity in the deployment and management of X10 Home Networks, which is one of the reasons such an old technology remains popular.

Keywords: 802.15.4, X10, Java, ZigBee, Domotics.

1   Introduction

X10 [1] is one of the oldest, yet still fairly popular, domotics technologies. Developed in 1975, it remains to date one of the references in home networking by using the Power Line as the Physical mean to communicate different modules. X10 has a very modest performance, close to just one command per second, and isn't reliable, this means there's no way to know if a command has reached destination or not. But still, X10 is a pretty cost effective solution and its functionality is enough for the modest needs of a small home: control over lights, shutters, alarms and even climate conditions.

However, X10 lacks a good wireless companion. There's no real standard for wireless communication using X10, and most solutions don't really offer a true

Please use the following format when citing this chapter:

Wallace, W., Moreno, J. I., Hidalgo, R., 2007, in IFIP International Federation for Information Processing, Volume 256, Home Networking, Al Agha, K., Carcelle, X., Pujolle, G., (Boston: Springer), pp. 255-265.

wireless network solution, but more the ability to act over wireless modules separately. Companies such as Insteon [2] do offer wireless compatibility, but still lack the strength of a real standard behind them. IEEE 802.15.4 [3] provides a cost effective, standard solution for this. 802.15.4 is a low cost, with extremely low power consumption and low data rate technology released in 2004, and has the strength of a standard defined by the IEEE organization. It's designed to work very well in sensor networks, which is an asset X10 lacks, because even if it is compatible with sensor networks, its limitations don't really allow it to manage complex sensor networks that could really improve the domotics service it provides [4]. Other technologies offer much better performance, or even lower cost, if deployed from scratch, but still many X10 networks already exist that could be greatly improved by using a simple and cost effective wireless solution.

2   X10 Overview

X10 is one of the oldest domotics technologies. Through the Power Line network, it allows the communication of up to 256 modules, divided in 16 Areas with 16 devices per Area. Therefore, a module's address is composed of an area code (ranging from A to P) and a device code (ranging from 1 to 16).

X10 isn't reliable, this means there's no way to know if a command has been correctly received or not. In order to avoid undesired effects (for example, a shutter going down when it shouldn't), each command is sent twice, and in case the copies don't match nothing is done. A command is divided in two parts before being sent. The first part addresses one to several modules and tells them to listen for the command to be sent afterwards. Then, the function these devices have to execute is sent. Since 3 cycles have to pass before the second part is sent, each is sent twice to avoid errors and 3 cycles have to go by before another command is sent, each command takes about 50 cycles.

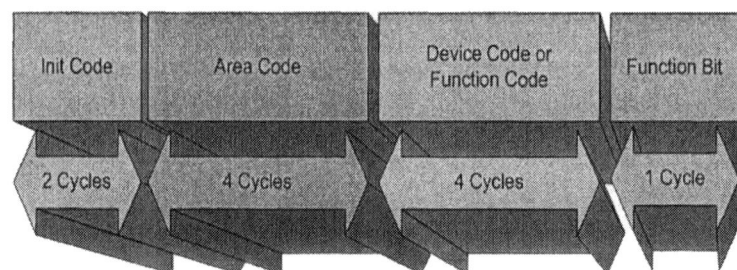

Fig. 1. X10 telegram structure

X10 has a very low performance by today's standards, since it sends "bits" of information on the zero crossing of the power line's AC signal. Since the AC signal's frequency in Europe is 50 Hz, and each simple command needs about 50 cycles, the performance is at best one command per second.

On the other hand, X10 is very inexpensive and simple, which is the rea-son many users still choose it as a solution for their home automation needs. In fact, X10 only supports up to 16 commands, of which 3 of them are extended commands (one for security, another one for sensor networks and advanced func-tionality and the last one is reserved for the manufacturer). However, only 13 commands are normally used:

- ON: Turns a device On.
- OFF: Turns a device Off.
- DIM: Dims a light or lowers the shutter by 5%.
- BRIGHT: Brightens a light or raises a shutter by 5%.
- ALL LIGHTS OFF: Turns off all light modules of an area code.
- ALL LIGHT ON: Turns on all light modules of an area code.
- ALL UNITS OFF: Turns off all units in an area code.
- STATUS ON.
- STATUS OFF.
- STATUS REQUEST.
- HAIL REQUEST.
- HAIL ACKNOWLEDGMENT.

3   IEEE 802.15.4 Overview

Released in 2004, the IEEE 802.15.4 standard defines a low cost, low data rate (up to 256Kbps) and very low power consumption communications technology. It's aimed at small devices, powered by batteries which should last up to several months or even years. Because of this, data communication must be brought to a minimum if batteries must last, so even if the data rate may be enough for the transmission of multimedia content, it's strongly recommended not to use 802.15.4 networks for this purpose, since the relatively high data rate is useful to bring the time the 802.15.4 antenna is powered to a minimum, thus greatly reducing power consumption.

802.15.4 allows up to 16 channels on the 2.4 GHz band, which is useful to avoid interference with widespread WiFi and Bluetooth / WiBree networks [5], which also use the same band to communicate.

Although 802.15.4 is specially useful in sensor networks, its application in other scenarios is also interesting. Take for example a 802.15.4 light switch, light switches are not activated extremely often, maybe just a dozen times a day or so. By using 802.15.4, a light switch may be placed wherever we want, at a very small cost (around 3 euros per 802.15.4 module, plus the cost of the switch itself). Compare this to the cost of placing a regular, power line connected, light switch. Its fairly obvious that by the use of this standard, not only new functionality may be achieved in domotics networks, but could also lower the cost of common home networking needs.

802.15.4 allows for two types of devices, Full Function Devices (FFDs), used as network coordinators and Bridges to other networks, and Reduced Function Devices (RFDs), that can only communicate with their assigned FFD. In a domotics environment, it is clear a star topology might be the best idea.

4   System Concept

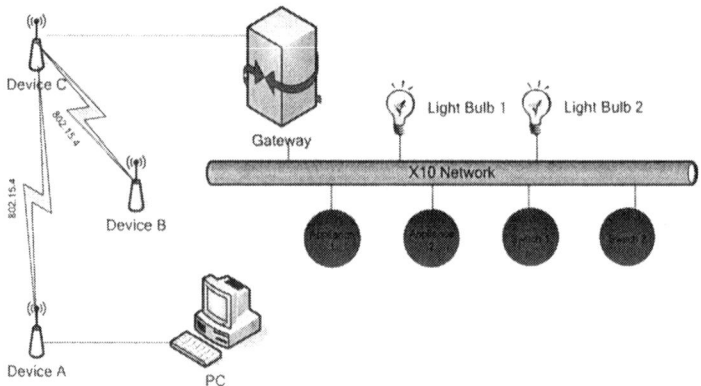

Fig. 2. Overview of the Network Structure

The network shown in figure 2 will allow us to illustrate how 802.15.4 devices may allow modules connected to them to communicate with X10 net-works as if they were directly plugged to them. In this scenario, Device B is equipped with four switches and four LED, and we will show how these switches can control X10 modules, and how the X10 Switches may act on the LED. Device C is the PAN coordinator, and acts as a bridge to the X10 wired network. Device A provides an 802.15.4 connection to the PC.

In order to implement this network, a simple X10 protocol has been developed to communicate wireless devices with the X10 wired network. This protocol allows modules connected to a 802.15.4 device to be treated as if they where directly connected to the Power Line, as well as allowing the PC to communicate with the Gateway as if it were directly connected to it, allowing network monitoring as well as device management.

5   A Simple X10 Protocol in 802.15.4

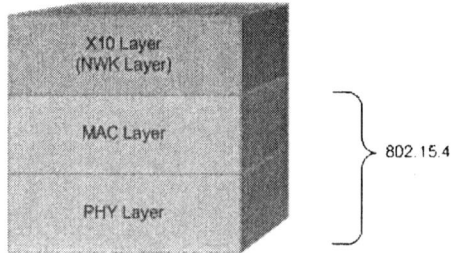

Fig. 3. Protocol Architecture in 802.15.4 X10 networks

The X10 protocol will be implemented directly over 802.15.4's MAC layer. This layer provides device discovery functionality, so all the upper X10 layer has to provide is the necessary logic in order to identify different modules connected to the same device. Since the protocol architecture is very simple, so will be the necessary software to be developed on 802.15.4 devices, and the data-grams to be sent are kept as small as possible in order to profit from 802.15.4 low power consumption.

Several protocols are set in place:

• Address assignment and device pairing protocol: it's used to add devices to the wireless network. The 802.15.4 device sends a message to its FFD asking it to assign an address to each of the modules connected to it. Modules connected to the device fall in one of two categories. First of all, they can need an address to be assigned to them in order to be able to receive commands from other X10 modules. Other modules might need to be paired to another device, such as light switches for example, and therefore need the PAN coordinator to tell them the address of the module they must send their commands to. A module type field is therefore included in the datagram in order to identify the type of module connected to the device. If the PAN coordinator isn't able to satisfy this request, it will forward this message to the corresponding X10 network coordinator.

• A CM11A [6] direct transport protocol. This is useful to establish a direct link between the PC and the Gateway (in our case, a CM11A module) in case they aren't directly connected through a RS-232 or USB link, but rather through the 802.15.4 network. In fact, in the chosen scenario, since the PC is connected through a RS-232 link to a 802.15.4 device, it will really "think" it is directly connected to the CM11A device.

• The X10 - 802.15.4 protocol. This protocol has the same functionality as the wired X10 protocol. For the sake of simplicity, and because the elements of the network we studied don't support extended commands, these are yet to be implemented.

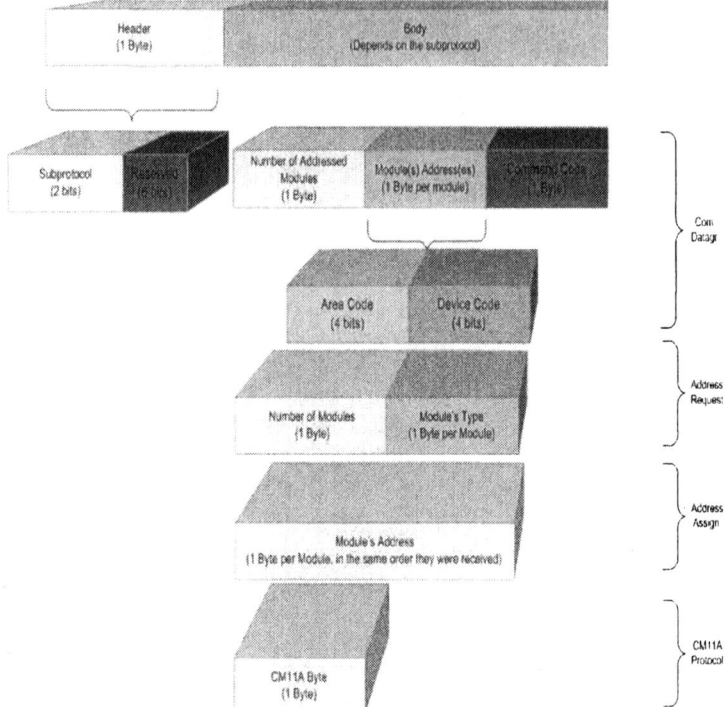

Fig. 4. Complete X10 - 802.15.4 Protocol

In this scenario, only two types of module will be used, however, by using a whole byte to identify the module's type we can differentiate up to 256 different types of modules, which should be more than enough in simple Home Networks. However, it's obvious that more bytes could be eventually used in case this was needed.

6   Management and Deployment of Hybrid Networks

As we've already said, this network structure is to be used only in scenarios with humble needs, in which control over shutters, lamps and simple appliances is enough. Deploying an X10 wired network is fairly easy, no software is needed to do this and plenty documentation is ready on the net that describes the process of running and installing regular X10 networks. In short, X10 modules usually come equipped with two dials. These dials are used to manually assign it an address (Area and Device Codes). This address is either the module's address, or its target's.

There are two options when adding 802.15.4 controlled modules to the domotic network. Either these modules can be "programmed" as regular X10 modules are, that is, their address (or destination address, in the case of switches for example) can be manually set, or they can use the protocol defined above. This protocol allows the dynamic pairing of different modules, but comes at a cost, you need a complex device (such as a PC) to manage the network.

To solve this issue, a set of software tools has been developed. A JAVA API allows the development of applications that need to communicate with the X10 network (wired and wireless devices alike). This software allows the control and monitoring of wired as well as hybrid networks alike, without adding too much complexity. Through the serial port, an 802.15.4 gateway device or a CM11A module may be connected, giving access to either the Hybrid or the wired network. The API allows the application to monitor X10 Commands as well as sending them, in order to act over a certain device (for example, turning off all lights in the living room). It also allows to create sets of devices that can be ad-dressed at the same time (for example, the lights in a room, or the shutters in an-other one).

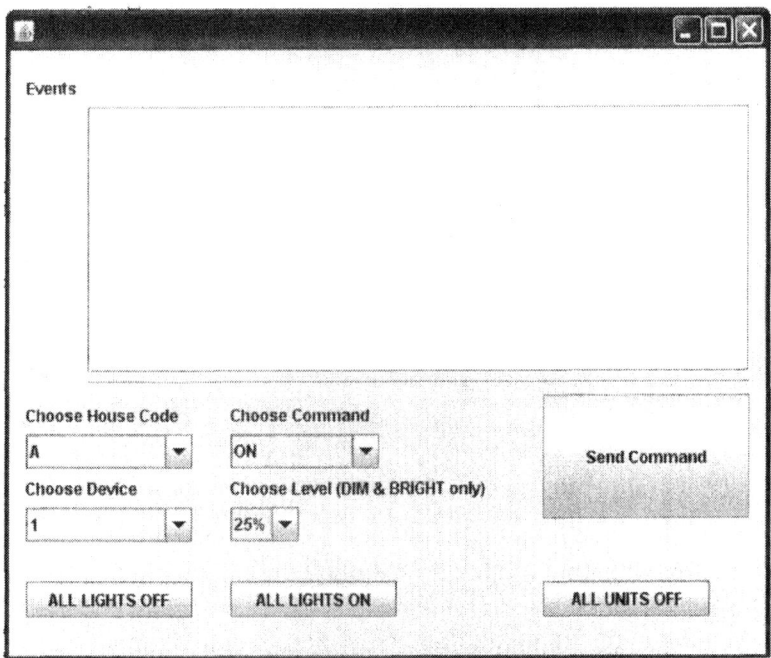

Fig. 5. Software interface to monitor and act over the devices of the X10 network.

The software also allows to assign addresses to different wireless modules that ask for one. This assignment may be done manually (by asking for direct input by the user), or automatically by using a database (in case the device lost power and needs to be reprogrammed, for example). This is specially useful in scenarios where some devices may act over different modules depending on the circumstances, such as, for example, a switch that could control shutters at day time, and lights at night.

The CM11A protocol over 802.15.4 allows the API to ignore if it's really directly connected to a CM11A gateway device or not, so except for the casual in-put request to pair devices or assign an address to a module, the management and monitoring of a

Hybrid network should appear to the user as almost equivalent to a regular wired X10 network. The CM11A protocol is not described in this docu-ment, although more information about may be found on the References section. Suffice to say, this protocol allows a computer, or any other device for that matter, to send commands to the X10 network as well as monitoring the commands other modules send through it. However, in some scenarios it might not be always pos-sible or desirable to physically connect the computer to the network, and using a wireless connection might be more useful, for example, if the user wishes to moni-tor and control the network from different or mobile devices such as PDAs, lap-tops, etcetera.

Finally, the JAVA API also allows remote devices to access the Hybrid network as if they were directly connected to it, through an Internet connection.

7   Application Scenario

The network is as shown in figure 2, where device B controls four switches and appliances (LEDs). In this section, we'll not cover how the wired X10 network is set in place, since it's very simple and widely explained in many documents over the Internet. We will, however, focus on how the Hybrid network is configured using an Application developed over the Java API described in the previous Section.

The following Hardware was used:

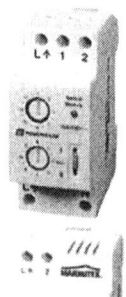

AD10D IN Switch by Marmitek [7]. Controlled by simple on and off commands. Two of these modules are used to control two LEDs. The modules are connected to the regular power line installation and are controlled by two switches.

LD11 DIM Dimmer by Marmitek. Allows the control of lighting devices, by turning them on, off, dimming or brightening them. Two switches control these two modules, which are connected to two light bulbs.

TMD4 Micro module by Marmitek. Converts up to four switches into X10 modules capable of transmitting on, off, dim and bright commands. Four switches are used in this network to control two light bulbs and two simple appliances (that just turn on or off).

Adding functionality to X10 networks with 802.15.4. Using 802.15.4 to
communicate and add functionality to X10 wired networks.

263

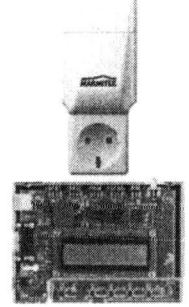

CM11A interface by **Marmitek**. Through a serial or USB port, this device allows the management and monitoring of X10 networks, as well as other advanced functions not covered in this paper.

1321XNSK-BDM by **Freescale [8]**. Allows 802.15.4 communications and has 4 LEDs, as well as four switches and an LCD panel. Programming of these devices was done using Metrowerks' CodeWarrior.

Therefore, the following network setup is used:

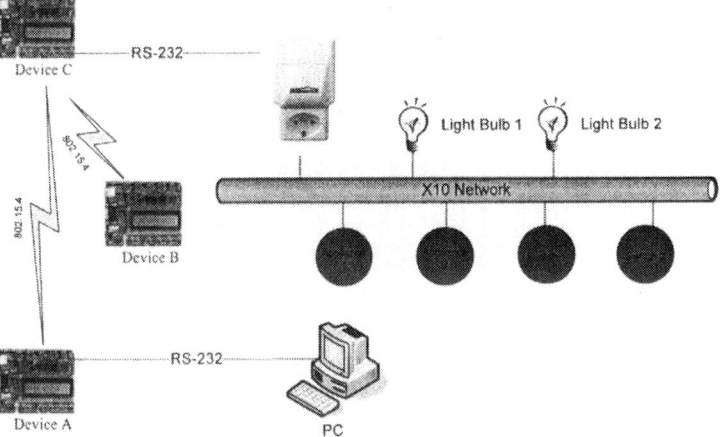

Fig. 6. Application Scenario network structure.

Device A allows the PC to communicate to the Hybrid network through a serial port. Device C allows the CM11A gateway module to communicate with 802.15.4 devices, and Device B will act as our only 802.15.4 device, which allows 4 switches and 4 leds to communicate with the rest of the network.

Once Device B is added to the Network, using the common 802.15.4 device discovery procedure, the following steps are taken:

1. Device B sends a Message requesting an address for each of the modules connected to it. The first four are announced as switches (so the received address will be the one of the module they should control) and the other four as simple appliances, which will only answer to ON, OFF and ALL UNITS OFF commands. Since the PAN coordinator isn't able to answer this request, it will forward the message to device A, which is connected to the network manager (the computer).

2. The PC - 802.15.4 gateway receives the message and asks the PC for in-put through the JAVA application.

3. The user inputs the information or the application automatically answers the request.
4. The PC - 802.15.4 gateway answers the request.
5. Device C receives the message and forwards it to Device B.
6. Device B stores the received data, modules are effectively paired.

The following Sequence Diagram sums up all of this process.

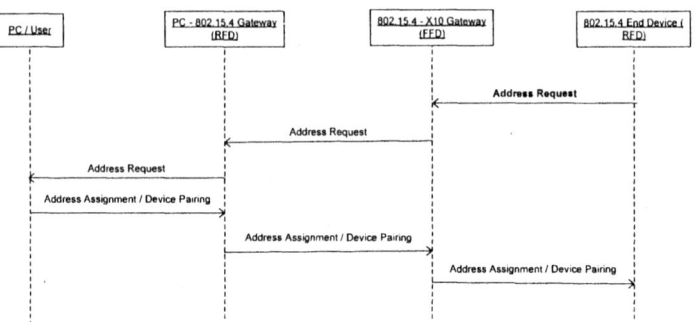

8   Conclusions and Future Work

As we've seen, adding functionality to X10 wired networks through 802.15.4 is very simple, yet extremely cheap, from an economic point of view as well as from a complexity point of view. Almost no complexity is added to the management and deployment of regular X10 networks, still, the ability to place a switch wherever we want, as well as controlling simple appliances not connected to the main power line (such as a turning on a sprinkler for example) at a very low cost proves that not only 802.15.4 is capable of bringing X10 networks to a whole new level, but that 802.15.4 or ZigBee's [9] Home Networking Profile could provide a perfect replacement for wired technologies such as this one at a very low cost.

Still, many X10 networks exist already, and many owners don't feel the need to upgrade them by throwing away there whole domotics installation. In those cases, the direct use of 802.15.4 may be a perfect solution to upgrade those old networks and still get a glimpse of what 802.15.4 can offer.

Future work will focus on bringing full sensor network functionality to these Hybrid Networks, by adding support for extended commands. Also, since security is a key concern, specially in wireless networks where physical access is very hard to forbid, data encryption is a must [10]. The next logical step will be to bring the same encryption tools ZigBee uses to Hybrid networks. This will probably increase power consumption and cost, but will provide the necessary security a domotics environment must have.

Because of the extremely limited functionality of X10 networks, which allow a small amount of modules very limited in functionality, large or even medium size

Adding functionality to X10 networks with 802.15.4. Using 802.15.4 to communicate and add functionality to X10 wired networks.

265

projects (such as a big house, for example) can't profit from such a low cost solution. In that case, other technologies such as KNX/EIB [11] or ZigBee are more suited. Future work will also focus on hybrid KNX/EIB ZigBee networks, since KNX/EIB RF doesn't allow data encryption and ZigBee's Home Networking Profile would be a perfect substitute for it.

Acknowledgments. This work was partly funded by Spanish Minister of Education (MEC) under CASERTEL-NGN project (TSI2005-07306-C02-02) and Madrid National Research Program e-Magerit (S-0505/TIC/000251).

References

1. X10 protocol description: ftp://ftp.x10.com/pub/manuals/xtcode.pdf.
2. Insteon's website: http://www.insteon.net/
3. 802.15.4 Standard Definition:
   http://standards.ieee.org/getieee802/download/802.15.4-2006.pdf
4. Ed Callaway, "Home Networking with IEEE 802.15.4: A developing standard for low rate wireless personal area networks", Aug 2002, IEEE Communications magazine.
5. Khaled Shuaib, Maryam Alnuami, Mohamed Boulmalf, Imad Jawhar, Farag Sallabi and Abderrahmane Lakas, "Performance Evaluation of IEEE 802.15.4: Experimental and Simulation Results", Journal of Communications, Vol. 2, No. 4, June 2007.
6. CM11A protocol description:
   http://mywebpages.comcast.net/ncherry/common/protocol.html
7. Marmitek's website: http://www.marmitek.com/
8. Freescale's web site: http://freescale.com/
9. ZigBee Alliance's web site: http://www.zigbee.org
10. Naveen Sastry, David Wagner, "Security Considerations for IEEE 802.15.4 Networks", University of California, Berkeley.
11. Konnex Association web site: http://www.knx.org/
12. Workgroup's site: http://panal.it.uc3m.es/zigbee/

IPv6 and Homenetworking

Tayeb Ben Meriem
European IPv6 Task Force Steering Committee member
tayeb.benmeriem@orange-ftgroup.com

Introduction

This submission focuses on highlighting the main benefits that IPv6 could bring to home networking services, based on wired and wireless architectures. Particularly wireless sensor networks (WSN) from the European IPv6 Task Force Steering Committee 's standpoint.

This work has been carried out within the "Applications" topic. The main objective being to identify the trends, for decision makers, from a business and technical perspective, as well as the role of applications, as an enabler in the acceleration of IPv6 deployment.

The chosen approach was to focus on a few relevant applications (Multi-play, home networking, M2M/RFID, Communicating Object Networks, Sensor Networks, Social Networks based on Web2.0, Emergency & Crisis, Transportation, Push applications).

These applications should be coupled to the access networks (Fixed & Mobile: xDSL, Cable, FTTH, ETTX, WIMAX, 3G, HSPA, DVB-H/T/S/SH,..). These applications are projected to be the potential "goldmine" of revenue growth in the coming years for ISPs and associated partners in the access value chain (content providers, vendors, software providers, handsets manufactures, home electronic devices manufacturers ..) [Euv6TF].

From a broadband penetration perspective, at least 6 European countries are ranked on the top 10 list. This suggests that Europe is ideally positioned to take advantage of applications & services deployment using IPv6. This is a significant outcome from the "eEurope 2005"[eEurope2005] initiative, with over 180 M€ invested in IPv6 projects during the last 6 years.

The European Commission's "i-2010" initiative [i-2010] is more focusing on concrete objectives hence, it is the foundational "next step" for IPv6 deployment and associated market development.

Therefore, we believe that Broadband access services and IPv6 technology presents a unique opportunity for all the value chain actors in fixed and mobile access networks, for developing the home applications market.

Please use the following format when citing this chapter:

Meriem, T. B., 2007, in IFIP International Federation for Information Processing, Volume 256, Home Networking, Al Agha, K., Carcelle, X., Pujolle, G., (Boston: Springer), pp. 267-273.

Within the European IPv6 Task Force Steering Committee work plan, the question related to Home network is a key topic.. It is for this reason, a study surveying the Home networking ecosystem from technical, industry, business and standardisation perspective has been carried out. [EUv6TF]

For the latter item, since 2004, the IPv6 Steering Committee has been working alongside the major fora addressing the issue of Home networking. Liaisons with CENELEC [CENELEC], SmartHouse Forum, HGI [HGI] , DLNA [DLNA], North American IPv6 Task Force [NAv6TF] and the IPv6 promotion Council China [IPv6China] were established.

Home IP services integrate Voice over IP or more generally Triple plays, on line gaming or remote controlling for instance. Since an ISP has to be able to provide a wide area of services to its customer, it has to think about the right solution for such networks. Indeed, the current solutions based on IPv4 protocol suffer limitations:

One of the requirements of IP home networks is to facilitate the installation and the configuration of devices.

The first step is to configure the device with an IP address. IPv4 protocols do not provide any stateless configuration service that permits a device to establish an external connection.

The following are the main technical challenges we identified that should be overcome in order to develop an attractive home network.

- How to allow users to connect and communicate regardless of device type, manufacturer, or network technology?
- How to do name resolution in the absence of DNS?
- How to auto-configure services?
- How to bridge between different network technologies (e.g. Bluetooth, 802.11b,)?
- How feasible is it to implement IPsec?
- How to implement QoS?
- Multicast?
- Multi-homing?
- Transition & Interoperability?

Therefore, it appears that IPv6 can fill in the gap!

How can IPv6 bring to Homenetworking: IPv6 Feature Set

IPv6 provides features that allow the set up of networks very easily and integrates characteristics that ease the deployment of value added services such as multicast or mobility.

Moreover, the security of communications and integrity of data in the home network, as well as authentication and confidentiality will be improved with the new version of IP protocol, thanks to the integration of IPsec within the protocol.

The auto-configuration of all home devices (plug & play manner) is also one of major features of IPv6. It is this auto-configuration that places the Internet within everyone's reach: "I hook up my terminal; it obtains an IP address automatically and is immediately operational" (no configuration needed).

IPv6's ability to introduce new services on a larger scale and at less cost through the simple integration of new features, without the need for additional equipment is another advantage it has over IPv4. The capacity for multi-homing (a client can be hooked up to several ISPs) through the IETF SHIM6 protocol (Site Multihoming by IPv6 Intermediation) [Shim6] provides a more efficient method of multihoming than what's available with IPv4.

From a user perspective, the Home should not be seen as an isolated area, but it should be included in its entire social and business environment. That means the home should be extended to the car, to the office, to the airport, to the train, as in real life.

Thus, this user case can be studied from a convergence perspective. Technically speaking, we need to implement IPv6 mobile protocols allowing host mobility (MIPv6) as well as network mobility (Nemo)along with the target operators network architecture NGN/IMSv6-based (New Generation Network/Internet Multimedia Subsystem)[NGN][IMS]. Indeed, this NGN access network will be directly connected to the home networks and the associated huge number of devices.

The IMS control plane SIPv6-oriented [SIP] will be at the heart of this architecture. From a services perspective, the application plane based on so called "Applications servers" or (SA) will open up new opportunities of development of advanced applications that the home market should be the main beneficiary.

The home networking cost model is another main challenge for user acceptance. It is linked to CAPEX & OPEX (the installation cost and operation/management cost). This cost can be reduced or overcome by eliminating cumbersome wired architecture. Thus, IPv6-based wireless sensor networks architectures will be progressively introduced in the home, reducing the CAPEX consequently. Moreover, the connectivity of the Home to Internet will allow the user to remotely manage its home services and reducing significantly the associated OPEX. .

Therefore, such cost effective solutions will open up new opportunities for the home networking market.

Consequently the effort is focusing on the wireless sensor home network. Indeed, they will raise new issues pertaining to IPv6 implementation from a sensor nodes constraints and routing perspective

Home sensors devices and sensor nodes at large, are constrained devices in terms of energy and CPU and the main challenge is how to port these constrained communication sensors to IPv6. Some platforms used by the academic world have been recently developed, with first commercial products made available (Archrock,…) .

Regarding routing angle, WSNs nodes in most cases have limited or no mobility whereas ad hoc network nodes are mostly mobile; therefore, ad hoc routing protocols [MANET] such as AODV: Ad-hoc On Demand Vector Routing, DSDV: Destination Sequenced Distance Vector, DSR: Dynamic Source Routing, OLSR: Optimized Link State Routing… are not adapted to the WSNs.

This is why; new protocols must be designed for this purpose.

In this context, IETF working Groups are actively working on these topics such as Manemo [Manemo], (IEEE 802.15.4,…).

How to move to IPv6?

According to the recent IANA's forecast [ ], IPv4 address blocks will be unavailable from 2012. We will all have to deal with the consequences.

So, the question for the Internet Community is no longer – "should we move to IPv6?" but rather, " how do we prepare for IPv6, ?" and we must start now !

Two key points lead to this situation.

1. The management of IPv4 addresses blocks in one hand and
2. The huge development and popularization of Internet services

The initial rules of IPv4 address attribution were established without proper controls.

Efficient measures were put into place during the 1990s:
- Decentralised management structures
- Management rules with economy of use in mind
- New address networking techniques (CIDR "Classless Inter-Domain Routing", NAT, etc.).

These measures only apply to new requests. Consequently, they do not place most of the spaces attributed before 1994, into jeopardy. This was the year that the regional registers appeared.

IPv6's coming of age, offers the opportunity to once again place all the players on an equal footing. The management of IPv6 address blocks is also based on the five national registers that manage the IPv4 address blocks (RIPE for Europe, APNIC for Asia/Pacific, ARIN for the United States and Northern America, LACNIC for Latina America and Caribbean, and AFRINIC for Africa).

For this reason, the question of IPv6 should be seen at a global level.

From a business standpoint, this large addressing capability will allow the development of flexible solutions to the mass markets such as Domestic devices, general public electronics, etc. as well as those of ADSL access networks, third generation mobile networks, communicating transportation (planes, trains, buses and cars), smart objects (sensor networks, Machine to Machine, etc.), audio or video-type interpersonal services (PtoP), aeronautics and military communications.

Conclusion

The current situation of the Internet can be described by two separate worlds, the "actual Internet", IPv4 based and its slow migration to IPv6, in one hand, and the "Internet of things" or M2M or communicating objects not IP based, on the other

Therefore, the challenge for the coming years is how to bridge these two worlds in order to include the huge number of devices and sensor networks in the global Internet.

IPv6 can be an appropriate instrument to help the development of this market in which home networking cases are the main driver.

References:

[Euv6TF]: http://www.ec.ipv6tf.org/PublicDocuments/Press_Release_IPv6TF.pd

[eEurope2005]: http://europa.eu.int/information_society/eeurope/news_library/documents/eeurope2005/eeurope2005_en.pdf

[i-2010]: ec.europa.eu/i2010

[CENELEC]: http://www.cenelec.org/Cenelec/CENELEC+in+action/News+Centre/Press+releases/Smart+House+IPv6+PR.htm

HGI]: www.homegatewayinitiative.org

[DLNA]: http://www.dlna.org

[NAv6TF]: www.nav6tf.org

[IPv6China]:: ww.conference.cn/ipv6/2007/Overview.asp

[Shim6]: www.ietf.org/html.charters/shim6-charter.html

[NEMO]: Ref: RFC 3963 - Network Mobility (NEMO) Basic Support Protocol

[NGN]: ITU-T WTSA-04

[IMS]: ETSI IMS TISPAN

[SIP]: http://www.freebit.com/english/index.html)

[Archrock]: www.archrock.com

[MANET]:www.ietf.org/html.charters/manet-charter.html

[Manemo]: draft-culler-rl2n-routing-reqs-01, draft-brandt-rl2n-home-routing-reqs-01),

[IANA]: www.iana.org

Hand-around on Seamless Services and Mobility in Home Networking

Pei-Yuan Qiu[1], Min-Shu Hung[1], Jen-yi Pan[1], Kuo-Pao Fan[2], and Jui-Wen Chen[2]

[1]Department of Communications Engineering National Chung Cheng University of Taiwan

dimhdp10@ant.comm.ccu.edu.tw

hungenter@hotmail.com

jypan@comm.ccu.edu.tw

[2]Industrial Technology Research Institute of Taiwan

{kpfan, RyanChen}@itri.org.tw

Abstract. In the age of technology, most of the network services originally run on large scale and base on complicated systems. When they're brought into our home, the migration could derive further technical problems due to the change of scale and cost. Home networking structure is often improvised and built up with several types of wireless technology, such as WiMedia and WiFi, inside several small rooms. In addition, people enjoy walking around at home and being served without constraints and service interruption, so the seamless services and mobility within home are a must. This paper describes a novel notion on the transition among wireless connectivities at home which is named Hand-around and efficiently provides seamless network services while moving in heterogeneous and improvised home networking. A developing technique in Mobile IPv6, called multiple care-of addresses (MCoA) registration, is the best candidate to accomplish such seamless services in an all-IP home network. Besides, it's a pure layer-3 mechanism and hence could more easily apply on and adapt to home services without massively changing the operational flow and system hierarchy, especially suited for services of multimedia, communication and entertainment. This notion also gives a new vision to some scenarios described in Home Gateway Initiative (HGI) document.

Keywords: Home networking, Home gateway, Seamless service, Mobile home service, Multiple care-of address registration, Heterogeneous networks.

Please use the following format when citing this chapter:

Qiu, P.-Y., Hung, M.-S., Pan, J.-Y., Fan, K.-P., Chen, J.-W., 2007, in IFIP International Federation for Information Processing, Volume 256, Home Networking, Al Agha, K., Carcelle, X., Pujolle, G., (Boston: Springer), pp. 275-294.

1. Introduction and Background

Nowadays, the performance of personal computers has been improved day by day, and the broadband network has also been introduced into home environments. These advancements have created a new type of service, which is inside a house serving just few people, rather than most internet applications that connect to a respectable number of users. It is important to bring the convenience and comfort of these applications right into home, after a day of working, and can even create new services like media center, and home IP-PBX, which provides an IP-based telephone system. That's what we called digital life is. This kind of service usually relies on many devices working simultaneously, including embedded systems and personal computers. These devices can be divided into three categories: the devices providing broadband, the devices providing the connectivity between devices, and the devices working for services in home networking. Figure 1 illustrates the location of digital devices inside a house. These devices are serving in their corresponding places. For example, there are televisions in the living room and parents' room. According to their requirements and characteristics, the devices have various kinds of connectiveties, like wireless headphones using Bluetooth [1], and laptops using Wi-Fi [2]. Hence, inside the house there may have diverse wireless connectivities, such as Wi-Fi, Bluetooth, ZigBee [3], IrDA [4], wireless USB [5], WiMedia [6], and so on. They may be deployed casually and without comprehensively planned so their coverage could be heavily overlapping. We've got convenience by using these wireless services, but uncertainties exist when it comes to mobility, especially on handoff issues.

Fig. 1. Home [7]

2. Home Networking Services with Mobility

Following subsections list some services that might have mobility concerns in HGI [7].

2.1 Communication

Voice over IP (VoIP) [8] is the main communication application. Many VoIP end-user device products have Wi-Fi or other wireless connectivity, and a laptop could be a VoIP client device, too. By carrying one of these devices, users could walk through doors from room to room while talking on VoIP. So, mobility is now a necessary part of communication at home.

2.2 Fix Mobile Convergence

Fix mobile convergence is based on the premise that the device has multiple network interfaces. For example, an unlicensed mobile access (UMA) [9] phone may have both GSM and Wi-Fi radio module. Also there are 3G/Wi-Fi scenarios that can switch to VoIP in home to reduce some expense. To seamlessly switch from one network to another without cutting off a living session needs a hand-off mechanism carried with mobility.

2.3 Entertainment & Information

2.3.1 Multimedia

Multimedia enjoyments are common entertainment in modern lives, especially at home, people expect to get some relax by listening to music, watching videos, or many other multimedia clips. Watching multimedia clips without lags when users roam around at home can be a relaxation after a whole day's working, and it can be achieved by carrying a playing device with multimedia contents stored inside. But when the contents or multimedia streams are on the Internet or simply in a home media center which cannot be easily carried about, the media continuity is certainly a different story especially when the users move around from a wireless coverage to another.

2.3.2   Gaming

Gaming is an industry growing explosively; it's about gaming type, platform, contents, multi-sense presentation, and also how players make control commands. Cordless game controllers have become burning to the touch instead of wired controllers. If the control commands can be transmitted via network to the game console with mobility and seamless design, the "gaming everywhere at anytime" dream, i.e. pervasive gaming [10], can be accomplished.

2.3.3   IPTV

IPTV [11] is a real-time delivery that broadcasts quality TV over IP. IPTV is also a kind of multimedia application. But with stricter quality definition and other extensions, such as encryption, multi-stream capability and IP-core design, bringing IPTV into mobility and keeping the contents played seamlessly creates technically issues.

2.4 Home Management & Security

Some home management and security devices also have wireless connectivity. A universal remote control must have the ability to access home network at every position at home. Also, there may have monitoring cameras moving inside the house. For example, a camera attached to a vivacious baby could help adults keep a watch on her. And of course the video content must be seamless.

3. Discussion of Handoff and Mobility Scenario

Here we discuss a scenario about mobile IP in home networking.

Cell phones are now small but powerful. There's a trend that they're equipped with several network interfaces including 3G/GSM, Wi-Fi, Bluetooth, IrDA, even WiMAX in a near future. Although the original design of mobile communicating function uses only 3G/GSM, but with VoIP technology, using other interfaces is possible and already commercialized, such as UMA.

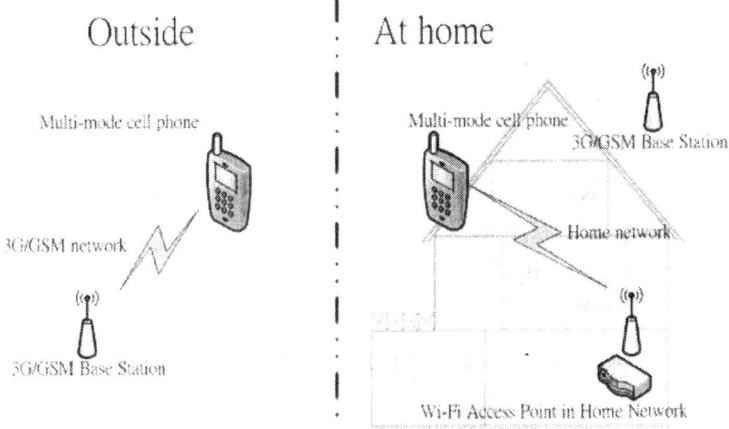

Fig. 2. Multi-mode Cell Phone

Fig. 2 shows the basic principle of the multi-mode cell phone. When in outdoors or somehow without other connectivity except 3G/GSM, a multi-mode cell phone works just like a single-mode one. However, when it's at home, it can establish several kinds of connections to the home network, and uses them to replace 3G/GSM on communicating purpose. The benefit is, when using non-3G/GSM network, the message flow goes through an IP-core network, communicating using VoIP. VoIP is considered cheaper than 3G/GSM, since the physical linkage is the home broadband instead of mobile networks. Also, when at home, that is, inside a modern building, the 3G/GSM signal quality may not be capable of communication, so switching to another network with stronger connectivity would be better. Nevertheless, signal quality is still an issue regardless of 3G/GSM. Because the wireless base stations (BS) or access points (AP) inside our home are usually deployed without projections, the multi-mode cell phone must have the ability to choose the right interface with better signal quality. Hence, handoff is still necessary even inside our home.

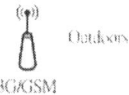

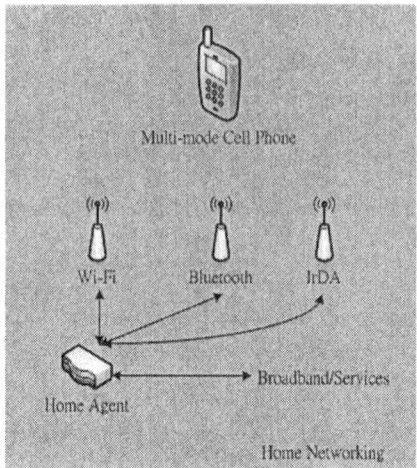

Fig. 3. Accessible Communicating Base Stations at Home

Fig. 3 illustrates the possible physical connections at home. Since signal quality may be altering when the multi-mode cell phone is moving, selection between these base stations would be necessary. Hence, a call session may maintained by switching from these connectivity. The handoff technology in 3G/GSM network has already come to maturity, but there's no widely acceptable handoff technology between these indoor connectivity based on IP-core network. Besides, the demand for communication quality is rigid when it comes to commercial services. Can VoIP handoff achieve seamless?

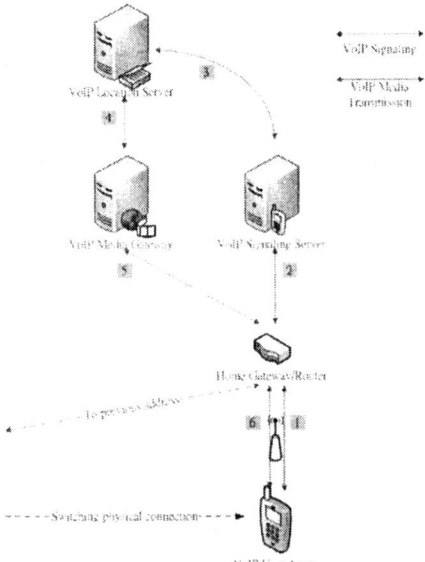

Fig. 4. VoIP Call Forwarding

A VoIP system must have call forwarding ability, and call forwarding can be a possible way to deal with handoffs between IP-core connections [12]. As illustrated in Fig. 4, a VoIP call forwarding action takes six procedures:

- Step 1 and step 2 : When switching connection, VoIP user agent informs the VoIP signaling server via the home gateway/router that the address of the VoIP user agent had been changed.
- Step 3 : Updating location information.
- Step 4 : Looking up new location.
- Step 5 and step 6 : The VoIP media gateway redirects the communication content again to reach the new address of the VoIP user agent.

However it's not a good solution at all. Since VoIP is based on application layer protocols, and the user agent informs the VoIP system after the active physical connection is changed, call forwarding would take a lot of time, and causes interruption in call sessions. That's not acceptable with commercialized telephone services.

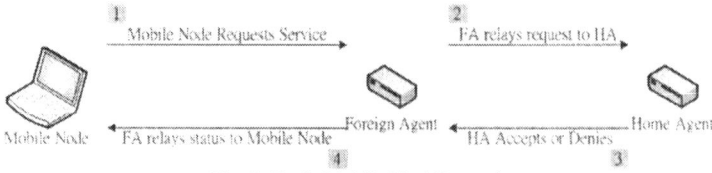

Fig. 5. Basic Mobile IPv4 Scenario

Fig. 5 is a basic scenario of mobile IPv4 (MIPv4). When a mobile node (MN) moves to a foreign network, it first send a request to the foreign agent, and then the foreign agent relays the request to the home agent of the mobile node. The home agent (HA) tells foreign agent (FA) whether the request is accepted or denied, and then the foreign agent relays the decision to the mobile node.

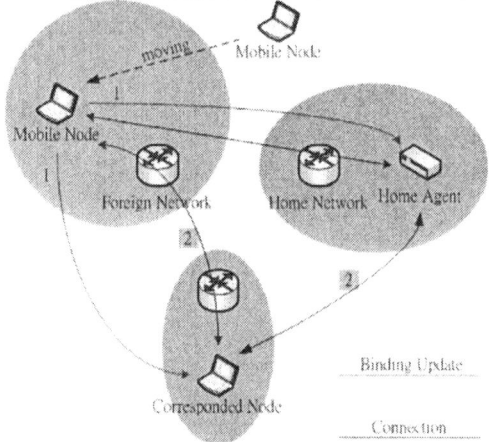

Fig. 6. Basic Mobile IPv6 Scenario

As shown in Fig. 6, the biggest difference between mobile IPv4 and mobile IPv6 (MIPv6) is that the MIPv6 does not require foreign agent because the router of the foreign network can assist the MN to form the care-of address, which is done by foreign agents in MIPv4. When a MN travels to a foreign network, it first gets a care-of address (CoA), and then the MN send binding update (BU) directly to the home agent and correspondent node (CN). So both HA and CN know the CoA of the MN. Thus, CN and MN may connect to each other with or without the tunneling by HA.

Mobile IP could be a solution. Since the connections are all based on IP-core network, the multi-mode cell phone must have an IP address. When handoff occurs, the VoIP user agent may still need to follow these procedures, but the home agent knows it. The home agent knows it right away when the VoIP user agent is taking a physical handoff changing the IP address, since mobile IP technology is a layer-3 method. So the home agent just simply tunnels the communicating media content to the new address regardless of the VoIP call forwarding. There's no longer need to wait for the VoIP system passively accepting requests from VoIP user agents and then taking VoIP switching procedures. Even if the VoIP system does no forwarding procedures, as long as the home agent handles the tunneling, the call session can be maintained. This method could avoid the interruption during call forwarding by VoIP system and satisfy users' expectation on voice quality.

We can learn from this VoIP scenario that by switching to another connection, applications could be effected and need to be recovered. Mobile IP is a layer-3 solution, which could be better than other solutions of upper-layers in the aspect of application independence, i.e. suiting any application without modification. A mobile IP environment is usually composed with good schemes and constructions. With wide coverage and low overlapping, the capitalized cost, the frequency of handoff, the signaling effect, all could be reduced. However, in home networking environment, wireless coverage is usually highly overlapped and with uncertainty due to the house-building structures. So handoffs could occur frequently, and uncertainties exist on when and how to do vertical handoffs, and how to determine the best foreign network since several kinds of foreign networks may be detected. These are the differences between traditional mobile IP and home mobile IP environment. Also, the handoff latency should be considered. As shown in Fig. 5 and Fig. 6, a handoff action consists of several steps, and the latency cannot be ignored. Now we address a notion named hand-around to cope with these concerns.

4. Hand-around

In this section, we will start from the motivation and definition of hand-around. Then we will discuss some issues and possible challenges in hand-around. At last, we will compare several techniques of connectivity transition and illustrate that Multiple Care-of Addresses registration (MCoA), which was produced by the IETF working group "Mobile Nodes and Multiple Interfaces in IPv6" (Monami6) [13], should be the most proper layer 3 mechanism for connectivity transition in heterogeneous wireless home networks with highly overlapped coverage per our simulation.

4.1 Motivation and definition

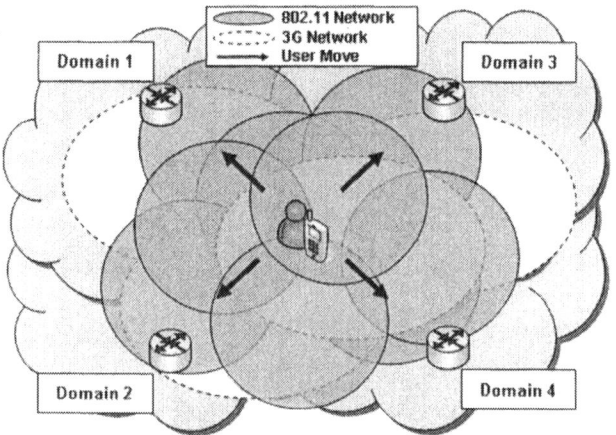

Fig. 7. Heterogeneous wireless networks with highly overlapped coverage [14]

Considering the scenario in Fig. 7, MN has multiple interfaces. The MN locates in wireless networks with heterogeneous layer 2 technologies and several IP domains. We observe that in this dense overlapping network the MN always has at least one interface staying connected while other interfaces' associations transit from one access point (or base station) to another, and thus keeps continuous online with hardly any disconnection caused by weak signals or connectivity transition. In this situation handoff latency nearly disappears according to the usual definition (i.e., the period between the last moment before disconnection and the next successful data transmission). We name this process of connectivity transition where at least one interface keeps working and hence the MN keeps continuous online without interruption caused by other interfaces' transition, as hand-around. Here are some observations and features about hand-around:

1. More than one IP domains probably overlap.

2. Base stations locate in high density, and wireless coverage areas are highly overlapped.

3. Users can transmit data through one or more interfaces concurrently.

In fact, many research projects and operators continuously develop related seamless integration technology of these networks with high degree of heterogeneity and highly overlapped coverage. For example in Ambient network [15, 16], users can have the best choice when the network condition varies in difference places, time, and even network loading. As fore-mentioned, the UMA is also a good example of such seamless integration technology. Hand-around already affects our daily life, and traditional assumption about handoffs should be reviewed. Some points of view in such environment will be discussed in the next subsection.

4.2 Discussion

We discuss several points about hand-around as follows.

- Construction and Decision: Formerly wireless network construction proceeds from using minimum number of base stations for maximum coverage, but it should be changed in heterogeneous wireless networks with highly overlap coverage, e.g., houses and hotels. Heavy-load sharing, seamless services or better transmission quality could be the primary consideration. Just maintaining access to Internet is not the only purpose in user's point of view. Issues like how to choose a suitable wireless network by user preference or enhance transmission efficiency by multi-interface are more important during hand-around.

- Handoff Target and Timing: We propose a new viewpoint of connectivity transition, called hand-around, which is different from traditional handoff. Hand-around doesn't specify a target access point or base station to attach to but a set of simultaneous access points or base stations during connectivity transition because of concurrent activations of multiple interfaces and dense overlap of heterogeneous wireless serving areas. Hand-around also doesn't identify specific timing and location of connectivity transition, but traditional handoffs do. In hand-around, the MN with the support of multiple interfaces, which activate at the same time and have at least one connected to base station or access point, can keep continuous transmission regardless of some interfaces proceeding transition from one access point or base station to another, and therefore the handoff latency doesn't need to be concerned anymore. Furthermore, users can enjoy a higher quality and seamless service if the connectivity may transit without the handoff latency.

- Handoff Latency and Link Stability: As far as we know, most MNs only use one network interface. In dense wireless environment, MNs may continuously receive wireless signals, but there must be distinguishable handoff latency without any technical enhancement. Meanwhile, because of the lack of the condition from the next wireless network that MNs will handoff to, the stability of next connectivity is unpredictable and then the quality of ongoing service may deteriorate. Soft handoff is one solution to eliminate handoff latency and possible instability if we use multi-interface techniques such as MCoA, or Simultaneous Mobility Binding (SB-MIP) [17] which means that MN may use simultaneous mobility binding with more than one network devices to avoid packet loss and discontinuity during the moving process. In addition, the MN can collect the quality information of the next network it might handoff to from the alternative interface, and then determine which access point or base station has better signal quality and whether the MN can obtain a better wireless link than current one after handoff [18, 19].

• Bandwidth Exhaustion: Considering handoff latency above, SB-MIP and MCoA seem to be the probable solution. If we use SB-MIP, MNs will concurrently use both interfaces for a long time and exhaust redundant bandwidths under high density network environment. As to MCoA, only one transmission path is in use during overlapped area. MNs can choose the proper BS more flexible and dramatically decrease bandwidth exhaustion.

• CoA Binding Trails:

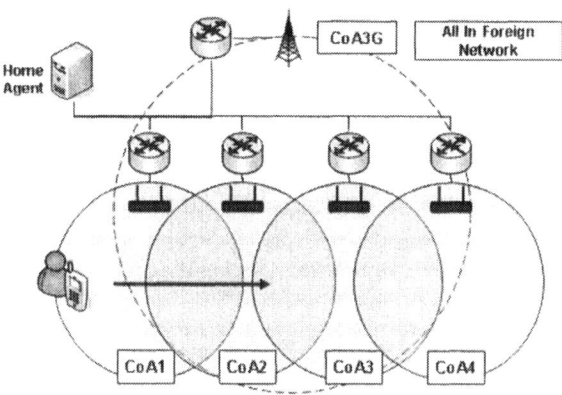

Fig. 8. Linking Map [14]

In Figure Fig. 8, suppose all networks are in different IP domains. MNs probably have an IP variation like CoA1->CoA2->CoA3->CoA4 or CoA1->CoA3G->CoA4 during the moving process. It makes no difference in SB-MIP due to simply IP address recording but distinguished by MCoA with layer 2 devices binding unique identification number (BID) which is an identification number to distinguish MN's multiple registrations that CoA3G binds an interface with distinct bandwidth. By this kind of linking characteristics, MN may choose CoA1->CoA3G->CoA4 IP variation for bandwidth conservation with more handoffs, or directly link to CoA3G to lower handoff frequency, and handaround may help us to achieve that. However, the performance comparison of these two binding trails is out of this paper's scope and also an open problem.

Hand-around will inevitably be one procedure in the future wireless network on the trend of denser BS' distribution. MNs with multi-interface may eliminate handoff latency. MCoA and SB-MIP are two mechanisms of multi-interface management. Moreover, next the following subsection will show MCoA can save more bandwidth than SB-MIP under highly overlapped wireless network environment. We suggest that MCoA, with the ability of interface identification, should be the better one.

4.3 SIMULATION AND RESULTS

We simply analyze the handoff latency and bandwidth exhaustion about MCoA. We use NS2-2.28 plus MobiWan module to simulate MCoA procedure and use IEEE 802.11b configuration for wireless network connection.

In the part of MCoA module, we modify MobiWan and refer to [20] about the BU message configuration. Since the draft doesn't define any interface switching timing guideline, we initiate interface switching procedure in the meanwhile moving into the wireless overlapped area.

Table 1. Simulation parameters of handoff latency

Network Simulator	NS2-2.28+MobiWan
Simulation Environment Scope	600 x 50 (m2)
BS Radius	109 (m)
BS1 Position	0 (m)
BS2 Position	150 (m)
Scope Between BSs	150 (m)
Simulation Time	75 (s)
MN Start Position	0 (m)
MN Speed	2 (m/s)
Wireless MAC	802.11b
Interface Queue	DropTail
Transport Layer	TCP
Application Layer	FTP
Packet Data Size	1000(bytes)
RA Interval	30~70 (ms)

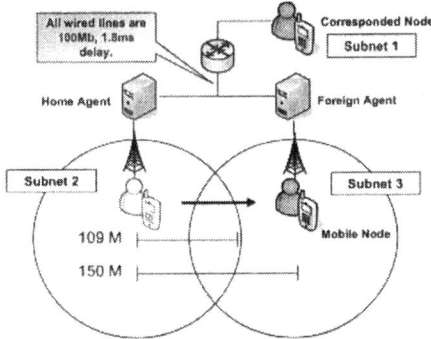

Fig. 9. Simulation scenario of handoff latency

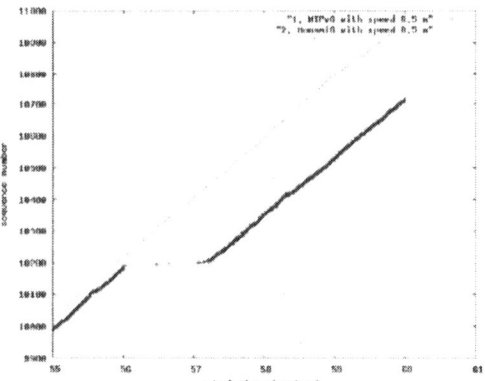

Fig. 10. Handoff Latency between MIPv6 and MCoA [14]

Table 1 and Fig. 9 are the arguments and environment for the Simulation scenario of handoff latency. In Fig. 10, MN processes a handoff procedure between two wireless overlapped BSs. We can figure out that MCoA has nearly no packet transmission delay resulted from the make-before-break handoff procedure. The MN with MIPv6 module has about 1.26s latency because MIPv6 detects and initiates handoff only when receiving routing advertisement from new V6 router or BU registration timeout. This handoff latency should add extra one second according to Duplicate Address Detection (DAD) [21] since MobiWan doesn't implement DAD operation. However, it makes no difference in MCoA benefited from soft handoff procedure. This means multi-interface mechanism really has better performance on handoff latency.

Table 2. Simulation parameters of bandwidth consumption

Network Simulator	NS2-2.28
Simulation Environment Scope	600 x 50 (m2)
BS Radius	109 (m)
BS1 Position	0 (m)
BS2 Position	200 (m)
Scope Between BSs	200 (m)
Simulation Time	40 (s)
MN Start Position	80 (m)
MN Speed	1 (m/s)
Wireless MAC	802.11b
Interface Queue	DropTail
Transport Layer	UDP
Application Layer	CBR
Packet Data Size	1500(bytes)
RA Interval	1 (s)

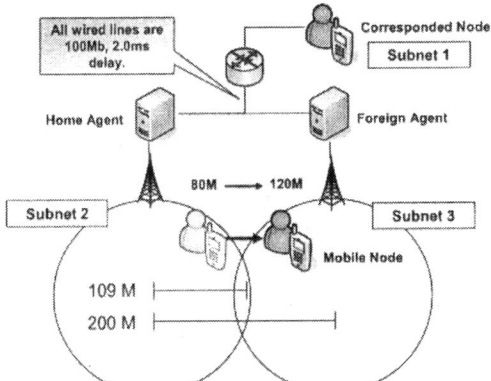

Fig. 11. Simulation scenario of bandwidth consumption

Table 2 and Fig. 11 are the parameters and environment for the Simulation scenario of bandwidth consumption. In Fig. 12, we compare bandwidth exhaustion between two BSs by measuring throughputs on MN. We modify the MIP module in NS2 for SB-MIP and duplicate the packets when moving into the overlapped area. The MN with SB-MIP module has twice bandwidth exhaustion of the original 1M/s constant bit rate (CBR) traffic at about 18 secs in the figure. The other MN with MCoA module has an unstable transmission bit rate during the handoff procedure but maintains a 1M/s bit rate most of the time. We conclude that SB-MIP exhausts more bandwidth in the overlapped area than MCoA.

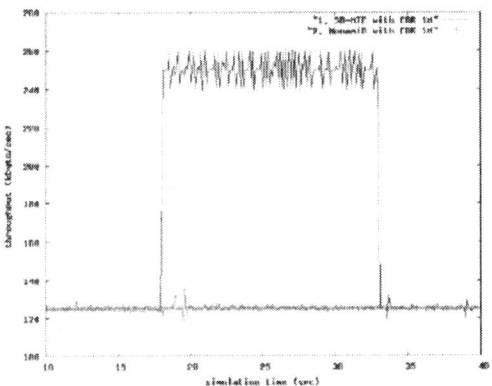

Fig. 12. Multi-interface bandwidth exhaustion between SB-MIP and MCoA[14]

Because MCoA has lower handoff latency than MIPv6 by using soft handoff method in our simulation and takes less bandwidth than SB-MIP in the overlapped area, we conclude that MCoA should be the most proper layer 3 mechanism for hand-around.

5. Hand-around in Home Networking

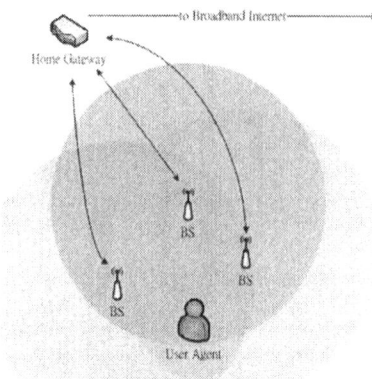

Fig. 13. Wireless Home Networking

Now we introduce multiple care-of address (MCoA) and hand-around notions to home networking. The home networking shown in Fig. 13 supports mobile IP with the two notions. By using MCoA, the mobile node can connect to foreign networks via base stations; and hand-around mobile IP techniques could handle the traffic tunneling. This design can achieve seamless handoff even if the application doesn't support. Moreover, home gateway is an important existence in home networking, and its standing is similar to home agent since they both play an administrative role. So we suggest that the home agent should be placed on the home gateway.

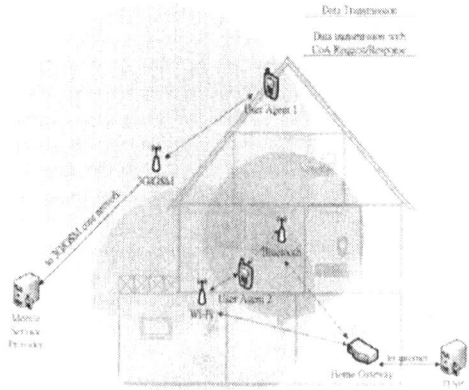

Fig. 14. UMA/Multi-mode Cell Phone Applications with MCoA

Fig. 14 shows two cases of using MCoA on UMA or multi-mode cell phones with Wi-Fi and Bluetooth capabilities. User agent 1 is not at home, or can't receive good wireless signals of home networking. So user agent 1 uses 3G/GSM network to establish or maintain call sessions. User agent 2, who has came back home in the house, receiving bad or even no signal from 3G/GSM base stations, uses internet and VoIP via Wi-Fi or Bluetooth with better signal quality to maintain the call session. In this case, User agent 2 can also switch between Wi-Fi and Bluetooth. User agent 2 is currently using Wi-Fi as shown in Fig. 14, but it also maintains a CoA with the Bluetooth network. And if the signal quality of Bluetooth becomes much better than Wi-Fi while moving, user agent 2 just simply switches to the CoA in the Bluetooth network instead of Wi-Fi. This kind of handoff, or what we called hand-around can achieve seamless. To the user who is talking on phone, the call session won't be disconnected or interrupted so the user don't even aware of handoffs; to the internet telephone service provider (ITSP) [22], the service protocols don't need to be substantially modified for mobility and seamless concerns, since these protocols are all based on IP, which is a layer-3 protocol and independent of the ITSP's protocols.

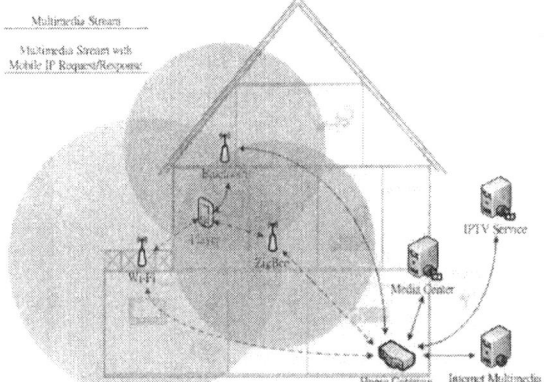

Fig. 15. Multimedia Applications with MCoA

Fig. 15 shows that multimedia services and applications can also be improved by MCoA and hand-around notions. Whether the multimedia clips and streams came from the internet or the media center at home, as long as the player carried by, or placed near the user, these media streams must go through the home gateway. On the other hand, since the home gateway could also be the home agent of mobile IP network, the media streams can be tunneled to the CoAs. We assume the media player with multiple connectivity uses Bluetooth to receive media streams in the beginning. When the signal of Bluetooth is turning too weak to maintain the media quality, the player should try another CoA that offers connectivity which could reach the quality and seamless requirements of multimedia. Thus, the user can enjoy the multimedia entertainment without breaking off and quality loss, even if the user is on the move in the house as long as wireless connectivity exists.

The multimedia service providers, such as the media center at home, IPTV, and other internet media sources, need no revision and redirection.

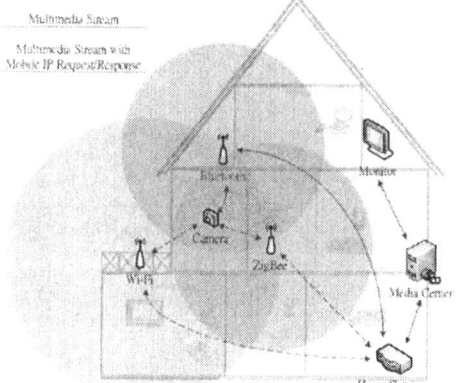

Fig. 16. Security Applications with MCoA

Fig. 16 shows a similar case comparing to Fig. 15, substituting the multimedia player to a camera. Just like we stated to the multimedia player in the last paragraph, the camera is enabled with mobility, so the changing of position won't affect the continuity of transmitting and recording. Furthermore, we can collocate with the multimedia playing applications, and create a security service by dynamic monitoring. For example, a baby can crawl all over the house to satisfy her curiosity, and may put herself in danger. Adults can attach the camera to the baby, and carry a multimedia player as the monitor. Wherever the baby goes, with available wireless connectivity, the adults can keep a watch on her every second even if the adults themselves are moving in the house. This is just an example. While putting MCoA and hand-around mobility notions into home networking, there must be further services and applications to invent, improving our lives from various aspects and dimensions.

6. Conclusions

Hand-around is a new paradigm of connectivity transition with heterogeneous networks and no handoff latency. It can manage multiple interfaces to accomplish seamless connections and mobility. Home networking has some characteristics matching the observations of hand-around, such as a small space crowded with wireless base stations, highly overlapped wireless coverage, and concurrent activation of multiple interfaces. So, to home networking, hand-around not only brings performance advancing but also provides support of seamless services and mobility. With hand-around, the picture of digital life will be more complete and convenient.

Acknowledgement

This work was supported partially by National Science Council of Republic of China under Grants NSC: 96-2219-E-194-008.

References

1. Bluetooth; http://www.bluetooth.com/ .
2. Wi-Fi; http://www.wi-fi.org/ .
3. ZigBee; http://www.zigbee.org/ .
4. IrDA; http://www.irda.org/ .
5. wireless USB; http://www.usb.org/developers/wusb/ .
6. WiMedia; http://www.wimedia.org/ .
7. Home Gateway Technical Requirements: Release 2; http://www.homegatewayinitiative.com .
8. VoIP; http://en.wikipedia.org/wiki/Voip .
9. UMA; http://www.umatoday.com/ .
10. pervasive gaming; http://en.wikipedia.org/wiki/Pervasive_game .
11. IPTV; http://www.itu.int/ITU-T/IPTV/ .
12. Elin Wedlund and Henning Schulzrinne, *Mobility support using SIP*, Pages: 76 – 82 (1999).
13. R. Wakikawa, T. Ernst, K. Nagami, *Multiple Care-of Addresses Registra-tion*, draft-ietf-monami6-multiplecoa-02.txt, March 5, 2007
14. Jing-Luen Lin and J.-Y. Pan,*Hand-around: A Handoff Evolution with Monami6*, (Wi-COM Shanghai 2007).
15. M. Johnsson, J. Sachs, T. Rinta-aho, and T. Jokikyyny, *Ambient Networks –A Frame-work for Multi-Access Control in Heterogeneous Networks*, IEEE 64th Vehicular Technology Conference, pp. 1-5 (2006).
16. N. Akhtar, M. A. Callejo, and J. A. Colas, *Ambient networks, an architecture for com-munication networks beyond 3G*, IEEE 61st Vehicular Technology   Conference, pp. 2974-2978 (2005).
17. C. Perkins, *IP Mobility Support for IPv4*, RFC 3344, Aug 2002.
18. T. Min, T. Lin, and K. Jianchu, *A seamless handoff approach of mobile IP based on dual-link*, Proceedings of the First International Conference on Wireless Internet, pp. 56-63 (2005).

19. R. Inayat, R. Aibara, and K. Nishimura, *A seamless handoff for dual-interfaced mobile devices in hybrid wireless access networks*, 18th International Conference on Advanced Information Networking and Applications, pp. 373-378 (2004).
20. M. Kuparinen, H. Mahkonen, and T. Kauppinen, *Multiple CoA Per-formance Analysis*, draft-kuparinen-monami6-mcoa-performance-00.txt, 2006.
21. T. Narten, E. Nordmark, and W. Simpson, *Neighbor Discovery for IP Version 6 (IPv6)*, RFC 2461, 1998.
22. ITSP; http://en.wikipedia.org/wiki/ITSP .

Dynamic Total Cost of Ownership Optimization for IPTV Service Provider

P. Goudarzi[*], M. Adeli[+], M.M. Azadfar[*] and F. Ayatollahi

[*] Multimedia Group, IT Faculty, Iran Telecom Research Center, Tehran-Iran
[+] Islamic Azad University of Dezful
Email: pgoudarzi@itrc.ac.ir

Please use the following format when citing this chapter:

Goudarzi, P., Adeli, M., Azadfar, M.M., Ayatollahi, F., 2007, in IFIP International Federation for Information Processing, Volume 256, Home Networking, Al Agha, K., Carcelle, X., Pujolle, G., (Boston: Springer), pp. 295-312.

1 Introduction

P. Goudarzi[*], M. Adeli[+], M.M. Azadfar[*] and F. Ayatollahi

[*] Multimedia Group, IT Faculty, Iran Telecom Research Center, Tehran-Iran

[+] Islamic Azad University of Dezful

Email: pgoudarzi@itrc.ac.ir

Abstract   *Total Cost of Ownership (TCO) for developing communication services comprises from two parts; CAPital EXpenditure (CAPEX) and OPerational EXpenditure (OPEX). These two types of costs are interrelated and affect any service provider's deployment strategy. In many traditional methods, selection of critical elements of a new service is performed in a heuristic manner aimed at reducing only the OPEX part of the TCO which is not necessarily optimal. In the current chapter, a brief review of the TCO for a communication service is proposed.*

Keywords— TCO, CAPEX, OPEX

Total cost of ownership (TCO) is a financial estimate designed to help consumers and enterprise managers assess direct and indirect costs commonly related to software or hardware. It is a form of full cost accounting. Middleware and other systems needed to provide video are also part of the total CAPEX. In a business case, CAPEX can be broken into fixed and variable parts; fixed being those costs to build the requisite system and infrastructure to deliver the services, and variable being those costs incurred with individual subscriber take rates. CPE and in home installation are considered variable costs, along with DSL line cards, since the CAPEX is incurred only when service is taken. Ideally, fixed CAPEX should be minimized since it is the "at risk" investment to enter into the business. Variable CAPEX, although directly related to actual service take rate and revenue, cannot be so excessive as to present a ROI (Rate of Investment) that it creates unacceptable ROI.

IPTV business cases as well as actual deployments have shown that the in home CPE and installation costs amount to 60% or more of the total installed cost for the IPTV system [1].

With CPE and in-home installation representing the largest portion of total installed cost, it is the area best targeted for cost reduction.

OPEX is composed of funds used by a company to acquire or upgrade physical assets such as property, industrial buildings or equipment.

This type of outlay is made by companies to maint-ain or increase the scope of their operation. These expenditures include everything from repairing a roof to building a brand new factory.

Video-on-Demand (VoD) is the next killer-app and a subset of the IPTV service. Initial trials have been well received by customers and network operators are deploying VoD to increase subscriber revenues and service profitability. VoD allows subscribers to request the programming of their choice, when they want where they want it. It is this flexibility that appeals to the broader customer base when compared with regularly scheduled network programming of broadcast video.

In most traditional methods, the only objective is to minimize the OPEX part of the TCO by selecting critical components of the service in a heuristic manner. But, this approach may not necessarily result in optimal solution for the service providers.

For example, in deploying the IPTV service in Iran, the service providers select the number of the required edge servers in order to minimize the OPEX part of the TCO [2].

Because of its static nature, this method doesn't consider the interrelations between OPEX and CAPEX which varies with time. For example, though choosing a specific initial number of edge servers may be optimal at the first stages of service deployment, this may not lead to an optimal solution for TCO minimization problem as time elapses.

Any solution for minimizing the TCO must take into the account the dynamic characteristics of the problem as time elapses.

In the current work, a mathematical approach is developed to minimize the

TCO. The proposed method tracks the dynamic changes in the number of subscribers and takes into the account the subscribers' geographical distributions and time.

2 IPTV service

P. Goudarzi[*], M. Adeli[+], M.M. Azadfar[*] and F. Ayatollahi

[*] Multimedia Group, IT Faculty, Iran Telecom Research Center, Tehran-Iran

[+] Islamic Azad University of Dezful

Email: pgoudarzi@itrc.ac.ir

Abstract *In the current chapter, an introduction about the basic components of an IPTV service scenario is developed. Then the various components delved in modeling of its TCO (including CAPEX and OPEX parts) are introduced.*

Keywords— TCO, IPTV, CAPEX, OPEX

Total cost of ownership modeling is a tool that systematically accounts for all costs related to an IT investment decision. TCO models were initially developed by Gartner Research Corporation in 1987 and are now widely accepted. Simply stated, TCO includes all costs, direct and indirect, incurred throughout the life cycle of an asset, including acquisition and procurement, operations and maintenance, and end-of-life management. TCO analysis originated with the Gartner group in 1987 and has since been developed in a number of different methodologies and software tools. A TCO assessment ideally offers a final statement reflecting not only the cost of purchase but all aspects in the further use and maintenance of the equipment, device, or system considered. This includes the costs of training support personnel and the users of the system, costs associated with failure or outage (planned and unplanned), diminished performance incidents (i.e. if users are kept waiting), costs of security breaches (in loss of reputation and recovery costs), costs of disaster preparedness and recovery, floor space, electricity, development expenses, testing infrastructure and expenses, quality assurance, boot image control, marginal incremental growth, decommissioning, e-waste handling, and more.

When incorporated in any financial benefit analysis TCO provides a cost basis for determining the economic value of that investment.

The TCO concept is widely used in the automobile industry. In this context, the TCO denotes the cost of owning a vehicle from the purchase, through its maintenance, and finally its sale as a used car. Comparative TCO studies between various models help consumers choose a car to fit their needs and budget. In [2] after extensive market research, an estimation about the CAPEX and OPEX of each IPTV component is derived from which we have developed a mathematical model for the TCO of IPTV service in Section III.

IPTV describes a system where a digital television service is delivered using the Internet Protocol over a network infrastructure, which may include delivery by a broadband connection [4].

For residential users, IPTV is often provided in conjunction with VoD and may be bundled with Internet services such as Web access and VoIP. The commercial bundling of IPTV, VoIP and Internet access is referred to as a Triple Play. Adding the mobile voice service leads to the Quadruple Play denomination.

IPTV is typically supplied by a broadband operator using a closed network infrastructure. This closed network approach is in competition with the delivery of TV content over the public Internet. This type of delivery is widely called TV over Internet or Internet Television.

In businesses, IPTV may be used to deliver television content over corporate LANs and business networks. Perhaps a simpler definition of IPTV would be television content that, instead of being delivered through traditional formats and cabling, is received by the viewer through the technologies used for computer networks.

Broadcast IPTV has two major architecture forms: free and fee based. This sector is growing rapidly and major television broadcasters worldwide are transmitting their broadcast signal over the Internet. IPTV channels require only an Internet connection and an Internet enabled device such as a personal computer, iPod, HDTV connected to a computer or even a 3G cell/mobile phone to watch the IPTV broadcasts.

A typical IPTV scenario is depicted in the Figure 1.

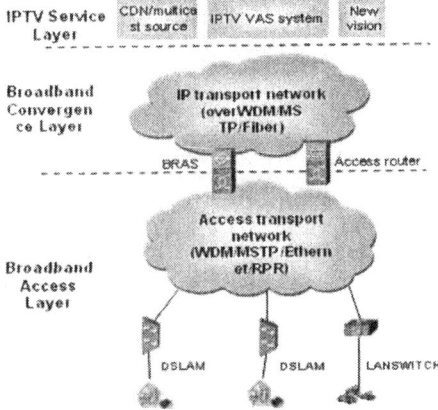

Figure 1. Typical IPTV service scenario

The basic components of IPTV service are, video streaming servers [5], edge streaming servers used for load balancing purposes, encoded content, transport and access QoS-enabled networks, BRAS (Broadband Remote Access Server), DSLAM (Digital Subscriber Line Access Multiplexer), STB (Set Top Box) and ADSL (Asymmetric DSL) modems.

Each IPTV component is associated with an incurred CAPEX and OPEX. Some components such as transport network are out of the service provider's control and impose only a long-term OPEX on the service provider's deployment strategy and some of the components such as content only consist of an initial CAPEX and don't impose any important OPEX on the service development.

In the following section, mathematical models for the CAPEX and OPEX of each IPTV component are developed and based on the proposed models; a dynamic solution for the TCO minimization problem is introduced.

3 Problem Formulation

P. Goudarzi[*], M. Adeli[+], M.M. Azadfar[*] and F. Ayatollahi

[*] Multimedia Group, IT Faculty, Iran Telecom Research Center, Tehran-Iran

[+] Islamic Azad University of Dezful

Email: pgoudarzi@itrc.ac.ir

Abstract   *In this chapter based on a project which was performed in the Iran Telecom Research Center, a mathematical model is introduced which can model the CAPEX and OPEX parts of the IPTV's TCO dynamically in terms of time and the number of service subscribers.*

Keywords— TCO, IPTV, CAPEX, OPEX

In order to minimize the TCO (CAPEX+OPEX) of an IPTV service, we have developed in a heuristic manner, the mathematical models associated with the CAPEX and OPEX of each component which is involved in the service.

DSLAM, STB, ADSL modem, Edge Server, Main server are among the devices which together build an IPTV solution. In this section, mathematical models for CAPEX and OPEX of these components are presented. To do so, we first make an estimation of the initial cost of each component individually based on the research accomplished in [2]. The initial cost of

STB, ADSL modem, DSLAM, BRAS, main server, edge server, content and infrastructure are denoted by x_{STB}, x_{MDM}, x_{DSLM}, x_{BRAS}, x_{MSRVR}, x_{ESRVR}, x_{CNT}, x_{INSTR} respectively.

Table 1 shows the initial cost of the devices normalized by the initial cost of ADSL modem.

Table 1. Initial cost of IPTV devices normalized by ADSL modem cost

DEVICE	COST	DEVICE	COST
x_{STB}	3.33	x_{MSRVR}	176
x_{MDM}	1	x_{ESRVR}	44.44
x_{DSLM}	128	x_{CNT}	11.11
x_{BRAS}	10	x_{INSTR}	100

It must be mentioned that the above normalized values in Table (1) are obtained from a survey on the prices of each IPTV component which was investigated about the Iran's IT market in [2].

In order to cover the dynamic nature of the mentioned components of the TCO, the mathematical models for CAPEX and OPEX are chosen to be functions of time t, number of subscribers n and number of edge servers m.

In the following equations, parameters beginning with 'C' represent CAPEX and those beginning with 'O' represent OPEX.

The CAPEX and OPEX are modeled as follows:

$$C_{STB}(n,t) = \left(x_{STB} + (y_{STB} - x_{STB})e^{-z_{STB}n} \right).$$
$$\left(2 - e^{-e_0 t} \right) \quad\quad (3.1)$$

$$O_{STB}(n,t) = x_{STB}\left(1 - e^{-e_1 n}\right)\left(1 - e^{-e_2 t}\right)$$

$$C_{MDM}(n,t) = \left(x_{MDM} + (y_{MDM} - x_{MDM})e^{-z_{MDM}n} \right)$$
$$\left(2 - e^{-e_0 t} \right) \quad\quad (3.2)$$
$$O_{MDM}(n,t) = x_{MDM}\left(1 - e^{-e_1 n}\right)\left(1 - e^{-e_2 t}\right)$$
$$C_{DSLM}(t) = x_{DSLM} \cdot \left(2 - e^{-e_0 t} \right)$$
$$O_{DSLM}(n,t) = x_{DSLM}\left(1 - e^{-e_1 n}\right)\left(1 - e^{-e_2 t}\right) \quad\quad (3.3)$$

$$C_{BRAS}(t) = x_{BRAS} \cdot \left(2 - e^{-e_0 t}\right) \qquad (3.4)$$

$$O_{BRAS}(n,t) = x_{BRAS}\left(1 - e^{-e_1 n}\right)\left(1 - e^{-e_2 t}\right)$$

$$C_{MSRVR}(t) = x_{MSRVR} \cdot \left(2 - e^{-e_0 t}\right)$$
$$O_{MSRVR}(n,t) = x_{MSRVR}\left(1 - e^{-e_2 t}\right) \qquad (3.5)$$

$$C_{ESRVR}(t) = x_{ESRVR} \cdot \left(2 - e^{-e_0 t}\right) \qquad (3.6)$$

$$O_{ESRVR}(n,t) = x_{ESRVR}\left(1 - e^{-e_1 n}\right)\left(1 - e^{-e_2 t}\right)$$

$$C_{CNT} = x_{CNT} \qquad (3.7)$$

$$O_{INSTR} = \left(x_{INSTR} + y_{INSTR}\, e^{-z_{INSTR} m}\right). \qquad (3.8)$$
$$\left(p_{INSTR} - q_{INSTR}\, e^{-s_{INSTR} n}\right).$$
$$\left(v_{INSTR} - w_{INSTR}\, e^{-u_{INSTR} t}\right)$$

Where we have [6]:

$$y_{STB} = 0.8 x_{STB};\ y_{MDM} = 0.8 x_{MDM};$$
$$y_{INSTR} = 0.11 y_{NSTR};\ e_1 = 3.22 \times 10^{-7};\ e_2 = 0.0053;$$
$$z_{STB} = z_{MDM} = 3 \times 10^{-6};$$
$$z_{INSTR} = 0.002231;\ u_{INSTR} = 0.00886;\ p_{INSTR} = q_{INSTR} = s_{INSTR} = 1;$$
$$v_{INSTR} = 1.1;\ w_{INSTR} = 0.1;$$

The value of e_0 and e_1 for each device is considered as $0.1x$.

As we see in the above equations, the CAPEX of each IPTV component is a decreasing function of the number of subscribers n and an increasing function of time t because it is assumed that the CAPEX can be reduced as the request (n) increases and can be increased for the sake of inflation as time (t) evolves.

The OPEX of each IPTV component is assumed initially to be null and can increase as time and number of subscribers increase.

From research adopted in [6], the OPEX associated with Infrastructure part of the network is assumed to be a decreasing function of m and an increasing function of both n and t.

Finally, TCO for an IPTV service is:

$$TCO(n,m,t) = n(C_{STB} + O_{STB}) + n(C_{MDM} + O_{MDM}) + \left\lceil \frac{n}{\theta} \right\rceil \cdot \tag{3.9}$$
$$(C_{DSLM} + O_{DSLM} + C_{BRAS} + O_{BRAS}) + C_{CNT} + 2$$
$$(C_{MSRVR} + O_{MSRVR}) + m(C_{ESRVR} + O_{ESRVR}) + O_{INSTR} + O_{INSTR}$$

Where, $\lceil x \rceil$ is the smallest integer number which is greater than or equal to x and θ is the number of DSLAM ports. In this paper we have assumed that $\theta = 128$.

In the current work, we have tried to track the changes which are imposed on the optimal TCO as time evolves by regulating the number of edge servers m as a function of time. By work presented in [6] it is resulted that the number of edge servers can be regarded as a major parameter affecting the TCO of the IPTV solution.

Thus, the objective is to choose the optimal value of m so that the TCO is minimized.

The so-called TCO minimization can be formulated as the following nonlinear programming problem [7]:

$$m^*(n,t) = \arg\min_{m \geq 0} TCO(n,m,t) \tag{3.10}$$

An appropriate numerical approach is used to solve the problem for the optimal m and this method leads to the time-varying minimized TCO[3].

4 Numerical results

P. Goudarzi[*], M. Adeli[+], M.M. Azadfar[*] and F. Ayatollahi

[*] Multimedia Group, IT Faculty, Iran Telecom Research Center, Tehran-Iran

[+] Islamic Azad University of Dezful

Email: pgoudarzi@itrc.ac.ir

Abstract   Tin the current chapter, based on a model which is similar to that which was proposed in [6] for IPTV service deployment in Iran, a numerical analysis is performed which can find dynamically the optimal number of edge servers in terms of the number of subscribers and time. Based on the results of this numerical analysis, the service provider can optimize the TCO of its service deployment dynamically.

Keywords— TCO, CAPEX, OPEX

We have used the scenario depicted in the Fig.2 which is similar to one adopted in [6] for deployment of the IPTV service in Iran. In order to minimize the total cost (TCO) of the IPTV service, the minimization was performed with respect to m (number of edge servers).

In other words, in equation 3.9, we have to determine the optimal value of m so that the total cost in this equation is minimized for a specific number of subscribers n and time t. Time means the number of years which have elapsed since IPTV service was first deployed ($t=0$).

In the scenario, it is assumed that the end-users are distributed uniformly in a circular geographical region and for each $\lceil n/\theta \rceil$ user there exist a BRAS and a DSLAM. Each edge server can be connected to at least one DSLAM for streaming more demanding contents.

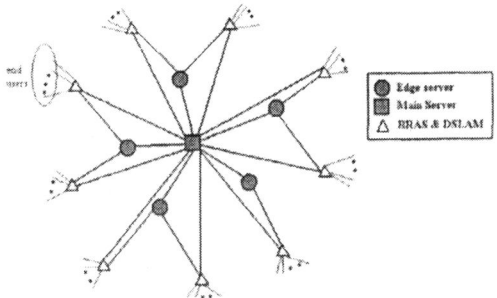

Figure 2. Sample IPTV service scenario

First, we supposed that the number of subscribers is constant and is equal to 5000 (n=5000). Then we calculated the m that minimizes the total cost at the first year of service deployment or t=0. The diagram of the total cost versus m for n=5000 and t=0 is shown in Fig.3.

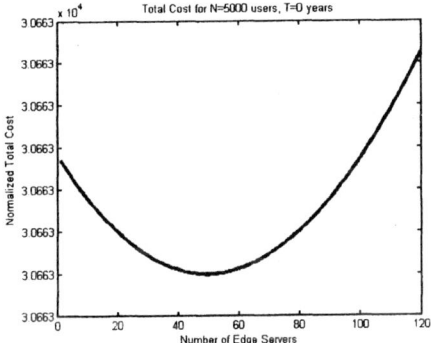

Figure 3. TCO for n=5,000 and t=0

As it is clear from Fig.3, total cost is minimum at m=49. To see the effect of time on the optimal m (the m which makes total cost minimum), we again calculated the optimal m for n=5000 subscribers and t=10 years. As the Fig.4 shows the optimal m is 53.

The Figs.5 and 6 show the diagrams of total cost for the cases (n=500000, t=0) and (n=500000, t=10). Optimal m in these cases is 1159 and 1163 respectively.

Figs.3-6 show that the value of m which minimizes the total cost of IPTV changes as either the number of subscribers or time changes.

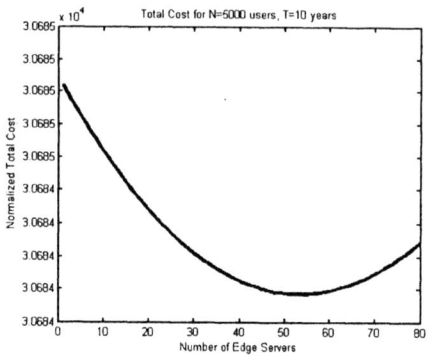

Figure 4. TCO for n=5,000 and t=10

Figure 5. TCO for n=500,000 and t=0

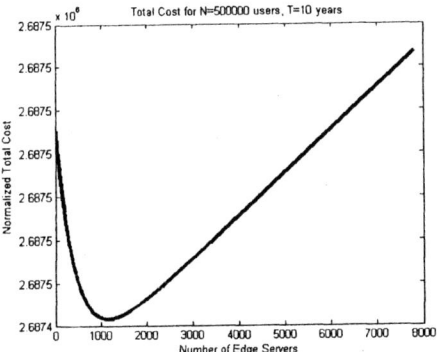

Figure 6. TCO for n=500,000 and t=10

To see the effect of time more clearly, we sketched the diagram of the total cost for n=500000 during the temporal period of t= [0 1 2 ... 20]. Fig.7 shows the result.

At last to see the changes of optimal m versus time and number of subscribers, we have calculated the optimal m for n= [5000 10000 15000 ... 1000000] subscribers and t= [0 1 2 ... 20] years. The result is shown in Fig.8.

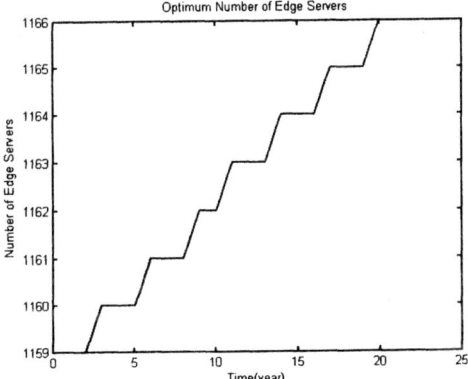

Figure 7. Optimal number of edge servers vs. time

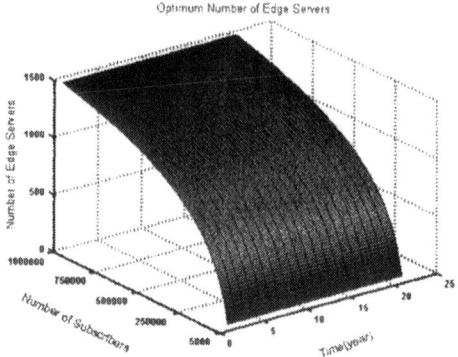

Figure 8. Optimal number of edge servers vs. time and number of subscribers

Fig.9 shows the variations occurring in the TCO of IPTV deployment with increasing time and number of subscribers.

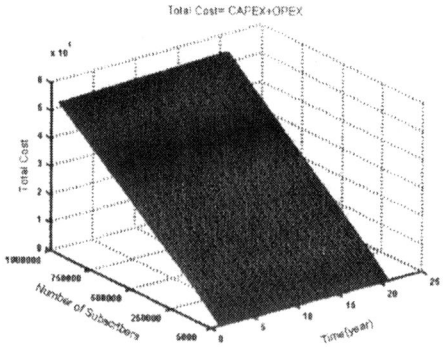

Figure 9. TCO vs. time and number of subscribers

5 Conclusion

Though IPTV and VOD services are very attractive to the end users, they are highly expensive and this has caused them to be developed with a very slow pace. Minimizing the TCO (CAPEX+ OPEX) of these services is a challenge to all IPTV and VOD service providers. In an IPTV scenario one of the major factors that determine the cost of the service is the number of edge servers. We used an algorithm to minimize the TCO using selection of an optimal number of edge servers in a typical IPTV scenario. This leads to the lowest cost of service deployment. The proposed algorithm has proved to be quite efficient and dynamic in minimizing the TCO of IPTV as the number of subscribers increases and time elapses.

6 References

1. Zhone technologies, *In-home triple play delivery*, white paper, USA, (2004).
2. Iran Telecom Research Center (ITRC), *Investigating the technical, regulatory and business requirements of ACS (Advanced Communication Services) deployment in Iran*, technical report, (2006).
3. D.G. Luenberger, *Linear and Nonlinear Programming*, 2nd Ed. Addison-Wesley Publishing Company, (1984).
4. ATIS IIF's *IPTV Architecture Requirements*, ATIS 0800002.
5. *Internet Streaming Media Alliance (ISMA)* Implementation Specification V.2 (2005).
6. Iran Telecom Research Center (ITRC), *Investigating the technical aspects of developing IPTV service in IRAN*, technical report, (2006).
7. D. P. Bertsekas, *Nonlinear Programming*: 2nd Edition. Athena Scientific, (1999).

Networked Appliances for Home Healthcare and Lifestyle Management

Paul Fergus, David Llewellyn-Jones, Madjid Merabti, Arshad Haroon

Networked Appliances Laboratory
School of Computing and Mathematical Sciences
Liverpool John Moores University,
Byrom Street, Liverpool L3 3AF, UK.
Email: {P.Fergus, D.Llewellyn-Jones, M.Merabti, Arshad Haroon}@ljmu.ac.uk;
A.Haroon@2006.ljmu.ac.uk

Abstract. Advances in technology and the increased use of home medical devices, will revolutionise the way public healthcare is administered. Homes and their associated networks in conjunction with such devices will take over many mundane healthcare tasks and manage new and enriched lifestyle choices that affect our overall quality of life. Through the combination of wireless and fixed networking infrastructures explicit links will form between the home and its devices and medical installations, such as hospitals. Through these interconnected networks new real-time healthcare management systems will emerge that continually provide information and react to adverse or unusual medical conditions received from occupants within the home. Achieving this will undoubtedly require a convergence between home networks and medical installations in order to harness the power afforded by both. We present a new approach using a working prototype to implement networked medical devices within the home capable of monitoring data received from an individual, which could then be accessed within the home and medical installations.

1. Introduction

Home networking has received considerable attention over the past decade with many research projects and blue chip organisations having tried to transform passive interaction within our homes to include interactive technology that helps attend to our every need. No longer is it acceptable to carefully configure home environments where such configurations restrict how and when we use technology. We have become more demanding, were we expect to use our technological solutions wherever we are. Moving from one room to the next, our preferences are expected to follow us, communications have to be ubiquitous, and multimedia access and control, as well as information services must be readily available. We are less

Please use the following format when citing this chapter:

Fergus, P., Llewellyn-Jones, D., Merabti, M., Haroon, A., 2007, in IFIP International Federation for Information Processing, Volume 256, Home Networking, Al Agha, K., Carcelle, X., Pujolle, G., (Boston: Springer), pp. 313-328.

tolerant towards the mundane interactions associated with home management. We want lights to automatically switch on as we enter a room and heating systems that self-adapt to environmental and physiological changes.

As such home environments have become superimposed with technology where intelligence is beginning to emerge to optimise the operation of such environments. This has made it possible to create complex configurations so that devices are networked and only operated given certain conditions. The health industry is beginning to ask questions about how such advances could be used to push secondary healthcare services into the patient's home. Many non-networked devices have been developed such as blood glucose meters, blood pressure monitors and heart monitors that can be used easily by patients within the home. Such solutions have prompted further investigation into whether providing such devices with networking capabilities could significantly reduce costs. Necessitated by the fact that such networked devices exist, the hope is that large overlay networks will emerge that provide ubiquitous healthcare and lifestyle monitoring services similar to that illustrated in Figure 1.

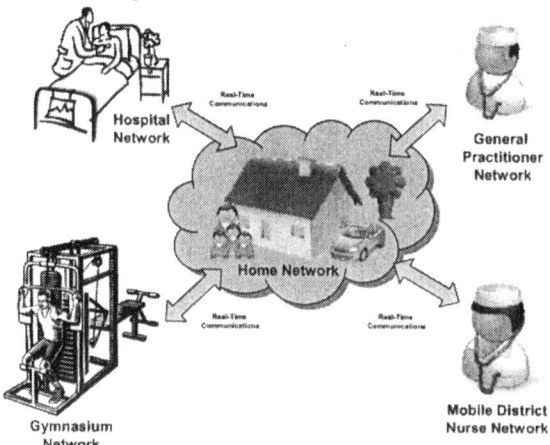

Fig. 1 Home, Healthcare, and Lifestyle Platform

Implementing such a solution could have many benefits. Perhaps it will help reduce unnecessary fatalities that could have been avoided if such technological solutions were available. In this sense networked medical devices will act to prevent adverse affects to home users by reacting to the detection of early symptoms. For example, many elderly people are not always aware that they are dehydrated. This can pose significant problems causing secondary conditions to develop, resulting in potential loss of life. For example, early detection could help reduce stress hormones called cortisol, which can suppress the production of white blood cells, which in turn may leave the patient susceptible to allergies. Here a very simple networked medical device could monitor hydration levels and prompt the person to take a drink. If the condition persists a healthcare practitioner could be notified via the home network.

Imagine an extension to this where lifestyle choices are carefully monitored and used to observe the short and long-term affects of such choices. On entering the gymnasium, medical devices automatically connect to the gymnasium network and begin collecting different biological and health related data, such as heart rate recovery information and the number of calories lost during a session. This could all be directly linked into personal profiles managed at your home, within your local hospital and by your general practitioner. Results from your recent gym sessions could determine what food you could have, with certain choices resulting in approval or a recommendation that alternative foods should be used. Tagging items with the use of sensor technology such as RFID make the implementation of such a system possible. The challenge is to overcome the many difficulties that currently exist within both the home networking and healthcare domains, such as interoperability and Food and Drug Administration (FDA) approval.

Addressing this challenge, we provide a platform that allows consumer devices and home medical devices to be more easily combined to meet the unique medical needs of the user and the environment. The proposed framework ensures users are not burdened with the details of this process; it simply happens unbeknown to them and without affecting their day-to-day home activities. For example, a user simply introduces new medical devices into the home and they automatically and wirelessly communicate and configure themselves with all other devices in the home without human intervention. We achieve this using a peer-to-peer network that consumes devices and the functions they provide, which themselves are abstracted as discoverable services. Using the peer-to-peer network these services can be automatically composed into any number of healthcare applications to administer healthcare solutions. In this way the integration and management of healthcare and lifestyle choices is achieved using these devices and services.

2. Background and Related Work

The home has been the focus of many research initiatives for several years and a great deal can be learnt from the existing work in this area.

More recently, industrial and academic efforts have given us many solutions resulting in the introduction of a wide spectrum of wired and wireless infrastructures and network protocols such as LonWorks, CEBus, SmartHouse, VHN, HomePHA, HomePnP, IEEE1394 (Firewire), X-10, IrDA, IEEE802.11b, IEEE802.15.4, Bluetooth and HyperLAN/2 [1]. However, despite the long list of advantages each provides, several challenges still remain to be addressed, most notably interoperability [2, 3] and the difficulties associated with the integration of combined functionalities, including the use of vocabularies to discover and describe devices and their operational capacity.

Lots of existing frameworks have been developed that aim to provide interoperability in the home environment such as the Digital Living Network Alliance

(DLNA) [4], the Open Services Gateway Initiative (OSGi) [5], Reconfigurable Ubiquitous Networked Embedded Systems (RUNES) [6], AMIDEN [7], and Universal Plug and Play [8]. None of these have specifically addressed the ad-hoc, functional capabilities that we believe will be of particular benefit in the medical domain.

Whilst many challenges still exist, enough advancement has been achieved within the home networking domain were the deployment of networked medical devices and services is now possible. Medical devices themselves will become increasingly network-enabled and support better capabilities. This will allow devices ranging from sensors to high-end multimedia appliances to form part of these networks, where the functions they provide can be pervasively distributed and used to create new and innovative home healthcare solutions. In support of this Lee *et al.* [9] make some interesting observations. They argue that realising such a complex integration will result in a ubiquitous heterogeneous overlay containing different protocols, different contexts, location and property independent device control, ad hoc device registration and updating, real-time data processing and alarm management, and high volumes of event traffic. Many of these issues have been the focus of much home networking research, consequently much can be learnt from these advances when integrated networked medical devices within the home.

Many have foreseen this gap in the market and are already building on the notion that the environment will become more finely augmented with information-bearing devices, such as sensors. For example, Stankovic *et al.* [10] believe that wireless sensor networks will play a big part in home healthcare provisioning. In what they refer to as in-home assistance and smart medical homes, this technology will help the aging population by providing memory enhancement; home appliance control; data collection; and emergency communication services. Wearable sensors will serve to collect data, which could be used by services and mined as a data source for next-generation clinical trials.

Sensor networking research is clearly a very active topic in both the home and medicine, with estimates already reaching $18 billion on BioMEMS research in 2005 as reported by Gupta *et al.* [11]. They argue that investment is significantly influenced by a drive to revolutionise healthcare to allow pervasive and continuous monitoring of real-time physiological conditions. There are many motivating factors for the use of biosensors. For example, sensors have already been designed for internal patient examination as is the case with SmartPill designed to monitor and transmit gastro-based information to a home computer. Furthermore, wireless sensors have been designed to collect routine data, such as Wireless ECGs, which would otherwise require trained medical practitioners. Using sensor technology to obtain biological data in this way is seen as a considerable cost saving to the medical organisation and at the same time an advanced means of processing and reacting to real-time data. Nonetheless, Gupta *et al.* report that implementation is plagued by many technical challenges. Specifically: heterogeneity between devices and sensors, interoperability between the numerous wireless protocols available, reliability, context, and real-time adaptation.

Despite the long list of challenges, we cannot ignore the potential benefits, and the fact that a new bread of networked medical device has great potential in moving from reactive to preventative medicine. Current practice means we tend to only visit a doctor when something has already gone wrong. Only at this point are technological advances used to diagnose – and if possible – rectify a problem. This is unacceptable given that many fatalities or serious illnesses could be prevented through early detection. For example, diabetes, if not treated, can result in the amputation of limbs. This could be addressed through the use of sensor technologies as discussed above using real-time pressure readings measured continuously and used to notify people that perhaps they need to put their feet up to avoid unnecessary risk to their health [12]. There are obviously many other preventative steps that could better utilise technology and significantly reduce health related risks. For example, Voss describes bandages that warn you when infection is detected, even identifying the bacterium and applying the appropriate antibiotic required to treat it.

This section has discussed two distinct research domains that are showing signs of convergence. Each approach in its own right provides benefits, but also suffers from drawbacks. The challenge is to capture the positive aspects from each to enable a new research strand allowing home networks to safely underpin the integration of networked home and medical devices.

3. Home Healthcare and Lifestyle Management Framework

As we have seen, many standards exist in home networking to provide a means of abstracting device functionality as services. Healthcare is beginning to turn to this domain in an attempt to capitalise on its benefits to offer home healthcare services. For example, Kin et al. have used OSGi as their deployment platform [13]. Coupled with the ability to create this abstraction, peer-to-peer technologies such as JXTA [14] have been used to provide a vehicle to dynamically disperse and discover healthcare services [15, 16]. Given the success of such approaches it is appropriate to build on these advances. Using networked appliances abstracted as peer-to-peer services we present an investigation detailing how medical devices can seamlessly interoperate within and across different networks.

The discussion describes how device operations are abstracted as services and deployed within the network, where interconnected medical devices are free to utilise these services. Given that all functionality is viewed as a collection of these services, compositions are automatically created based on shared characteristics. For example, a service (implemented on a device) that outputs multimedia streams may be composed with services that consume multimedia data. Given such compositions exist, mechanisms responsible for creating relationships can manage their execution allowing medical devices to self-adapt to unforeseen changes that occur within and between services and the environment. Combining these principles allows high-level applications to be automatically created through device and service interactions. This reduces the difficulties associated with combining medical devices making it easier for healthcare specialists and home users alike to simply use the devices without having to define how applications are created beforehand.

3.1 Approach Overview

The design goals provide the system requirements for a suitable scheme as described in this paper. The principle goals are as follows.

- Peer-to-Peer. Home and medical devices and services are published and utilised using peer-to-peer technologies.
- Abstraction. Device functionality is abstracted as services, which can be discovered and utilised by other devices or services within the network.
- Service Architecture. Devices have the ability to offer zero or more framework services. If a service is not hosted by the device then it discovers and uses the required service remotely within the network.
- Ad hoc Services. Home and medical devices offer and discover services without third-party intervention. Once devices are switched on they can offer their services without having to register them with a third-party registry.
- Semantic Descriptions. Services are described and discovered using semantic annotations. Semantic interoperability between different ways of describing services is achieved using an ontology (a shared understanding of some subject) [17].
- Automatic Device and Service Composition. Devices and services are automatically composed using semantic annotations and service capability models, i.e. devices that provide the same functionality may redundantly co-exist, and consequently it may be desirable to select devices that support the best configuration.
- Device and Service Management. Devices and services self-adapt and extend the functionality they provide beyond that which they were initially designed to do. Conflicts are detected and rectified as and when they occur.

The approach presented in this paper can be seen as an important step towards networked medical device research where the line of enquiry is likely to prove fruitful. The remainder of this paper explains how the principal goals have been incorporated within the framework and highlights the novelty of our approach.

3.2 Device Interoperation

The proposed scheme provides a middleware that operates between medical devices and services contained within different networks and the different applications created that use such devices and services. Figure 2 illustrates how all communication between compositions passes through the service integration framework and the technology adapters used to communicate with devices. Not all appliances are network-enabled. Consequently, technology adapters may be required to integrate legacy devices. Nonetheless, networked-enabled appliances may choose to bypass these adapters and interact with the framework directly.

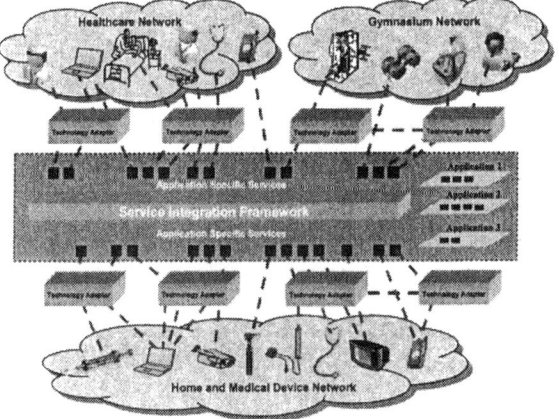

Fig. 2 Proposed Framework

As devices connect to the network they perform four tasks. First, they either publish the framework services they implement and/or discover and use framework services provided by other devices. Devices with varied capabilities must be accommodated. In this sense the framework needs to be flexible enough to allow devices to implement some, all, or none of the framework services. For example, a personal computer might implement the entire collection of framework services because it is capable of doing so, whereas a biofeedback sensor might not due to its limited capabilities. In the latter instance the sensor may discover and use framework services remotely (for example, services provided by a personal computer). Second, devices publish their operational capabilities (e.g. a blood pressure device may abstract the functionality it provides as services). Third, devices form relationships with each other and services within the network. This is not to be confused with step one which describes how a device implements framework services; this step relates to how devices are connected together. Fourth, devices self-adapt to connections between each other and services, as well as environmental changes.

Many home networking standards utilise message-based approaches to dynamically discover resources. Adopting a simplified viewpoint, discovery approaches such as the simple service discovery protocol [18], as used in UPnP, provide an oversimplified means of discovering content based on keyword matching. The problems associated with this approach are well documented, resulting in the use of semantics to try and address these limitations. Consequently, the approach taken in this paper extends message-oriented techniques to include the use of semantics to describe services and device capabilities.

The rules governing semantics differ significantly over keyword matching where logical constructs interconnect semantic elements. This does have problems of its own where heterogeneity exists between the ways concepts are defined. Given this limitation, semantic information does however provide a conceptual net in which a larger number of queries can be handled that would otherwise be missed. Whilst promoting the unconstrained use of different vocabularies, there is a need to provide semantic interoperability mechanisms to help resolve conflicts. Techniques used by the Semantic Web [19] and the Semantic Web Services communities can help to address this issue. We can therefore use unconstrained vocabularies in line with semantic interoperability mechanisms to help interconnect devices and services. In achieving this, the approach adopted by Paouluci et al [20], is extended to not only discover services, but also to help automatically compose services with little or no human intervention [21]. However, the precise nature of medical terminology means that particular care must be taken in this area to avoid inappropriate semantic matching.

Building on peer-to-peer technologies, the extension of such approaches to incorporate the use of semantics and self-adaptation enriches them to better enable devices to automatically interoperate. Using semantically annotated service advertisements devices can advertise the functionality they provide by publishing them within peer-to-peer networks. Depending on the technology, advertisements are likely to have a time-to-live value that expires after a given time period – consequently, advertisements have to be periodically re-published to keep the service alive. Devices may fail unexpectedly. In this case, service advertisements would no longer be re-published and would eventually be purged from the network. Early results suggest that our approach, based on these principles, helps improve medical device and service deployment as well as provide additional benefits that allow devices to self-adapt.

Devices can join the network as specialised or as simple networked medical devices. Specialised devices may have the ability to host services, store and evolve semantic information used to describe and discover services, as well as propagate service requests within the network. A simple networked appliance by definition may not have these capabilities. This type of device would typically join the network, propagate queries and invoke discovered services, or simply just be controlled. An example of such devices might be a sensor or an X-10 enabled lamp [22]. This would enable any device, irrespective of its capabilities, to effectively choose how it wants to interact within the network.

The Primary service is the only compulsory service each medical device is required to implement. This service is responsible for marshalling all communications between framework services (Secondary Services) and Application Peer Services (APS), whether they reside locally or remotely within the network. Simple networked medical devices, such as a Doppler tester, classed as a sensor (has very limited capabilities), could use the secondary services provided by a more general device (e.g. a personal computer). The Primary service on the sensor marshals communications to the hardware of the sensor and the Primary service located on specialised devices. The Secondary services themselves provide framework functionality, whilst Application Peer Services provide abstractions to the operational functions devices provide such as readings provided by the Doppler tester.

When devices initially join the network the goal is to try and discover devices they may have relationships with. For example, a treadmill machine in a gymnasium may discover all the equipment used by someone during a training session. This configuration may also include a medical interface used to submit information to the user's general healthcare practitioner and their mobile phone could be used to synchronise data readings with healthcare services on the user's home PC used to monitor fitness levels.

By managing references to external services (relationships), devices can adapt to changes that occur. For example, if the user's mobile phone becomes unavailable for some reason, the treadmill could detect this change and automatically select an alternative device, such as an Internet information processing service, provided by another device or the gymnasium. Looking at another example, we are able to monitor the osmolality of bodily fluids, which may be obtained using blood serum, urine or saliva sensors, to inform a person if they are dehydrated. This could be achieved via any audio device in the person's immediate vicinity. This has the potential to provide a breakthrough in all aspects of healthcare and lifestyle management where early detection can minimise the effects dehydration may have, which can often result in headaches and cramps [23]. Obviously the difference here is the ability to allow the sensors themselves to form relationships with other home devices and decipher how best to inform the user as and when required using appropriate services. In particular, care must be taken during the composition of services to ensure that the most appropriate functionality is chosen amongst ostensibly similar devices or services. In this instance compositions between devices and services need to be based on the best resources available. "Best" could mean resources that provide the best functionality, or resources that are free to use. Whatever the definition, the term needs to be identified and adhered to. In this paper, it refers to the service and the ability of the device to provide that service.

As a result, it is beneficial for devices to describe their capabilities in terms of how well they execute the services they provide. This means that devices would benefit from providing a corresponding device capability model describing how capable it is. By processing these capability models, a device can determine other devices' suitability before including them in a composition. For example, a mobile phone may be connected to the gymnasium's satellite system allowing a user to listen to a music channel. If the user moves to a different location a plasma display may be selected because it provides a better entertainment experience (audio and video). If the user moves location (to alternative gymnasium equipment) where the plasma display is no longer visible, the configuration may adapt to re-direct the satellite signal back to the mobile phone.

4. Secondary Framework Services

We turn our attention now to describing how the Secondary services extend the Primary service functionality discussed in the previous section to allow devices to be dynamically composed. The process requires the automatic resolution of terminology differences between vocabularies, and the assessment of device capabilities. Importantly the framework is not limited to these services but has the ability to accommodate any new functionality that may be required as the framework evolves.

4.1 Dynamically Composing Devices

To address the issue of increasing complexity, it is important to ensure that management tasks are considered in parallel with device development. We believe the management of devices and services to be perhaps one of the most important aspects of medical device research. For this reason, devices must be equipped with management techniques to automatically integrate and adapt services used in high-level applications. For example, when a networked-enabled dehydration device is connected to a home network, it must automatically advertise its services and form relationships with notification devices, such as those that provide audio capabilities, so that the person can be notified when signs of dehydration are detected. Underpinning this dispersed operational functionality, management services need to react to adverse environmental conditions and composite conflicts, such as the unavailability of services [21]. This requires a collaborative 'intelligence' allowing devices to negotiate these interactions and composite conflicts.

One approach is to enable machine-to-machine negotiation using service ontologies [24], to semantically describe functionality so that such functionality can be discovered and composed to create high-level tasks or applications (service compositions). Using the concept of Inputs, Outputs, Preconditions, and Effects (IOPEs) devices and services are composed by matching similarities between the service request and the service ontologies. Service ontologies, in conjunction with domain ontologies are used to match vocabularies that may be syntactically different but semantically equivalent. This approach overcomes many of the limitations associated with simple syntactic attribute-value pair matching.

Whilst using semantics in this way provides an interesting line of enquiry, it is well documented that automatically composing devices is problematic. This can be attributed to the variation in how service interfaces are defined and described, where one single difference in the parameters used in the signature can render the service inappropriate for the composition. To accommodate this, mechanisms could be adopted similar to constructors used in object-oriented programming where a base constructor could be used and then extended to include the different ways the object can be created. Whilst this is one possible solution, it is not scalable. A more effective way may be to extend the concept of automatic service composition to enable signatures to be composed, resulting in new signatures emerging. We achieve this using intermediary services and extended interfaces. For a more detailed description of this please refer to [21].

4.2 Enhancing the User Experience

To fully utilise devices we need to determine what functionality is available and how effectively devices providing those functions can execute them. For example, a plasma television and a video-enabled mobile phone are both able to process video information. However, the quality of these services will differ. A plasma television may be considered better equipped to process high definition video compared to a mobile phone. Given these different capabilities selecting and composing devices must be dependent on quality of service and application specific requirements. To address this, devices have the ability to select devices and services based on how well they can execute a service [21]. This can be achieved using metadata models, dynamically generated to assess device capabilities. Each model contains information about every resource the device manufacturer deems important. Using this information will allow a device to rank functionality based on ordered capabilities where the top of the list provides highly capable devices and the bottom those that are less capable. For an in-depth discussion of this algorithm the reader is referred to [21]

This section has considered all of the secondary services that comprise our proposed framework. The following section demonstrates their practical use in an intelligent home environment.

5. Implementation

Our framework has been designed to equip medical devices with plug and play capabilities, and aid interoperability between heterogeneous services they provide that can self-adapt to environmental changes. Although still at an early stage, we have built a prototype to evaluate the design, which demonstrates how state changes in the human body can be used to discover and control networked devices or alert a healthcare practitioner of the event. To achieve this we use an ECG sensor, a camera, a mobile device and a high-end visual display unit. The ECG sensor provides a service capable of taking ECG readings and making that data available within the network. The camera is used to stream images of the patient to either the mobile device or the visual display. The mobile device is carried by a medical practitioner, whilst the visual display is located in the practitioner's place of work.

When devices are initially switched on they perform three tasks. First, they publish the services they provide using the Primary Service discussed above. Second, they try to discover devices within the environment they have a relationship with (in the prototype the sensor service discovers the ECG service, the camera service, the mobile device and the visual display) using the Second Services to compose service interfaces and determine device capabilities. Third, they monitor the communication links they have with other devices and using our framework devices self-adapt to changes that occur.

The prototype demonstrates how high-level applications can be altered at runtime when exceptions occur within compositions. For example, when the healthcare practitioner moves out of the immediate vicinity of the visual display, an event is triggered to inform the framework that this device should no longer be used as part of the composition, and an alternative visual display should be used, such as that provided by a mobile phone.

The Primary and Secondary services have been developed using the JXTA protocols. JXTA allows any device to be connected to the network independent of platform, programming language, or transport protocol. This includes simple medical devices such as our Doppler tester. Framework services (Primary and Secondary) are predetermined and each device understands how to discover and invoke them. Bindings between devices and Secondary services are achieved using pipe advertisements. Pipes are used by services and applications to send and receive information between the two. Through the abstraction provided by JXTA they can be viewed as virtual communication channels, much like sockets programming, except pipes exist independent of location and network topology.

Application-specific services are used to expose the operational capabilities of all devices. Many functions may exist, consequently pipe advertisements used are not known by devices beforehand. As discussed above, service ontologies describe device functionality by mapping high-level semantics onto low-level service interfaces. This is achieved using the service ontologies [24].

We used a BIOPAC MP150 data acquisition workstation [25] to read the electrical activity produced by the heart in real-time, which was received using electrode sensors (LEAD1102-R, LEAD110S-W and LEAD11), connected to a MEC110C extension cable [25]. The electrode sensors themselves are connected to a Biopotential amplifier (ECG100C Electrocardiogram Amplifier) and the human body using Vermed SilverRest Electrodes.

Communication between the MP150 and the heart monitoring service is achieved using a standard straight through RJ45 Ethernet cable. The heart monitoring service communicates with a TINI microcontroller [26] in ad hoc mode using a wireless 802.11b access point. The access point is directly connected to the TINI board using a straight through RJ45 cable, which simulates an on-board wireless interface, which to date is not implemented natively on TINI microcontroller boards. The microcontroller is connected to a PC via its serial port, where a service is used to turn the camera on or off and receive AV streams. This is achieved using the JXTA pipes and the Real-time Transmission Protocol. These streams are piped towards the visual display or the mobile device, dependent on where the medical practitioner is. For example, if on call and out on a visit, the mobile phone is used; if at work the visual display is used. The described configuration is illustrated in Figure 3.

In a situation where the medical practitioner is away from the visual display, the actions require that the screen resolution be adapted to support a mobile device, the media format set to 3gp and the content is transcoded from H.264 to 3gp. The configuration is dependent on where the medical practitioner resides and our framework can dynamically change which device the medical practitioner is using. The framework provides self-adaptation functions to detect such changes and reconfigure compositions to best suite the medical practitioner's context.

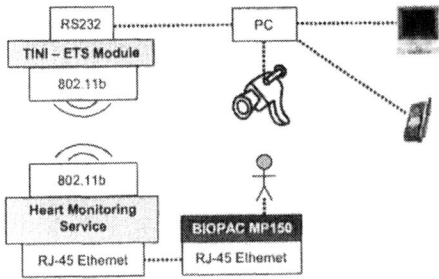

Fig. 3 Prototype Hardware Configuration

In the prototype the human body is connected to the BIOPAC MP150 via the heart monitoring electrode sensors. The values received from the sensors are analogue values between 0 and +10 volts. These are measured by the ECG 100C device and converted into digital values using the MP150. This digital data is transmitted to the Heart Monitoring Service, via the RJ45 connection and processed using two algorithms. The first algorithm analyses the digital data received from the BIOPAC and calculates the global maximum in the heart beat signal as illustrated in Figure 4. When processing the data we avoid local maximums by only processing peaks above 5 volts. The peaks in the data are determined by calculating the increasing values; when the value starts to decrease we know that we have reached the maximum point.

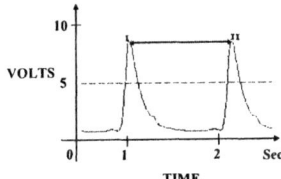

Fig. 4 Heat beats signals received from the ECG 100C

The second algorithm calculates the time between two peaks (also illustrated in Figure 4) and calculates the number of beats per minute (bpm). The bpm value is then used to determine if an alarm state has been reached. For experimental purposes, values between 50bpm and 75bpm are classed as normal heartbeat activity and values above or below this range indicate an alarm state has occurred. In this case a counter is invoked and incremented by one for each heartbeat out of range. If this counter reaches a predetermined value (for experimental purposes this value was set to 5), the Heart Monitoring Service generates an "enable-alarm-message" and sends it to the TINI microcontroller. If the heartbeats remain within range for 5 consecutive beats an "alarm-disable-message" is sent to the TINI microcontroller. Using a counter in this way enables the service to avoid triggering alarm conditions if spurious spikes in the data occur. For example it is possible for a spurious heartbeat to spike above 75bpm, therefore counting 5 consecutive beats ensures that an alarm condition is definitely present.

Messages are sent to the TINI microcontroller using 802.11b communications and are processed by an Ethernet to Serial (ETS) converter service written in Java, in order to control the underlying functions provided by the camera. In reality the TINI microcontroller and the camera would be one self-contained unit, however in the prototype the TINI microcontroller is connected to the camera via a PC. Upon receiving control messages from the Heart Monitoring Service the TINI microcontroller instructs the camera to activate. This results in the audio and video received from the camera being streamed to either the visual display or the mobile device.

Stankovic et al. [10] describe several application areas where wireless sensor networks could be used – sleep apnea, journal support, and cardiac health. We have successfully implemented within our framework mechanisms to obtain data through EEG and ECC sensors building on the ideas Stankovic et al. provide.

6. Conclusions

In recent years significant advances have been made independently in the areas of medical technology and networked appliance research. We believe that by combining elements from each of these domains there is the potential to provide further benefit, notably in relation to monitoring and preventative medicine.

We present a framework as an initial attempt to provide such capabilities. The framework has been tested using a prototype heart monitoring service able to stream video to a medical practitioner in the event that an alert is triggered, and which is able to react dynamically to real time changes in the situation and environment.

Whilst the medical devices and service framework used have each been proven effective in their own respective domains, this work represents a novel combination that provides additional benefits. We believe the direction represents a potentially crucial advance in medical technology that can – for example – build upon ongoing developments in home networking. However, although a working prototype has been achieved, we acknowledge that significant challenges remain, particularly in the areas of guaranteeing safety and satisfying regulatory requirements. We do not underestimate the importance of these, and aim to focus on these areas in our future work.

Acknowledgements

The authors would like to thank Lorna Bracegirdle from the NHS North Liverpool Primary Care Trust in the United Kingdom, for providing her valuable experience and understanding of medical device usage and healthcare provisioning within the home.

References

[1]   B. Rose, Home Networks: A Standards Perspective. IEEE Communications Magazine, 2001. 39(12): p. 78-85.

[2]   O. Abuelma'atti, M. Merabti, and B. Askwith, Internetworking the Wireless Domain. Proceedings of the 3rd International Symposium in Communication Systems, Networks and Digital Signal Processing (CSNDSP), 2002, Staffordshire, UK, p. 344 - 348.

[3]   T. Zahariadis and K. Pramataris, Multimedia home networks: standards and interfaces. Computer Standards and Interfaces, 2002. 24(5): p. 425-235.

[4]   DLNA: Overview and Vision. 2004, DLNA, Accessed: October 2006, http://www.dlna.org/about/DLNA_Overview.pdf.

[5]   The OSGi Service Platform - Dynamic services for networked devices. 2005, OSGi Alliance, Accessed: 2006, http://www.osgi.org/.

[6]   C. Koumpis, L. Hanna, M. Anderson, and M. Johansson, Wireless Industrial Control and Monitoring beyond Cable Replacement. 2nd Profibus International Conference, 2005, Warwickshire, UK.

[7]   M. Minoh and T. Kamae, Networked Appliances and their Peer-to-Peer Architecture AMIDEN. IEEE Communications Magazine, 2001. 39(10): p. 80-84.

[8]   UPnP Forum. 2005, Microsoft Corp., Accessed: 2006, http://www.upnp.org/.

[9]   M. Lee and S. Kang, Multimedia Room Gateway for Integration and Management of Distributed Medical Devices Workshop on High Confidence Medical Device Software and Systems (HCMDSS), 2005, University of Pennsylvania, Philadelphia, PA, USA: University of Pennsylvania.

[10]   J. A. Stankovic, Q. Cao, T. Doan, L. Fang, Z. He, R. Kiran, S. Lin, S. Son, R. Stoleru, and A. Wood, Wireless Sensor Networks for In-Home Healthcare: Potential and Challenge. Workshop on High Confidence Medical Device Software and Systems (HCMDSS), 2005, University of Pennsylvania, Philadelphia, PA, USA: University of Pennsylvania.

[11]   S. K. S. Gupta and L. Schwiebert, Dependable Pervasive Health Monitoring. Workshop on High Confidence Medical Device Software and Systems (HCMDSS), 2005, University of Pennsylvania, Philadelphia, PA, USA: University of Pennsylvania.

[12]   D. Voss, Smart Home Care: New diagnostic devices could save an ER visit. The MIT Technology Review, 2001: p. 31.

[13]   N. Kin, Y. Jeong, S. Song, and D. Shin, Middleware Interoperability based Mobile Healthcare System. The 9th IEEE International Conference on Advanced Communication Technology, 2007, Phoenix Park, Gangwon-Do, Republic of Korea: IEEE Computer Society, p. 209 - 213.

[14]   L. Gong, JXTA: A Network Programming Environment. IEEE Internet Computing, 2001. 5(3): p. 88-95.

[15]   B. Lim, K. Choi, and D. Shin, A Secure Peer-to-Peer Group Collaboration Scheme for Healthcare System. 5th International Conference on Computational Science, 2005, Atlanta, GA, USA: Springer, p. 346 - 349.

[16]   B. Lin, K. Choi, and D. Shin, A JXTA-based Architecture for Efficient and Adaptive Healthcare Services. International Conference on Convergence in Broadband and Mobile Networking, 2005, Jeju Island, Korea: Springer, p. 776 - 785.

[17]   M. Uschold and M. Gruninger, Ontologies: Principles, Methods and Applications. The Knowleddge Engineering Review, 1996. 11(2): p. 93-155.

[18]   Y. Y. Goland, T. Cai, P. Leach, J. Gu, and S. Albright, Simple Service Discovery Protocol/1.0, I. E. T. Force, Editor. 1999, Internet Engineering Task Force: Internet Engineering Task Force. p. 1 - 18.

[19]   T. Berners-Lee, J. Hendler, and O. Lassila, The Semantic Web. Scientific America, 2001. 284(5): p. 34-43.

[20]   M. Paolucci and K. Sycara, Autonomous Semantic Web Services. Internet Computing, 2003. 7(5): p. 34 - 41.

[21]   M. Merabti, P. Fergus, O. Abuelma'atti, Y. Heather, and C. Judice, Managing Distributed Networked Appliances in Home Networks. To appear in the Proceedings of the IEEE, 2008.

[22]   Z. Yuejun and W. Mingguang, Design of Wireless Remote Module in X-10 Intelligent Home. IEEE International Conference on Industrial Technology, 2005, Hong Kong: IEEE Computer Society, p. 1349 - 1353.

[23]   R. L. Gunter, W. D. Delinger, T. L. Porter, R. Steward, and J. Reed, Hydration level monitoring using embedded piezoresistive microcantilever sensors. Medical Engineering & Physics, 2005. 27(3): p. 215 - 220.

[24]   OWL-S 1.0 Release. 2003, DAML, Accessed: 2006, http://www.daml.org/services/owl-s/1.0/.

[25]   BIOPAC Systems, Inc. 2004, BIOPAC Systems Inc., Accessed: 13 May 2004, http://www.biopac.com/.

[26]   Introducing TINI: Tiny InterNet Interface. 2003, Dallas Semiconductor, Accessed: 18-11-2005, http://www.maxim-ic.com/.

Remote Access VPNs Performance Comparison between Windows Server 2003 and Fedora Core 6

Ahmed A. Joha, Fathi Ben Shatwan, Majdi Ashibani

The Higher Institute of Industry

Misurata, Libya

goha_99@yahoo.com

Abstract - A Virtual Private Network (VPN) can be defined as a way to provide secure communication between members of a group through use of the public telecommunication infrastructure, maintaining privacy through the use of a tunneling protocol and security procedures. This work examines and empirically evaluates the remote access VPNs, namely Point to Point Tunneling Protocol (PPTP), Layer 2 Tunneling Protocol over Internet Protocol Security (L2TP/IPSec), and Secure Socket Layer (SSL). We explore the impact of these VPNs on end-to-end user application performance using metrics such as throughput, RTT, jitter, and packet loss. All experiments were conducted using a window XP SP/2 host (VPN Client) connected to a windows server 2003 host (VPN Server) and to a fedora core 6 host (VPN Server).

Keywords- VPN; PPTP; L2TP; IPSec; SSL; OpenVpn; tunneling; encapsulation; performance evaluation

1. INTRODUCTION

In the past, organizations or enterprises would physically install lines over large distances to ensure secure data transfer. However, this system is impractical for every enterprise and everyday users due to the cost, space, and time required for such installations. The concept of Virtual Private Network (VPN) is not new – technologies such as Frame Relay (FR) or Asynchronies Transfer Mode (ATM) have been used over the last decades as a basis for the implementation of this concept. Whatever the format or the technology behind it, a VPN provides a service functionally equivalent to a private network using resources of a public network. In recent years, with the exponential growth of the Internet, the landscape of telecommunications has changed radically and the Internet has become part of almost every aspect of the developed world including education, banking, business, and politics. Over the past two decades the public Internet has been found to be vulnerable to attackers seeking sensitive information. The most recent solution to this problem has been IP-based Virtual Private Network (IPVPN). A Virtual Private Network (VPN) can be defined as a way to provide secure communication between members of a group through use of the public telecommunication infrastructure, maintaining privacy through the use of a tunneling protocol and security procedures. VPN systems provide users with the illusion of a completely private network. An IP Virtual Private Network (IPVPN) can be

Please use the following format when citing this chapter:

Joha, A. A., Shatwan, F. B., Ashibani, M., 2007, in IFIP International Federation for Information Processing, Volume 256, Home Networking, Al Agha, K., Carcelle, X., Pujolle, G., (Boston: Springer), pp. 329-343.

defined as a VPN implementation that uses public or shared IP network resources to emulate the characteristics of an IP-based private network.

2. TUNNELING BASICS

Tunneling is a method of using an internetwork infrastructure to transfer data for one network over another network. The data to be transferred (or payload) can be the frames (or packets) of another protocol. Instead of sending a frame as it is produced by the originating node, the tunneling protocol encapsulates the frame in an additional header. The additional header provides routing information so that the encapsulated payload can traverse the intermediate internetwork. The encapsulated packets are then routed between tunnel endpoints over the internetwork. The logical path through which the encapsulated packets travel through the internetwork is called a tunnel. Once the encapsulated frames reach their destination on the internetwork, the frame is decapsulated and forwarded to its final destination. Tunneling includes this entire process (encapsulation, transmission, and decapsulation of packets) as shown in "Figure. 1".

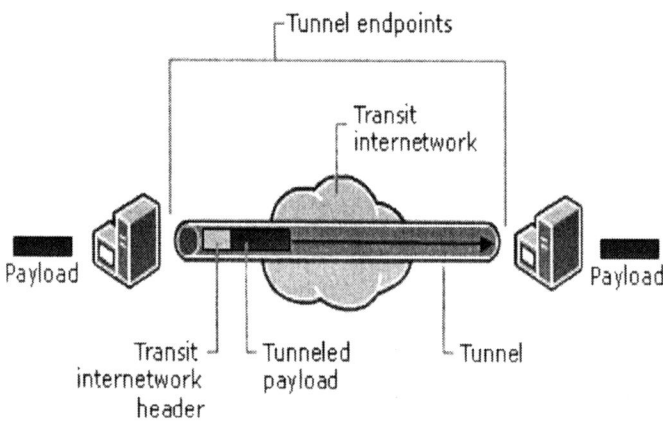

Figure1. Tunneling

3. SECURITY OF VPN

A VPN should provide the following critical functions to ensure security of the data.

3.1 Authentication

AUTHENTICATION ENSURES THAT THE DATA IS COMING FROM THE SOURCE FROM WHICH IT CLAIMS TO COME.

3.2 Access Control

Access control concept relates to the accepting or rejecting of a particular requester to have access to some service or data in any given system. It is therefore necessary to define a set of access rights, privileges, and authorizations, and assign these to appropriate people within the domain of the system under analysis.

3.3 Confidentiality

Confidentiality ensures the privacy of information by restricting an unauthorized users from reading data carried on the public network.

3.4 Data Integrity

Data Integrity verifies that a data has not been altered during its travel over the public network.

3.5 Non-Repudition

Non-repudiation ensures that the originator of a message cannot deny having sent the message.

4. THE BENFITES OF VPN

The main purpose of a VPN is to give enterprises the same capabilities, or even better in some cases as the list below shows, as in private networks, but at a much lower cost. Enterprises benefit from VPN in the following ways [1]:

4.1 Cost

When using VPN, cost is reduced in many ways. Most importantly, VPN eliminate the fixed monthly charge of dedicated leased lines. The cost is even higher if the lines are purchased.

4.2 Scalability

VPN offers better scalability. An enterprise with only two branch offices can connect the two offices with just one leased line. But as the enterprise grows, full-mesh connectivity might be required between the different offices. This means that the number of leased lines, and the total cost associated with deploying them, increases exponentially. In addition, if an enterprise wants to scale globally, the cost associated with deploying leased lines will be even higher, if it is even possible to reach the same global connectivity with leased lines. VPN that utilizes the Internet avoid this problem by simply using the infrastructure already available.

4.3 Security

Security is not impaired when using VPN since transmitted data is either encrypted or, if sent unencrypted, forwarded through trusted networks.

4.4 Productivity

In addition to cost savings, VPN increases profits by improving productivity. The improved productivity results from the ability to access resources from anywhere at anytime (i.e. more business can be conducted).

5. ARCHITECTURE OF VPN

A VPN should typically support the following architecture "Figure. 2". A main LAN at the headquarters of an enterprise, other LANs at remote offices, partner or customer company LANs, and individual users connecting from out in the field. There are basically two types of VPNs, remote access VPN and site-to-site VPN. Site to site VPN can be further divided into intranet VPN and extranet VPN.

5.1 Remote Access VPN

The remote access VPN is a user-to-LAN connection used by enterprises that have employees who need to connect to their private network from various remote locations (e.g. homes, hotel rooms, airports). Since users access the network over the Internet, the remote access VPN is a low-cost solution, compared to the dial-up solution which often results in costly phone bills.

5.2 Site to Site VPN

By using dedicated equipment, enterprises can connect multiple sites over a public network such as the Internet, thus creating a site-to-site VPN. Site-to-site VPNs can be one of two types.

5.2.1 Intranet Site to Site VPN

If an enterprise has one or more branch offices that they wish to join in a single private network, they can create an intranet VPN. This is a low-cost solution compared to maintaining dedicated leased lines.

5.2.2 Extranet Site to Site VPN

When an enterprise has a close relationship with another enterprise (for example, a partner, supplier or customer), it can build an extranet VPN which connects LANs together. By doing so, the partner companies can work in a shared environment.

5.3 VPN within an Intranet

Intranets can also utilize VPN technology to implement controlled access to subnets on the private network. Even though a public network is not involved in this case, the security features (e.g. encryption, authentication) of secure VPN technology are taken advantage of.

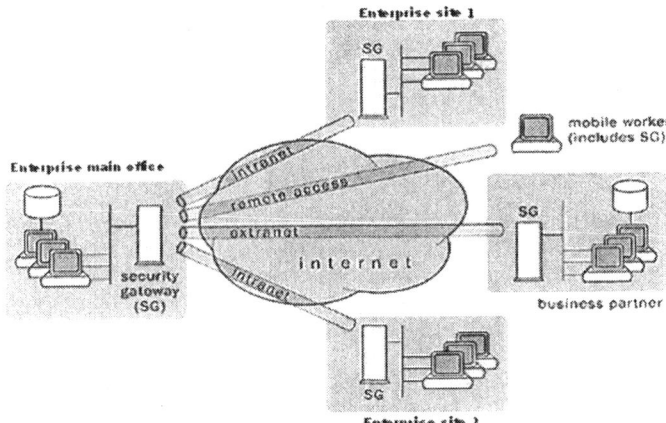

Figure2. VPN architecture

6. REMOTE ACCESS VPN PROTOCOLS

For a connection to be established, both the client and the server must be using the same VPN protocol [2].

6.1 Point to Point Tunneling Protocol (PPTP)

PPTP is a standard tunneling protocol developed by PPTP Forum which consists of Microsoft and some other remote access vendors. Basically, PPTP is an extension of Point to Point Protocol (PPP), which encapsulates PPP frames in IP datagrams for transmission over an IP-based network, such as the Internet or over a private intranet. PPTP is described in RFC 2637 in the IETF RFC Database [3]. Microsoft has included PPTP clients in all versions of Windows since Windows 95 and PPTP servers in all its server products since Windows NT 4.0, PPTP clients and servers are supported in Linux. PPTP has been very popular, especially on Windows systems, because it is widely available, free and easy to set up.

6.2 Layer Two Tunneling Protocol (L2TP)

L2TP is a combination of PPTP and Layer Tow Forwarding (L2F). Rather than having two incompatible tunneling protocols competing in the marketplace and causing customer confusion, the IETF mandated that the two technologies be combined into a single tunneling protocol that represents the best features of both. L2TP is described in RFC 2661 in the IETF RFC Database [4]. L2TP alone does not provide any security. In order to have strong security in place the L2TP must be run over IPSec.

6.3 Internet Protocol Security (IPSec)

IPSec is a framework of IETF open standards aim at securing traffic on the network layer. It does not specify the authentication and encryption protocol to use. This makes it flexible and able to support new authentication and encryption methods as they are developed. IPSec is described in RFCs 2401-2411 and 2451 in the IETF RFC Database [5]. IPSec is supported in Windows XP, 2000, 2003 and Vista, in Linux 2.6 and later. Many vendors supply IPSec VPN servers and clients.

L2TP/IPSec combines L2TP's tunnel with IPSec's secure channel. Microsoft has provided a free L2TP/IPSec VPN client for Windows 98, ME and NT since 2002, and ships an L2TP/IPSec VPN client with Windows XP, 2000, 2003 and Vista. Windows Server 2003 and Windows 2000 Server include L2TP/IPSec servers. There are several open-source implementations of L2TP/IPSec for Linux

6.4 Secure Socket Layer (SSL)

SSL is a higher-layer security protocol developed by *Netscape*. SSL is commonly used with HTTP to enable secure Web browsing, called HTTPS. Most browser and servers currently use SSL 3.0. However, SSL can also be used to create a VPN tunnel. For example, OpenVpn is an open-source VPN package, which uses SSL to provide encryption of both the data and control channels.

7. EXPERIMENTAL TEST BED AND MEASUREMENT PROCEDURES

The work in this paper is based on the test bed, that was built to evaluate the performance of remote access VPNs on both windows server 2003 VPN server and fedora core 6 VPN server. The hardware components of this test bed are listed in the "Table 1.", The software components of this test bed are listed in the "Table 2.", and the connections of these components are shown in the "Figure 1".

Table1. TEST BED HARD WARE COMPONENTS

Node	Description
dc01Server	Desktop equipped with double Genuine Intel 2600 MHz processor, 512 Mbytes of RAM, and VIA Rhine II Compatible Fast Ethernet Adapter built-in NIC. It is act as a domain controller server.
vpn01Server	Desktop equipped with double Genuine Intel 3000 MHz processor, 512 Mbytes of RAM, Broadcom Extreme Gigabit Ethernet built-in NIC, and VIA VT6105 Rhine III Compatible Fast Ethernet Adapter NIC. It is act as a domain client and VPN server.
vpn01Client	Laptop equipped with Genuine Intel 1866 MHz processor, 512 Mbytes of RAM, and Broadcom 440x 10/100 Integrated controller built-in NIC. It is act as a VPN client.
HUB	LANTECH, Ethernet 10 BASE-T HUB.

Table2. TEST BED SOFTWARE COMPONENTS

Node	Description
dc01Server	This node is loaded with windows server 2003. Configure your server wizard is used to configure this node to act as a domain controller server [6].
vpn01Server	This node is loaded with windows server 2003. Configure your server wizard is used to configure this node to act as PPTP and L2TP/IPSec VPN servers [6] and OpenVpn-2.0.9.exe is installed to configure this node to act as SSL VPN server [7]. In addition, this node is loaded with fedora core 6. Pptpd-1.3.3-1.fc6.i386.rpm is installed to configure this node to ac as PPTP VPN server [8], xl2tpd-1.1.09-1.i386.fc6.rpm and OpensWan-2.4.5-2.1 are installed to configure this node to act as L2TP/IPSec VPN server [9][10], and OpenVpn-2.0.9.tar is installed to configure this node to act as SSL VPN server [7].
vpn01Client	This node is loaded with windows XP SP/2. New connection wizard is used to configure this node to act as PPTP VPN client that is connected to vpn01Server node with MS-CHAPv2 authentication algorithm, MPPE encryption algorithm, and no compression algorithm [6]. New connection wizard is used to configure this node to act as L2TP/IPSec VPN client that is connected to vpn01Server node with preshared key, MS-CHAPv2 authentication algorithm (windows server 2003) or MD5-CHAP authentication algorithm (fedora core 6), ESP-3DES encryption algorithm, and no compression algorithm [6]. OpenVpn-2.0.9.exe is installed to configure this node to act as SSL client that is connected to vpn01Server node with preshared key, SHA1 authentication algorithm, 3DES encryption algorithm, and no compression algorithm [7].

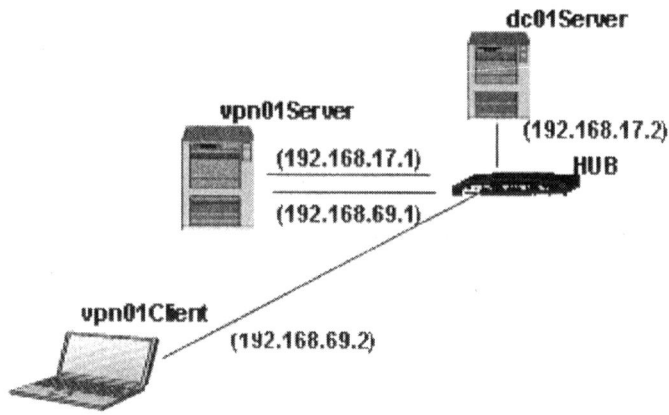

Figure3. Test bed connections

We measure some performance metrics like Throughput, RTT, Jitter, and packet loss in both TCP and UDP mode. These metrics are used in our experiments as they have a direct impact on the ultimate performance perceived by end user applications. During our experiments, the following parameters were used to quantify the QoS services provided [11]:

- Throughput is the rate at which bulk of data transfers can be transmitted from one host to another over a sufficiently long period of time.

- Round Trip Time (RTT) is the amount of time it takes one packet to travel from one host to another and back to the originating host.

- Packet delay variation (Jitter) is measured for packets belonging to the same packet stream and shows the difference in the one-way delay that packets experience in the network. Jitter occurs when packets are sent and received with timing variations. Jitter is effectively a variation of packet delay where delays actually impact the quality of service.

- Packet loss is measured as the portion of packets transmitted but not received in the destination compared to the total number or packets transmitted.

8. EXPERIMENTAL RESULTS

Iperf tool is used to measure TCP Throughput in TCP mode and UDP throughput, jitter, and packet loss in UDP mode [12]. Hrping tool is also used to measure RTT [13].

The following results were collected from the test bed was illustrated in section 7.

8.1 TCP Throughput

TCP throughput is measured according to tcp window size, time of test, and the number of flows (parallel streams). The same experiments were repeated number of times to find the average TCP throughput.

The results of these experiments are presented in "Figure 4", "Figure 5", and "Figure 6".

These figures indicate clearly that the PPTP on windows server 2003 has produced the best TCP throughput value, the PPTP on fedora core 6 has produced the second TCP throughput value, the OpenVpn on fedora core 6 has produced the third TCP throughput value, the L2TP/IPSec on fedora core 6 has produced the forth TCP throughput value, the L2TP/IPSec on windows server 2003 has produced the fifth TCP throughput value, and the OpenVpn on windows server 2003 has produced the lowest TCP throughput value.

8.2 Round Trip Time (RTT)

RTT can be measured by sending packets with a variant packet size from a client to the server. The same experiments were repeated a number of times to find the average RTT. The results of these experiments are presented in "Figure 7". This figure indicates clearly that the PPTP on windows server 2003 has produced the best RTT value, the PPTP on fedora core 6 has produced the second RTT value, the L2TP/IPSec on windows server 2003 has produced the third RTT value, the OpenVpn on fedora core 6 has produced the forth RTT value, the OpenVpn on windows server 2003 has produced the fifth RTT value, and the L2TP/IPSec on fedora core 6 has produced the last RTT value.

8.3 UDP throughput

UDP throughput is measured according to transmission rate of packets. The same experiments were repeated a number of times to find the average UDP throughput. The results of these experiments are presented in "Figure 8". This figure indicates clearly that the UDP throughput values of the PPTP on windows server 2003, the PPTP on fedora core 6, the L2TP/IPSec on windows server 2003, and the L2TP/IPSec on fedora core 6 are equal to the transmission rate if the transmission rate is less than 8000 kbits/sec and less than the transmission rate if the transmission rate is more than 8000 kbits/sec. In addition, this figure indicates clearly that the UDP throughput values of the OpenVpn on windows server 2003 and the OpenVpn on fedora core 6 are equal to the transmission rate if the transmission rate is less than 200 kbits/sec and less than the transmission rate if the transmission rate is more than 200 kbits/sec. Also, this figure indicates that the UDP throughput values of the OpenVpn on windows server 2003 and the OpenVpn on fedora core 6 are always less than 500 kbits/sec.

8.4 Jitter

Jitter is measured according to the transmission rate of packets. The same experiments were repeated a number of times to find the average Jitter. The results of these experiments are presented in "Figure 9". This figure indicates clearly that the PPTP on windows server 2003, the PPTP on fedora core 6, the L2TP/IPSec on windows server 2003, and the L2TP/IPSec on fedora core 6 have produced a low Jitter values. Also, this figure indicates clearly that the OpenVpn on windows server 2003 and the OpenVpn on fedora core 6 have produced a high Jitter values if the transmission rate is more than 200 kbits/sec.

8.5 Packet loss

Packet loss is measured according to the transmission rate of packets. The same experiments were repeated a number of times to find the average Packet loss. The results of these experiments are presented in "Figure 10". This figure indicates clearly that both PPTP and L2TP/IPSec on both windows server 2003 and fedora core 6 have produced a low Packet loss values. Also, this figure indicates clearly that the OpenVpn on both windows server 2003 and fedora core 6 have produced a high Packet loss values if the transmission rate is more than 200 kbits/sec.

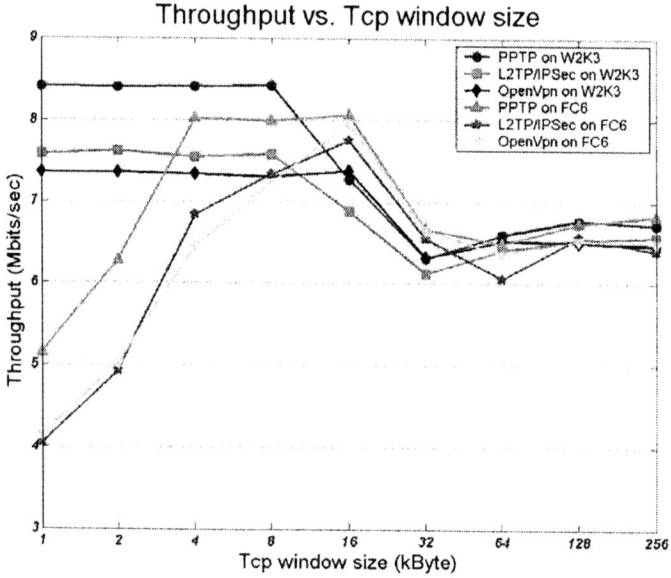

Figure4. TCP throughput according to the window size

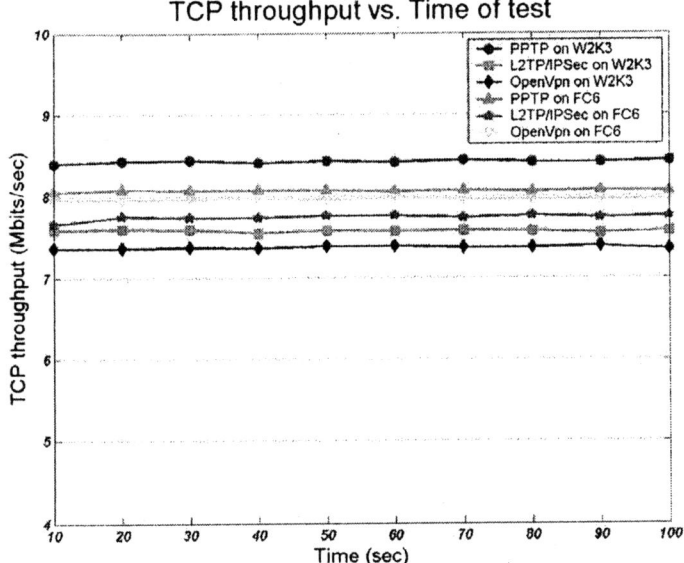

Figure5. TCP throughput according to thetime of test

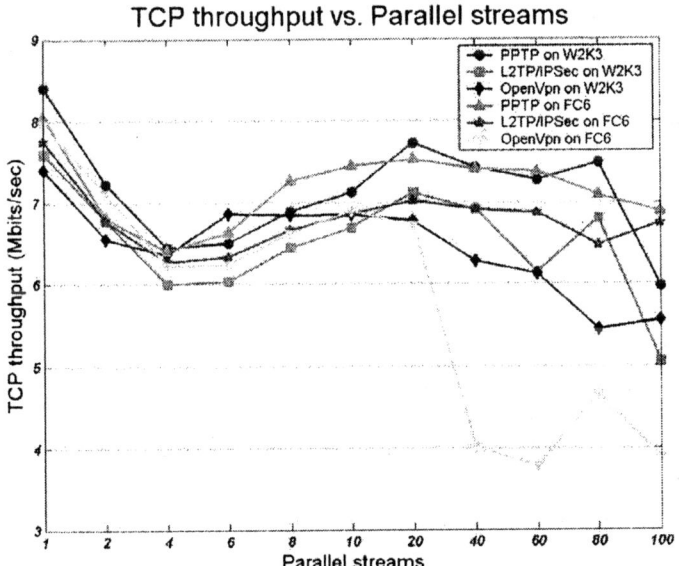

Figure6. TCP throughput according to the parallel streams

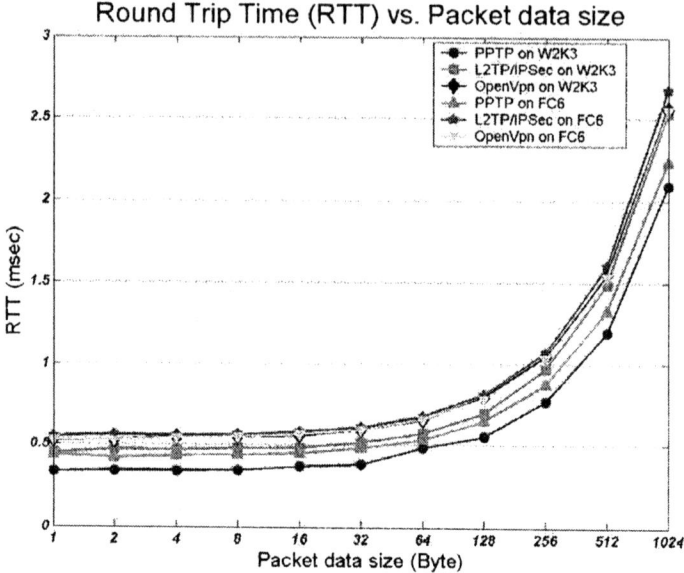

Figure7. RTT according to the packet data size

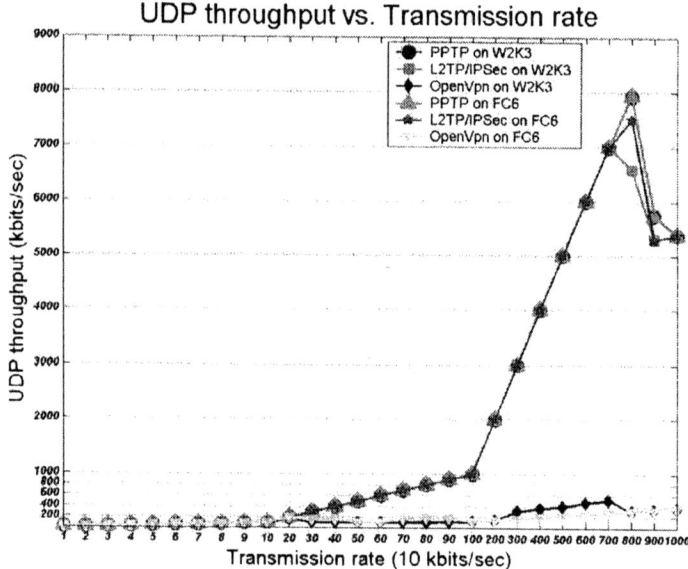

Figure8. UDP throughput according to the transmission rate

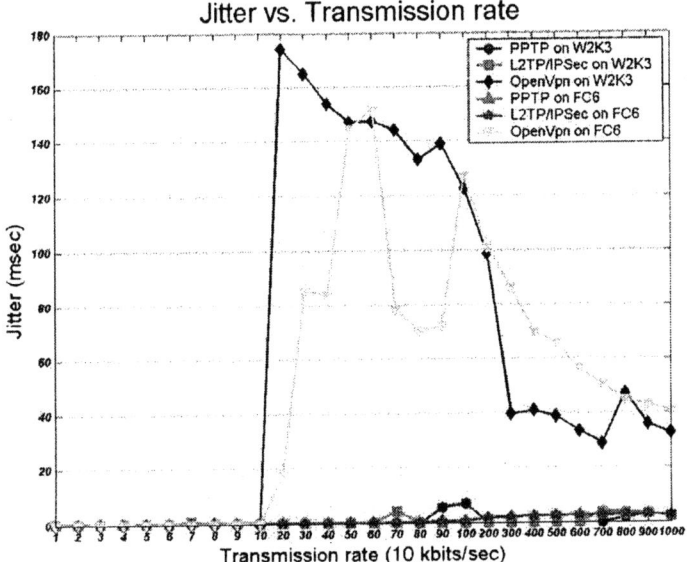

Figure9. Jitter according to the transmission rate

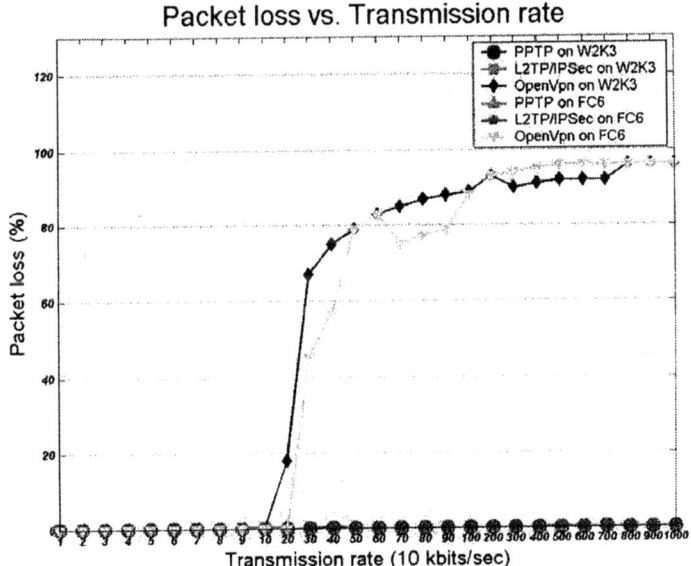

Figure10. Packet loss according to the transmission rate

The test bed experimental results are summarized in the "Table III.".

Table3. SUMMARY OF THE EXPERIMENTAL RESULTS

TCP throughput					
Best	**2nd**	**3rd**	**4th**	**5th**	**lowest**
PPTP on W2k3	PPTP on FC6	OpenVpn on FC6	L2TP/IPSec on FC6	L2TP/IPSec on W2K3	OpenVpn on W2K3
Round Trip Time (RTT)					
Best	**2nd**	**3rd**	**4th**	**5th**	**last**
PPTP on W2k3	PPTP on FC6	L2TP/IPSec on W2k3	OpenVpn on FC6	OpenVpn on W2K3	L2TP/IPSec on FC6
UDP throughput					
High				**Low**	
PPTP on W2k3	PPTP on FC6	L2TP/IPSec on W2K3	L2TP/IPSec on FC6	OpenVpn on W2K3	OpenVpn on FC6
Jitter					
Low				**High**	
PPTP on W2k3	PPTP on FC6	L2TP/IPSec on W2K3	L2TP/IPSec on FC6	OpenVpn on W2K3	OpenVpn on FC6
Packet loss					
Low				**High**	
PPTP on W2k3	PPTP on FC6	L2TP/IPSec on W2K3	L2TP/IPSec on FC6	OpenVpn on W2K3	OpenVpn on FC6

9. CONCLUSION AND FUTURE WORK

This paper has presented an experimental performance evaluation for the remote access VPNs, namely PPTP, L2TP/IPSec, and OpenVpn on both windows server 2003 and fedora core 6 VPN servers. From the results that were collected from the test bed and the user applications requirements, the following conclusion remarks are gained:

- Due to the smallest overhead packets that have been introduced by PPTP, PPTP on both windows server 2003 and fedora core 6 have produced the best performance values for both TCP and UDP-based user applications.

- In order to have strong security, L2TP/IPSec combines L2TP's tunnel with IPSec's secure channel which increases the overhead packets. So, L2TP/IPSec on both windows server 2003 and fedora core 6 have produced a good performance values for both TCP and UDP-based user applications.

- Because OpenVpn was written as a user space daemon rather than a kernel module, OpenVpn on both windows server 2003 and fedora core

6 have produced a low performance values in high traffic environments for the UDP-based user applications.

- The performance values of both PPTP and L2TP/IPSec on windows server 2003 are better than the performance values of both PPTP and L2TP/IPSec on fedora core 6.

This work should be extended to include performance evaluation of the remote access VPNs on other software and hardware VPN servers.

The OpenVpn needs to be manipulated to improve it's performance with UDP-based user applications.

REFERENCES

[1] Rezan Fisli, "Secure Corporate Communications over VPN-Based WANs," Master's Thesis in Computer Science at the School of Computer Science and engineering, Royal Institute of Technology, sweden, 2005.

[2] Jon C. Snader, "VPNs ILLUSTRATED: Tunnels, VPNs, and IPSec," Addison-Wesley, 2006.

[3] RFC 2637, "PPTP," IETF, ftp://ftp.isi.edu/in-notes/rfc2637.txt, 1999.

[4] RFC 2661, "L2TP,"IETF, ftp://ftp.isi.edu/in-notes/rfc2661.txt, 1999.

[5] RFCs 2401-2411, and 2451, "IPSec," IETF, ftp://ftp.isi.edu/in-notes/, 1999.

[6] http://www.microsoft.com, 2007.

[7] http://openvpn.net/download.html, 2007.

[8] http://sourceforge.net/project/showfiles.php?group_id=44827, 2007.

[9] http://www.xelerance.com/software/xl2tpd, 2007.

[10]http://www.openswan.org,2007.

[11]IP Performance Metrics (IPPM) Working Group, IETF, http://www.ietf.org /html.charters/ippm-charter.html.

[12]http://dast.nlanr.net/projects/IPerf, 2007.

[13]http://www.cfos.de, 2007.

We disregard the other two states arising from the same configurations but having different symmetry; they are the odd state of the triplets $1s\sigma 2p\sigma^3\Sigma_u$ which is unstable and has already been considered by HEITLER and LONDON and, with some approximation, the $1s\sigma 2p\sigma^1\Sigma_u$ state that belongs to the singlets but is equally odd. The states y_1 and y_2 that appear in (1) are not orthogonal but the ground state $(1s\sigma)^{2\,1}\Sigma_g$ and the anomalous state $(2p\sigma)^{2\,1}\Sigma_g$ should result from their orthogonal combinations. The secular equation for determining the eigenvalues is(*):

$$(2) \qquad \begin{vmatrix} I_0 + I_1 - (1+S)E & 2M - 2QE \\ 2M - 2QE & L_0 + L_1 - (1+R)E \end{vmatrix} = 0$$

where, if the eigenfunctions are real:

$$(3) \qquad \begin{cases} I_0 = \displaystyle\int \varphi_1\psi_2 H \varphi_1\psi_2 d\tau \\[2mm] I_1 = \displaystyle\int \varphi_2\psi_1 H \varphi_1\psi_2 d\tau \\[2mm] L_0 = \displaystyle\int \Phi_{12} H \Phi_{12} d\tau \\[2mm] L_1 = \displaystyle\int \Phi_{12} H \Psi_{12} d\tau \\[2mm] M = \displaystyle\int \varphi_1\psi_2 H \Phi_{12} d\tau \\[2mm] S = \displaystyle\int \varphi_1\psi_1 \varphi_2\psi_2 d\tau \\[2mm] R = \displaystyle\int \Phi_{12} \Psi_{12} d\tau \\[2mm] Q = \displaystyle\int \varphi_1\psi_2 \Phi_{12} d\tau \end{cases}$$

If, for example, we set the energy of the separate neutral atoms equal to zero, we can consider H as a perturbation; the difference between the energies of $H^+ + H^-$ and of $H + H$ naturally appears then as a perturbation when H is applied to Φ_{12} or to Ψ_{12}.

2.   Some of the integrals (3) can be found in HEITLER and LONDON[3] and SUGIURA[4]; to evaluate the other integrals we have to find an approximate expression for Φ_{12}. This eigenfunction, describing the ion H^-, is not exactly known but its eigenvalue, which is related to the electronic affinity of hydrogen, has been calculated with

---

(*) In "Rendiconti dell'Accademia dei Lincei" the term "= 0"of eq. (2) is erroneously missing. (Note of the Editor, see also E. AMALDI, *op. cit.*)
[3] W. HEITLER and F. LONDON, loc. cit.
[4] Y. SUGIURA, "Z. Physik", *45*, 484 (1927).

great precision by several Authors[5]. This simplifies the evaluation of the integrals (3) since H reduces to a finite operator. For Φ_{12} we can approximately take the product $\Phi_1 \, \Phi_2$ of two eigenfunctions depending on the single electrons. The best solution in the sense of the minimum energy is then, as is well known, the one given by HARTHREE'S method which in our case is, with great approximation,

$$\Phi_1 = \frac{c}{r_1} \left(e^{-0.29 \frac{r_1}{a_0}} - e^{-1.68 \frac{r_1}{a_0}} \right)$$

and similarly for Φ_2. The whole calculation, using this eigenfunction, though feasible, is too cumbersome; we have therefore preferred to use the simpler expression

$$\Phi_1 = c \, e^{-\frac{11}{16} \frac{r_1}{a_0}}$$

that has already been used by HYLLERAAS in his theory of solid lithium hydride[6]. Using the approximate eigenfunction Φ_{12} and the conventional meaning for $H\Phi_{12}$, we obtain for M two different values:

$$M = \int \varphi_1 \psi_2 H \Phi_{12} d\tau \qquad \text{and} \qquad M = \int \Phi_{12} H \varphi_1 \psi_2 d\tau.$$

We prefer the first expression that is simpler and possibly more exact; however since the second does not allow simple calculations, we cannot control this statement except for the limiting cases. The largest of the eigenvalues of (2) that belongs to $(2p\sigma)^{2}{}^{1}\Sigma_g$ reaches its minimum at a distance that is in disagreement with the equilibrium distance of the term X (approximately 2 Å instead of 1.35). However, the energy is 7.5 volts above the energy of the neutral atoms when they are separated and in the ground state, *i.e.* approximately $27000 \, \text{cm}^{-1}$ below the normal limit of H_2 (the experimental value for the X term being $22000 \, \text{cm}^{-1}$). This result is even too favourable as, with the method we followed, we could have expected a value considerably smaller than the true one. We cannot definitely exclude that WEIZEL's interpretation is wrong and that the term $(2p\sigma)^{2}{}^{1}\Sigma_g$, which is certainly stable and relatively deep, is, instead of the X term, rather the K term or some other term not yet observed. Nevertheless it is perhaps possible to attribute the error in the determination of the equilibrium point and the too favourable result in the calculation of the energy to the use for H^- of a non-properly correct eigenfunction. A quantitative evaluation is difficult but it is plausible that such an approximation tends to produce errors compatible with the discrepancies ascertained between calculation and experiment.

---

[5] H. BETHE, "Z. Physik", *57*, 815 (1929); E. A. HYLLERAAS, ivi, *60*, 624 (1930); P. STARO-DUBROSKI, ivi, *65*, 806 (1930).
[6] E. A. HYLLERAAS, "Z. Physik", *63*, 771 (1930).

Comment on the Scientific Paper no. 4 : *"Pseudopolar reaction of hydrogen atoms".*

This paper, no. 4 of the Majorana production, is "technically" similar to paper no. 2 on the chemical bond of the He_2^+ ion. Although Majorana is a theoretician, his interest always arouses from considerations of experimental kind. Hence, also the motivation of this work is not a purely academic exercise, but it is aimed to explain an unexplained phenomenon observed in the spectrum of the H_2 molecule (the so-called X term). While for an atomic system the frequency corresponding to the transition $2p\,2p{-}1s\,2p$ (involving two excited optical electrons) is quite close to that of the transition $1s\,2p - 1s\,2s$ (where only one optical electron is excited) this behaviour is no longer valid for the analogous molecular system as observed in the spectrum of H_2 where the excited $(2p\sigma)^2\ {}^1\Sigma_g$ state decays toward the state $1s\sigma\,2p\sigma\ {}^1\Sigma_u$ in the infrared spectral region (anomalous X term). As already done in paper no. 2, Majorana makes use of the concept based on the resonance force.

His approach assumes the molecule formation to be the result of the interaction between two ions, H^+ and H^- (*pseudopolar binding*), and considers the possibility that one electron can jump from one nucleus to the other at a given frequency. Coherently with this idea, Majorana chooses combinations of electronic eigenfunctions of the $(H^+ + H^-)$ (where one electron can oscillate between the two protons) and $(H + H)$ (where instead each electron is associated to one proton) systems and selects two even functions which give rise to bound states. In such a way he finds the ground state $(1s\sigma)^2\ {}^1\Sigma_g$ (already contained in the theory of Heitler and London) and the excited state $(2p\sigma)^2\ {}^1\Sigma_g$.

To reach this result once again Majorana demonstrates his capability to remarkably master the use of wave functions (see, for instance, the discussion on the configuration space for the electron density distribution, the comment on the nodal surfaces, and the motivation for selecting the singlet states). Moreover, in order to obtain quantitative results he manages to overcome the limits imposed by analytical non-integrability using, with artfulness, appropriate simplifications. As the starting point of his study is connected with experimental facts, similarly the data reported in the literature are always used as a feedback for his calculations.

In this respect it is worth to underline the style of Majorana in making this comparison. In the presence of a good agreement with the experimental data Majorana does not hesitate to almost diminish its importance by commenting: *"...it is perhaps possible to attribute... the too favourable result in the calculation of the energy to the use for H^- of a non properly correct eigenfunction."* Similar comments are also present at the end of paper no. 2 and denote an intellectual honesty and, at the same time, a spirit inclined to astonishment which, especially nowadays, are quite rare virtues.

ANTONIO SASSO
Università di Napoli

NOTA SCIENTIFICA n. 5   —   SCIENTIFIC PAPER no. 5

Teoria dei tripletti P' incompleti

Nota di Ettore Majorana

"Il Nuovo Cimento", vol. 8, 1931, pp. 107-113.

Sunto. — I più noti tripletti anomali posti sopra il limite delle serie normali sono stabili se si trascurano le correzioni relativistiche. La presenza dei momenti magnetici intrinseci determina una leggera instabilità che solo in circostanze eccezionali può assumere importanza quantitativa. Le condizioni a ciò necessarie sono soddisfatte per la componente $j = 2$ dei tripletti anomali di Zn, Cd e Hg; l'esperienza conferma che la componente $^3P_2$ di questi tripletti è assente o indebolita.

Nello spettro del calcio sono noti cinque gruppi ciascuno di sei linee che sono combinazioni del termine $1s2p\,^3P_{012}$ (numeri correnti empirici) con una successione di tripletti $^3P'_{012}$ che si lasciano ordinare in serie; ma il limite di questa serie corrisponde a Ca$^+$ con l'elettrone esterno nell'orbita $3d$ e non nell'orbita fondamentale $1s$, come accade per le serie normali, e questa ed altre circostanze obbligano ad attribuire ai tripletti P' del calcio la configurazione $3dnd\,^3P_{012}$ ($n = 3, 4, 5, \ldots$). Si tratta dunque di stati con entrambi gli elettroni eccitati. Ciò che vogliamo qui rilevare a proposito di tali termini anomali del calcio, è solo che parte di essi stanno al di sopra del potenziale di ionizzazione, nel campo dello spettro continuo, e ciò nonostante sono stabili, non danno luogo cioè a una ionizzazione spontanea apprezzabile. Questo fatto non ha nulla di strano, poiché sarebbe facile dimostrare che nell'approssimazione non relativistica i detti termini hanno tali caratteri di simmetria che le transizioni allo spettro continuo sono rigorosamente vietate. Ma in altri elementi e precisamente in Zn, Cd e Hg sono conosciuti tripletti P' oltre il potenziale di ionizzazione che dovrebbero essere stabili per le stesse ragioni, ma nei quali

manca la componente P'_2, mentre P'_1 e P'_0 sono state osservate. Questi termini di Zn, Cd e Hg sono analoghi a quelli del calcio ora ricordati, benché derivino da configurazioni differenti (pp in luogo di dd), e perché in quelli manchi una componente, e precisamente P'_2, è quanto qui ci proponiamo di studiare. L'ipotesi affacciata da FOOTE, TAKAMINE e CHENAULT([1]), limitatamente a Cd, e anche per spiegare certe anomalie di intensità, che il termine P'_2 esista, ma sia accidentalmente così prossimo a P'_1 da rendere impossibile la risoluzione, non mi sembra sostenibile, sia perché di troppo contraddice alle regole dell'accoppiamento normale, sia perché è smentita dalla mancanza dei termini analoghi, di Zn e Hg. Voglio ancora notare che per Zn, esattamente al posto delle righe mancanti $^3P'_2 - {}^3P_2$ e $^3P'_2 - {}^3P_1$ SAWYER([2]) pose due linee $^1D_2 - {}^3P_2$ e $^1D_2 - {}^3P_1$ più deboli e di aspetto differente da quello delle quattro linee restanti del gruppo $P\ P'$, essendo $^1D_2$ uno degli stati che derivano da due orbite $2p$; secondo la presente teoria le righe di SAWYER sono invece precisamente le righe $^3P'_2 - {}^3P_2$ e $^3P'_2 - {}^3P_1$ che completano il gruppo PP', indebolite perché il termine $^3P'_2$ è instabile per effetto AUGER, e questo è dovuto all'interazione fra *spin* e orbita; al contrario righe che fanno capo al termine $^1D_2$ non devono essere osservabili perché la instabilità di questo termine è assai maggiore, non ostandovi i suoi caratteri di simmetria anche se si prescinde dal momento magnetico degli elettroni.

1. Da due orbite $2p$ equivalenti derivano senza elettrone rotante i termini ^1D, ^3P e ^1S (gli indici di molteplicità indicano solo simmetria o antisimmetria delle autofunzioni dei baricentri) la cui separazione dipende in prima approssimazione da un unico parametro e può calcolarsi con il metodo di SLATER([3]); si trova che ^3P è il più profondo, ^1S il più alto, e che la distanza $^1S - {}^1D$ vale 3/2 della distanza $^1D - {}^3P$. Per ciò che riguarda il valore assoluto della separazione, possiamo stimarne l'ordine di grandezza, usando autofunzioni approssimate. I risultati di questo metodo si accordano bene con quanto si osserva, ad esempio, nei termini profondi del silicio; ma vi sono dei casi in cui la prima approssimazione è insufficiente, e citiamo il magnesio dove sono conosciuti il termine $(2p)^2\ {}^3P_{012}$ e, se un'interpretazione di SAWYER([4]) è corretta, anche il termine $(2p)^2\ {}^1D_2$. Qui il termine $^1D_2$ è effettivamente più alto di $^3P_{012}$ come vuole il metodo di SLATER, ma la separazione è solo di alcune centinaia di cm^{-1} non di alcune migliaia come quel metodo farebbe prevedere; l'anomalia può forse essere spiegata con l'influenza prevalente dello spettro continuo, specie dello "stato virtuale" $(3d)^2\ {}^1D_2$ sul termine $(2p)^2\ {}^1D_2$. Ragioni analoghe possono valere per i termini $(2p)^2\ {}^3P_{012}$ e $(2p)^2\ {}^1D_2$ di Zn, Cd e Hg, ma si tratta di termini che sono sopra il limite di ionizzazione, e non considerando il momento magnetico dell'elettrone, solo il primo è stabile, perché è un termine *riflesso*([5]) mentre gli stati dello spettro continuo appartenenti alla stessa energia hanno simmetria normale;

([1]) P. D. FOOTE, T. TAKAMINE e R. L. CHENAULT, "Phys. Rev.", *26*, 174 (1925).

([2]) R. A. SAWYER, "J. Opt. Soc. Am.", *13*, 431 (1926).

([3]) J. C. SLATER, "Phys. Rev.", *34*, 1293 (1929).

([4]) R. A. SAWYER, loc. cit.

([5]) E. WIGNER, "Z. Physik", *43*, 624 (1927).

$(2p)^2\,{}^1D_2$ è al contrario esso stesso uno "stato virtuale" nel senso di Beck[6], e la sua energia, non esattamente definita, è poco maggiore di quella di $(2p)^2\,{}^3P_{012}$. L'interazione fra momento intrinseco e orbitale di ciascuno dei due elettroni stabilisce però una mutua influenza fra lo stato virtuale $(2p)^2\,{}^1D_2$ e quella componente di $(2p)^2\,{}^3P_{012}$ che appartiene allo stesso valore del quanto interno $(j = 2)$; e la conseguenza è che anche ${}^3P_2$ diviene instabile, potendo dar luogo a una ionizzazione spontanea che significa passaggio *senza radiazione* da tripletti a singoletti. La vicinanza di uno stato virtuale con opportuni caratteri di simmetria è necessaria solo perché l'effetto Auger assuma importanza quantitativa, ma anche quando quello manca come per la componente ${}^3P_1$, o è abbastanza lontano, come lo stato virtuale $(2p)^2\,{}^1S_0$ per la componente ${}^3P_0$, dobbiamo aspettarci una leggera instabilità, e questo può spiegare le anomalie di intensità osservate nelle righe superstiti del gruppo PP'. Premettiamo pertanto alcune considerazioni generali sull'influenza dei momenti magnetici intrinseci di tutti gli stati ${}^1D_2\,{}^3P_2\,{}^3P_1\,{}^3P_0\,{}^1S_0$ che derivano da due orbite $2p$. Trascurando, come è lecito per numeri atomici sufficientemente alti, l'interazione magnetica fra i due elettroni, e solo portando[*] in conto l'interazione fra il campo elettrico costante dovuto al resto atomico e i momenti magnetici degli elettroni in movimento, cioè il cosidetto accoppiamento fra *spin* e orbita, la perturbazione si può far dipendere dalla hamiltoniana:

$$(1) \qquad\qquad H = f(r_1)(s_1, M_1) + f(r_2)(s_2, M_2)$$

essendo s_1, s_2 e M_1, M_2 i momenti intrinseci e orbitali dei due elettroni, che per semplicità supporremo misurati in unità $h/2\pi$, e $f(r)$ una funzione del raggio proporzionale a $\frac{1}{r}\frac{dV}{dr}$. Scegliamo come sistema di coordinate quello in cui l'energia impertubata è diagonale e ammettiamo ancora che con sufficiente approssimazione le autofunzioni imperturbate possano essere espresse come combinazioni lineari di prodotti di autofunzioni dei singoli elettroni, rappresentanti stati stazionarii individuali in un conveniente campo centrale. Giova allora rappresentare la matrice di H come somma di prodotti delle matrici $f(r_1)$ e $f(r_2)$, facilmente valutabili mediante quadrature, per le matrici (s_1, M_1) e (s_2, M_2), le quali ultime sono in detta approssimazione matrici costanti, che legano cioè solo stati con uguale energia, poiché tali sono separatamente s_1, M_1, s_2 e M_2; ma è da notare che funzioni dipendenti dalle coordinate di *un solo* elettrone, quali $f(r_1)$, s_1, M_1, etc. non sono grandezze fisiche, e possono formalmente riguardarsi come tali, ed esprimersi con matrici, solo se si rinuncia al principio di Pauli e si considerano anche autofunzioni complete non antisimmetriche. La complicazione che ne risulta non è eccessiva nel caso di due soli elettroni, poiché qui un solo carattere di simmetria non Paulistico resta da considerare: quello delle autofunzioni simmetriche. Ai termini già indicati dobbiamo ancora, ad esempio, aggiungere i seguenti che derivano da due orbite $2p$, e che chiudo in parentesi per indicare che non soddisfano al principio di Pauli $({}^3D_{123})\,({}^1P_1)\,({}^3S_1)$. In

---

[6] G. Beck, "Z. Physik", *62*, 331 (1930).
[*] Ne "Il Nuovo Cimento" è stampato "pertanto", ma dal manoscritto risulta "portando". (Nota del Curatore in E. Amaldi, *op. cit.*)

tutto per i singoli valori di j troviamo:

(2)
$$\begin{cases} j = 3 : (^3D_3) \\ j = 2 : {}^1D_2, {}^3P_2, (^3D_2) \\ j = 1 : {}^3P_1, (^3D_1), (^1P_1), (^3S_1) \\ j = 0 : {}^3P_2, {}^1S_0. \end{cases}$$

Poiché ognuno di questi stati è degenerato $(2j+1)$ volte abbiamo in tutto naturalmente 36 stati, ogni elettrone potendo essere in 3 (degenerazione orbitale) $\times 2$ (degenerazione instrinseca) = 6 stati differenti, e il principio di esclusione è inattivo. Le matrici (s_1, M_1) e (s_2, M_2) che legano fra loro, e in prima approssimazione soltanto fra loro, gli stati (2), si costruiscono direttamente con artifici su cui lo spazio mi vieta di fermarmi. Se riferiamo righe e colonne ai vari stati nello stesso ordine in cui questi sono riportati in (2), tali matrici sono

$j = 3$
$$(s_1, M_1) = (s_2, M_2) = \frac{1}{2}$$

$j = 2$

$$(s_1, M_1) = \begin{vmatrix} 0 & \dfrac{1}{2\sqrt{2}} & -\dfrac{\sqrt{3}}{2\sqrt{2}} \\[2mm] \dfrac{1}{2\sqrt{2}} & \dfrac{1}{4} & \dfrac{\sqrt{3}}{4} \\[2mm] -\dfrac{\sqrt{3}}{2\sqrt{2}} & \dfrac{\sqrt{3}}{4} & -\dfrac{1}{2} \end{vmatrix} \qquad (s_2, M_2) = \begin{vmatrix} 0 & \dfrac{1}{2\sqrt{2}} & \dfrac{\sqrt{3}}{2\sqrt{2}} \\[2mm] \dfrac{1}{2\sqrt{2}} & \dfrac{1}{4} & -\dfrac{\sqrt{3}}{4} \\[2mm] \dfrac{\sqrt{3}}{2\sqrt{2}} & -\dfrac{\sqrt{3}}{4} & -\dfrac{1}{4} \end{vmatrix}$$

$j = 1$

$$(s_1, M_1) = \begin{vmatrix} -\dfrac{1}{4} & \dfrac{\sqrt{5}}{4\sqrt{3}} & \dfrac{1}{2\sqrt{2}} & -\dfrac{1}{\sqrt{3}} \\[2mm] \dfrac{\sqrt{5}}{4\sqrt{3}} & -\dfrac{3}{4} & \dfrac{\sqrt{5}}{2\sqrt{6}} & 0 \\[2mm] \dfrac{1}{2\sqrt{2}} & \dfrac{\sqrt{5}}{2\sqrt{6}} & 0 & \dfrac{1}{\sqrt{6}} \\[2mm] -\dfrac{1}{\sqrt{3}} & 0 & \dfrac{1}{\sqrt{6}} & 0 \end{vmatrix}$$

$$(s_2, M_2) = \begin{vmatrix} -\dfrac{1}{4} & -\dfrac{\sqrt{5}}{4\sqrt{3}} & -\dfrac{1}{2\sqrt{2}} & \dfrac{1}{\sqrt{3}} \\[2mm] -\dfrac{5}{4\sqrt{3}} & -\dfrac{3}{4} & \dfrac{\sqrt{5}}{2\sqrt{6}} & 0 \\[2mm] -\dfrac{1}{2\sqrt{2}} & \dfrac{\sqrt{5}}{2\sqrt{6}} & 0 & \dfrac{1}{\sqrt{6}} \\[2mm] \dfrac{1}{\sqrt{3}} & 0 & \dfrac{1}{\sqrt{6}} & 0 \end{vmatrix}$$

$$j = 0 \qquad\qquad (s_1, M_1) = (s_2, M_2) = \begin{vmatrix} -\dfrac{1}{2} & \dfrac{1}{\sqrt{2}} \\[2mm] \dfrac{1}{\sqrt{2}} & 0 \end{vmatrix}.$$

Queste equazioni devono intendersi ripetute per ogni valore permesso del quanto magnetico. Deduciamo le seguenti espressioni di $H\psi$ per le componenti del tripletto P':

$$(3) \quad \begin{cases} H\,{}^3P_2 = \dfrac{f(r_1) + f(r_2)}{4}\,{}^3P_2 + \dfrac{f(r_1) + f(r_2)}{2\sqrt{2}}\,{}^1D_2 + \sqrt{3}\,\dfrac{f(r_1) - f(r_2)}{4}\,({}^3D_2) \\[3mm] H\,{}^3P_1 = -\dfrac{f(r_1) + f(r_2)}{4}\,{}^3P_1 + \sqrt{5}\,\dfrac{f(r_1) - f(r_2)}{4\sqrt{3}}\,({}^3D_1) + \\[3mm] \qquad\qquad + \dfrac{f(r_1) - f(r_2)}{2\sqrt{2}}\,({}^3P_1) - \dfrac{f(r_1) - f(r_2)}{\sqrt{3}}\,({}^3S_1) \\[3mm] H\,{}^3P_0 = -\dfrac{f(r_1) + f(r_2)}{2}\,{}^3P_0 + \dfrac{f(r_1) + f(r_2)}{\sqrt{2}}\,{}^1S_0. \end{cases}$$

I quadrati dei coefficienti dello sviluppo di $H\psi$ che si riferiscono a stati dello spettro continuo aventi la stessa energia di ψ sono proporzionali, in valore assoluto e in *prima approssimazione*, alla probabilità di ionizzazione spontanea, secondo la formula di Wentzel[7]. I vari addendi nei secondi membri di (3) sono funzioni *pari* e quelli che appartengono a $L = l$ sono ortogonali agli stati dello spettro continuo aventi l'energia del tripletto P', perché tali stati risultano da un elettrone $1s$ e uno in un'orbita iperbolica e possono essere, o pari con $L = 0, 2, 4, \dots$, o dispari con $L = 1, 3, 5, \dots$ Gli altri termini nei secondi membri di (3) sono *normalmente* quasi ortogonali agli stessi stati dello spettro continuo, a causa della diversa dipendenza angolare, e lo sarebbero esattamente trascurando la polarizzazione; oltre a ciò portano a fattore $f(r)$ che è dell'ordine degli effetti relativistici, e poiché l'effetto Auger dipende dal quadrato delle componenti utili di H, concludiamo che esso è *ordinariamente* assai debole per termini del nostro tipo. Le cose cambiano se è presente uno stato virtuale con energia poco diversa, come ${}^1D_2$ per la componente ${}^3P_2$. Anche ${}^1S_0$ è uno stato virtuale che potrebbe influire sulla stabilità di ${}^3P_0$, ma è troppo lontano e la distanza è accresciuta dagli effetti relativistici. Tornando a ${}^1D_2$ questo stato può essere descritto con una autofunzione la cui dipendenza dal tempo è della forma $e^{-\frac{2\pi i}{h}E_0 t}e^{-\frac{t}{2T}} = e^{-\frac{2\pi i}{h}Et}$ essendo $E = E_0 + \frac{h}{4\pi iT}$ un autovalore *complesso*; questa espressione di ψ vale naturalmente solo se entrambi gli elettroni si trovano in una regione dell'ordine delle dimensioni atomiche. Supponiamo ora che l'indeterminazione $a = \frac{h}{4\pi T}$ dell'energia di ${}^1D_2$(*) e la distanza d fra E_0 e l'energia di ${}^3P_2$ (incluso il termine diagonale della perturbazione H) siano piccoli rispetto al valore (negativo) del termine; introduciamo ancora $\Delta = \frac{3}{2}\overline{f(r)}$, essendo il valore medio $\overline{f(r)}$ preso su un'orbita $2p$, che rappresenta la separazione energetica fra le componenti

---

(7) G. Wentzel, "Z. Physik", *43*, 524 (1927).
(*) Ne "Il Nuovo Cimento" è erroneamente stampato ${}^3P_2$. (Nota del Curatore.)

estreme del tripletto normale $1s2p\,{}^3P_{012}$ o, ciò che in prima approssimazione è lo stesso, la separazione del tripletto anomalo $(2p)^2\,{}^3P_{012}$. Supponiamo ancora Δ piccolo nello stesso senso. Allora si può usare un formalismo assai semplice, la cui giustificazione non sarebbe difficile fondare sulle proprietà di quelle soluzioni periodiche appartenenti a una stretta regione dello spettro continuo, secondo cui lo stato virtuale ${}^1D_2$ arbitrariamente limitato è praticamente sviluppabile; lo studio dell'influenza di ${}^1D_2$ su ${}^3P_2$ è ridotto ad un ordinario problema di perturbazione, e si tratta di trovare gli autovalori (complessi) e gli autovettori (non ortogonali) della matrice:

$$
\begin{array}{c}
{}^1D_2 \\
{}^3P_2
\end{array}
\left|
\begin{array}{cc}
d - ai & \dfrac{\sqrt{2}}{3}\Delta \\[2mm]
\dfrac{\sqrt{2}}{3}\Delta & 0
\end{array}
\right| .
$$

Il coefficiente dell'immaginario nell'autovalore perturbato di ${}^3P_2$ misura con il suo valore assoluto l'indeterminazione dell'energia (semilarghezza) di questo stato, e diviso per $h/4\pi$ dà la probabilità di ionizzazione spontanea nell'unità di tempo. Se Δ è abbastanza piccolo di fronte a $\sqrt{d^2 + a^2}$, e questo potrebbe anche non essere il caso reale, la semilarghezza del termine ${}^3P_2$ vale $\frac{2}{9}\frac{\Delta^2}{d^2+a^2}a(^*)$; per $a \to 0$ questa formula è evidente perché indica che per avere la probabilità di ionizzazione di ${}^3P_2$ basta moltiplicare quella di ${}^1D_2$ per il rapporto in cui ${}^1D_2$ entra in ${}^3P_2$ perturbato, secondo la comune teoria delle perturbazioni. Per grandi valori di a, cioè per grande instabilità di ${}^1D_2$, l'instabilità indotta in ${}^3P_2$ torna a diminuire dopo aver toccato un massimo, e questo è da intendere nel senso che uno stato ${}^1D_2$ eccessivamente instabile cessa di essere "uno stato virtuale", la cui presenza è in ogni caso necessaria perché l'effetto Auger del termine $(2p)^2\,{}^3P_2$ assuma importanza quantitativa.

(*) Ne "Il Nuovo Cimento" è erroneamente stampato $\frac{2}{9}\frac{\Delta^2}{d^2+a^2}a^2$. (Nota del Curatore.)

Commento alla Nota Scientifica n. 5 : *"Teoria dei tripletti P' incompleti".*

Questo articolo, pubblicato da Majorana mentre rimane a Roma dopo la discussione della propria tesi di laurea, tratta un problema di spettoscopia atomica, la caratterizzazione degli spettri ottici d'atomi con due elettroni nell'orbita più esterna. Il lavoro di Majorana fu stimolato dalle osservazioni sperimentali pubblicate nel 1925, rif. (1) del lavoro originale, da un gruppo di ricerca del *National Bureau of Standard* (il predecessore dell'attuale *US National Institute of Standards and Technology*). L'importante risultato sperimentale di P. Foote *et al.* era la mancata osservazione di alcune righe previste nello spettro d'assorbimento degli atomi di Hg, Cd e Zn. Più precisamente, fra le sei righe previste per le transizioni ai livelli di tripletto $p^2\ {}^3P_{0,1,2}$ più bassi in energia, quelle associate al livello ${}^3P_2$ non erano presenti nello spettro di nessuno dei tre atomi. Majorana presenta una spiegazione dell'assenza di tali righe introducendo un nuovo processo spettroscopico che chiama *ionizzazione spontanea*.

A quel tempo, era ben noto che le serie di righe spettrali associate ad atomi (o ioni) con più elettroni nell'orbita più esterna presentavano deviazioni nella posizione dei livelli d'energia e nell'intensità delle righe previste dalle relazioni matematiche valide per gli spettri atomici più semplici. Tali deviazioni erano note come perturbazioni. Le perturbazioni sono prodotte da un processo di risonanza dove due (o più) livelli atomici sono quasi degeneri in energia, e gli autostati sono mescolati dalle interazioni fra gli elettroni. Come conseguenza, le nuove autofunzioni sono soluzioni dell'equazione di Schrödinger che tiene conto del mescolamento prodotto dalle interazioni, con nuovi autovalori in energia e nuove probabilità di transizione per l'assorbimento di luce. Majorana introduce un nuovo tipo di perturbazione, proponendo che i livelli $p^2\ {}^3P_{0,1,2}$ siano perturbati da livelli degeneri posizionati nel continuo sopra il livello di ionizzazione per l'eccitazione di un singolo elettrone. Ipotizza quindi un mescolamento tra livelli discreti e livelli nel continuo. A causa della perturbazione tali livelli discreti acquistano alcune caratteristiche tipiche delle transizioni ottiche associate al continuo: grandi larghezze di riga, asimmetrie nella forma di riga ed intensità anomale nell'emissione ed assorbimento di radiazione. Per esempio, i livelli discreti che sono mescolati al continuo possono decadere attraverso un processo di transizione non radiativa, che converte l'energia dell'atomo eccitato in un elettrone libero ed uno ione positivo. Questo processo costituisce il processo di *ionizzazione spontanea* definito da Majorana e rappresenta l'equivalente nel campo ottico del processo Auger ben noto nel caso dei raggi X, processo menzionato alla fine dell'articolo.

Per le molecole un processo simile, discusso da R. de L. Kronig alcuni anni prima[1], è la predissociazione senza emissione di radiazione quando la somma delle energie vibrazionali ed elettronica della molecola risulta maggiore dell'energia necessaria alla dissociazione in una configurazione elettronica con un'energia più bassa.

Il processo di ionizzazione spontanea per gli spettri ottici atomici fu introdotto in maniera indipendente lo stesso anno da A. G. Shenstone dell'Università di Princeton in una pubblicazione su *The Physical Review*[2]. Shenstone analizza il livello $^3P_2^0$ dell'atomo di mercurio che era stato scoperto poco prima da T. Takamine e T. Suga[3], con l'osservazione confermata da F. Paschen[4]. Shenstone identifica lo stesso processo introdotto da Majorana, ma lo chiama *auto-ionizzazione*, termine che è rimasto standard nella letteratura di spettroscopia atomica, usualmente scritto *autoionizzazione*. In realtà l'attenzione di Shenstone era concentrata sull'atomo di rame il cui spettro ottico è realmente unico in quanto l'autoionizzazione è la regola invece di essere l'eccezione, come affermato nella sua dettagliata descrizione dello spettro di tale elemento pubblicata nel 1936[5].

In un'importante pubblicazione del 1935[6], H. Beutler dell'Università di Berlino pubblicò un'analisi dettagliata dello spettro d'assorbimento dei gas nobili per livelli atomici che si trovano sopra il limite di ionizzazione. Nel suo studio Beutler interpreta le osservazioni di forti modulazioni asimmetriche nello spettro d'assorbimento come prodotte dal processo di autoionizzazione e cita i lavori di Kroning e di Shenstone, ma non quello di Majorana. Invece il libro *The Theory of Atomic Spectra* di E. U. Condon e G. H. Shortley nel 1935[7], spesso indicato come la "Bibbia" della spettroscopia atomica, riconosce il contributo simultaneo ed indipendente di Majorana e Shenstone al concetto di autoionizzazione. Ancora nello stesso anno il lavoro di Beutler attrae l'attenzione di E. Fermi a Roma, che suggerisce al suo giovane collaboratore U. Fano di trovare un'adeguata spiegazione per le forme di riga ottenute da Beutler. Infatti, come osservato dallo stesso Fano, l'ipotesi d'autoionizzazione da sola non forniva la spiegazione delle forme di riga allargate in maniera asimmetrica. Rapidamente Fano produsse una precisa descrizione teorica per il mescolamento di un livello discreto con un continuo, pubblicata in un articolo nel 1935[8]. Questo lavoro, e l'analisi di Fano più dettagliata pubblicata nel 1961[9], introdussero il profilo di autoionizzazione di Beutler-Fano, una formula per la forma di riga che ha trovato larga applicazione in molti campi della fisica. La ricerca

[1] R. de L. Kronig, *Z. Phys.* **50** (1928) 347.
[2] A. G. Shenstone, *Phys. Rev.* **38** (1931) 873.
[3] T. Takamine e T. Suga, *Sci. Pap. Inst. Phys. and Chem. Res. Tokyo* **13** (1930) 1.
[4] F. Paschen, *Ann. Phys. (Leipzig)* **6** (1930) 47.
[5] A. G. Shenstone, *Philos. Trans. Roy Soc. London* **235** (1936) 195.
[6] H. Beutler, *Z. Phys.* **93** (1935) 177.
[7] E. U. Condon e G. H. Shortley, *"Theory of Atomic Spectra"* (Cambridge University Press), 1935.
[8] U. Fano, *Nuovo Cimento* **12** (1935) 154.
[9] U. Fano, *Phys. Rev.* **124** (1961) 1866.

svolta da Fano al NIST negli anni '60, e lo sviluppo parallelo di tecniche sperimentali per la spettroscopia nell'ultravioletto estremo, di nuovo soprattutto al NIST, ha condotto le forme di riga Beutler-Fano alla frontiera del progresso nella fisica atomica, come descritto concisamente da C. W. Clark nel 2001[10]. Il concetto d'autoionizzazione ha giocato un importante ruolo nello sviluppo della spettroscopia, poiché è osservata in una grande varietà di spettri atomici e molecolari, e risultati molto differenti sono ottenuti per l'energia e le probabilità dei livelli mescolati dalle pertubazioni.

L'analisi di Majorana del 1931 non esamina lo spettro dell'assorbimento associato all'autoionizzazione. Invece di descrivere il continuo attraverso una distribuzione continua di stati come nelle analisi di Fano, Majorana calcola il mescolamento tra un livello che presenta un decadimento radiativo trascurabile ed un singolo livello che simula il continuo attraverso una larghezza di riga grande, descritta dalla quantità "a" introdotta in fondo a pagina 95. Infine Majorana non deriva l'espressione per la probabilità di transizione del processo di assorbimento che termina nel livello mescolato dalla pertubazione. Anche se la descrizione di Majorana non è completa, dalla diagonalizzazione della matrice di pertubazione che scrive nella pagina finale del suo articolo si potrebbe derivare una espressione per la forma di riga di assorbimento riproducente la caratteristica forma a dente di sega associata al profilo di autoionizzazione. Tale derivazione della forma di riga è stata fatta da B. W. Shore nel 1968[11].

Il mescolamento degli stati discreti e del continuo introdotto da Majorana che produce il processo di autoionizzazione è molto complesso. Il mescolamento della autoionizzazione può avvenire se un livello discreto con energia sopra quella del limite di ionizzazione è quasi risonante con un continuo che possiede la stessa parità e lo stesso momento angolare. Per il caso dei livelli $p^2\ ^3P_2$ di Hg, Cd e Zn, non esiste un continuo con carattere $^3P_2$ e simmetrico per parità che possa contribuire al mescolamento di autoionizzazione. Pertanto Majorana decide di introdurre un accoppiamento diverso fra gli elettroni dell'orbita più esterna, un accoppiamento non corrispondente al tipico caso LS di Russell-Saunders. Grazie a questo diverso accoppiamento i livelli discreti acquistano caratteristiche miste di termini $p^2\ ^3P_2$ e $sd\ ^1D_2$ e quindi possiedono un contributo di singoletto necessario ad autoionizzare facilmente nel continuo $sd\ ^1D_2$. Come giustamente fa notare Majorana, questo complicato schema di mescolamento di livelli, prima fra i livelli discreti e poi fra i livelli discreti così mescolati a quelli del continuo, non è strettamente necessario per produrre l'ionizzazione spontanea. Tuttavia in assenza del mescolamento fra carattere tripletto e singoletto per i livelli discreti, la autoionizzazione sarebbe molto debole e quindi non in grado di spiegare la sparizione delle righe associate al livello p^2 $^3P_2$. Condon e Shortley nel loro libro del 1935 affermano che la discussione di Majorana non è molto convincente, poiché un simile processo di autoionizzazione, con sparizione delle righe di assorbimento, dovrebbe applicarsi anche al livello $p^2\ ^3P_0$. Di conseguenza

[10] C. W. CLARK, in *"A Century of Excellence in Measurements, Standards, and Technology"* NIST Special Publication 958, a cura di David R. Lide (Washington, DC USA) 2001, p. 116.
[11] B. W. SHORE, *Phys. Rev.* **171** (1968) 43.

le identificazioni spettroscopiche e lo schema di autoionizzazione di Majorana non sono state accettate per un lungo tempo. La storia delle linee spettrali mancanti termina nel 1955 quando W. R. S. Garton e A. Rajaratnam[12] furono capaci di identificare nello spettro di Zn le deboli righe di assorbimento terminanti nel livello $p^2\ ^3P_2$ ed allargate per autoionizzazione. In seguito, nel 1970, W. C. Martin e V. Kaufman[13] confermarono la correttezza degli assegnamenti spettroscopici fatti da Majorana. Infine nel 1986[14] e nel 1988[15] due gruppi di ricercatori ad Orsay e Caen misurarono le larghezze di riga associate alla autoionizzazione utilizzando la rivelazione optogalvanica. Gli stessi gruppi di ricercatori fecero anche una precisa trattazione teorica del mescolamento fra i livelli discreti e quelli continui. Pertanto, tutte le righe che appartengono alla configurazione p^2 subiscono perturbazioni dovute alla autoionizzazione, grandi o piccole, seguendo precisamente lo schema previsto da Majorana.

In conclusione, il lavoro di Majorana contiene tre risultati importanti per il progresso della spettroscopia atomica: i) l'identificazione di righe spettrali in Hg, Cd e Zn; ii) un trattamento dell'accoppiamento fra gli elettroni diverso da quello LS di Russell-Saunders; iii) l'introduzione del processo di autoionizzazione.

ENNIO ARIMONDO
NIST, Gaithersburg, MD (USA)

[12] W. R. S. GARTON e A. RAJARATNAM, Proc. Phys. Soc. A **68** (1955) 1107.
[13] W. C. MARTIN e V. KAUFMAN, J. Opt. Soc. Am. **60** (1970) 1096.
[14] M. AYMAR, E. LUC-KOENING, M. CHANTEPIE, J. L. COJAN, J. LANDAIS e B. LANIEPCE, J. Phys. B: At. Mol. Phys. **19** (1986) 3881.
[15] M. CHANTEPIE, B. CHERON, J. L. COJAN, J. LANDAIS, B. LANIEPCE e M. AYMAR, J. Phys. B: At. Mol. Phys. **21** (1988) 1379.

Theory of the incomplete P' triplets(*)

Ettore Majorana

Summary. — Most of the anomalous triplets above the limit of the normal series are stable if relativistic corrections are neglected. The presence of intrinsic magnetic moments produces a small instability that only in exceptional cases can have a quantitative importance. The necessary conditions for such a case to occur are satisfied by the component $j=2$ of the anomalous triplets of Zn, Cd and Hg. Experimentally the component $^3P_2$ of these triplets seems absent or weak.

Five groups of terms, each one with six lines, are known in the calcium spectrum that can be attributed to combinations of the term $1s2p\,^3P_{012}$ (current empirical numbers) with a succession of triplets $^3P'_{012}$ that can be ordered as a series. However the limit of this series corresponds to Ca^+ with the external electron in the orbit $3d$ and not in the fundamental orbit $1s$ as happens in normal series. This fact, together with some other indications, suggests to attribute to the P' triplets of calcium the configuration $3dnd\,^3P_{012}$ ($n = 3, 4, 5, \ldots$). These states therefore correspond to excitation of two electrons. What we want to point out, apropos of these anomalous terms of calcium, is that only some of them are above the ionization potential in the continuous spectrum and nevertheless are stable, *i.e.* they do not give rise to an appreciable spontaneous ionization. There is nothing strange in this as it would be easy to prove that in the non-relativistic approximation such terms have a symmetry character which rigorously forbids transitions to the continuous spectrum. In other elements however, in particular in Zn, Cd and Hg, P' triplets are known above the ionization potential that should be stable for the same

---

(*) Translated from "Il Nuovo Cimento", vol. 8, 1931, pp. 107-113, by P. Radicati di Brozolo.

reasons; however the component P_2' is absent, whereas P_1' and P_0' have been observed. These terms of Zn, Cd and Hg are analogous to those of calcium mentioned above, even though they arise from different configurations (pp instead of dd). Here we want to study why in this case the component P_2' is absent. FOOTE, TAKAMINE and CHENAULT[1] have suggested, only for the case of Cd and to explain some anomalies in the intensities, that the term P_2' exists but is accidentally so close to P_1' to make it impossible to separate the two. This looks to me difficult to believe both because it violently contradicts the rules of the normal coupling and also because it is disproved by the lack of analogous terms in Zn and Hg. I also want to point out that SAWYER[2] has suggested that for Zn, at exactly the same position of the non-existing lines $^3P_2' - {}^3P_2$ and $^3P_2' - {}^3P_1$, two lines $^1D_2 - {}^3P_2$ and $^1D_2 - {}^3P_1$ exist and that both are weaker and of a different aspect from those of the remaining four lines of the group PP' (here $^1D_2$ is one of the states arising from two orbits $2p$). According to the present theory, the lines of SAWYER are instead precisely the lines $^3P_2' - {}^3P_2$ and $^3P_2' - {}^3P_1$ that complete the PP' group. These lines are weaker since the term $^3P_2'$ is unstable because of the AUGER effect; this is due to spin-orbit interaction. Instead the lines that arise from term $^1D_2$ should not be observable because the instability of this term is much larger, as it is not contrasted by its symmetry characters even if we disregard the electron magnetic moment.

1. Without electron rotation, from two equivalent orbits $2p$ we obtain the terms ^1D, ^3P and ^1S (the multiplicity indices only denote the symmetry or antisymmetry of the center-of-mass eigenfunction). Their separation depends, in the first approximation, upon a single parameter and can be calculated with SLATER's method[3]. One finds that ^3P is the deepest state, ^1S the highest and the distance $^1S - {}^1D$ is 3/2 of the distance $^1D - {}^3P$. The order of magnitude of the absolute value of the separation can be estimated by using approximate eigenfunctions. The results of this method are in good agreement with the observed values, for example for the deep terms of silicon. However in some cases the first approximation is insufficient, as for example for magnesium, where the term $(2p)^2\,^3P_{012}$ is known and, if SAWYER's[4] interpretation is correct, also the $(2p)^2\,^1D_2$ one. The term $^1D_2$ is actually higher than $^3P_{012}$ as it follows from SLATER's method but the separation is only a few hundred cm^{-1} and not several thousand as the method would predict. The anomaly can perhaps be attributed to the predominant influence of the continuous spectrum and in particular to the influence of the "virtual state" $(3d)^2\,^1D_2$ on the term $(2p)^2\,^1D_2$. The same reasoning could apply to the terms $(2p)^2\,^3P_{012}$ and $(2p)^2\,^1D_2$ of Zn, Cd and Hg. In this case however the terms are above the ionization limit and, if we disregard the magnetic moment of the electron, only the first one is stable because it is a *reflected* term[5], whereas the states in the continuous

[1] P. D. FOOTE, T. TAKAMINE and R. L. CHENAULT, "Phys. Rev.", *26*, 174 (1925).
[2] R. A. SAWYER, "J. Opt. Soc. Am.", *13*, 431 (1926).
[3] J. C. SLATER, "Phys. Rev.", *34*, 1293 (1929).
[4] R. A. SAWYER, loc. cit.
[5] E. WIGNER, "Z. Physik", *43*, 624 (1927).

spectrum belonging to the same energy have a normal symmetry. The term $(2p)^2\,{}^1D_2$ is instead a "virtual state" in the sense of BECK[6] and its energy, which is not exactly defined, is slightly greater than that of $(2p)^2\,{}^3P_{012}$. However, the interaction between the intrinsic momentum and the orbital one of each of the two electrons establishes a mutual influence between the virtual state $(2p)^2\,{}^1D_2$ and the component of $(2p)^2\,{}^3P_{012}$ that belongs to the same value of the internal quantum ($j = 2$). As a consequence also ${}^3P_2$ becomes unstable and can give rise to a spontaneous ionization which means a transition *without radiation* from triplets to singlets. The closeness of a virtual state with appropriate symmetry characters is necessary only if the AUGER effect has to acquire a sizable importance; but even when that is absent, as is the case for the component ${}^3P_1$, or when it is sufficiently far away, as the virtual state $(2p)^2\,{}^1S_0$ for the component ${}^3P_0$, we can expect a weak instability which can explain the anomalies of the intensities that one observes in the remaining lines of the group PP'. Let us then premise a few general considerations on the influence of the intrinsic magnetic moment in all the states ${}^1D_2\,{}^3P_2\,{}^3P_1\,{}^3P_0\,{}^1S_0$ arising from two orbits $2p$. For sufficiently high atomic numbers, we can neglect the magnetic interaction between the two electrons and only take into account the interaction between the constant electric field arising from the remaining atomic cloud and the magnetic moment of the moving electrons which is the so-called spin-orbit coupling. The perturbation is thus described by the Hamiltonian

$$(1) \qquad\qquad H = f(r_1)(s_1, M_1) + f(r_2)(s_2, M_2),$$

where s_1, s_2 and M_1, M_2 are the intrinsic and orbital momenta of the two electrons measured in units of $h/2\pi$ and $f(r)$ is a function of the radius proportional to $\frac{1}{r}\frac{dV}{dr}$. Let us choose the coordinate system so that the unperturbed energy be diagonal and let us further suppose that the unperturbed eigenfunctions can, with sufficient approximation, be expressed as linear combinations of products of the eigenfunctions of the single electrons; these functions represent individual stationary states in an appropriate central field. Then the matrix of H can be conveniently represented as a sum of products of the matrices $f(r_1)$ and $f(r_2)$, that can be easily evaluated through quadratures, times the matrices (s_1, M_1) and (s_2, M_2). In this approximation the latter are constant matrices, *i.e.* that link only states with equal energies, because so are the matrices s_1, M_1, s_2 and M_2, separately. However the functions that depend upon the coordinates of a *single* electron, as $f(r_1)$, s_1, M_1 etc. are not physical quantities. We can formally consider them as such and express them by matrices only if we renounce PAULI's principle and include also complete non-antisymmetrical eigenfunctions. In the case of only two electrons the resulting complication is not too great because we need to consider only one symmetry character that does not follow PAULI's principle, *i.e.* that of symmetrical eigenfunctions. For example we should further add to the terms already considered the following terms arising from two orbits $2p$: we shall write them in brackets to recall that they do not satisfy PAULI's principle $({}^3D_{123})\,({}^1P_1)\,({}^3S_1)$. For each individual value of j all terms are

---

[6] G. BECK, "Z. Physik", *62*, 331 (1930).

listed below:

$$(2) \qquad \begin{cases} j = 3 : (^3D_3) \\ j = 2 : {}^1D_2, {}^3P_2, (^3D_2) \\ j = 1 : {}^3P_1, (^3D_1), (^1P_1), (^3S_1) \\ j = 0 : {}^3P_2, {}^1S_0. \end{cases}$$

Each of these terms is $(2j + 1)$ times degenerate. Therefore we naturally have all together 36 states since each electron can be in 3 (orbital degeneration) $\times 2$ (intrinsic degeneration) $= 6$ different states with no effect of the exclusion principle. The matrices (s_1, M_1) and (s_2, M_2), that in first approximation interconnect only the states of (2), can be constructed directly but we will not enter the details of the calculation. If we refer the rows and columns to the various states in the order in which these appear in (2) the matrices are:

$$j = 3 \qquad\qquad (s_1, M_1) = (s_2, M_2) = \frac{1}{2}$$

$$j = 2 \quad (s_1, M_1) = \begin{vmatrix} 0 & \dfrac{1}{2\sqrt{2}} & -\dfrac{\sqrt{3}}{2\sqrt{2}} \\[2mm] \dfrac{1}{2\sqrt{2}} & \dfrac{1}{4} & \dfrac{\sqrt{3}}{4} \\[2mm] -\dfrac{\sqrt{3}}{2\sqrt{2}} & \dfrac{\sqrt{3}}{4} & -\dfrac{1}{2} \end{vmatrix} \qquad (s_2, M_2) = \begin{vmatrix} 0 & \dfrac{1}{2\sqrt{2}} & \dfrac{\sqrt{3}}{2\sqrt{2}} \\[2mm] \dfrac{1}{2\sqrt{2}} & \dfrac{1}{4} & -\dfrac{\sqrt{3}}{4} \\[2mm] \dfrac{\sqrt{3}}{2\sqrt{2}} & -\dfrac{\sqrt{3}}{4} & -\dfrac{1}{4} \end{vmatrix}$$

$$j = 1 \qquad\qquad (s_1, M_1) = \begin{vmatrix} -\dfrac{1}{4} & \dfrac{\sqrt{5}}{4\sqrt{3}} & \dfrac{1}{2\sqrt{2}} & -\dfrac{1}{\sqrt{3}} \\[2mm] \dfrac{\sqrt{5}}{4\sqrt{3}} & -\dfrac{3}{4} & \dfrac{\sqrt{5}}{2\sqrt{6}} & 0 \\[2mm] \dfrac{1}{2\sqrt{2}} & \dfrac{\sqrt{5}}{2\sqrt{6}} & 0 & \dfrac{1}{\sqrt{6}} \\[2mm] -\dfrac{1}{\sqrt{3}} & 0 & \dfrac{1}{\sqrt{6}} & 0 \end{vmatrix}$$

$$(s_2, M_2) = \begin{vmatrix} -\dfrac{1}{4} & -\dfrac{\sqrt{5}}{4\sqrt{3}} & -\dfrac{1}{2\sqrt{2}} & \dfrac{1}{\sqrt{3}} \\[2mm] -\dfrac{5}{4\sqrt{3}} & -\dfrac{3}{4} & \dfrac{\sqrt{5}}{2\sqrt{6}} & 0 \\[2mm] -\dfrac{1}{2\sqrt{2}} & \dfrac{\sqrt{5}}{2\sqrt{6}} & 0 & \dfrac{1}{\sqrt{6}} \\[2mm] \dfrac{1}{\sqrt{3}} & 0 & \dfrac{1}{\sqrt{6}} & 0 \end{vmatrix}$$

$$j = 0 \qquad\qquad (s_1, M_1) = (s_2, M_2) = \begin{vmatrix} -\dfrac{1}{2} & \dfrac{1}{\sqrt{2}} \\ \dfrac{1}{\sqrt{2}} & 0 \end{vmatrix}.$$

These equations are valid for each allowed value of the magnetic quantum. We obtain in this way the following expressions of $H\psi$ for the components of the triplets P':

(3)
$$\begin{cases} H\,^3P_2 = \dfrac{f(r_1) + f(r_2)}{4}\,^3P_2 + \dfrac{f(r_1) + f(r_2)}{2\sqrt{2}}\,^1D_2 + \sqrt{3}\,\dfrac{f(r_1) - f(r_2)}{4}\,(^3D_2) \\[2mm] H\,^3P_1 = -\dfrac{f(r_1) + f(r_2)}{4}\,^3P_1 + \sqrt{5}\,\dfrac{f(r_1) - f(r_2)}{4\sqrt{3}}\,(^3D_1) + \\[2mm] \qquad\qquad + \dfrac{f(r_1) - f(r_2)}{2\sqrt{2}}\,(^3P_1) - \dfrac{f(r_1) - f(r_2)}{\sqrt{3}}\,(^3S_1) \\[2mm] H\,^3P_0 = -\dfrac{f(r_1) + f(r_2)}{2}\,^3P_0 + \dfrac{f(r_1) + f(r_2)}{\sqrt{2}}\,^1S_0. \end{cases}$$

According to WENTZEL's formula[7] the squares of the coefficients in the expansion of $H\psi$ for states in the continuous spectrum having the same energy as ψ are proportional, in absolute value and in *first approximation*, to the probability of spontaneous ionization. The various terms in the second members of (3) are *even* functions and those that belong to $L = l$ are orthogonal to the states of the continuous spectrum having the same energy as the triplet P', because those states come from one electron $1s$ and one in a hyperbolic orbit and can be even for $L = 0, 2, 4, \ldots$, or odd for $L = 1, 3, 5, \ldots$ The other terms in the right-hand sides of (3) are *usually* almost orthogonal to the same states in the continuous spectrum because of the different angular dependence. They would be exactly orthogonal if one were to neglect the polarization. Furthermore, they all have a common $f(r)$ factor which is of the order of the relativistic effects; since the AUGER effect depends upon the square of the relevant components of H, we can conclude that the effect is *usually* very weak for the terms we are considering. The situation is different if a virtual state is present with almost the same energy, as $^1D_2$ for the component $^3P_2$. Also $^1S_0$ is a virtual state that could influence the stability of $^3P_0$; however it is too far and the distance is increased by relativistic effects. Coming back to $^1D_2$ this state could be described as an eigenfunction whose time dependence is of the form $e^{-\frac{2\pi i}{h} E_0 t} e^{-\frac{t}{2T}} = e^{-\frac{2\pi i}{h} Et}$, where $E = E_0 + \frac{h}{4\pi i T}$ is a *complex* eigenvalue. This expression for ψ is valid of course only if both electrons are in a region of the order of the atomic dimensions. Let us now suppose that the uncertainty $a = \frac{h}{4\pi T}$ of the $^1D_2(*)$ energy and the distance d between E_0 and the energy of $^3P_2$ (including the diagonal term of the perturbation H) are small compared to the (negative) value of the term. Let us further define $\Delta = \frac{3}{2} f(r)$, with the

---

[7] G. WENTZEL, "Z. Physik", *43*, 524 (1927).
(*) Note that in the original text of "Il Nuovo Cimento" it is erroneously printed $^3P_2$. (Note of the Editor.)

average value $\overline{f(r)}$ calculated on an orbit $2p$, which represents the difference between the energies of the extreme components of the normal triplet $1s2p$, $^3P_{012}$ or, which is the same in first approximation, the separation of the anomalous triplet $(2p)^2$ $^3P_{012}$. Let us further suppose that also Δ be small in the same sense. Then one can use a very simple formalism whose justification can easily be based on the properties of those periodic solutions that belong to a narrow region of the continuous spectrum in terms of which the arbitrarily limited virtual state $^1D_2$ can in practice be expanded. The study of the influence of $^1D_2$ on $^3P_2$ is thus reduced to an ordinary perturbation problem and one has to determine the (complex) eigenvalues and the (non-orthogonal) eigenvectors of the matrix:

$$
\begin{array}{c|cc}
 & ^1D_2 & ^3P_2 \\
^1D_2 & d - ai & \dfrac{\sqrt{2}}{3}\Delta \\
^3P_2 & \dfrac{\sqrt{2}}{3}\Delta & 0
\end{array}.
$$

The absolute value of the imaginary coefficient of the perturbed eigenvalue of $^3P_2$ is a measure of the energy uncertainty (half-width) of this state. If we divide it by $h/4\pi$ we obtain the probability per unit time of spontaneous ionization. If Δ is sufficiently small compared to $\sqrt{d^2 + a^2}$, which is not necessarily true, the half-width of the term $^3P_2$ is $\frac{2}{9}\frac{\Delta^2}{d^2+a^2}a(^*)$. When $a \to 0$ this formula has a simple meaning: it says that to obtain the probability of ionization of $^3P_2$, it is enough to multiply the probability for $^1D_2$ by the contribution of $^1D_2$ in the perturbed $^3P_2$, according to common perturbation theory. For large values of a, which means for great instability of $^1D_2$, the instability induced in $^3P_2$ decreases again after having reached a maximum: this should be interpreted in the sense that an exceedingly unstable state $^1D_2$ ceases to be "a virtual state" whose presence is in any case necessary for the AUGER effect of the term $(2p)^2$ $^3P_2$ to become quantitatively relevant.

(*) Note that in the original text of "Il Nuovo Cimento" it is erroneously printed $\frac{2}{9}\frac{\Delta^2}{d^2+a^2}a^2$. (Note of the Editor.)

Comment on the Scientific Paper no. 5 : *"Theory of the incomplete P' triplets".*

This paper, published in 1931 while Majorana was in Rome after receiving his doctoral degree, deals with an atomic spectroscopy problem, the characterization of spectra of different atoms with two electrons in the outer shell. The study was stimulated by experimental observations published in 1925 by P. Foote *et al.* of the *National Bureau of Standards of the US Department of Commerce, Washington DC* (the predecessor of the *US National Institute of Standards and Technology*), see ref. (1) of the original paper. The experimental finding was that some predicted lines in the absorption spectra of Hg, Cd and Zn atoms were missing. More precisely, of the three lines expected for transitions to the lowest $p^2\ {}^3P_{0,1,2}$ triplet levels, those associated with the ${}^3P_2$ level were not observed in any of these spectra. Majorana presented a theoretical explanation of those results introducing a new process he designates as *spontaneous ionization*.

At that time, deviations of energy levels and line intensities from the simple formulas for ordinary atomic series were already known for line series belonging to atoms (or ions) with several electrons in the outer shell. These deviations are known as perturbations. The perturbations are produced by a resonance process where two (or more) energy levels are nearly degenerate, and their wave functions are mixed up by the interactions between electrons. As a consequence, the new mixed wave functions are the solutions of the Schrödinger equation, with new energy eigenvalues and new transition probabilities for absorption of light. Majorana introduced a new kind of perturbation, proposing that the $p^2\ {}^3P_{0,1,2}$ levels are modified by the interaction with levels in the continuum. Thus, level mixing takes place between discrete and continuum levels. Owing to the perturbation the discrete levels acquire features ordinarily seen only in continuum transitions: large natural linewidths, line asymmetries and intensity anomalies in emission or absorption of radiation. For instance, the mixed discrete level may decay through a radiationless transition process, which converts the excited atom into a free electron and a positive ion. This decay constitutes the "spontaneous ionization" process identified by Majorana. It is equivalent to the Auger process then known in X-ray emissions, which is mentioned at the end of Majorana's paper. A similar process, discussed by R. de L. Kronig a few years earlier[1], is the radiationless dissociation of a molecule when the sum of its vibrational and electronic energies exceeds the energy necessary for dissociation in a lower energy electronic configuration.

---

(1) R. de L. KRONIG, *Z. Phys.* **50** (1928) 347.

The spontaneous ionization process in optical spectra of atoms was introduced independently in the same year by A. G. Shenstone of Princeton University in a publication in *The Physical Review*[2]. Shenstone analyzed a $^3P_2^0$ level of mercury that had been recently discovered by T. Takamine and T. Suga[3] and confirmed by F. Paschen[4]. Shenstone identified the same process as Majorana, but called it *auto-ionization*, a name which has since become standard in the literature of atomic spectroscopy (usually as *autoionization*). The attention of Shenstone was really concentrated on copper whose spectrum is unique with autoionization being the rule rather than the exception, as stated in his detailed report of 1936[5].

In an important later work in 1935[6], H. Beutler of the University of Berlin published a detailed investigation of the absorption spectra of noble gases for levels above the ionization limit. In that study, Beutler ascribes the observed strong asymmetric modulations of the absorption lines to the autoionization process, and refers to Kronig's and Shenstone's previous work, but not to Majorana's. *The Theory of Atomic Spectra*, published by E. U. Condon and G. H. Shortley in 1935[7], often called the "bible" of atomic spectroscopy, recognizes the simultaneous and independent contributions of Majorana and Shenstone in identifying the autoionization concept yet. In the same year, Beutler's work caught the attention of E. Fermi in Rome, who suggested to a junior associate, U. Fano, that he find a specific explanation for the line shapes seen by Beutler. In fact, as described by Fano himself, the hypothesis of autoionization alone does not provide a description of the asymmetrically broadened lines. Fano soon produced a theoretical analysis of the mixing of a discrete level with a continuum published in 1935[8]. This work, and Fano's more complete analysis published in 1961[9], introduced the Beutler-Fano autoionization profile, a lineshape formula that has found wide applicability in many branches of physics. Fano's work at NIST in the 1960s, and the contemporaneous development in experimental techniques for extreme ultraviolet spectroscopy, again mainly at NIST, elevated the Beutler-Fano lineshapes to a frontier research topic in atomic physics, as described in a short report by C. W. Clark in 2001[10]. Autoionization has played an important role in the progress of spectroscopy, because it is observed in a large variety of atomic and molecular spectra, and very different results are obtained for the energy and probabilities of the mixed levels.

[2] A. G. SHENSTONE, *Phys. Rev.* **38** (1931) 873.
[3] T. TAKAMINE and T. SUGA, *Sci. Pap. Inst. Phys. and Chem. Res. Tokyo* **13** (1930) 1.
[4] F. PASCHEN, *Ann. Phys. (Leipzig)* **6** (1930) 47.
[5] A. G. SHENSTONE, *Philos. Trans. Roy Soc. London* **235** (1936) 195.
[6] H. BEUTLER, *Z. Phys.* **93** (1935) 177.
[7] E. U. CONDON and G. H. SHORTLEY, *"Theory of Atomic Spectra"* (Cambridge University Press) 1935.
[8] U. FANO, *Nuovo Cimento* **12** (1935) 154.
[9] U. FANO, *Phys. Rev.* **124** (1961) 1866.
[10] C. W. CLARK, in *"A Century of Excellence in Measurements, Standards, and Technology"* NIST Special Publication 958, edited by David R. Lide (Washington, DC USA) 2001, p. 116.

The 1931 Majorana analysis does not calculate the autoionization absorption spectra. Moreover, instead of describing the continuum through a continuous distribution of states as in the Fano analyses, Majorana mixes a discrete level having a negligible decay rate with a single level that simulates the continuum through its large linewidth, denoted by the quantity "a" introduced at the bottom of page 105. Furthermore, Majorana does not derive the transition probability for the absorption process. Even if the description by Majorana is not complete, the diagonalization of the perturbation matrix he writes down on the last page of his paper would produce an expression for the absorption lineshape having the characteristic sawthooth profile of autoionization. Such a lineshape derivation was reported by B. W. Shore in 1968([11]).

The mixing of discrete and continuum states introduced by Majorana and leading to autoionization is complex. Autoionization mixing may occur whenever a discrete level above the ionization limit is embedded in a continuum with the same parity and angular momentum. For the case of the $p^2 \, {}^3P_2$ levels of Hg, Cd and Zn, no ${}^3P_2$ continuum of even parity is available for the autoionization mixing. Therefore, Majorana argued that the electron coupling is sufficiently removed from the strict LS Russell-Saunders case, so that the discrete levels share $p^2 \, {}^3P_2$ and $sd \, {}^1D_2$ characteristics. Thus, the discrete level acquires the singlet character necessary to autoionize readily into the $sd \, {}^1D_2$ continuum. As pointed out by Majorana, this complicated double interaction mixing, between discrete states and between discrete and continuum states, is not strictly required to produce the spontaneous ionization. However, in the absence of a singlet admixture in the triplet state, the autoionization mixing would not have been large enough to explain the disappearance of the lines associated with the $p^2 \, {}^3P_2$ level. In their 1935 book, Condon and Shortley stated that the Majorana argument is not entirely convincing, because a similar autoionization process should apply also to the $p^2 \, {}^3P_0$ level. Therefore, for a long time the spectroscopic assignments and the autoionization scheme proposed by Majorana remained under scrutiny. The story of the missing lines ended in 1955 when W. R. S. Garton and A. Rajaratnam([12]) were able to identify the weak autoionization-broadened absorption lines of Zn terminating on the $p^2 \, {}^3P_2$ level. In 1970, W. C. Martin and V. Kaufman([13]) pointed out the correctness of Majorana's spectroscopic assignments. Finally, between 1986 and 1988 research groups in Orsay and Caen measured the Cd([14]) and Zn([15]) autoionization linewidths using optogalvanic detection and produced a precise derivation of the perturbation mixing for the discrete and continuum levels. Therefore, all the lines belonging to the p^2 configuration suffer perturbations by autoionization, large or small, following precisely the scheme predicted by Majorana.

([11]) B. W. SHORE, *Phys. Rev.* **171** (1968) 43.
([12]) W. R. S. GARTON and A. RAJARATNAM, *Proc. Phys. Soc.* A **68** (1955) 1107.
([13]) W. C. MARTIN and V. KAUFMAN, *J. Opt. Soc. Am.* **60** (1970) 1096.
([14]) M. AYMAR, E. LUC-KOENING, M. CHANTEPIE, J. L. COJAN, J. LANDAIS and B. LANIEPCE, *J. Phys. B: At. Mol. Phys.* **19** (1986) 3881.
([15]) M. CHANTEPIE, B. CHERON, J. L. COJAN, J. LANDAIS, B. LANIEPCE and M. AYMAR, *J. Phys. B: At. Mol. Phys.* **21** (1988) 1379.

In conclusion, the Majorana paper contains three remarkable steps for the progress of atomic spectroscopy: i) an identification of spectral lines in Hg, Cd and Zn; ii) a treatment of the electron coupling for a case other than the LS Russell-Saunders case; iii) the introduction of the autoionization process.

* * *

EA is grateful to W. C. CLARK for carefully reading the English translation of the original paper and of his comment, and for useful suggestions.

ENNIO ARIMONDO
NIST, Gaithersburg, MD (USA)

NOTA SCIENTIFICA n. 6 — SCIENTIFIC PAPER no. 6

Atomi orientati in campo magnetico variabile

Nota di Ettore Majorana

"Il Nuovo Cimento", vol. 9, 1932, pp. 43-50.

Sunto. — L'autore calcola la probabilità che abbiano luogo processi non adiabatici quando un raggio di vapore orientato passa in prossimità di un punto in cui il campo magnetico si annulla.

Un atomo orientato in un campo magnetico lentamente variabile segue, come è noto, adiabaticamente la direzione, supposta variabile, del campo. A ciò si deve il fatto recentemente posto in evidenza che sottoponendo un raggio molecolare proveniente da una esperienza di Stern e Gerlach a una seconda esperienza di Stern e Gerlach non si ottiene una nuova divisione del raggio, perché tutti gli atomi hanno la stessa orientazione, avendo seguito esattamente il campo vagante, difficilmente eliminabile, nel tratto compreso fra le espansioni polari destinate a produrre il raggio orientato e quelle che devono saggiarne l'orientazione dopo un certo percorso. Tuttavia Phipps ha intrapreso delle esperienze per rivelare una variazione non adiabatica del campo in detta regione; la condizione a ciò necessaria è che il campo sia sufficientemente debole e la variazione della sua direzione sufficientemente rapida perché la sua frequenza di rotazione divenga comparabile con la frequenza di Larmor. Poiché è difficile abbassare l'intensità del campo al disotto di alcuni gauss[1], è necessario, per una velocità del raggio di 10^5 cm/sec, che la direzione del campo vari di molto entro una frazione di millimetro; si tratta quindi di esperienze delicate che non hanno dato finora esito conclusivo.

---

[1] T. E. Phipps e O. Stern, "Z. Physik", *73*, 185 (1932).

Il problema è stato trattato teoricamente da GÜTTINGER([2]) per il caso di un campo rotante uniformemente e di intensità costante. In questa nota supporremo invece che il raggio molecolare passi in prossimità di un punto in cui il campo magnetico si annulli; questo caso è particolarmente importante perché se il raggio passasse esattamente per un punto di campo nullo tutti gli atomi invertirebbero la loro orientazione.

D'altra parte un punto di campo nullo non può essere portato sul percorso del raggio molecolare che per tentativi, disponendo, ad esempio, di due campi ausiliari ortogonali indipendentemente regolabili, così che è difficile realizzare l'esperienza fino a che non si disponga di mezzi rapidi per la rivelazione del raggio. Ne anticipiamo tuttavia la discussione anche per meglio chiarire la natura del problema dinamico offerto dalla rotazione di un atomo magnetico in campo comunque variabile. Risulterà da quanto segue che la trattazione del problema secondo la meccanica classica o secondo la meccanica quantistica richiede l'integrazione delle stesse equazioni differenziali, cosicché quando la soluzione classica è nota, come nel caso di un campo uniforme rotante con velocità angolare costante, particolarmente considerato da GÜTTINGER, la soluzione quantistica può esserne dedotta immediatamente. Per il problema che studieremo più avanti, passaggio in prossimità di un punto di campo nullo con gradiente di campo lentamente variabile, l'impostazione quantistica è matematicamente più conveniente; ma anche qui basta risolvere il caso più semplice, $j = 1/2$, per dedurne la soluzione generale.

1. Uno stato rotazionale di un atomo con quanto interno $j = 1/2$ può essere rappresentato come combinazione lineare dei due stati ortogonali $\psi_{1/2}$ e $\psi_{-1/2}$ aventi momento $\pm 1/2$ in direzione dell'asse z:

$$\psi = C_{1/2}\psi_{1/2} + C_{-1/2}\psi_{-1/2}$$

ed è essenzialmente definito dal rapporto $\frac{C_{-1/2}}{C_{1/2}}$.

Se le fasi di $\psi_{1/2}$ e $\psi_{-1/2}$(*) sono scelte in modo da dare la rappresentazione ordinaria dei momenti angolari, lo stato ψ può essere rappresentato, come è noto, in modo invariante da un punto P su una sfera unitaria, le cui coordinate sferiche ϑ, φ sono definite da(**)

$$\tan \frac{\vartheta}{2} e^{i\varphi} = \frac{C_{-1/2}}{C_{1/2}}.$$

([2]) P. GÜTTINGER, "Z. Physik", *73*, 169 (1932).
(*) Ne "Il Nuovo Cimento" è erroneamente stampato $\psi_{1/2}$. (Nota del Curatore, si veda anche E. AMALDI, *op. cit.*)
(**) Ne "Il Nuovo Cimento" è erroneamente stampato $\tan \frac{\vartheta}{z}$ qui e successivamente in eq. (3). (Nota del Curatore, si veda anche E. AMALDI, *op. cit.*)

Il raggio vettore OP, essendo O il centro della sfera, dà allora la direzione secondo la quale il momento nello stato ψ ha il valore $1/2$. Nel caso $j = 1/2$ il più generico stato rotazionale corrisponde quindi ad atomi orientati con momento $\frac{1}{2}\frac{h}{2\pi}$ in una direzione arbitraria. La probabilità d'accordo fra due stati rappresentati dai punti P e P' è data da

$$W(P, P') = \cos^2 \frac{1}{2}\alpha$$

se α è l'angolo POP'; essa si annulla, cioè i due stati sono ortogonali, quando P e P' sono diametralmente opposti. Per $j > 1/2$ non esiste in generale una direzione secondo cui l'atomo è orientato, ha cioè un valore determinato dal momento angolare, ma una rappresentazione geometrica intrinseca, simile alla precedente, è ancora possibile. Solo ogni stato sarà rappresentato da $2j$ punti sulla sfera unitaria, anzi che da uno solo. Consideriamo infatti uno stato generico:

$$\psi = C_j\psi_j + C_{j-1}\psi_{j-1} + \cdots + C_{-j}\psi_{-j}$$

e siano $\zeta_1, \zeta_2, \ldots, \zeta_{2j}$ le radici dell'equazione:

(1) $$a_0\zeta^{2j} + a_1\zeta^{2j-1} + \cdots + a_{2j} = 0$$

essendo

(2) $$a_r = (-1)^r \frac{C_j - r}{\sqrt{(2j-r)!\,r!}}.$$

Lo stato ψ può allora essere rappresentato dai punti $P_1, P_2, \ldots, P_{2j}$ sulla sfera unitaria, le coordinate sferiche ϑ_s, φ_s di P_s essendo date da

(3) $$\text{tang}\,\frac{\vartheta_s}{2}e^{i\varphi_s} = \zeta_s.$$

Si verifica senza difficoltà che questa rappresentazione geometrica non dipende dal sistema di coordinate. La disposizione dei punti rappresentativi è a priori arbitraria, ma diviene particolarmente semplice se si considerano atomi orientati. A uno stato orientato con componente del momento angolare m nella direzione OP corrispondono infatti $j + m$ punti coincidenti in P e $j - m$ nel punto diametralmente opposto a P, *come se ognuno dei punti rappresentativi indicasse la direzione di un piccolo giroscopio con momento angolare* $\frac{1}{2}\frac{h}{2\pi}$. La probabilità di accordo fra due stati *orientati*, l'uno con momento m nella direzione OP, l'altro con momento m' nella direzione OP' formante con la prima

l'angolo α, è data da

$$(4) \qquad W(P, P'; m, m') = \left(\cos \frac{\alpha}{2}\right)^{4j} (j+m)!(j-m)!(j+m')!(j-m')!$$

$$\left[\sum_0{}_r \frac{(-1)^r \left(\tan g \frac{\alpha}{2}\right)^{2r-m+m'}}{r!(r-m+m')!(j+m-r)!(j-m'-r)!}\right]^2$$

ed è naturalmente simmetrica in m e m'.

Consideriamo ora la rotazione dell'atomo in un campo magnetico $H(t)$ comunque variabile nel tempo. Supponiamo perciò che l'atomo possieda un momento magnetico $-gj\mu_0$ così che per campo sufficientemente debole si può assumere come Hamiltoniana $g\mu_0(j, H)$. Le equazioni del movimento saranno allora:

$$\dot{C}_m = -\frac{2\pi i}{h} g\mu_0 \left[mH_z C_m + \sqrt{(j+m)(j-m+1)}\, \frac{H_x - iH_y}{2} C_{m-1} + \right.$$

$$\left. + \sqrt{(j+m+1)(j-m)}\, \frac{H_x + iH_y}{2} C_{m+1}\right].$$

Sostituendo mediante (2) abbiamo

$$\dot{a}_r = -\frac{2\pi i}{h} g\mu_0 \left[(j-r)H_z a_r - (r+1)\frac{H_x - iH_y}{2} a_{r+1} - \right.$$

$$\left. -(2j-r+1)\frac{H_x + iH_y}{2} a_{r-1}\right].$$

Uguagliando a zero la derivata temporale del primo membro di (1) troviamo, dopo facili riduzioni, per una generica radice ζ_i di detta equazione:

$$\dot{\zeta}_i = \frac{2\pi i}{h} g\mu_0 \left(H_z \zeta_i + \frac{H_x - iH_y}{2}\zeta_i^2 - \frac{H_x + iH_y}{2}\right)$$

da cui seguono mediante la (3) le variazioni temporali di ϑ_i, φ_i relative al punto rappresentativo P_i di cui ζ_i è la proiezione stereografica sul piano complesso $x + iy$:

$$\dot{\vartheta}_i = \frac{2\pi}{h} g\mu_0 (H_y \cos \varphi_i - H_x \sin \varphi_i),$$

$$\dot{\varphi}_i = \frac{2\pi}{h} g\mu_0 \left(H_z - \frac{H_x \cos \varphi_i + H_y \sin \varphi_i}{\tan g\, \vartheta_i}\right).$$

Queste equazioni esprimono che ciascuno dei punti rappresentativi sulla sfera unitaria precede intorno al campo con frequenza $g \cdot o$, essendo o la frequenza di Larmor, come accadrebbe nella meccanica classica se uno qualsiasi dei raggi vettori OP_i indicasse la direzione di un giroscopio di autoimpulso $j\frac{h}{2\pi}$ e momento magnetico $-gj\mu_0$. Si può del

resto provare che la validità di questo risultato è implicita nell'invarianza della nostra rappresentazione geometrica, e viceversa.

Da quanto si è detto risulta anche che la posizione relativa dei $2j$ punti rappresentativi resta invariata nel corso del tempo, cosicché se inizialmente l'atomo è orientato con componente del momento angolare m in direzione del campo, esso sarà ancora orientato al tempo t con momento m secondo una direzione formante un angolo $\alpha(t)$ con il campo. La conoscenza dell'angolo di sbandamento $\alpha(t)$, che può essere calcolato indifferentemente con la meccanica classica o con la meccanica quantistica ed è indipendente da j e da m permette di calcolare mediante la (4) la probabilità che la componente del momento angolare nella direzione del campo abbia al tempo t il valore generico m'.

2. Supponiamo ora che un raggio di atomi orientati passi in prossimità di un punto Q in cui $H_x = H_y = H_z = 0$; in vicinanza di Q le componenti del campo saranno funzioni lineari delle coordinate cartesiane x, y, z, e, in un sistema solidale con l'atomo in movimento, che con grande approssimazione possiamo ritenere rettilineo e uniforme, le componenti del campo agente sull'atomo stesso saranno funzioni lineari del tempo. Scegliamo l'asse x nella direzione che ha il campo quando esso raggiunge la minima intensità, ciò che accadrà in generale a non grande distanza da Q, e l'asse z nella direzione della derivata temporale, cambiata di segno, del campo magnetico, che è naturalmente normale alla precedente. Assumiamo inoltre come origine dei tempi, l'istante in cui il campo è minimo. Le componenti del campo a cui l'atomo è sottoposto in un istante generico avranno la forma:

$$H_x = A; \qquad H_y = 0; \qquad H_z = -Ct.$$

Supponiamo $j = 1/2$ ponendo $\psi = \xi\psi_{1/2} + \eta\psi_{-1/2}(^*)$; le equazioni del moto saranno

$$\dot{\xi} = -\frac{\pi i}{h}\, g\mu_0\big(-Ct\xi + A\eta\big),$$

$$\dot{\eta} = -\frac{\pi i}{h}\, g\mu_0\big(A\xi + Ct\eta\big).$$

A fine di operare con variabili prive di dimensioni, introduciamo una nuova misura del tempo(**):

$$\tau = \sqrt{\frac{\pi}{2h}\, g\mu_0 C} \cdot t$$

(*) Ne "Il Nuovo Cimento" $\frac{1}{2}$ e $-\frac{1}{2}$ sono erroneamente stampati in linea. (Nota del Curatore, si veda anche E. AMALDI, *op. cit.*)
(**) Ne "Il Nuovo Cimento" è erroneamente stampato $\frac{\pi}{zh}$. (Nota del Curatore, si veda anche E. AMALDI, *op. cit.*)

e la grandezza numerica

$$k = \frac{2\pi g \mu_0 A^2}{hC}$$

che dà il rapporto fra la frequenza di precessione dell'atomo e la frequenza di rotazione della direzione del campo quando questo rapporto ha il valore minimo, cioè per $\tau = 0$. Se il raggio di vapore passa con velocità v a una distanza d dal punto Q, nelle cui vicinanze regnano gradienti di campo dell'ordine di G gauss per cm, $k(^*)$ risulterà dell'ordine di $10^7 G \frac{d^2}{v}$; per es., per $v = 10^5$ e $G \sim 1$ sarà $k \sim 100\,d^2$ e così $k \sim 1$ per $d = 1\,\mathrm{mm}$. Nelle nuove variabili avremo:

$$\frac{d\xi}{d\tau} = -i\left(-2\tau\xi + \sqrt{k}\,\eta\right)$$
$$\frac{d\eta}{d\tau} = -i\left(\sqrt{k}\,\xi + 2\tau\eta\right)$$

che possiamo semplificare con la posizione:

$$\xi = e^{i\tau^2} f\,; \qquad \eta = e^{-i\tau^2} g$$

da cui segue:

(5)
$$\begin{cases} \dfrac{df}{d\tau} = -i\sqrt{k}\,e^{-2i\tau^2} g \\ \dfrac{dg}{d\tau} = -i\sqrt{k}\,e^{2i\tau^2} f. \end{cases}$$

Eliminando g troviamo:

(6)
$$\frac{d^2 f}{d\tau^2} + hi\tau \frac{df}{d\tau} + kf = 0.$$

Delle soluzioni di questa equazione differenziale possiamo dare una rappresentazione integrale che permette di determinarne l'espressione asintotica per grandi valori, positivi o negativi, di τ; questo è appunto quanto ci occorre, poiché noi supponiamo che per $\tau = -\infty$ l'atomo sia orientato rispetto al campo e vogliamo determinarne l'orientazione per $\tau \to \infty$.

(*) Ne "Il Nuovo Cimento" è erroneamente stampato K, come anche a pagina 120, sei righe dal fondo. (Nota del Curatore, si veda anche E. Amaldi, *op. cit.*)

Poiché tutto si riduce a calcolare l'angolo α più sopra definito, basta considerare una sola soluzione della (6). Essa ci è data da

$$f(\tau) = \frac{\sqrt{k}\, e^{-k\pi/8}}{2(1+i)\sqrt{\pi}} \int s^{(k/4i)-1} e^{(s^2/8i)+s\tau}\, ds$$

log s avendo il suo valore principale e la condizione ai limiti

$$\left| s^{k/4i} e^{(s^2/8i)+s\tau} \right._{\mathrm{C}} = 0$$

essendo soddisfatta se il cammino di integrazione ha la forma indicata nella figura, dove si sono distinti i due casi $\tau < 0$ e $\tau > 0$.

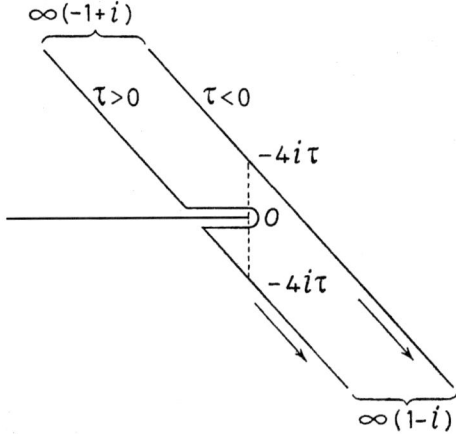

La parte negativa dell'asse reale è linea di discontinuità nella funzione integranda e non può essere attraversata; inoltre, a fine di permettere la valutazione delle espressioni asintotiche i cammini di integrazione si sono fatti passare per il punto di sella $s = -4i\tau$ nella direzione della massima pendenza.

Per $\tau \to -\infty$ tutto l'integrale proviene dalle vicinanze del punto $s = -4i\tau$ e mediante la sostituzione

$$s = -4i\tau + (1-i)p$$

si calcolano facilmente i primi termini dello sviluppo asintotico di f e, attraverso la prima delle (5), di g. Si trova, trascurando termini che tendono a zero:

$$\tau \to -\infty; \qquad f = 0; \qquad g = (-4\tau)^{k/4i}.$$

Per $\tau \to \infty$ l'espressione asintotica dell'integrale proviene in parte dalle vicinanze del punto di sella $s = -4i\tau$ e in parte da quelle del punto di diramazione O. Si trova in

questo caso:

$$\tau \to \infty: \qquad f = -\frac{1-i}{2\sqrt{\pi}}\sqrt{k}\,e^{-k/4i}e^{-k\pi/8}\sinh\left(\frac{k\pi}{4}\right)\Gamma\left(\frac{k}{4i}\right)$$

$$g = (4\tau)^{k/4i}e^{-k\pi/4}.$$

Badando che per a reale[3]

$$|\Gamma(ai)| = \sqrt{\frac{\pi}{a\sinh(\pi a)}}$$

oppure tenendo presente la costanza di $|f^2|+|g^2|$ troviamo le seguenti espressioni per $|f|$ e $|g|$:

$$\tau \to -\infty: \qquad |f| = 0; \qquad |g| = 1$$

$$\tau \to \infty: \qquad |f| = \sqrt{1-e^{-k\pi/2}}\,; \qquad |g| = e^{-k\pi/4}.$$

Per $\tau \to -\infty$ il campo è diretto secondo l'asse z, cosicché all'inizio del fenomeno l'atomo ha nella direzione del campo il momento $-\frac{1}{2}\frac{h}{2\pi}$; per $\tau \to \infty$ il campo è diretto invece secondo $-z$ e il valore limite di $|g^2|$ segna quindi la probabilità che l'atomo inverta la propria orientazione, si trovi cioè ad avere, dopo essere passato nelle vicinanze di Q, un momento $\frac{1}{2}\frac{h}{2\pi}$ nella direzione del campo. Tale probabilità è quindi

$$W\left(-\frac{1}{2},\frac{1}{2}\right) = e^{-k\pi/2}.$$

Così per $k=1$ il 21% e per $k=2$ il 4,3% degli atomi si capovolgono.

La soluzione generale del problema per j qualsiasi e transizioni da m a m' si avrà dalla (4) sostituendovi il valore dell'angolo α di sbandamento. E poiché nel nostro caso

$$W\left(-\frac{1}{2},\frac{1}{2}\right) = \sin^2\frac{\alpha}{2}$$

risulta confrontando con l'espressione precedente

$$\alpha = 2\arcsin e^{-k\pi/4}.$$

---

[3] Vedi per es. Whittaker e Watson, *Modern Analysis*, IV ed., p. 259.

Commento alla Nota Scientifica n. 6: "Atomi orientati in campo magnetico variabile".

In questo lavoro Majorana calcola la probabilità che gli atomi di un fascio polarizzato in movimento in un campo magnetico variabile invertano il loro spin (*spin-flip*). Si tratta dello studio quantitativo di cosa accade se la variazione della direzione del campo non è adiabatica. Il problema che Majorana trova "particolarmente importante" è cosa succeda quando la variazione del campo magnetico avviene nell'intorno di un valore nullo: "tutti gli atomi invertirebbero la loro orientazione". La questione gli era stata posta da E. Segré, come ricorda E. Amaldi[1].

Infatti E. Segré, insieme a R. Frisch[2], stava mettendo a punto un esperimento che generalizzasse le famose indagini di Stern e Gerlach sulla quantizzazione spaziale che erano state compiute con gradienti di campi magnetici statici ed in situazione adiabatica. Si voleva misurare quali fossero gli stati finali di momento magnetico di un atomo inizialmente preparato in uno stato definito e sottoposto ad un campo magnetico che variasse rapidamente. Nell'apparato di Segré e Frisch, la transizione non adiabatica veniva indotta facendo passare il fascio atomico vicino ad un punto dove il campo magnetico si annullava. Le loro misure furono interpretate utilizzando la teoria quantitativa sviluppata da Majorana, che nell'articolo dimostra come l'effetto globale di un campo magnetico variabile su di un corpuscolo con un dato momento angolare ed una data componente m lungo l'asse z possa venir descritto come una brusca rotazione del momento angolare stesso. Risolvendo rigorosamente l'equazione di Schrödinger dipendente dal tempo, Majorana ricava l'angolo di rotazione e dimostra che questo dipende dal fattore giromagnetico e dal campo, ma non dal valore m di partenza. Ne segue che, dopo che ha avuto luogo la rotazione, il sistema non è più in uno stato di ben definita quantizzazione spaziale rispetto alla direzione originale del campo, ma deve essere descritto a mezzo di un pacchetto d'onde costituito dalla sovrapposizione di stati con diversi m'. Nell'articolo viene calcolata esplicitamente l'ampiezza di probabilità di transizione da un livello m ad un livello m'. Majorana individua subito nel problema fisico due frequenze caratteristiche:

---

[1] E. Amaldi, *op. cit.* e la traduzione in inglese *Ettore Majorana, man and scientist* in *Strong and Weak Interactions, Present Problems, International School of Physics Ettore Majorana, Erice, June 19th - July 4th 1966*, a cura di Zichichi A. (Academic Press, New York and London) 1966.

[2] R. Frisch e E. Segrè, "Ricerche sulla quantizzazione spaziale", *Nuovo Cimento* **10** (1933) 78; "Über die Einstellung der Richtungsquantelung" *Z. Phys.*, **80** (1933) 610.

la frequenza di precessione di Larmor del dipolo magnetico atomico e la frequenza di rotazione del campo magnetico vista dall'atomo in movimento. Quando le due frequenze diventano comparabili l'atomo ha un'alta probabilità di cambiare sottostato magnetico e invertire la direzione del dipolo, cioè di compiere uno *spin-flip*. Majorana dimostra che la probabilità di *spin-flip* dipende proprio dal rapporto k tra le due frequenze ed è data da $e^{-k\pi/2}$. Come scrive E. Amaldi, il problema "fu in realtà trattato e risolto da Majorana con estrema eleganza e concisione per il caso $J = 1/2$". L'estensione al caso di momento angolare J qualsiasi fu sviluppata da F. Bloch e I. I. Rabi, che nel loro celebre articolo del 1945[3] citano ampiamente il lavoro di Majorana individuandolo come il lavoro fondamentale per la soluzione del problema. La trattazione di Majorana dei processi di ribaltamento di spin resta un classico, è utilizzata in testi di meccanica quantistica[4], è stata recentemente ripresa anche nel contesto della fisica delle collisioni atomiche e molecolari a bassa energia[5], ha applicazioni anche al di fuori della fisica atomica e molecolare ed è ad esempio utilizzata per manipolare fasci polarizzati in spettroscopia neutronica.

Discutiamo due campi di indagine sperimentale in cui il lavoro di Majorana ha trovato applicazione ed è tuttora di attualità: la spettroscopia di doppia risonanza e la condensazione di Bose-Einstein. Nei primi anni '50 la fisica atomica sviluppa una tecnica di spettroscopia di doppia risonanza (ottica-radiofrequenze) per indagare le strutture atomiche. In particolare, Brossel e Bitter[6] studiano la polarizzazione della fluorescenza dal livello $^3P_1$ più basso del mercurio eccitato dallo stato fondamentale con luce polarizzata in modo da popolare solo il sottolivello $m = 0$. Nell'esperimento gli atomi sono immersi in un campo magnetico che separa i sottolivelli Zeeman $m = -1, 0, +1$. Una radiazione a radiofrequenza viene utilizzata per indurre transizioni da $m = 0$ a $m = +1$ o $m = -1$, il che altera la polarizzazione della radiazione di fluorescenza. La forma di riga osservata ha un comportamento atipico, infatti al crescere della potenza a radiofrequenza si osserva uno sdoppiamento con un marcato minimo centrale. Brossel e Bitter interpretano tale comportamento come risultato di "risonanze di Majorana" ed usano proprio la formula di Majorana per riprodurre perfettamente i dati sperimentali. Tale forma di riga è oggi universalmente nota come "curva di Majorana-Brossel". L'analisi del fenomeno è tuttora di grande interesse ed è stata ripresa da C. Cohen-Tannoudji nel suo corso al *Collège de France* del 2003[7]. Egli interpreta la forma di riga con un minimo centrale come

[3] F. BLOCH e I. I. RABI, "Atoms in Variable Magnetic Fields", *Rev. Mod. Phys.* **17** (1945) 237.
[4] L. D. LANDAU e E. M. LIFSHITZ, *Quantum Mechanics: Non-relativistic Theory* (Nauka, Moscow) 1974; (Pergamon Press, Oxford) 1977.
[5] F. DI GIACOMO e E. E. NIKITIN, "The Majorana formula and the Landau-Zener-Stuckelberg treatment of the avoided crossing problem", *Phys. Usp.* **48** (2005) 515.
[6] J. BROSSEL e F. BITTER, "A New Double Resonance Method for Investigating Atomic Energy Levels. Application to Hg $^3P_1$", *Phys. Rev.* **86** (1952) 308; vedi anche: J. BROSSEL, Thesis, Faculté des Sciences de l'Université de Paris (1952).
[7] C. COHEN-TANNOUDJI, lezioni pubblicate in rete all'indirizzo `http://www.phys.ens.fr/cours/college-de-france/`.

conseguenza dell'interferenza quantistica con un processo a tre fotoni dove l'atomo dal sottolivello $m = 0$, prima di transire al sottolivello $m = +1$, opera una transizione di andata e ritorno al sottolivello $m = -1$.

Tornando al problema del ribaltamento del momento angolare degli atomi in movimento in un campo magnetico variabile attorno ad un punto di zero, è interessante osservare che la comprensione di questo effetto ha reso possibile la realizzazione sperimentale della condensazione di Bose-Einstein in un gas di atomi. Perché questa avvenga, il campione atomico deve essere raffreddato a temperature dell'ordine dei microkelvin e questo è stato realizzato utilizzando trappole magnetiche per atomi orientati e preraffreddati con radiazione laser. Il raffreddamento finale verso la condensazione avviene per evaporazione forzata dalla trappola magnetica degli atomi più energetici e conseguente termalizzazione dei restanti. A questo proposito sono cruciali i processi collisionali, che richiedono un'alta densità atomica. Agitandosi in una trappola che è realizzata con un gradiente di campo magnetico, gli atomi in moto sono sottoposti ad un campo variabile: più freddi sono, più lentamente si muovono e più lento è il loro spostamento attorno al minimo. Nei primi tentativi sperimentali di raggiungere la condensazione venivano utilizzate delle trappole magnetiche di quadrupolo, realizzate con un gradiente uniforme di campo a partire da uno zero di minimo: esattamente la configurazione esaminata da Majorana nel suo articolo. In tal caso all'attraversamento del minimo lo spin si inverte, gli atomi non vengono più confinati e la formula di Majorana consente un'analisi quantitativa del fenomeno, con k che dipende dal gradiente di campo, dalla distanza dallo zero e dalla velocità degli atomi, cioè dalla loro temperatura. Lo zero di campo costituisce una sorta di "buco" di perdita che abbassa la densità atomica sino a rendere inefficiente il raffreddamento. E. A. Cornell, C. E. Wieman e W. Ketterle, che per primi hanno realizzato sperimentalmente la condensazione di Bose-Einstein nel 1995, erano ben consapevoli della drammaticità del problema tanto che del "Majorana hole" parlano diffusamente e ripetutamente nelle loro relazioni per il premio Nobel[8][9]. Il problema da risolvere era quello di creare delle trappole con un minimo diverso da zero. Il primo ad aver successo fu il gruppo di Boulder con una trappola piuttosto sofisticata (TOP), dove il minimo veniva fatto ruotare ed i vari parametri erano scelti avendo presente l'espressione quantitativa dello *spin-flip*. È interessante riportare quanto Cornell e Wieman scrivono: *"This zero represents a hole in the trap, a site at which atoms can undergo Majorana transitions and thus escape from the trap. . . . the TOP design worked well, and the samples were cooled far colder, in fact too cold . . . "*. Ketterle ricorse invece alla soluzione di tenere lontani gli atomi dal punto di campo zero focalizzando radiazione laser. Oggigiorno, avendo capito a fondo il fenomeno, è possibile utilizzare varie configurazioni statiche con minimo diverso da zero. Fra le tante si cita quella che F. S. Cataliotti ha in funzione nella Catania di Majorana, dove l'intrappolamento degli atomi avviene su un microcircuito elettronico.

---

[8] E. A. Cornell e C. E. Wieman, "Bose-Einstein condensation in a dilute gas", *Rev. Mod. Phys.* **74** (2002) 875.

[9] W. Ketterle, "When atoms behave as waves", *Rev. Mod. Phys.* **74** (2002) 1173.

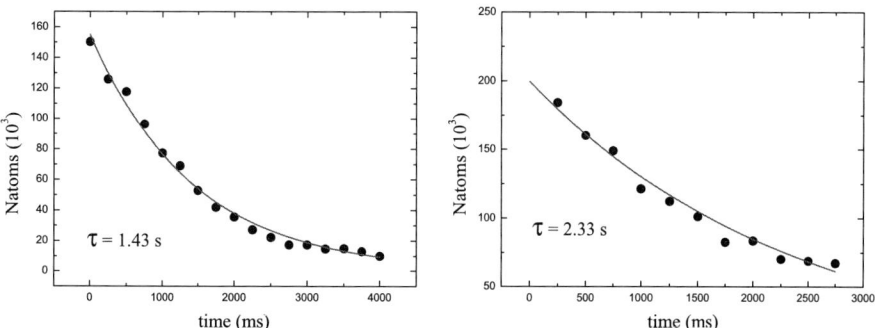

Fig. 1. – Atomi polarizzati e confinati con gradienti magnetici a pochi microkelvin sulla via della condensazione di Bose-Einstein. Il grafico a sinistra si riferisce a una configurazione in cui il campo magnetico ha un minimo uguale a zero, per cui si hanno perdite di atomi a causa dello *spin-flip* di Majorana. Il grafico a destra si riferisce a una trappola appositamente progettata con un minimo diverso da zero per controllare il fenomeno di ribaltamento dello spin[10].

Si riporta in Fig. 1 l'andamento nel tempo del numero di atomi intrappolati a una temperatura di poche decine di microkelvin in presenza di un minimo uguale a zero (a sinistra) ed in una situazione in cui il "buco" viene tappato con l'aggiunta di un ulteriore campo magnetico (a destra): come si osserva, l'eliminazione dello *spin-flip* di Majorana porta ad un aumento significativo del tempo di vita degli atomi intrappolati[10].

Una volta realizzato il condensato, transizioni di *spin-flip*, indotte in maniera controllata, possono rivelarsi utili per ulteriori sviluppi nel campo della fisica atomica a bassissime temperature. Recentemente, X. Chen dell'Università di Pechino[11] ha utilizzato le previsioni teoriche di Majorana per sviluppare un nuovo metodo per estrarre atomi coerenti da un condensato e realizzare così un *laser atomico* impulsato.

MASSIMO INGUSCIO
Università di Firenze

[10] Per gentile concessione di F. S. Cataliotti, Università di Catania (2006).
[11] X. MA *et al.*, "Population oscillation of the multicomponent spinor BEC induced by nonadiabatic transitions", *Phys. Rev. A* **73** (2006) 013624.

Oriented atoms in a variable magnetic field(*)

Ettore Majorana

Summary. — The author calculates the probability of non-adiabatic processes when an oriented atomic beam passes close to a point where the magnetic field vanishes.

As is well known, an oriented atom in a slowly varying magnetic field follows adiabatically the direction, assumed to be variable, of the field. This is the cause of a phenomenon that has recently been observed: if a molecular beam emerging from a Stern-Gerlach experiment is passed through another Stern-Gerlach experiment, one does not observe any further splitting of the beam. The reason is the following: all the atoms have the same orientation since all of them have followed exactly the stray field inevitably existing in the region between the pole-pieces which are meant to produce the orientation of the beam and those which should test this orientation after a certain distance. However, Phipps has undertaken some experiments to observe a non-adiabatic variation of the field in this region; this requires that the field be sufficiently weak and the variation of its direction sufficiently fast so that its rotational frequency be comparable with the Larmor frequency. Since it is difficult to reduce the intensity of the field below a few gauss([1]), it is necessary, with a velocity of the beam of the order of 10^5 cm/sec, that the direction of the field changes appreciably over a distance of a fraction of a millimeter. These are, therefore, very delicate experiments that have not yet produced any decisive result.

(*) Translated from "Il Nuovo Cimento", vol. 9, 1932, pp. 43-50, by P. Radicati di Brozolo.
([1]) T. E. Phipps and O. Stern "Z. Physik", 73, 185 (1932).

The problem has been discussed theoretically by GÜTTINGER[2] in the case of a uniformly rotating field with constant intensity. In this paper we will suppose instead that the molecular beam passes close to a point where the magnetic field vanishes. This case is of special importance because, if the beam were to pass exactly by a point of zero field, all the atoms would invert their orientation.

On the other hand, we cannot obtain a zero field in a point on the trajectory of the molecular beam except by several trials, for example by using two orthogonal auxiliary fields that can be regulated independently; this makes it difficult to perform the experiment until fast means to detect the beam are available. Nevertheless we anticipate the discussion to better clarify the nature of the dynamical problem arising from the rotation of a magnetic atom in an arbitrarily varying magnetic field. Our calculations will show that both the classical and the quantum-mechanical treatment require the integration of the same differential equations. It follows that when the classic solution is known, as in the case of a uniformly rotating field with constant angular velocity —which is the problem treated by GÜTTINGER—, the quantum solution can be immediately derived. For the problem that we will study later, namely the passing close to a point of vanishing field with a slowly varying gradient, the quantum treatment is mathematically more convenient. Also in this case to obtain the general solution it is enough to solve the simplest case $j = 1/2$.

1. A rotational state of an atom with internal quantum $j = 1/2$ can be represented as a linear combination of two orthogonal states $\psi_{1/2}$ and $\psi_{-1/2}$ with projection $\pm 1/2$ in the z-direction:

$$\psi = C_{1/2}\psi_{1/2} + C_{-1/2}\psi_{-1/2}.$$

The state is therefore essentially defined by the ratio $\frac{C_{-1/2}}{C_{1/2}}$.

If the phases of $\psi_{1/2}$ and $\psi_{-1/2}$(*) are chosen so as to obtain the normal representation of angular momenta, the state ψ can be represented, as is known, in an invariant way by a point P on a unit sphere whose spherical coordinates ϑ and φ are defined by(**)

$$\text{tang}\,\frac{\vartheta}{2}e^{i\varphi} = \frac{C_{-1/2}}{C_{1/2}}.$$

If O is the center of the sphere, the vector radius OP defines the direction along which the momentum in the state ψ has value $1/2$. In the case $j = 1/2$ the most generic rotational state then corresponds to oriented atoms with momentum $\frac{1}{2}\frac{h}{2\pi}$ in an arbitrary

---

[2] P. GÜTTINGER, "Z. Physik", **73**, 169 (1932).
(*) In "Il Nuovo Cimento" it is erroneusly printed $\psi_{1/2}$. (Note of the Editor, see also E. AMALDI, *op. cit.*)
(**) In "Il Nuovo Cimento" it is erroneously printed tang $\frac{\vartheta}{z}$ here and in the following eq. (3). (Note of the Editor, see also E. AMALDI, *op. cit.*)

direction. The probability of agreement for two states represented by the points P and P' is given by

$$W(P, P') = \cos^2 \frac{1}{2}\alpha\,,$$

where α is the angle POP'. The probability vanishes, *i.e.* the two states are orthogonal, when P and P' are diametrically opposite. For $j > 1/2$ there is in general no direction along which the atom is oriented, *i.e.* with a value determined by angular momentum. In spite of this, an intrinsic geometric representation similar to the previous one is still possible. The only difference is that every state, rather than being represented by a single point, is represented by $2j$ points on the unit sphere. Indeed let us consider a generic state:

$$\psi = C_j\psi_j + C_{j-1}\psi_{j-1} + \cdots + C_{-j}\psi_{-j}$$

and let $\zeta_1, \zeta_2, \ldots, \zeta_{2j}$ be the roots of the equation

(1) $$a_0\zeta^{2j} + a_1\zeta^{2j-1} + \cdots + a_{2j} = 0\,,$$

where

(2) $$a_r = (-1)^r \frac{C_j - r}{\sqrt{(2j - r)!\, r!}}\,.$$

The state ψ can then be represented by the points $P_1, P_2, \ldots, P_{2j}$ on the unit sphere where the spherical coordinates ϑ_s, φ_s of P_s are given by

(3) $$\text{tang}\,\frac{\vartheta_s}{2} e^{i\varphi_s} = \zeta_s\,.$$

It is not difficult to verify that this geometric representation is independent of the choice of the coordinate system. The distribution of the representative points is *a priori* arbitrary but becomes particularly simple in the case of oriented atoms. To an oriented state with angular momentum component m in the direction OP, there actually correspond $j + m$ points that coincide in P and $j - m$ in the point diametrically opposite to P, *as if each of the representative points indicated the direction of a little gyroscope with angular momentum* $\frac{1}{2}\frac{h}{2\pi}$. The probability of agreement for two *oriented* states, one with momentum m in the direction OP, the other with momentum m' in the direction OP' forming with OP an angle α, is given by

(4) $$W(P, P'; m, m') = \left(\cos\frac{\alpha}{2}\right)^{4j} (j + m)!(j - m)!(j + m')!(j - m')!$$

$$\left[\sum_r^0 \frac{(-1)^r \left(\text{tang}\,\frac{\alpha}{2}\right)^{2r-m+m'}}{r!(r - m + m')!(j + m - r)!(j - m' - r)!}\right]^2$$

which is obviously symmetric in m and m'.

Let us now consider the rotation of the atom in a magnetic field $H(t)$ varying arbitrarily with time; hence let us suppose that the atom has a magnetic moment $-gj\mu_0$ so that for a sufficiently weak field we can assume that the Hamiltonian is $g\mu_0(j, H)$. The equations of motion are therefore:

$$\dot{C}_m = -\frac{2\pi i}{h}g\mu_0\left[mH_zC_m + \sqrt{(j+m)(j-m+1)}\frac{H_x - iH_y}{2}C_{m-1}+\right.$$
$$\left. +\sqrt{(j+m+1)(j-m)}\frac{H_x + iH_y}{2}C_{m+1}\right].$$

Using relation (2) we obtain

$$\dot{a}_r = -\frac{2\pi i}{h}g\mu_0\left[(j-r)H_za_r - (r+1)\frac{H_x - iH_y}{2}a_{r+1}-\right.$$
$$\left. -(2j-r+1)\frac{H_x + iH_y}{2}a_{r-1}\right].$$

Setting the time derivative of the left-hand side of (1) equal to zero, we easily find that the time derivative of a generic root ζ_i is:

$$\dot{\zeta}_i = \frac{2\pi i}{h}g\mu_0\left(H_z\zeta_i + \frac{H_x - iH_y}{2}\zeta_i^2 - \frac{H_x + iH_y}{2}\right).$$

The time derivatives of ϑ_i, φ_i relative to the point P_i of which ζ_i is the stereographic projection on the complex plane $x + iy$ follow from equation (3):

$$\dot{\vartheta}_i = \frac{2\pi}{h}g\mu_0(H_y\cos\varphi_i - H_x\sin\varphi_i),$$
$$\dot{\varphi}_i = \frac{2\pi}{h}g\mu_0\left(H_z - \frac{H_x\cos\varphi_i + H_y\sin\varphi_i}{\tang\vartheta_i}\right).$$

These equations mean that each of the representative points on the unit sphere precedes around the field direction with frequency $g \cdot o$, where o is the LARMOR frequency. This is what would happen in classical mechanics if any of the radii OP_i denoted the direction of a gyroscope with self-momentum $j\frac{h}{2\pi}$ and magnetic moment $-gj\mu_0$. It is actually possible to prove that the validity of this result is implicit in the invariance of the geometric representation. The converse is also true.

From what has been said so far, it follows that the relative positions of the $2j$ representative points are invariant in time; as a consequence, if the atom is initially oriented with angular momentum component m in the direction of the field, at time t it will still be oriented with momentum m along a direction forming an angle $\alpha(t)$ with the field. Knowing the rotation angle $\alpha(t)$ that can be calculated both with classical and quantum mechanics, and is independent of j and m, we can calculate with (4) the probability that the angular momentum component in the direction of the field takes at time t the generic value m'.

2. Let us now suppose that a beam of oriented atoms passes close to a point Q where $H_x = H_y = H_z = 0$. Close to Q the field components are linear functions of the Cartesian coordinates x, y, z; in a coordinate system centred on a moving atom whose motion we can assume with large approximation to be rectilinear and uniform, the components of the field acting on the atom are then linear functions of time. Let the x-axis be in the same direction of the field when it reaches the minimum intensity, which will in general happen not too far from Q and the z-axis in the direction opposite to the time derivative of the magnetic field, which is obviously orthogonal to the previous one. Let us further suppose that the origin of time coincides with the instant when the field is minimum. The components of the field acting on the atom at a given time t will be:

$$H_x = A; \qquad H_y = 0; \qquad H_z = -Ct.$$

If $j = 1/2$ let us set $\psi = \xi\psi_{1/2} + \eta\psi_{-1/2}(^*)$; the equations of motion will then be

$$\dot{\xi} = -\frac{\pi i}{h} g\mu_0\left(-Ct\xi + A\eta\right),$$

$$\dot{\eta} = -\frac{\pi i}{h} g\mu_0\left(A\xi + Ct\eta\right).$$

To work with dimensionless variables let us introduce a new time measure$(^{**})$:

$$\tau = \sqrt{\frac{\pi}{2h}\, g\mu_0 C} \cdot t$$

and the numerical quantity

$$k = \frac{2\pi g\mu_0 A^2}{hC}$$

which gives the ratio of the atom precession frequency to the rotation frequency of the field direction when this ratio reaches its minimum value, *i.e.* for $\tau = 0$. If v is the vapour-beam velocity at distance d from point Q close to which the field gradient is of the order of G gauss per cm, $k(\star)$ will be of the order of $10^7 G\frac{d^2}{v}$. For example for $v = 10^5$ and $G \sim 1$, k will be $\sim 100\, d^2$ and therefore $k \sim 1$ for $d = 1\,\mathrm{mm}$. With the above new variables we obtain:

$$\frac{d\xi}{d\tau} = -i\left(-2\tau\xi + \sqrt{k}\,\eta\right),$$

$$\frac{d\eta}{d\tau} = -i\left(\sqrt{k}\,\xi + 2\tau\eta\right).$$

$(^*)$ In "Il Nuovo Cimento" $\frac{1}{2}$ and $-\frac{1}{2}$ are erronously printed in line. (Note of the Editor, see also E. AMALDI, *op. cit.*)

$(^{**})$ In "Il Nuovo Cimento" it is erroneously printed $\frac{\pi}{zh}$. (Note of the Editor, see also E. AMALDI, *op. cit.*)

$(\star)$ In "Il Nuovo Cimento" it is erroneously printed K, here and also in the first line of p. 132. (Note of the Editor, see also E. AMALDI, *op. cit.*)

These equations can be simplified by setting:

$$\xi = e^{i\tau^2} f; \qquad \eta = e^{-i\tau^2} g$$

from which it follows:

(5)
$$\begin{cases} \dfrac{df}{d\tau} = -i\sqrt{k}\,e^{-2i\tau^2} g \\[2mm] \dfrac{dg}{d\tau} = -i\sqrt{k}\,e^{2i\tau^2} f. \end{cases}$$

Eliminating g, we obtain:

(6)
$$\frac{d^2 f}{d\tau^2} + hi\tau \frac{df}{d\tau} + kf = 0.$$

We can derive an integral representation of the solutions of this differential equation that allows to determine the asymptotic expression for large positive or negative values of τ. This is indeed what we need since we assume that for $\tau = -\infty$ the atom is oriented with respect to the field and we want to determine its orientation for $\tau \to \infty$.

Since everything reduces to the calculation of the angle α defined above, it is enough to consider only one solution of eq. (6). This is given by

$$f(\tau) = \frac{\sqrt{k}\,e^{-k\pi/8}}{2(1+i)\sqrt{\pi}} \int s^{(k/4i)-1} e^{(s^2/8i)+s\tau}\,ds$$

with $\log s$ assuming its principal value, and the boundary condition

$$\left| s^{k/4i} e^{(s^2/8i)+s\tau} \right|_C = 0$$

being satisfied if the integration path has the form shown in the figure for the two cases $\tau < 0$ e $\tau > 0$.

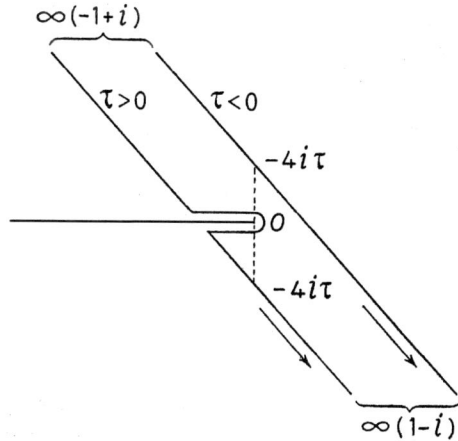

The negative part of the real axis is a line of discontinuity for the function to be integrated and cannot be crossed. Moreover, to evaluate the asymptotic expressions, the integration paths are drawn through the saddle point $s = -4i\tau$ in the direction of maximum slope.

For $\tau \to -\infty$ the whole integral comes from the vicinity of the point $s = -4i\tau$. With the substitution

$$s = -4i\tau + (1-i)p$$

we can easily calculate the first terms in the asymptotic expansion of f and, with the help of the first equation (5), of g. Neglecting the terms that tend to zero we find

$$\tau \to -\infty; \qquad f = 0; \qquad g = (-4\tau)^{k/4i}.$$

For $\tau \to \infty$ the asymptotic expression of the integral comes partly from the neighbourhoods of the saddle point $s = -4i\tau$, and partly from the branching point O. In this case the result is

$$\tau \to \infty: \qquad f = -\frac{1-i}{2\sqrt{\pi}}\sqrt{k}e^{-k/4i}e^{-k\pi/8}\sinh\left(\frac{k\pi}{4}\right)\Gamma\left(\frac{k}{4i}\right)$$

$$g = (4\tau)^{k/4i}e^{-k\pi/4}.$$

Since for real $a(^3)$

$$|\Gamma(ai)| = \sqrt{\frac{\pi}{a\sinh(\pi a)}},$$

or keeping in mind the constancy of $|f^2| + |g^2|$ we find the following expressions for $|f|$ and $|g|$:

$$\tau \to -\infty: \qquad |f| = 0; \qquad |g| = 1$$

$$\tau \to \infty: \qquad |f| = \sqrt{1 - e^{-k\pi/2}}; \qquad |g| = e^{-k\pi/4}.$$

For $\tau \to -\infty$ the field is directed along the z-axis and therefore at the beginning of the phenomenon the momentum of the atom is $-\frac{1}{2}\frac{h}{2\pi}$ in the direction of the field. For $\tau \to \infty$ the field is instead directed along $-z$, hence the limiting value of $|g^2|$ provides the probability that the atom reverses its orientation, *i.e.* that, once it has passed in the vicinity of Q it acquires a momentum $\frac{1}{2}\frac{h}{2\pi}$ in the direction of the field. This probability is therefore

$$W\left(-\frac{1}{2},\frac{1}{2}\right) = e^{-k\pi/2}.$$

(^{3}) See, *e.g.*, Whittaker and Watson, *Modern Analysis*, IV ed., p. 259.

In this way, 21% of the atoms turn over for $k = 1$ and 4.3% for $k = 2$.

The general solution of the problem for an arbitrary j and for transitions from m to m' can be obtained from eq. (4) with the appropriate value of the rotation angle α. Since in our case

$$W\left(-\frac{1}{2}, \frac{1}{2}\right) = \sin^2 \frac{\alpha}{2},$$

by comparison with the previous expression, we obtain

$$\alpha = 2 \arcsin e^{-k\pi/4}.$$

Comment on the Scientific Paper no. 6: *"Oriented atoms in a variable magnetic field"*.

In this work Majorana evaluates the probability of spin-flip for atoms in a polarized beam in the presence of a varying magnetic field. It is a quantitative study of the non-adiabatic situation. The problem, "particularly important" to Majorana, is what happens close to a zero of the magnetic field: "all the atoms would invert their spin orientation". The problem had been proposed to Majorana by E. Segré, as E. Amaldi recalls[1]. Indeed E. Segré, together with R. Frisch[2], were setting up an experiment to generalize the famous Stern and Gerlach work on spatial quantization. The latter observations had been done in static magnetic gradient and adiabatic conditions. The goal of the new experiment was to measure the final state of an atomic magnetic moment initially prepared in a definite state in the presence of a rapidly varying field. In Segré and Frisch apparatus the non-adiabatic transition was induced by having the atomic beam close to a zero of the magnetic field. Their measurements were explained using Majorana's quantitative predictions. In his paper Majorana shows how to interpret the total effect of a varying magnetic field on an object with a given angular momentum and a component m along the z-axis in terms of a sudden rotation of the angular momentum itself. By a rigorous solution of the time-dependent Schrödinger equation, Majorana obtains the rotation angle showing that there is a dependence on the gyromagnetic factor but not on the initial m value. As a consequence, after the rotation the system is not in a well-defined quantum state with respect to the original field direction but has to be described as wavepacket composed by a superposition of states with different m'. In the paper the probability amplitude for a transition between m and m' is explicitly calculated.

Majorana immediately singles out two characteristic frequencies of the problem: Larmor precession frequency of the atomic dipole moment and the frequency of rotation of the magnetic field as seen by the atom. When the two frequencies become comparable the atom has a high probability of changing its magnetic substate, *i.e.* to undergo a spin-flip. Majorana demonstrates that the spin-flip probability depends on the ratio k

---

[1] E. AMALDI, *op. cit.* and the English translation *Ettore Majorana, man and scientist* in *Strong and Weak Interactions, Present Problems, International School of Physics Ettore Majorana, Erice, June 19th - July 4th 1966*, edited by Zichichi A. (Academic Press, New York and London) 1966.
[2] R. FRISCH and E. SEGRÈ, "Ricerche sulla quantizzazione spaziale", *Nuovo Cimento* **10** (1933) 78; "Über die Einstellung der Richtungsquantelung", *Z. Phys.*, **80** (1933) 610.

between the two frequencies and is given by $e^{-k\pi/2}$. As E. Amaldi points out "the problem was really solved by Majorana with extreme elegance and conciseness for the case $J = 1/2$". The generalization to the case of any J was done by F. Bloch e I. I. Rabi who, in their celebrated work of 1945[3], cite the work of Majorana as seminal for the solution of the problem. Majorana's treatment for spin-flips is used in quantum mechanics textbooks[4] and has recently been rediscovered in atomic and molecular collision physics at low energy[5]; it is also widely applied outside atomic and molecular physics, *e.g.* to manipulate polarized beams in neutron physics.

Let us discuss here two experimental fields were Majorana's work has found an application and is still quite useful: namely double-resonance spectroscopy and Bose-Einstein condensation. In the early 1950s in atomic physics double-resonance spectroscopy (optics+radiofrequency) has been developed to investigate atomic structures. In particular, Brossel and Bitter[6] have studied the polarization state of fluorescence from the lowest $^3P_1$ level of mercury excited with polarized light in order to populate only the sublevel $m = 0$. In the experiment the atoms are subjected to a magnetic field to separate Zeeman sublevels $m = -1, 0, +1$. A radiofrequency radiation is used to induce transition between $m = 0$ and $m = +1$ or $m = -1$. As a consequence, the polarization state of the fluorescence radiation is altered. The observed lineshape has a peculiar behaviour, indeed by increasing the radiofrequency power one observes a doubling of line with an evident central minimum. Brossel and Bitter interpret such behaviour as "Majorana transitions" and use Majorana's formula to perfectly explain the experimental data. Nowadays such lineshape is known as "Majorana-Brossel". The explanation of the experiment is still of great interest and has been treated by C. Cohen-Tannoudji in his course at *Collège de France* in 2003[7]. He interprets the lineshape as a consequence of the quantum interference with a three-photon process where the atoms from sublevel $m = 0$, before making a transition to sublevel $m = +1$, undergo a transition to and from sublevel $m = -1$.

Coming back to the problem of the spin-flip of atoms moving in a magnetic quadrupole field, it is interesting to note that the understanding of this effect has made the experimental realization of Bose-Einstein condensation in an atomic gas possible. In order to observe condensation, atoms must be cooled to the microkelvin regime and this has been achieved by using magnetic traps for atoms oriented and pre-cooled with laser radiation.

---

[3] F. BLOCH and I. I. RABI, "Atoms in Variable Magnetic Fields", *Rev. Mod. Phys.* **17** (1945) 237.

[4] L. D. LANDAU and E. M. LIFSHITZ, *Quantum Mechanics: Non-relativistic Theory* (Nauka, Moscow) 1974; (Pergamon Press, Oxford) 1977.

[5] F. DI GIACOMO and E. E. NIKITIN, "The Majorana formula and the Landau-Zener-Stuckelberg treatment of the avoided crossing problem", *Phys. Usp.* **48** (2005) 515.

[6] J. BROSSEL and F. BITTER, "A New Double Resonance Method for Investigating Atomic Energy Levels. Application to Hg $^3P_1$", *Phys. Rev.* **86** (1952) 308; see also: J. BROSSEL, Thesis, Faculté des Sciences de l'Université de Paris (1952).

[7] C. COHEN-TANNOUDJI, lessons available online at `http://www.phys.ens.fr/cours/college-de-france/`

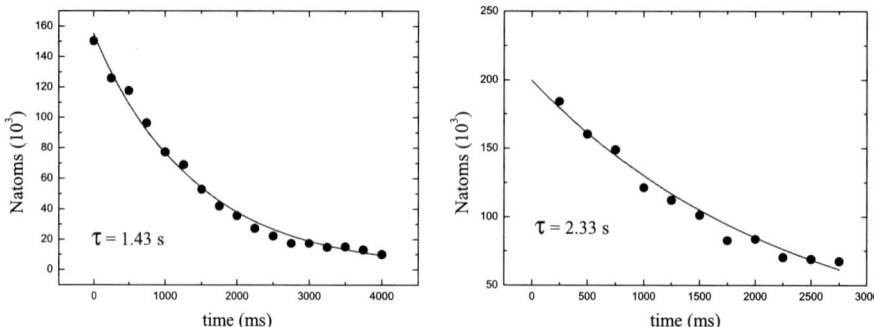

Fig. 1. – Atoms polarized and confined with magnetic field gradients on the route to Bose-Einstein condensation. The graph on the left refers to a quadrupole trap where there are losses due to Majorana spin-flip. The graph on the right refers to a trap specifically designed to avoid spin-flips([10]).

The final cooling towards condensation is performed by forced evaporation of the hottest atoms from the magnetic trap and by the consequent thermalization of the remaining atoms. To this aim collision processes are fundamental requiring a large atomic density. By moving in a magnetic trap the atoms are exposed to a varying magnetic field; the coldest they are the slowest they move around the magnetic-field minimum. In the first attempts quadrupole magnetic traps were used; *i.e.* the configuration Majorana has studied in his paper. When the atoms undergo a spin-flip they are no longer confined and Majorana's formula allows a quantitative analysis in terms of the magnetic field gradient and of the atomic temperature. The zero in the magnetic field is a sort of "hole" that reduces the atomic density thus preventing the evaporative cooling. E. A. Cornell, C. E. Wieman and W. Ketterle, who have first realized Bose-Einstein condensation in 1995, were perfectly aware of the problem. Indeed in their Nobel Lectures([8])([9]) they often mention the "Majorana hole". The problem to be solved was to create traps with a non-zero minimum. The first solution came from the Boulder group using a quite sophisticate trap where the minimum was rotated (TOP) and the parameters were chosen using the quantitative expression for the spin-flip. It is interesting to report what Cornell and Wieman write: "This zero represents a hole in the trap, a site at which atoms can undergo Majorana transitions and thus escape from the trap. ...the TOP design worked well, and the samples were cooled far colder, in fact too cold ...". Ketterle, on the other hand, solved the problem by using a focused laser beam to "plug the hole". Nowadays, having completely understood the problem, it is possible to use different static configurations with a non-zero minimum. Among the others we here cite the one used in the very town —Catania— of Majorana by F. S. Cataliotti where the atoms are trapped on a micro-electronic circuit. Figure 1 shows the temporal behaviour of the atomic number trapped

([8]) E. A. Cornell and C. E. Wieman, "Bose-Einstein condensation in a dilute gas", *Rev. Mod. Phys.* **74** (2002) 875.
([9]) W. Ketterle, "When atoms behave as waves", *Rev. Mod. Phys.* **74** (2002) 1173.

at a temperature of a few microkelvin in the presence of a zero (left) and of a situation where the "hole" is plugged by adding a magnetic field (right): as can be observed by removing Majorana spin-flip the atomic-trap lifetime is significantly enhanced[10].

Once the condensate is realized, spin-flip transitions, this time induced in a controlled fashion, can be used for further developments in atomic physics at ultra-low temperatures. Recently, X. Chen in Beijing University[11] has used Majorana's theoretical predictions to develop a new method to extract coherent atoms from a condensate and realize a pulsed *atom laser*.

MASSIMO INGUSCIO
Università di Firenze

---

[10] Courtesy of F. S. Cataliotti, Università di Catania (2006).
[11] X. MA *et al.*, "Population oscillation of the multicomponent spinor BEC induced by nona-diabatic transitions", *Phys. Rev. A* **73** (2006) 013624.

NOTA SCIENTIFICA n. 7 — SCIENTIFIC PAPER no. 7

Teoria relativistica di particelle con momento intrinseco arbitrario

Nota di Ettore Majorana

"Il Nuovo Cimento", vol. 9, 1932, pp. 335-344.

Sunto. — L'autore stabilisce equazioni d'onda lineari nell'energia e relativistica-mente invarianti per particelle aventi momento angolare intrinseco comunque pre-fissato.

La teoria di Dirac dell'elettrone fa uso, come è noto, di una funzione d'onda a quattro componenti delle quali, quando si considerino movimenti lenti, due hanno valori trascurabili mentre le altre due obbediscono in prima approssimazione all'equazione di Schrödinger.

In modo analogo una particella con momento angolare intrinseco $s\frac{h}{2\pi}$ ($s = 0, \frac{1}{2}, 1, \frac{3}{2}, \ldots$) è descritta nella meccanica quantistica mediante un complesso di $2s + 1$ funzioni d'onda che soddisfano separatamente alla equazione di Schrödinger. Tale rappresentazione è naturalmente valida finché si trascurano gli effetti relativistici, e ciò è lecito per particelle mobili con velocità piccola di fronte a quella della luce. Un altro caso in cui la teoria elementare è ancora utilizzabile è ovviamente quello in cui la velocità della particella pur essendo comparabile con c rimane quasi costante in direzione e grandezza, poiché allora è possibile ricondursi allo studio di movimenti lenti scegliendo opportunamente il sistema di riferimento.

Il caso invece in cui la velocità delle particelle pur essendo quasi costante entro regioni sufficientemente estese del continuo spazio-tempo varia da una regione all'altra

lentamente ma fra valori estremi lontani, sotto l'azione di campi esterni deboli, non si lascia trattare immediatamente con l'equazione non relativistica di SCHRÖDINGER.

Una generalizzazione relativistica della teoria precedente deve soddisfare successivamente alle condizioni seguenti al crescere del suo grado di accuratezza:

(a) La teoria permette lo studio di particelle aventi velocità quasi determinata in grandezza e direzione, dando risultati equivalenti alla teoria non relativistica, senza tuttavia la necessità di scegliere un sistema particolare di riferimento.

(b) La teoria permette inoltre di studiare processi in cui la velocità delle particelle varia lentamente, ma entro limiti comunque estesi, per l'azione di campi esterni deboli.

(c) La teoria è valida in generale comunque indeterminata sia la velocità delle particelle.

È probabile che una teoria rigorosa soddisfacente alla condizione (c) sia incompatibile con il mantenimento dell'attuale schema quantistico. La teoria di DIRAC dell'elettrone che pure ha dimostrato la sua fecondità nello studio di fenomeni schiettamente relativistici come la diffusione di raggi γ duri, soddisfa certo imperfettamente alla (c), come prova la nota difficoltà delle transizioni a stati di energia negativa. Al contrario è verosimile che una teoria soddisfacente a (b) e solo parzialmente a (c) non urti in difficoltà sostanziali, il suo contenuto fisico potendo essere essenzialmente quello stesso che giustifica l'equazione di SCHRÖDINGER. L'esempio più notevole di tali generalizzazioni relativistiche ci è dato appunto dalla teoria di DIRAC, ma poiché questa è applicabile soltanto a particelle con momento intrinseco $s = 1/2$, ho cercato equazioni analoghe nella forma a quelle di DIRAC, sebbene alquanto più complicate, le quali permettono la considerazione di particelle con momento angolare arbitrario, e in particolare nullo.

L'equazione d'onda, in assenza di campo, di una particella materiale, deve avere secondo DIRAC la forma:

$$(1) \qquad \left[\frac{W}{c} + (\alpha, p) - \beta mc\right] \psi = 0.$$

Equazioni di questo tipo presentano una difficoltà di principio. L'operatore β(*) deve infatti trasformarsi come la componente temporale di un quadrivettore e così β non può essere semplicemente multiplo della matrice unità ma deve avere almeno due autovalori differenti, supponiamo β_1 e β_2; ma da ciò segue che l'energia di riposo della particella, che si ottiene da (1) ponendo $p = 0$ deve avere almeno due valori differenti, cioè $\beta_1 mc^2$ e $\beta_2 mc^2$. Secondo le equazioni di DIRAC i valori possibili della massa di riposo sono, come è noto, $+m$ e $-m$ dal che segue per l'invarianza relativistica che l'energia può avere due valori differenti per il segno per ogni valore di p: $W = \pm\sqrt{m^2c^4 + c^2p^2}$.

L'indeterminazione nel segno dell'energia può essere in realtà superata, usando equazioni del tipo fondamentale (1), solo se la funzione d'onda ha infinite componenti che *non* si lasciano spezzare in tensori o spinori finiti.

(*) Ne "Il Nuovo Cimento" è stampato erroneamente $^{-1}$ al posto di β. (Nota del Curatore, si veda anche E. AMALDI, *op. cit.*)

1. L'equazione (1) può essere dedotta dal principio variazionale

$$(2) \qquad \delta \int \tilde{\psi} \left[\frac{W}{c} + (\alpha, p) - \beta mc \right] \psi \, dV \, dt = 0.$$

Una delle condizioni dell'invarianza relativistica è ovviamente che sia invariante la forma $\tilde{\psi}\beta\psi$.

Se ora vogliamo che l'energia di riposo risulti sempre positiva, gli autovalori di β devono essere tutti positivi e la forma $\tilde{\psi}\beta\psi$ sarà definita positiva. È allora possibile mediante una trasformazione *non* unitaria $\psi \to \varphi$ ridurre detta forma alla forma unità:

$$(3) \qquad \tilde{\psi}\beta\psi = \tilde{\varphi}\varphi.$$

Sostituendo in (2) a ψ la sua espressione mediante φ si avrà

$$(4) \qquad \delta \int \tilde{\varphi} \left[\gamma_0 \frac{W}{c} + (\gamma, p) - mc \right] \varphi \, dV \, dt = 0,$$

da cui seguono le equazioni equivalenti alla (1):

$$(5) \qquad \left[\gamma_0 \frac{W}{c} + (\gamma, p) - mc \right] \varphi = 0.$$

Dobbiamo ora determinare la legge di trasformazione di φ di fronte a una rotazione di Lorentz e l'espressione delle matrici γ_0, γ_x, γ_y, γ_z in modo che sia rispettata l'invarianza relativistica del principio variazionale (4) e quindi che sia ivi invariante la funzione integranda.

Cominciamo con lo stabilire la legge di trasformazione di φ osservando anzitutto che l'invarianza di $\tilde{\varphi}\varphi$ significa che dobbiamo considerare solo trasformazioni unitarie. Per evitare complicazioni esagerate diamo inoltre la legge di trasformazione solo per trasformazioni di Lorentz infinitamente piccole, una trasformazione finita potendo ottenersi per integrazione di quelle. Introduciamo le trasformazioni infinitesime nelle variabili ct, x, y, z;

$$(6) \quad \begin{cases} S_x = \begin{vmatrix} 0 & 0 & 0 & 0 \\ 0 & 0 & 0 & 0 \\ 0 & 0 & 0 & -1 \\ 0 & 0 & 1 & 0 \end{vmatrix} ; \ S_y = \begin{vmatrix} 0 & 0 & 0 & 0 \\ 0 & 0 & 0 & 1 \\ 0 & 0 & 0 & 0 \\ 0 & -1 & 0 & 0 \end{vmatrix} ; \ S_z = \begin{vmatrix} 0 & 0 & 0 & 0 \\ 0 & 0 & -1 & 0 \\ 0 & 1 & 0 & 0 \\ 0 & 0 & 0 & 0 \end{vmatrix} ; \\[4em] T_x = \begin{vmatrix} 0 & 1 & 0 & 0 \\ 1 & 0 & 0 & 0 \\ 0 & 0 & 0 & 0 \\ 0 & 0 & 0 & 0 \end{vmatrix} ; \ T_y = \begin{vmatrix} 0 & 0 & 1 & 0 \\ 0 & 0 & 0 & 0 \\ 1 & 0 & 0 & 0 \\ 0 & 0 & 0 & 0 \end{vmatrix} ; \ T_z = \begin{vmatrix} 0 & 0 & 0 & 1 \\ 0 & 0 & 0 & 0 \\ 0 & 0 & 0 & 0 \\ 1 & 0 & 0 & 0 \end{vmatrix} . \end{cases}$$

e poniamo

(7)
$$\begin{cases} a_x = iS_x; & a_y = iS_y; & a_z = iS_z \\ b_x = -iT_x; & b_y = -iT_y; & b_z = -iT_z. \end{cases}$$

Gli operatori a e b devono essere Hermitiani in una rappresentazione unitaria, e viceversa; inoltre perché le trasformazioni infinitesime siano integrabili devono soddisfare a certe relazioni di scambio che si deducono da (6) e (7):

(8)
$$\begin{cases} (a_x, a_y) = ia_z \\ (a_x, b_x) = 0 \\ (a_x, b_y) = ib_z \\ (a_x, b_z) = -ib_y \\ (b_x, b_y) = -ia_z \end{cases}$$

e le altre che si ottengono per permutazione circolare di x, y, z.

La più semplice soluzione delle (8) mediante operatori Hermitiani è data dalle seguenti matrici infinite in cui gli elementi diagonali sono numerati con due indici j e m e bisogna distinguere due possibilità, secondo che si faccia $j = 1/2, 3/2, 5/2, \ldots$; $m = j, j - 1, \ldots, -j$, oppure $j = 0, 1, 2, \ldots$; $m = j, j - 1, \ldots, -j$:

(9)
$$\begin{cases} (j, m | a_x - ia_y | j, m+1) = \sqrt{(j+m+1)(j-m)} \\ (j, m | a_x + ia_y | j, m-1) = \sqrt{(j+m)(j-m+1)} \\ (j, m | a_z | j, m) = m \\ (j, m | b_x - ib_y | j+1, m+1) = -\frac{1}{2}\sqrt{(j+m+1)(j+m+2)} \\ (j, m | b_x - ib_y | j-1, m+1) = \frac{1}{2}\sqrt{(j-m)(j-m-1)} \\ (j, m | b_x + ib_y | j+1, m-1) = \frac{1}{2}\sqrt{(j-m+1)(j-m+2)} \\ (j, m | b_x + ib_y | j-1, m-1) = -\frac{1}{2}\sqrt{(j+m)(j+m-1)} \\ (j, m | b_z | j+1, m) = \frac{1}{2}\sqrt{(j+m+1)(j-m+1)} \\ (j, m | b_z | j-1, m) = \frac{1}{2}\sqrt{(j+m)(j-m)}. \end{cases}$$

Se assumiamo che per riflessione nell'origine le $\varphi_{j,m}$(*) restano inalterate o cambiano segno alternativamente al variare di j, b risulta un vettore polare, mentre a è un vettore assiale.

Chiameremo le grandezze su cui operano a e b tensori o spinori infiniti di indice zero secondo che j è intero o mezzo. La denominazione "di indice zero" significa che è nullo l'invariante:

$$(10) \qquad\qquad Z = a_x b_x + a_y b_y + a_z b_z .$$

Spinori o tensori infiniti più generali possono definirsi per qualunque valore di Z. Gli spinori possono essere ottenuti semplicemente nel modo seguente. Si consideri una soluzione generica $\psi(q,t)$ delle equazioni di Dirac senza campo e la si assoggetti a una trasformazione relativistica:

$$(11) \qquad\qquad \psi(q,t) \to \psi'(q,t).$$

Allora la trasformazione nello spazio:

$$(12) \qquad\qquad \psi(q,0) \to \psi'(q,0)$$

è unitaria, e se invece di funzioni arbitrarie $\psi(q,0)$ consideriamo solo quelle che appartengono a un determinato autovalore z_0 dell'operatore (10), che ha uno spettro continuo che si estende da $-\infty$ a $+\infty$, noi troviamo funzioni che si trasformano mediante (12) come spinori infiniti, ognuno di questi ottenendosi esattamente due volte.

Gli operatori a_x e b_x hanno nella rappresentazione (12) la forma:

$$a_x = \frac{2\pi}{h}\left(y p_z - z p_y\right) + \frac{1}{2}\sigma_x$$

$$b_x = \frac{2\pi}{h} x \frac{H}{c} + \frac{i}{2}\alpha_x$$

e analogamente a_y, a_z, b_y, b_z.

2. Dobbiamo ora determinare gli operatori γ_0, γ_x, γ_y, γ_z in modo che (4) sia invariante. Poiché consideriamo solo trasformazioni unitarie, detti operatori si trasformano come le forme Hermitiane ad essi collegate ed è quindi necessario per l'invarianza della funzione integranda in (4) che essi costituiscano un vettore covariante ($\gamma_0, \gamma_x, \gamma_y, \gamma_z \sim ct, -x, -y, -z$).

(*) Ne "Il Nuovo Cimento" è stampato erroneamente $\varphi j, m$. (Nota del Curatore, si veda anche E. Amaldi, *op. cit.*)

È ovvia l'interpretazione di $\tilde{\varphi}\gamma_0\varphi$ e $-\tilde{\varphi}\gamma\varphi$ come densità di carica e di corrente. Gli operatori γ devono soddisfare alle relazioni di scambio:

(13)
$$\begin{cases}
(\gamma_0, a_x) = 0 \\
(\gamma_0, b_x) = i\gamma_x \\
(\gamma_x, a_x) = 0 \\
(\gamma_x, a_y) = i\gamma_z \\
(\gamma_x, a_z) = -i\gamma_y \\
(\gamma_x, b_x) = i\gamma_0 \\
(\gamma_x, b_y) = 0 \\
(\gamma_z, b_z) = 0
\end{cases}$$

e alle altre che si ottengono per permutazione circolare di x, y, z. Le relazioni di scambio (13) determinano, come è facile dimostrare, γ_0, γ_x, γ_y, γ_z a meno di un fattore costante. Si trova

(14)
$$\begin{cases}
\gamma_0 = j + \dfrac{1}{2} \\[2mm]
(j, m|\gamma_x - i\gamma_y|j + 1, m + 1) = -\dfrac{i}{2}\sqrt{(j + m + 1)(j + m + 2)} \\[2mm]
(j, m|\gamma_x - i\gamma_y|j - 1, m + 1) = -\dfrac{i}{2}\sqrt{(j - m)(j - m - 1)} \\[2mm]
(j, m|\gamma_x + i\gamma_y|j + 1, m - 1) = \dfrac{i}{2}\sqrt{(j - m + 1)(j - m + 2)} \\[2mm]
(j, m|\gamma_x + i\gamma_y|j - 1, m - 1) = \dfrac{i}{2}\sqrt{(j + m)(j + m - 1)} \\[2mm]
(j, m|\gamma_z|j + 1, m) = \dfrac{i}{2}\sqrt{(j + m + 1)(j - m + 1)} \\[2mm]
(j, m|\gamma_z|j - 1, m) = -\dfrac{i}{2}\sqrt{(j + m)(j - m)}.
\end{cases}$$

Le componenti non indicate di γ_x, γ_y, γ_z essendo nulle. Si noti che la forma Hermitiana $\varphi\gamma_0\varphi$ è definita positiva come richiede l'interpretazione fisica.

Vogliamo ora passare dalle equazioni scritte nella forma (5) alle equazioni (1). Basta per ciò porre

(15)
$$\varphi_{j,m} = \frac{\psi_{j,m}}{\sqrt{j + \frac{1}{2}}}$$

poiché allora la forma collegata a γ_0 si riduce alla forma unità. Otteniamo così equazioni della forma desiderata

(16)
$$\left[\frac{W}{c} + (\alpha, p) - \beta mc\right]\psi = 0$$

in cui $\beta = \frac{1}{j+\frac{1}{2}}$ mentre le componenti diverse da zero di α_x, α_y, α_z sono date da

(17)
$$
\begin{cases}
(j,m|\alpha_x - i\alpha_y|j+1, m+1) = -\frac{i}{2}\sqrt{\dfrac{(j+m+1)(j+m+2)}{\left(j+\frac{1}{2}\right)\left(j+\frac{3}{2}\right)}} \\[16pt]
(j,m|\alpha_x - i\alpha_y|j-1, m+1) = -\frac{i}{2}\sqrt{\dfrac{(j-m)(j-m-1)}{\left(j-\frac{1}{2}\right)\left(j+\frac{1}{2}\right)}} \\[16pt]
(j,m|a_x + i\alpha_y|j+1, m-1) = \frac{i}{2}\sqrt{\dfrac{(j-m+1)(j-m+2)}{\left(j+\frac{1}{2}\right)\left(j+\frac{3}{2}\right)}} \\[16pt]
(j,m|\alpha_x + i\alpha_y|j-1, m-1) = \frac{i}{2}\sqrt{\dfrac{(j+m)(j+m-1)}{\left(j-\frac{1}{2}\right)\left(j+\frac{1}{2}\right)}} \\[16pt]
(j,m|\alpha_z|j+1, m) = \frac{i}{2}\sqrt{\dfrac{(j+m+1)(j-m+1)}{\left(j+\frac{1}{2}\right)\left(j+\frac{3}{2}\right)}} \\[16pt]
(j,m|\alpha_z|j-1, m) = -\frac{i}{2}\sqrt{\dfrac{(j+m)(j-m)}{\left(j-\frac{1}{2}\right)\left(j+\frac{1}{2}\right)}} \, .
\end{cases}
$$

Quando si cercano le soluzioni di (16) corrispondenti a onde piane con massa positiva si trovano tutte quelle che derivano per trasformazione relativistica delle onde di momento nullo. Per queste l'energia è data da

(18)
$$
W_0 = \frac{mc^2}{j+\frac{1}{2}} \, .
$$

Abbiamo così per valori mezzi di j stati corrispondenti a valori della massa: $m, m/2, m/3, \ldots$, e per j intero: $2m, 2m/3, 2m/5, \ldots$.

È da notare che particelle con massa differente hanno momento angolare intrinseco differente, il momento angolare intrinseco avendo un valore determinato solo nel sistema in cui le particelle sono in riposo.

Se si considera il complesso degli stati appartenenti al valore $\frac{m}{s+\frac{1}{2}}$ della massa di riposo come realizzato in natura, tutti gli altri stati non avendo significato, otteniamo una teoria invariante di particelle con momento angolare s che in assenza di campo può riguardarsi come soddisfacente. Si verifica senza difficoltà che per movimenti lenti e particelle di momento intrinseco s solo le $\psi_{s,m}$ sono sensibilmente diverse da zero e obbediscono all'equazione di Schrödinger con il valore $M = \frac{m}{s+\frac{1}{2}}$ della massa, mentre le $\psi_{s+1,m}$ e $\psi_{s-1,m}$ sono dell'ordine di v/c, le $\psi_{s+2,m}$ e $\psi_{s-2,m}$ dell'ordine di v^2/c^2, e così via.

Otteniamo così solo due delle equazioni d'onda di cui l'una è adatta per la descrizione di particelle con momento angolare non intero e l'altra per particelle senza momento angolare o con momento intero.

Oltre agli stati appartenenti a valori positivi della massa, ve ne sono altri in cui l'energia è legata al momento da una relazione del tipo

$$(19) \qquad W = \pm\sqrt{c^2 p^2 - k^2 c^4}$$

e ne esistono per tutti i valori positivi di k ma solo per $p \geq kc$.

Questi stati possono riguardarsi come appartenenti al valore immaginario ik della massa.

Le funzioni di *spin* appartenenti a onde piane con $p \neq 0$ hanno una espressione particolarmente semplice nel caso di particelle senza momento intrinseco se $p_x = p_y = 0$, $p_z = p$.

Per queste si trova a meno di un fattore di normalizzazione

$$(20) \qquad \begin{cases} \psi_{j,0} = \sqrt{\left(j + \dfrac{1}{2}\right)} \left(i \dfrac{\eta - j}{\varepsilon}\right)^j \\[2mm] \psi_{j,m} = 0 \quad \text{per} \quad m \neq 0 \end{cases} \qquad (j = 0, 1, 2, \ldots)$$

essendo

$$(21) \qquad \varepsilon = \frac{p}{Mc}, \qquad \eta = \frac{\sqrt{M^2 c^2 + p^2}}{Mc}$$

e $M = 2m$ la massa di riposo.

3. Vogliamo ora considerare brevemente l'introduzione del campo elettromagnetico nell'equazione (16).

Il passaggio dalle equazioni senza campo alle equazioni con campo esterno avviene nel modo più semplice sostituendo a W e p, $W - e\varphi$ e $p - \frac{e}{c}A$, se e è la carica della particella e φ e A i potenziali scalare e vettore. Ma altre possibilità sono aperte. Possiamo ad esempio aggiungere dei termini invarianti, analoghi a quelli introdotti da Pauli[3] nella teoria del neutrone magnetico, che portano a fattore le forze del campo in luogo dei potenziali elettromagnetici così da non turbare l'invarianza delle equazioni di fronte all'indeterminazione dei potenziali.

Tale artificio permette di attribuire a particelle con momento angolare non nullo un momento magnetico comunque prefissato. Nel caso dell'elettrone per esempio si trova mediante la semplice sotituzione $W, p \rightarrow W - e\varphi, p - \frac{e}{c}A$ un momento magnetico $+\frac{1}{2}\mu_0$ in luogo di $-\mu_0$.

---

[3] Citato da Oppenheimer, "Phys. Rev.", *41*, 763 (1932).

Se si vuole specializzare la nostra teoria in una teoria dell'elettrone che si accordi fin dove è possibile con i dati sperimentali dobbiamo quindi modificare il momento magnetico con termini aggiunti. Ma la teoria dell'elettrone così ottenuta è un doppione inutile della teoria di DIRAC che resta assolutamente da preferire in grazia della sua semplicità e del largo suffragio della esperienza. Il vantaggio della presente teoria è per contro la sua applicabilità a particelle con momento angolare differente da $1/2$.

Le equazioni con il campo e termini aggiunti per modificare il momento magnetico intrinseco hanno la forma

$$(22) \qquad \left[\left(\frac{W}{c} - \frac{e}{c}\varphi \right) + \left(a, p - \frac{e}{c}A \right) - \beta mc + \lambda(a', H) + \lambda(b', E) \right] \psi = 0$$

in cui a' sta per (a'_x, a'_y, a'_z) e b' per (b'_x, b'_y, b'_z) mentre E e H rappresentano il campo elettrico e magnetico.

La matrice a'_x si deduce da a_x (9) mediante la regola

$$(23) \qquad \left(j, m | a'_x | j', m' \right) = \frac{1}{\sqrt{\left(j + \frac{1}{2} \right) \left(j' + \frac{1}{2} \right)}} \left(j, m | a_x | j', m' \right)$$

e analogamente a'_y, a'_z, b'_y, b'_z.

Per particelle con momento angolare intrinseco $s = 1/2$ si deve porre $\lambda = \frac{2}{c}\mu$ se μ è il momento magnetico che si vuole aggiungere a quello che sorge naturalmente dall'introduzione dei potenziali elettromagnetici nell'equazione d'onda. Quest'ultimo vale in tal caso, come si è detto, $-\frac{1}{2}\frac{eh}{4\pi mc}$. Per particelle senza momento angolare intrinseco è naturale porre $\lambda = 0$.

Per quanto riguarda la soluzione pratica dell'equazione d'onda ricordiamo che per movimenti lenti sono finite e obbediscono all'equazione di SCHRÖDINGER solo le $\psi_{j,m}$ per il valore di j che misura il momento angolare intrinseco in unità $h/2\pi$.

Per particelle senza momento, ad esempio si ha una sola componente grande e cioè $\psi_{0,0}$, mentre le $\psi_{1,m}$ sono dell'ordine di v/c, se v la è velocità della particella, le $\psi_{2,m}$ dell'ordine di v^2/c^2 e così via. Si riesce così a eliminare per successive approssimazioni le componenti piccole e in particolare si giunge a espressioni molto semplici per il calcolo della prima correzione relativistica.

$$* \ * \ *$$

Ringrazio particolarmente il prof. E. FERMI per la discussione della presente teoria.

Commento alla Nota Scientifica n. 7: "Teoria relativistica di particelle con momento intrinseco arbitrario".

Il problema principale che affligge la costruzione di una estensione relativistica della equazione di Schrödinger nel quadro della meccanica ondulatoria è l'esistenza di soluzioni ad energia negativa. Anche assumendo che solo le soluzioni ad energia positiva siano fisicamente significative è difficile escludere transizioni verso stati ad energia negativa. Dirac tentò di risolvere il problema con una equazione alle derivate prime,

$$(1) \qquad i\frac{d\psi}{dt} = \left(-i\vec{\alpha}\cdot\vec{\nabla} + \beta m\right)\psi, \quad \text{ovvero:} \quad (i\gamma^{\mu}\frac{\partial}{\partial x_{\mu}} - m)\psi = 0.$$

Se seguendo Dirac assumiamo le regole di anticommutazione $\{\gamma^{\mu}, \gamma^{\nu}\} = 2g^{\mu\nu}$, l'equazione descrive una particella di massa m, ma ammette soluzioni con energia sia positiva che negativa. Dirac propose di risolvere il problema assumendo che tutti gli stati di energia negativa siano occupati, di modo che grazie al principio di Pauli una particella di energia positiva non possa saltare in uno stato di energia negativa. In questa versione la teoria va ben oltre i limiti della meccanica ondulatoria, ed è essenzialmente equivalente alla moderna formulazione di teoria dei campi, ammirevolmente presentata nella "Teoria simmetrica dell'elettrone e del positrone" di Majorana.

In questo lavoro su particelle di spin arbitrario Majorana tentò di costruire una generalizzazione relativistica della meccanica ondulatoria che eliminasse completamente le soluzioni ad energia negativa. Nel lavoro mostrò che una condizione *necessaria* per l'assenza di stati a energia negativa è che l'operatore β abbia solo autovalori positivi, e da questo segue che $\varphi = \beta^{1/2}\psi$ si trasforma secondo una rappresentazione unitaria del gruppo di Lorentz. Majorana mostra una assoluta padronanza della teoria dei gruppi. E. Amaldi[1] racconta l'ammirazione di Majorana per i lavori di H. Weyl e di E. Wigner sull'applicazione della teoria dei gruppi alla meccanica quantistica. In questo lavoro troviamo tracce della discussione di Weyl dell'algebra di Lie del gruppo delle rotazioni, qui estesa al gruppo di Lorentz, ad esempio quando presenta le regole di commutazione dei generatori del gruppo come "condizioni di integrabilità". Partendo dalle regole di commutazione, Majorana costruisce le "più semplici" rappresentazioni unitarie ad infinite dimensioni del gruppo di Lorentz, una per momenti angolari interi, l'altra per momenti

---

[1] E. Amaldi, *op. cit.*

angolari semi-interi, e costruisce esplicitamente le corrispondenti rappresentazioni delle matrici $\vec{\alpha}$ e β.

La versione di Majorana dell'equazione (1) ha soluzioni che descrivono una sequenza di stati di spin j crescente (intero o semi-intero nei due casi), con massa

$$(2) \qquad\qquad M_j = \frac{m}{j + \frac{1}{2}}.$$

Evitare gli stati di energia negativa ha un costo elevato, l'esistenza di una sequenza infinita di stati di spin crescente e massa decrescente. Non potendo accettare questa conclusione Majorana lascia aperta la possibilità che la sua teoria possa essere usata per descrivere particelle di spin arbitrario j_0 dichiarando non fisiche le soluzioni con $j \neq j_0$, e discute in qualche dettaglio il caso di particelle di spin nullo. Si rende tuttavia conto che in presenza di interazioni sarebbe difficile garantire l'assenza di transizioni a stati di spin differente. In un contesto differente questo è esattamente il problema che affliggeva la interpretazione ondulatoria dell'equazione di Dirac. Il problema è qui ancora più serio per la presenza, cui il lavoro accenna solo brevemente, di soluzioni che oggi diremmo "tachioniche" che corrispondono a valori immaginari della massa, ik, con energia $E = \pm\sqrt{c^2\vec{p}^2 - k^2 c^4}$, che esistono per $|\vec{p}| > k$ e qualunque k.

Il lavoro, scritto all'inizio dell'estate del 1932, appena prima l'annuncio della scoperta dell'elettrone positivo che segnò il trionfo della teoria di Dirac, non ebbe alcun successo malgrado i risultati brillanti e originali sulle rappresentazioni unitarie del gruppo di Lorentz, riscoperti solo dopo alcuni anni da Wigner. Per una discussione dei successivi sviluppi in questo campo si veda la rassegna di questo lavoro da parte di D. M. Fradkin[2].

Se questo lavoro non fosse stato totalmente dimenticato esso si potrebbe considerare un precursore di alcuni degli sviluppi della teoria delle particelle attivamente perseguiti negli ultimi decenni. Negli anni sessanta lo studio dei poli di Regge e la scoperta di stati adronici di spin elevato riaccese brevemente l'interesse per teorie basate su campi che trasformano secondo rappresentazioni infinito-dimensionali del gruppo di Lorentz, che descrivono una sequenza di particelle di spin e massa crescente. Questi tentativi trovarono la loro espressione più alta nei modelli duali, che però, come era stato per la teoria di Majorana, soffrivano della presenza di stati tachionici che si potevano solo evitare in uno spazio-tempo con un numero elevato di dimensioni. Per queste difficoltà, ma anche per l'affermazione della Cromodinamica Quantistica, l'applicazione di queste idee alla fisica degli adroni fu abbandonata, ma idee simili riapparvero più tardi nelle moderne teorie di stringa.

Nicola Cabibbo
Università di Roma "La Sapienza"

[2] D. M. Fradkin, *Am. J. Phys.* **34** (1966) 314.

Relativistic theory of particles with arbitrary intrinsic angular momentum(*)

Ettore Majorana

Summary. — The author establishes wave equations for particles having arbitrary given intrinsic angular momentum. Such equations are linear in the energy and relativistically invariant.

As is well known, Dirac's theory of the electron makes use of a four-component wave function. When slow movements are considered, two of the components acquire negligible values, while the remaining two, at least in a first approximation, satisfy the Schrödinger equation.

In a similar fashion, a particle having intrinsic angular momentum $s\frac{h}{2\pi}$ ($s = 0, \frac{1}{2}, 1, \frac{3}{2}, \ldots$) is described in quantum mechanics by a set of $2s+1$ wave functions which separately satisfy the Schrödinger equation. Of course, such a representation is valid as long as the relativistic effects are neglected, and this is allowed for a particle moving with speed much smaller than the speed of light. A different case in which the elementary theory retains its validity is, of course, the one in which the velocity of the particle is comparable with c but remains approximately constant in direction and magnitude. In fact, this case can be reduced to the study of slow movements by means of a suitable choice of the frame of reference.

(*) Translated from "Il Nuovo Cimento", vol. 9, 1932, pp. 335-344, by C. A. Orzalesi in Technical Report no. 792, 1968, University of Maryland. (Courtesy of E. Recami.)

On the other hand, the following situation cannot be easily dealt with by means of the nonrelativistic SCHRÖDINGER equation: a particle with speed which retains an almost constant value within fairly large regions in the space-time continuum, but for which the speed is also slowly varying between very different extremum values from one such region to another, as an effect of weak external fields.

A relativistic generalization of the preceding theory should satisfy the following hierarchy of conditions, as it becomes more and more accurate:

(a) The theory should allow the study of particles having an almost constant velocity (in direction and magnitude), and the results should be equivalent to those given by the nonrelativistic theory; however, there should be no need to specify any particular reference frame.

(b) The theory should allow the study of processes where the speed of the particles is slowly varying, but within arbitrarily separated limits, under the effect of weak external fields.

(c) The theory should retain its validity in general, even when the velocities of the particles vary arbitrarily.

It is likely that a rigorous theory satisfying condition (c) might be incompatible with the present-day quantum scheme. [For instance,] DIRAC's theory of the electron has largely proved its fruitfulness in the study of genuine relativistic phenomena, e.g., scattering of hard γ-rays; however, this theory certainly satisfies condition (c) only incompletely as is shown by the well-known difficulties coming from the transitions to states having negative energy. On the contrary, it is probably true that a theory satisfying condition (b), and only partially satisfying condition (c), should not meet essential difficulties since its physical content might be essentially the same as that which justifies the SCHRÖDINGER equation, The most remarkable example of this type of generalization is provided precisely by Dirac's theory. However, since this theory can be applied to particles with intrinsic [angular] momentum $s = 1/2$, I have investigated equations formally similar to the ones by DIRAC, although considerably more involved; these equations allow us to consider particles with arbitrary (and, in particular, zero) angular momentum.

According to DIRAC, the wave equation of a material particle in the absence of external fields must have the following form:

(1)
$$\left[\frac{W}{c} + (\alpha, p) - \beta mc \right] \psi = 0.$$

Equations of this kind present a difficulty in principle. Indeed, the operator $\beta(^*)$ has to transform as the time component of a four-vector, and thus β cannot be simply a

---

(*) In "Il Nuovo Cimento" it is erroneously printed $^{-1}$ instead of β. (Note of the Editor, see also E. AMALDI, *op. cit.*)

multiple of the unit matrix, but must have at least two different eigenvalues, say β_1 and β_2. However, this implies that the energy of the particle at rest, obtained from Eq. (1) by taking $p = 0$, shall have at least two different values, *i.e.* $\beta_1 mc^2$ and $\beta_2 mc^2$. According to DIRAC's equations, the allowed values of the mass at rest are, as well known, $+m$ and $-m$; from this it follows by relativistic invariance that for each value of p the energy can acquire two values differing in sign: $W = \pm\sqrt{m^2c^4 + c^2p^2}$.

As a matter of fact, the indeterminacy in the sign of the energy can be eliminated by using equations of the type (1), only if the wave function has infinitely many components that cannot be split into finite tensors or spinors.

1. Equation (1) can be derived from the following variational principle:

$$(2) \qquad \delta \int \tilde{\psi} \left[\frac{W}{c} + (\alpha, p) - \beta mc \right] \psi \, dV \, dt = 0$$

(one of the conditions imposed by relativistic invariance is, of course, that the form $\tilde{\psi}\beta\psi$ has to be invariant).

If now we require the energy at rest to be always positive, all the eigenvalues of β have to be positive so that the form $\tilde{\psi}\beta\psi$ will be positive definite. By means of a *nonunitarity* transformation $\psi \to \varphi$ it is then possible to reduce the expression at hand to the form unity:

$$(3) \qquad \tilde{\psi}\beta\psi = \tilde{\varphi}\varphi.$$

By substituting in Eq. (2) ψ with its expression in terms of φ one obtains:

$$(4) \qquad \delta \int \tilde{\varphi} \left[\gamma_0 \frac{W}{c} + (\gamma, p) - mc \right] \varphi \, dV \, dt = 0,$$

from which the equations equivalent to Eq. (1): follow:

$$(5) \qquad \left[\gamma_0 \frac{W}{c} + (\gamma, p) - mc \right] \varphi = 0.$$

We have now to determine the transformation law of φ under a LORENTZ rotation, as well as the expressions for the matrices γ_0, γ_x, γ_y, γ_z, in such a way as to respect the relativistic invariance of the variational principle (4), and thus to have an invariant integrand function in Eq. (4).

We begin by establishing the transformation law of φ and we note, first of all, that the invariance of $\tilde{\varphi}\varphi$ implies that we must restrict ourselves to unitary transformations. Moreover, in order to avoid exaggerated complications, we will give the transformation law only for infinitesimal LORENTZ transformations, since any finite transformation can

be obtained by integration of the former ones. We introduce the infinitesimal transformations in the variables ct, x, y, z;

$$(6) \begin{cases} S_x = \begin{vmatrix} 0 & 0 & 0 & 0 \\ 0 & 0 & 0 & 0 \\ 0 & 0 & 0 & -1 \\ 0 & 0 & 1 & 0 \end{vmatrix}; \quad S_y = \begin{vmatrix} 0 & 0 & 0 & 0 \\ 0 & 0 & 0 & 1 \\ 0 & 0 & 0 & 0 \\ 0 & -1 & 0 & 0 \end{vmatrix}; \quad S_z = \begin{vmatrix} 0 & 0 & 0 & 0 \\ 0 & 0 & -1 & 0 \\ 0 & 1 & 0 & 0 \\ 0 & 0 & 0 & 0 \end{vmatrix}; \\[4em] T_x = \begin{vmatrix} 0 & 1 & 0 & 0 \\ 1 & 0 & 0 & 0 \\ 0 & 0 & 0 & 0 \\ 0 & 0 & 0 & 0 \end{vmatrix}; \quad T_y = \begin{vmatrix} 0 & 0 & 1 & 0 \\ 0 & 0 & 0 & 0 \\ 1 & 0 & 0 & 0 \\ 0 & 0 & 0 & 0 \end{vmatrix}; \quad T_z = \begin{vmatrix} 0 & 0 & 0 & 1 \\ 0 & 0 & 0 & 0 \\ 0 & 0 & 0 & 0 \\ 1 & 0 & 0 & 0 \end{vmatrix}. \end{cases}$$

We also define

$$(7) \quad \begin{cases} a_x = iS_x; & a_y = iS_y; & a_z = iS_z; \\ b_x = -iT_x; & b_y = -iT_y; & b_z = -iT_z. \end{cases}$$

The operators a and b must be Hermitian operators in a unitary representation, and *vice versa*; furthermore, in order for the infinitesimal transformations to be integrable, they must satisfy certain relationships under commutation, as can be deduced from Eqs. (6) and (7):

$$(8) \quad \begin{cases} (a_x, a_y) = ia_z \\ (a_x, b_x) = 0 \\ (a_x, b_y) = ib_z \\ (a_x, b_z) = -ib_y \\ (b_x, b_y) = -ia_z \end{cases}$$

the remaining relations can be obtained by cyclic permutations of x, y, z.

The simplest solution of Eqs. (8) by means of Hermitian operators is given by the following infinite matrices, where the diagonal elements are labelled by two indices j and m; we have to distinguish two possibilities according to the assumption $j = 1/2, 3/2, 5/2, \ldots$;

$m = j, j - 1, \ldots, -j$, or $j = 0, 1, 2, \ldots$; $m = j, j - 1, \ldots, -j$:

(9)
$$
\begin{cases}
(j, m|a_x - ia_y|j, m + 1) = \sqrt{(j + m + 1)(j - m)} \\[4pt]
(j, m|a_x + ia_y|j, m - 1) = \sqrt{(j + m)(j - m + 1)} \\[4pt]
(j, m|a_z|j, m) = m \\[4pt]
(j, m|b_x - ib_y|j + 1, m + 1) = -\dfrac{1}{2}\sqrt{(j + m + 1)(j + m + 2)} \\[4pt]
(j, m|b_x - ib_y|j - 1, m + 1) = \dfrac{1}{2}\sqrt{(j - m)(j - m - 1)} \\[4pt]
(j, m|b_x + ib_y|j + 1, m - 1) = \dfrac{1}{2}\sqrt{(j - m + 1)(j - m + 2)} \\[4pt]
(j, m|b_x + ib_y|j - 1, m - 1) = -\dfrac{1}{2}\sqrt{(j + m)(j + m - 1)} \\[4pt]
(j, m|b_z|j + 1, m) = \dfrac{1}{2}\sqrt{(j + m + 1)(j - m + 1)} \\[4pt]
(j, m|b_z|j - 1, m) = \dfrac{1}{2}\sqrt{(j + m)(j - m)}.
\end{cases}
$$

If we assume that, by reflection with respect to the origin, the $\varphi_{j,m}$ either remain unchanged or change in sign as j varies, b turns out to be a polar vector while a has axial properties.

The entities to which a and b apply will be called infinite tensors (or spinors) of zero index, for integer (respectively, half-integer) j. The nomenclature of "zero index" comes from the fact that the invariant

(10)
$$Z = a_x b_x + a_y b_y + a_z b_z$$

vanishes.

More general infinite spinors or tensors can be introduced for any value of Z. A simple way to obtain the spinors is as follows. Let us consider a general solution $\psi(q, t)$ of the DIRAC equation with no external field and transform it relativistically:

(11)
$$\psi(q, t) \rightarrow \psi'(q, t).$$

Thus, the transformation in the space variables:

(12)
$$\psi(q, 0) \rightarrow \psi'(q, 0)$$

is unitary. Now, if instead of general functions $\psi(q, 0)$ we consider only those belonging to a fixed eigenvalue z_0 so of the operator (10), which has a spectrum extending from $-\infty$ to $+\infty$, we obtain functions which transform under (12) as infinite spinors, each function appearing twice.

In the representation (12), the operators a_x and b_x have the following form:

$$a_x = \frac{2\pi}{h}(yp_z - zp_y) + \frac{1}{2}\sigma_x$$

$$b_x = \frac{2\pi}{h}x\frac{H}{c} + \frac{i}{2}\alpha_x$$

and similarly for a_y, a_z, b_y, b_z.

2. We have now to determine the operators γ_0, γ_x, γ_y, γ_z in such a way as to make Eq. (4) invariant. Since we consider only unitary transformations, these operators transform in the same way as the Hermitian forms related to them; thus, in order for the integrand fraction in (4) to be invariant, it is necessary that the operators in question form a covariant vector $(\gamma_0, \gamma_x, \gamma_y, \gamma_z) \sim ct, -x, -y, -z)$.

The interpretation of $\tilde{\varphi}\gamma_0\varphi$ and $-\tilde{\varphi}\gamma\varphi$ as charge and current densities is immediate. The γ operators must satisfy the following commutation relations:

(13)
$$\begin{cases} (\gamma_0, a_x) = 0 \\ (\gamma_0, b_x) = i\gamma_x \\ (\gamma_x, a_x) = 0 \\ (\gamma_x, a_y) = i\gamma_z \\ (\gamma_x, a_z) = -i\gamma_y \\ (\gamma_x, b_x) = i\gamma_0 \\ (\gamma_x, b_y) = 0 \\ (\gamma_z, b_z) = 0 \end{cases}$$

and the others obtained by cyclic permutation of x, y z. As can be easily checked, the commutation relations (13), determine γ_0, γ_x, γ_y, γ_z to within a constant factor. One finds:

(14)
$$\begin{cases} \gamma_0 = j + \frac{1}{2} \\ (j, m|\gamma_x - i\gamma_y|j+1, m+1) = -\frac{i}{2}\sqrt{(j+m+1)(j+m+2)} \\ (j, m|\gamma_x - i\gamma_y|j-1, m+1) = -\frac{i}{2}\sqrt{(j-m)(j-m-1)} \\ (j, m|\gamma_x + i\gamma_y|j+1, m-1) = \frac{i}{2}\sqrt{(j-m+1)(j-m+2)} \\ (j, m|\gamma_x + i\gamma_y|j-1, m-1) = \frac{i}{2}\sqrt{(j+m)(j+m-1)} \\ (j, m|\gamma_z|j+1, m) = \frac{i}{2}\sqrt{(j+m+1)(j-m+1)} \\ (j, m|\gamma_z|j-1, m) = -\frac{i}{2}\sqrt{(j+m)(j-m)}. \end{cases}$$

The omitted matrix elements of γ_x, γ_y, γ_z vanish. It should be noticed that the Hermitian form $\varphi\gamma_0\varphi$ is positive definite, as the physical interpretation requires.

We now want to translate the equations written in the form (5) into the form of Eq. (5). For this, it suffices to write

$$(15) \qquad \qquad \varphi_{j,m} = \frac{\psi_{j,m}}{\sqrt{j + \frac{1}{2}}},$$

since then the form related to γ_0 reduces to the unit form. In this way we obtain equations having the desired form

$$(16) \qquad \qquad \left[\frac{W}{c} + (\alpha, p) - \beta mc\right]\psi = 0,$$

where $\beta = \frac{1}{j + \frac{1}{2}}$ and the non-vanishing components of α_x, α_y, α_z are, given as follows:

$$(17) \quad
\begin{cases}
(j, m|\alpha_x - i\alpha_y|j + 1, m + 1) = -\frac{i}{2}\sqrt{\dfrac{(j + m + 1)(j + m + 2)}{\left(j + \frac{1}{2}\right)\left(j + \frac{3}{2}\right)}} \\[12pt]
(j, m|\alpha_x - i\alpha_y|j - 1, m + 1) = -\frac{i}{2}\sqrt{\dfrac{(j - m)(j - m - 1)}{\left(j - \frac{1}{2}\right)\left(j + \frac{1}{2}\right)}} \\[12pt]
(j, m|\alpha_x + i\alpha_y|j + 1, m - 1) = \frac{i}{2}\sqrt{\dfrac{(j - m + 1)(j - m + 2)}{\left(j + \frac{1}{2}\right)\left(j + \frac{3}{2}\right)}} \\[12pt]
(j, m|\alpha_x + i\alpha_y|j - 1, m - 1) = \frac{i}{2}\sqrt{\dfrac{(j + m)(j + m - 1)}{\left(j - \frac{1}{2}\right)\left(j + \frac{1}{2}\right)}} \\[12pt]
(j, m|\alpha_z|j + 1, m) = \frac{i}{2}\sqrt{\dfrac{(j + m + 1)(j - m + 1)}{\left(j + \frac{1}{2}\right)\left(j + \frac{3}{2}\right)}} \\[12pt]
(j, m|\alpha_z|j - 1, m) = -\frac{i}{2}\sqrt{\dfrac{(j + m)(j - m)}{\left(j - \frac{1}{2}\right)\left(j + \frac{1}{2}\right)}}.
\end{cases}$$

In looking for solutions of Eq. (16) corresponding to plane waves with positive mass, one finds all those which can be derived by means of a relativistic transformation from a zero-momentum plane wave. For these, the energy is given by

$$(18) \qquad \qquad W_0 = \frac{mc^2}{j + \frac{1}{2}}.$$

For half-integer values of j we thus obtain states corresponding to the values $m, m/2, m/3, \ldots$, of the mass, while for integer j one has $2m, 2m/3, 2m/5, \ldots$.

It should be emphasized that particles having different masses also have different intrinsic angular momentum, the latter having a determined value only in the system where the particle is at rest.

If we consider the set of all states belonging to the value $\frac{m}{s+\frac{1}{2}}$ of the rest mass, as is realized in nature, all other states having no significance, we obtain an invariant theory for particles of angular momentum s; in the absence of an external field, this theory can be regarded as satisfactory. One can easily verify that in the case of slow movements and for particles having intrinsic angular momentum s, only the functions $\psi_{s,m}$ are appreciably different from zero and satisfy the SCHRÖDINGER equation with mass $M = \frac{m}{s+\frac{1}{2}}$; the functions $\psi_{s+1,m}$ and $\psi_{s-1,m}$ are then of order v/c, while $\psi_{s+2,m}$, and $\psi_{s-2,m}$ are of order v^2/c^2, and so on.

In this way we obtain only two equations; the one suitable for the description of particles with noninteger angular momentum and the other pertinent to zero or integer angular momentum.

Besides the states pertinent to positive values of the mass, there are other states for which the energy is related to the momentum by a relation of the following type:

$$(19) \qquad W = \pm\sqrt{c^2 p^2 - k^2 c^4};$$

such states exist for all positive values of k but only for $p \geq kc$, and can be regarded as pertaining to the imaginary value ik of the mass.

The "spin" functions belonging to plane waves with $p \neq 0$ have a particularly simple expression in the case of particles with no intrinsic angular momentum if $p_x = p_y = 0$, $p_z = p$. Apart from a normalization factor for these functions, one finds

$$(20) \qquad \begin{cases} \psi_{j,0} = \sqrt{\left(j + \dfrac{1}{2}\right)} \left(i\dfrac{\eta - j}{\varepsilon}\right)^j & (j = 0, 1, 2, \ldots) \\ \psi_{j,m} = 0 \quad \text{for} \quad m \neq 0, \end{cases}$$

where

$$(21) \qquad \varepsilon = \frac{p}{Mc}, \qquad \eta = \frac{\sqrt{M^2 c^2 + p^2}}{Mc}$$

and $M = 2m$ is the mass at rest.

3. We want now to discuss briefly the introduction of the electromagnetic field into Eq. (16).

The simplest way to perform the transition from the field equations without external field to those with an external field is to substitute for W and p, the quantities $W - e\varphi$ and $p - \frac{e}{c}A$, respectively, e being the charge of the particle and φ and A being the scalar and vector potentials. However, other possibilities are also open. For instance, one can

add other invariant terms, analogous to those introduced by Pauli[2] in the theory of
the magnetic neutron. Those additional terms contain as a factor the field forces instead
of the electromagnetic potentials and thus do not destroy the invariance of the field
equations coming from the indeterminacy of the potentials.

This artifice allow us to ascribe an arbitrarily fixed magnetic moment to particles
having a non-vanishing angular momentum. For instance, in the case of the electron, by
means of the simple substitutions $W, p \to W - e\varphi, p - \frac{e}{c}A$, one finds a magnetic moment
equal to $+\frac{1}{2}\mu_0$, instead of $-\mu_0$.

Thus, if we want to specialize our theory to a theory for the electron and maintain
as far as possible good agreement with the experimental data, we have to modify the
magnetic moment by introducing additional terms. However, the electron theory obtained in this way is a useless copy of Dirac's theory, the latter remaining completely
preferable thanks to its simplicity and to the wide support from experiment. On the
other hand, the advantage of the present theory lies in its applicability to particles with
angular momentum different from $1/2$.

The equations, including both the external field and the additional terms which modify the intrinsic magnetic moment, have the following form:

$$(22) \qquad \left[\left(\frac{W}{c} - \frac{e}{c}\varphi \right) + \left(a, p - \frac{e}{c}A \right) - \beta mc + \lambda(a', H) + \lambda(b', E) \right] \psi = 0,$$

where a' stands for (a'_x, a'_y, a'_z) and b' for (b'_x, b'_y, b'_z), while E and H represent the electric
and magnetic field.

The matrix a'_x can be deduced from a_x of Eq. (9) by means of the rule

$$(23) \qquad \left(j, m \left| a'_x \right| j', m' \right) = \frac{1}{\sqrt{\left(j + \frac{1}{2} \right) \left(j' + \frac{1}{2} \right)}} \left(j, m \left| a_x \right| j', m' \right)$$

and similarly for a'_y, a'_z, b'_y, b'_z.

For particles having intrinsic angular momentum $s = 1/2$ the choice $\lambda = \frac{2}{c}\mu$ should
be made if μ is the magnetic moment which one wants to add to the one which naturally
arises from the introduction of the electromagnetic potentials into the wave equation.
As seen before, the latter magnetic moment has in this case, the value $-\frac{1}{2}\frac{eh}{4\pi mc}$. For
particles having no intrinsic magnetic moment it is natural to choose $\lambda = 0$.

Regarding the practical solutions of the wave equations, we recall that for slow movements they are finite and that those $\psi_{j,m}$ which satisfy to the Schrödinger equations
are only those which have j equal to the intrinsic angular momentum in units $h/2\pi$.

For instance, for particles having no intrinsic momentum, one is left with one component only, namely $\psi_{0,0}$, while $\psi_{1,m}$ are of order v/c, v being the speed of the particle,

---

[2] Quoted by Oppenheimer, "Phys. Rev.", *41*, 763 (1932).

$\psi_{2,m}$ are of order v^2/c^2, and so on. In this way one succeeds in eliminating, by successive approximations, the small components and in particular one arrives at very simple expansions for the calculation of the first relativistic corrections.

* * *

I particularly thank Prof. E. FERMI for discussions of the present theory.

Comment on the Scientific Paper no. 7: *"Relativistic theory of particles with arbitrary intrinsic angular momentum."*

The central problem in constructing a purely wave-mechanical relativistic generalization of Schrödinger's equation is the emergence of negative-energy solutions. Even if we assume that only positive-energy states are physically meaningful, the resulting theory would be unstable with respect to transitions to negative-energy states. Dirac tried to avoid this problem by writing a first order-wave equation

$$(1) \qquad i\frac{d\psi}{dt} = \left(-i\vec{\alpha}\cdot\vec{\nabla} + \beta m\right)\psi, \quad \text{or:} \quad (i\gamma^{\mu}\frac{\partial}{\partial x_{\mu}} - m)\psi = 0.$$

If, following Dirac we assume anticommutation relations, $\{\gamma^{\mu},\gamma^{\nu}\} = 2g^{\mu\nu}$, this equation describes a particle of mass m, but admits both positive and negative energy solutions. Dirac's solution for this problem was to assume that all negative-energy states are occupied, so that thanks to the Pauli esclusion principle a positive-energy particle cannot jump into a negative-energy state. In this version Dirac's theory goes far beyond wave mechanics, and is essentially equivalent to the modern field-theoretical formulation, admirably presented in Majorana's "Teoria simmetrica dell'elettrone e del positrone".

In his paper on particles of arbitrary spin, Majorana tried to construct a fully relativistic *wave mechanics* that completely avoids the negative-energy states. He was able to show that a *necessary* condition for the absence of negative-energy states is that the operator β has only positive eigenvalues, and in turn this implies that $\phi = \beta^{1/2}\psi$ transforms according to a unitary representation of the Lorentz group. In this paper Majorana displays a complete mastery of the theory of groups. E. Amaldi([1]) recalls Majorana's admiration for the work of H. Weyl and E. Wigner on the application of group theory to quantum mechanics. In this paper we can find traces of Weyl's discussion of the Lie

---

([1]) E. AMALDI, *op. cit.*

algebra of the rotation group, extended here to the case of the Lorentz group, in particular when he introduces the commutation rules of the group generators as "integrability
conditions". Starting from the commutation relations, Majorana builds the "simplest"
infinite-dimensional unitary representations of the Lorentz group, one for integer angular
momentum and one for semi-integer angular momentum, and constructs explicitly the
corresponding infinite-dimensional representations of the $\vec{\alpha}$ and β matrices that appear
in Dirac's equation.

The Majorana versions of equation (1) have solutions that respectively describe particles of arbitrary integer or semi-integer spin angular momentum j , with mass

$$(2) \qquad\qquad\qquad M_j = \frac{m}{j + \frac{1}{2}}.$$

The avoidance of negative-energy solutions has a very high price: the existence of an
infinite sequence of states with increasing spin and decreasing mass. Majorana could not
accept this conclusion and leaves open the posssibility that his equation could describe
a single particle of arbitrary spin j_0 by declaring that all solutions with $j \neq j_0$ are
to be considered as "unphysical". He mentions in particular the possibility of using
the integer-spin version of the equation to describe a spinless particle. He, however,
realizes that in the presence of interactions it would be difficult to ensure the absence
of transitions to states of different spin. In a different context this is the same problem
that plagued the wave mechanics interpretation of Dirac's equation. The disease is made
worse here by the presence, briefly mentioned in Majorana's paper, of what we now call
"tachyonic" solutions, that would correspond to states with imaginary mass ik, with
$E = \pm\sqrt{c^2\vec{p}^2 - k^2c^4}$, that exist for $|\vec{p}| > k$ and for any value of k.

Majorana's paper was written in the early summer of 1932, just before Anderson
announced the discovery of the positive electron, thus sealing the triumph of Dirac's
electron theory. It received little attention, in spite of the brilliant and original results
on the unitary representations of the Lorentz group that were rediscovered years later by
Wigner. Extensive references to the successive developments in this field can be found
in the review of Majorana's paper by D. M. Fradkin[2].

If Majorana's paper on particles with arbitrary spin had not been totally forgotten, it
could be considered a precursor of some of the most actively pursued recent developments
in theoretical physics. In the sixties the study of Regge-poles and the discovery of high-
spin hadrons briefly rekindled the interest for theories, based on fields that transform
according to infinite-dimensional representations of the Lorentz group, that describe a
sequence of particles with increasing spin and increasing mass. These attempts had
their highest expression in the dual models of hadrons but, as in the case of Majorana's
theory, were plagued by the existence of tachyonic states that could only be avoided

---

[2] D. M. FRADKIN, *Am. J. Phys.* **34** (1966) 314.

in a space-time with a large number of dimensions. In view of these difficulties and of the emergence of Quantum Chromo Dynamics the application of these ideas to hadron physics was abandoned, but they resurfaced later in modern string theories.

NICOLA CABIBBO
Università di Roma "La Sapienza"

NOTA SCIENTIFICA n. 8 — SCIENTIFIC PAPER no. 8

Über die Kerntheorie

Von Ettore Majorana, zur Zeit in Leipzig
Mit 3 Abbildungen (Eingegangen am 3 März 1933)

"Zeitschrift für Physik", Bd. 82, 1933, pp. 137-145.

Es wird eine Neubegründung der Heisenbergschen Kerntheorie diskutiert, die zu einer etwas abweichenden Hamiltonfunktion führt. Dementsprechend wird eine statistische Behandlung der Kerne entwickelt.

Die Entdeckung des Neutrons, d. h. eines schweren und ladungslosen Elementarteilchens, hat die Möglichkeit geboten, eine Kerntheorie aufzubauen, die, ohne allerdings die grundsätzlichen mit dem β-Zerfall verbundenen Schwierigkeiten aufzulösen, wohl aber die Begriffe der Quantenmechanik in einem Bereich zu benutzen gestattet, der geschlossen schien. Nach Heisenberg[1] ist es möglich, für viele Zwecke die Kerne als aus Protonen und Neutronen bestehend, d. h. aus Teilchen mit fast der gleichen Masse, die den Drehimpuls $\frac{1}{2}\frac{h}{2\pi}$ haben und der Fermischen Statistik gehorchen, zu betrachten. Das Studium der Kerne ist also zurückgeführt auf die Aufsuchung einer geeigneten Hamiltonfunktion, die für ein solches System materieller Punkte gültig sei, und zwar in nichtrelativistischer Näherung, da die Geschwindigkeiten der Teilchen vermutlich ziemlich klein im Vergleich zur Lichtgeschwindigkeit sind ($v \sim \frac{c}{10}$). Um eine zweckmäßige Wechselwirkung zwischen den Bausteinen der Kerne aufzustellen, hat sich Heisenberg von einer offenbaren Analogie leiten lassen. Das Neutron wird als aus einem Proton und einem Elektron

---

[1] W. Heisenberg, "Z. Physik", 77, 1 (1932); 78, 156 (1933).

bestehend, also wie ein nach einem den jetzigen Theorien unzugänglichen Prozeß konzentriertes Wasserstoffatom gedacht und zwar so, daß es seine statistischen Eigenschaften und seinen Drehimpuls verändere. HEISENBERG nimmt nun an, daß zwischen Protonen und Neutronen Austauschkräfte wirken denjenigen ähnlich, die für die Molekularbindung von H und H$^+$ vor allem verantwortlich sind. Zu einer solchen Wechselwirkung zwischen Neutronen und Protonen, die als maßgebend für die Kernstabilität betrachtet wird, fügen sich die Coulombabstoßungskräfte zwischen Protonen, Anziehungskräfte vom van der Waals-Typus zwischen Neutronen und eine Art von "elektrostatischer" Wechselwirkung zwischen Protonen und Neutronen[2].

Man kann natürlich an der Gültigkeit dieser Analogie zweifeln, denn einerseits gibt die Theorie keine Auskunft über die innere Struktur des Neutrons, andererseits scheint die Wechselwirkung zwischen Neutron und Proton groß im Vergleich zum Massendefekt des Neutrons, wie er von CHADWICK bestimmt worden ist, zu sein. Ich glaube also, es sei nicht ohne Interesse zu zeigen, wie man zur Aufstellung einer der von HEISENBERG betrachteten sehr ähnlichen Hamiltonfunktion gelangen kann, wenn man nur die allgemeinsten und offenbarsten Kerneigenschaften am einfachsten wiedergeben will. Wir werden dafür ein statistisches Verfahren zu benutzen haben, an dessen Zulässigkeit für Größenordnungsbestimmungen kaum zu zweifeln ist. Ich möchte noch darauf aufmerksam machen, daß infolge des von mir festgelegten Kriteriums für die Auswahl der Hamiltonfunktion jetzt die Austauschkräfte das umgekehrte Vorzeichen wie in der Heisenbergschen Theorie haben, daher, sind die Symmetriecharaktere der Eigenfunktionen, die zum Normalzustand gehören, und die ganze statistische Behandlung verschieden von der in HEISENBERGS Arbeit.

1. Die ziemlich zahlreichen Auskunftquellen, die wir über die Kernstruktur besitzen, d. h. radioaktive Zerfälle, künstliche Zerfälle und Anregungen, anomale Streuung von α-Teilchen, Massendefektmessungen usw., scheinen einstimmig darauf hinzudeuten, daß den Kernen keine stark unitäre, den Atomen ähnliche Organisation zuzuschreiben ist. Im Gegenteil sieht es so aus, als ob die Kerne aus ziemlich unabhängigen Konstituenten bestehen, die nur bei unmittelbarer Berührung aufeinander wirken. Man findet so im Zentrum des Atoms eine Art von Materie wieder, die mit denselben Eigenschaften von Ausdehnung und Undurchdringlichkeit versehen ist wie die makroskopische Materie. Aus einer solchen Materie sind die leichten und schweren Kerne ebenfalls konstituiert und der Unterschied zwischen den einen und den anderen hängt vor allem von ihrem verschiedenen Inhalt von "Kernmaterie" ab. Eine solche Vorstellung kann natürlich nur richtig sein, wenn die Coulombabstoßung zwischen den positiven Konstituenten der Kerne keine sehr große Rolle spielt; das ist sicher der Fall für ziemlich leichte Kerne: für die schwereren Kerne muß infolgedessen eine gewisse Korrektur eingeführt werden.

Nehmen wir nach dem oben Gesagten an, daß die Kerne aus Protonen und Neutronen bestehen, so ist unser Problem, das einfachste Wechselwirkungsgesetz zwischen diesen

---

[2] W. HEISENBERG, ebenda *80*, 587 (1933).

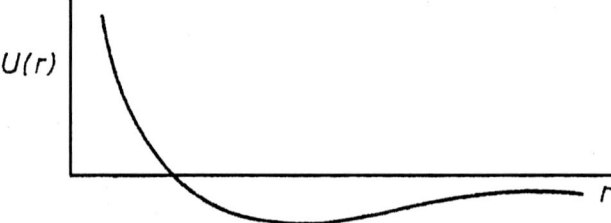

Fig. 1. – Potentielle Energie zwischen zwei Atomen.

Teilchen, aufzustellen, welches, sofern die elektrostatische Abstoßung vernachlässigbar ist, zur Definition einer undurchdringlichen Materie führt. Es handelt sich eigentlich darum, drei Wechselwirkungsgesetze aufzustellen, und zwar zwischen Protonen, zwischen Protonen und Neutronen und zwischen Neutronen. Wir werden aber der Einfachheit halber annehmen, daß zwischen jedem Paar von Protonen nur die Coulombsche Kraft wirke; diese Annahme kann sich darauf einigermaßen stützen, daß der klassische Radius der Protonen viel kleiner als der mittlere Abstand der Teilchen innerhalb des Kernes ist. Ferner kommt der Coulombschen Kraft keine große Wichtigkeit für leichte Kerne zu, und da diese aus beinahe ebensovielen Neutronen wie Protonen bestehen, liegt es nahe, als wichtigste Ursache der Kernstabilität eine besondere Wechselwirkung zwischen Protonen und Neutronen zu betrachten; zwischen den Neutronen aber nehmen wir an, daß keine merkliche Wechselwirkung sich abspiele, da kein sicherer Grund für das Gegenteil vorliegt. Also müssen wir nunmehr nur eine geeignete Kopplung zwischen Protonen und Neutronen aufstellen. Infolge der schon hervorgehobenen, scheinbaren Ähnlichkeit zwischen der Kernstruktur und derjenigen der festen Körper oder der Flüssigkeiten könnte es plausibel scheinen, eine Wechselwirkung von demselben Typus wie für Atome und Moleküle, d. h. Anziehungskräfte bei großem Abstand und stark abstoßende Kräfte bei kleinem Abstand festzulegen, so daß die "Undurchdringlichkeit" der Teilchen gesichert ist (siehe Fig. 1). Außerdem müßte man aber noch Abstoßungskräfte zwischen Neutronen bei kleiner Entfernung annehmen, um die gewünschte Proportionalität zwischen Teilchenzahl und Kernvolumen zu erhalten. Eine solche Lösung des Problems ist aber vom ästhetischen Standpunkt aus unbefriedigend, denn man muß nicht nur Anziehungskräfte von unbekanntem Ursprung zwischen den Elementarteilchen annehmen sondern noch, bei kleinem Abstand, Abstoßungskräfte von ungeheurer Größenordnung, die von einem Potential von etwa einigen hundert Millionen Volt abhängen. Wir wollen deshalb einen anderen Weg einschlagen, mit Einführung von so wenigen willkürlichen Elementen, wie es möglich ist. Die Hauptschwierigkeit, die zu überwinden ist, besteht in der Frage, wie man zu einer von der Masse des Kernes unabhängigen Dichte gelangen kann, ohne die freie Beweglichkeit der Teilchen durch eine künstliche Undurchdringlichkeit zu hindern. Wir dürfen z.B. nach einem Typus von Wechselwirkung suchen, bei dem die mittlere Energie pro Teilchen nie eine gewisse Grenze überschreiten kann, wie groß auch die Dichte sein mag; das könnte eintreten infolge irgendeiner Absättigungserscheinung, die der Valenzsättigung einigermaßen analog sein dürfte. Eine solche Wechselwirkung zwi-

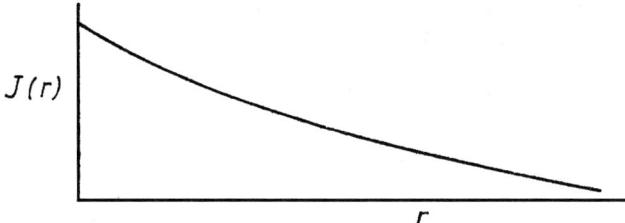

Fig. 2. – Gang der Resonanzkräfte.

schen Neutronen und Protonen wird, wie wir beweisen werden, durch folgenden Ausdruck gegeben:

(1) $$\left(Q', q' | J | Q'', q''\right) = -\delta\left(q' - Q''\right)\delta\left(q'' - Q'\right)J(r).$$

Hierbei ist $r = |q' - Q'|$ gesetzt worden und Q und q sind die Koordinaten eines Neutrons bzw. eines Protons. Die Funktion $J(r)$ ist positiv und sie darf den in Fig. 2 bezeichneten Gang aufweisen. Der Ausdruck (1) bedeutet, daß zwischen dem Neutron und dem Proton Anziehung bzw. Abstoßung stattfindet, je nachdem die Wellenfunktion ungefähr symmetrisch oder antisymmetrisch in den beiden Teilchen ist. Um der besonderen Stabilität des α-Teilchens Rechnung zu tragen, werden wir noch annehmen, daß Q und q in (1) nur die Schwerpunktskoordinaten mit Ausschließung des Spins sein sollen. So erhält man, daß auf jedes Proton im α-Teilchen beide Neutronen statt eins wirken und umgekehrt, da wir eine symmetrische Funktion in den Schwerpunktskoordinaten aller Protonen und Neutronen (was streng bei Vernachlässigung der Coulombschen Energie der Protonen gilt) annehmen können. Im α-Teilchen sind alle vorhandenen vier Partikeln in demselben Zustand, so daß es eine abgeschlossene Schale in höherem Sinne als das Heliumatom ist. Geht man vom α-Teilchen zu schwereren Kernen über, so kann man nicht mehr, wegen des Pauliverbots, weitere Teilchen in demselben Zustand ansetzen, und da außerdem die Austauschenergie (1) nur dann im allgemeinen groß ist, wenn Proton und Neutron sich in demselben Zustand befinden, muß man erwarten, was genau der Erfahrung entspricht, daß bei schweren Kernen der Massendefekt pro Partikel nicht wesentlich größer als beim α-Teilchen sein dürfte.

Wir wollen jetzt den Ausdruck (1) der Wechselwirkungsenergie zwischen Proton und Neutron mit demjenigen vergleichen, den man aus dem Resonanzglied der Heisenbergschen Hamiltonfunktion herleiten kann, wenn man durch Betrachtung der Neutronen und Protonen als verschiedener Teilchen die unbequeme ρ-Spinkoordinate eliminiert. Dann findet man einen zu (1) ähnlichen Ausdruck, aber mit zwei grundsätzlichen Unterschieden. Erstens nach Heisenbergschem Ausdruck sollen Q und q in (1) alle Koordinaten einschließlich des Spins bezeichnen. Zweitens nimmt HEISENBERG für die Resonanzkräfte das umgekehrte Vorzeichen an, was für die statistischen Folgen am wichtigsten ist, denn infolgedessen sind die Symmetriecharaktere der Eigenfunktionen bei der Heisenbergschen Theorie solche, daß keine Absättigung stattfindet und noch Abstoßungskräfte

bei kleinen Entfernungen notwendig sind([3]). Wir werden jetzt näher untersuchen, in welcher Weise diejenige Absättigung eintritt, die zur experimentellen Erscheinung der Undurchdringlichkeit der Kernkonstituenten führt.

2. In erster Näherung betrachten wir die Eigenfunktion des Kernes als durch ein Produkt zweier Funktionen darstellbar, die von den Koordinaten der n_1, Neutronen, bzw. der n_2, Protonen, abhängen:

$$(2) \qquad \psi = \psi_N(Q_1, \Sigma_1, \ldots, Q_{n_1}, \Sigma_{n_1}) \psi_P(q_1, \sigma_1, \ldots, q_{n_2}, \sigma_{n_2})$$

und denken wir uns ψ_N und ψ_P als aus Produkten von individuellen, orthogonalen Eigenfunktionen durch Antisymmetrisierung erhalten:

$$(3) \qquad \begin{cases} \psi_N = \frac{1}{\sqrt{n_1!}} \sum_R \pm R \psi_N'(Q_1, \Sigma_1) \cdots \psi_N^{n_1}(Q_{n_1}, \Sigma_{n_1}), \\ \psi_P = \frac{1}{\sqrt{n_2!}} \sum_R \pm R \psi_P'(q_1, \sigma_1) \cdots \psi_P^{n_2}(q_{n_2}, \sigma_{n_2}). \end{cases}$$

Im Falle einer großen Anzahl von Teilchen dürfen die individuellen Wellenfunktionen ψ mit freie Teilchen darstellenden Wellenpaketen identifiziert werden. Aus der Rechnung wird es sich ergeben, daß jedes Proton im Mittel der Wirkung einer keinen Anzahl (eins oder zwei) Neutronen unterliegt und umgekehrt; daher führt die Annahme von zu freien Teilchen gehörenden Wellenfunktionen infolge merklicher Polarisationseffekte einen gewissen Fehler ein. Die Methode ist aber für Größenordnungsbestimmungen ohne Zweifel anwendbar.

Wir müssen also den über die Eigenfunktion (2) genommenen Mittelwert der gesamten Energie berechnen und nach den Bedingungen suchen, unter denen er minimal wird. Die Energie besteht aus drei Teillen:

$$(4) \qquad W = T + E + A,$$

wobei T die kinetische Energie, E die elektrostatische Energie der Protonen und A die Austauschenergie bezeichnen sollen. Wir nehmen der Einfachheit halber an, daß alle individuellen im Schwerpunkt festgesetzten Zustände entweder frei oder zweimal mit entgegengesetzter Spinrichtung besetzt seien. Dann sind n_1 und n_2 gerade Zahlen. Wir führen noch die Diracschen Dichtenmatrizen ein:

$$(5) \qquad \begin{cases} (q'|\rho_N|q'') = \sum_{\sigma_i=1}^{2} \sum_{i=1}^{n_1} \psi_N^i(q', \sigma_i) \bar{\psi}_N^i(q'', \sigma_i), \\ (q'|\rho_P|q'') = \sum_{\sigma_i=1}^{2} \sum_{i=1}^{n_2} \psi_P^i(q', \sigma_i) \bar{\psi}_P^i(q'', \sigma_i). \end{cases}$$

([3]) W. HEISENBERG, "Z. Physik", *80*, 587 (1933). Für die Möglichkeit, diese Arbeit vor der Publikation zu sehen, bin ich Herrn Prof. HEISENBERG zum größten Dank verpflichtet.

Es gelten die Gleichungen:

$$(6) \qquad \rho_N^2 = 2\rho_N, \qquad \rho_P^2 = 2\rho_P,$$

wobei der Faktor 2 vom Spin herrührt, und daraus folgt:

$$(7) \qquad \rho_N = \begin{array}{c} 2 \\ \diagdown \\ 0 \end{array}, \qquad \rho_P = \begin{array}{c} 2 \\ \diagdown \\ 0 \end{array}.$$

Wenn M die Masse jedes Teilchens, näherungsweise dieselbe für Neutronen und Protonen, ist, wird sich ergeben:

$$(8) \qquad T = \frac{1}{2M} \operatorname{Spur}\left[(\rho_N + \rho_P)p^2\right],$$

$$(9) \qquad E = \frac{e^2}{2} \int (q'|\rho_P|q') \frac{1}{|q' - q''|} (q''|\rho_P|q'')\mathrm{d}q'\mathrm{d}q'' + \cdots.$$

Wir haben in (9) ein Glied, das im wesentlichen die *gewöhnliche*, von der Coulombschen Wechselwirkung der Protonen abhängige Austauschenergie darstellt, weggelassen. Dieses Glied ist von DIRAC[4] berechnet worden, und es ist nicht sehr wichtig, wenn die Anzahl der Teilchen groß ist.

Wir haben schließlich:

$$(10) \qquad A = - \int (q'|\rho_N|q'')J|q' - q''|(q''|\rho_P|q')\mathrm{d}q'\mathrm{d}q''.$$

Wenn die Zahl der Teilchen groß ist, dürfen ρ_N und ρ_P als fast diagonale Matrizen und sogar als klassische Funktionen von p und q betrachtet werden, und zwar ist die beste Bindung zwischen Matrizen und klassischen Funktionen[5] durch folgende Beziehungen gegeben:

$$(11) \qquad \begin{cases} \left(q - \dfrac{v}{2}|\rho_N|q + \dfrac{v}{2}\right) = \dfrac{1}{h^3} \int \rho_N(p,q)e^{-\frac{2\pi i}{h}(p,v)}\mathrm{d}p, \\[2mm] \left(q - \dfrac{v}{2}|\rho_P|q + \dfrac{v}{2}\right) = \dfrac{1}{h^3} \int \rho_P(p,q)e^{-\frac{2\pi i}{h}(p,v)}\mathrm{d}q \end{cases}$$

und durch diejenige, die man aus Umkehrung der Fourierschen Integrale erhält.

---

[4] P. A. M. DIRAC, "Proc. Cambridge Phil. Soc.", *26*, 376 (1930).
[5] Siehe z. B. DIRAC, ebenda.

Wenn man in die vorigen Ausdrücke (11) einsetzt, bekommt man(*):

$$(12) \qquad T = \frac{1}{2M} \int \frac{\rho_N(p,q) + \rho_P(p,q)}{h^3} p^2 \, dp \, dq,$$

$$(13) \qquad E = \frac{e^2}{2} \int \frac{\rho_N(p,q)\rho_P(p',q')}{h^6} \frac{1}{|q-q'|} \, dp \, dq \, dp' \, dq',$$

$$(14) \qquad A = \int \frac{\rho_N(p,q)V_N(p,q)}{h^3} \, dp \, dq = \int \frac{\rho_P(p,q)V_P(p,q)}{h^3} \, dp \, dq,$$

wobei $V_N(p,q)$ und $V_P(p,q)$ die klassischen Funktionen, die den Matrizen

$$(15) \qquad \begin{cases} (q'|V_N|q'') = -(q'|\rho_P|q'')J|q'-q''|, \\ (q'|V_P|q'') = -(q'|\rho_N|q'')J|q'-q''| \end{cases}$$

entsprechen, bezeichnen sollen.

Wir nehmen nun an, daß in der Nähe eines Punktes q die Zustände kleiner Energie besetzt seien, sowohl von den Neutronen wie von den Protonen. Es wird dann einen maximalen Wert des Impulses $P_N(q)$ für die Neutronen und einen solchen für die Protonen geben; und als Folge von (7) wird sein:

$$(16) \qquad \rho_N(p,q) = \begin{cases} 2, & \text{wenn } p < P_N(q), \\ 0, & \text{wenn } p > P_N(q), \end{cases}$$

$$(17) \qquad \rho_P(p,q) = \begin{cases} 2, & \text{wenn } p < P_P(q), \\ 0, & \text{wenn } p > P_P(q). \end{cases}$$

Betrachten wir zunächst einen Grenzfall, d. h. den Fall sehr hoher Dichte, so daß h/p_N, und h/p_P, die der Größenordnung nach der gegenseitigen Entfernung der Teilchen im Kern entsprechen, klein im Vergleich zum Wirkungsradius der Resonanzkräfte sind. Nehmen wir noch an, daß $P_N > P_P$, also die Dichte der Neutronen größer als diejenige der Protonen sei, und bemerken wir, daß man in der zweiten Gleichung (15) infolge der praktischen Diagonalität von $\rho_N J|q'-q''|$ durch den Grenzwert $J(0)$ ersetzen kann, wenn $J(0)$ endlich ist, so wird diese Gleichung einfach

$$(q'|V_P|q'') = -J(0)(q'|\rho_N|q''),$$

(*) In "Zeitschrift für Physik" ist die gleichung (13) irrtümlich ohne des Integral-Zeichen gedruckt worden. (Fußnote des Herausgebers.)

woraus folgt

(18) $$V_P(p, q) = -J(0)\rho_N(p, q).$$

Wenn wir nun in (14) diese einsetzen und bemerken, daß, wenn $\rho_P(p, q) > 0$, auch immer $\rho_N = 2$ ist, bekommen wir

(19) $$A = -2J(0) \int \frac{\rho_P(p, q)}{h^3}\, dp\, dq = -2J(0)n_2.$$

Das bedeutet, daß die von den Austauschkräften abhängige Bindungsenergie pro Proton im Falle sehr hoher Teilchendichte bloß gleich $-2J(0)$ ist, wenn die Neutronendichte nur größer ist als die Protonendichte. Vernachlässigen wir zunächst die Coulombsche gegenseitige Abstoßung zwischen den Protonen, was für leichte Kerne mit einer gewissen Näherung zulässig ist, und setzen wir das Verhältnis n_1/n_2, aber nicht die Dichte fest: dann wird die potentielle Energie pro Teilchen eine gewisse Funktion der gesamten Dichte:

(20) $$a = a(\mu), \quad \mu = \frac{8\pi}{3h^3}\left(P_N^3 + P_P^3\right),$$

die natürlich für $\mu = 0$ verschwindet und sich dem konstanten Wert $-\frac{2n_2}{n_1+n_2}J(0)$ für $\mu \to \infty$ nähert. Dieser Grenzwert wird das Minimum $-J(0)$ erreichen, wenn $n_1 = n_2$ ist. Für mittlere Dichten ist der allgemeine Ausdruck von $a(\mu)$ wegen (10) und (11) durch(*)

(21) $$a = \frac{1}{\mu(q)} \iint \frac{\rho_N(p, q)\rho_P(p', q)}{h^6}\, G(p, p')\mathrm{d}p\, \mathrm{d}p'$$

gegeben, wobei $G(p, p')$ eine Funktion von $|p - p'|$ ist, die folgendermaßen mit $J(r)$ zusammenhängt:

(22) $$G(p, p') = \int e^{-\frac{2\pi i}{h}(p-p', v)} J|v|\mathrm{d}v.$$

Die kinetische Energie pro Teilchen wird die Form haben:

$$t = \kappa\mu^{2/3}$$

und die gesamte Energie $a + t$ kann ein Minimum für einen gewissen, nur vom Verhältnis n_1/n_2 abhängigen Wert erreichen (Fig. 3). Man erhält also eine konstante, von der Masse des Kernes unabhängige Dichte, und so ein Kernvolumen und einen Energieinhalt bloß proportional der Anzahl der Teilchen, wie die Erfahrung verlangt. Man kann

---

(*) In "Zeitschrift für Physik" ist im Nenner von gleichung (21) irrtümlich h^σ gedruckt worden. (Fußnote des Herausgebers.)

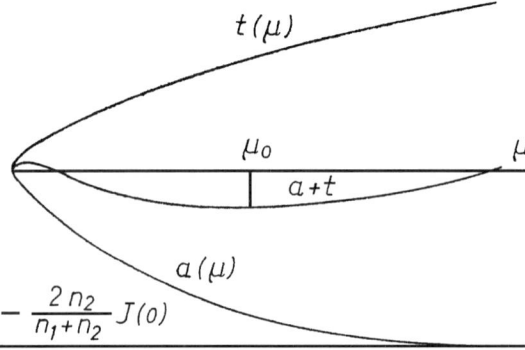

Fig. 3. – Kinetische und potentielle Energie pro Teilchen.

versuchen, die Funktion $J(r)$ so zu bestimmen, daß die experimentellen Angaben am besten wiedergegeben werden. Der Ausdruck(*)

$$J(r) = \lambda \frac{e^2}{r}$$

z. B. mit einer willkürlichen Konstante ist zweckmäßig, wenn er auch unendlich bei $r = 0$ wird. Er ist aber bei großem Abstand zu modifizieren, da er einen unendlichen Wirkungsquerschnitt für den Zusammenstoß zwischen Proton und Neutron gibt; außerdem scheint er ein zu kleines Verhältnis für die Massendefekte vom α-Teilchen und vom Wasserstoffisotop zu liefern. So muß man einen Ausdruck mit mindestens zwei Konstanten benutzen, z. B. eine Exponentialfunktion, $J(r) = Ae^{-\beta r}$. Wir werden aber auf diese Untersuchung nicht näher eingehen, denn, wie schon hervorgehoben, kann die erste statistische Näherung zu erheblichen Fehlern führen, wie groß auch die Anzahl der Teilchen ist. Für schwere Kerne spielt die Coulombsche Kraft eine wichtige Rolle, und sie hat zur Folge, daß die Kernausdehnung etwas anwächst, und auch die Dichte, sowohl der Neutronen wie der Protonen, nicht mehr örtlich konstant ist. Die Austauschbindungsenergie wird jetzt nicht bloß vom Verhältnis n_1/n_2 abhängen, sie wird sogar etwas kleiner als im Falle leichter Kerne sein, infolge der von den Coulombschen Kräften verursachten Verminderung der Dichte.

$$* * *$$

Ich möchte Herrn Prof. HEISENBERG für zahreiche Ratschläge und Erörterungen herzlich danken. Auch Herrn Prof. EHRENFEST sei für wertvolle Diskussion bestens gedankt. Endlich danke ich noch dem Consiglio Nazionale delle Ricerche für die Ermöglichung meines Aufenthaltes in Leipzig.

(*) In "Zeitschrift für Physik" ist der erste Ausdruck der gleichung irrtümlich als $J(n)$ gedruckt worden. (Fußnote des Herausgebers.)

Sulla teoria dei nuclei

ETTORE MAJORANA

"La Ricerca Scientifica", vol. 4 (1) 1933, pp. 559-563.

Riassunto. — L'autore propone alcune correzioni alla teoria di HEISENBERG di cui sono particolarmente discussi i fondamenti sperimentali. Viene inoltre descritto un procedimento di carattere statistico per l'applicazione della teoria ai nuclei pesanti.

La scoperta del neutrone, cioè di una particella elementare pesante e senza carica elettrica, ha offerto la possibilità di edificare una teoria della struttura nucleare che, senza risolvere le difficoltà connesse con lo spettro continuo dei raggi β, permette tuttavia di utilizzare largamente i concetti della meccanica quantistica in un campo che sembrava loro estraneo. Secondo HEISENBERG[1] è possibile per molti scopi considerare i nuclei come costituiti da protoni e da neutroni, particelle provviste del momento meccanico intrinseco $\frac{1}{2}\frac{h}{2\pi}$ che obbediscono alla statistica di FERMI e hanno all'incirca la stessa massa. La velocità media di queste particelle all'interno dei nuclei è presumibilmente abbastanza piccola di fronte a quelle della luce ($v \sim \frac{c}{10}$) e si può pertanto ritenere che siano applicabili con grande approssimazione i metodi ordinari della meccanica quantistica non relativistica. Rimane da stabilire la legge di interazione fra i costituenti nucleari, e a questo fine HEISENBERG si è lasciato guidare, in mancanza di altri criteri direttivi, dall'analogia che sussisterebbe fra il comune atomo neutro di idrogeno e il neutrone se questo è costituito, come generalmente si suppone, da un protone e da un elettrone. HEISENBERG suppone

---

[1] W. HEISENBERG, "Z. Physik", 77, 1 (1932); 78, 156 (1933).

pertanto che l'interazione fra i protoni e i neutroni sia qualitativamente simile a quella che effettivamente si esercita fra protoni e atomi neutri di idrogeno e dipenda principalmente da una specie di "energia di scambio". Similmente per ogni coppia di neutroni si introducono forze attrattive del tipo di Van der Waals.

L'uso di tale analogia è difficile a giustificarsi, poiché se il neutrone è realmente composto da un protone e da un elettrone, il modo in cui viene realizzata la loro unione è però affatto inaccessibile alle teorie attuali che porterebbero ad attribuire al neutrone la statistica di Bose-Einstein e un momento meccanico multiplo intero di $\frac{h}{2\pi}$, contrariamente alle ipotesi fondamentali. Queste sono d'altra parte direttamente appoggiate alle proprietà empiriche dei nuclei e non è possibile rinunziarvi. È pertanto preferibile, allo stato attuale delle nostre conoscenze, tentare di stabilire la legge di interazione fra le particelle elementari in base a soli criteri di semplicità, ma in modo che vengano riprodotte le proprietà più generali e più caratteristiche dei nuclei.

1. Le varie fonti di informazioni che possediamo sulla struttura dei nuclei, come disintegrazioni radioattive, disgregazioni ed eccitazioni artificiali, misure dei difetti di massa, diffusione anomala delle particelle α, e così via, sembrano indicare concordemente che non si può attribuire ai nuclei un'organizzazione fortemente centrale simile a quella degli atomi. Sembra al contrario che i nuclei siano costituiti da una specie di materia estesa e impenetrabile le cui parti agiscono reciprocamente solo per immediato contatto. La differenza fra i nuclei pesanti e quelli leggeri si riduce così essenzialmente al differente contenuto di "materia nucleare". Tale rappresentazione può essere naturalmente valida solo finché la repulsione coulombiana fra i protoni contenuti nei nuclei non ha grande importanza di fronte alle altre forze in gioco; e questo è certamente il caso per i nuclei più leggeri, mentre per i più pesanti bisogna introdurre per questo motivo notevoli correzioni.

Il nostro problema, è dunque di trovare la più semplice legge di interazione fra tutte le particelle elementari, protoni, e neutroni, che conduca, finché è trascurabile la repulsione coulombiana alla definizione di una materia impenetrabile. Assumiamo anzitutto, per semplicità, che fra ogni coppia di protoni agisca soltanto l'ordinaria repulsione elettrostatica, questa ipotesi potendosi in qualche modo appoggiare al fatto che il raggio classico dei protoni è assai piccolo rimetto alle dimensioni nucleari. Le forze elettrostatiche non possono avere, come si è detto, grande influenza sulla struttura dei nuclei leggeri e poiché questi risultano costituiti all'incirca da un numero uguale di protoni e di neutroni, si presenta spontanea l'ipotesi che la causa principale della stabilità nucleare debba risiedere in una particolare azione mutua dei protoni e dei neutroni, mentre in mancanza di sicuri indizi in contrario assumeremo che sia trascurabile l'interazione fra i neutroni.

Il nostro problema è così ridotto alla ricerca di un conveniente accoppiamento fra protoni e neutroni. Per l'apparente analogia, già rilevata, fra la struttura dei nuclei e quella dei corpi solidi o liquidi, può apparire naturale introdurre un'interazione del tipo che in modo affatto generale è realizzato per ogni coppia di atomi o molecole, cioè forze attrattive a grande distanza e intensamente repulsive a piccola distanza in modo che sia assicurata la "impenetrabilità" delle particelle. Oltre a ciò occorrerebbe però assumere anche forze repulsive fra i neutroni, per distanze piccole, per ottenere la desiderata pro-

porzionalità fra il numero delle particelle costituenti e il volume dei nuclei. Una tale soluzione del problema è però insoddisfacente, poiché bisogna ammettere l'esistenza non solo di forze attrattive di origine sconosciuta, ma anche a piccola distanza di forze repulsive aventi un ordine di grandezza eccezionalmente elevato e un'origine altrettanto sconosciuta. Dobbiamo quindi tentare un'altra via per spiegare come la densità nucleare possa essere indipendente dalla massa totale senza che sia impedita la libera mobilità delle particelle elementari mediante un'artificiosa impenetrabilità. Possiamo ricercare, per es., un tipo di accoppiamento siffatto che l'energia media per particella non possa mai superare un limite determinato, comunque grande sia la densità, e ciò in conseguenza di qualche fenomeno di saturazione che potrebbe essere in certo modo analogo alla saturazione delle valenze. Un'interazione di questo tipo ci è data in realtà nello schema di DIRAC dalla seguente espressione, come dimostreremo più avanti:

$$(1) \qquad (Q', q'|I|Q'', q'') = -\delta(q' - Q'')\delta(q'' - Q')I(r)$$

in cui si è posto $r = |q' - Q'|$ e Q, q sono le coordinate rispettivamente di un neutrone e di un protone. La funzione $I(r)$ è positiva e decresce rapidamente con la distanza. Per tener conto però della particolare stabilità della particella α assumeremo inoltre che Q e q in (1) rappresentino solo le coordinate dei baricentri con esclusione dello "spin". Si ottiene così che su ogni protone nella particella α agiscano entrambi i neutroni invece di uno solo, e viceversa, poiché possiamo assumere un'autofunzione simmetrica nelle coordinate dei baricentri di tutti i protoni e i neutroni (ciò che vale rigorosamente se si trascura l'energia coulombiana dei protoni). Nella particella α tutti i corpuscoli elementari sono nello stesso stato, così che essa costituisce un "anello chiuso" in un senso più alto che l'atomo di elio. Se si passa dalla particella α a nuclei più complessi, non si può a causa del principio di PAULI aggiungere altre particelle elementari nello stesso stato, e poiché oltre a ciò l'energia di scambio (1)[2] è grande in generale solo quando protone e neutrone si trovano in uno stesso stato, bisogna prevedere, ciò che corrisponde esattamente all'esperienza, che l'energia di legame per ogni corpuscolo non possa essere presso i nuclei pesanti essenzialmente più grande che presso la particella α.

Vogliamo ora paragonare l'espressione (1) dell'energia di scambio con quella che si può derivare dal termine di risonanza dell'Hamiltoniana di HEISENBERG[2] eliminando l'incomoda coordinata di "ρ-spin", ciò che è possibile se si riguardano, anche formalmente, i protoni e i neutroni come particelle differenti. Si trova allora un'espressione simile a (1) ma con due essenziali differenze. Anzitutto Q e q rappresentano secondo l'espressione di HEISENBERG tutte le coordinate, incluso lo "spin". In secondo luogo HEISENBERG assume per $I(r)$ il segno opposto, ciò che ha particolare importanza per le conseguenze statistiche poiché a causa di ciò i caratteri di simmetria delle autofunzioni risultano secondo la teoria di HEISENBERG tali che non ha luogo alcun fenomeno di saturazione e bisogna ancora introdurre a piccola distanza quelle forze repulsive che ci siamo preoccupati di evitare[3].

---

[2] W. HEISENBERG, "Z. Physik", 77, 1 (1932).
[3] W. HEISENBERG, "Z. Physik", 80, 587 (1933)

Vogliamo ora brevemente esaminare l'applicazione, secondo un metodo statistico, della nostra teoria ai nuclei pesanti che sono composti da un numero assai elevato di protoni e di neutroni.

2. - In prima approssimazione consideriamo l'autofunzione di un nucleo come rappresentabile mediante un prodotto di due funzioni che dipendono rispettivamente dalle coordinate di n_1 neutroni e di n_2 protoni:

$$(2) \qquad \Psi = \Psi_N\big(Q_1,\ldots,Q_{n_i};\Sigma_1,\ldots,\Sigma_{n_1}\big)\Psi_P\big(q_1,\ldots,q_{n_2};\sigma_1,\ldots,\sigma_{n_2}\big)$$

e supponiamo che Ψ_N e Ψ_P siano ottenute mediante antisimmetrizzazione da prodotti di autofunzioni individuali ortogonali:

$$(3) \qquad \begin{cases} \Psi_N = \frac{1}{\sqrt{n_1!}}\sum_R \pm R\Psi_N^1(Q_1,\Sigma_1)\,\Psi_N^2(Q_2,\Sigma_2)\cdots\Psi_N^{n_1}(Q_{n_1},\Sigma_{n_1}), \\[2mm] \Psi_P = \frac{1}{\sqrt{n_2!}}\sum_R \pm R\Psi_P^1(q_1,\sigma_1)\,\Psi_P^2(q_2,\sigma_2)\cdots\Psi_P^{n_2}(q_{n_2},\sigma_{n_2}). \end{cases}$$

Nel caso di un gran numero di particelle le autofunzioni individuali Ψ si possono naturalmente identificare con pacchetti d'onda rappresentanti particelle libere. L'uso delle autofunzioni di prima approssimazione introduce un certo errore a cause di notevoli effetti di polarizzazione, ma il metodo è certamente utilizzabile per determinazioni d'ordine di grandezza.

Dobbiamo ora calcolare il valore medio dell'energia totale preso sull'autofunzione (2) e ricercare sotto quali condizioni esso diventa minimo. L'energia è composta da tre parti:

$$(4) \qquad\qquad W = T + E + A$$

essendo T l'energia cinetica, E l'energia elettrostatica dei protoni e A l'energia di scambio.

Assumiamo per semplicità che tutti gli stati individuali definiti nei centri di gravità siano, o liberi, o occupati due volte con opposta direzione dello "spin". Introduciamo ancora le matrici di Dirac[4]:

$$(5) \qquad \begin{cases} \big(q'|\rho_N|q''\big) = \displaystyle\sum_{\sigma_i=1}^{2}\sum_{i=1}^{n_1} \Psi_N^i\big(q',\sigma_i\big)\,\bar{\Psi}_N^i\big(q'',\sigma_i\big), \\[4mm] \big(q'|\rho_P|q''\big) = \displaystyle\sum_{\sigma_i=1}^{2}\sum_{i=1}^{n_2} \Psi_P^i\big(q',\sigma_i\big)\,\bar{\Psi}_P^i\big(q'',\sigma_i\big). \end{cases}$$

Valgono le relazioni:

$$(6) \qquad\qquad \rho_N^2 = 2\rho_N; \qquad \rho_P^2 = 2\rho_P$$

---

[4] P. A. M. Dirac, "Proc. Cambridge Phil. Soc.", *26*, 376 (1930).

in cui il fattore (2) dipende dallo spin. Segue:

(7)
$$\rho_N = \diagdown\!\!\begin{smallmatrix}2\\[4pt]0\end{smallmatrix} \quad ; \quad \rho_P = \diagdown\!\!\begin{smallmatrix}2\\[4pt]0\end{smallmatrix} \, .$$

Se M è la massa di ogni particella, approssimativamente la stessa per i protoni e per i neutroni, risulta(*):

(8)
$$T = \frac{1}{2M} \, \mathrm{Spur} \left[(\rho_N + \rho_P) p^2 \right],$$

(9)
$$E = \frac{e^2}{2} \int (q'|\rho_P|q') \frac{1}{|q' - q''|} (q''|\rho_P|q'') \, dq' dq'' + \cdots .$$

Abbiamo trascurato in (9) un termine che rappresenta essenzialmente l'*ordinaria* energia di scambio dipendente dall'interazione elettrostatica dei protoni. Questo termine è stato calcolato da DIRAC[5] e non ha grande importanza quando il numero delle particelle è grande.

Abbiamo infine:

(10)
$$A = - \int (q'|\rho_N|q'') (q''|\rho_N|q') I|q' - q''| \, dq' dq''.$$

Quando il numero delle particelle è sufficientemente elevato si possono riguardare ρ_N e ρ_P come matrici quasi diagonali, anzi come funzioni classiche di p e q, e precisamente il migliore legame fra matrici e funzioni classiche ci è dato da[6](**):

(11)
$$\left(q - \frac{v}{2}|\rho|q + \frac{v}{2} \right) = \frac{1}{h^3} \int \rho(p, q) e^{-\frac{2\pi i}{h}(p, v)} dp,$$

e attraverso la formula che si ottiene rovesciando l'integrale di Fourier. Sostituendo mediante (11) nelle formole precedenti si trova:

(12)
$$T = \frac{1}{2M} \int \frac{\rho_N(p, q) + \rho_P(p, q)}{h^3} p^2 dp \, dq,$$

(13)
$$E = \frac{e^2}{2} \int \frac{\rho_N(p, q) \rho_P(p', q')}{h^6} \frac{1}{|q - q'|} dp \, dq \, dp' dq',$$

(14)
$$A = \int \frac{\rho_N(p, q) V_N(p, q)}{h^3} dp \, dq = \int \frac{\rho_P(p, q) V_P(p, q)}{h^3} dp \, dq,$$

(*) Nel testo originale in eq. (8) è mantenuta la dizione tedesca "Spur" per traccia, Tr. (Nota del Curatore.)
[5] P. A. M. DIRAC, *loc. cit.*
[6] V., p. es., DIRAC, *loc. cit.*
(**) Ne "La Ricerca Scientifica" è erroneamente stampato V nella parentesi dell'esponenziale. (Nota del Curatore.)

in cui $V_N(p,q)$ e $V_P(p,q)$ sono le funzioni classiche che corrispondono alle matrici:

(15)
$$\begin{cases} (q'|V_N|q'') = -(q'|\rho_P|q'')I(|q'-q''|), \\ (q'|V_P|q'') = -(q'|\rho_N|q'')I(|q'-q''|). \end{cases}$$

Assumiamo ora che nell'intorno di ogni punto q siano occupati gli stati di minore energia cinetica, così dai neutroni, come dai protoni. Esisterà allora un valore massimo $P_N(q)$ per i neutroni e analogamente per i protoni, e a causa di (7) sarà:

(16)
$$\rho_N(p,q) = \begin{cases} 2 & \text{per} \quad p < P_N(q) \\ 0 & \text{per} \quad p > P_N(q) \end{cases}$$

(17)
$$\rho_P(p,q) = \begin{cases} 2 & \text{per} \quad p < P_P(q) \\ 0 & \text{per} \quad p > P_P(q). \end{cases}$$

Consideriamo dapprima il caso limite che la densità sia molto elevata, così che h/P_N e h/P_P, che nell'ordine di grandezza corrispondono alla mutua distanza media delle particelle nel nucleo, siano piccole di fronte al raggio d'azione della forze di risonanza. Assumiamo ancora che sia $P_N(q) > P_P(q)$, e quindi la densità dei neutroni maggiore di quella dei protoni, e osserviamo che nella seconda delle (15) a causa della pratica diagonalità di ρ_N si può sostituire $I(|q'-q''|)$ con il valore limite $I(0)$, almeno se $I(0)$ è finito; allora quell'equazione si riduce a:

$$(q'|V_P|q'') = -I(0)(q'|\rho_N|q''),$$

da cui segue:

(18)
$$V_P(p,q) = -I(0)\rho_N(p,q).$$

Sostituendo con questa nella (14) e tenendo presente che per $\rho_P(p,q) > 0$, è anche sempre $\rho_N = 2$, troviamo:

(19)
$$A = -2I(0) \int \frac{\rho_P(p,q)}{h^3} \, dp \, dq = -2I(0)n_2.$$

Questo significa che l'energia di legame dipendente dalle forze di risonanza è per ogni protone, nel caso di densità molto alta, semplicemente uguale a $-2I(0)$, purché la densità dei neutroni superi in ogni punto quella dei protoni. Se trascuriamo per un momento la repulsione elettrostatica fra i protoni e fissiamo il rapporto n_2/n_1, lasciando indeterminata la densità, l'energia potenziale per particella sarà una certa funzione della densità totale:

(20)
$$a = a(\mu), \quad \mu = \frac{8\pi}{3h^3}(P_N^3 + P_P^3),$$

che naturalmente per $\mu = 0$ si annulla e per $\mu \to \infty$ si approssima al valore costante $-\frac{2n_2}{n_1+n_2}I(0)$. Questo valore limite raggiunge il minimo $-I(0)$ quando $n_2 = n_1$. Per medie densità l'espressione generale di $a(\mu)$ risulta a causa di (10) e (11)

$$(21) \qquad\qquad a = \frac{1}{\mu} \int \frac{\rho_N(p,q)\rho_P(p',q)}{h^6} \, G(p,p') \mathrm{d}p \, \mathrm{d}p'$$

essendo $G(p,p')$ una funzione di $|p - p'|$ connessa nel modo seguente con $I(r)$:

$$(22) \qquad\qquad G(p,p') = \int e^{-\frac{2\pi i}{h}(p-p',v)} I(|v|) \mathrm{d}v.$$

L'energia cinetica per particella avrà la forma

$$(23) \qquad\qquad t = \kappa\mu^{2/3}$$

e l'energia totale $a + t$ può raggiungere un minimo per un certo valore della densità che dipende solo dal rapporto n_2/n_1. Si ottiene così una densità costante indipendente della massa del nucleo, e quindi un volume nucleare e un contenuto energetico semplicemente proporzionati al numero delle particelle come richiede l'esperienza.

Si può tentare di determinare la funzione $I(r)$ in modo che i dati sperimentali siano riprodotti con la maggiore esattezza. L'espressione

$$(24)\,(^*) \qquad\qquad I(r) = \lambda\frac{e^2}{r}$$

p. es., con una costante arbitraria è adatta allo scopo, sebbene essa divenga infinita per $r = 0$. Essa deve essere però modificata per grandi valori di r poiché fornisce una sezione efficace infinita per l'urto fra protone e neutrone; inoltre sembra che conduca a un rapporto troppo piccolo per i difetti di massa della particella α e dell'isotopo dell'idrogeno. Così bisogna utilizzare un'espressione con almeno due costanti arbitrarie, p. es. una funzione esponenziale $I(r) = Ae^{-sr}$. Noi non entreremo però in questa indagine poiché, come si è già rilevato, la prima approssimazione statistica può condurre a errori notevoli comunque grande sia il numero delle particelle. Per nuclei pesanti acquista grande importanza la repulsione coulombiana, ed essa ha per effetto di accrescere alquanto le dimensioni dei nuclei e di rendere variabile dal centro alla periferia la densità, così dei protoni, come dei neutroni. L'energia di legame dovuta alle forze di scambio non dipende ora soltanto dal rapporto n_2/n_1, ed è, a parità di detto rapporto, alquanto minore che nel caso di nuclei leggeri, a causa della diminuzione di densità dovuta alle forze elettrostatiche.

Lipsia, 11 *maggio* 1933-XI

(*) Ne "La Ricerca Scientifica" è erroneamente ripetuto (23). (Nota del Curatore.)

Commento alla Nota Scientifica n. 8: "Über die Kerntheorie - Sulla teoria dei nuclei".

È questo il primo e unico articolo di Majorana sulla fisica nucleare[1]; esso contiene un modello di forze di scambio fra neutroni (n) e protoni (p) più elegante e del resto più profondo di quello suggerito da Heisenberg nel luglio del 1932 (Z. Phys., 77, 1 (1932)).

Majorana arrivò a Lipsia il 20 gennaio 1933 usufruendo di una borsa di studio del Consiglio Nazionale delle Ricerche. Nella domanda per la borsa egli aveva affermato di voler studiare "sotto la guida del professor W. Heisenberg la struttura dei nuclei e la formulazione relativistica di una nuova teoria dei quanti". Certamente Heisenberg era allora la migliore e più originale guida allo studio del misterioso mondo nucleare: infatti, meno di quattro mesi dopo la scoperta dei neutroni da parte di Chadwick (Febbraio 1932) Heisenberg aveva inviato alla rivista "Zeitschrift für Physik" un articolo dal titolo "Sulla struttura dei nuclei atomici" che si può considerare come l'inizio della fisica nucleare teorica. Majorana fu uno dei primi fisici a rendersi rapidamente conto dell'importanza di tale articolo.

In esso Heisenberg suggeriva che "i nuclei atomici sono composti di protoni e neutroni, ma non contengono elettroni. Se quest'idea è corretta essa porta a una notevole semplificazione della teoria nucleare". Secondo Heisenberg un nucleo di numero di massa A e di numero di carica Z è composto di Z protoni e $A - Z$ neutroni. Poiché i neutroni hanno una massa dello stesso ordine della massa dei protoni (in effetti lievemente maggiore) i loro moti sono non-relativistici come quelli dei protoni e perciò la meccanica quantistica non-relativistica è valida per tutti i componenti del nucleo senza che occorra invocare la presenza di nessun elettrone. Come scrisse Heisenberg a Bohr il 20 giugno 1932 "l'idea fondamentale [della mia teoria] è di scaricare tutte le difficoltà fondamentali sul neutrone e di trattare in maniera quantomeccanica tutti i componenti del nucleo". Naturalmente questa estensione della validità della meccanica quantistica al nucleo non poteva che fare piacere a Heisenberg.

Il punto di vista di Heisenberg rappresentava una frattura netta con il modello nucleare comunemente accettato all'epoca che supponeva esistessero nel nucleo A protoni e $A - Z$ elettroni. Si noti che i protoni e gli elettroni erano, prima della scoperta del neutrone, le uniche particelle elementari conosciute.

---

[1] La tesi di laurea di Majorana discussa nel luglio 1929, nonostante il suo titolo "Sulla meccanica dei Nuclei Radioattivi", non riguarda esplicitamente la struttura nucleare ma è uno studio assai interessante della penetrazione quantistica di una barriera di potenziale.

Ci volle un po' di tempo prima che il modello di Heisenberg fosse accettato. Invero più di sei mesi dopo la scoperta sperimentale dei neutroni, Fermi, alla Conferenza Internazionale sull'Elettricità a Parigi (1932), discuteva ancora le difficoltà inerenti all'esistenza di elettroni all'interno dei nuclei. Come spiegava nel suo discorso, il principio d'indeterminazione implicava che gli elettroni, per rimanere confinati entro una sfera del raggio di 10^{-13} cm, dovevano avere un'energia cinetica media di oltre $60 \, \text{MeV}$, cioé assai più elevata di quella di qualunque raggio beta conosciuto. Inoltre, secondo il modello nucleare fatto di protoni ed elettroni, il nucleo ^{14}N doveva contenere 14 protoni e 7 elettroni, cioè un numero dispari di fermioni; pertanto, come dimostrato da Ehrenfest e Oppenheimer, il suo spin doveva essere semi-intero e la statistica doveva essere quella di Fermi. Gli esperimenti invece mostravano che lo spin era intero e la statistica quella di Bose. Fermi concludeva *"Ceci semble indiquer encore une fois que les conceptions de la mécanique quantique ordinaire, ne sont pas applicable à l'étude de la dinamique des électrons du noyau atomique"* (Rapport 22, p. 798, alla Conferenza di Parigi del 1932. Il rapporto era stato certamente scritto prima della conferenza, ma il testo pubblicato non contiene nessuna correzione). Anziché rigettare il modello basato su protoni ed elettroni e accettare l'esistenza di una nuova particella elementare neutra, sembra che Fermi fosse pronto ad abbandonare la meccanica quantistica la cui validità, come egli sottolineava, era stata verificata soltanto alla scala atomica ma poteva fallire alla scala nucleare che è 100000 volte più piccola. La relatività e la meccanica quantistica avevano insegnato ai fisici che le leggi della natura possono cambiare quando cambia la scala dei fenomeni: la fisica nucleare insegnerà loro che *"there are more things in heaven and earth, Horatio, than are dreamt of in your philosophy"* (W. Shakespeare, Hamlet, I, 5).

La forza di scambio di Heisenberg era l'unico modello quantomeccanico del nucleo quando Majorana arrivò a Lipsia il 20 gennaio 1933. È lecito domandarsi se egli sia davvero andato a Lipsia con l'idea di studiare sotto la guida del professor Heisenberg, come aveva affermato nella domanda per la borsa di studio, o se non invece sia arrivato con già la propria versione di forze di scambio ben chiara nella sua mente e, anziché la guida del famoso professore, non abbia piuttosto voluto sentire il suo parere sulla versione modificata sviluppata da lui stesso. Per quanto non vi sia traccia negli archivi di Majorana di alcun lavoro, o appunti per un lavoro, sulla struttura dei nuclei fatto a Roma e ispirato dal lavoro di Heisenberg del 1932, la velocità con cui egli completò il suo articolo mi sembra piuttosto favorire la seconda alternativa. In una lettera del 18 febbraio 1933 a suo padre, Majorana afferma di aver già scritto "un articolo sulla struttura dei nuclei che a Heisenberg è piaciuto molto, sebbene contenga qualche correzione alla sua [di Heisenberg] teoria". L'approvazione di Heisenberg è menzionata nuovamente in una lettera di Majorana alla madre del 22 febbraio in cui scrive "Heisenberg [nel colloquio settimanale] ha parlato della teoria nucleare; ha fatto una grande reclame dell'articolo che ho scritto qui. Ora siamo in rapporti molto amichevoli, grazie a numerose discussioni scientifiche e a qualche partita a scacchi".

In cosa consistono le correzioni che Majorana fece al modello di Heisenberg? Ambedue sono d'accordo sul fatto che i nuclei siano composti esclusivamente da neutroni e protoni. Inoltre essi suppongono che non vi siano forze n-n o al massino che esse siano del tutto

trascurabili; le uniche forze p-p sono quelle dovute all'interazione coulombiana e in prima approssimazione possono essere trascurate almeno per nuclei leggeri. Pertanto le uniche forze responsabili della stabilità nucleare sono quelle fra n e p. Per determinare tali forze Heisenberg era partito dall'analogia della coppia (n, p) con lo ione molecolare H_2^+ costituito da un atomo di idrogeno H e da un atomo di idrogeno ionizzato $H^+ = p$. Come era stato dimostrato da Heitler e London, H_2^+ è tenuto insieme dallo scambio di un elettrone

$$(H, H^+) \quad \Leftrightarrow \quad (H^+, H).$$

L'analogia non significa che Heisenberg pensasse che il neutrone sia uno stato legato di un protone e di un elettrone. Egli intendeva semplicemente che la coppia (n, p) fosse tenuta assieme dallo scambio della "carica" che egli definisce come l'autovalore di un operatore ρ^ς che rappresenta la carica elettrica dove ρ^ς assume il valore $+1$ su n e -1 su p. ρ^ς è la terza componente di un operatore ρ simile all'operatore σ che rappresenta lo spin e che egli chiama spin-ρ e che noi chiamiamo isospin e che denotiamo con τ. I neutroni e i protoni possono dunque venir considerati come due stati diversi di una singola particella che oggi chiamiamo nucleone. Come Heisenberg dice "ogni particella in un nucleo è caratterizzata da cinque grandezze, le tre coordinate di posizione (x, y, z), lo spin σ_z lungo l'asse z e un quinto numero ρ^ς che può valere ± 1".

Nel suo discorso alla Conferenza Solvay sulla Fisica Nucleare a Brussels (ottobre 1933) Heisenberg rappresentò graficamente l'operatore di scambio carica P_c fra n e p con il seguente diagramma

$$
\begin{array}{cccccc}
x_1 & x_2 & P_c & x_1 & x_2 \\
\leftarrow \bullet & \circ \rightarrow & \Leftrightarrow & \leftarrow\circ & \bullet \rightarrow,
\end{array}
$$

dove $\bullet$ rappresenta un protone a x_1 e $\circ$ un neutrone a x_2; le frecce rappresentano l'orientamento degli spin. L'operatore P_c inverte il segno dell'autovalore di ρ^ς ma non quello dell'operatore di spin.

Per Majorana invece l'analogia della coppia (n, p) con H_2^+ è di dubbio significato probabilmente poiché egli pensava che l'analogia implicasse necessariamente che il neutrone sia una particella composta, $n = (p, e)$. Inoltre non gli piaceva il concetto astratto di carica introdotto da Heisenberg come l'autovalore di ρ^ς che considerava "incomodo" (in tedesco: *umbequem*) e insisteva nel trattare n e p come particelle diverse. Suggeriva che la forza n-p sia dovuta allo scambio, rappresentato da un operatore P_x, delle coordinate spaziali x_1, x_2:

$$
\begin{array}{cccccc}
x_1 & x_2 & P_x & x_1 & x_2 \\
\leftarrow \bullet & \circ \rightarrow & \Leftrightarrow & \circ\rightarrow & \leftarrow \bullet.
\end{array}
$$

A causa di qualche "fenomeno di saturazione" questa forza di scambio conduce all'indipendenza della densità nucleare dalla massa totale. Si verifica facilmente che gli operatori di scambio di Majorana e di Heisenberg sono legati dalla relazione

$$P_x = P_s P_c,$$

dove P_s è l'operatore che inverte il segno dello spin ordinario. Lo scambio delle coordinate spaziali è dunque equivalente allo scambio delle coordinate di spin e di ρ-spin. Lo scambio di Majorana impedisce il collasso del nucleo senza la necessità di introdurre alcuna forza repulsiva a breve distanza come voleva Heisenberg purché si inverta però il segno della funzione potenziale di Heisenberg $J(r)$.

Majorana giustifica il suo modello di forze di scambio rispetto a quello di Heisenberg osservando che esso è compatibile con la costanza della densità nucleare e che assicura la "particolare stabilità della particella α" prodotta da "un fenomeno di saturazione più o meno analogo alla saturazione delle valenze". In effetti nella particella α "tutti e due i neutroni agiscono su ciascun protone invece che su uno solo [come nel modello di Heisenberg] poiché possiamo supporre che la funzione delle coordinate spaziali di tutti i neutroni e i protoni sia simmetrica (cosa che è vera se si trascura l'energia coulombiana del protoni). Nella particella α tutte le quattro particelle sono nello stesso stato che è perciò un guscio chiuso" (nel testo tedesco: *"so das es eine abgeschlossene Schale in höhere Sinne as das Heliumatom ist"*; *abgeschlossene Schale* significa, nel linguaggio di spin e di spin-isotopico, che il guscio è chiuso quando sia lo spin che l'isospin sono in stati antisimmetrici).

Fu questa saturazione delle forze nucleari a $A = 4$ che convinse immediatamente Heisenberg della superiorità del modello di Majorana rispetto al suo di modello. Il discorso di Heisenberg alla Conferenza Solvay nell'ottobre del 1933 rappresentò la migliore consacrazione del lavoro del suo giovane collega.

Nei loro articoli, Heisenberg e Majorana, discutevano soltanto la stabilità dei nuclei, cioé degli effetti di quelle che oggi chiamiamo interazioni forti. Pertanto essi non risolsero il mistero dell'origine dei raggi beta, cioé degli elettroni emessi dai nuclei radioattivi. Il problema fu risolto da Fermi nel suo celebre lavoro del 1934 ("Z. Phys." 88, 161 (1934)) che segna l'inizio della teoria delle interazioni deboli.

Dopo il 1933 lo studio delle forze nucleari fece rapidi progressi. Si scoprirono rapidamente le forze n-n che risultarono essere uguali a quelle n-p e a quelle p-p a parte le interazioni coulombiane. Si scoprì così l'indipendenza delle interazioni forti dalla carica e, con buona pace di Majorana, il formalismo di Heisenberg dell'isospin fu riconosciuto essere il vero modo di esprimere questa importante proprietà delle interazioni forti.

Nel 1937 Wigner osservò che una combinazione di forze di Majorana e di forze dipendenti soltanto dalla distanza (che oggi chiamiamo forze di Wigner) sono invarianti non solo rispetto allo spin e isospin, ma anche rispetto a un gruppo più grande $SU(4)$. È questa la cosidetta teoria dei super-multipletti che conduce a una degenerazione dei livelli nucleari, e che è più o meno in accordo con i dati empirici dei nuclei leggeri.

Dopo questo lavoro del 1933, Majorana sembra aver perso interesse nella fisica nucleare o addirittura per tutta la fisica forse a causa della sua cattiva salute.

* * *

Voglio ringraziare sentitamente Nadia ROBOTTI e Francesco GUERRA per le molte e illuminanti discussioni e per avermi permesso di leggere (e di fare ampio uso di) una versione preliminare di un lavoro storico sui primi sviluppi della fisica nucleare a Roma.

L. A. RADICATI di BROZOLO
Scuola Normale Superiore, Pisa

On nuclear theory(*)

ETTORE MAJORANA

Summary. — We discuss a new interpretation of HEISENBERG's nuclear theory which leads to a slightly different Hamiltonian function. Accordingly we treat the nuclei statistically.

The discovery of the neutron, a heavy and uncharged elementary particle, made it possible to develop a nuclear theory using ideas of quantum mechanics without, however, removing the fundamental difficulties that are connected with β-decay. According to HEISENBERG[1], we can think of nuclei for many purposes as consisting of protons and neutrons, *i.e.* of particles of almost the same mass, with spin $\frac{1}{2}\frac{h}{2\pi}$ and obeying FERMI statistics. The problem is thus reduced to finding a suitable Hamiltonian which holds for this system of particles, and we need a non-relativistic approximation since the speed of the particles is presumably rather small compared with the speed of light ($v \sim \frac{c}{10}$). In order to find a suitable interaction between the components of the nuclei HEISENBERG was guided by an obvious analogy. He treats the neutron as a combination of a proton and an electron, *i.e.* like a hydrogen atom bound by a process not fully understood by present theories, in such a way that it changes its statistical properties and its spin. He further assumes that there are exchange forces between protons and neutrons similar to those responsible for the molecular binding of H and H^+. In addition to this interaction

---

(*) Translated from "Zeitschrift für Physik", Bd. 82, 1933, pp. 137-145, by Verena Wehrli-Brink. (Courtesy of D. M. Brink.)
[1] W. HEISENBERG, "Z. Physik", 77, 1 (1932); 78, 156 (1933).

between protons and neutrons considered essential for the stability of the nucleus there are COULOMB repulsion between protons, VAN DER WAALS attraction between neutrons and some sort of electrostatic interaction between protons and neutrons([2]).

One may doubt the validity of this analogy as the theory does not explain the inner structure of the neutron, and the interaction between neutron and proton seems rather big compared with the mass-defect of the neutron as determined by CHADWICK. We think, therefore, that it may be quite interesting to find a Hamiltonian very similar to HEISENBERG's which represents in the simplest way the most general and most obvious properties of the nucleus. We shall use a statistical method which should be permissable for determining orders of magnitude. We should also like to point out the exchange forces must have the opposite sign to HEISENBERG's forces because of the criterium we fixed for the Hamiltonian. Therefore, the symmetry characteristics of the eigenfunctions belonging to the normal state and the whole statistical treatment are different from HEISENBERG's.

1. The numerous sources of information we have on nuclear structure, *i.e.* radioactive decay, artificial decay, anomalous scattering of α-particles, mass-defect measurements etc. seem to indicate that nuclei, unlike atoms, are not uniformly organized. On the contrary, it looks as though nuclei consist of rather independent components which react only on immediate contact, *i.e.* of some sort of matter with the same properties of size and impenetrability as macroscopic matter. Light and heavy nuclei are built up of this matter and the difference between them depends mainly on their different content of "nuclear matter". This theory can only be correct if the COULOMB repulsion between the positive components of nuclei is not very important. This certainly holds for rather light nuclei, whereas we have to have a slight correction for heavy nuclei.

If we assume that nuclei consist of protons and neutrons we have to formulate the simplest law of interaction between them which will lead if the electrostatic repulsion is negligible, to a constant density for nuclear matter. We have to find three laws of interaction: One between protons, one between protons and neutrons and one between neutrons. We shall assume, however, that only COULOMB's force acts between each pair of protons. This can be justified to a certain extent by the fact that the classical radius of protons is much smaller than the average distance between the particles in the nucleus. Also, the COULOMB force is not very important for light nuclei and, as they contain almost the same number of neutrons and protons, it seems reasonable to think that a special interaction between protons and neutrons is the main cause of nuclear stability. We assume that there is no noticeable interaction between the neutrons for there is no proof of the contrary.We now have to find a suitable interaction between protons and neutrons. Nuclear structure and the structure of solids and liquids seem to be somewhat similar and it mightbe possible to have an interaction of the same type as between atoms and molecules, *i.e.* attraction for large distances and strong repulsion for small distances

---

([2]) W. HEISENBERG, "Z. Physik", *80*, 587 (1933).

Fig. 1. – Potential energy between two atoms.

so that the particles do not penetrate each other (see Fig. 1). We would also have to assume repulsive forces between neutrons with small separations in order to obtain the desired ratio between the number of particles and the nuclear volume. Such a solution would be aesthetically unsatisfactory, however, since we would have not only attractive forces of unknown origin between the particles, but also, for short distances, repulsive forces of enormous magnitude corresponding to a potential of several million volts. We shall, therefore, try to find another solution and introduce as few arbitrary elements as possible. The main problem is this: How can we obtain a density independent of the nuclear mass without obstructing the free movement of the particles by an artificial impenetrability? We must try to find an interaction whose average energy per particle never exceeds a certain limit however great the density. This might occur through a sort of saturation phenomenon more or less analogous to valence saturation. Such an interaction is given, as we shall prove, by

$$(1) \qquad\qquad \left(Q', q' | J | Q'', q''\right) = -\delta\left(q' - Q''\right)\delta\left(q'' - Q'\right)J(r),$$

where $r = |q' - Q'|$ and Q and q are the coordinates of a neutron and proton, respectively. The function $J(r)$ is positive, and a possible form of it is shown in Fig. 2. Expression (1) implies that there is an attraction or a repulsion respectively between the neutron and the proton depending on whether the wave-function is approximately symmetrical or anti-symmetrical in the two particles. In order to account for the special stability of the α-particle we shall assume that Q and q in equation (1) are only the position coordinates

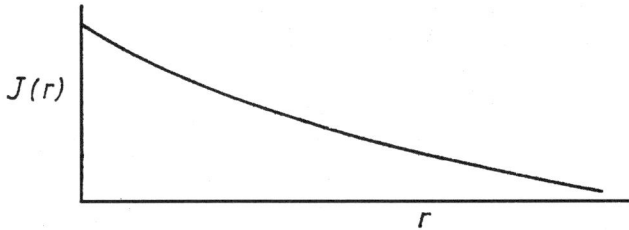

Fig. 2. – Curve of the resonance forces.

without spin. Thus we find that both neutrons act on each proton in the α-particle instead of only one and vice versa, since we assume a symmetrical function in the position coordinates of all protons and neutrons (which is true only if we neglect the COULOMB energy of the protons). In the α-particle all four particles are in the same state so that it is a closed shell. If we proceed from an α-particle to heavier nuclei we can have no more particles in the same state because of the PAULI principle. Also, the exchange energy (1) is usually large only if a proton and a neutron are in the same state and we may expect, which agrees with experiments, that in heavy nuclei the mass defect per particle is not noticeably bigger than in the α-particle.

Let us now compare expression (1) for the interaction between a proton and a neutron with the interaction deduced from the resonance term of HEISENBERG's Hamiltonian by distinguishing between neutrons and protons and by eliminating the troublesome ρ-spin-coordinate.

We find an expression similar to (1) which is, however, fundamentally different in two respects: Firstly, in HEISENBERG's expression Q and q stand for all coordinates including the spin. Secondly, HEISENBERG assumes the opposite sign for the resonance forces. Statistically this is most important as there is no saturation because of the symmetry character of HEISENBERG's eigenfunctions and repulsive interactions at short distances are necessary([3]). We shall now investigate the saturation that leads to the uniform density of the nuclear components found experimentally.

2. In a first approximation we take the eigenfunction of the nucleus as a product of two functions which depend on the coordinates of the n_1 neutrons and n_2 protons respectively:

$$(2) \qquad \psi = \psi_N(Q_1, \Sigma_1, \ldots, Q_{n_1}, \Sigma_{n_1})\psi_P(q_1, \sigma_1, \ldots, q_{n_2}, \sigma_{n_2})$$

and we assume that ψ_N and ψ_P can be obtained by anti-symmetrizing products of individual orthogonal single-particle eigenfunctions:

$$(3) \qquad \begin{cases} \psi_N = \frac{1}{\sqrt{n_1!}} \sum_R \pm R\psi'_N(Q_1, \Sigma_1) \cdots \psi_N^{n_1}(Q_{n_1}, \Sigma_{n_1}), \\ \psi_P = \frac{1}{\sqrt{n_2!}} \sum_R \pm R\psi'_P(q_1, \sigma_1) \cdots \psi_P^{n_2}(q_{n_2}, \sigma_{n_2}). \end{cases}$$

For many particles the individual-particle wave-function ψ may be identified with free-particle wave-packets. We can show that each proton is subject on the average to the interaction of a small number (one or two) of neutrons and vice versa, and the assumption of free-particle wave-functions introduces a slight error because of polarization effects. This method is, suitable for order-of-magnitude calculations.

([3]) W. HEISENBERG, "Z. Physik", *80*, 587 (1933). I would like to thank Professor HEISENBERG very much for being able to see his paper before it was published.

We have to calculate the mean value of the total energy using the wave-function (2) and find its minimum. This energy consists of three parts:

$$(4) \qquad\qquad\qquad W = T + E + A,$$

where T is the kinetic energy, E the electrostatic energy of the protons and A the exchange energy. We assume that all individual particle states are either free or occupied twice with opposite spin direction. Then, n_1 and n_2 are even. We also introduce DIRAC's density matrices:

$$(5) \qquad \begin{cases} (q'|\rho_N|q'') = \displaystyle\sum_{\sigma_i=1}^{2}\sum_{i=1}^{n_1} \psi_N^i(q',\sigma_i)\bar\psi_N^i(q'',\sigma_i), \\[2mm] (q'|\rho_P|q'') = \displaystyle\sum_{\sigma_i=1}^{2}\sum_{i=1}^{n_2} \psi_P^i(q',\sigma_i)\bar\psi_P^i(q'',\sigma_i). \end{cases}$$

and have

$$(6) \qquad\qquad\qquad \rho_N^2 = 2\rho_N, \qquad \rho_P^2 = 2\rho_P,$$

where the factor 2 comes from the spin. The eigenvalues of the density matrices are

$$(7) \qquad\qquad\qquad \rho_N = \begin{matrix} 2 \\ \diagdown \\ 0 \end{matrix} \;, \qquad \rho_P = \begin{matrix} 2 \\ \diagdown \\ 0 \end{matrix} \;.$$

If the mass M of each particle is approximately the same for neutrons and protons we obtain

$$(8) \qquad\qquad\qquad T = \frac{1}{2M}\, \mathrm{Tr}\left[(\rho_N + \rho_P)p^2\right],$$

$$(9) \qquad\qquad E = \frac{e^2}{2}\int (q'|\rho_P|q')\frac{1}{|q'-q''|}(q''|\rho_P|q'')\mathrm{d}q'\mathrm{d}q'' + \cdots .$$

In equation (9) we have left out a term which is essentially the COULOMB exchange energy of the protons. This term has been calculated by DIRAC([4]) and is not very important when there are many particles. Finally we obtain:

$$(10) \qquad\qquad A = -\int (q'|\rho_N|q'')\,J|q'-q''|\,(q''|\rho_P|q')\mathrm{d}q'\mathrm{d}q''.$$

([4]) P. A. M. DIRAC, "Proc. Cambridge Phil. Soc.", *26*, 376 (1930).

If the number of particles is large ρ_N and ρ_P are almost diagonal matrices and even classical functions of p and q([5]). The best relation between the matrices and the classical functions is given by

(11)
$$
\begin{cases}
\left(q - \dfrac{v}{2}\Big|\rho_N\Big|q + \dfrac{v}{2}\right) = \dfrac{1}{h^3} \int \rho_N(p, q) e^{-\frac{2\pi i}{h}(p,v)} dp, \\[3mm]
\left(q - \dfrac{v}{2}\Big|\rho_P\Big|q + \dfrac{v}{2}\right) = \dfrac{1}{h^3} \int \rho_P(p, q) e^{-\frac{2\pi i}{h}(p,v)} dq
\end{cases}
$$

and by an inversion of the FOURIER integrals. If we put equation (11) in the above expression we obtain

(12)
$$
T = \frac{1}{2M} \int \frac{\rho_N(p, q) + \rho_P(p, q)}{h^3} p^2 dp\, dq,
$$

(13)
$$
E = \frac{e^2}{2} \int \frac{\rho_N(p, q)\rho_P(p', q')}{h^6} \frac{1}{|q - q'|} dp\, dq\, dp'\, dq',
$$

(14)
$$
A = \int \frac{\rho_N(p, q)V_N(p, q)}{h^3} dp\, dq = \int \frac{\rho_P(p, q)V_P(p, q)}{h^3} dp\, dq,
$$

where $V_N(p, q)$ and $V_P(p, q)$ are the classical functions corresponding to the matrices

(15)
$$
\begin{cases}
(q'|V_N|q'') = -(q'|\rho_P|q'')\, J\big|q' - q''\big|, \\[2mm]
(q'|V_P|q'') = -(q'|\rho_N|q'')\, J\big|q' - q''\big|.
\end{cases}
$$

We now assume that near a point q the states of low energy are occupied by neutrons as well as by protons. There will be a maximum value of the momentum $P_N(q)$ for the neutrons and the protons, and from equation (7) it follows that

(16)
$$
\rho_N(p, q) = \begin{cases} 2, & \text{if } p < P_N(q), \\ 0, & \text{if } p > P_N(q), \end{cases}
$$

(17)
$$
\rho_P(p, q) = \begin{cases} 2, & \text{if } p < P_P(q), \\ 0, & \text{if } p > P_P(q). \end{cases}
$$

We first investigate a limiting case, *i.e.* a case of very high density when h/p_N and h/p_P, which are of the order of magnitude of the mutual distance between the particles in the nucleus, are small compared with the range of the resonance forces. We also assume that $P_N > P_P$, *i.e.* that the density of the neutrons is larger than the density of the protons.

([5]) See, P. A. M. DIRAC, ibidem.

We note that in the second equation of (15) ρ_N is almost diagonal and $J|q' - q''|$ can be substituted by $J(0)$ if $J(0)$ is finite. The equation then reads

$$\left(q'|V_P|q''\right) = -J(0)\left(q'|\rho_N|q''\right),$$

and from this follows

(18) $$V_P(p, q) = -J(0)\rho_N(p, q).$$

We put this in equation (14) and note that $\rho_N = 2$ if $\rho_P(p, q) > 0$ and obtain

(19) $$A = -2J(0) \int \frac{\rho_P(p, q)}{h^3} \, dp \, dq = -2J(0)n_2.$$

This means that the binding energy per proton due to the exchange forces is only $-2J(0)$ if the particle density is high and the density of neutrons larger than that of protons. We neglect for the time being the COULOMB repulsion of the protons (which is approximately true for light nuclei) and fix the ratio n_1/n_2, but not the density. Then the potential energy per particle is a certain function of the total density

(20) $$a = a(\mu), \qquad \mu = \frac{8\pi}{3h^3}\left(P_N^3 + P_P^3\right).$$

This vanishes for $\mu = 0$ and approaches a constant value $-\frac{2n_2}{n_1+n_2}J(0)$ for $\mu \to \infty$. This limiting value will reach the minimum $-J(0)$ if $n_1 = n_2$. For intermediate densities the general expression of $a(\mu)$ follows from equations (10) and (11) and is

(21) $$a = \frac{1}{\mu(q)} \iint \frac{\rho_N(p, q)\rho_P(p', q)}{h^6} G(p, p') dp \, dp',$$

where $G(p, p')$ is a function of $|p - p'|$ which depends on $J(r)$ in the following way

(22) $$G(p, p') = \int e^{-\frac{2\pi i}{h}(p-p', v)} J|v| dv.$$

The kinetic energy per particle is

$$t = \kappa \mu^{2/3}$$

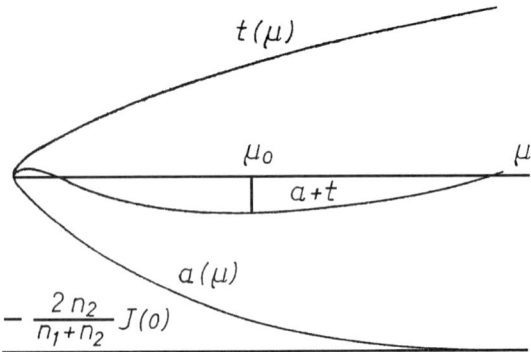

Fig. 3. – Kinetic and potential energy per particle.

and the total energy $a + t$ reaches a minimum for a certain value dependent only on the ratio n_1/n_2 (Fig. 3). We obtain a constant density independent of the nuclear mass and thus a nuclear volume and binding energy proportional only to the number of particles, as is found by experiment. We can try to determine the function $J(r)$ in a way that best represents the experimental results. The expression

$$J(r) = \lambda \frac{e^2}{r} \,,$$

for instance, with an arbitrary constant is suitable even though it becomes infinite if $r = 0$. For great distances, however, it must be modified as it gives an infinite cross section for the collision between protons and neutrons. Also, it seems to provide too small a ratio for the mass defects of the α-particle and the hydrogen isotope. Thus, we have to use an expression with at least two constants, $e.g.$ an exponential function, $J(r) = Ae^{-\beta r}$. We shall not follow this up since it has been shown that the first statistical approximation can lead to considerable errors however large the number of particles. For heavy nuclei COULOMB's force is very important which means that the nuclear extension increases slightly and the density of neurons and protons is no longer constant locally. The exchange binding energy not only depends on the ratio n_1/n_2, it is even slightly smaller than for light nuclei because of the smaller density caused by COULOMB forces.

* * *

I would like to thank Professor HEISENBERG very much for his advice and numerous discussions. My thanks are due to Professor EHRENFEST for many valuable discussions and also to the Consiglio Nazionale delle Ricerche for making my stay in Leipzig possible.

Comment on the Scientific Paper no. 8: *"On nuclear theory"*.

This is Majorana's first and only article on nuclear physics([1]); it contains a version of exchange forces between neutrons (n) and protons (p) more elegant and deeper than the one suggested by Heisenberg in July 1932 (Z. Phys., 77, 1 (1932)).

Majorana arrived in Leipzig on January 20, 1933, with a research grant from the Italian "Consiglio Nazionale delle Ricerche". In the application for the grant he had stated that his plan was to study "under the guidance of Professor W. Heisenberg the structure of nuclei and the relativistic formulation of the new quantum theory". Surely Heisenberg was at that time the best and most original guide to the mysterious world of nuclear structure. Indeed less than four months after Chadwick's discovery of neutrons (February 1932) Heisenberg had sent to "Zeitschrift für Physik" an article "On the Structure of Atomic Nuclei" which marked the beginning of nuclear theory. Majorana was one of the first physicists to quickly realize its importance.

In that paper Heisenberg suggested that "atomic nuclei are composed of protons and neutrons but do not contain electrons. If this is correct it means a very considerable simplification of nuclear theory". According to Heisenberg a nucleus with mass number A and charge number Z is made up of Z protons and $A - Z$ neutrons. Since neutrons have a mass of the same order as that of the protons (actually a little larger) their motions would be non-relativistic as that of the protons. Hence quantum mechanics would hold for all the components of the nucleus without the need of any electrons. As Heisenberg wrote to Bohr on June 20, 1932 "the basic idea [of my theory] is to shove all fundamental difficulties onto the neutron and to do quantum mechanics in the nucleus". Obviously this was much to Heisenberg's satisfaction.

Heisenberg's point of view represented a profound departure from the traditional nuclear model which was supposed to contain A protons and $A - Z$ electrons. Protons and electrons were, before the discovery of the neutron, the only known elementary particles.

Heisenberg's model took some time to be accepted. Indeed more than six months after the experimental discovery of neutrons, Fermi, at the International Conference on Electricity in Paris (1932), was still discussing in details the difficulties posed by the existence of electrons inside the nuclei. As he explained in his talk, the uncertainty prin-

---

([1]) Majorana's unpublished doctoral dissertation (discussed in July 1929), in spite of its title "Sulla meccanica dei Nuclei Radioattivi" ("On the mechanics of the radioactive nuclei") does not really concern nuclear structure. It is an interesting study of the quantum potential barrier.

ciple implied that electrons confined within a sphere of radius 10^{-13} cm would have an average kinetic energy of more than 60 MeV, much higher than that of any known β-ray. Moreover, according to the proton-electron model the nucleus ^{14}N was supposed to contain 14 protons and 7 electrons, *i.e.* an odd number of fermions; therefore, as proved by Ehrenfest and Oppenheimer, its spin should have been half-integer and the nucleus should have followed Fermi's statistics. Experiment instead showed that the spin was integer and the statistics was that of Bose. Fermi concluded: *"Ceci semble indiquer encore une fois que les conceptions de la mécanique quantique ordinaire, ne sont pas applicable à l'étude de la dinamique des électrons du noyau atomique"* (Rapport 22, p. 798, at the Paris Conference, 1932). The report was certainly written before the conference, but in the published text there was no correction). Rather than discarding the proton-electron model and accepting the existence of a new neutral elementary particle, Fermi seems to have been ready to give up quantum mechanics whose validity, he emphasized, had only been tested at the atomic scale but might well fail at the nuclear scale which is 100000 times smaller. Relativity and quantum mechanics had taught physicists that the laws of physics may change when the scale of phenomena changes: nuclear physics was going to teach them that "there are more things in heaven and earth, Horatio, than are dreamt of in your philosophy" (W. Shakespeare, Hamlet, I, 5).

Heisenberg's charge exchange force was the only purely quantum-mechanical model of the nucleus when Majorana arrived in Leipzig on January 20, 1933. Did he really go there to study the structure of nuclei under the guidance of Professor Heisenberg, as he had stated in the application for the research grant, or did he arrive there with his own version of exchange forces in mind and, rather than guidance, did he only want to ask the famous Professor his opinion on ideas that he, Majorana, had already developed? There is no record in Majorana's archives of any work on nuclear structure that he might have done in Rome inspired by Heisenberg's 1932 paper. However, the speed with which Majorana completed his paper seems to me to favour the second alternative. In a letter of February 18, 1933, to his father, Majorana states that he had already written "an article on the structure of nuclei that Heisenberg liked very much, even though it contains some corrections to his [Heisenberg's] theory". Heisenberg's approval of the paper is mentioned again in a letter to his mother of February 22: "Heisenberg has spoken [in the weekly colloquium] of nuclear theory: he did a lot of advertising for a paper I have written here. We are now on friendly terms, thanks to many scientific discussions and some chess games".

What are the corrections that Majorana made to Heisenberg's model? Both agree that nuclei are composed exclusively of neutrons and protons. They assume that there are no n-n forces or at most they are negligible; p-p forces are only due to Coulomb interactions and can be neglected in a first approximation at least for light nuclei. Hence the only forces responsible for nuclear stability are those between n and p. To determine these forces, Heisenberg started from the analogy of the (n, p) pair with the molecular ion H_2^+ made up of a hydrogen atom H and a ionized hydrogen $H^+ = p$. As Heitler and London had proved, H_2^+ is held together by the exchange of an electron

$$(\mathrm{H}, \mathrm{H}^+) \quad \Leftrightarrow \quad (\mathrm{H}^+, \mathrm{H}).$$

The analogy does not mean that Heisenberg thought that the neutron is a bound state of a proton and an electron. He simply meant that the pair (n, p) is held together by the exchange of "charge" which he defines as the eigenvalue of an operator ρ^ς representing the electric charge, where ρ^ς takes the value $+1$ on n and -1 on p. ρ^ς is the third component of a spin-like operator ρ that he calls ρ-spin, which we now call isospin and denote by τ. Neutrons and protons are thus to be thought of as two different states of one single particle that we now call nucleon. As Heisenberg says "each particle in a nucleus is characterised by 5 quantities: the three position coordinates (x, y, z), the spin σ_z along the z-axis and a fifth number ρ^ς which can be ± 1".

In his rapporteur talk at the Solvay Conference on Nuclear Physics in Brussels (October 1933) Heisenberg represented graphically the charge exchange operator P_c between n and p with the following diagram

$$
\begin{array}{ccccc}
x_1 & x_2 & P_\mathrm{c} & x_1 & x_2 \\
\leftarrow \bullet & \circ \rightarrow & \Leftrightarrow & \leftarrow \circ & \bullet \rightarrow,
\end{array}
$$

where $\bullet$ represents a proton at x_1 and $\circ$ a neutron at x_2; the arrows represent the orientation of the spins. The operator P_c reverses the sign of the eigenvalue of ρ^ς but not that of the spin operator.

Majorana instead considered the analogy of the pair (n, p) with H_2^+ of dubious significance probably because he thought it implied necessarily that the neutron is a composite particle, $n = (p, e)$. Moreover, he disliked Heisenberg's abstract conception of charge as the eigenvalue of ρ^ς which he termed "troublesome" (German: *umbequem*; Italian: *incomodo*) and insisted in treating n and p as different particles. He suggested that the n-p force is due to the exchange of the space coordinates x_1, x_2, represented by an operator P_x:

$$
\begin{array}{ccccc}
x_1 & x_2 & P_x & x_1 & x_2 \\
\leftarrow \bullet & \circ \rightarrow & \Leftrightarrow & \circ \rightarrow & \leftarrow \bullet.
\end{array}
$$

Owing to some "saturation phenomenon", this exchange force leads to the independence of nuclear density of the total mass. One easily verifies that Majorana and Heisenberg's exchange are related by

$$P_x = P_\mathrm{s} P_\mathrm{c},$$

where P_s is the operator that reverses the sign of the ordinary spin. Thus the exchange of space coordinates is equivalent to exchanging spin and ρ-spin coordinates. Majorana's exchange prevents the collapse of the nucleus without the need of any repulsive force at short distance provided one inverts the sign of Heisenberg's potential function $J(r)$.

Majorana motivates his own model of exchange forces in preference to Heisenberg's one by noticing that it is compatible with the constancy of the nuclear density and that it ensures the "particular stability of the α-particle" arising from a "saturation phenomenon more or less analogous to valence saturation". Indeed in the α-particle "both neutrons

act on each proton instead of only one [as in Heisenberg's model] and vice-versa since we can assume a symmetrical function in the position coordinates of all protons and neutrons (which is true if we neglect the Coulomb energy of the protons). In the α-particle all four particles are in the same state so that it is a closed shell" (German: *"so das es eine abgeschlossene Schale in höhere Sinne as das Heliumatom ist"*; abgeschlossene Schale means in the language of spin and isospin that the shell is closed when both spin and isospin functions are anti-symmetrical).

It was this saturation of nuclear forces at $A = 4$ that immediately convinced Heisenberg that Majorana's model was preferable to his own. Heisenberg's talk at the Solvay Conference on nuclei in October 1933 was the best advertisement for the work of his younger colleague.

In their papers Heisenberg and Majorana were only concerned with nuclear stability, *i.e.* with what we now call strong interactions. Therefore they did not solve the mystery of the origin of β-rays, *i.e.* of the origin of the electron emitted by radioactive nuclei. The problem was finally solved by Fermi in his celebrated 1934 article (Z. Phys. *88*, 161 (1934)) which marks the beginning of the theory of weak interactions.

After 1933 the study of nuclear forces advanced very rapidly. The n-n forces were soon found to be equal to the n-p forces and to the p-p forces, apart from the Coulomb interaction. The charge independence of the strong interactions was thus established, and Heisenberg's isospin formalism was recognised (*pace* to Majorana) to be the correct way to describe it.

In 1937 Wigner noticed that a combination of Majorana forces with his own forces (that depend only upon the space distance) are not only spin and isospin independent but are invariant under a larger symmetry group, $SU(4)$. This is the so-called super-multiplets theory which leads to a degeneracy of nuclear levels in very rough agreement with empirical evidence for light nuclei.

After his 1933 paper Majorana seems to have lost interest in nuclear physics or in physics all together, perhaps owing to poor health.

$*$ $*$ $*$

I wish to thank Nadia ROBOTTI and Francesco GUERRA for many enlightening discussions and for letting me read (and make ample use of) the preliminary version of a historical paper on the early developments of nuclear physics in Rome.

L. A. RADICATI DI BROZOLO
Scuola Normale Superiore, Pisa

NOTA SCIENTIFICA n. 9   —   SCIENTIFIC PAPER no. 9

Teoria simmetrica dell'elettrone e del positrone

Nota di Ettore Majorana

"Il Nuovo Cimento", vol. 14, 1937, pp. 171-184.

Sunto. — Si dimostra la possibilità di pervenire a una piena simmetrizzazione formale della teoria quantistica dell'elettrone e del positrone facendo uso di un nuovo processo di quantizzazione. Il significato delle equazioni di Dirac ne risulta alquanto modificato e non vi è più luogo a parlare di stati di energia negativa; né a presumere per ogni altro tipo di particelle, particolarmente neutre, l'esistenza di "antiparticelle" corrispondenti ai "vuoti" di energia negativa.

L'interpretazione dei cosidetti "stati di energia negativa" proposta da Dirac[1] conduce, come è ben noto, a una descrizione sostanzialmente simmetrica degli elettroni e dei positroni. La sostanziale simmetria del formalismo consiste precisamente in questo, che fin dove è possibile applicare la teoria girando le difficoltà di convergenza, essa fornisce realmente risultati del tutto simmetrici. Tuttavia gli artifici suggeriti per dare alla teoria una forma simmetrica che si accordi con il suo contenuto, non sono del tutto soddisfacenti; sia perché si parte sempre da una impostazione asimmetrica, sia perché la simmetrizzazione viene in seguito ottenuta mediante tali procedimenti (come la cancellazione di costanti infinite) che possibilmente dovrebbero evitarsi. Perciò abbiamo tentato una nuova via che conduce più direttamente alla meta.

---

[1] P. A. M. Dirac, "Proc. Camb. Phil. Soc.", *30*, 150 (1924). V. anche W. Heinsenberg, "Z. Physik", *90*, 209 (1934).

Per quanto riguarda gli elettroni e i positroni, da essa si può veramente attendere soltanto un progresso formale; ma ci sembra importante, per le possibili estensioni analogiche, che venga a cadere la nozione stessa di stato di energia negativa. Vedremo infatti che è perfettamente possibile costruire, nella maniera più naturale, una teoria delle particelle neutre elementari senza stati negativi.

1. L'elettrodinamica quantistica si può dedurre, come si sa, mediante un processo di quantizzazione da un sistema di equazioni che comprende, da una parte, le equazioni d'onda dell'elettrone di Dirac, dall'altra le equazioni di Maxwell in cui le densità di carica e di corrente sono rappresentate da certe espressioni formate mediante la funzione d'onda elettronica. La forma che si dà a queste espressioni aggiunge in realtà qualcosa di nuovo alle equazioni di Dirac e soltanto da essa può derivare quella asimmetria rispetto al segno della carica che nelle equazioni di Dirac non esiste. Ma poiché tali espressioni risultano automaticamente dall'applicazione di un principio variazionale da cui si deducono insieme le equazioni di Maxwell e quelle di Dirac, il nostro problema sarà dunque di esaminare il fondamento di questo principio e la possibilità di sostituirlo con altro più appropriato.

Le grandezze che figurano nelle equazioni di Maxwell-Dirac sono notoriamente di due specie: da una parte si hanno i potenziali elettromagnetici, suscettibili entro i limiti del principio di corrispondenza di interpretazione classica, dall'altra le onde materiali che rappresentano particelle obbedienti alla statistica di Fermi e che hanno significato solo come grandezze quantistiche. In queste condizioni appare poco soddisfacente che le equazioni e tutto il processo di quantizzazione si facciano dipendere da un principio variazionale che è soltanto suscettibile di interpretazione classica. Sembra più naturale il cercare una generalizzazione dei metodi variazionali tale che le variabili le quali figurano nella funzione Lagrangiana abbiano, come è desiderabile, fin dal principio il loro significato finale; e rappresentino quindi delle grandezze non necessariamente commutabili. È questa appunto la via che seguiremo. Essa ha importanza sopra tutto per i campi legati alla statistica di Fermi, mentre per quanto riguarda il campo elettromagnetico ragioni di semplicità possono far presumere che nulla sia da aggiungere ai vecchi metodi. Non affronteremo del resto lo studio sistematico delle possibilità logiche offerte dal nuovo punto di vista in cui ci poniamo, ma ci limiteremo a descrivere un processo di quantizzazione dell'onda materiale che solo sembra avere attualmente importanza applicativa; esso si presenta come una naturale generalizzazione del metodo di Jordan-Wigner[2] e permette non solo di dare una forma simmetrica alla teoria degli elettroni-positroni, ma anche di costruire una teoria sostanzialmente nuova per le particelle senza carica elettrica (neutroni e ipotetici neutrini). Per quanto non sia forse ancora possibile chiedere all'esperienza una decisione fra questa nuova teoria e quella consistente nella semplice estensione delle equazioni di Dirac alle particelle neutre, va tenuto presente che la prima introduce, in questo campo ancora poco esplorato, un minor numero di entità ipotetiche.

(²) P. Jordan e E. Wigner, "Z. Physik", 47, 631 (1928).

Lasciando al lettore l'ovvia estensione delle formole seguenti ai sistemi continui di cui dovremo occuparci in seguito, esponiamo per maggiore chiarezza il metodo di quantizzazione con riferimento ai sistemi discreti. Sia dunque un sistema fisico descritto dalle variabili *reali* (matrici simmetriche Hermitiane) $q_1 q_2, \ldots, q_n$. Definiamo una funzione Lagrangiana

$$(1) \qquad L = i \sum_{r,s} \left(A_{rs} q_r \dot{q}_s + B_{rs} q_r q_s \right),$$

e poniamo

$$(2) \qquad \delta \int L dt = 0,$$

intendendo che in queste formule A_{rs} e B_{rs} sono numeri reali ordinari, costanti i primi ed eventualmente dipendenti dal tempo i secondi, e che soddisfano alle relazioni

$$(3) \qquad A_{rs} = A_{sr}; \qquad B_{rs} = -B_{sr},$$

essendo inoltre $\det \| A_{rs} \| \neq 0$.

Se le q fossero grandezze commutabili, il principio variazionale (2) non avrebbe alcun significato essendo identicamente verificato. Per grandezze non commutabili la (2) implica invece l'annullarsi in ogni istante della matrice Hermitiana

$$i \sum_r \left[\delta q_r \left(\sum_s A_{rs} \dot{q}_s + B_{rs} q_s \right) - \sum_s (A_{rs} \dot{q}_s + B_{rs} q_s) \delta q_r \right] = 0,$$

comunque si scelgano le variazioni δq_r. Questo è possibile solo se le espressioni $\sum_s (A_{rs} \dot{q}_s + B_{rs} q_s)$ sono multiple della matrice unità, in modo che con qualche opportuna aggiunta al principio variazionale (2) (per es. imponendo l'annullarsi della somma dei termini diagonali[3] in tali espressioni) si possono considerare le seguenti come equazioni del movimento

$$(4) \qquad \sum_s \left(A_{rs} \dot{q}_s + B_{rs} q_s \right) = 0 \qquad r = 1, 2, \ldots, n.$$

Vogliamo ora mostrare che queste equazioni possono farsi dipendere nel modo consueto

$$\dot{q}_r = -\frac{2\pi i}{h} \left(q_r H - H q_r \right)$$

---

[3] L'applicazione fisica che è esposta più avanti suggerisce la restrizione più rigorosa che in qualunque combinazione lineare delle q_r e $\dot{q}_r$ con ogni autovalore debba presentarsene un altro uguale e opposto.

dall'Hamiltoniana

(5) $$H = -i \sum_{r,s} B_{rs} q_r q_s,$$

la cui forma esatta sarà meglio giustificata in seguito, purché si stabiliscano fra le q_r opportune relazioni di *anticommutabilità*. Sostituendo nelle (4) mediante le equazioni successive si trova infatti(*)

$$\sum_s B_{rs} q_s = \frac{2\pi}{h} \sum_{s,l,m} A_{rs} B_{lm} (q_s q_l q_m - q_l q_m q_s) =$$

$$= \frac{2\pi}{h} \sum_{s,l,m} A_{rs} B_{lm} \left[(q_s q_l + q_l q_s) q_m - q_l (q_s q_m + q_m q_s) \right] =$$

$$= \frac{2\pi}{h} \sum_{lm} B_{lm} \left\{ q_m \left[\sum_s A_{rs} (q_s q_l + q_l q_s) \right] + \left[\sum_s A_{rs} (q_s q_l + q_l q_s) \right] q_m \right\},$$

e basta porre

(6) $$\sum_s A_{rs} (q_s q_l + q_l q_s) = \frac{h}{4\pi} \delta_{rl},$$

perché le (4) siano soddisfatte. Indicando con $\|A_{rs}^{-1}\|$ la matrice inversa di $\|A_{rs}\|$ la (6) può scriversi

(6') $$q_r q_s + q_s q_r = \frac{h}{4\pi} A_{rs}^{-1}.$$

Nel caso speciale che A sia ridotta a forma diagonale

$$A_{rs} = a_r \delta_{rs},$$

si avrà dunque

(7) $$q_r q_s + q_s q_r = \frac{h}{4\pi a_r} \delta_{rs}.$$

Passiamo ora ad applicare questo schema alle equazioni di Dirac.

(*) Ne "Il Nuovo Cimento", nell'ultimo termine dell'equazione prima della parentesi graffa finale compare erroneamente una parentesi quadra di troppo. (Nota del Curatore.)

2. Dalle equazioni di Dirac senza campo esterno

$$(8) \qquad \left[\frac{W}{c} + (\alpha, p) + \beta mc\right]\psi = 0,$$

può notoriamente essere eliminata l'unità immaginaria (e in modo relativisticamente invariante) con un'opportuna scelta degli operatori α e β. Noi ci riferiremo appunto ad un sistema di coordinate intrinseche tale che renda le (8) reali, avvertendo espressamente che le formole a cui perverremo non sono valide, senza opportune modificazioni, in coordinate generali. Indicando come di consueto, con σ_x, σ_y, σ_z e ρ_1, ρ_2, ρ_3 due terne indipendenti di matrici di Pauli, porremo:

$$(9) \qquad \alpha_x = \rho_1\sigma_x; \qquad \alpha_y = \rho_3; \qquad \alpha_z = \rho_1\sigma_z; \qquad \beta = -\rho_1\sigma_y;$$

con che dividendo le (9) per $-\frac{h}{2\pi i}$ e ponendovi $\beta' = -i\beta$, $\mu = \frac{2\pi mc}{h}$ si hanno le equazioni reali

$$(8') \qquad \left[\frac{1}{c}\frac{\partial}{\partial t} - (\alpha, \mathrm{grad}) + \beta'\mu\right]\psi = 0.$$

In conseguenza le (8) si scindono in due gruppi distinti, di cui l'uno agisce sulla parte reale, l'altro sulla parte immaginaria di ψ. Poniamo $\psi = U + iV$ e consideriamo le equazioni reali (8') in quanto agiscono sulle U:

$$(10) \qquad \left[\frac{1}{c}\frac{\partial}{\partial t} - (\alpha, \mathrm{grad}) + \beta'\mu\right]U = 0.$$

Queste equazioni *da sole*[4], cioè senza considerare le equazioni identiche che legano le V, possono essere ricondotte al principio variazionale esposto anteriormente ed assoggettate al processo di quantizzazione già descritto, mentre nulla di simile potrebbe farsi con i metodi elementari.

Come principio variazionale da cui dedurre le (10) assumiamo il seguente:

$$(11) \qquad \delta\int i\frac{hc}{2\pi}U^*\left[\frac{1}{c}\frac{\partial}{\partial t} - (\alpha, \mathrm{grad}) + \beta'\mu\right]U\,dq\,dt = 0.$$

È facile riconoscere che le condizioni (3) nella loro naturale estensione ai sistemi continui sono verificate. Seguono in base alle (7) le relazioni di anticommutabilità

$$(12) \qquad U_i(q)U_k(q') + U_k(q')U_i(q) = \frac{1}{2}\delta_{ik}\delta(q - q'),$$

---

[4] Il comportamento delle U per riflessione in un punto dello spazio si può definire convenientemente tenendo presente che, già per altre ragioni, un cambiamento simultaneo di segno delle U_r non ha significato fisico. Nel nostro schema: $U'(q) = RU(-q)$ con $R = i\rho_1\sigma_y$ e quindi $R^2 = -1$. Similmente se si inverte l'asse del tempo: $U'(q, t) = i\rho_2 U(q, -t)$.

mentre l'energia diviene, per la (5):

(13)
$$H = \int U^* \left[-c(\alpha, p) - \beta mc^2 \right] U dq.$$

L'invarianza relativistica di (12) e (13) non richiede particolare dimostrazione, poiché completando tali equazioni con quelle analoghe che si riferiscono alle V, nonché con le relazioni di anticommutabilità fra le U e le V : $U_r(q)V_s(q') + V_s(q')U_r(q) = 0$, si riottiene null'altro che l'ordinario schema di Jordan-Wigner applicato alle equazioni di Dirac senza campo. Ma è notevole che la parte di tale formalismo che si riferisce alle U (o alle V) possa *da sola* essere considerata come descrizione teorica, in armonia con i metodi generali della meccanica quantistica, di un qualche sistema materiale. Il fatto che tale formalismo ridotto non si adatti alla descrizione degli elettroni positivi e negativi, può bene essere dovuto alla presenza della carica elettrica e non impedisce l'affermazione che allo stato attuale delle nostre conoscenze le (12) e (13) costituiscono la più semplice rappresentazione teorica di un sistema di particelle neutre. Il vantaggio di questo procedimento rispetto alla interpretazione elementare delle equazioni di Dirac è (come vedremo meglio fra poco) che non vi è più nessuna ragione di presumere l'esistenza di antineutroni o antineutrini. Questi ultimi vengono in realtà utilizzati nella teoria dell'emissione β positiva[5], ma tale teoria può essere, ovviamente, modificata in modo che l'emissione β, sia negativa che positiva, venga sempre accompagnata dall'emissione di un neutrino.

In ragione dell'interesse che l'ipotesi suddetta conferisce alle equazioni (12) e (13), crediamo utile esaminarne da vicino il significato. Sviluppiamo perciò le U nell'interno di un cubo di lato L secondo il sistema di funzioni periodiche

(14)
$$f_\gamma(q) = \frac{1}{L^{3/2}} e^{2\pi i(\gamma, q)},$$

$$\gamma = (\gamma_x, \gamma_y, \gamma_z); \qquad \gamma_x = \frac{n_1}{L}, \qquad \gamma_y = \frac{n_2}{L}, \qquad \gamma_z = \frac{n_3}{L} :$$

$$n_1, n_2, n_3 = 0, \pm 1, \pm 2, \ldots$$

ponendo

(15)
$$U_r(q) = \sum_\gamma a_r(\gamma) f_\gamma(q).$$

In conseguenza della realità delle U, sarà

(16)
$$a_r(\gamma) = \bar{a}_r(-\gamma).$$

---

[5] Cfr. G. Wick, "Rend. Accad. Lincei", 21, 170 (1935).

Ponendoci nel caso generale $\gamma \neq 0$, segue dalle (12)

(17)
$$\begin{cases} a_r(\gamma)\bar{a}_s(\gamma) + \bar{a}_s(\gamma)a_r(\gamma) = \dfrac{1}{2}\delta_{rs}, \\ a_r(\gamma)a_s(\gamma) + a_s(\gamma)a_r(\gamma) = 0, \\ \bar{a}_r(\gamma)\bar{a}_s(\gamma) + \bar{a}_s(\gamma)\bar{a}_r(\gamma) = 0. \end{cases}$$

Tutte queste grandezze sono inoltre anticommutabili con le $a(\gamma')$ e $\bar{a}(\gamma')$ per γ' diverso sia da γ che da $-\gamma$.

L'energia risulta per la (13):

(18)
$$H = \sum_\gamma \sum_{r,s=1}^{4} \left[-hc(\gamma, \alpha^{rs}) - mc^2\beta^{rs} \right] \bar{a}_r(\gamma)a_s(\gamma).$$

La quantità di moto secondo x corrisponde, come sempre, a meno del fattore $\frac{h}{2\pi}i$ allo spostamento unitario in tale direzione

(19)
$$M_x = \int U^* p_x U \, dq = \sum_\gamma \sum_{r=1} h\gamma_x \bar{a}_r(\gamma)a_k(\gamma),$$

e analogamente per M_y e M_z.

Per ogni valore di γ figura in (18) una forma Hermitiana che ha notoriamente due autovalori positivi e due negativi, tutti uguali in valore assoluto a $c\sqrt{m^2c^2 + h^2\gamma^2}$.

Possiamo quindi porre in luogo di (18)

(18')
$$H = \sum_\gamma c\sqrt{m^2c^2 + h^2\gamma^2} \left[\bar{b}_1(\gamma)b_1(\gamma) + \bar{b}_2(\gamma)b_2(\gamma) - \bar{b}_3(\gamma)b_3(\gamma) - \bar{b}_4(\gamma)b_4(\gamma) \right]$$

essendo le b_r opportune combinazioni lineari delle a_r ottenute per trasformazione unitaria. Risulta inoltre dalla (16) che le $b_r(\gamma)$ sono esprimibili linearmente mediante le $\bar{b}_r(-\gamma)$.

Dal fatto poi che la forma Hermitiana che figura in (18) per un dato valore di γ resta invariata in virtù di (16) e (17) quando si cambia γ in $-\gamma$ segue tenendo ancora conto di (17) che si può porre:

(20)
$$b_3(\gamma) = \bar{b}_1(-\gamma); \qquad b_4(\gamma) = \bar{b}_2(-\gamma).$$

Introducendo per semplicità le nuove variabili

(21)
$$B_1(\gamma) = \sqrt{2}b_1(\gamma); \qquad B_2(\gamma) = \sqrt{2}b_2(\gamma),$$

otteniamo così

$$(22) \qquad H = \sum_{\gamma} c\sqrt{m^2c^2 + h^2\gamma^2} \sum_{r=1}^{2} \left[n_r(\gamma) - \frac{1}{2} \right],$$

$$(23) \qquad M_x = \sum_{\gamma} h\gamma_x \sum_{r=1}^{2} \left[n_r(\gamma) - \frac{1}{2} \right],$$

essendosi posto

$$n_r(\gamma) = \bar{B}_r(\gamma)B_r(\gamma) = \underset{1}{\overset{0}{\diagdown}}$$

ed essendo(*) inoltre

$$(24) \qquad \begin{cases} B_r(\gamma)\bar{B}_s(\gamma') + \bar{B}_s(\gamma')B_r(\gamma) = \delta_{\gamma\gamma'}\delta_{rs}, \\ B_r(\gamma)B_s(\gamma') + B_s(\gamma')B_r(\gamma) = 0, \\ \bar{B}_r(\gamma)\bar{B}_s(\gamma') + \bar{B}_s(\gamma')\bar{B}_r(\gamma) = 0, \end{cases}$$

come si otterrebbe formalmente per i coefficienti dello sviluppo di un'onda materiale *a due componenti* secondo lo schema di Jordan-Wigner.

Queste formole sono completamente analoghe, salvo la diversa statistica, a quelle che si ottengono dalla quantizzazione delle equazioni di Maxwell. In luogo di quanti immateriali si hanno particelle con una massa di riposo finita e anche esse con due possibilità di polarizzazione. Anche qui *come nel caso della radiazione*, sono presenti i mezzi quanti di riposo della energia e della quantità di moto, salvo che il loro segno è opposto in apparente relazione con la diversa statistica. Essi non costituiscono pertanto una difficoltà specifica e allo stato attuale della teoria debbono anche qui essere considerati come semplici costanti additive prive di significato.

La descrizione mediante autofunzioni di queste particelle, così come dei quanti di luce, non riesce in modo conveniente, ma nel nostro caso l'esistenza di una massa di riposo permette di considerare l'*approssimazione non relativistica*, nella quale sono naturalmente valide tutte le nozioni della meccanica quantistica elementare. Questa approssimazione può avere interesse pratico sopra tutto nel caso di particelle pesanti (neutroni).

Il mezzo più semplice per passare allo spazio delle configurazioni consiste nell'associare a un generico oscillatore l'onda piana

$$\frac{1}{L^{3/2}} e^{2\pi i(\gamma, q)} \delta_{\sigma\sigma_r}, \qquad (r = 1, 2),$$

(*) Ne "Il Nuovo Cimento" è in realtà scritto "essendosi" e non essendo. (Nota del Curatore in E. Amaldi, *op. cit.*)

corrispondente allo stesso valore della quantità di moto e con due possibilità di polarizzazione per tenere conto della molteplicità degli oscillatori. Possiamo andare oltre e
rappresentare con l'autofunzione complessa a due valori $\Phi = (\Phi_1, \Phi_2)$ non più una sola
particella ma un sistema che ne contenga in numero indeterminato secondo il metodo di
Jordan-Wigner. Basterà allora porre

(25)
$$\begin{cases} \Phi_1(q) = \sum_\gamma \frac{1}{L^{3/2}} e^{2\pi i(\gamma, q)} B_1(\gamma), \\ \Phi_2(q) = \sum_\gamma \frac{1}{L^{3/2}} e^{2\pi i(\gamma, q)} B_2(\gamma). \end{cases}$$

Nell'approssimazione non relativistica ($|\gamma| \ll \frac{mc}{h}$) le costanti $b_r(\gamma)$ che figurano
in (18') sono combinazioni lineari della $a_r(\gamma)$ con *coefficienti indipendenti da γ*.
Tali coefficienti dipendono solo dagli elementi di β e in virtù di (9) si può porre

$$b_1(\gamma) = \frac{a_3(\gamma) - i a_2(\gamma)}{\sqrt{2}}; \qquad b_3(\gamma) = \frac{a_3(\gamma) + i a_2(\gamma)}{\sqrt{2}},$$

$$b_2(\gamma) = \frac{a_4(\gamma) + i a_1(\gamma)}{\sqrt{2}}; \qquad b_4(\gamma) = \frac{a_4(\gamma) - i a_1(\gamma)}{\sqrt{2}},$$

con che anche le (20), a causa di (16), sono soddisfatte. Dalle (15) e (25) segue dunque
per l'approssimazione non relativistica:

(26)
$$\begin{cases} \Phi_1(q) = U_3(q) - i U_2(q), \\ \Phi_2(q) = U_4(q) + i U_1(q). \end{cases}$$

Notiamo la circostanza, di interesse puramente formale, che $\Phi = (\Phi_1, \Phi_2)$ coincide a
meno del fattore $\sqrt{2}$ con la coppia di componenti *grandi* delle autofunzioni appartenenti
alle equazioni (10), interpretate nel modo consueto, senza cioè restrizioni di realtà. Per
dimostrarlo basta verificare che la trasformazione $\psi = \frac{1 - \rho_2 \sigma_y}{\sqrt{2}} U$ permette di passare dallo
schema (9) a quello usuale di Dirac ($\alpha = \rho_1 \sigma$; $\beta = \rho_3$) e che risulta effettivamente

$$\psi_3 = \frac{1}{\sqrt{2}} \Phi_1, \qquad \psi_4 = \frac{1}{\sqrt{2}} \Phi_2;$$

in tale schema sono infatti notoriamente ψ_3 e ψ_4 le componenti grandi. Questo avvici-
namento, se chiarisce la legge di trasformazione di Φ di fronte alle rotazioni nello spazio,
cessa naturalmente di avere significato in rapporto alle trasformazioni generali di Lorentz.

L'esistenza di formole semplici come le (26), potrebbe fare ritenere superfluo, almeno
fino a una certa approssimazione, il passaggio attraverso le onde piane. In realtà tale
passaggio è sempre concettualmente necessario per ottenere la cancellazione dei *mezzi*

quanti di riposo. Dopo tale cancellazione l'espressione dell'energia è infatti naturalmente in prima approssimazione

$$(27) \qquad H = \int \tilde{\Phi} \left(mc^2 + \frac{1}{2m} p^2 \right) \Phi dq,$$

e differisce quindi in modo essenziale dalla (13).

3. Come abbiamo già detto, lo schema (12) non è sufficiente per la descrizione di particelle cariche; ma l'aggiunta di una seconda quaterna di grandezze reali V_r analoghe alle U_r permette di riottenere l'ordinaria elettrodinamica in una forma simmetrica rispetto all'elettrone e al positrone. Consideriamo dunque due serie di grandezze reali rappresentanti rispettivamente le particelle materiali e il campo elettromagnetico. Le grandezze della prima specie vanno interpretate secondo lo schema esposto al n. 1, mentre quelle della seconda serie, e cioè i potenziali elettromagnetici φ e $A = (A_x, A_y, A_z)$ possono intendersi come grandezze classiche quantizzate secondo la regola di Heisenberg fondata sul principio di corrispondenza. L'insieme delle equazioni di Maxwell e Dirac si potrà ottenere (con l'accennata restrizione per quanto riguarda le seconde) da un principio variazionale(*)

$$\delta \int L dq dt = 0$$

risultando L dalla somma di tre termini

$$L = L' + L'' + L'''$$

di cui il primo è relativo all'onda materiale

$$(28) \qquad L' = i \frac{hc}{2\pi} \left\{ U^* \left[\frac{1}{c} \frac{\partial}{\partial t} - (\alpha, \mathrm{grad}) + \beta' \mu \right] U + \right.$$
$$\left. + V^* \left[\frac{1}{c} \frac{\partial}{\partial t} - (\alpha, \mathrm{grad}) + \beta' \mu \right] V \right\},$$

e il secondo si riferisce al campo di radiazione che supponiamo quantizzato secondo il metodo di FERMI([6])

$$(29) \qquad L'' = \frac{1}{8\pi} \left(E^2 - H^2 \right) - \frac{1}{8\pi} \left(\frac{1}{c} \dot{\varphi} + \mathrm{div}\, A \right)^2.$$

(*) Ne "Il Nuovo Cimento" manca erroneamente il membro di destra dell'equazione "= 0". (Nota del Curatore, si veda anche E. Amaldi, *op. cit.*)
([6]) E. FERMI, "Rend. Accad. Lincei", *9*, 881 (1929).

Bisogna quindi imporre la condizione aggiunta

(30) $$\frac{1}{c}\dot{\varphi} + \text{div}\, A = 0.$$

L'espressione (29) differisce in realtà da quella usata originariamente da FERMI, ma solo per termini integrabili. Essa conduce a una definizione del momento P_0 coniugato a φ tale da permettere l'immediata eliminazione di una delle due onde longitudinali senza passare per lo sviluppo secondo le onde piane; è a questo riguardo del tutto indifferente che il secondo termine nell'espressione (29) di L'' venga moltiplicato per una costante arbitraria diversa da zero.

Quanto al termine L''', esso va scelto in modo che $\psi = U + iV$ obbedisca alle equazioni di Dirac (8) completate con l'introduzione del campo esterno, cioè alle equazioni:

$$\left[\frac{W}{c} + \frac{e}{c}\varphi + \left(\alpha, p + \frac{e}{c}A\right) + \beta mc\right]\psi = 0.$$

Questo praticamente obbliga a porre

(31) $$L''' = ieU^*[\varphi + (\alpha, A)]V - ieV^*[\varphi + (\alpha, A)]U.$$

Dalla variazione dei potenziali elettromagnetici si deducono allora le seguenti espressioni per le densità di carica e di corrente

(32) $$\begin{cases} \rho = -ie(U^*V - V^*U) = -e\dfrac{\tilde{\psi}\psi - \psi^*\bar{\psi}}{2}, \\[3mm] I = ie(U^*\alpha V - V^*\alpha U) = e\dfrac{\tilde{\psi}\alpha\psi - \psi^*\alpha\bar{\psi}}{2}. \end{cases}$$

Queste espressioni differiscono da quelle consuete solo per *costanti infinite*. La cancellazione di tali costanti infinite è richiesta dalla simmetrizzazione della teoria che è già implicita nella forma scelta per il principio variazionale; infatti lo scambio di U_r e V_r, che entrano simmetricamente in L', equivale appunto a un cambiamento di segno della carica elettrica.

Le U e V obbediscono alle relazioni di anticommutabilità

$$U_r(q)U_s(q') + U_s(q')U_r(q) = \frac{1}{2}\delta(q - q')\delta_{rs},$$

$$V_r(q)V_s(q') + V_s(q')V_r(q) = \frac{1}{2}\delta(q - q')\delta_{rs},$$

$$U_r(q)V_s(q') + V_s(q')U_r(q) = 0,$$

equivalenti all'ordinario schema di Jordan-Wigner quando si faccia $\psi = U + iV$. I potenziali elettromagnetici φ, A_x, A_y, A_z e i loro momenti coniugati soddisfanno invece alle

ordinarie relazioni di commutabilità, ad esempio $P_0(q)\varphi(q') - \varphi(q')P_0(q) = \frac{h}{2\pi i}\delta(q - q')$ essendo ora

$$(33) \qquad \begin{cases} P_0 = -\dfrac{1}{4\pi c}\left(\dfrac{1}{c}\dot\varphi + \operatorname{div} A\right), \\[3mm] P_x = -\dfrac{1}{4\pi c}E_x; \qquad P_y = -\dfrac{1}{4\pi c}E_y; \qquad P_z = -\dfrac{1}{4\pi c}E_z. \end{cases}$$

L'energia consta di tre parti: $H = H' + H'' + H'''$. Il primo termine H' si deduce da L' secondo le regole già esposte. Il secondo si ottiene secondo le regole classiche $H'' = \int[P_0\dot\varphi + (P, A) - L'']dq$, essendosi posto $P = (P_x, P_y, P_z)$. Quanto al termine H''', esso si può dedurre da L''' seguendo indifferentemente l'uno o l'altro metodo (nel nostro caso $H''' = -\int L'''dq$) e così deve essere dato che L''' è funzione tanto delle grandezze di campo materiali che di quelle elettromagnetiche. Questo prova d'altronde la necessità della posizione (5). L'equazione di continuità (30) è valida sempre purché sia soddisfatta inizialmente insieme con l'equazione della divergenza $\operatorname{div} E = 4\pi\rho$. Segue, per le (33), che la cinematica definita dalle relazioni di scambio deve essere ridotta mediante le equazioni

$$(34) \qquad \begin{cases} P_0(q) = 0, \\[3mm] \operatorname{div} P + \dfrac{1}{c}\rho = 0, \end{cases}$$

e quindi mediante la fissazione di due grandezze di campo e conseguente indeterminazione delle coniugate. *La prima* delle (34) importa dunque l'eliminazione di P_0 e di φ dall'espressione di H. Tale eliminazione si ottiene facilmente facendo uso delle (33) e si giunge così alla formola

$$(35) \qquad H = \int\left\{\tilde\psi[-c(\alpha, p) - \beta mc^2]\psi - (A, I) + 2\pi cP^2 + \frac{1}{8\pi}\left|\operatorname{rot} A\right|^2\right\}dq.$$

Circa la questione dell'invarianza relativistica, osserviamo che le $\psi = U + iV$ soddisfano alle equazioni di Dirac, mentre le equazioni di Maxwell continuano anche esse a valere con espressioni delle densità di carica e di corrente che obbediscono alla legge di trasformazione relativistica. Queste due circostanze assicurano che la dimostrazione completa dell'invarianza della teoria è già implicita nei risultati di HEISENBERG e PAULI[7]. Passiamo ora all'interpretazione del formalismo.

4. Sviluppando la U, e analogamente la V, secondo il sistema di funzioni periodiche già considerato, troviamo come ovvia estensione della (22), dopo la cancellazione dei

---

[7] W. HEISENBERG e W. PAULI, "Z. Physik", *56*, 1 (1929); *59*, 168 (1930).

mezzi quanti di riposo

$$(36) \qquad H' = \sum_\gamma c\sqrt{m^2c^2 + h^2\gamma^2} \sum_{r=1}^{2} \left[\bar{B}_r(\gamma) B_r(\gamma) + \bar{B}'_r(\gamma) B'_r(\gamma) \right],$$

riferendosi le B_r e B'_r rispettivamente allo sviluppo delle U e V; le B_r e B'_r e le loro coniugate obbediscono alle consuete relazioni di anticommutabilità. Introducendo, per ogni valore di γ, quattro opportune funzioni di spin $\xi_s(\gamma)$ ($s = 1, 2, 3, 4$) a quattro valori complessi e formanti un sistema unitario, si potrà porre

$$(37) \quad \begin{cases} U = \dfrac{1}{\sqrt{2}} \sum_\gamma \left\{ B_1(\gamma)\xi_1(\gamma) + B_2(\gamma)\xi_2(\gamma) + \bar{B}_1(-\gamma)\xi_3(\gamma) + \bar{B}_2(-\gamma)\xi_4(\gamma) \right\} f_\gamma(q), \\[2mm] V = \dfrac{1}{\sqrt{2}} \sum_\gamma \left\{ B'_1(\gamma)\xi_1(\gamma) + B'_2(\gamma)\xi_2(\gamma) + \bar{B}'_1(-\gamma)\xi_3(\gamma) + \bar{B}'_2(-\gamma)\xi_4(\gamma) \right\} f_\gamma(q), \end{cases}$$

essendo inoltre soddisfatte le relazioni

$$(38) \qquad \begin{cases} \xi_3(\gamma) = \bar{\xi}_1(-\gamma), \\ \xi_4(\gamma) = \bar{\xi}_2(-\gamma). \end{cases}$$

Dall'espressione (32) della densità di elettricità segue per la carica totale

$$(39) \qquad Q = -\frac{ie}{2} \int \left[U^*(q)V(q) - V^*(q)U(q) \right] dq =$$

$$= -\frac{ie}{2} \sum_\gamma \sum_{r=1}^{2} \left[B_r(\gamma)\bar{B}'_r(\gamma) + \bar{B}_r(\gamma)B'_r(\gamma) - \bar{B}'_r(\gamma)B_r(\gamma) - B'_r(\gamma)\bar{B}_r(\gamma) \right].$$

Se si pone

$$(40) \qquad C^{\mathrm{el}}_r = \frac{B_r + iB'_r}{\sqrt{2}}; \qquad C^{\mathrm{pos}}_r = \frac{B_r - iB'_r}{\sqrt{2}}$$

le espressioni (36) e (39) dell'energia e della carica si possono portare nella forma

$$(41) \qquad H' = \sum_\gamma c\sqrt{m^2c^2 + h^2\gamma^2} \sum_{r=1}^{2} \left(\bar{C}^{\mathrm{el}}_r C^{\mathrm{el}}_r + \bar{C}^{\mathrm{pos}}_r C^{\mathrm{pos}}_r \right)$$

$$(42) \qquad Q = e \sum_\gamma \sum_{r=1}^{2} \left[-\left(\bar{C}^{\mathrm{el}}_r C^{\mathrm{el}}_r - \frac{1}{2} \right) + \bar{C}^{\mathrm{pos}}_r C^{\mathrm{pos}}_r - \frac{1}{2} \right] =$$

$$= e \sum_\gamma \sum_{r=1}^{2} \left(- \bar{C}^{\mathrm{el}}_r C^{\mathrm{el}}_r + \bar{C}^{\mathrm{pos}}_r C^{\mathrm{pos}}_r \right).$$

L'eliminazione dei *mezzi quanti di riposo di elettricità* avviene dunque automaticamente purché, bene inteso, si esegua prima la sommatoria interna. L'insieme di (41) e (42) rappresenta oscillatori equivalenti a un doppio sistema di particelle obbedienti alla statistica di Fermi con la massa di riposo m e la carica $\pm e$; le variabili C_r^{pos} si riferiscono ai positroni e le C_r^{el} agli elettroni.

L'eliminazione del campo elettrico longitudinale mediante la seconda delle (34) presenta difficoltà in una teoria simmetrica per l'impossibilità di porre ρ, quale risulta da (32), in forma diagonale. Il risultato dell'eliminazione è ben noto (per quanto parzialmente illusorio per difficoltà di convergenza) nell'elettrodinamica ordinaria in cui si pone $\rho = -e\tilde{\psi}\psi$; ma esso è egualmente noto se si parte da $\rho = e\psi^*\bar{\psi}$ poiché quest'ultima posizione equivale interamente a invertire l'ufficio dell'elettrone e del positrone, considerando quest'ultimo come particella reale e l'elettrone come "vuoto" di positrone. Sembra plausibile che quegli elementi di matrice che risultassero della stessa forma in tali teorie opposte, si debbono conservare nella teoria simmetrica. Supponiamo dunque di aver proceduto alla eliminazione della parte irrotazionale di A e P.

L'espressione (35) di H verrà modificata in due modi: in primo luogo intendendo che A e P in questa espressione rappresentino solo la parte priva di divergenza di tali vettori; e in secondo luogo aggiungendo un termine che rappresenta l'energia elettrostatica. Questo termine ha una forma differente nella teoria ordinaria (elettrone-vuoto di elettrone) e in quella opposta. Nella prima si ha conservando l'interazione di ogni particella con se stessa

$$H_{\text{els}} = \frac{e^2}{2} \iint \frac{1}{|q - q'|} \tilde{\psi}(q)\psi(q)\tilde{\psi}(q')\psi(q')\,dq\,dq',$$

e nella seconda

$$H_{\text{els}} = \frac{e^2}{2} \iint \frac{1}{|q - q'|} \psi^*(q)\bar{\psi}(q)\psi^*(q')\bar{\psi}(q')\,dq\,dq'.$$

Mediante le (37) e (40) si può esprimere l'energia elettrostatica in funzione delle C. I soli termini elettrostatici che hanno ricevuto applicazione fisica sono peraltro identici nelle due teorie; essi sono quelli che dal punto di vista corpuscolare si lasciano interpretare come repulsione o attrazione fra particelle distinte della stessa specie o di specie differente.

Per quanto infine concerne l'interazione con il campo di radiazione, l'unica differenza fra la teoria simmetrica e quella ordinaria riguarda la cancellazione di costanti di risultante indeterminata, relative ai singoli oscillatori, nell'espressione della densità di corrente; anche qui rimangono invariate le formole di interesse applicativo.

Commento alla Nota Scientifica n. 9 : *"Teoria simmetrica dell'elettrone e del positrone".*

Scritto nel 1937, un anno prima della sua tragica scomparsa, questo lavoro rappresenta probabilmente il contributo più duraturo di Ettore Majorana alla Fisica moderna. Il lavoro è scritto in un italiano elegante e conciso (la traduzione in inglese è risultata più lunga del testo originale) ed affronta il problema di formulare la teoria di Dirac eliminando del tutto l'armamentario degli stati ad energia negativa.

Nella usuale formulazione, si parte da una situazione altamente asimmetrica tra elettroni e positroni, per arrivare solo alla fine a scoprire che le due particelle sono perfettamente simmetriche tra loro. La simmetria elettrone-positrone è talmente poco evidente che lo stesso Dirac, nella sua prima formulazione, aveva proposto di identificare le particelle positive, le lacune, con il protone.

Riferendosi alla formulazione originale, Majorana nota che

"... gli artifici suggeriti per dare alla teoria una forma simmetrica che si accordi con il suo contenuto, non sono del tutto soddisfacenti; sia perché si parte sempre da una impostazione asimmetrica, sia perché la simmetrizzazione viene in seguito ottenuta mediante tali procedimenti (come la cancellazione di costanti infinite) che possibilmente dovrebbero evitarsi. Perciò abbiamo tentato una nuova via che conduce più direttamente alla meta."

Partendo da queste premesse, Majorana delinea una teoria di campo basata su variabili anticommutanti, prive quindi di analogia classica, e deriva l'equazione di Dirac da un principio variazionale.

L'elettrone è rappresentato da un campo complesso, che si può decomporre in parte reale e parte immaginaria. Tuttavia, nella particolare rappresentazione delle matrici di Dirac in cui esse sono tutte immaginarie (da allora nota come rappresentazione di Majorana) ciascuna delle due componenti può, separatamente, *"essere considerata come una descrizione teorica, in armonia con i metodi generali della meccanica quantistica, di un qualche sistema materiale"*.

Naturalmente, Majorana riconosce prontamente che per l'elettrone, che possiede una carica elettrica conservata, non si può fare a meno di considerare le due componenti allo stesso tempo. Ma l'economicità dello schema lo porta naturalmente a supporre che esso possa trovare applicazione per le particelle neutre.

"Il vantaggio di questo procedimento... è che non vi è più nessuna ragione per presumere l'esistenza di antineutroni o antineutrini. Questi ultimi vengono in realtà utiliz-

zati nella teoria dell'emissione β positiva, ma tale teoria può essere ovviamente modificata in modo che l'emissione β, sia positiva sia negativa, venga sempre accompagnata dall'emissione di un neutrino."

Majorana si riferisce qui alla teoria dei raggi β positivi, formulata appena due anni prima, sempre a Roma, da Giancarlo Wick.

Dalla riformulazione della teoria di Dirac emerge una possibilità fisica del tutto inattesa, che da allora è stata oggetto di scrutinio sperimentale e teorico, ed alla quale non siamo riusciti ancora a dare una risposta.

La proposta del neutrino di Majorana ha avuto sorti alterne e si è intrecciata con la "teoria a due componenti" del neutrino formulata da Herman Weyl qualche anno prima, nel 1929.

È un fatto che le particelle emesse nei decadimenti β negativi e in quelli β positivi si comportano diversamente: nella loro interazione con i nuclei atomici i primi producono solo positroni, ed i secondi solo elettroni. Tuttavia, la forma $V - A$ dell'interazione e la teoria di Weyl permettono di associare questa differenza alla differenza di elicità delle due particelle.

Poiché l'elicità è conservata per una particella di massa nulla, deviazioni da questo comportamento si avrebbero solo per termini dell'ordine del rapporto (massa del neutrino)/(energia del neutrino), che assume valori completamente trascurabili nelle reazioni iniziate da neutrini.

La natura di Majorana del neutrino si può mettere alla prova con l'osservazione dei decadimenti *doppio-β senza neutrino*. Sono processi di secondo ordine nell'interazione di Fermi. Nel primo passo viene emesso, insieme ad un elettrone, un neutrino virtuale con elicità positiva, che successivamente viene assorbito come se fosse un neutrino (elicità negativa), con emissione di un secondo elettrone. Il processo complessivo, $N^* \rightarrow N + 2e$, viola la conservazione del numero leptonico ed ha un'ampiezza proporzionale alla massa di Majorana del neutrino. La sua esistenza sarebbe la prova evidente che *"non vi è alcuna ragione per presumere... l'esistenza di... antineutrini."*

Rimasta a lungo come una possibilità alquanto esotica, il neutrino di Majorana è emerso, ai nostri giorni, come la spiegazione più naturale della piccolissima massa del neutrino.

Inoltre, l'assenza di un numero leptonico conservato, L, analogo alla carica dell'elettrone, permette di speculare che proprio il decadimento di neutrini di Majorana super-pesanti abbia dato luogo, nell'Universo primordiale, ad un'asimmetria in L, trasformata poi, in virtù della stretta conservazione della combinazione $B - L$ ($B =$ numero barionico), nell'asimmetria materia-antimateria del nostro Universo.

In diversi laboratori sotterranei in giro per il mondo si è cercato di mettere in evidenza il decadimento doppio-β senza neutrini, finora senza successo. Presso i Laboratori del Gran Sasso dell'INFN è in preparazione un esperimento di dimensioni mai raggiunte prima, CUORE, che dovrebbe porre limiti molto stringenti al processo doppio β,... oppure osservarlo.

Mi piace pensare che proprio nel nostro Paese si possa rispondere affermativamente alla domanda posta sul tappeto da Majorana più di mezzo secolo fa, e dare allo stesso tempo una possibile spiegazione alla preponderanza della materia sull'antimateria nell'Universo, da cui è dipesa la nostra stessa esistenza.

LUCIANO MAIANI
Università di Roma "La Sapienza"

A symmetric theory of electrons and positrons(*)

Ettore Majorana

Summary. — It is shown that it is possible to achieve complete formal symmetrization in the electron and proton quantum theory by means of a new quantization process. The meaning of Dirac equations is somewhat modified and there is no longer any reason to speak of negative-energy states nor to assume, for any other types of particles, especially neutral ones, the existence of antiparticles, corresponding to the "holes" of negative energy.

The interpretation of the so-called "negative energy states" proposed by Dirac[1] leads, as is well known, to a substantially symmetric description of electrons and positrons. The substantial symmetry of the formalism consists precisely in that the theory itself gives completely symmetric results, whenever it is possible to apply it while overcoming divergence problems.

The prescriptions needed to cast the theory into a symmetric form, in conformity with its content, are however not entirely satisfactory, because one always starts from an asymmetric form or because symmetric results are obtained only after one applies appropriate procedures, such as the cancellation of divergent constants, that one should

---

(*) Translated from "Il Nuovo Cimento", vol. 14, 1937, pp. 171-184, by Luciano Maiani in "Soryushiron Kenkyu", *63* (1981) 149-462. (Courtesy of L. Maiani.) The present translation has been revised by the Editor with the addition of the summary which was missing in "Soryushiron Kenkyu".
(1) P. A. M. Dirac, "Proc. Camb. Phil. Soc.", *30*, 150 (1924). See also W. Heinsenberg, "Z. Physik", *90*, 209 (1934).

possibly avoid. For these reasons, we have attempted a new approach, which leads more directly to the desired result.

In the case of electrons and positrons, we may anticipate only a formal progress; but we consider it important, for possible extensions by analogy, that the very notion of negative energy states can be avoided. We shall see, in fact, that it is perfectly, and most naturally, possible to formulate a theory of elementary neutral particles which do not have negative (energy) states.

1. It is well known that quantum electrodynamics can be deduced by quantizing a system of equations which include the DIRAC wave equations for the electron and the MAXWELL equations. In the latter, the charge density and current are represented by certain expressions containing the electron wave function. The form given to these expressions adds, in reality, something new because it allows to derive the asymmetry with respect to the sign of the electric charge, an asymmetry which is not present in the Dirac equations. These expressions can be derived directly from a variational principle, which yields the Maxwell and the Dirac equations at the same time. Therefore, our first problem will be to examine the foundation of the variational principle itself, and the possibility of replacing it with a more appropriate one.

The Maxwell-Dirac equations contain quantities of two different types. On the one side, we have the electromagnetic potentials, which can be given a classical interpretation, within the limits posed by the correspondence principle. On the other side, there are the matter waves, which represent particles obeying the FERMI Statistic, and which have only a quantum interpretation. In this respect, it seems little satisfactory that the equations as well as the whole quantization procedure have to be derived from a variational principle which can be given only a classical interpretation. It seems more natural to search for a generalization of the variational method, such that the variables appearing in the Lagrange function assume, from the very beginning, their final significance, and, therefore, represent not necessarily commuting quantities.

This is the approach we shall follow. This approach is most important for fields obeying the Fermi statistics; reasons of simplicity may indicate, on the other hand, that nothing has to be added to the old method in the case of the electromagnetic field. In fact, we shall not perform a systematic study of all the logical possibilities offered by the new point of view we are adopting. Rather, we limit ourselves to the description of a quantization procedure for the matter-waves, which is the only important case for applications, at present; this method appears as a natural generalization of the JORDAN-WIGNER method[2], and it allows not only to cast the electron-positron theory into a symmetric form, but also to construct an essentially new theory for particles not endowed with an electric charge (neutrons and the hypothetical neutrinos). Even though it is perhaps not yet possible to ask experiments to decide between the new theory and a simple extension of the Dirac equations to neutral particles, one should keep in mind

---

[2] P. JORDAN and E. WIGNER, "Z. Physik", *47*, 631 (1928).

that the new theory introduces a smaller number of hypothetical entities, in this yet unexplored field.

Leaving to the reader the obvious extension of the formulae to the continuous systems, which we shall consider later on, we illustrate in the following the quantization procedure for discrete systems. Let a physical system be described by the real variables $q_1 q_2, \ldots, q_n$ (symmetric, Hermitian matrices). We define a Lagrange function:

$$(1) \qquad\qquad L = i \sum_{r,s} \left(A_{rs} q_r \dot{q}_s + B_{rs} q_r q_s \right),$$

and set:

$$(2) \qquad\qquad \delta \int L dt = 0,$$

we understand that A_{rs} and B_{rs} are ordinary real numbers, constant the former and, eventually, time-dependent the latter, which obey the relations:

$$(3) \qquad\qquad A_{rs} = A_{sr}; \qquad B_{rs} = -B_{sr},$$

and, furthermore, with $\det \|A_{rs}\| \neq 0$.

If the q's were ordinary, commuting, variables, the variational principle (2) would have no meaning because it would be identically satisfied. In the case of non-commuting variables, eq. (2) implies the vanishing, at any time, of the Hermitian matrix:

$$i \sum_r \left[\delta q_r \left(\sum_s A_{rs} \dot{q}_s + B_{rs} q_s \right) - \sum_s \left(A_{rs} \dot{q}_s + B_{rs} q_s \right) \delta q_r \right] = 0,$$

for arbitrary variations δq_r. This is only possible if the expression $\sum_s (A_{rs} \dot{q}_s + B_{rs} q_s)$ are multiple of the unit matrix so that, after some appropriate modification of the variational principle (2) (*e.g.* by requiring the sum of the diagonal terms in the above expressions to vanish([3])) we may consider the following equations of motion:

$$(4) \qquad\qquad \sum_s \left(A_{rs} \dot{q}_s + B_{rs} q_s \right) = 0 \qquad r = 1, 2, \ldots, n.$$

We now show that these equations can be derived, following the usual procedure:

$$\dot{q}_r = -\frac{2\pi i}{h} \left(q_r H - H q_r \right)$$

([3]) The physical application which will be illustrated later on suggests the more rigorous restriction that, in any linear combination of q_r and $\dot{q}_r$ to any given eigenvalue there corresponds another one, equal in absolute value and opposite in sign.

from the Hamiltonian:

$$(5) \qquad H = -i \sum_{r,s} B_{rs} q_r q_s,$$

(whose exact form will be better justified in the following) provided we assume suitable *anticommutation* relations for the q_r. Substituting in eq. (4) the successive equations, one finds:

$$\sum_s B_{rs} q_s = \frac{2\pi}{h} \sum_{s,l,m} A_{rs} B_{lm} (q_s q_l q_m - q_l q_m q_s) =$$

$$= \frac{2\pi}{h} \sum_{s,l,m} A_{rs} B_{lm} \big[(q_s q_l + q_l q_s) q_m - q_l (q_s q_m + q_m q_s) \big] =$$

$$= \frac{2\pi}{h} \sum_{lm} B_{lm} \left\{ q_m \left[\sum_s A_{rs} (q_s q_l + q_l q_s) \right] + \left[\sum_s A_{rs} (q_s q_l + q_l q_s) \right] q_m \right\},$$

so that it suffices to set:

$$(6) \qquad \sum_s A_{rs} (q_s q_l + q_l q_s) = \frac{h}{4\pi} \delta_{rl},$$

for eqs. (4) to be satisfied. Denoting by $\|A_{rs}^{-1}\|$ the inverse matrix of $\|A_{rs}\|$, eq. (6) can be written as:

$$(6') \qquad q_r q_s + q_s q_r = \frac{h}{4\pi} A_{rs}^{-1}.$$

In the special case where A is reduced to the diagonal form:

$$A_{rs} = a_r \delta_{rs},$$

we have therefore:

$$(7) \qquad q_r q_s + q_s q_r = \frac{h}{4\pi a_r} \delta_{rs}.$$

We shall now apply the present scheme to the Dirac equations.

2. It is well known that one can eliminate the imaginary unit from the Dirac equations with no external field:

$$(8) \qquad \left[\frac{W}{c} + (\alpha, p) + \beta mc \right] \psi = 0,$$

with an appropriate choice of the operators α and β (and this can be done in a relativistically invariant fashion). We shall, in fact, refer to a system of intrinsic coordinates such

as to make eqs. (8) real, keeping explicitly in mind that the formulae we shall derive are not valid, without suitable modification, in a more general coordinate system. Denoting, as usual, with σ_x, σ_y, σ_z and ρ_1, ρ_2, ρ_3 two independent sets of Pauli matrices, we set:

(9) $$\alpha_x = \rho_1 \sigma_x; \qquad \alpha_y = \rho_3; \qquad \alpha_z = \rho_1 \sigma_z; \qquad \beta = -\rho_1 \sigma_y.$$

Dividing eqs. (9) by $-\frac{h}{2\pi i}$ and defining $\beta' = -i\beta$, $\mu = \frac{2\pi mc}{h}$, we obtain the real equations:

(8') $$\left[\frac{1}{c} \frac{\partial}{\partial t} - (\alpha, \mathrm{grad}) + \beta' \mu \right] \psi = 0.$$

As a consequence, eqs. (8) separate into two independent sets of equations, one for the real and one for the imaginary part of ψ. We set $\psi = U + iV$ and consider the real equations (8') as acting on U:

(10) $$\left[\frac{1}{c} \frac{\partial}{\partial t} - (\alpha, \mathrm{grad}) + \beta' \mu \right] U = 0.$$

The latter equations, *by themselves*[4], *i.e.* without the similar equations involving V, can be derived from the variational principle previously illustrated and quantized, as indicated above. Nothing similar could be done with elementary methods. Equation (10) can be obtained from the variational principle:

(11) $$\delta \int i \frac{hc}{2\pi} U^* \left[\frac{1}{c} \frac{\partial}{\partial t} - (\alpha, \mathrm{grad}) + \beta' \mu \right] U \, dq \, dt = 0.$$

It is easy to verify that the conditions (3), in their natural extension to a continuous system, are obeyed. Following eqs. (7) the anticommutation relations hold:

(12) $$U_i(q) U_k(q') + U_k(q') U_i(q) = \frac{1}{2} \delta_{ik} \delta(q - q'),$$

while the energy, according to (5) is:

(13) $$H = \int U^* \left[-c(\alpha, p) - \beta mc^2 \right] U \, dq.$$

The relativistic invariance of (12) and (13) does not require a separate demonstration. If one adds to these equations the analogous ones involving V, as well as the anticommutation relations: $U_r(q) V_s(q') + V_s(q') U_r(q) = 0$, one reobtains the usual Jordan-Wigner scheme, applied to the Dirac equations without external field.

---

[4] The behaviour of U under space reflection can be conveniently defined taking into account that a simultaneous change of sign of U_r has no physical significance, as already implied by other reasons. In our scheme: $U'(q) = RU(-q)$ with $R = i\rho_1 \sigma_y$ and $R^2 = -1$. Similarly, for a time reflection: $U'(q,t) = i\rho_2 U(q, -t)$.

It is remarkable, however, that the part of the formalism which refers to U (or V) can be considered, in itself, as the theoretical descriptions of some material system, in conformity with the general methods of quantum mechanics. The fact that the reduced formalism cannot be applied to the description of positive and negative electrons may well be attributed to the presence of the electric charge, and it does not invalidate the statement that, at the present level of knowledge, eqs. (12) and (13) constitute the simplest theoretical representation of neutral particles. The advantage, with respect to the elementary interpretation of the Dirac equation, is that there is now no need to assume the existence of antineutrons or antineutrinos (as we shall see shortly). The latter particles are indeed introduced in the theory of positive β-ray emission([5]); the theory, however, can be obviously modified so that the β-emission, both positive and negative, is always accompanied by the emission of a neutrino.

Considering the interest that the above-mentioned hypothesis gives to eqs. (12) and (13), it seems useful to examine their meaning more closely. To this aim, we developed U, inside a cube of side L, over the system of periodical functions:

(14)
$$f_\gamma(q) = \frac{1}{L^{3/2}} e^{2\pi i(\gamma, q)},$$

$$\gamma = (\gamma_x, \gamma_y, \gamma_z); \qquad \gamma_x = \frac{n_1}{L}, \qquad \gamma_y = \frac{n_2}{L}, \qquad \gamma_z = \frac{n_3}{L};$$

$$n_1, n_2, n_3 = 0, \pm 1, \pm 2, \ldots$$

setting:

(15)
$$U_r(q) = \sum_\gamma a_r(\gamma) f_\gamma(q).$$

As a consequence of the reality of U, we have:

(16)
$$a_r(\gamma) = \bar{a}_r(-\gamma).$$

In the general case, $\gamma \neq 0$, it follows from (12) that:

(17)
$$\begin{cases} a_r(\gamma)\bar{a}_s(\gamma) + \bar{a}_s(\gamma)a_r(\gamma) = \frac{1}{2}\delta_{rs}, \\ a_r(\gamma)a_s(\gamma) + a_s(\gamma)a_r(\gamma) = 0, \\ \bar{a}_r(\gamma)\bar{a}_s(\gamma) + \bar{a}_s(\gamma)\bar{a}_r(\gamma) = 0. \end{cases}$$

Furthermore, these quantities anticommute with $a(\gamma')$ and $\bar{a}(\gamma')$, when γ' differs both from γ and from $-\gamma$.

([5]) See G. Wick, "Rend. Accad. Lincei", *21*, 170 (1935).

The expression of the energy resulting from (13) is:

$$(18) \qquad H = \sum_{\gamma} \sum_{r,s=1}^{4} \left[-hc(\gamma, \alpha^{rs}) - mc^2 \beta^{rs} \right] \bar{a}_r(\gamma) a_s(\gamma).$$

The x component of the linear momentum corresponds to the unit translation along x, up to the factor $\frac{h}{2\pi} i$, as usual:

$$(19) \qquad M_x = \int U^* p_x U \, dq = \sum_{\gamma} \sum_{r} h\gamma_x \bar{a}_r(\gamma) a_k(\gamma),$$

and similarly for M_y and M_z.

For any value of γ we have in (18) a Hermitian form which has, notoriously, two positive and two negative eigenvalues, all equal in absolute value to $c\sqrt{m^2c^2 + h^2\gamma^2}$.

We can thus replace (18) by:

$$(18') \qquad H = \sum_{\gamma} c\sqrt{m^2c^2 + h^2\gamma^2} \left[\bar{b}_1(\gamma) b_1(\gamma) + \bar{b}_2(\gamma) b_2(\gamma) - \bar{b}_3(\gamma) b_3(\gamma) - \bar{b}_4(\gamma) b_4(\gamma) \right]$$

b_r being appropriate linear combinations of the a_r, obtained by a unitary transformation. Furthermore, it follows from (16) that $b_r(\gamma)$ are linearly related to $\bar{b}_r(-\gamma)$.

The Hermitian form (18), for a given value of γ, remains invariant under the exchange of γ with γ, as a consequence of (16) and (17). From this, and keeping again (17) into account, it follows that we can set:

$$(20) \qquad b_3(\gamma) = \bar{b}_1(-\gamma); \qquad b_4(\gamma) = \bar{b}_2(-\gamma).$$

We introduce, for simplicity, the new variables:

$$(21) \qquad B_1(\gamma) = \sqrt{2} b_1(\gamma); \qquad B_2(\gamma) = \sqrt{2} b_2(\gamma),$$

and we obtain:

$$(22) \qquad H = \sum_{\gamma} c\sqrt{m^2c^2 + h^2\gamma^2} \sum_{r=1}^{2} \left[n_r(\gamma) - \frac{1}{2} \right],$$

$$(23) \qquad M_x = \sum_{\gamma} h\gamma_x \sum_{r=1}^{2} \left[n_r(\gamma) - \frac{1}{2} \right],$$

where we have set:

$$n_r(\gamma) = \bar{B}_r(\gamma) B_r(\gamma) = {\Large\lbrace}{\begin{matrix} 0 \\ 1 \end{matrix}}$$

considering, furthermore, that the following relations hold:

(24)
$$\begin{cases} B_r(\gamma)\bar{B}_s(\gamma') + \bar{B}_s(\gamma')B_r(\gamma) = \delta_{\gamma\gamma'}\delta_{rs}, \\ B_r(\gamma)B_s(\gamma') + B_s(\gamma')B_r(\gamma) = 0, \\ \bar{B}_r(\gamma)\bar{B}_s(\gamma') + \bar{B}_s(\gamma')\bar{B}_r(\gamma) = 0, \end{cases}$$

as it would follow formally, in the Jordan-Wigner scheme, for the coefficients in the development of a *two-component* matter-wave.

The preceding formulae are entirely analogous to those obtained in the quantization of the Maxwell equations, except for the different statistic. In the place of massless quanta, we have particles with a finite mass and also for them we have two available polarization states. In the present case, *as in the case of the electromagnetic radiation*, the half-quanta of rest energy and momentum are present, except that they appear with the opposite sign, in apparent connection with the different statistic. They do not constitute a specific difficulty, and they must be considered simply as additive constants, with no physical significance.

Similarly to the case of light quanta, it is not possible to describe with eigenfunctions the states of such particles. In the present case, however, the presence of a rest mass allows one to consider the *non-relativistic approximation*, where all the notions of elementary quantum mechanics apply, obviously. The non-relativistic approximation may be useful primarily in the case of the heavy particles (neutrons).

The simplest way to go to the configuration space representation is to associate the following plane wave to each oscillator:

$$\frac{1}{L^{3/2}}e^{2\pi i(\gamma,q)}\delta_{\sigma\sigma_r}, \qquad (r = 1, 2),$$

corresponding to the same value of the momentum, and with two possible polarization states, to keep into account the multiplicity of oscillators. We can go further, and describe not a simple particle, but a system with an indefinite number of particles with the two-valued, complex eigenfunction $\Phi = (\Phi_1, \Phi_2)$, according to the Jordan-Wigner method. It is sufficient to set:

(25)
$$\begin{cases} \Phi_1(q) = \sum_\gamma \frac{1}{L^{3/2}}e^{2\pi i(\gamma,q)}B_1(\gamma), \\ \Phi_2(q) = \sum_\gamma \frac{1}{L^{3/2}}e^{2\pi i(\gamma,q)}B_2(\gamma). \end{cases}$$

In the non-relativistic approximation ($|\gamma| \ll \frac{mc}{h}$) the constants $b_r(\gamma)$ in (18') are linear combinations of $a_r(\gamma)$, *with γ-independent coefficients.*

The latter coefficients depend only upon the elements of γ and, according to (9), we have:

$$b_1(\gamma) = \frac{a_3(\gamma) - ia_2(\gamma)}{\sqrt{2}} \; ; \qquad b_3(\gamma) = \frac{a_3(\gamma) + ia_2(\gamma)}{\sqrt{2}} \, ,$$

$$b_2(\gamma) = \frac{a_4(\gamma) + ia_1(\gamma)}{\sqrt{2}} \; ; \qquad b_4(\gamma) = \frac{a_4(\gamma) - ia_1(\gamma)}{\sqrt{2}} \, ,$$

which satisfy also eq. (20), as a consequence of (16). From eqs. (15) and (25) we have, in the non-relativistic approximation:

(26)
$$\begin{cases} \Phi_1(q) = U_3(q) - iU_2(q), \\ \Phi_2(q) = U_4(q) + iU_1(q). \end{cases}$$

On the purely formal side, we note that $\Phi = (\Phi_1, \Phi_2)$ coincides, up to a $\sqrt{2}$ factor, with the pair of *large* eigenfunctions of eqs. (10), when interpreted in the usual way, that is with no reality restriction.

To prove this, it is enough to verify that the transformation $\psi = \frac{1 - \rho_2 \sigma_y}{\sqrt{2}} U$ allows one to go from the scheme (9) to the usual Dirac scheme ($\alpha = \rho_1 \sigma; \; \beta = \rho_3$), so that, effectively:

$$\psi_3 = \frac{1}{\sqrt{2}} \Phi_1, \qquad \psi_4 = \frac{1}{\sqrt{2}} \Phi_2;$$

notoriously, in the latter scheme, ψ_3 and ψ_4 are the large components. This relation clarifies the transformation law of Φ with respect to space rotations, but it has no meaning, obviously, with respect to general Lorentz transformations.

The existence of simple formulae such as (26) could lead one to suspect that, to a certain extent, the passage through plane waves is superfluous. As a matter of fact, such a passage is conceptually needed to obtain the cancellation of the *rest-energy half-quanta*. In fact, after such cancellation, the method of the energy is naturally given by:

(27)
$$H = \int \tilde{\Phi} \left(mc^2 + \frac{1}{2m} p^2 \right) \Phi dq,$$

to first approximation, and it differs in an essential way from (13).

3. As we have already said, the scheme (12) is not sufficient to describe charged particles; but, upon the introduction of a further quadruplet of real quantities V_r, analogous to the U_r, one re-obtains the usual electrodynamics, in a form symmetric with respect to the electron and positron. We consider, therefore, two sets of real quantities, representing the matter particles and the electromagnetic field, respectively. Quantities of the first kind are to be interpreted according to the scheme described in Sect. 1. Quantities of the second kind, *i.e.* the electromagnetic potentials φ and $A = (A_x, A_y, A_z)$, can be

interpreted as classical quantities, and have to be quantized according to the Heisenberg rule, based on the correspondence principle. The Maxwell and Dirac equations (with the above-mentioned restriction for the latter) can be obtained from a variational principle:

$$\delta \int L \, dq \, dt = 0$$

L being the sum of three terms:

$$L = L' + L'' + L'''.$$

The first term refers to the matter wave:

$$(28) \qquad L' = i\frac{hc}{2\pi} \left\{ U^* \left[\frac{1}{c}\frac{\partial}{\partial t} - (\alpha, \mathrm{grad}) + \beta'\mu \right] U + \right.$$

$$\left. + V^* \left[\frac{1}{c}\frac{\partial}{\partial t} - (\alpha, \mathrm{grad}) + \beta'\mu \right] V \right\},$$

while the second describes the radiation field, which we suppose to be quantized according to the method of FERMI[6]:

$$(29) \qquad L'' = \frac{1}{8\pi}(E^2 - H^2) - \frac{1}{8\pi}\left(\frac{1}{c}\dot{\varphi} + \mathrm{div}\, A \right)^2.$$

We must therefore impose the auxiliary condition

$$(30) \qquad \frac{1}{c}\dot{\varphi} + \mathrm{div}\, A = 0.$$

The expression given in (29) differs from the one used by Fermi, but for integrable terms only. It leads to a definition of the momentum P_0, conjugate to φ, such as to allow one to eliminate immediately one of the two longitudinal waves, without having to go through the plane-wave development; in this respect, it is completely immaterial whether the second term in the expression (29) for L'' is multiplied by an arbitrary, non-vanishing constant. As for L''' it must be so chosen that $\psi = U + iV$ obeys the Dirac equation (8) completed with the external field, i.e. the equation:

$$\left[\frac{W}{c} + \frac{e}{c}\varphi + \left(\alpha, p + \frac{e}{c}A \right) + \beta mc \right] \psi = 0.$$

In practice, this requirement leads to:

$$(31) \qquad L''' = ieU^*[\varphi + (\alpha, A)]V - ieV^*[\varphi + (\alpha, A)]U.$$

---

[6] E. FERMI, "Rend. Accad. Lincei", **9**, 881 (1929).

Upon variation of the electromagnetic potentials, we obtain the following expressions for the charge and current densities:

(32)
$$
\begin{cases}
\rho = -ie(U^*V - V^*U) = -e\dfrac{\tilde{\psi}\psi - \psi^*\bar{\psi}}{2}, \\[2mm]
I = ie(U^*\alpha V - V^*\alpha U) = e\dfrac{\tilde{\psi}\alpha\psi - \psi^*\alpha\bar{\psi}}{2}.
\end{cases}
$$

These expressions differ from the usual ones for *infinite constants* only. The cancellation of such infinite constants is required by the symmetry of the theory, which is already implicit in the form chosen for the variational principle; in fact, the exchange of U_r and V_r, which appear symmetrically in L', is equivalent to changing sign to the electric charge.

U and V obey the anticommutation relations:

$$
U_r(q)U_s(q') + U_s(q')U_r(q) = \frac{1}{2}\delta(q - q')\delta_{rs},
$$

$$
V_r(q)V_s(q') + V_s(q')V_r(q) = \frac{1}{2}\delta(q - q')\delta_{rs},
$$

$$
U_r(q)V_s(q') + V_s(q')U_r(q) = 0,
$$

which are equivalent to the usual Jordan-Wigner scheme, if we set $\psi = U + iV$. The electromagnetic potentials φ, A_x, A_y, A_z, on the other side, obey to the usual commutation relations with their conjugate momenta, e.g. $P_0(q)\varphi(q') - \varphi(q')P_0(q) = \frac{h}{2\pi i}\delta(q - q')$, with:

(33)
$$
\begin{cases}
P_0 = -\dfrac{1}{4\pi c}\left(\dfrac{1}{c}\dot{\varphi} + \mathrm{div}\,A\right), \\[3mm]
P_x = -\dfrac{1}{4\pi c}E_x; \quad P_y = -\dfrac{1}{4\pi c}E_y; \quad P_z = -\dfrac{1}{4\pi c}E_z.
\end{cases}
$$

The energy is made up of three terms: $H = H' + H'' + H'''$ is derived from L', according to the rules already illustrated. The second term is obtained from the classical rules: $H'' = \int[P_0\dot{\varphi} + (P, A) - L'']dq$, where $P = (P_x, P_y, P_z)$. As for H''', it can be obtained from L''', following either methods (in our case $H''' = -\int L'''dq$) as it must be, since L''' is a function of both the matter and the electromagnetic field variables. This, by the way, proves the necessity of the ansatz (5). The continuity equation (30), is obeyed at any time, if it holds initially together with the divergence equation $\mathrm{div}\,E = 4\pi\rho$. It follows from (33) that the kinematics defined by the exchange rules has to be reduced by the use of the equations:

(34)
$$
\begin{cases}
P_0(q) = 0, \\[2mm]
\mathrm{div}\,P + \dfrac{1}{c}\rho = 0,
\end{cases}
$$

and therefore by assigning fixed values to two field quantities, with the corresponding indeterminacy in the conjugate variables. The *first* of (34) implies therefore, the elimination of P_0 and φ from the expression of H. The elimination is easily obtained by making use of (33), and one arrives, in this way, at the expression:

$$(35) \qquad H = \int \left\{ \tilde{\psi}\left[- c(\alpha, p) - \beta mc^2 \right]\psi - (A, I) + 2\pi cP^2 + \frac{1}{8\pi}\left| \text{rot } A \right|^2 \right\} dq.$$

As for relativistic invariance, we note that $\psi = U + iV$ obeys the Dirac equations, and that the Maxwell equations also hold, with charge and current densities which obey the relativistic transformation law. These two facts guarantee that the complete proof of the invariance of the theory is already implicit in the results of HEISENBERG and PAULI([7]). We turn now to the interpretation of the formalism.

4. Upon developing the U in the basis of the periodical functions considered before, and similarly for the V, we find as the obvious extension of (22), and after cancellation of the rest-energy half-quanta:

$$(36) \qquad H' = \sum_{\gamma} c\sqrt{m^2c^2 + h^2\gamma^2} \sum_{r=1}^{2} \left[\bar{B}_r(\gamma)B_r(\gamma) + \bar{B}'_r(\gamma)B'_r(\gamma) \right],$$

where B_r and B'_r refer to the development of U and V, respectively; B_r and B'_r and their conjugate variables obey the usual anticommutation relations. If, for each value of γ, we introduce four appropriate spin functions $\xi_s(\gamma)$ $(s = 1, 2, 3, 4)$ assuming four complex values and forming a unitary system, we can set:

$$(37) \quad \begin{cases} U = \dfrac{1}{\sqrt{2}} \sum_{\gamma} \left\{ B_1(\gamma)\xi_1(\gamma) + B_2(\gamma)\xi_2(\gamma) + \bar{B}_1(-\gamma)\xi_3(\gamma) + \bar{B}_2(-\gamma)\xi_4(\gamma) \right\} f_\gamma(q), \\[2mm] V = \dfrac{1}{\sqrt{2}} \sum_{\gamma} \left\{ B'_1(\gamma)\xi_1(\gamma) + B'_2(\gamma)\xi_2(\gamma) + \bar{B}'_1(-\gamma)\xi_3(\gamma) + \bar{B}'_2(-\gamma)\xi_4(\gamma) \right\} f_\gamma(q), \end{cases}$$

the following relations being, furthermore, satisfied:

$$(38) \qquad \begin{cases} \xi_3(\gamma) = \bar{\xi}_1(-\gamma), \\ \xi_4(\gamma) = \bar{\xi}_2(-\gamma). \end{cases}$$

([7]) W. HEISENBERG and W. PAULI, "Z. Physik", *56*, 1 (1929); *59*, 168 (1930).

It follows from the expression (32) for the electric charge density that the total charge is given by:

$$(39) \qquad Q = -\frac{ie}{2} \int \left[U^*(q)V(q) - V^*(q)U(q) \right] dq =$$

$$= -\frac{ie}{2} \sum_{\gamma} \sum_{r=1}^{2} \left[B_r(\gamma)\bar{B}'_r(\gamma) + \bar{B}_r(\gamma)B'_r(\gamma) - \bar{B}'_r(\gamma)B_r(\gamma) - B'_r(\gamma)\bar{B}_r(\gamma) \right].$$

If we set:

$$(40) \qquad C_r^{\text{el}} = \frac{B_r + iB'_r}{\sqrt{2}} ; \qquad C_r^{\text{pos}} = \frac{B_r - iB'_r}{\sqrt{2}}$$

we can transform the expressions (36) and (39) for the energy and charge into the form:

$$(41) \qquad H' = \sum_{\gamma} c\sqrt{m^2c^2 + h^2\gamma^2} \sum_{r=1}^{2} \left(\bar{C}_r^{\text{el}} C_r^{\text{el}} + \bar{C}_r^{\text{pos}} C_r^{\text{pos}} \right)$$

$$(42) \qquad Q = e \sum_{\gamma} \sum_{r=1}^{2} \left[-\left(\bar{C}_r^{\text{el}} C_r^{\text{el}} - \frac{1}{2} \right) + \bar{C}_r^{\text{pos}} C_r^{\text{pos}} - \frac{1}{2} \right] =$$

$$= e \sum_{\gamma} \sum_{r=1}^{2} \left(-\bar{C}_r^{\text{el}} C_r^{\text{el}} + \bar{C}_r^{\text{pos}} C_r^{\text{pos}} \right).$$

The elimination of the *half-quanta of electricity* is, therefore, automatic, provided we perform the internal sum first. Equations (41) ans (42) represent a set of oscillators which are equivalent to a double system of particles obeying the Fermi statistic, with rest mass m and charge $\pm e$; the variables C_r^{pos} refer to positrons and the C_r^{el} to electrons.

The elimination of the longitudinal electric field by the second equation in (34) is somewhat different in a symmetric theory because it is not possible to cast ρ, as it results from (32), in a diagonal form. The result of the elimination is well known in ordinary electrodynamics (though partially illusory because of convergence difficulties) where $\rho = -e\bar{\psi}\psi$; but it is equally known if one starts from $\rho = e\psi^*\bar{\psi}$ because the latter position is fully equivalent to exchange the role of electron and positron, considering the latter as a real particle and the former as a positron "hole". It seems plausible that those matrix elements which mantain the same form in the two opposite theories remain the same in the symmetric theory.

We thus assume to have already eliminated the irrotational part of A and P. The expression (35) for H is modified in two ways: first by assuming that A and P in this expression represent only the divergence free part of such vectors; secondly by adding a term which represents the electrostatic energy. The latter term takes a different form in the ordinary theory (electron-electron hole) and in the opposite theory. Keeping the

interaction of each particle with itself, one has in the first theory:

$$H_{els} = \frac{e^2}{2} \iint \frac{1}{|q - q'|} \tilde{\psi}(q)\psi(q)\tilde{\psi}(q')\psi(q')dqdq',$$

while in the second theory:

$$H_{els} = \frac{e^2}{2} \iint \frac{1}{|q - q'|} \psi^*(q)\bar{\psi}(q)\psi^*(q')\bar{\psi}(q')dqdq'.$$

Using (37) and (40) one can express the electrostatic energy as a function of the C's. The only terms which have given rise to physical applications are identical in the two theories: they are those which can be interpreted, from the particle viewpoint, as repulsion or attraction between distinct particles of the same or of the opposite type.

For what concerns the interaction with the radiation field, the only difference between the symmetric and the ordinary theory lies in the cancellation of undetermined constants, relative to the single oscillators, in the expression for the current density; again the formulae of interest for the applications remain unchanged.

Comment on the Scientific Paper no. 9 : *"A symmetric theory of electrons and positrons".*

Written in 1937, one year before his tragic disappearence, in a concise and elegant Italian language, this article probably represents the best long-lasting contribution of Ettore Majorana to particle physics.

The article tackles the problem of formulating the Dirac theory without the cumbersome sea of negative-energy states. In the usual formulation one would start from a highly asymmetric situation, to discover only at the end that there is a perfect symmetry between electrons and positrons. The symmetry is so little evident that Dirac himself tried at first to identify the positively charged particles, the holes, with protons!

Referring to the usual formulation, M. notes that:

"the prescriptions needed to cast the theory into a symmetric form, in conformity to its content, are however not entirely satisfactory because one always starts from an asymmetric form or because symmetric results are obtained after one applies appropriate procedures, such as the cancellation of divergent constants, that one should possibly avoid. For these reasons, we have attempted a new approach, which leads more directly to the desired result."

From these premises, M. formulates a field theory based on anticommuting variables, hence without classical interpretation, and derives the Dirac equation from a variational principle.

The electron is represented by a complex field, which can be divided into Hermitian and anti-Hermitian components. However, in the representation where the Dirac matrices are all imaginary (henceforth called the M. representation) each component *"can be considered, in itself, as the theoretical description of some material system, in conformity with the general methods of quantum mechanics."*

M. promptly recognizes, of course, that we cannot avoid introducing both components for the electron, which admits a conserved charge. But the simplicity of the scheme leads him to speculate that his theory can find application to the case of electrically neutral particles.

"The advantage... is that there is no reason now to infer the existence of antineutrons or antineutrinos. The latter particles are introduced in the theory of positive β-ray emission; the theory, however, can be obviously modified so that the β-emission, both positive and negative, is always accompanied by the emission of a neutrino."

M. refers here to the theory of positive β-rays formulated two years before, in Rome, by Giancarlo Wick.

Unexpectedly, from a reformulation of the Dirac theory, a novel physical possibility emerges, which has since been the object of theoretical and experimental scrutiny. We have not succeeded, yet, to find a definitive answer to M.'s proposal.

The M. neutrino has met with alternating fortunes, somehow superimposing to the "two-component neutrino" theory, formulated by Herman Weyl a few years before, in 1929.

It is a fact that the neutral particles emitted in negative or positive β-decays behave differently: in the interaction with atomic nuclei, the former particles produce invariably positrons, the latter electrons. However, with a $V - A$ interaction, we can associate the different behaviour to the different helicity of the emitted neutral particle.

Since helicity is strictly conserved for massless particles, deviations from this pattern are due to terms in the amplitude of the order of the ratio: (neutrino mass)/(neutrino energy), which is unobservably small in all neutrino-induced reactions.

The Majorana nature of the neutrino can be tested in the so-called *neutrinoless double β-decays*. These are second-order processes in the Fermi theory, whereby a virtual neutrino of positive elicity is emitted, together with an electron, and reabsorbed as if it were a neutrino (negative elicity), with emission of a second electron. The overall process: $N^* \rightarrow N + 2e$, violates lepton number conservation and is proportional to the Majorana mass of the neutrino. The observation of neutrinoless double β-decay would be an evident proof that: *"there is no reason to infer... the existence of... antineutrinos."*

Long considered as an exotic possibility, the M. neutrino has emerged, in our times, as the most natural explanation for the surprisingly small value of neutrino masses.

In addition, the non-conservation of a lepton number, L, leads to speculate that the decay of supermassive M. neutrinos in the primordial Universe may have given rise to an asymmetry in L, transformed in the presently observed baryon number asymmetry by virtue of $B - L$ conservation.

Several laboratories around the world host experiments to detect neutrinoless double β-decay, thus far with no success.

A new-generation experiment, CUORE, is in preparation in the INFN laboratory below the Gran Sasso Mountain in Central Italy. With dimensions never reached before, CUORE should put very stringent limits to the process... or maybe observe it.

I like to think that the answer to the question posed by Majorana more than half a century ago may be found precisely in our country giving, at the same time, a possible explanation to the dominance of matter over antimatter in our Universe, on which our very same existence depends.

LUCIANO MAIANI
Università di Roma "La Sapienza"

Il valore delle leggi statistiche nella fisica e nelle scienze sociali(*)

NOTA DI ETTORE MAJORANA

"Scientia", vol. 36, 1942, pp. 58-66.

Sunto. — La concezione deterministica della natura racchiude in sé una reale causa di debolezza nell'irrimediabile contradizione che essa incontra con i dati più certi della nostra coscienza. G. SOREL tentò di comporre questo dissidio con la distinzione tra *natura artificiale* e *natura naturale* (quest'ultima acausale), ma negò così l'unità della scienza. D'altra parte l'analogia formale tra le leggi statistiche della fisica e quelle delle scienze sociali accreditò l'opinione che anche i fatti umani sottostassero a un rigido determinismo. È importante, quindi, che i principî della meccanica quantistica abbiano portato a riconoscere (oltre ad una certa assenza di oggettività nella descrizione dei fenomeni) il carattere statistico delle leggi ultime dei processi elementari. Questa conclusione ha reso sostanziale l'analogia tra fisica e scienze sociali, tra le quali è risultata un'identità di valore e di metodo.

(*) Questo articolo di ETTORE MAJORANA —l'insigne fisico teorico dell'Università di Napoli scomparso senza lasciar traccia di sé il 25 Marzo 1938— fu scritto originariamente per una rivista di sociologia. Ma non fu pubblicato, forse per quella scontrosa reticenza che aveva l'A. ad aprirsi con gli altri e che lo persuadeva troppo spesso a chiudere nel cassetto lavori anche importanti. Questo articolo c'è stato conservato dall'amorosa cura del fratello e viene qui presentato non solo per l'interesse in sé dell'argomento, ma anche sovra tutto perché ci mostra un lato della ricca personalità del MAJORANA, che tanto attraeva coloro che lo conoscevano. Pensatore che univa a un acuto senso realistico uno spirito estremamente critico, ma non scettico, egli assume qui una chiara posizione di fronte al dibattuto problema del valore statistico delle ultime leggi fisiche. Questo che a molti sembra un difetto, come una denuncia d'indeterminismo nel divenire della natura, è invece per il MAJORANA un motivo per rivendicare l'intrinseca importanza del metodo statistico, sinora nella sua essenza applicato solo nelle scienze sociali e che nella nuova interpretazione delle leggi fisiche ritrova intero il suo significato originario.

GIOVANNI GENTILE jr.

Lo studio dei rapporti, veri o supposti, che passano fra la fisica e le altre scienze, ha sempre rivestito un notevole interesse in ragione dell'influenza speciale che la fisica ha esercitato nei tempi moderni sul generale indirizzo del pensiero scientifico. È noto che le leggi della meccanica, in modo particolare, sono apparse lungamente come il tipo insuperabile delle nostre conoscenze della natura, e si è anzi creduto da molti che a tal tipo, in ultima si sarerebbero dovute ricondurre anche le nozioni imperfette fornite dalle altre scienze. Valga ciò di giustificazione allo studio che intraprendiamo.

1. LA CONCEZIONE DELLA NATURA SECONDO LA FISICA CLASSICA

Il credito eccezionale goduto dalla fisica deriva evidentemente dalla scoperta delle così dette leggi esatte, consistenti in formule relativamente semplici che, escogitate originariamente inbase a indicazioni frammentarie e approssimative dell'esperienza, si rivelano in seguito di universale validità, sia che vengano applicate a nuovi ordini di fenomeni, sia che il progressivo affinamento dell'arte sperimentale le sottoponga a un controllo sempre più rigoroso. È a tutti noto che secondo la concezione fondamentale della meccanica classica il movimento di un corpo materiale è interamente determinato dalle condizioni iniziali (posizione e velocità) in cui il corpo si trova e dalle forze che agiscono su di esso. Sulla natura e misura delle forze che si possono creare nei sistemi materiali, le leggi generali della meccanica stabiliscono però naturalmente solo qualche condizione, o limitazione, che deve essere sempre soddisfatta. Tale carattere ha per esempio il principio dell'uguaglianza fra l'azione e la reazione al quale si sono aggiunte, in epoca meno remota, altre regole generali, come quelle riguardanti i sistemi vincolati (principio dei lavori virtuali) o le reazioni elastiche, e ancora più recentemente con l'interpretazione meccanica del calore, anche il principio della conservazione dell'energia in quanto principio generale della meccanica. A parte tali indicazioni generali, è però compito della fisica speciale lo scoprire volta per volta quanto occorre per l'uso effettivo dei principî della dinamica, cioè la conoscenza di tutte le forze in gioco.

In un caso tuttavia è stato possibile trovare l'espressione generale delle forze che nascono fra i corpi materiali: nel caso cioè che questi siano isolati e agiscano quindi reciprocamente solo a *distanza*. In questo caso, a prescindere dalle forze elettromagnetiche scoperte posteriormente e che si manifestano però solo in particolari condizioni, l'unica forza agente si riduce alla gravitazione universale, la cui nozione fu suggerita a NEWTON dall'analisi matematica delle leggi di KEPLERO. La legge di NEWTON è tipicamente applicabile allo studio dei movimenti degli astri che, essendo separati da immensi spazi vuoti, possono effettivamente influenzarsi a vicenda solo per un'apparente azione a distanza. Come è noto, tale legge è realmente sufficiente per prevedere in ogni aspetto e con esattezza meravigliosa tutto il complesso svolgimento del nostro sistema planetario. Una sola minuta eccezione, riguardante lo spostamento secolare che subisce il perielio di Mercurio, costituisce una delle maggiori prove sperimentali della recente teoria della relatività generale.

Il successo sensazionale della meccanica applicata all'astronomia ha incoraggiato naturalmente la supposizione che anche i fenomeni più complicati dell'esperienza comune debbono infine ricondursi a un meccanismo simile e solo alquanto più generale della legge di gravitazione.   Secondo tale modo di vedere, che ha dato luogo alla concezione meccanicistica della natura, tutto l'universo materiale si svolge obbedendo a una legge inflessibile, in modo che il suo stato in un certo istante è interamente determinato dallo stato in cui si trovava nell'istante precedente; segno che tutto il futuro è implicito nel presente, nel senso che può essere previsto con assoluta certezza purché lo stato attuale dell'universo sia interamente noto.   Tale concezione pienamente deterministica della natura ha avuto in seguito numerose conferme; gli sviluppi ulteriori della fisica, dalla scoperta delle leggi dell'elettromagnetismo fino alla teoria della relatività, hanno suggerito infatti un progressivo allargamento dei principî della meccanica classica, ma hanno, d'altra parte, vigorosamente confermato il punto essenziale, cioè la completa causalità fisica.   Non è contestabile che si debba al determinismo il merito principale e quasi esclusivo di aver reso possibile il grandioso sviluppo moderno della scienza, anche in campi lontanissimi dalla fisica.   Eppure il determinismo, che non lascia alcun posto alla libertà umana e obbliga a considerare come illusori, nel loro apparente finalismo, tutti i fenomeni della vita, racchiude una reale causa di debolezza: la contraddizione immediata e irrimediabile con i dati più certi della nostra coscienza.   Come il suo effettivo e, secondo ogni verosimiglianza, definitivo superamento sia avvenuto proprio nella fisica in questi ultimi anni, diremo solo più innanzi; sarà anzi nostro scopo ultimo l'illustrare il rinnovamento che il concetto tradizionale delle leggi statistiche deve subire in conseguenza del nuovo indirizzo seguito dalla fisica contemporanea.   Ma per il momento vogliamo ancora attenerci alla concezione classica della fisica; non solo per il suo enorme interesse storico, ma anche perché essa è ancora la sola largamente conosciuta oltre la cerchia degli specialisti.

Prima di chiudere questa parte introduttiva, crediamo opportuno ricordare che le critiche al determinismo si sono moltiplicate, sopratutto in tempi a noi abbastanza vicini.   La reazione filosofica, quando è stata felice, non è uscita dal suo campo, lasciando sostanzialmente intatto, se pur circoscritto nella sua importanza, il problema propriamente scientifico.   Un tentativo di risolvere quest'ultimo troviamo invece in G. Sorel[1] che rappresenta la corrente pragmatistica o pluralistica.   Secondo i partigiani di questo movimento una effettiva eterogeneità dei fenomeni naturali esclude che se ne possa avere una conoscenza unitaria.   Ogni principio scientifico sarebbe quindi applicabile a un determinato ambito di fenomeni, senza poter mai aspirare ad una validità universale. G. Sorel svolge in modo particolare la critica del determinismo affermando che questo riguarderebbe soltanto i fenomeni che egli chiama della *natura artificiale*, caratterizzati dal fatto che non sono accompagnati da una apprezzabile *degradazione* di energia (nel senso del secondo principio della termodinamica).   Tali fenomeni hanno luogo talvolta spontaneamente in natura, specie nel campo astronomico, e costituiscono allora materia di semplice osservazione; ma più frequentemente vengono provocati nei laboratori dagli

---

[1] G. Sorel, *De l'utilité du pragmatisme*, Cap. IV, Parigi 1921.

sperimentatori i quali pongono una cura particolare nell'eliminazione delle resistenze passive. Gli altri fenomeni, quelli cioè dell'esperienza comune o della *natura naturale*, nei quali entrano in gioco le resistenze passive, non sarebbero dominati da leggi definite, ma dipenderebbero in misura più o meno ampia dal caso. Il SOREL si richiama esplicitamente ad un principio metafisico di G. B. VICO. Non vogliamo qui discutere l'accentuazione arbitraria data a un particolare aspetto della scienza quale si presentava in un'epoca che non è più la nostra; dobbiamo invece rilevare che il principio pragmatista di giudicare le dottrine scientifiche in base alla loro reale utilità, non giustifica in alcun modo la pretesa di condannare l'ideale dell'unità della scienza che si è rivelata più volte un efficace stimolo al progresso delle idee.

2. IL SIGNIFICATO CLASSICO DELLE LEGGI STATISTICHE E LE STATISTICHE SOCIALI

Per bene intendere il significato delle leggi statistiche secondo la meccanica, bisogna richiamarsi ad una ipotesi sulla struttura della materia che, già familiare agli antichi, entrò effettivamente nel dominio della scienza ai primi del secolo scorso per opera di DAL-TON; questi riconobbe per primo in tale ipotesi la naturale spiegazione delle leggi generali della chimica da poco messe in luce. Secondo la moderna teoria atomica che è stata definitivamente confermata con i metodi propri della fisica, esistono in natura tante specie di particelle elementari indivisibili, o *atomi*, quanti sono i corpi chimici semplici; dall'unione di due o più atomi di specie uguale o diversa, talvolta da atomi isolati, risultano le *molecole* le quali sono le ultime particelle capaci di una esistenza indipendente in cui si può suddividere una sostanza chimicamente definita. Le singole molecole (e talvolta anche gli atomi all'interno delle molecole) lungi dall'occupare una posizione fissa, sono animate da un movimento rapidissimo di traslazione e di rotazione su se stesse. La struttura molecolare dei corpi gassosi è particolarmente semplice. Infatti nei gas in condizioni ordinarie le singole molecole si possono considerare come particolarmente indipendenti e a distanze reciproche, considerevoli rispetto alle loro ridottissime dimensioni; segue, per il principio di inerzia, che il loro moto di traslazione è rettilineo e uniforme, subendo modificazioni quasi istantanee nella direzione e nella misura della velocità solo in occasione di urti reciproci. Se supponiamo di conoscere esattamente le leggi che regolano l'influenza mutua delle molecole, dobbiamo attenderci, secondo i principî generali della meccanica, che basti *inoltre* conoscere nell'istante iniziale la disposizione di tutte le molecole e le loro velocità di traslazione e di rotazione, per poter prevedere *in principio* (se anche cioè a mezzo di calcoli troppo complessi per venire praticamente realizzati) quali saranno le esatte condizioni del sistema dopo un certo tempo. L'uso dello schema deterministico proprio della meccanica subisce tuttavia una reale limitazione di principio quando teniamo conto che i metodi *ordinari* di osservazione non sono in grado di farci conoscere esattamente le condizioni istantanee del sistema, ma ci danno solo un certo numero di informazioni globali. Dato, ad esempio, il sistema fisico risultante da una certa quantità di un determinato gas, basta conoscerne la pressione e la densità perché risultino determinate tutte quelle altre grandezze, come temperatura, coefficiente di viscosità, ecc., che potrebbero essere

oggetto di particolari misure. In altri termini il valore della pressione e della densità bastano in questo caso a determinare interamente lo stato del sistema *dal punto di vista macroscopico*, pur non essendo evidentemente sufficienti a stabilire in ogni istante la sua esatta struttura interna, cioè la distribuzione delle posizioni e velocità di tutte le molecole.

Per esporre con chiarezza e brevità e senza alcun apparato matematico, la natura del rapporto che passa fra *stato macroscopico* (A) e stato reale (a) di un sistema, e per trarne alcune deduzioni, dobbiamo sacrificare alquanto la precisione, pur evitando di alterare in modo essenziale la vera sostanza dei fatti. Dobbiamo dunque intendere che allo stato apparente o macroscopico A corrisponda un gran numero di possibilità effettive $a, a', a'' \ldots$ tra le quali le nostre osservazioni non ci permettono di distinguere. Il *numero* N di queste possibilità interne secondo le concezioni propriamente classiche sarebbe naturalmente infinito, ma la teoria dei quanti ha introdotto nella descrizione dei fenomeni naturali un'essenziale discontinuità in virtù della quale il numero (N) di tali possibilità nella struttura intima di un sistema materiale è realmente *finito*, sebbene naturalmente grandissimo. Il valore di N dà una misura del grado di indeterminazione *nascosta* del sistema; è però praticamente preferibile considerare una grandezza proporzionale al suo logaritmo

$$S = K \log N$$

K essendo la costante universale di Boltzmann determinata in modo che S coincida con una grandezza fondamentale, già nota, della termodinamica: l'*entropia*. L'entropia si presenta in realtà come una grandezza fisica al pari del peso, dell'energia ecc., sopra tutto perché come queste altre grandezze gode della proprietà additiva: cioè la entropia di un sistema risultante da più parti indipendenti è uguale alla somma delle entropie delle singole parti. Per dimostrarlo, basta osservare che il numero di possibilità latenti di un sistema composto è uguale evidentemente al prodotto dei numeri analoghi relativi alle parti costituenti; e tener presente d'altra parte la nota regola elementare che stabilisce la corrispondenza fra il prodotto di due o più numeri e la somma dei rispettivi logaritmi.

Sul modo di determinare il complesso di configurazioni interne $a, a', a'' \ldots$ che corrisponde allo stato macroscopico A, non sorgono in genere difficoltà. Si può invece discutere se tutte le singole possibilità $a, a', a'' \ldots$ si debbano o no riguardare come egualmente probabili. Orbene, secondo l'ipotesi ergodica o quasi ergodica, che si ha ragione di credere generalmente verificata, se un sistema persiste *indefinitamente* in uno stato A, allora si può affermare che esso passa un'eguale frazione del suo tempo in ciascuna delle configurazioni $a, a', a'' \ldots$; si è così condotti a considerare effettivamente come egualmente probabili tutte le possibili determinazioni interne. È questa in realtà una nuova ipotesi, poiché l'universo, lungi dal permanere indefinitamente nello stesso stato, va soggetto a trasformazioni continue. Ammetteremo dunque come ipotesi di lavoro estremamente plausibile, ma le cui conseguenze lontane potrebbero anche talvolta non essere verificate, che tutti i possibili stati interni di un sistema in condizioni fisiche determinate siano a priori egualmente probabili. Risulta così interamente definito il *complesso statistico* associato ad ogni stato macroscopico A.

Il problema generale della meccanica statistica si può così riassumere: essendo definito statisticamente, come si è detto, lo stato A iniziale del sistema quali previsioni sono possibili in riguardo al suo stato al tempo t? Può apparire a prima vista che questa definizione sia troppo ristretta, poiché oltre al problema propriamente dinamico altri se ne possono considerare di carattere *statico*; ad es. qual'è la temperatura di un gas di cui siano noti le pressioni e la densità? E così in tutti i casi che si voglia da alcune caratteristiche di un sistema, sufficienti a definirne lo stato, dedurne altre che possano interessare. La distinzione si può peraltro formalmente ignorare; incorporando infatti nel sistema appropriati strumenti di misura, ci si può sempre ricondurre al caso precedente.

Supponiamo dunque che lo stato iniziale del sistema in esame risulti da un complesso statistico $A = (a, a', a'' \ldots)$ di casi possibili e, per quanto si è detto, egualmente probabili. Ciascuna di queste determinazioni concrete si modifica nel corso del tempo secondo una legge che, in accordo con i principî generali della meccanica, dobbiamo ancora ritenere rigidamente causale, cosicché dopo un certo tempo si passa dalla serie $a, a', a'' \ldots$ a un'altra serie ben determinata $\beta, \beta', \beta'' \ldots$; il complesso statistico $(\beta, \beta', \beta'' \ldots)$, che è anch'esso costituito di N elementi egualmente probabili come il complesso originario A (teorema di Liouville), definisce tutte le possibili previsioni sullo svolgimento del sistema. Per ragioni che solo un'analisi matematica complessa potrebbe precisare, accade in generale che tutti i casi semplici appartenenti alla serie $\beta, \beta', \beta'' \ldots$ *salvo un numero del tutto insignificante di eccezioni*, costituiscono *in tutto o in parte* un nuovo complesso statistico B definito come A da uno stato *macroscopicamente* ben determinato. Possiamo allora enunciare la *legge statistica* secondo la quale vi è la pratica certezza che il sistema debba passare da A in B. Per quanto si è detto, il complesso statistico B è almeno così ampio come A, cioè contiene un numero di elementi non inferiore a N; segue che l'entropia di B è uguale a quella di A *o maggiore*. Durante qualunque trasformazione che si compia *in accordo con le leggi statistiche* si ha quindi costanza o aumento di entropia, mai diminuzione; è questo il fondamento statistico del famoso secondo principio della termodinamica.

È notevole che dal punto di vista pratico il passaggio da A a B si può considerare come certo; ciò che spiega come storicamente le leggi statistiche siano state considerate dapprima altrettanto fatali delle leggi della meccanica e solo per il progresso dell'indagine teorica se ne sia in seguito riconosciuto il vero carattere. Le leggi statistiche abbracciano gran parte della fisica. Fra applicazioni più note ricordiamo: l'equazione di stato dei gas, la teoria della diffusione, della conducibilità termica, della viscosità, della pressione osmotica e molte altre consimili. Un posto a parte merita la teoria statistica dell'irraggiamento che introduce per la prima volta nella fisica il *discontinuo* simboleggiato della costante di PLANCK. Ma vi è inoltre una intera branca della fisica, la *termodinamica*, i cui principî benché fondati direttamente sull'esperienza, si possono ricondurre alle nozioni generali della meccanica statistica. Per quanto abbiamo fatto finora si può così riassumere il significato delle leggi statistiche secondo la fisica classica: 1°) i fenomeni naturali obbediscono ad un determinismo assoluto; 2°) l'osservazione *ordinaria* non permette di riconoscere esattamente lo stato interno di un corpo ma solo di stabilire un complesso innumerevole di possibilità

indistinguibili; 3°) stabilite delle ipotesi plausibili sulla probabilità delle diverse possibilità e supposte valide le leggi della meccanica, il calcolo delle probabilità permette la previsione più o meno certa dei fenomeni futuri. Possiamo ormai esaminare il rapporto che passa fra le leggi stabilite dalla meccanica classica e quelle regolarità francamente empiriche che sono note con lo stesso nome in modo particolare nelle scienze sociali.

Bisogna anzitutto convincersi che l'analogia formale non potrebbe essere più stretta. Quando si enuncia, ad es., la legge statistica: "In una società moderna di tipo europea il coefficiente annuo di nuzialità è prossimo a 8 per 1000 abitanti", è abbastanza chiaro che il sistema su cui dobbiamo eseguire le nostre osservazioni è definito solo in base a certi caratteri globali rinunziando deliberatamente a indagare tutti quei dati ulteriori (come per es. la biografia di tutti gli individui che compongono la società in esame) la cui conoscenza sarebbe indubbiamente utile per prevedere il fenomeno con maggiore precisione e sicurezza di quanto non consenta la generica legge statistica; non altrimenti allorché si definisce lo stato di un gas semplicemente dalla pressione e dal volume, si rinunzia deliberatamente a investigare le condizioni iniziali di tutte le singole molecole. Una differenza sostanziale si potrebbe invece scorgere nel carattere matematicamente definito dalle leggi statistiche della fisica a cui fa riscontro quello chiaramente empirico delle leggi statistiche sociali; ma è plausibile attribuire l'empirismo delle statistiche sociali (intendiamo precisamente l'incostanza dei loro risultati *oltre la parte spettante al caso*) alla complessità dei fenomeni che essi considerano, per cui non è possibile definire esattamente le condizioni o il contenuto della legge. D'altra parte anche la fisica conosce le leggi empiriche quando studia fenomeni di puro interesse applicativo; tali ad es., le leggi sull'attrito fra corpi solidi, o sulle proprietà magnetiche dei vari tipi di ferro e altri simili. Infine si potrebbe dare speciale importanza alla differenza nei metodi di rilevazione che nella fisica sono globali (così basta la lettura di uno strumento di misura per conoscere la pressione di un gas benché essa derivi dalla somma degli impulsi indipendenti che le singole molecole trasmettono alle pareti) mentre nelle statistiche sociali si registrano di solito i fatti individuali; non è però neanche questa un'antitesi assoluta, come prova la possibilità dei metodi più vari di rilevazione indiretta. Ammesse così le ragioni che fanno credere all'esistenza di una reale analogia fra le leggi statistiche fisiche e sociali, siamo indotti a ritenere plausibile che, come le prime presuppongono logicamente un rigido determinismo, così le ultime siano da parte loro la prova più diretta che il più assoluto determinismo governa anche i fatti umani; argomento che ha avuto tanto miglior fortuna in quanto, come abbiamo detto in principio, si era già manifestata per ragioni indipendenti la tendenza a vedere nella causalità della fisica classica un modello di valore universale. Sarebbe qui fuor di luogo riprendere discussioni antiche e mai concluse, ma crediamo di potere ricordare, come fatto generalmente ammesso, che la non avvenuta conciliazione fra le nostre contrastanti intuizioni della natura ha lungamente pesato sul pensiero moderno e sui valori morali. Non va quindi accolto semplicemente come una curiosità scientifica l'annunzio che negli ultimissimi anni la fisica è stata costretta ad abbandonare il suo indirizzo tradizionale rigettando, in maniera verosimilmente definitiva, il determinismo assoluto della meccanica classica.

3. LE NUOVE CONCEZIONI DELLA FISICA

È impossibile esporre con qualche compiutezza in poche righe lo schema matematico e il contenuto sperimentale della meccanica quantistica[2]. Ci limiteremo pertanto a qualche accenno. Vi sono dei fatti sperimentali noti da gran tempo (fenomeni di interferenza) che depongono irrefutabilmente a favore della teoria ondulatoria della luce; altri fatti scoperti di recente (effetto Compton) suggeriscono, al contrario, non meno decisamente l'opposta teoria corpuscolare. Tutti i tentativi di comporre la contraddizione nel quadro della fisica classica sono rimasti assolutamente infruttuosi; il che può anche sembrare poco significativo. Senonché di tali fatti inesplicabili, e di altri non meno inesplicabili e della più diversa natura, e infine di *quasi tutti* i fenomeni noti ai fisici e finora insufficientemente spiegati si è trovata realmente da pochi anni la spiegazione unica e meravigliosamente semplice: quella contenuta nei principî della meccanica quantistica. Questa straordinaria teoria è dunque così solidamente fondata nell'esperienza come forse nessun'altra fu mai; le critiche a cui essa fu ed è assoggettata non possono quindi concernere in alcun modo la legittimità del suo uso per l'effettiva previsione dei fenomeni, ma soltanto l'opinione, condivisa dai più, che il nuovo indirizzo da essa segnato debba conservarsi, e anzi ancora accentuarsi, nei futuri sviluppi della fisica. Gli aspetti caratteristici della meccanica quantistica, in quanto essa si differenzia dalla meccanica classica sono i seguenti:

a) non esistono in natura leggi che esprimano una successione fatale di fenomeni; anche le leggi ultime che riguardano i fenomeni elementari (sistemi atomici) hanno carattere statistico, permettendo di stabilire soltanto la *probabilità* che una misura eseguita su un sistema preparato in un dato modo dia un certo risultato, e ciò qualunque siano i mezzi[*] di cui disponiamo per determinare con la maggior esattezza possibile lo stato iniziale del sistema. Queste leggi statistiche indicano un reale difetto di determinismo e non hanno nulla di comune con le leggi statistiche classiche nelle quali l'incertezza dei risultati deriva dalla volontaria rinunzia, per ragioni pratiche, a indagare nei più minuti particolari le condizioni iniziali dei sistemi fisici. Vedremo più avanti un esempio ben noto di questo nuovo tipo di leggi naturali.

b) una certa mancanza di *oggettività* nella descrizione dei fenomeni. Qualunque esperienza eseguita in un sistema atomico esercita su di esso una perturbazione finita che non può essere, per ragioni di principio, eliminata o ridotta. Il risultato di qualunque misura sembra perciò riguardare piuttosto lo stato in cui il sistema viene portato nel corso dell'esperienza stessa che non quello inconoscibile in cui si

---

[2] Il lettore che desideri approfondire le sue conoscenze in tale materia girando, finché si può, lo scoglio matematico, può consultare W. HEISENBERG, *Die Physikalischen Prinzipien der Quantentheorie*, Lipsia 1930.
[*] In "Scientia" è erroneamente stampato "prezzi". (Nota del Curatore, vedi anche E. AMALDI, *op. cit.*)

trovava prima di essere perturbato. Questo aspetto della meccanica quantistica è senza dubbio più inquietante, cioè più lontano dalle nostre intuizioni ordinarie, che non la semplice mancanza di determinismo.

Fra le leggi probabilistiche riguardanti i fenomeni elementari è nota da più antica data quella che regola i processi radioattivi.

Ogni atomo di una sostanza radioattiva ha una probabilità definita mdt di trasformarsi nel tempuscolo dt in seguito all'emissione, o di una particella α (nucleo di elio) ovvero in altri casi di una particella β (elettrone). Il *tasso di mortalità m* è costante, cioè indipendente dalla *età* dell'atomo, ciò che dà una forma particolare (esponenziale) alla *curva di sopravvivenza*; la vita media vale $1/m$ e in modo elementare si può determinare analogamente la *vita probabile*, chiamata talvolta *periodo di trasformazione*. Entrambe sono indipendenti dall'età dell'atomo che non manifesta del resto per alcun altro segno un reale invecchiamento con il progredire del tempo. Esistono vari metodi per l'osservazione, o anche per la registrazione automatica delle singole trasformazioni che avvengono nel seno di una sostanza radioattiva, ed è stato quindi possibile verificare, mediante dirette rivelazioni statistiche e applicazioni del calcolo della probabilità, che i singoli atomi radioattivi non subiscono alcuna influenza reciproca o esterna per quanto riguarda l'istante della trasformazione; infatti il numero delle disintegrazioni che hanno luogo in un certo intervallo di tempo è soggetto a fluttuazioni dipendenti esclusivamente dal caso, cioè dal carattere probabilistico della legge individuale di trasformazione.

La meccanica quantistica ci ha insegnato a vedere nella legge esponenziale delle trasformazioni radioattive una legge elementare non riducibile ad un più semplice meccanismo causale. Naturalmente anche le leggi statistiche note alla meccanica classica e riguardanti *sistemi complessi*, conservano la loro validità secondo la meccanica quantistica. Questa modifica peraltro le regole per la determinazione delle configurazioni interne, e in due modi diversi, a seconda della natura dei sistemi fisici, dando luogo rispettivamente alle teorie statistiche di Bose-Einstein, o di Fermi. Ma l'introduzione nella fisica di un nuovo tipo di legge statistica, o meglio semplicemente probabilistica, che si nasconde, in luogo del supposto determinismo, sotto le leggi statistiche ordinarie obbliga a rivedere le basi dell'analogia che abbiamo stabilita più sopra con le leggi statistiche sociali. È indiscutibile che il carattere statistico di queste ultime deriva almeno in parte dalla maniera in cui vengono definite le condizioni dei fenomeni: maniera generica, cioè propriamente statistica, e tale da permettere un complesso innumerevole di possibilità concrete differenti. D'altra parte se ricordiamo quanto si è detto più sopra sulle *tavole di mortalità* degli atomi radioattivi siamo indotti a chiederci se non esista anche qui un'analogia reale con i fatti sociali che si descrivono con linguaggio alquanto simile.

Qualche cosa a prima vista sembra escluderlo; la disintegrazione di un atomo è un fatto semplice, imprevedibile, che avviene improvvisamente e isolatamente dopo un'attesa talvolta di migliaia e perfino di miliardi di anni; mentre niente di simile accade per i fatti registrati dalle statistiche sociali. Questa non è però un'obiezione insormontabile.

La disintegrazione di un atomo radioattivo può obbligare un contatore automatico a registrarlo con effetto meccanico, reso possibile da adatta amplificazione. Bastano

quindi comuni artifici di laboratorio per preparare una catena comunque complessa e vistosa di fenomeni che sia *comandata* dalla disintegrazione accidentale di un solo atomo radioattivo. Non vi è nulla dal punto di vista strettamente scientifico che impedisca di considerare come plausibile che all'origine di avvenimenti umani possa trovarsi un fatto vitale ugualmente semplice, invisibile e imprevedibile. Se è così, come noi riteniamo, le leggi statistiche delle scienze sociali vedono accresciuto il loro ufficio che non è soltanto quello di stabilire empiricamente la risultante di un gran numero di cause sconosciute, ma sopratutto di dare della realtà una testimonianza immediata e concreta. La cui interpretazione richiede un'arte speciale, non ultimo sussidio dell'arte di governo.

Commento alla Nota Scientifica n. 10: *"Il valore delle leggi statistiche nella fisica e nelle scienze sociali".*

Majorana pubblicò nove articoli prima della sua scomparsa mentre un decimo articolo, il cui manoscritto fu trovato dal fratello di Majorana tra le sue carte, fu pubblicato nel 1942 dopo la sua scomparsa nella rivista internazionale *Scientia* grazie all'interessamento del suo amico Giovanni Gentile jr.

Questo articolo è piuttosto speciale sotto diversi aspetti. Nella presentazione fatta per *Scientia*, Giovanni Gentile jr. affermò che l'articolo era stato originariamente scritto per una rivista di sociologia. Questo articolo intendeva quindi presentare il punto di vista di un fisico circa il valore delle leggi statistiche in fisica e nelle scienze sociali a studiosi di altre discipline come la sociologia e l'economia. Nel suo articolo, Majorana presenta la meccanica quantistica come una teoria fondamentale e di completo successo nel descrivere i processi che coinvolgono particelle ed atomi. Egli considera la meccanica quantistica una teoria statistica irriducibile in quanto la teoria non è in grado di descrivere ad un livello deterministico l'evoluzione di una *singola* particella (o di un *singolo* atomo) caratterizzata in una precisa condizione. Come esempio di impossibilità di una descrizione deterministica nell'evoluzione temporale di un singolo sistema fisico, Majorana discute il caso del decadimento di un atomo radioattivo. Questa mancanza di determinismo a livello di un sistema fisico elementare motiva Majorana a suggerire una analogia formale fra le leggi statistiche osservate in fisica e nelle scienze sociali. Nel suo articolo egli afferma che "Questa conclusione ha reso sostanziale l'analogia tra fisica e scienze sociali, tra le quali è risultata un'identità di valore e di metodo".

Nella nota biografica e scientifica pubblicata nel testo a cura di Edoardo Amaldi[1], l'Autore afferma che probabilmente Majorana scrisse questo articolo nel periodo tra il 1933 ed il 1937 dopo il suo viaggio a Lipsia e Copenhagen del 1933. Sappiamo dai ricordi di Amaldi che dopo il ritorno a Roma nell'autunno del 1933 il suo coinvolgimento nella fisica teorica declinò fino al 1937. Durante questo periodo Ettore Majorana si interessava

---

[1] E. AMALDI, *op. cit.*

di economia politica, di politica, delle flotte di diversi paesi e dei loro rapporti di forza e di problematiche filosofiche.

In questo articolo è presente una natura pionieristica sia da una prospettiva fisica che economica. Dal punto di vista della fisica, Majorana asserisce che la meccanica quantistica impone una descrizione statistica ad eventi che coinvolgono singole entità elementari. Egli prende una chiara posizione circa la natura statistica della teoria che ritiene irriducibile in termini di una sottostante teoria deterministica. Dal punto di vista dell'economia e delle scienze sociali, c'è l'osservazione che le leggi statistiche costituiscono strumenti d'indagine nella modellizzazione economica e sociale e sono caratterizzate dallo stesso stato epistemologico di leggi probabilistiche irriducibili come la meccanica quantistica. Va notato che questa posizione culturale non era certamente maggioritaria fra gli studiosi del secolo scorso in entrambe le discipline considerate. Infatti durante gli anni trenta del secolo scorso, le interazioni fra gli studiosi di economia e fisica erano sviluppate sotto il paradigma della meccanica dei corpi celesti e quindi sotto un paradigma di completo determinismo (la sola eccezione a questo approccio fu quello perseguito da Louis Bachelier con la descrizione stocastica dell'evoluzione temporale dei prezzi di un bene finanziario che in quel periodo non ebbe alcun impatto sull'accademia[2]). Questa interazione ha riguardato lo sviluppo della teoria dell'equilibrio generale perseguita da Walras, Pareto, Schlesinger e Wald. L'enfasi di Majorana sulla natura intrinsecamente statistica dei processi che descrivono fenomeni quantistici lo ha portato a supportare l'idea che leggi statistiche possano essere incorporate nel processo di modellizzazione scientifica di fenomeni sociali.

La fisica può certamente beneficiare di una più profonda comprensione di ruolo, necessità e peculiarità delle leggi statistiche presenti in questa disciplina. Alcune delle leggi statistiche sono in seguito reinterpretate in termini di leggi deterministiche più fondamentali. Tuttavia ci sono casi dove una tale riduzione sembra essere impossibile. Uno di questi casi è proprio quello della meccanica quantistica e altri esempi, successivi all'epoca che vide Majorana attivo, riguardano argomenti della teoria dei sistemi dinamici e della teoria dei fenomeni critici.

Riassumendo, il decimo articolo di Majorana solleva la necessità di focalizzare l'attenzione di varie discipline sul valore e sulla natura delle leggi statistiche. Dalla fisica alla biologia ed alle scienze sociali, diverse discipline scientifiche presentano leggi statistiche e gli studiosi hanno la necessità di riflettere circa il loro ruolo e valore in ogni disciplina. Majorana prese il punto di vista che la meccanica quantistica implica che una descrizione scientifica senza leggi di natura statistiche è impossibile a livello di descrizione di processi elementari. Oggi si sente ancora la necessità di valutare lo stato delle leggi statistiche nelle diverse discipline e di considerare le procedure di validazione che sono più appropriate per questo tipo di leggi e per il loro contenuto di conoscenza.

---

[2] L. Bachelier, *Thèorie de la spèculation*, Ph.D. Thesis in mathematics, *Annales Scientifiques de l'Ecole Normale Supèrieure*, **III-17** (1900) 21–86.

Desideriamo concludere questa breve nota affermando che, a nostro parere, Ettore Majorana merita oggi un profondo tributo ed una attenzione non solo per i suoi eccezionali risultati ottenuti nella fisica teorica ma anche per le sue opinioni ancora originali e attuali sugli aspetti essenziali, sull'importanza e sul ruolo delle leggi statistiche in fisica ed in altre discipline come le scienze sociali.

R. N. MANTEGNA
Università di Palermo

The value of statistical laws in physics and social sciences(*)(**)

Ettore Majorana

Summary. — The deterministic conception of nature implies in itself a real cause of weakness in the irremediable contradiction that it faces with the most certain data of our consciousness. G. Sorel attempted to compose this disagreement with the distinction between *artificial nature* and *natural nature* (this last acausal), but in this way he denied the unity of science. On the other hand, the formal analogy between the statistical laws of physics and the ones of social sciences credited the opinion that human facts also undergo a rigid determinism. It is therefore important that quantum mechanics principles have brought to recognize the statistical character of basic laws of elementary processes, in addition to a certain absence of objectiveness in the description of phenomena. This conclusion has made essential the analogy between physics and social sciences, between which it turned out an identity of value and method.

(*) This article of Ettore Majorana —the great theoretical physicist of Naples University who went missing on 25 March 1938— was originally written for a sociology journal. It was not published perhaps due to the reticence that the author had in interacting with others. Reticence that convinced him to put important papers inside a drawer too often. This article has been conserved by the dedicated care of his brother and it is presented here not only for the intrinsic interest of the topic but above all because it shows us one aspect of the rich personality of Majorana which so much impressed people who knew him, a thinker with a sharp realistic sense and with an extremely critical but not skeptical mind. He takes here a clear position concerning the debated problem of the statistical value of the basic physics law. This aspect was considered by several scholars as a defect similar to a charge of indeterminism in the evolution of nature; it is indeed for Majorana a reason to claim the intrinsic importance of the statistical method. Up to now this method has been applied only to social sciences and in the new interpretation of physics laws it fully recovers its original meaning.

Giovanni Gentile jr, 1942.

(**) Translated from "Scientia", vol. 36, 1942, pp. 58-66, by R. N. Mantegna in "Quantitative Finance" **5** (2005) 133-140. Reproduced by kind permission of Taylor and Francis Ltd. (http://www.tandf.co.uk/journals).

1. The concept of nature according to classical physics

The study of the true or hypothetical relations between physics and other sciences has always been of notable interest due to the special influence that physics has played on the general course of scientific thought in modern times. It is known that the laws of mechanics have been seen for a long time as the ultimate kind of human knowledge about nature. Many scholars have also believed that the imperfect notions of other sciences should eventually be related back to the kind of notions observed in mechanics. The above concept justifies the study we consider here.

The exceptional credit of physics evidently comes from the discovery of the so-called exact laws. These laws consist of relatively simple formulas, originally "excogitated" starting from fragmentary and approximate empirical indications, which turn out to be of universal validity both when these laws are applied to new orders of phenomena and when the progressive improvement of the art of experiments allows one to verify them in a more and more rigorous way. It is known to everybody that according to the fundamental concept of classical mechanics the motion of a physical body is completely determined by the initial conditions (position and velocity) of the body and by the forces that are applied to it. On the nature and size of forces that may be present in material systems, the general laws of mechanics state only some condition, or limitation, that always must be verified. Such a characteristic, for example, has the principle of action and reaction. To this principle one has added, more recently, other general rules such as the ones concerning constrained systems (principle of virtual work) or elastic reactions and, even more recently, the mechanical interpretation of heat and also the energy conservation principle, which is seen as a general principle of mechanics. Apart from these general indications, it is however a special task of physics to discover, case by case, all that is needed to effectively apply the principles of dynamics, which is the knowledge of all forces acting in the system being investigated.

In one case, however, it has been possible to find the general expression for forces that are present between material bodies. This occurs in the case where material bodies are isolated one from the other and therefore the forces are reciprocally acting at distance only. In this last case, if we do not consider electromagnetic forces, which were discovered in the XIX century and which manifest themselves only under specific conditions, the only force acting is the force of gravitation, whose notion was suggested to Newton from the mathematical analysis of the Keplero laws. The Newton law is typically applicable to the study of the motion of celestial bodies which being separated by immense empty spaces, can indeed influence each other only through action at a distance As is known, this law is indeed sufficient to predict in any aspect and with a beautiful accuracy the complex dynamics of our planetary system. Only one minute exception, the secular displacement that undergoes Mercury's perihelion, constitutes one of the major experimental proofs of the recent theory of general relativity.

The sensational success of mechanics applied to astronomy has encouraged the assumption that more complicated phenomena of common experience must also be in the end reconducted to a similar mechanism, albeit more general than the gravitational law.

According to this point of view, which has produced the mechanistic conception of nature, the entire material universe evolves obeying an inflexible law, where the state of the universe at a given instant of time is completely determined from its state at the previous instant of time. This is a sign of the fact that the future is implicit in the present. In other words, the future can be predicted with absolute certainty provided that the actual state of the universe is completely known. This fully deterministic conception of nature has had numerous confirmations since its introduction. Further developments of physics, from the discovery of the electromagnetism laws to the ones for the theory of relativity, have suggested a progressive enlargement of the principles of classical mechanics. On the other hand, they have vigorously confirmed an essential point, namely, the complete causality in physics. It is not disputable that determinism has the principal and almost exclusive merit of having made possible the magnificent modern development of science, and also in fields very far removed from physics. Determinism, which does not leave any rule to human freedom and forces one to consider all the phenomena of life as illusory, implicates a real cause of weakness. This is the irremediable and immediate contradiction with the most certain data of our conscience. Indeed, how the effective and, most probably, definitive overtaking of determinism has occurred in the physics of recent years will be discussed later. Indeed our final aim will be to illustrate the renovation that the traditional concept of statistical laws must undertake as a consequence of the new direction followed by contemporary physics. At the present stage we still wish to keep the classical conception of physics. This is done not only for its enormous historical interest but also because classical physics is still the only physics largely known except to specialists.

Before ending this introductory part, we wish to point out that criticism of determinism has been raised in recent times. The philosophical reaction, when appropriate, did not extend beyond the philosophical field and essentially it has left the scientific problem untouched. An attempt devoted to solve this specific scientific problem can be found in the work of G. SOREL[1]. He is an author representing the pragmatism or philosophical current in pluralism. According to the followers of this movement, an effective heterogeneity of natural phenomena excludes that a unitary knowledge of them might exist. Each scientific principle should be applied to a delimited ambit of phenomena without the possibility of achieving universal validity. G. SOREL develops the criticism of determinism by stating that this concept would apply only to phenomena which he calls *artificial nature*. These phenomena are characterized by the fact that they do not occur in the presence of an appreciable *degradation* of energy (in the sense of the second principle of thermodynamics). These phenomena sometimes occur spontaneously, especially in astronomy, where they constitute phenomena of simple observation. However, more often these phenomena are investigated in laboratories by experimenters. They devote special care to eliminating all possible passive resistances. The other phenomena, which belong to the common experience or to *natural nature* and occur in the presence of

---

[1] G. SOREL, *De l'utilité du pragmatisme*, Cap. IV, Paris 1921.

passive resistances, would not be controlled by precise laws but they should be affected by chance to a various degree. SOREL explicitly uses a metaphysical principle of G. B. VICO. We do not want to discuss here the arbitrary accentuation given to a specific aspect of science as it has been represented in an epoch which is no longer ours. Here we have to note that the pragmatist principle of judging the scientific doctrines on the basis of their effective usefulness does not justify the attempt of condemning the ideal of the unity of science. This idea has acted as a powerful stimulus to the progress of science many times.

2. THE CLASSICAL MEANING OF STATISTICAL LAWS AND SOCIAL STATISTICS

To fully understand the meaning of statistical laws according to mechanics, one needs to recall a hypothesis about the structure of matter, which was already familiar to the ancients and entered the domain of science due to DALTON at the beginning of the 19th century. He first recognized in the atomic hypothesis the natural explanation for the general laws of chemistry, which had been recently discovered. According to modern atomic theory, which has been definitively confirmed with specific methods of physics, there exists an amount of species of indivisible elementary particles, or *atoms*, of the same number of simple chemical elements. The union of two or more atoms of the same or different species forms the *molecules*. Molecules are the last particles in which one can divide a definite chemical substance, which are capable of independent existence. Single molecules (and sometimes also atoms within molecules) are not located in a fixed position but rather they undergo a very fast movement of translation and rotation around themselves. The molecular structure of gases is very simple. Indeed single molecules of gases can be considered as rather independent in common conditions. The relative distances between molecules are very large with respect to their extremely limited dimensions. By applying the inertial principle one concludes that their motion is rectilinear and uniform most of the time. The motion undergoes abrupt changes of direction and speed only when impacts occur. Supposing we exactly know the laws governing the mutual influence of molecules we should expect, in terms of general principles of mechanics, that it is enough to know the position of all molecules and their translational and rotational velocities *in addition* in order to predict *in principle* the exact state of the system after a certain time interval (although these calculations could be too complex to be effectively realized in practice). The use of the deterministic scheme, which is specific to mechanics, is however subject to a real limitation of principle when we take into account the fact that the *usual* methods of observation are not able to provide us with the exact instantaneous conditions of the system. They provide us only with a certain number of global observables. For example, by considering the physical system given by a certain amount of gas, it is sufficient to know the gas pressure and density to determine other variables, such as the temperature, the viscosity coefficient, etc., that could be the object of specific measurements. In other words, in the present example the values of pressure and density are sufficient to fully determine the state of the system *from a macroscopic point of view*, although they are evidently not sufficient to establish the exact internal structure of the gas at each time, *i.e.* the distribution of position and velocity of all molecules.

To discuss with clarity and conciseness and without any mathematical apparatus, the nature of the relationship between a *macroscopic state* (A) and a real state (a) of a system, we need to relax precision to a certain degree, although we avoid altering the true nature of the facts in an essential way. We therefore need to understand that the observed *macroscopic state* (A) corresponds to a large number of possibilities $a, a', a'' \ldots$ Our observations do not allow us to distinguish among them. The *number N* of these internal possibilities would be infinite within the framework of classical theory, but quantum theory has introduced an essential discontinuity in the description of natural phenomena, so that the number (N) of these possibilities in the structure of a system is indeed finite although huge. The value of N gives a measure of the degree of hidden indeterminacy of the system. It is however practically preferable to consider a quantity proportional to its logarithm

$$S = K \log N$$

K being the Boltzmann universal constant, which has been determined by imposing that S coincides with the entropy, which is a known quantity of thermodynamics. Indeed entropy is a physical quantity with the same importance as weight, energy, etc. This is mainly because entropy is an additive quantity in the same manner as the others. In other words, the entropy of a system composed of several independent parts is equal to the sum of the entropy of each single part. To prove this, it is enough to observe that the number of potential possibilities of a composed system is evidently equal to the product of analogous numbers describing the constituent parts together with the known elementary rule establishing the correspondence between the product of two or more numbers and the sum of their logarithms.

In general, there are no difficulties in how to determine the ensemble of internal configurations $a, a', a'' \ldots$ corresponding to a macroscopic state A. However one can discuss if all the distinct possibilities $a, a', a'' \ldots$ should be considered as equally probable. According to the ergodic or quasi-ergodic hypothesis, which is widely believed to be verified, whether a system persists in a state A indefinitely, then one can state that it spends an equal fraction of its time in each of the configurations $a, a', a'' \ldots$ Therefore one considers all possible internal determinations as equally probable. This is indeed a new hypothesis because the universe, which is far from being in the same state indefinitely, is subjected to continuous transformations. We will therefore admit as an extremely plausible working hypothesis, whose far reaching consequences could sometime not be verified, that all the internal states of a system are *a priori* equally probable for specific physical conditions. Under this hypothesis, the *statistical ensemble* associated with each macroscopic state A turns out to be completely defined.

The general problem of statistical mechanics can be summarized as follows: suppose the initial state A has been statistically defined; which predictions, therefore, are possible about its state at time t? At first sight, it may seem that this definition is too limited because other *static* problems can be considered in addition to the dynamic problem. For example, what is the temperature of a gas whose pressure and density are known? Similarly this applies in all cases when one wishes to determine a quantity of interest

from certain known characteristics of the system, which are sufficient to define its state. The distinction can be formally ignored because by incorporating appropriate measuring instruments in the system one can always go back to the previous case.

Let us suppose that the initial state of the considered system is described by a statistical ensemble $A = (a, a', a'' \ldots)$ of possible cases which are, as stated before, equally probable. Each of these specific determinations changes during time according to a law that we have to consider strictly causal in agreement with the general principles of mechanics. Therefore the system moves from the series $a, a', a'' \ldots$ to another specific series $\beta, \beta', \beta'' \ldots$ after a certain time. The statistical ensemble $(\beta, \beta', \beta'' \ldots)$; which is also constituted of N equally probable elements as the original ensemble A (Liouville theorem), defines all the possible predictions for the system evolution. Due to reasons that only a complex mathematical analysis could make precise, in general it turns out that all simple cases belonging to the series, $\beta, \beta', \beta'' \ldots$ *except a negligible number of exceptions, wholly* or *in part* constitute a new statistical ensemble B defined from a well-determined macroscopic state as in A. We can therefore state the *statistical law* according to which there is the practical certainty that the system should move from A to B. Due to the above discussion, the statistical ensemble B is at least as large as A. It contains a number of elements not less than N. It therefore follows that the entropy of B is equal to or larger than that for A. In the presence of any transformation occurring in *agreement with statistical laws* one therefore has a constant or increasing entropy, never a decrease. This is the statistical foundation of the famous second principle of thermodynamics.

It is worth noting that the transition from A to B can be considered certain from a practical point of view. This explains why historically the statistical laws have been originally considered as accurate as the laws of mechanics and only because of the progress of theoretical investigation one has subsequently recognized their true character. The statistical laws include a large amount of physics. Among the most widespread applications, we cite: the gas state equation, the diffusion theory, the theory of thermal conductance, of viscosity, of osmotic pressure and several other similar ones. A specific mention is deserved for the statistical theory of irradiation, which introduces the *discontinuum* symbolized by the PLANCK constant for the first time in physics. Moreover there is an entire area of physics, thermodynamics, whose principles, although directly based on experience, can be related to the general notions of statistical mechanics. On the basis of what has been done before, one can summarize the meaning of statistical laws within classical physics in the following way: 1) natural phenomena obey a complete determinism; 2) the *customary* observation of a system does not allow one to identify the internal state of the system but only the ensemble of very large possibilities which are macroscopically indistinguishable; 3) by establishing a plausible hypothesis for the probability of different possibilities and by assuming valid the laws of mechanics, the probability calculus allows the probabilistic prediction of future phenomena. We are now ready to examine the relation present between the laws established by classical mechanics and the empirical regularities, which are known by the same name especially in social sciences.

First of all, one should realize that the formal analogy could not be more stringent. For example, when one states the statistical law: "In a modern European society the annual

marriage rate is about 8 for 1000 inhabitants". It is clear enough that the investigated system is defined only with respect to certain global characters by deliberately renouncing the investigation of additional information, such as, for example, the biography of all individuals composing the society under investigation. This knowledge would certainly be useful in predicting the phenomenon with a precision and an accuracy higher than in the case for a generic statistical law. This is not different from when one defines the state of a gas by simply using pressure and volume and by deliberately renouncing investigation of the initial conditions for all single molecules. A substantial difference could indeed be detected in the definite mathematical character of the physics statistical laws, which has to be compared with the empirical character of social statistical laws. It is however plausible to attribute the empirism of social statistics (with the term empirism we precisely mean the lack of reproducibility of their results *in addition to the random part*) to the complexity of the considered phenomena. This last aspect implies that it is not possible to precisely define the conditions or the content of the law. On the other hand, physics also has empirical laws when it is studying phenomena of applied interest. Examples are the laws of friction among solid bodies or the magnetic properties of several types of iron and other similar materials. Lastly, one could express the special importance of the difference in the measurement methods, which are global in physics (it is sufficient to read a measurement instrument to know the pressure of a gas in spite of the fact that pressure arises from the sum of independent pulses that single molecules transmit to the walls) whereas in social statistics individual facts are recorded. This difference is however not an absolute antithesis as it is proved by the possibility of various indirect methods of detection. By admitting the arguments that suggest the existence of a real analogy between physics and statistical laws, we are induced to assume as plausible that the social statistical laws are the most direct proof that an absolute determinism also governs human facts in a way similar as physics statistical laws imply a rigid determinism. This is an argument that has had much better fortune because, as said before, one has detected the tendency to see the causality of classical physics as a model of universal value for independent reasons. Here it would be out of place to reopen old and never concluded discussions, but we wish to recall as a generally admitted fact that the absence of conciliation among contrasting intuitions of nature has for a long time played a role in modern thought and in moral values. It is therefore not just a scientific curiosity the announcement that physics has been forced to abandon its traditional course by rejecting the absolute determinism of classical mechanics in a definitive manner in recent years.

3. THE NEW CONCEPTS OF PHYSICS

It is impossible to present with some completeness in a few lines the mathematical apparatus and the experimental content of quantum mechanics([2]). We will therefore

---

([2]) The reader desiring to study thoroughly the knowledge in this matter by avoiding where possible the mathematical difficulty can consult W. HEISENBERG, *Die Physikalischen Prinzipien der Quantentheorie*, Lipsia, 1930.

limit ourselves to some short description. There are experimental facts, known for a long time (interference phenomena), which undoubtedly support in favour of an undulatory theory of light. Conversely, other recently discovered facts (Compton effect) suggest, no less convincingly, the opposite corpuscular theory. All attempts of settling this contradiction within classical physics have been unsuccessful. This may not seem so relevant except that these inexplicable facts and others no less inexplicable and those of the most differing nature and lastly almost all phenomena known to physicists, and up to now insufficiently understood, have been explained with a unique and wonderful simple explanation. This is the one contained in the principles of quantum mechanics. This extraordinary theory is so solidly founded on experience in as much, perhaps, any other one has never been. The criticism that it has received and is receiving are not concerned at all with the legitimacy of its use for effective prediction of phenomena, but rather the widespread opinion that the new approach should be conserved and perhaps even grow in future developments of physics. The specific aspects of quantum mechanics as compared with classical mechanics are as follows.

a) There are no laws in nature which express a fatal succession of phenomena. Basic laws governing elementary phenomena (atomic systems) have a statistical character. They establish only the *probability* that a measure performed in a prepared system will give a certain result. This occurs in spite of the means by which we are disposed to determine the initial state of the system with the highest possible accuracy. These statistical laws indicate a real deficiency of determinism. They have nothing in common with the classical statistical laws where uncertainty of results derives from a voluntary renunciation for practical reasons to investigate the initial conditions of physical systems in the most minute aspects. Below we will see a well-known example of this new kind of natural law.

b) A certain lack of *objectiveness* in the description of phenomena. Any experiment performed on an atomic system exerts a finite perturbation on it that cannot be eliminated or reduced for principle reasons. The result of any measure seems, therefore, to be concerned with the state where the system is led during the same measurement rather than the undetectable state in which the system was before the perturbation. This aspect of quantum mechanics is without doubt more disquieting, *i.e.* farther from our customary intuitions, than the simple lack of determinism.

Among the probabilistic laws concerning basic phenomena, the one governing radioactive processes has been known for a long time. Any atom of radioactive matter has a probability mdt in a time interval dt of transforming itself after the emission of an α particle (a helium nucleus) or, in other cases, of a β particle (an electron). The *mortality rate* m is constant, *i.e.* independent of the atom age. This gives a specific form to the *survival curve*, which is exponential. The mean lifetime is $1/m$ and one can estimate the *probable lifetime*, sometimes called the *transformation period*, in an elementary way. Both

quantities are independent of the atom age. Indeed the atom does not manifest any sign of real aging when time elapses. Several methods of observation and automatic recording of the single transformation occurring within a radioactive matter exist. It has been therefore possible to verify through direct statistical measurements and applications of probability calculus that single radioactive atoms do not undergo any reciprocal influence or any external influence concerning the instant of transformation. Indeed the number of disintegrations occurring in a certain time interval is subject to random fluctuations, *i.e.* to the probabilistic character of the individual law of transformation.

Quantum mechanics has taught us to see in the exponential law of radioactive transformations a basic law which is not reducible to a simpler causal mechanism. Of course the statistical laws concerning complex systems known in classical mechanics retain their validity according to quantum mechanics. Quantum mechanics modifies the rules of the determination for internal configurations in two different ways, depending on the nature of the physical systems, ending up with the statistical theories of BOSE-EINSTEIN and FERMI. However the introduction in physics of a new kind of statistical law or, better, simply a probabilistic law, which is hidden under the customary statistical laws, forces us to reconsider the basis of the analogy with the above-established statistical social laws. It is indisputable that the statistical character of social laws derives at least in part from the manner in which the conditions for phenomena are defined. It is a generic manner, *i.e.* strictly statistical, allowing a countless complex of different concrete possibilities. On the other hand, by remembering what has been said above on the *mortality tables* of radioactive atoms, we are induced to ask ourselves whether there also exists here a real analogy with social facts, which are described with a somewhat similar language.

At first sight something seems to exclude this. The disintegration of an atom is a simple fact, which is unpredictable and which occurs abruptly and in isolation after a wait of thousands and even billions of years, whereas nothing similar occurs for facts which are recorded from social statistics. However, this is not an insurmountable objection.

The disintegration of a radioactive atom can force an automatic counter to detect it with a mechanical effect, which is possible thanks to a suitable amplification. Common laboratory set-ups are therefore sufficient to prepare for whatever complex chain of rich phenomena which is *produced* from an accidental disintegration of a single radioactive atom. From a scientific point of view nothing prevents one from considering that an equally simple, invisible and unpredictable vital fact could be found at the origin of human events. If this is so, as we believe it is, the statistical laws of social sciences increase their function. Their function is not only of empirically establishing the resultant of a great number of unknown causes, but, above all, it is to provide an immediate and concrete evidence of reality. The interpretation of this evidence requires a special skill, which is an important support of the art of government.

Comment on the Scientific Paper no. 10: *"The value of statistical laws in physics and social sciences".*

Majorana published nine articles before his disappearance and a 10th article, whose manuscript was found by Majorana's brother among his files, was published in 1942, after his disappearance, in the international Italian journal *Scientia*, through the interest of his friend Giovanni Gentile jr.

The article is a rather special article in several respects. In the original presentation for *Scientia*, Giovanni Gentile jr. wrote that the article was originally written for a sociology journal. This article was therefore intended to present the point of view of a physicist about the value of statistical laws in physics and social sciences to scholars of a broad spectrum of different disciplines such as sociology and economics. In his article, Majorana considers quantum mechanics as a fundamental and successful theory able to describe the basic processes involving particles and atoms. He explicitly considers quantum mechanics as an irreducible statistical theory because theory is not able to describe the time evolution of a *single* particle or atom in a precise environment at a deterministic level. As an example of the lack of determinism in the time evolution of a single system he discusses the case of the decay of a radioactive atom. This lack of determinism at the level of an elementary physical system motivated him to suggest a formal analogy between statistical laws observed in physics and in social sciences. In his article, he states that: "This conclusion has made essential the analogy between physics and social sciences, between which it turned out an identity of value and method".

According to the biographical and scientific note published in the book edited by Edoardo Amaldi[1], Majorana most probably wrote this article during the period from 1933 to 1937 after his 1933 travel to Lipsia and Copenhagen. According to Amaldi's recollection, after his return to Rome during the fall of 1933 Majorana's involvement in theoretical physics research declined until 1937. During this period Ettore Majorana was studying economics, politics, naval fleets of different countries and their relative strength and philosophical problems.

There is a pioneering nature of this article both from the perspective of physics and of economics. From the physics point of view, Majorana stated that quantum mechanics forces scientists to use a statistical description down to events involving single entities. He took a clear position about the statistical nature of quantum mechanics by considering

[1] E. Amaldi, *op. cit.*

this property as irreducible in terms of an underlying deterministic theory. From the point of view of economics and social sciences, there is the observation that statistical laws are investigation tools to be used in economic and social modeling and are characterized by the same epistemological status of irreducible probabilistic laws as quantum mechanics. It should be noted that this position was not that of the majority of scholars working in the thirties of the XX century in both the disciplines considered. In fact, during the thirties of the last century the interaction between economics and physics was developed under the paradigm of celestial mechanics and therefore under a complete determinism (the only exception to this approach was the one pursued by Louis Bachelier with the stochastic description of the time evolution of the price of a financial asset that, at that time, had no impact on the academy[2]). This interaction goes back to the development of the general equilibrium theory pursued by Walras, Pareto, Schlesinger and Wald. The emphasis of Majorana on the intrinsic statistical nature of quantum phenomena motivated him to support the idea that statistical laws should be incorporated into the scientific modeling of social phenomena.

Physics might certainly benefit from a deeper understanding of the role, necessity and peculiarity of statistical laws in physics. Some of the statistical laws are eventually reinterpreted in terms of more fundamental and deterministic laws. However there are cases when a reduction seems to be impossible. One of these cases is indeed quantum mechanics and other more recent examples, in years when Majorana was not active any longer, concern topics of dynamical systems and critical-phenomena theory.

In summary, the 10th article of Majorana raised the necessity of focusing the attention of several disciplines on the value and nature of statistical laws. From physics, to biology and to social sciences, several scientific disciplines present statistical laws and scholars need to reflect about their role and value within each discipline. Majorana took the view that quantum mechanics implies that a scientific description without statistical laws is impossible as far as the description of elementary processes is concerned. Today there is still the need to assess the status of statistical laws in different disciplines and to consider the validation procedures that are most appropriate to these sorts of laws and to their knowledge content.

We wish to conclude this short note by saying that we believe Ettore Majorana today deserves a great tribute not only for his exceptional achievements in theoretical physics but also for his fresh and original views on the essential aspects, importance and role of statistical laws in physics and in other disciplines such as social sciences.

R. N. MANTEGNA
Università di Palermo

---

[2] L. BACHELIER, *Thèorie de la spèculation*, Ph.D. Thesis in mathematics, *Annales Scientifiques de l'Ecole Normale Supèrieure*, **III-17** (1900) 21–86.

LA LEZIONE INAUGURALE   —   THE INAUGURAL LECTURE

Gli appunti per la lezione inaugurale

Ettore Majorana

Università di Napoli, 13 gennaio 1938

In questa prima lezione di carattere introduttivo illustreremo brevemente gli scopi della fisica moderna e il significato dei suoi metodi, soprattutto in quanto essi hanno di più inaspettato e originale rispetto alla fisica classica.

La fisica atomica, di cui dovremo principalmente occuparci, nonostante le sue numerose e importanti applicazioni pratiche —e quelle di portata più vasta e forse rivoluzionaria che l'avvenire potrà riservarci—, rimane anzitutto una scienza di enorme interesse *speculativo*, per la profondità della sua indagine che va veramente fino all'ultima radice dei fatti naturali. Mi sia perciò consentito di accennare in primo luogo, senza alcun riferimento a speciali categorie di fatti sperimentali e senza l'aiuto del formalismo matematico, ai caratteri generali della concezione della natura che è accettata nella nuova fisica.

$$* * *$$

La *fisica classica* di Galileo e Newton all'inizio del nostro secolo è interamente legata, come si sa, a quella concezione *meccanicistica* della natura che dalla fisica è dilagata non solo nelle scienze affini, ma anche nella biologia e perfino nelle scienze sociali, informando di sé quasi tutto il pensiero scientifico e buona parte di quello filosofico in tempi a noi abbastanza vicini; benché, a dire il vero, l'utilità del metodo matematico che ne costituiva la sola valida giustificazione sia rimasta sempre circoscritta esclusivamente alla fisica.

Questa concezione della natura poggiava sostanzialmente su due pilastri: l'esistenza oggettiva e indipendente della materia, e il determinismo fisico. In entrambi i casi si tratta, come vedremo, di nozioni derivate dall'esperienza comune e poi generalizzate e rese universali e infallibili soprattutto per il fascino irresistibile che anche sugli spiriti più profondi hanno in ogni tempo esercitato le leggi esatte della fisica, considerate veramente

come il segno di un assoluto e la rivelazione dell'essenza dell'universo: i cui segreti, come già affermava Galileo, sono scritti in caratteri matematici.

L'*oggettività* della materia è, come dicevo, una nozione dell'esperienza comune, poiché questa insegna che gli oggetti materiali hanno un'esistenza a sé, indipendente dal fatto che essi cadano o meno sotto la nostra osservazione. La fisica matematica classica ha aggiunto a questa constatazione elementare la precisazione o la pretesa che di questo mondo oggettivo è possibile una rappresentazione mentale completamente adeguata alla sua realtà, e che questa rappresentazione mentale può consistere nella conoscenza di una serie di grandezze numeriche sufficienti a determinare in ogni punto dello spazio e in ogni istante lo stato dell'universo fisico.

Il *determinismo* è invece solo in parte una nozione dell'esperienza comune. Questa dà infatti al riguardo delle indicazioni contraddittorie. Accanto a fatti che si succedono fatalmente, come la caduta di una pietra abbandonata nel vuoto, ve ne sono altri —e non solo nel mondo biologico— in cui la successione fatale è per lo meno poco evidente. Il determinismo in quanto principio universale della scienza ha potuto perciò essere formulato solo come generalizzazione delle leggi che reggono la meccanica celeste. È ben noto che un *sistema* di punti —quali, in rapporto alle loro enormi distanze, si possono considerare i corpi del nostro sistema planetario— si muove e si modifica obbedendo alla legge di Newton. Questa afferma che l'accelerazione di uno di questi punti si ottiene come somma di tanti vettori quanti sono gli altri punti:

$$\overset{..}{\overrightarrow{P_r}} \propto \Sigma_s \frac{m_s}{R_{rs}^2} \overrightarrow{e_{rs}},$$

essendo m_s la massa di un punto generico e $\overrightarrow{e_{rs}}$ il vettore unitario diretto da $\overrightarrow{P_r}$ a $\overrightarrow{P_s}$. Se in tutto sono presenti n punti, occorreranno $3n$ coordinate per fissarne la posizione e la legge di Newton stabilisce fra queste grandezze altrettante equazioni differenziali del secondo ordine il cui integrale generale contiene $6n$ costanti arbitrarie. Queste si possono fissare assegnando la posizione e le componenti della velocità di ciascuno dei punti all'istante iniziale. Ne segue che la configurazione futura del *sistema* può essere prevista con il calcolo purché se ne conosca lo stato iniziale cioè l'insieme delle posizioni e velocità dei punti che lo compongono. Tutti sanno con quale estremo rigore le osservazioni astronomiche abbiano confermato l'esattezza della legge di Newton; e come gli astronomi siano effettivamente in grado di prevedere con il suo solo aiuto, e anche a grandi distanze di tempo, il minuto preciso in cui avrà luogo un'eclisse, o una congiunzione di pianeti o altri avvenimenti celesti.

* * *

Per esporre la *meccanica quantistica* nel suo stato attuale esistono due metodi pressoché opposti. L'uno è il cosiddetto metodo storico: ed esso spiega in qual modo, per indicazioni precise e quasi immediate dell'esperienza, sia sorta la prima idea del nuovo formalismo; e come questo si sia successivamente sviluppato in una maniera obbligata assai più dalla necessità interna che non dal tenere conto di nuovi decisivi fatti sperimentali. L'altro metodo è quello matematico, secondo il quale il formalismo quantistico

viene presentato fin dall'inizio nella sua più generale e perciò più chiara impostazione, e solo successivamente se ne illustrano i criteri applicativi. Ciascuno di questi due metodi, se usato in maniera esclusiva, presenta inconvenienti molto gravi.

È un fatto che, quando sorse la meccanica quantistica, essa incontrò per qualche tempo presso molti fisici sorpresa, scetticismo e perfino incomprensione assoluta, e ciò soprattutto perché la sua consistenza logica, coerenza e sufficienza appariva, più che dubbia, inafferrabile. Ciò venne anche, benché del tutto erroneamente, attribuito a una particolare oscurità di esposizione dei primi creatori della nuova meccanica, ma la verità è che essi erano dei fisici, e non dei matematici, e che per essi l'evidenza e giustificazione della teoria consisteva soprattutto nell'immediata applicabilità ai fatti sperimentali che l'avevano suggerita. La formulazione generale, chiara e rigorosa, è venuta dopo, e in parte per opera di cervelli matematici. Se dunque noi rifacessimo semplicemente l'esposizione della teoria secondo il modo della sua apparizione storica, creeremmo dapprima inutilmente uno stato di disagio o di diffidenza, che ha avuto la sua ragione d'essere ma che oggi non è più giustificato e può essere risparmiato. Non solo, ma i fisici —che sono giunti, non senza qualche pena, alla chiarificazione dei metodi quantistici attraverso le esperienze mentali imposte dal loro sviluppo storico— hanno quasi sempre sentito a un certo momento il bisogno di una maggiore coordinazione logica, di una più perfetta formulazione dei princípi, e non hanno sdegnato per questo compito l'aiuto dei matematici.

Il secondo metodo, quello puramente matematico, presenta inconvenienti ancora maggiori. Esso non lascia in alcun modo intendere la genesi del formalismo e in conseguenza il posto che la meccanica quantistica ha nella storia della scienza. Ma soprattutto esso delude nella maniera più completa il desiderio di intuirne in qualche modo il significato fisico, spesso così facilmente soddisfatto dalle teorie classiche. Le applicazioni, poi, benché innumerevoli, appaiono rare, staccate, perfino modeste di fronte alla sua soverchia e incomprensibile generalità.

Il solo mezzo di rendere meno disagevole il cammino a chi intraprende oggi lo studio della fisica atomica, senza nulla sacrificare della genesi storica delle idee e dello stesso linguaggio che dominano attualmente, è quello di premettere un'esposizione il più possibile ampia e chiara degli strumenti matematici essenziali della meccanica quantistica, in modo che essi siano già pienamente familiari quando verrà il momento di usarli e non spaventino allora o sorprendano per la loro novità: e si possa così procedere speditamente nella derivazione della teoria dai dati dell'esperienza.

Questi strumenti matematici in gran parte preesistevano al sorgere della nuova meccanica (come opera disinteressata di matematici che non prevedevano un così eccezionale campo di applicazione), ma la meccanica quantistica li ha "sforzati" e ampliati per soddisfare alle necessità pratiche; così essi non verranno da noi esposti con criteri da matematici, ma da fisici. Cioè senza preoccupazioni di un eccessivo rigore formale, che non è sempre facile a raggiungersi e spesso del tutto impossibile.

La nostra sola ambizione sarà di esporre con tutta la chiarezza possibile l'uso effettivo che di tali strumenti fanno i fisici da oltre un decennio, nel quale uso —che non ha mai condotto a difficoltà o ambiguità— sta la fonte sostanziale della loro certezza.

Commento su "Gli appunti per la lezione inaugurale".

1. Le procedure della chiamata e della *lectio magistralis* a Napoli

Il 5 giugno del 1224 Federico II, re di Germania ed imperatore dei Romani, inviava da Siracusa a tutte le autorità del Regno una circolare (*generales licterae*) che esordiva con:

"Col favore di Dio, per il quale viviamo e regniamo, al quale riferiamo quanto di bene facciamo, desideriamo che, mediante una fonte di scienza ed un semenzaio di dottrina, nel Regno nostro molti diventino savi ed accorti, i quali, resi abili dallo studio e dalla meditazione del diritto, servano a Dio, al quale tutte le cose servono, e piacciano a noi per il culto della giustizia, ai cui precetti ordiniamo a tutti di obbedire. Abbiamo perciò disposto che, nell'amenissima città di Napoli, s'insegnino le arti e si coltivino gli studi di ogni professione, affinché i digiuni ed affamati di dottrina trovino dentro il Regno stesso di che soddisfare le loro brame, e non sieno costretti, per procurare d'istruirsi, a imprendere lunghi viaggi, e mendicare in terre straniere."

Nella stessa circolare annunziava che *"uno dei maestri da lui scelti sarebbe stato il dottissimo Roffredo di Benevento"*, e stabiliva che *"si farà prestito agli scolari..."*; come riferito da Torraca([1]), le lezioni allo "Studio" sarebbero cominciate nell'ottobre del 1224.

La nomina dei professori e la durata della stessa erano quindi prerogativa dell'imperatore. Tale procedura fu mantenuta da Corrado e Manfredi e, dopo una breve interruzione succeduta alla battaglia di Benevento (1266), dagli Angioini (1266-1442) e successivamente dagli Aragonesi (1442-1503). È nel 1503 che ha inizio il periodo spagnolo con Ferdinando il Cattolico. All'inizio lo Studio rimase chiuso per qualche anno, ma fu riaperto il giorno di S. Luca (18 Ottobre) del 1507. Va notato che era in tale giorno che l'Università di Salamanca, fondata sei anni prima dello Studio, usava riaprire i battenti; peraltro, come vedremo più avanti, lo Studio di Salamanca fu sempre un riferimento per Napoli.

La persona che portò un significativo contributo fu senz'altro il vicerè D. Pietro Fernandez de Castro, conte di Lemos. Questi, infatti, non solo fece edificare un grande edificio fuori della porta di Costantinopoli, ora sede del Museo Archeologico, che fu occupato dallo Studio dal 1615 fino all'inizio del secolo XVIII, ma realizzò, fra il 1614 e il 1616, una profonda riforma nella procedura per il reclutamento dei professori. Tale riforma copia sostanzialmente la regola sancita per l'Università di Salamanca nel 1561, in cui si

---

([1]) Stamperia di Giovanni de Simone, Napoli MDCCLIV.

stabilisce che il reclutamento avviene con una procedura di concorso bandito dal Governo e dopo un pubblico esame davanti ad una commissione composta da professori e lettori, anche di collegi religiosi. A Salamanca, dopo il pubblico esame gli aspiranti attendevano in una cappella la chiamata del vincitore e l'invito ad unirsi al consesso dei professori.

Come riportato da Giangiuseppe Origlia nella sua *Istoria dello Studio di Napoli*(²), il pubblico esame consisteva *"in porre al concorrente l'obbligo di pubblicamente sporre a viva voce e per lo continuo spazio di un'ora e senza l'aiuto de' scritti ..., quei punti della materia, ..., li quali 24 ore prima"* gli erano stati assegnati *"dal Prefetto in presenza de' testimoni."*

A dimostrazione dell'interesse con cui queste lezioni erano seguite, Origlia precisa che il pubblico presente era costituito dai *"lettori e tutti quelli che avevano la facoltà di dare il suffragio alla Cattedra, ch'era da conferirsi, non che d'uno stuolo infinito de' scolari, o d'altri, che desideravano in simili giostre essere presenti".*

Il Lemos stabilì anche le regole per l'apertura dell'Anno Accademico (la prima il 14 giugno 1615). Secondo una testimonianza di un contemporaneo, la cerimonia iniziò con un corteo in cui *"andavano prima i legisti con mozzetta*(*) *di drappo verde e cappello con fiocco di seta verde, quindi i medici con mozzetta di drappo torchino e cappello con fiocco dello stesso colore, quindi i teologi con mozzetta di drappo bianco e cappello dello stesso colore."*

Una volta giunti al palazzo dello Studio, ebbe luogo la cerimonia con una *lectio magistralis* letta da Gio. Lorenzo di Rogiero.

Le acconciature incontrarono l'irrisione del popolo; ciò nonostante furono mantenute per le successive analoghe circostanze.

In (²), Nino Cortese descrive le occasioni in cui veniva letta una lezione con carattere ufficiale nel seguente modo: *"L'anno scolastico si apriva solennemente con un'orazione di uno dei lettori; inoltre si continuò un uso già in voga nel secolo precedente, pel quale questi ultimi, all'atto di prendere possesso della cattedra, pronunciavano una vera e propria prolusione."*

Questa prolusione inaugurale era una usanza seguita anche a Salamanca e divenne una tradizione che in Spagna trovò una formalizzazione in un Decreto Real del 20 agosto 1859, ma a Napoli rimase interna all'Ateneo.

Tornando alla procedura di reclutamento, va detto che non sempre avvenne per concorso tant'è che il vicerè marchese di Villena dovette, nel 1703, ribadire che i concorsi erano assolutamente necessari ed obbligò coloro che erano stati nominati lettori senza aver sostenuto un concorso a sottomersi a tale procedura. Nella stessa prammatica, il Villena ordina che ogni cattedratico esponga durante il corso una conclusione generale della materia che legge (si tenga presente che la lezione era divisa in due parti; nella prima il lettore dettava, nella seconda spiegava).

(²) F. TORRACA, *Storia della Università di Napoli* (Riccardo Ricciardi Editore, Napoli) MCMXXIV.
(*) Corta mantellina; i papi, nelle cerimonie, ne indossano una bianca.

Lo Studio seguì queste regole sino al 1707, quando il regno venne occupato dagli Austriaci per ventisette oscuri anni e il Palazzo dello Studio fu occupato dalle truppe austriache. Le lezioni tornarono a tenersi nel chiostro del convento di S. Domenico Maggiore, come usava prima del 1615. La ristrettezza dello spazio rese difficile lo svolgimento della didattica, ma la situazione non cambiò, nonostante le suppliche del Cappellano Maggiore alle Autorità(^{3}).

Nel 1735 il Regno riacquistò l'indipendenza, il Re ordinò di restaurare la sede dello Studio ed il 4 Novembre 1736 fu inaugurato l'anno accademico con una prolusione di Giovan Battista Vico, lettore regio della scienza della Retorica. Tutte le *lectiones magistrales* di cui si è detto erano rigorosamente in latino.

Nel 1754 ci fu un evento che dette una svolta a questa regola. Un matematico toscano, Bartolomeo Infieri, vivente a Napoli, amministratore di beni dei Medici e dei Corsini, propose alla Corte di istituire una cattedra finanziata con una rendita di 300 ducati, frutto di un capitale in banca di 7500 ducati, a condizione che l'insegnamento fosse impartito in lingua italiana. Questa proposta incontrò varie difficoltà, ma alla fine fu approvata e il 5 novembre 1754 Antonio Genovese potè salire sulla cattedra di filosofia economica e di economia civile, che fu la prima cattedra di economia pubblica in Europa, tenendo una *lectio magistralis* alla presenza di un pubblico straordinariamente folto.

Nella seconda metà del '700 non ci furono particolari novità, salvo una leggerissima apertura alle discipline scientifiche, il trasferimento dello Studio nel 1777 nei notevoli spazi resisi liberi dopo la cacciata dei gesuiti del 1767, e la temporanea chiusura dello Studio nel 1799 dopo l'ingresso della *gloriosa armata cristiana* del cardinal Ruffo di Calabria che represse la Rivoluzione Napoletana, con sette professori afforcati ed undici arrestati.

Il passaggio ad una Università moderna si ebbe con la venuta dei francesi nel 1806 al seguito di Giuseppe Bonaparte, che ripartì l'Università degli Studi di Napoli nelle classi di diritto, teologia, medicina, scienze naturali, e filosofia: quest'ultima associata alle cattedre di logica e metafisica, matematica semplice, matematica trascendentale, meccanica, fisica sperimentale e astronomia; c'era infine una classe di cattedre diverse. Ancora più moderna l'innovazione introdotta da Gioacchino Murat, che, sulla base di una accurata analisi condotta da una commissione di cui fu relatore Vincenzo Cuoco, con decreto del 1811, introdusse le Facoltà, fra cui quella di scienze fisiche e matematiche, con le cattedre di matematica sintetica, matematica analitica, calcolo degl'infiniti, arte euristica o dell'invenzione matematica, meccanica, fisica sperimentale (con un gabinetto di macchine e un aggiunto), zoologia, botanica (con un giardino botanico), fisiologia vegetale, storia naturale (con l'obbligo del corso di anatomia comparata e con un museo curato da un professore cui era affidato il corso di iconografia naturale), mineralogia (con un gabinetto mineralogico ed un laboratorio), chimica (con un gabinetto ed un aggiunto cui era affidato il corso di farmacia) e di astronomia (con un osservatorio e due aggiunti).

(^{3}) I. Ascione, *L'Università di Napoli nei documenti del '700 (1690-1734)* (Edizioni Scientifiche Italiane) 1997.

Con lo stesso decreto Murat riformò i concorsi sulla base delle seguenti regole:
– le commissioni d'esame non vedevano più insieme tutti i professori, ma questi venivano accorpati (ad esempio, scienze era accorpata a medicina);
– i candidati inviavano al Cancelliere uno scritto con l'esposizione della propria esperienza e delle proprie idee in un plico contenente una busta al cui interno c'era il proprio nome;
– questo scritto veniva esaminato da un segretario; se lo scritto era disapprovato, la busta veniva bruciata;
– gli autori degli scritti approvati venivano sottoposti ad un esame analogo a quelli in uso nel passato;
– al termine i commissari esprimevano il loro voto segreto ed il risultato veniva trasmesso alle autorità di governo e quindi al Re che firmava il decreto di nomina.

Certamente era mantenuta la regola secondo cui il nuovo professore pronunciava la sua lezione inaugurale, detta anche *lectio magistralis*, alla presenza della facoltà e di invitati.

Quest'ultima tradizione è sicuramente durata fino alla seconda guerra mondiale, ma è stata man mano abbandonata (a Salamanca già nel 1973). Ad esempio, nessuno dei fisici che sono andati in cattedra dopo Majorana l'ha tenuta, mentre risulta che, nella nostra facoltà di lettere, ne siano state ancora tenute nel 1992 e nel 1993.

2. Majorana: Il conferimento della cattedra e la sua *lectio magistralis*

Dopo il concorso del 1926, in cui ottennero la cattedra Fermi, Persico e Pontremoli, passarono dieci anni prima che si aprisse, nel 1937, un nuovo concorso per la fisica teorica, richiesto dall'università di Palermo per iniziativa di Emilio Segré. A questo nuovo concorso volle partecipare Ettore Majorana (o per propria iniziativa o perché invitato da amici). Per chi conosce il carattere di Majorana, così lontano da interessi accademici, questa decisione può sembrare strana. Ma una spiegazione ci è giunta nei mesi scorsi. Premettiamo il ricordo che, dopo il rientro da Lipsia della fine del 1933, Ettore si allontanò dal gruppo di Fermi, ma non dalla fisica, come testimoniano molti documenti[4]. Per di più De Gregorio[5] ha recentemente scoperto presso l'Università di Roma "La Sapienza", che, negli anni di isolamento, e precisamente per gli AA. AA. 1933/34, 1934/35 e 1935/36, il Majorana aveva chiesto di potere tenere presso l'Istituto di via Panisperna dei corsi universitari "liberi", cosa cui aveva diritto possedendo egli la libera docenza. Il direttore Corbino fece approvare tali domande, ma pare che il Nostro non tenne mai le desiderate lezioni, probabilmente per la mancanza, allora, di studenti capaci di comprenderne la importanza.

Majorana era molto interessato, quindi, all'insegnamento di quanto la sua mente prodigiosa andava scoprendo delle leggi della natura. Ed è probabile che partecipò volentieri al concorso del 1937 proprio per avere finalmente degli allievi (ai quali prestò

[4] E. Recami, *Il Caso Majorana: Epistolario, Documenti, Testimonianze* (Mondadori, Milano) 1987, 1991; si veda la IV edizione ampliata (Di Renzo Editore, Roma) 2002.

[5] A. De Gregorio e S. Esposito, in *Sapere*, no. 3, Giugno 2006, 56; e *Teaching theoretical physics: The cases of E. Fermi and E. Majorana*, preprint `arXiv:phisics/0602146`.

molta attenzione, come stiamo per vedere). Come sappiamo, su proposta della Commissione preposta al concorso, presieduta da Fermi, il 2 novembre 1937 il ministro Bottai emette il decreto di nomina di Ettore Majorana a professore ordinario di fisica teorica, presso la Regia Università di Napoli, fuori concorso; e alla fine del 1937 tale nomina viene partecipata dal Ministero a Ettore, presso la sua abitazione di viale Regina Margherita 37 in Roma, *"per l'alta fama di singolare perizia cui Ella è pervenuta nel campo degli studi riguardanti la detta disciplina, con decorrenza dal 16 novembre 1937-XVI"*. Majorana si reca a Napoli dopo l'Epifania (verso il 10 gennaio 1938), e il 12 scrive dalla sua sede universitaria al ministro Bottai asserendo, tra l'altro, *"... tengo ad affermare che darò ogni mia energia alla scuola e alla scienza italiane, oggi in così fortunata ascesa"*[6].

Le lettere del 1938 di Ettore Majorana, aventi rilevanza anche per le circostanze della sua scomparsa, sono contenute in bibliografia [4]. Accenniamo brevemente solo a quelle che qui ci interessano. Nella lettera dell'11 gennaio 1938 da Napoli, alla madre, Ettore scrive: *"Ho annunziato l'inizio del corso per giovedì 13 alle ore nove. Ma non è stato possibile verificare se vi sono sovrapposizioni d'orario, così che è possibile che gli studenti non vengano e che si debba rimandare. Ho visto il preside con cui ho concordato di evitare ogni carattere ufficiale all'apertura del corso, e anche per questo non vi consiglierei di venire..."*. La famiglia, invece, si presentò puntuale il giovedì 13 gennaio 1938, alle ore nove, per assistere alla prolusione di Ettore. Alla lezione assistettero i professori della Facoltà, fra cui sicuramente Antonio Carrelli e Renato Caccioppoli, molto amici tra loro; come ricorda Gilda Senatore, gli studenti non furono invitati.

Gli appunti per la prolusione al corso, o lezione inaugurale, sono stati rinvenuti da uno di noi [E.R.] verso il 1972 e resi noti per la prima volta dieci anni dopo[7][8]: essi sono più sopra riportati. In essi traspare l'interesse dello scienziato, non solo per le questioni generali e di fondo che animano la ricerca scientifica, ma anche per il migliore *metodo didattico* da seguire per trasmettere il sapere agli allievi (per i quali nutriva, ripetiamo, profondo interesse).

Una lettura degli appunti di Majorana per la sua prolusione può riuscire rivelatrice riguardo a vari aspetti del carattere scientifico ed umano del Nostro; avvertiamo solo che in essi ci si riferisce alla fisica classica e alla meccanica quantistica, trascurando in questa prima fase gli aspetti relativistici: aspetti che verranno trattati dal Majorana solo

---

[6] I documenti, scoperti, raccolti, e per primo pubblicati, da E. Recami, sono contenuti in bibliografia [4]. Essi (fotografie incluse) sono coperti da copyright a favore di Recami, della famiglia Majorana, ed, ora, dell'editore Di Renzo, ed abbisognano del permesso scritto degli aventi diritto per la loro riproduzione. Ovviamente ne sono escluse tutte le carte *scientifiche*.

[7] E. Recami, in *Corriere della Sera* (Milano), 19 Ottobre 1982. Si vedano anche le bibliografie [4] e [8].

[8] B. Preziosi (Curatore), *Ettore Majorana – Lezioni all'Università di Napoli*, (Bibliopolis, Napoli) 1987. Questo volume contiene, oltre a un commento di N. Cabibbo, anche un articolo di E. Recami contenente il già citato testo della lezione inaugurale e il catalogo dei manoscritti scientifici inediti del Nostro (ad opera di M. Baldo, R. Magnani e E. Recami); per questo catalogo si veda anche E. Recami, *Quaderni di Storia della Fisica*, no. **5** (1999) 19-68.

nella seconda parte del corso, come rivelato dagli appunti delle sue ultime sei lezioni recentemente scoperti. Majorana era particolarmente sedotto dalla descrizione antimeccanicistica e "probabilistica" della meccanica quantistica, tanto da trattarla ampiamente anche nel suo articolo[9], pubblicato postumo, nel 1942, da Giovannino Gentile. Già il 27 luglio 1934, da Monteporzio Catone (RM), Majorana aveva scritto allo stesso Gentile: *"Credo che il maggior merito del libro di Jeans[10] sia quello di anticipare le reazioni psicologiche che il recente sviluppo della fisica dovrà fatalmente produrre quando sarà generalmente compreso che la scienza ha cessato di essere una giustificazione per il volgare materialismo...".*

Poiché il mito ha associato la scomparsa di Ettore con timori circa la possibile costruzione della bomba atomica, osserviamo subito che, fin dagli inizi della sua lezione inaugurale, Ettore dichiara esplicitamente: *"... La fisica atomica, di cui dovremo principalmente occuparci, nonostante le sue numerose e importanti applicazioni pratiche —e quelle di portata più vasta e forse rivoluzionaria che l'avvenire potrà riservarci—, rimane anzitutto una scienza di enorme interesse speculativo, per la profondità della sua indagine che va veramente fino all'ultima radice dei fatti naturali...".* Il periodare di Majorana lascia intendere che, anche di fronte alle applicazioni forse "rivoluzionarie" alle quali la fisica atomica e nucleare avrebbero potuto portare, il loro interesse (in particolare per lui) è essenzialmente quello speculativo.

3. Le lezioni del suo corso di fisica teorica

Come testimoniato da Gilda Senatore e Sebastiano Sciuti, gli alunni del corso, che iniziò il 15 gennaio, furono, oltre a loro due, Nella Altieri, Laura Mercogliano, Nada Minghetti e Savino Coronato, allievo di Caccioppoli, che dopo l'ultima lezione non frequentò più l'Istituto Fisico e che si laureò in Matematica lo stesso anno. A loro testimonianza nessun altro partecipò, salvo, molto sporadicamente, Mario Cutolo, già laureato in fisica.

Ai propri studenti il Majorana dedicava la più grande attenzione; e ne era soddisfatto. Invero, il 2 marzo 1938, nella sua ultima lettera all'amico e collega Giovanni Gentile jr, scrive: *"... Sono contento degli studenti, alcuni dei quali sembrano risoluti a prendere la fisica sul serio...".* Quando prendeva in mano il gesso, la sua timidezza scompariva ed Ettore, come è facile immaginare, si trasfigurava, mentre dalla sua mano uscivano con facilità intere, eleganti lavagne di simboli fisici e matematici. Ciò è stato ricordato da Gilda Senatore di fronte alla telecamera di Bruno Russo, e più di recente, in occasione del 60mo anniversario dalla sua scomparsa, in un convegno organizzato dall'Università Federico II di Napoli.

L'intera serie degli appunti autografi di lezione redatti con ogni cura da Majorana, a

---

[9] E. Majorana, "Il valore delle leggi statistiche nella fisica e nelle scienze sociali", *Scientia* **36** (1942) 58-66.
[10] J. Jeans, *I Nuovi Orizzonti della Scienza* (Sansoni, Firenze) 1934, traduzione italiana a cura di G. Gentile jr.

beneficio dei propri allievi (e forse Ettore stava pensando di scrivere un libro per studenti, così come aveva pensato ad un libro nello stendere i suoi originalissimi appunti di studio, i *Volumetti*[11])) fu consegnata alla prediletta studentessa Gilda Senatore insieme con altri scritti, che non sono stati ritrovati, il giorno prima di partire per Palermo. Come queste carte arrivarono, tra la fine del '38 ed i primi del '39, a Carrelli e in che occasione Carrelli le trasmise ad Amaldi, prive di sei lezioni riguardanti l'elettrodinamica e la relatività speciale, è descritto in ([12]) e in una lettera di Preziosi a "Le Scienze" (settembre 2002). È interessante notare che nel 1939-40 Carrelli tenne un corso di relatività speciale, con le relative dispense pubblicate dal GUF nel 1940. Le dieci lezioni trasmesse ad Amaldi, e da lui depositate alla Domus Galilaeana, furono pubblicate anastaticamente in ([8]). Recentemente, S. Esposito([13]) ed Antonino Drago hanno rinvenuto, fra le carte lasciate alla famiglia da Eugenio Moreno, uno studente di Matematica che si laureò con Caccioppoli nel 1941, la trascrizione, di pugno del Moreno, di tutti gli appunti manoscritti da Majorana, incluse la parte di relatività che non c'è tra i documenti depositati nella Domus, ma che, a memoria di Gilda Senatore, *c'era* fra gli appunti consegnatile da Majorana. Tali appunti completi sono in ([14]).

Bruno Preziosi
Università di Napoli

Erasmo Recami
Università di Bergamo

([11]) S. Esposito, E. Majorana jr, A. van der Merwe e E. Recami, *Ettore Majorana - Notes on Theoretical Physics,* (Kluwer Academic Press, Dordrecht, Boston e New York) 2003. (Edizione nella lingua originale italiana: Majorana E., *Appunti inediti di fisica teorica,* a cura di S. Esposito e E. Recami (Zanichelli, Bologna) 2006).
([12]) *L'eredità di Fermi e Majorana ed altri temi* (Bibliopolis, Napoli) 2006.
([13]) S. Esposito, *Nuovo Saggiatore,* **21** No. 1-2 (2005) 21-41.
([14]) S. Esposito (Curatore), *Ettore Majorana - Lezioni di Fisica Teorica* (Bibliopolis, Napoli) 2006.

Preliminary notes for the inaugural lecture

Ettore Majorana

University of Naples, 13 January 1938

In this first introductory lecture I will briefly discuss the aims of modern physics and the significance of its methods, with particular emphasis on their most unexpected and original aspects with respect to classical physics.

Atomic physics, which will be the main subject of my discussion, despite its important and numerous practical applications —together with those of a wider and perhaps revolutionary impact that the future may have in store—, is first of all a science of immense *speculative* interest for the depth of its investigation that really reaches the extreme roots of natural facts. Let me first mention, without referring to any specific category of experimental facts and without the help of mathematical formalism, the general characters of the conceptions of nature that the new physics has introduced.

$$* * *$$

As is well known, at the beginning of our century the *classical physics* of Galileo and Newton is entirely founded on a *mechanistic* conception of nature that from physics has spread out not only to the sciences that are closer to it but also to biology and even to social sciences. This conception was extended in very recent times to almost all the scientific thinking and to a good extent also to the philosophical one, even though, to tell the truth, the usefulness of the mathematical method, which represented the only valid justification of the mechanistic conception, has always been limited only to physics.

This conception of nature rested essentially on two pillars: the objective and independent existence of matter, and physical determinism. As we shall see, in both cases these notions were based on common experience and were then generalized and given a universal and infallible character mostly because of the irresistible fascination that the exact laws of physics have always had even on the deepest thinkers: they were considered

as a sign of the absolute and the revelation of the essence of the universe whose secrets, as Galileo already proclaimed, are written in mathematical characters.

The *objectivity* of matter derives, as I have said, from common experience which teaches us that material objects have their own existence independently of the fact that they are or are not observed. Classical mathematical physics has added to this elementary observation the further statement or requirement that it is possible to give a mental representation of this objective world which is perfectly adequate to explain reality; and that such a mental representation can consist in the knowledge of a series of numerical quantities sufficient to determine at every point in space and at every instant of time the state of the physical universe.

Determinism instead only partially derives from common experience. In fact this common experience gives contradictory indications: besides facts that inevitably occur, as for example the free fall of a body in vacuum, there are others —and not only in the biological world— for which the inevitable occurrence is at least little evident. Determinism, as a universal principle of science, could therefore be formulated only as a generalization of the laws of celestial mechanics. It is well known that a *system* of points —as the bodies of our planetary system can be considered because of their enormous distances— moves and changes according to Newton's law This law states that the acceleration of one of these points is obtained from the sum of as many vectors as the other points are:

$$\overset{\cdots}{\overrightarrow{P}_r} \propto \Sigma_s \frac{m_s}{R_{rs}^2} \overrightarrow{e_{rs}},$$

m_s being the mass of a generic point and $\overrightarrow{e}_{rs}$ the unit vector with direction from $\overrightarrow{P}_r$ to $\overrightarrow{P}_s$. If we have a total of n points, $3n$ coordinates will be necessary to fix their position, and Newton's law establishes among these quantities as many second-order differential equations whose general integrals contain $6n$ arbitrary constants. These constants can be determined by assigning the position and the velocity components of each point at the initial time. Hence it follows that the future configuration of the *system* can be predicted by calculation, provided we know its initial state, *i.e.* the set of positions and velocities of the points which compose it. Everyone knows the extreme accuracy with which astronomical observations have confirmed the exactness of Newton's law and how astronomers can actually predict with its help only, and even in the distant future, the precise instant of an eclipse or a conjunction of planets or other celestial events.

* * *

To illustrate the present state of *quantum mechanics* there exist two almost opposite methods. One is the so-called historical method: It explains how, starting from precise and almost immediate experimental indications, the first idea of the new formalism was born; and how its subsequent development was compulsorily determined more by its internal consistency than by newly discovered fundamental experimental phenomena. The other method is the mathematical one, according to which the quantum formalism

is presented right from the beginning in its most general and therefore clearest structure and only later its criteria of application are discussed. Each one of these two methods, if exclusively applied, has very serious drawbacks.

It is a fact that, when quantum mechanics was born, for some time is was looked at by many physicists with surprise, skepticism and even considered as completely incomprehensible. This was mainly due to the fact that its logical consistency, internal coherence and sufficiency appeared dubious and even elusive. This was also attributed, though in a completely wrong way, to a special obscurity of exposition by the first founders of the new mechanics. But the truth is that they were physicists and not mathematicians and for them the evidence and justification of the theory rested essentially on the immediate applicability to the experimental facts that had suggested it. The general formulation, clear and rigorous, came later partly thanks to mathematical minds. If we were then to simply repeat the exposure of the theory according to its historical appearance, we would unnecessarily create at first an uncomfortable or distrustful feeling that was justified in the old days but which can no longer be accepted and can be spared. Furthermore physicists —who have managed to clarify, not without trouble, the quantum methods by means of conceptual experiments imposed by their own historical progress— have, not rarely, felt the need for a greater logical coordination and a more perfect formulation of the principles, and have not refused the help of mathematicians in this effort.

The second method, the purely mathematical one, presents even greater inconveniences. It does in no way allow to understand the origin of the formalism and as a consequence the place that quantum mechanics has in the history of science. Moreover it does not fulfil at all the desire to somehow perceive by intuition its physical significance, often so easily satisfied by classical theories; finally its applications, though quite numerous, appear few and disconnected, and even modest compared to its overwhelming and incomprehensible generality.

The only way to make life easier for those who begin today the study of atomic physics, without any sacrifice of the historical origin of the ideas and even of the language we use today, is to start with an ample and clear discussion of the mathematical tools that are essential to quantum mechanics. Then the student will be already familiar with such tools, when the time will come to use them, and will no longer be frightened or surprised by their novelty: at this stage, one will be thus able to proceed rapidly to derive the theory from the experimental data.

Most of these mathematical tools already existed before the beginning of the new mechanics (they had been without specific interests introduced by mathematicians who did not forecast such an exceptionally wide field of application); but quantum mechanics has "forced" and extended them to satisfy its practical needs. Thus we will expose them not as mathematicians but rather as physicists would do, *i.e.* with the criterion not to worry about an excessive formal rigour, which is not always easy and often totally impossible to achieve.

Our only ambition will be to discuss as clearly as possible the effective way in which physicists have been using those tools for over a decade: It is this use, that has never led to any difficulty or ambiguity, that constitutes the essential source of their certainty.

Comment on the "Preliminary notes for the inaugural lecture."

1. The procedures for the chair assignment and for the *lectio magistralis* in Naples

On June 5th 1224, Fredric II, king of Germany and emperor of the Romans, sent forth from Siracuse to all authorities in the Kingdom a circular letter (*generales licterae*) which commenced:

"With God's blessing, for whom we live and reign, to whom we report all the good we do, we wish that, in our Kingdom, through a source of science and a breeding ground of erudition, many may become wise and shrewd, who, made skilful by the meditation and the study of law, may serve God, to whom all things serve, and be useful to us for the worship of justice, whose commands we order all of you to obey. Therefore we have provided that, in the most pleasant city of Naples, arts may be taught and studies of all professions may be cultivated, thus those who are thirsty and greedy for erudition may find within the Kingdom itself how to satisfy their thirst, not being forced to procure education, by embarking on long journeys and begging in foreign lands."

In the same circular he announced that *"one of the scholars he meant to choose was the well learned Roffredo di Benevento"* and stated that *"loans will be allowed to pupils..."*; as referred by Torraca([1]), lectures at the "Studium" began in October 1224.

The appointment of the professors was then a privilege of the Emperor. This procedure was kept by Corrado and Manfredi and, after a brief interruption following the battle of Benevento (1226), by the Angevins (1266-1442) and later by the Aragoneses (1442-1503). In 1503, with Ferdinand the Catholic, the Spanish period started. At the beginning the Studium was closed for a few years, but it was reopened on St. Luca's day (October 18) in 1507. It is interesting to point out that the University of Salamanca, funded six years earlier than the Studium, used to open on the same day; moreover, as we shall see further down, the University of Salamanca was always taken as a reference institution.

The person who brought important innovation was certainly the viceroy D. Pietro Fernandez de Castro, Earl of Lemos. Not only did he order that a big building was built outside Costantinopoli gate —the building hosted the Studium from 1615 till the beginning of the XVIII century and at present it hosts the archaeological museum—, but he also made a deep reform in the way professors were recruited between 1614 and 1616.

([1]) Stamperia di Giovanni de Simone, Napoli MDCCLIV.

The reform is basically the same as the rule sanctioned by the University of Salamanca in 1561, which states that the assignment is carried out through a competition announced by the government and after a public examination in front of a commission made of professors and lecturers even belonging to religious orders, but, contrary to Salamanca's procedure, there were no students. In Salamanca, after the public examination, the competitors were invited to wait in a chapel for the call of the winner and the invitation to join the professor board.

As Giangiuseppe Origlia reports in his *Istoria dello Studio di Napoli*(²), in the public exam the applicant was *"imposed to explain publicly and loudly for the duration of one whole hour without the help of any written paper... those topics of the subject... which had been given to him 24 hours earlier by the Prefect in the presence of witnesses."*

To underline the interest with which these lessons were attended, Origlia says that the people who attended the lessons were *"lecturers and all those who had the right to vote for the chair which was to be assigned, as well as a crowd of students, and others, who wished to attend such 'jousts'."*

Earl of Lemos also fixed the rules for the opening of the academic year (the first time on June 14th 1615). According to the testimony of a person of the time, the ceremony started with a procession *"opened by the jurists, wearing a green brocade 'mozzetta'(*) and a hat with a green flock; the physicians, with a blue brocade 'mozzetta' and a hat with a blue flock were in the middle; at the end the theologians with a white brocade 'mozzetta' and a hat with a white flock."*

Once the procession reached the palace of the Studium, the ceremony started with a *lectio magistralis* read by Gio. Lorenzo Rogiero.

Although the clothes provoked the people's derision, they were used also in the following analogous ceremonies.

In ref. (²), Nino Cortese describes the occasions in which an official lecture was read: *"The academic year commenced solemnly with an oration of one of the lecturers; moreover, a custom which was common in the previous century was saved according to which when one of the lecturers was appointed to a chair he had to read a real opening lecture."*

The opening lecture was a custom common in Salamanca too and it became a tradition which was formalised in Spain with a Royal Decree on 20th August 1859, whereas in Naples it remained an internal rule of the University.

Going back to the assignment procedure, we must say that it did not always take place through a public competition; in fact, in 1703 the viceroy, marquis of Villena, ought to state again that public competitions were absolutely necessary and obliged those who had been appointed lecturers without a regular competition to undergo such a procedure. In the same occasion, Villena ordered that every professor expounded during the competition a general conclusion on the subject he would read (one must recall that the lesson was

---

(²) F. TORRACA, *Storia della Università di Napoli* (Riccardo Ricciardi Editore, Napoli) MCMXXIV.
(*) Short cloack; the popes, in ceremonies, use a white one.

divided into two parts; in the first the lecturer dictated, in the second one he explained).

The Studium followed these rules until 1707, when the reign was occupied by Austrians for twenty-seven dark years and the palace of the Studium was occupied by the Austrian Army troops. The lectures went back to be given again in the cloister of the monastery of St. Domenico Maggiore, as it used to be before 1615. The limited space made the didactics difficult but, despite the Major Chaplain's petitions to the authorities([3]), the situation did not change.

In 1735 the Reign got its independence again, the king ordered that the seat of the Studium had to be restored, and in November 1736 the academic year was opened with an inaugural lecture given by Giovan Battista Vico, royal lecturer of the science of rhetoric. All the *lectiones magistrales* we mentioned were given in Latin.

In 1754 something happened which changed this rule. A Tuscan mathematician, Bartolomeno Infieri, who was living in Naples, as administrator of the possessions of the Medici and Corsini families, offered to the court to establish and finance a chair with a salary of 300 ducats, gained from a bank capital of 7500 ducats, on condition that the teaching language were Italian. The proposal met several difficulties, but in the end it was approved and on 5th November 1754 Antonio Genovese obtained the chair of economic philosophy and civil economy, which was the first chair of public economy in Europe, giving a *lectio magistralis* in front of a very large number of people.

In the second half of the XVIII century no special changes occurred, apart from a very slight opening to the scientific disciplines. In 1777 the Studium was moved to bigger spaces that had been made available after the expulsion of the Jesuits in 1767. In 1799 the Studium was temporarily closed after the "glorious" Christian army of the Cardinal Ruffo di Calabria entered Naples and repressed the Neapolitan revolution when seven professors were hung and eleven arrested.

The transition to a modern university was performed in 1806, when the French arrived, by Giuseppe Bonaparte who established in the University of Naples the classes of law, theology, medicine, natural sciences, different chairs, and philosophy —the latter associated with the chairs of logic and metaphysics, of elementary mathematics, transcendental mathematics, mechanics, experimental physics and astronomy; there was finally a class of different chairs.

Even more modern was the innovation introduced by Gioacchino Murat, who on the basis of an accurate analysis carried out by a committee of which Vincenzo Cuoco was a member, introduced, with a decree in 1811, the Faculties, among which physical and mathematical sciences, with the chairs of synthetic mathematics, analytical mathematics, calculus of the infinities, heuristic art or art of the mathematical invention, mechanics, experimental physics (with a laboratory and an assistant), zoology, botany (with a botanic garden), vegetal physiology, natural history (with a compulsory course of compared anatomy and with a museum kept by a professor who was in charge of the

---

([3]) I. ASCIONE, *L'Università di Napoli nei documenti del '700 (1690-1734)* (Edizioni Scientifiche Italiane) 1997.

class in natural iconography), mineralogy (with a mineralogical cabinet and a laboratory), chemistry (with a cabinet and an assistant in charge of the class of pharmacy) and
astronomy (with an observatory and two assistants).

In the same decree Murat reformed the competitions in the following way:

– different boards of examiners were formed according to the disciplines' type: for instance, science was joined to medicine (formerly there was only one board of examiners
for all the disciplines);

– applicants sent the Chancellor a written paper, in which they explained their experiences and ideas, put inside a folder containing a sealed envelope with their name;

– the written paper was examined by a secretary: if the paper was disapproved the envelope was burnt;

– the authors of the approved papers had to undergo an examination similar to those
which were used in the past;

– in the end, the members of the commission wrote their secret mark and the result
was sent to the governmental authorities and from them to the king who signed the
nomination decree.

It was certainly kept the rule according to which the new professor read his inaugural
lesson (*lectio magistralis*) in front of the members of the faculty and invited people. This
tradition has been kept until the second world war, but it was gradually abandoned (in
Salamanca already in 1973). For instance, no one of the physicists who won the chair
after Majorana read the inaugural lesson, whereas in the humanistic faculty some were
still given in 1992 and 1993.

2. Majorana: the appointment to the chair and his *lectio magistralis*

After the 1926 competition, in which Fermi, Persico and Pontremoli were appointed
professors, ten years passed before a new competition for theoretical physics was announced in 1937; it was required by the University of Palermo on the initiative of Emilio
Segrè. Ettore Majorana too decided to apply to the competition (either on his own initiative or because he was invited to do so by his friends). This decision may appear strange
to those who know Majorana's temper, who was so far away from academic interests.
However, we got an explanation during the last few months. Let us first recall that when
Majorana came back from Leipzig at the end of 1933, he took the distances from Fermi's
group, but not from physics, as testified by a large number of documents[4]. Moreover, De Gregorio[5] has recently discovered, at the University of Rome "La Sapienza",
that during the time when he lived in isolation, namely in the academic years 1933/34,
1934/35 and 1935/36, Majorana had asked for the opportunity to deliver a "free" university course at the Institute in via Panisperna, which was his right since he was "Libero
Docente", namely qualified for university teaching. His requests were approved by the

---

[4] E. RECAMI, *Il Caso Majorana: Epistolario, Documenti, Testimonianze* (Mondadori, Milan)
1987, 1991; see the IV updated edition (Di Renzo Editore, Rome) 2002.
[5] A. DE GREGORIO and S. ESPOSITO, in *Sapere*, no. 3, June 2006, 56; see also *Teaching
theoretical physics: The cases of E. Fermi and E. Majorana*, preprint arXiv:physics/0602146.

Director Corbino, but Majorana never gave any lecture, probably because of the lack of students able, at that time, to understand the importance of his lectures.

Majorana was very interested in teaching what his prodigious mind was discovering about the laws of nature. It is likely that he applied to the competition just to finally have his own students (whom he always took care of, as we are going to see). As we know, after the proposal of the commission in charge of the competition, chaired by Fermi, on November 2nd 1937, the Minister Bottai issued the act of appointment for Majorana as full professor of theoretical physics, at the Royal University of Naples, out of competition. At the end of 1937, Majorana was informed by the Minister of this appointment at his dwelling place in viale Regina Margherita 37, in Rome, with this explanation: *"for the high reputation You achieved in the study of the mentioned discipline, as from November 16th 1937-XVI."* Majorana went to Naples after the Epiphany (around January 10th 1938), and on January 12th he writes from his university seat to Minister Bottai saying, among other things, *"I wish to affirm that I shall devote all my energies to the Italian school and science, today in such a successful ascension[6]."*

Majorana's letters, which are relevant also for the circumstances in which Majorana disappeared, are contained in ref. [4]. We will briefly mention only those which are of interest in this section. In his letter to his mother dated January 11th 1938 from Naples, Majorana wrote: *"I announced the beginning of the course for next Thursday 13th at nine. But it hasn't been possible to check if there is overlapping with other classes, thus it is likely that students will not come and we will need to postpone the beginning of the course. I spoke to the dean and we agreed on avoiding any formal character to the inauguration of the course, also for this reason I should suggest you not to come...".* Majorana's family, on the contrary, was punctual on Thursday January 13th 1938, at nine, at Majorana's inaugural lecture. The professors of the faculty were present at the lesson, among whom certainly Antonio Carrelli and Renato Caccioppoli, who were very good friends; as Gilda Senatore recalls, students were not invited.

The notes for the opening address to the course, or inaugural lecture, have been discovered by one of us [E.R.] about 1972 and have been made public for the first time ten years later[7][8]. In the mentioned notes all the interest of the scientist appears, not only for the general and basic issues which animate the scientific research, but also for the best *didactic method* to follow in order to pass on his knowledge to the students (for

---

[6] The documents, discovered and published for the first time by E. Recami are present in ref. [4]. They all are protected by copyright (including the photographs) held by E. Recami, the Majorana family and presently by the publisher Di Renzo. Any reproduction of these documents is forbidden without written permission of the copyright holders (exception is obviously made for the *scientific* papers).

[7] E. RECAMI, in *Corriere della Sera* (Milano), 19 Ottobre 1982. See also refs. [4] and [8].

[8] B. PREZIOSI (Editor), *Ettore Majorana - Lezioni all'Università di Napoli* (Bibliopolis, Napoli) 1987. The volume contains, besides a comment by N. Cabibbo, also an article by E. Recami which includes the notes for the inaugural lecture and a catalogue of all the unpublished scientific papers by Majorana (edited by M. Baldo, R. Magnani and E. Recami); for the catalogue see also E. RECAMI, in *Quaderni di Storia della Fisica*, no. **5** (1999), 19-68.

whom he had a deep care).

The notes of Majorana's inaugural lecture reveal several aspects of his scientific and human qualities. We wish to warn that they concern classical physics and quantum mechanics: in this first stage relativistic aspects were neglected. These aspects are examined in the second half of Majorana's course, as revealed by the notes of his last six lessons which have been recently discovered. Majorana was so particularly fascinated by the antimechanicistic and probabilistic description of quantum mechanics, that he discusses it widely also in his posthomous article[9] published in 1942 by Giovannino Gentile. On July 27th 1934 from Monteporzio Catone (Rome) he had written to Gentile himself: *"I think that the major merit of Jeans' book[10] is to anticipate the psychological reactions which the new development of physics will fatally produce when everybody understands that science has stopped being a justification for the vulgar materialism."*

Since the myth has associated the death of Majorana with the fear of the construction of the atomic bomb, we can say immediately that from the very beginning of his inaugural lecture Ettore says openly: *"Atomic physics, which will be the main subject of my discussion, despite its important and numerous practical applications —together with those of a wider and maybe revolutionary impact that the future may have in store—, is first of all a science of immense speculative interest for the depth of its investigation that really reaches the extreme roots of natural facts."* Majorana's words make us understand that, despite the probable "revolutionary" applications which nuclear and atomic physics could have led to, they interested him mainly from the speculative point of view.

3. Lectures in his theoretical physics course

As testified by Gilda Senatore and Sebastiano Sciuti, his course was attended, from January 15th onwards, by themselves and by Nella Altieri, Laura Mercogliano, Nada Minghetti and Savino Coronato, the latter being one of Caccioppoli's students; after the last lecture he no longer attended the Physics Institute and took his degree in mathematics in the same year. Nobody else attended his lectures, apart from a few occasional presences of Mario Cutolo, who had already graduated in physics.

Majorana took much care of his students, and appreciated them. In fact, in the last letter to his friend and colleague Giovanni Gentile jr, he wrote: *"I am satisfied with my students; some of them seem determined in approaching physics seriously."* When the chalk was in his hands, his bashfulness disappeared and entire blackboards were easily filled with elegant physical and mathematical symbols. This behaviour has been recalled by Gilda Senatore in a TV interview performed by Bruno Russo, and, more recently, at the meeting organized by the University of Naples Federico II on the occasion of the 60th anniversary of his disappearance.

---

[9] E. MAJORANA, "Il valore delle leggi statistiche nella fisica e nelle scienze sociali", *Scientia* **36** (1942) 58-66.
[10] J. JEANS, *I Nuovi Orizzonti della Scienza* (Sansoni, Firenze) 1934, Italian translation by G. Gentile jr.

All the autograph notes of his lectures, written with care by Majorana, as aids for his students (maybe Ettore had in mind to write a book for his students, in the same way as he did when he wrote his original study notes, the *"Volumetti"*[11])), were left in safekeeping, the day before going to Palermo, to his favorite pupil Gilda Senatore, together with some other writings which were no more found. A letter by Preziosi published in "Le Scienze" (September 2002) and ref. ([12]) explain how those lecture notes happened to be in Carrelli's hands between the end of 1938 and the beginning of 1939, and in which occasion were then sent to E. Amaldi, unfortunately without six lessons on electrodynamics and special relativity. It is interesting to notice that in 1939-1940 Carrelli taught special relativity and the related notes were published by GUF in 1940. The notes sent to Amaldi and deposited at the Domus Galilaeana were published anastatically in ref. ([8]).

Recently, S. Esposito[13] and A. Drago have found, among the papers left by Eugenio Moreno, a student in Mathematics who took his degree with Caccioppoli in 1941, a personally handwritten copy of all Majorana's manuscripts, including the part relative to special relativity, absent in the papers deposited at the Domus Galilaeana. Indeed, Gilda Senatore recalls that this part was present in the original notes given to her by Majorana himself. Such notes, now, are all present in ref. ([14]).

BRUNO PREZIOSI
Università di Napoli

ERASMO RECAMI
Università di Bergamo

([11]) S. ESPOSITO, E. MAJORANA jr, A. VAN DER MERWE and RECAMI E., *Ettore Majorana - Notes on Theoretical Physics* (Kluwer Academic Press, Dordrecht, Boston e New York) 2003. (Edition in the original Italian language: E. MAJORANA, *Appunti inediti di fisica teorica*, edited by Esposito S. e Recami E. (Zanichelli, Bologna) 2006.).
([12]) *L'eredità di Fermi e Majorana ed altri temi* (Bibliopolis, Napoli) 2006.
([13]) S. ESPOSITO, *Nuovo Saggiatore*, **21** No. 1-2 (2005) 21-41.
([14]) S. ESPOSITO (Editor), *Ettore Majorana - Lezioni di Fisica Teorica* (Bibliopolis, Napoli) 2006.

Finito di stampare
nel mese di novembre 2006
Monograf S.r.l. – Bologna